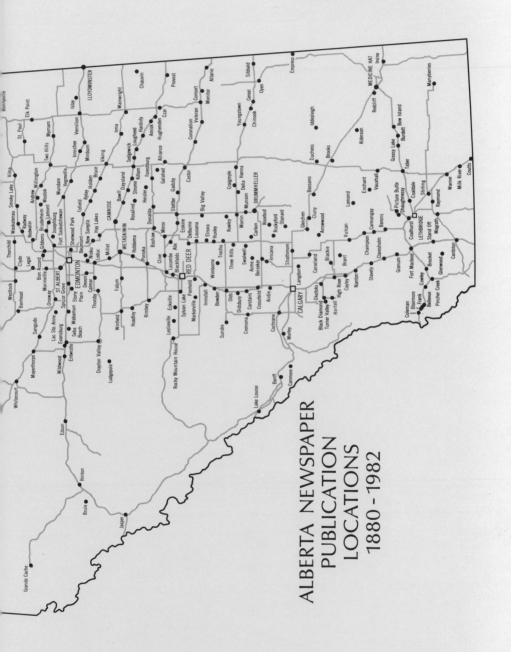

ALBERTA NEWSPAPER
PUBLICATION
LOCATIONS
1880 – 1982

GLORIA M. STRATHERN

Alberta Newspapers

1880-1982

AN HISTORICAL
DIRECTORY

GLORIA M. STRATHERN

Alberta Newspapers

1880-1982

AN HISTORICAL DIRECTORY

THE UNIVERSITY OF ALBERTA PRESS

First published by
The University of Alberta Press
Athabasca Hall
Edmonton, Alberta, Canada
T6G 2E8
1988

ISBN 0-88864-137-0 cloth
      0-88864-138-9 paper

Canadian Cataloguing in Publication Data

Strathern, Gloria M (Gloria Margaret)
    Alberta newspapers, 1880-1982: an historical
directory

    ISBN 0-88864-137-0 (bound). — ISBN 0-88864-
138-9 (pbk.)

    1. Canadian newspapers — Alberta — Directories. *
2. Canadian newspapers — Alberta — Bibliography. *
I. Title.
Z6954.C2S87 1988   015.7123'035   C88-091159-X

REF.

61,516

Typesetting by Dianne Green
Printed by Hignell Printers, Winnipeg, Manitoba, Canada

Contents

Foreword

ix

Introduction

xiii

Users Guide

xix

Historical Directory

1

Indexes

261

Bibliography

545

Foreword

by Bruce B. Peel

FOREWORD

The first newspaper published in Alberta was the Edmonton *Bulletin* which appeared in 1880, a quarter of a century before the establishment of the Province. It was followed by the *Fort Macleod Gazette* in 1882 and the *Calgary Herald* in 1883. Before 1982, some one thousand and ninety identified papers were published in a sparsely populated territory. Another twenty-three titles may also have been published and are listed in the Fugitive Titles section of the *Directory*.

Although the Canadian Pacific Railway arrived in Calgary in 1883, settlement was slow to develop, while many communities were isolated from the railways. As new settlements were established, newspapers appeared to supply information ranging from exclusively local to national and international news. The quality and content of these papers depended on the publisher, often a jobbing-printer in smaller centres. However, there were more sophisticated and experienced newspaper men, including the legendary R.C. (Eye-Opener Bob) Edwards.

A useful feature of the *Directory* is the Biographical Index which identifies individuals involved in the newspapers, with notes on their activities in Alberta and elsewhere. Other indexes provide a chronological review of the papers, subject access and titles, including bi-lingual and alternative titles.

My own *Bibliography of the Prairie Provinces* and Professor Strathern's *Alberta, 1954-1979* have documented monographic publications. However, until now, there has been no guide to the newspaper press which had a significant influence on public opinion and settlement patterns. It is very gratifying to see the documentation of Alberta history has been extended by this new study. Not only does it fill an important gap in the historical record but it should encourage the preservation of these fragile and irreplaceable archives.

The *Directory* is organized under place of publication with titles arranged in chronological order, so that an historical perspective is provided. Many papers had complicated histories, involving changes of title and ownership, relocations, amalgamations, splits, and relationships to other papers. All these developments are documented in the Notes Sections of title entries, while, as already noted, the extensive indexes provide alternative access to the papers.

Only those who have laboured on bibliographical work which requires the exploration of new areas of investigation can truly appreciate the time and effort involved in such an undertaking. Professor Strathern has made a signal contribution to the history of the printed word in the province and provided a key to further studies, not only of the press, but to other aspects of Alberta's history.

Bruce B. Peel,
Edmonton, Alberta,
June, 1987

Introduction

INTRODUCTION

It is almost impossible to properly estimate the far-reaching power and influence of the press in this Western country where there are fewer social attractions than in more thickly populated countries to direct the attentions of a farmer from the chief recreation of rural life, namely, reading, and where the local paper is probably more widely and carefully read than anywhere else in Canada. (Deputy Commissioner Peterson, Department of Agriculture, N.W.T., *Publisher and Printer*, v9no8 Ag, 1902, p.11).

Events, opinions, the temper of the times — all these are reflected more completely in the pages of newspapers than in any other single source of information. For this reason old files are being used more and more not only by historians, but by research workers in a wide variety of subject fields. Journalists, script writers, economists, psychologists, sociologists, biologists, and others are all finding, sometimes to their great surprise, that data essential to them are frequently hidden away in old newspapers. Unless the more important files are preserved, a great deal of interest and significance in Canada's past will be lost to us. (W. Kaye Lamb, Introduction to *Canadian Newspapers on microfilm catalogue*. Ottawa: Canadian Library Association, 1954, p.1)

The values of newspapers to the reader of the day and to the researcher of today are identified in these two quotations. In 1982, when work on this *Directory* began, information about Alberta newspapers existed in Checklists of the holdings of Institutions, Directories and Union Lists. These sources, published and unpublished, differed in their definitions of the term "newspaper," consequently, inclusions or exclusions varied and no listing was comprehensive. Fewer than half the titles now identified were recorded and information about publishing history was not included.

This *Directory* lists and describes all identified newspapers published in Alberta between 1880 and 1982. Newspapers issued for the first time subsequent to December 31, 1982, are not included. Information regarding newspapers continuing after that date is as complete as possible up to the end of 1982. Changes that occurred after that date are noted only when supplied by informants.

Publications eligible for inclusion were determined after an acceptable definition of the term "newspaper" was established. An extensive literature search confirmed Jean Whiffen's observation:

There is no internationally accepted definition of a newspaper, but this kind of serial is usually printed originally on newsprint, in a format of not less than four columns of type per page, is issued at least once a month, without a cover, and has a masthead. It usually contains general news coverage, rather than being oriented towards specific subject matter, but certain special types such as financial, student, ethnic, etc. are common to many countries. (Union Catalogues of Serials, *Serials Librarian* v8no1, Fall, 1983, p.73).

Not all newspapers published in Alberta meet these criteria: some were published less frequently than once a month, a few were handwritten in a single copy, while others had no masthead, though all had a banner title on the first page.

Papers included in this *Directory* are those considered by their publishers to be newspapers or so identified by examination or through secondary sources. Papers excluded are: church bulletins; community league organs; election campaign papers; papers published by and for juveniles, including college and school organs; bulletins and newsletters of companies, organizations and professional and trade associations; shoppers that comprise 75% or more advertising content and are not eligible for second class mail as defined by the *Canada Postal Guide*; and tourist papers comprised solely of advertising and information about tourist attractions. It was not always possible to establish that a publication met the definition of a newspaper, while occasionally only the discovery of a specimen issue late in the research revealed the nature of the item. In marginal cases, arbitrary decisions for inclusion were made on the basis of content, format and research value.

The first task in compiling the *Directory* was to establish a basic working file of titles from Checklists, Directories, Union Lists and Newspaper Indexes. The search was then widened by an extensive examination of secondary sources such as local histories, biographies and studies of the Canadian Press. The resultant file was then arranged by geographic areas and these areas clustered into counties, improvement districts, towns and cities. This approach revealed connections between papers published in a particular place and those published in neighboring areas. It was a common practice for a publisher to issue newspapers for a number of centres from one locality or to move a press from one place to another as economic conditions fluctuated. Additionally, a publisher might absorb, merge or split two or more papers for economic reasons.

The files of newspapers held in some twenty-one institutions were examined. Photocopies of titles held elsewhere in Canada were obtained wherever possible and an extensive correspondence was conducted with archivists, librarians, publishers and editors, including a questionnaire mailed to over three hundred informants. Many papers were either not located in any institution or were represented by minimal holdings. Moreover, secondary sources proved to be contradictory or unreliable, as errors were copied from one source to another without attribution, while other errors occurred owing to the faulty memories of elderly informants on long past events. Collating these contradictory references involved some bibliographic detective work and further delving into new sources. A list of titles found in one secondary source, with no confirmatory reference or surviving copies, was established. Further investigation pruned this list substantially as garbled references were untangled. The remaining doubtful titles may have been periodicals or publications projected but not realized. To assist further research, these titles are provided in a short list entitled Fugitive Titles.

Unfortunately for the historical record, unlike some other provinces, such as neighboring Saskatchewan, Alberta had no legislation requiring newspaper publishers to provide annual returns from proprietors, publishers and editors. An extensive search of the Corporate Registry of the Alberta

Department of Consumer and Corporate Affairs revealed little information about newspapers published by registered companies.

As work progressed, a Biographical Index of editors and publishers was established. This information revealed new titles and clarified others, so that the working file was revised. This Index is also intended to serve as a source for researchers interested in the origins of those who affected public opinion through the press and their overall contributions to newspaper publishing in Alberta and elsewhere. Regrettably, this record is very uneven. Although information was gathered from a wide variety of sources, in some cases, almost nothing could be discovered but a starting point for further exploration now exists.

Two factors influencing the nature of Alberta newspapers should be noted for the benefit of future researchers. The first is the extensive use of ready-print or boiler-plate printed elsewhere, usually in Winnipeg, by such firms as the Western Ready Print Service of the Winnipeg Saturday Post Limited or the Toronto Type Foundry Company, later purchased by the Prairie Publishers Co-operative Ltd. in Regina. These ready-print sections comprised the inner pages, usually six or eight, of a paper and contained serialized melodramatic stories, syndicated health columns, advertisements and world-wide gossip. These sections were sent by rail. Consequently, the expansion of the railways and the vagaries of railway services affected local publishing significantly.

The second factor was the practice of contract newspapers, whereby such papers printed records of minutes prepared and supplied by a local government such as a County Council in return for the publishers' guaranteed blanket circulation to ratepayers and sometimes reduced or free advertising rates for that government. The first such paper was the *Strathmore Standard* published in 1912. Alberta is the only province in Canada which includes provision in its legislation for contract papers.

Although every effort has been made to make the *Directory* complete within its stated limitations, it is almost inevitable in a work of this nature that some titles have not been identified or that the information obtained from secondary sources is incorrect or incomplete. While I owe much to all those who have contributed to the record, the responsibility for errors and omissions is, of course, mine. It is my earnest wish that such limitations will be corrected by those aware of additional information and that the *Directory* will stimulate further attention to Alberta newspapers, including efforts to preserve surviving issues of these indispensable historical documents.

A work of this nature can only be achieved with generous assistance from many sources. It is hoped that none of these have been overlooked, though it is impossible to list all individuals and institutions who patiently answered numerous enquiries over seven years of investigation. I am particularly grateful to Mr. B.B. Peel who kindly agreed to write the Foreword, to Mrs. Priscilla Rushton who undertook a major task in compiling the basic check-list of titles and much of the preparation of the master file of newspaper entries, to Miss Charlotte Landry who compiled the master file of titles in languages other than English, and to Miss Anna Bombak who documented Ukrainian newspapers. In addition, recognition must be given to those institutions who provided courteous assistance over periods of lengthy examination of their files, especially the Alberta Legislature Library, the Provincial

Archives of Alberta and the Glenbow Archives and Library. I am also indebted to Miss Noeline Bridge who edited the Biographical Index, in itself a major task, and to Mr. David Kales who undertook the final check of holdings in the Alberta Legislature Library.

For financial assistance, I am grateful to the University of Alberta's Small Faculties Endowment Fund for the Advancement of Scholarship and The Western Canada Publications Project of that University which funded the Pilot Project on a test file of newspapers to develop the methodology for the *Directory*. Most especially, I thank Alberta Culture and The Social Sciences and Humanities Research Council of Canada's Strategic Grants Division, who funded the study so generously. Finally I acknowledge my indebtedness to the University of Alberta which granted me a study leave for the academic year 1986/87 to complete the project and to my publishers, the University of Alberta Press.

Gloria M. Strathern
Faculty of Library Science
University of Alberta
May 30, 1987

User's Guide

Sample Entries xix
Arrangement xx
Descriptive Elements of Entries xx
  A. Item Number xx
  B. Title xx
  C. Publication Dates xx
  D. Frequency xx
  E. Special Interest or Ethnic Group Affiliations . xx
  F. Language xxi
  G. Notes xxi
Special Features xxi
  Supplements xxi
  Sections xxi
  Special and Anniversary Issues xxii
Relationships Between Newspapers xxii
  Absorptions xxii
  Amalgamations and Mergers xxii
  Continued/Continued By xxii
  Splits xxii
  Superseded/Superseded By xxii
Holdings xxii

Abbreviations Used xxiii
    Publication Dates: Months xxiii
    Publication Dates: Inclusive Dates xxiii
    Frequency xxiii
    Language Abbreviations xxiv
    Native Language Abbreviations xxiv
    Notes: Publishers and Editors xxiv
    Holdings xxiv
List of Geographical Names xxv
List of Locations with Symbols Used xxix

Sample Entries

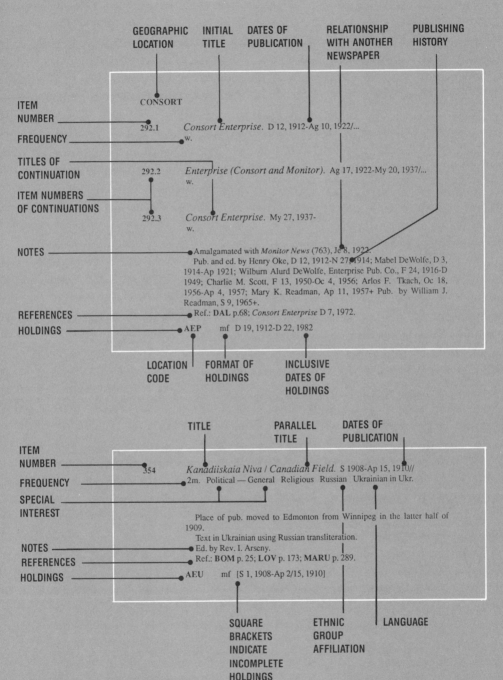

GEOGRAPHIC LOCATION

INITIAL TITLE

DATES OF PUBLICATION

RELATIONSHIP WITH ANOTHER NEWSPAPER

PUBLISHING HISTORY

ITEM NUMBER

FREQUENCY

TITLES OF CONTINUATION

ITEM NUMBERS OF CONTINUATIONS

NOTES

REFERENCES

HOLDINGS

CONSORT

292.1   *Consort Enterprise.* D 12, 1912-Ag 10, 1922/...
w.

292.2   *Enterprise (Consort and Monitor).* Ag 17, 1922-My 20, 1937/...
w.

292.3   *Consort Enterprise.* My 27, 1937-
w.

Amalgamated with *Monitor News* (763), Je 8, 1922.
Pub. and ed. by Henry Oke, D 12, 1912-N 27, 1914; Mabel DeWolfe, D 3,
1914-Ap 1921; Wilburn Alurd DeWolfe, Enterprise Pub. Co., F 24, 1916-D
1949; Charlie M. Scott, F 13, 1950-Oc 4, 1956; Arlos F. Tkach, Oc 18,
1956-Ap 4, 1957; Mary K. Readman, Ap 11, 1957+ Pub. by William J.
Readman, S 9, 1965+.
Ref.: **DAL** p.68; *Consort Enterprise* D 7, 1972.
AEP   mf   D 19, 1912-D 22, 1982

LOCATION CODE

FORMAT OF HOLDINGS

INCLUSIVE DATES OF HOLDINGS

TITLE

PARALLEL TITLE

DATES OF PUBLICATION

ITEM NUMBER

FREQUENCY

SPECIAL INTEREST

NOTES

REFERENCES

HOLDINGS

354   *Kanadiiskaia Niva / Canadian Field.* S 1908-Ap 15, 1910//
2m. Political — General Religious Russian Ukrainian in Ukr.

Place of pub. moved to Edmonton from Winnipeg in the latter half of
1909.
Text in Ukrainian using Russian transliteration.
Ed. by Rev. I. Arseny.
Ref.: **BOM** p. 25; **LOV** p. 173; **MARU** p. 289.
AEU   mf   [S 1, 1908-Ap 2/15, 1910]

SQUARE BRACKETS INDICATE INCOMPLETE HOLDINGS

ETHNIC GROUP AFFILIATION

LANGUAGE

xix

Arrangement

Newspapers are arranged chronologically by first date of issue under the name of the geographic area or place that they principally served. The geographic areas are arranged alphabetically, and where necessary, cross references are provided from earlier or related place names. If the place of printing or publication differed from the area served this information is provided in the Notes Section of the entry.

Descriptive Elements of Entries

Each newspaper title entry consists of a number of elements in order of appearance as follows (see sample entries):

A. Item Number Each newspaper has a unique item number, e.g. 352 *West-Land*. Ja 2, 1908-5 1913// If the same paper was published under a number of titles, all such titles have been identified by subordinate numbers, e.g. 353.1 *Alberta Homestead*, Ja 8? 1908-Ap 19, 1911/... 353.2 *Homestead* Ap 26, 1911-N 28, 1913//?

These item numbers are used to cross reference newspapers and to locate variant titles in the Title Index.

B. Title

Titles were taken from the front-page banner. Where a masthead title differed from the banner title, this information is included in the Notes. All titles under which a newspaper was published are included in the Title Index, while title variations are recorded in the Notes. Bi-lingual banner titles are indicated as follows: *Kanadiiskaia Niva / Canadian Field* and both titles are included in the Title Index. Subtitles are also included in the Notes.

C. Publication dates

Whenever possible, full dates (day, month, year) are supplied for the first and last issues of a newspaper.

D. Frequency

The frequency element records how often a newspaper was published. This may vary over the period of publication. (See Abbreviations Used).

E. Special Interest or Ethnic Group Affiliations

This element is provided when a newspaper had a special audience, e.g. agriculture, business or labour, was directed towards a specific ethnic group or has a specific political affiliation. The political affiliation of an editor or publisher was noted when it appeared in an editorial policy statement of the newspaper or in a reference source. A Subject Index for Special Interest papers and an Ethnic Index are provided.

F. Language

A newspaper was published in the English language unless otherwise stated. In the case of bi-lingual titles, the language stated first was the predominant one. If one of the languages was used infrequently, this information is enclosed in parentheses. Any variations or additional information regarding the languages of a newspaper is provided in the Notes

G. Notes

The Notes provide information on the publishing history of a newspaper, including any explanation of irregularities and discrepancies and any additional sources of information obtained. This information is arranged in the following order and may include statements on all or some of the following:

1. Relationships between the paper and other titles such as continuations, supersessions, amalgamations and mergers, absorptions and splits.

2. Publication variations: title, frequency, suspensions, voluming and numbering, format and place of publication.

3. Publishing history: The names of publishers, editors, contributors, and affiliations with organizations and associations.

4. Special features: Supplements, Sections, Special and Anniversary Issues.

5. References

Information given in the Notes may be established or confirmed in a secondary source. In such cases, a source reference in provided, e.g. Ref: CAN 1912. Citations for source references are listed in the Bibliography.

Special features

Supplements: These are considered to be an additional but separate part of a newspaper and may or may not be published by the newspaper with which it was distributed. If a supplement had separate voluming and numbering from the parent newspaper, it is described as a separate item and cross references are provided. Inclusive dates, whenever available, are provided for supplements.

Sections: These are usually integral parts of a newspaper (without separate voluming and numbering) which may serve a special interest group or a different geographic area from the parent newspaper. Cross references are made from the geographic areas served and inclusive dates, whenever available, are provided.

Special and Anniversary Issues: These are noted with dates of publication.

Relationships between newspapers

Absorptions: One newspaper was taken over by another as a result of the financial collapse of one, or simply the bringing together of subscription lists in order to serve a wider geographic area. Absorptions may have resulted in a title change or a voluming and numbering change. Whenever possible, full dates for absorptions are supplied.

Amalgamations and mergers: Two or more newspapers were consolidated to form one newspaper, usually a new one. Such an occurrence may have resulted in a title change or a voluming and numbering change. Whenever possible, full dates for amalgamations and mergers are supplied.

Continued/continued by: This relationship indicates an unbroken association between uniquely itemized newspapers, although changes may have occurred in title, place of publication, or geographic area served. The voluming and numbering is continuous between the linked newspapers.

Splits: One newspaper split to become two or more newspapers. Such an occurrence usually resulted in the creation of new titles and new voluming and numbering. Whenever possible, full dates for such splits are provided.

Superseded/superseded by: This relationship indicates that one newspaper ceased publication and was replaced by another, although an association remained between the newspapers either by sharing the same title or by having the same owner and publisher. The new newspaper started publication with a new voluming and numbering series.

Holdings

The holdings element notes those institutions possessing copies of the newspaper, the extent of their holdings and the physical format of those files. Where holdings are in an archival file with an accession number, this number is noted. Where no copies of a newspaper could be located in any institution, the entry records "No issues located."

An entry showing a continuous series of files for a newspaper does not necessarily mean that the repository possesses every single issue for the stated period. When the holdings of an institution are sparse over a particular time period, the inclusive dates are placed in square brackets, e.g. [1950-1962].

Institutions are cited by the code assigned in *Symbols of Canadian Libraries*. (Ottawa: National Library of Canada.) Institutions not included in that list have been coded to be consistent with it. A List of Locations with Symbols used is provided.

Finally, it should be noted that the *Directory* is not a Union List of institutional holdings. Only significant or unique holdings have been recorded.

Abbreviations Used

Publication Dates: Months

Ja	January	Jl	July
F	February	Ag	August
Mr	March	S	September
Ap	April	Oc	October
My	May	N	November
Je	June	D	December

Publication Dates: Inclusive Dates

-	Publication continues
/...	Publication continued under another title
//	Publication ceased
?	Information provided is not certain
F 6, 1928-	Publication continues
F 6, 1928-Mr 9, 1935/...	Publication under one title occurred during the inclusive dates and continued under another title
F 6, 1928-Mr 9,1935//	Publication began on February 6, 1928, and ceased on March 9, 1935
F 6, 1928-? 1935//	Precise date of final issue is uncertain
F 6, 1928-Mr 9, 1935?//	Publication may have continued after final date
F 6, 1928-1935?//	Final year of publication is uncertain
1928//	Publication is known only to have begun and ended within the year
1928-?//	Publication is known only to have begun in 1928 and final year of publication is unknown

Frequency:

d.	daily (five or more issues per week)
am	morning edition
pm	evening edition
w.	weekly
2w.	two issues per week
3w.	three issues per week
bw.	one issue every two weeks
m.	monthly
2m.	two issues per month
3m.	three issues per month
bm.	one issue every two months
q.	quarterly
/yr.	number of issues per year
irreg.	irregular and infrequent
?	frequency uncertain

Language Abbreviations:

Ara.	Arabic
Chi.	Chinese
Cro.	Croatian
Czech.	Czechoslovakian
Dan.	Danish
Engl.	English
Fin.	Finnish
Fr.	French
Ger.	German
Hung.	Hungarian
Icld.	Icelandic
Ital.	Italian
Kor.	Korean
Lat.	Latvian
Norw.	Norwegian
Pol.	Polish
Por.	Portuguese
Rus.	Russian
Slov.	Slovak
Span.	Spanish
Swed.	Swedish
Ukr.	Ukrainian

Native Language Abbreviations

Bl	Blood
Cr	Cree
Pe	Peigan
St	Stoney

Notes: Publishers and Editors

Bus. mgr.	Business Manager
Ed.	Edited/editor
Mgr.	Manager
Prop.	Proprietor
Pub.	Published/publisher

Holdings:

or	original files
mf	microform files
CY	current year only retained
2M + CM	2 months + current month retained
CM	current issue(s) only retained
[ ]	holdings very incomplete during time period given
Ja 6 1973+	indicates that files were examined up to the current year

List of Geographic Names

Headings are arranged alphabetically except in the case of counties which have the same name as towns, e.g. Lac Ste Anne County, Lac Ste Anne. In these instances, the larger geographic area precedes the town.

Acadia Valley See Cereal	Camrose
Acme	Canmore
Airdrie	Carbon
Alderson	Cardston
Alix	Carlstadt See Alderson
Alliance	Carmangay
Altario	Carseland
Amisk	Carstairs
Andrew	Castor
Arrowwood	Cayley
Athabasca	Cereal
Banff	Champion
Barons	Chauvin
Barrhead	Chinook
Bashaw	Clairmont
Bassano	Claresholm
Bawlf	Clive
Beaverlodge	Cluny
Beiseker	Clyde
Bellevue	Coaldale
Beverly See Edmonton	Coalhurst
Big Valley	Cochrane
Black Diamond	Cold Lake
Blackfalds	Coleman
Blackie	Colinton
Blairmore	Consort
Bon Accord	Coronation
Bonnyville	Coutts
Bow City	Cowley
Bow Island	Craigymle
Bowden	Cremona
Bowness See Calgary	Crossfield
Boyle	Czar
Bragg Creek	Daysland
Brant	Delburne
Brocket	Delia
Brooks	Devon
Bruce	Didsbury
Bruderheim	Dogpound See Cremona
Brule	Donalda
Buffalo Lake	Drayton Valley
Burdett	Drumheller
Calgary	Eckville
Calmar	Edgerton See Chauvin and Wainwright

Edmonton
Edson
Elk Point
Elnora
Empress
Enchant
Entwistle
Erckine
Evansburg
Fairview
Falher
Forestburg
Fort Chipewyan
Fort Macleod
Fort McMurray
Fort Saskatchewan
Fort Vermilion
Forty Mile County
Frank
Gadsby
Galahad
Gibbons
Gleichen
Glendon
Glenwood
Grand Centre
Grande Cache
Grande Prairie
Granam
Grassy Lake
Grimshaw
Grouard
Hanna
Hardisty
Harfell See Turner Valley
Hay Lakes
Heisler
High Level
High Prairie
High River
Hinton
Hoadley
Hobbema
Holden
Horburg
Hughenden
Hussar
Huxley
Hythe
Improvement District 1

Improvement District 23
Innisfail
Innisfree
Irma
Irricana
Irvine
Islay
Jarrow
Jasper
Jasper Place See Edmonton
Kathyrn
Keoma
Killam
Lac La Biche
Lac Ste Anne County
Lac Ste Anne
Lacombe
LaCrete
Lake Louise
Lake Saskatoon
Lakeview
Lamont County
Lamont
Langdon
Leavings See Granum
Leduc
Legal
Leslieville
Lethbridge County
Lethbridge
Lloydminster
Lodgepole
Lomond
Lougheed
Lousana
Macklin, Saskatchewan
Madden
Magrath
Manning
Mannville
Manyberries
Mayerthorpe
Medicine Hat
Milk River
Millet
Minburn County
Minburn
Mirror
Monitor
Morinville

Morley
Morrin
Mundare
Munson
Myrnam
Nanton
Naptha
New Sarepta
Nisku
Okotoks
Olds
Onoway
Oyen
Parkland County
Peace River
Pembina Municipal District
Penhold
Picture Butte
Pincher City
Pincher Creek
Ponoka County
Ponoka
Poplar Lake
Prairie Grange See Rocky Mountain House
Priddis
Provost
Radway
Raymond
Red Deer County
Red Deer
Redcliff
Redwater
Redwood Meadows See Cochrane
Retlaw
Rimbey
Rocky Mountain House
Rocky View Municipal District
Rockyford
Rosalind
Rosebud See Carbon
Rosebud Creek
Rowley
Rycroft
Ryley
St. Albert
St. Paul
Sangudo
Scotts Coulee
Sedgewick
Sexsmith

Sharples See Carbon
Sherwood Park
Sibbald
Slave Lake
Smoky River Municipal District
Spirit River
Springbank See Cochrane
Spruce Grove
Stand Off
Standard
Starland Municipal District
Stavely
Stettler
Stirling
Stony Plain Municipal District
Stony Plain
Strathcona See Edmonton
Strathcona County
Strathmore
Strome
Sturgeon Municipal District
Sundre
Sunnyslope
Swalwell
Swan Hills
Sylvan Lake
Taber
Thorhild County
Thorhild
Thorsby
Three Hills
Tofield
Travers
Trochu
Turner Valley
Two Hills County
Valleyview
Vauxhall
Vegreville
Vermilion
Vermilion River County
Veteran
Viking
Vilna
Vulcan
Wabamun
Wainwright
Warner County
Warner
Waskatenau

Water Valley
Waterhole See Fairview
Waterways See Fort McMurray
Westlock
Wetaskiwin County
Wetaskiwin
Whitecourt
Whitefish Lake
Wildwood
Willingdon
Wimborne
Winfield
Winnifred
Wostok
Youngstown

List of Locations With Symbols Used

ABA	Archives of the Canadian Rockies, Peter and Catharine Whyte Foundation, Banff, AB
ABOM	Bowden Pioneer Museum, Bowden, AB
AC	Calgary Public Library, Calgary AB
ACG	Archives, Glenbow-Alberta Institute, Calgary, AB
ACGL	Library, Glenbow-Alberta Institute, Calgary, AB
ACOM	Cochrane Municipal Library, Cochrane, AB
ACU	University of Calgary Library, Calgary, AB
ACUA	University of Calgary Archives, Calgary, AB
ACUCES	Research Centre for Canadian Ethnic Studies, University of Calgary, Calgary, AB
ADOD	Donalda and District Museum, Donalda, AB
AE	Edmonton Public Library, Edmonton, AB
AEA	Alberta Historical Resources Library, Edmonton, AB
AEAG	Alberta Agriculture Library, Edmonton, AB
AEPAA	Provincial Archives of Alberta, Edmonton, AB
AEC	Concordia College Library, Edmonton, AB
AECL	Alberta Culture Library, Edmonton, AB
AEEA	City of Edmonton Archives and Library, Edmonton, AB
AEMA	Alberta Municipal Affairs Library, Edmonton, AB
AEML	Alberta Labour Library, Edmonton, AB
AEP	Alberta Legislature Library, Edmonton, AB
AEU	University Libraries, University of Alberta, Edmonton, AB
AEUA	University Archives, University of Alberta, Edmonton, AB

AEUB	Boreal Institute for Northern Studies, University of Alberta, Edmonton, AB
AEUCA	Ukrainian Canadian Archives and Museum of Alberta, Edmonton, AB
AEUS	Bruce Peel Special Collections Library, University of Alberta, Edmonton, AB
AEUSJ	Faculté Saint-Jean, Bibliothèque, Edmonton, AB
AEVC	Learning Resources Centre, Alberta Vocational Centre, Edmonton, AB
AFMM	Heritage Park, Fort McMurray, AB
AHPD	High Prairie and District Centennial Museum, High Prairie, AB
ALU	University of Lethbridge Library, Lethbridge, AB
ALUA	University Archives, University of Lethbridge, Lethbridge, AB
AMHM	Medicine Hat Museum and Art Gallery, Medicine Hat, AB
AYOCM	Crossroads Museum, Oyen, AB
APROM	Fort Ostell Museum, Ponoka, AB
ARDA	Red Deer and District Museum and Archives, Red Deer, AB
AREM	Redcliff Museum, Redcliff, AB
AREDM	Redwater Museum, Redwater, AB
AVIHS	Viking Historical Museum, Viking, AB
AWCA	Wetaskiwin City Archives, Wetaskiwin, AB
BVAU	University of British Columbia Library, Vancouver, BC
LC	Library of Congress, Washington, D.C.
MWP	Legislative Library of Manitoba, Winnipeg, MB
MWPA	Provincial Archives of Manitoba, Winnipeg, MB
OOA	National Archives of Canada, Ottawa, ON
OOG	Geological Survey of Canada Library, Ottawa, ON
OOL	Labour Canada Library, Ottawa, ON

OONL	National Library of Canada, Ottawa, ON
OTAR	Archives of Ontario, Toronto, ON
SRA	Saskatchewan Archives Board, University of Regina, Regina, SK
WHL	State Historical Society of Wisconsin Library, Madison, WI.

Historical Directory

Supplement 246
Fugitive Titles 255
Fugitive Titles Listed by Place 258

ACME

1 *Acme News.* N? 1909-F 4, 1914?//
w. Political — Liberal

Superceded by *Telegram-Tribune,* Acme (2).
Pub. by Schooley Bros. F.H. Schooley, prop., Liberal, N 1909-D 1913;
Harold H. Schooley and Charles H. Schooley, Liberal, D 24, 1913-F 1914.
Pub. a section entitled *Sunnyslope Sun.*
Ref.: **DAL** p.60.

AEP   mf Ag 19 1910-F 4, 1914

2 *Telegram-Tribune.* F 11, 1914-Ap 22, 1914?//
w. Political — Liberal

Superceded *Acme News* (1).
Pub. by Schooley Bros. Pub. by Charles H. and Harold H. Schooley,
Liberal.

AEP   mf F 11-Ap 22, 1914

3.1 *Acme Sentinel.* Je 10, 1914-Oc 26, 1951/...
w.

3.2 *Sentinel.* N 2, 1951-S? 1973//
w.

Absorbed *Carbon Chronicle* (238.3), S 16, 1960.
Subtitle S 16, 1960-S? 1973: "With Which is Incorporated the Carbon
Chronicle."
Pub. by Arthur Wheeler, Je 10, 1914-F 25, 1949. Leased to Charles C.
Segrave, Je 13, 1919-My 18, 1934. Pub. by George Wheeler, Mr 4, 1949-
1973? Ed. by Arthur Wheeler, Mr 4, 1949-1973?
Alberta Golden Jubilee Edition, S 2, 1955.
Ref.: **DAL** p.62.

AEP   mf Je 10, 1914-D 30, 1921; Ja 6, 1926-D 24, 1965; My 17, 1968-
           Ap 17/24, 1970

4 *Valley News.* D 30, 1953-Ja 5, 1955?//
w.

Continued *Valley News,* Wimborne (1037).
Pub. by George Wheeler and ed. by George E. Smith.

AEP   or D 30, 1953
           mf Ja 6, 1954-Ja 5, 1955

Five Village Weekly. N 6, 1975-D 30? 1980
    See **ROCKY VIEW MUNICIPAL DISTRICT.** *Rocky View-Five
Village Weekly* (862).

AIRDRIE

5   *Airdrie News.* Jl 16, 1908-1911?//
           w.

           Pub. and ed. by James Mewhort.
           Ref.: **CAN**, 1912.

           AEP   mf Jl 16, 1908-D 31, 1909

6   *Airdrie Recorder.* 1921-Ja 14, 1926?//
           w.

           Ed. by H.A. English, 1921-1923, A.L. Harvey, 1923-1925; James Bailey,
           1925-1926? (Ref: **MK** 1922, 1923, 1925, 1926; **WILK** p.282).

           ACG   or My 18, 1922; D 13, 1923; My 8, N 27-D 18, 1924;
                        [Ja 15, 1925-Ja 14, 1926]

7   *Tri-Neighbour Press.* Oc 4, 1972-Je 1974?//
           w.

           Ref: **CNLU** p.1; **CAN** 1975.

           OONL   or Oc 4, 1972

8.1   *Airdrie and District Echo.* N 26, 1975-D 1, 1977/...
           w.

8.2   *Rocky View Times and Airdrie Echo.* D 7, 1977-S 19, 1979/...
           w.

8.3   *Airdrie and District Echo.* S 26, 1979-
           w.

           Amalgamated with *Rocky View Times* (9) D 7, 1977. Split S 26, 1979 into
           Rocky View Times (10) and *Airdrie and District Echo* (8.3).
           Pub. by Andy Marshall, Airdrie and District Echo Ltd. Ed. by John
           Groarke. Sold Jl 23, 1980 to Jack Tennant, pub. and ed.
           Ref.: *Calgary Herald,* Ja 7, 1978.

           AEP   mf My 12, 1976-D 29, 1982
                        or Ja 1983+

9   *Rocky View Times.* N 16, 1977-N 23, 1977//
           w.

           Amalgamated D 7, 1977 with *Airdrie and District Echo* (8.1) to form
           Rocky View Times and Airdrie Echo (8.2).
           Pub. by Andy Marshall, Airdrie and District Echo Ltd. Only 2 issues pub.
           (Ref.: *Airdrie and District Echo* N 9, 1977).

           No issues located

10 *Rocky View Times.* S 26, 1979-
w.

Split from *Rocky View Times and Airdrie Echo* (8.2).
Pub. by Andy Marshall, District Echo Pub. Co. Ltd. Ed. by John Groarke.
Sold Jl 23, 1980 to Jack Tennant, pub. and ed.
Ref.: **ALB** Ag 22, 1980:15.

AEP or S 26, 1979+

ALDERSON

11 *Times-Reporter.* 1911//
w.

Pub. by Carlstadt-Suffield Pub. Co. (Ref.: **MK** 1911).

No issues located

12.1 *Carlstadt Progress.* D 28, 1911-Jl 25, 1912/...
w. Political — Liberal

12.2 *Carlstadt News.* Ag 1, 1912-Je 24, 1915/...
w.

12.3 *Alderson News.* Jl 1, 1915-Jl 25, 1918//
w.

Town of Carlstadt changed name to Alderson Jl 1, 1915.
Pub. and ed. by Calvin Goss, Liberal, D 28, 1911-Jl 25, 1912; Herbert S.
Ketchum and Will D. MacKay, Ag 8, 1912-My 8, 1913; Will D. MacKay,
My 15-Oc 1, 1913; C.C. Stuart, mgr. and ed., Oc 15, 1913-My 6, 1914; H.S.
Ketchum, My 14, 1914-F 18, 1915; W.D. MacKay, F 25, 1915-Oc 22, 1917;
R.H. Thornton, N 1, 1917-Jl 25, 1918.

AEP or D 28, 1911-Jl 25, 1918

13 *Farmers Tribune.* Oc 6, 1914-D8, 1914?//
w. Agriculture

Printed by Herbert S. Ketchum at Carlstadt, Alta. for Farmers' Combined
Irrigation Committee.

ACG or Oc 6-D8, 1914

ALIX

14.1 *Alix Free Press.* Mr 12, 1909-Ja 27, 1933/...
w.

14.2   *Alix Free Press Mirror News-Record.* F 3, 1933-F 12, 1948/...
        w.

14.3   *Alix Free Press.* F 19, 1948-My 5, 1949/...
        w.

14.4   *Alix Free Press Mirror News Record.* My 12, 1949-Je 1, 1950/...
        w.

14.5   *Alix-Mirror Free Press.* Je 8, 1950-D 21, 1950/...
        w.

14.6   *Alix Free Press.* Mr 1, 1951-Ag 18, 1953//
        w.

        Pub. and ed. by Charles W. Frederick, Mr 12, 1909-Oc 5, 1911; S. Arnold
        Gill, with G.E. Rice, Oc 6-Oc 20? 1911; S.C. Andrews, N 3, 1911-Jl 31,
        1936; Ed. V. Chambers, Ag 7, 1936-Je? 1942; F.V. Richards, Je? 1942-My 5,
        1949; Robert C. Oldring, My 12-D 22, 1949; V.F. Oldring, Ja 5-Mr 30, 1950;
        Charles L. Kee, Ap 6, 1950-F? 1951; C.J. Thompson, Mr 1, 1951-Ja 30,
        1952; Thomas W. Pue, Community Publications of Alberta, Edmonton, F 7,
        1952-Ag 18, 1953.
        Pub. section entitled *Mirror News Record* Oc 16, 1931-Ja 27, 1933; My
        12-Ag 11, 1949.

        AEP   or Mr 2, 1909-Ag 27, 1920; Ja 7-D 30, 1921; Jl 3, 1925-Ag
                   18, 1953

15   *Alix Promoter.* Ja 10? 1957-Mr 1959//
        w.

        Amalgamated with *Bashaw Star* (56.1), Ap 1, 1959 to form *Bashaw Star
        and the Alix Promoter* (56.2).
        Pub. by *Bashaw Star.*
        Ref.: *Bashaw Star,* Ja 9 1957:1; **CNLU** p.2.

        No issues located

ALLIANCE

16.1   *Alliance Times.* S 23, 1916-Oc 13, 1939/...
        w. Political — Social Credit

16.2   *Enterprise.* Oc 20, 1939-
        w.

        Absorbed by *Community Press* (890.2), Sedgewick, S 3, 1980 and pub. as
        supplement of *Community Press* for Daysland, Heisler, Forestburg and
        Galahad, S 3, 1980+

Printed and pub. in Edmonton Oc 26, 1936-Oc 13, 1939.
Pub. and ed. by John W. Johnston, S 23, 1916-Ja 20, 1933; Alex J. Allnutt, Social Credit, Ja 21, 1933-Ag? 1939; Ernie Chabot, S 1-Oc 13, 1939; Wilburn Alurd DeWolfe, Oc 20, 1939-Je 22, 1945. Ed. by Randolph E. Matthews, Oc 20, 1939-Je 22, 1945. Pub. by R.E. Matthews, Je 29, 1945-1961; Vera Matthews, Ap 5, 1962-Oc 7, 1965; Raymond E. Matthews, Oc 14, 1965-F? 1976; Monte G. Keith, Sedgewick Community Press, F 18? 1976-Ap 1981; Rick Truss, My 1981+
Alberta Golden Jubilee Edition, N 3, 1955.
Ref.: **DAL** p.60.

AEP   mf S 23, 1916-D 16, 1986
         or Ja 1987+

17   *Argus.* 1920//
        w.

Pub. by the merchants in Alliance in opposition to *Alliance Times* (Ref.: ALC pp.127-128).
Ref.: **CAN** 1921.

No issues located

ALTARIO

18   *Arrow.* 1919//
        w.

Arrow Pub. Co., pubs. (Ref.: **MK** 1920). Ed. by J.A. Seabury (Ref.: **CPP** v28no12 D 1918).

No issues located

19   *Recorder.* 1921-1923?//
        w.

Pub. by F.M. Tarr, 1921-1922; G.W. McLeod, 1922-1923 (Ref.: **MK** 1922, 1923; **CAN** 1924).

No issues located

AMISK

20   *Amisk Advocate.* Mr 11, 1921-Mr 28 1951//
        w.

Amalgamated with *Hughenden Record* (636.3) (Ref.: **PUB** v32no710 Ap/My 1951).
Suspended S 13, 1945-Ag 22, 1946.
Place of pub. varies: Hughenden, 1921-1931; Hardisty, 1931-1945; Killam, 1946-1949; Edmonton, 1949-1951.
Pub. by H.W. Betts, 1921-S 13, 1945; Thomas William Pue, Community Publications of Alberta, Ag 22, 1946-Mr 28, 1951.

Ref.: **CAN** 1953; **AY** 1952.

AEP   or   Mr 11-D 30, 1921; My 5, 1922-S 13, 1945; Ag 22, 1946-
Mr 28, 1951

ANDREW

21   *Weekly Advance.* 1931//
w.

Pub. and ed. by Mr. S. Stewart, C.P.R. agent in Andrew (Ref.: **AND** p.67).

No issues located

22.1   *Andrew News.* D 6, 1934-Ja 11, 1935/...
w.

Pub. and ed. by Thomas Tomashevsky, Economy Printing Co., Edmonton.
Ref.: **AND** p.68; **MK** 1935, 1936; **MARU** pp.485-486.

22.2   *District Press.* Ja 19, 1935-1946?//
w.

"Successor to *Andrew News.* Published weekly in interest of towns along
Edmonton-Lloydminster C.P.R. Line" (Ap 26, 1940).

AEU   mf   N 19, 1937
AEPAA   or   Ap 26, 1940, Jl 11, 1941 (75.74/1301)
AEP   or   Ag 1-D 12, 1941; F 13, Je 12, 1942.

23   *Andrew Advocate.* My 1951-Ja 31, 1953//
w.

Pub. and ed. by Thomas W. Pue, Community Publications of Alberta,
Edmonton.

AEP   or   Je 23, 1951-Ja 31, 1953

ARROWWOOD

Bow River News. 1927-?//
See Supplement (1045).

24   *Bow Valley Resource.* Ag 20, 1931-D 3, 1936//
w.

Pub. and ed. by Norman G. Cary and his son Floyd. N.G. Cary moved the
plant to Bassano and started the *Bassano Recorder* (59).
Ref.: **CAN** 1938; **FUR** p.71.

AEP   or   Ag 20, 1931-D 3, 1936.

ATHABASCA

25
    Northern Light. N 28, 1908-D 26? 1908//
    w.

    Pub. at Athabasca Landing by Rev. F.W. Moxhay (Ref.: **LAN** p.15; *Northern News*, Athabasca, Ja 7, 1909).

    AEPAA or N 28, D 12, 1908 (71.419)
    AEEA   or D 5, 1908 (MS 133)

26
    Northern News. Ja 7, 1909-F? 1916//
    w.

    Succeeded by *Athabasca Herald* (28).
    Suspended pub. Ag 14-N 18, 1910; about F, 1916 suspended pub. due to depression (Ref.: **CPP** v25no3 Mr 1916).
    Pub. by Northern News Printing and Pub. Co., Ja 7, 1909-Ag 1910. Ed. by J.C. Macquarrie, Ja 7, 1909-Ag 13, 1910; Fred M. Watt, mgr. Pub. by Robert F. Truss, Northern News Co. Ltd., N 19, 1910-Ag 31, 1912; John M. Millar, S 7, 1912-My 2, 1913; H.S. French, My 9, 1913-Ap 17, 1914; A.M. Nicol F 6, 1914-F? 1916.
    Ref.: **CAN** 1917.

    AEP   mf Ja 7, 1909-D 31, 1915

27
    Athabasca Times. My 14, 1913-1915?//
    w.

    Pub. and ed. by R.W. Bruce, Athabasca Times Co. Ltd., My 14-Jl 10, 1913; E.A. Blow, Jl 17-D 4, 1913; A.M. Nicol, D 11, 1913-Ja 15, 1914.
    Ref.: **CAN** 1915.

    AEP   mf My 14, 1913-S 4, 1914

28
    Athabasca Herald. S 21? 1916-1919?//
    w.

    Succeeded *Northern News* (26) (Ref.: **CPP** v25no11 N 1916).
    Ed. by Robert F. Truss; George Mills, bus. mgr.
    Ref.: **CAN** 1919.

    AEP   mf Oc 12, 1916-D 13, 1917

29
    Athabasca Herald. Ap 30, 1920-Mr 19, 1921//
    w.

    Pub. and ed. by H. Oxley.

    AEP   mf Ap 30, 1920-Mr 19, 1921

30.1
    Athabasca Echo. Jl 12, 1928-D 30, 1970/...
    w.

30.2   *Athabasca Echo and Slave Lake Centennial Press.* Ja 6, 1971-Ap
          12, 1978/...
          w.

30.3   *Athabasca Echo.* Ap 19, 1978-Jl 15, 1986//
          w.

          Absorbed *Slave Lake Centennial Press* (900), Ja 6, 1971.
          Suspended S 26, 1941-Ap 3, 1942; Ap 17-Je 5, 1942.
          Pub. and ed. by William Conquest, Jl 12, 1928-Ap 17, 1942; Byron
          Webster (Bart) Bellamy, Jl 1, 1942-Ap 16, 1954; Evelyn Rogers, My 7,
          1954-Ap 5, 1978; Robert W. MacGregor, Ap 12, 1978-Jl 15, 1986.
          Alberta Golden Jubilee Edition, Ag 26, 1955.

          AEP   mf   Jl 12, 1928-D 30, 1981
                       or   Ja

31   *Athabasca Advance.* Ja 2, 1956-Je 5, 1957//
          w.

          Pub. and ed. by Thomas W. Pue, Sun Pub. Co., Edmonton.

          AEP   mf   Ja 2, 1956-Je 5, 1957

32   *Athabasca Call.* Ap 12, 1975-My 21, 1977//
          w.

          Pub. by Thomas W. Pue, Sun Colorpress Ltd., Edmonton. Ed. by Ken
          Coach, Ap 30-My 1977.

          AEP   mf   Ap 17, 1976-My 21, 1977.

33   *Advocate.* Oc 6, 1982-
          w.

          Pub. and ed. by James (Jiggs) Geisinger. Pub. and printed by Barrhead
          Printers and Stationers Ltd. (Ref.: Correspondence with Publisher, S 12,
          1984).

          No issues located

BANFF

34   *Hot Springs Record.* Je 21, 1887//
          w.

          One issue published. Intended to be pub. as a weekly.
          Pub. by William Findlay & Co., Calgary. Ed. by Mr. Newman, an ex-
          railroad conductor (Ref.: *Banff Crag and Canyon* D 14, 1923; F 19, 1958).
          Ref.: **ABA** M 241.

          ABA   or   Je 21, 1887.

35   *National Park Life.* Ap 1888-F 1889//
          w.

Oc 19, 1888 issue entitled *Mountain Echoes,* pub. by Charles B. Halpin and ed. by John C. Innes.
Pub. by Charles B. Halpin. Burned out in less than a year after starting. Revived by John C. Innes, but ceased after a few issues (Ref.: *Banff Crag and Canyon* D 14, 1923). The *Calgary Herald,* F 27, 1889, reported the *Mountain Echoes* was burned out the previous week.

ACG   or   My 3, Oc 19, 1888

56.1   *Banff Echoes.* Ap 1893-Je? 1893/...
w.

56.2   *Rocky Mountain Echoes.* Je 17? 1893-? 1893//
w.

Weekly newspaper devoted to social topics, literature, and general news. Ed. by photographer W. Hanson Boorne.

ACG   or   Ap, Je 17, 1893

57   *National Park Gazette.* Ap 26, 1900-D 25, 1900?//
w., m.

Pub. and ed. by Ike Byers, Ap 26, My 5, 1900. (Ref.: *Banff Crag and Canyon* D 14, 1923); suspended for the summer months. Purchased by Dr. Whyte. (Ref.: *Kicking Horse Chronicle* Ja 26, 1962 ABA M70f63).
Next issue to be a monthly magazine (S 29, 1900).

ABA   or   Ap 26, My 5 1900
ACG   or   Ap 26-S 29, 1900

58.1   *Crag and Canyon.* D 8, 1900-My 27, 1901/...
w.

58.2   *Crag and Canyon and National Park Gazette.* Je 3, 1901-S 27, 1902/...
w.

58.3   *Crag and Canyon.* My 2, 1903-N 14, 1957/...
w.

58.4   *Banff Crag and Canyon.* N 20, 1957-
w.

Suspended publication during winter months (S-My) from 1900 to 1923 except for the period My 4, 1912-S 1918 when pub. year-round. Began continuous pub. My 5, 1923.
Suspended pub. D 12, 1941-F 27, 1942; My 12-Je 23, 1944.
Pub. by Norman K. Luxton, D 8, 1900-Jl 1, 1951. Luxton leased the newspaper to a number of eds. and mgrs., including: R.J. Burde, 1903; Will H. Kidner, Ap 1905-S 1906, My 1909-Ap 1913, Oc 1927-Mr 1928; E.J. Brabyn,

My 1907-S 1908; P.W. Stone, Ag 1917-S 1918; W.F. Stanley, My 1920-Je
1923; C.W. Barnes, Jl 1923-Mr 1925; Victor W.R.B. Ball, Ap-S 1925, F
1942-N 1943; Leonard C. Newsom, N 1925-Jl 1927; Norman T.J. Frost, Mr-
Ag 1928; E.S. Duncan, Ag 1928-Mr 1938; N.L. Duncan, Ag 1938-Je 1940;
Frank S.Leska, Je 1940-Mr 1941; Percy B. Stead, Mr-Oc 1941; Stephen
Dillingham, Oc-D 1941; Tom C. Mewburn, D 1943-D 1944; Lin Spiller, Je
1944-Je 1951. Sold Jl 1, 1951 to William I. Clark, pub., Jl 1951-Oc 1957.
Sold N 1, 1957 to W.B. (Bill) McCusker, pub., N 1957-Mr 1974. Sold Mr 15,
1974 to Pat and Stephanie Boswell, Banff Crag and Canyon Ltd., pub., Mr
15, 1974+
    Ref.: **DAL** p.62; *Banff Crag and Canyon* My 2, 1956.

AEP   mf D 8, 1900-D 1983
           or 1984+

39   *Climber.* Je 23, 1906//
    w.

    Pub. and ed. by W.H. Footner (Ref.: *Calgary Herald*, d. ed. Jl 4, 1906).
    Ref.: Archives of the Canadian Rockies M 417, f.1.

ABA   or Je 23, 1906

40   *Rocky Mountain Courier.* Ap 1914-Oc 11, 1918//
    w.

    Superceded by *Banff Advocate and Rocky Mountain District Recorder*
    (41).
    Pub. by Robert W. Lipsett and Robert Campbell, 1914 (Ref.: *Kicking
    Horse Chronicles* Ja 19, 1962). Ed. by P.W. Stone until Je 19, 1915. Went
    defunct in Mr 1916 and was taken over by Brewster Transport Ltd. in Ap
    1916. Ed. by Thomas G. Jenkyns, 1916-1918.
    Ref.: **HART** pp.61-63.

AEP   mf Ap 19, 1915; Ja 5, 1917-Oc 11, 1918

41   *Banff Advocate and Rocky Mountains Park District Recorder.*
    N? 1918-1922//
    w.

    Superceded *Rocky Mountain Courier* (40).
    Incorporated with *Rocky Mountain Courier* (42).
    Plant was bought from the Brewster Transport Co. when the *Rocky
    Mountain Courier* (40) went defunct in Oc 1918. Pub. and ed. by Thomas G.
    Jenkyns.
    Ref.: **CAN** 1922; **HART** p.63.

AEP   mf Ja 17, My 23, 30, Je 13, S 12, 19, 26, Oc 3, 1919; Ap 2, 1920

42   *Rocky Mountain Courier.* Ja 20, 1922-Mr 3, 1922?//
    w.

    Subtitle: "With Which is Incorporated the Banff Advocate and Rocky
    Mountains Park District Recorder."

Continued voluming of *Rocky Mountain Courier* (40).
Pub. and ed. by Thomas G. Jenkyns.

AEU   mf Ja 20-Mr 3, 1922

3   *Banff Mercury.* My 3, 1928-Oc 18, 1928?//
w.

Pub. by Banff Printing Presses. Ed. by Will H. Kidner; Victor W.R.B. Ball, bus. mgr.
Lasted less than a year. (Ref.: *Banff Crag and Canyon* Mr 5, 1943).

AEP   mf My 10-Ag 23, Oc 4-18, 1928

4   *Banff News.* 1929-1951?//
w.; m.

Pub. by T.V. and C. Papers of Alberta, Edmonton to 1940, and Wade Papers of Alberta, Calgary, 1940-1951 (Ref.: **MK** 1937-1942).

AEP   mf Ap 24-Oc 24, 1930; Mr 30, 1931; D 1939; Ja 1944; Mr 1951

5   *Banff Summit News.* Oc 5, 1967-S 30, 1970//
w.

Pub by Herb Hildebrandt, Jim Achenbach, Jack Gorman. Ed. by Jack Gorman.

ACG   or Oc 5, 12, 1967
ABA   or Oc 5, 1967-S 30, 1970

6   *Mountain Merchandiser.* 1968-?//
w.

No information available regarding pub. or ed.

ABA   or F 22-My 2, 1968

7   *Scree.* Jl 16, 1971-Ag 12, 1971?//
w.

Ed. by Brian Morgan.

ABA   or Jl 16-Ag 12, 1971

BARONS

Barons Beacon. Oc 13, 1909-?//
See Supplement (1046)

8   *Barons Enterprise.* S 12, 1911-Je 20, 1912?//
w.

Printed in Claresholm, by *Claresholm Review*, S 12-D, 1911.
Pub. by Harwood Duncan, S 12, 1911-Je 1912; ed. by K.D. Duncan, Ja 11-Je 1912.

AEP   or   S 12, 1911-Je 20, 1912

49   *Barons Weekly.* 1918?//
        w.

        Satellite of Calgary Western Standard (142.5). (Ref.: **CPP** v28no5 My
        1918). Pub. by Standard Newspaper Syndicate, Calgary (Ref.: **MK** 1918;
        CAN 1919).

        No issues located

50   *Barons Globe.* Jl? 1919-Ag 4, 1921?//
        w.

        Pub. by G.A. Dunning, 1919-Mr 4, 1920; ed. by Vin. C. Dunning, 1919-
        Oc 16, 1920. Leased to C. Hermanson, ed., Mr 11, 1920-Jl 3, 1921. G.A.
        Dunning, prop., Jl 15-Jl 29? 1921; James Mewhort, prop., Ag 4, 1921.
        Issue of Ag 4, 1921 reported that the former publisher had just moved the
        operation to Carmangay where the paper was being produced with difficulty.
        Ref.: **MK** 1921; **CAN** 1923.

        AEP   or   Ag 13, 1920-Ag 4, 1921

BARRHEAD

51   *Barrhead News.* S? 1927-F 26, 1931?//
        w.

        Pub. and ed. by Edward Brice, S? 1927-S 27? 1928. Pub. by William Wor-
        ton, Oc 4? 1928-F 1931. Ed. by H.H. Rumball, Oc 4?-N 15, 1928; Mrs. C.N.
        Bateman, N 22, 1928-Ap 3, 1930; J.C. McCaig, Ap 10, 1930-F 1931.

        AEP   mf   Mr 1, 1928-F 26, 1931

52.1   *Barrhead Leader.* Ap 21, 1932-Ja 29, 1969/...
        w.

52.2   *Leader.* F 5, 1969-Oc 5, 1976/...
        w.

52.3   *Barrhead Leader.* Oc 12, 1976-
        w.

        Absorbed *Bulletin* (53), Barrhead, Ap 1, 1964.
        Pub. and ed. by W.C.R. Garrioch, Ap 1932-Je 1, 1939; A.E. Larkins and
        Son, Je 8, 1939-Oc 5, 1960; E.A. (Ed) Larkins, Oc 12, 1960-Ja 29, 1969;
        Barrhead Printers and Stationers Ltd., pub., F 5, 1969+ Ed. by Ed P.
        Hornsby, F 5-Oc 22, 1969; Gina Nisbet, N 12, 1969-Mr 28, 1972; James
        Geisinger, Ap 4, 1972-Ja 1976; Barry Marshall, Mr 2-Jl 20, 1976; Jan
        Michaud, Jl 27, 1976-Jl 4, 1978; James Geisinger, Jl 11, 1978-F 10, 1981;
        Terry Clements, F 17-Oc 5, 1981; Phil Rutherford, Ja 26-Oc 27, 1982; Al
        Blackmere, N 10, 1982+

Pub. section entitled *North of the Athabasca*. ed. by Gary A. Utas, N 1, 1967-F 28, 1968.

50th Anniversary of Barrhead Edition, Je 28, 1977.

AEP　　　mf　Je 16, 1932-D 21, 1976
　　　　　　　　or　Ja 4, 1977+

53　　　　*Bulletin*. My 3? 1961-Mr 1964//
　　　　　w.

Sold to and absorbed by *Barrhead Leader* (52.1), Ap 1, 1964.
Pub. by Ed P. Hornsby.
Ref.: **CNLU** p.1.

OONL　　or　Jl 12, 1961

54　　　　*Barrhead Star*. My 15, 1971-My 14? 1977//
　　　　　w.

Title varied: *Barrhead County Star*.
Pub. by Thomas W. Pue, Sun Colorpress Ltd., Edmonton.
Ref.: **CAN** 1977.

OONL　　or　My 15, 1971
AEP　　　mf　F 2, 1974-D 31, 1975

BASHAW

55　　　　*Bashaw Record*. My 19, 1911-F? 1913//
　　　　　w.

S.C. Andrews, Alix, owner; J.C. Mundy, mgr. (Ref.: **CPP** v20no8 Ag, 1911).

Had a short lease of life and is now no more (Ref.: **CPP** v22no3 Mr 1913).

AEP　　　or　My 19, 1911-Jl 5, 1912

56.1　　　*Bashaw Star*. My 7, 1915-Mr 25, 1959/...
　　　　　w.

56.2　　　*Bashaw Star and the Alix Promoter*. Ap 1, 1959-Oc 9, 1963/...
　　　　　w.

56.3　　　*Bashaw Star and Alix Promoter*. Oc 16, 1963-Ap 19, 1972/...
　　　　　w.

56.4　　　*Bashaw Star*. Ap 26, 1972-Ag 1, 1973/...
　　　　　w.

56.5   *Bashaw Star and Alix Promoter.* Ag 8, 1973-My 4, 1977/...
        w.

56.6   *Bashaw Star.* My 11, 1977-
        w.

        Amalgamated with *Alix Promoter* (15), Ap 1, 1959 to form *Bashaw Star
        and Alix Promoter* (56.2).
        Pub. and ed. by Charles A. Roulston, My 7, 1915-Mr 30, 1916; Charles H.
        Leathley, Ap 1-? 1916; George W. Armstrong,? 1916-F 28, 1918; R.S.
        Burns, Mr 7, 1918-My 30, 1929; Melville Leathley, Je 1, 1929-Mr 15, 1939;
        T.M. Brinsmead, Mr 22, 1939-Oc 2, 1957; W.R. (Ronnie) Newsom, Oc 15,
        1957-Ag 1, 1973; Elmer R. Schroeder, Ag 1, 1973-My 26, 1982; Alan R.
        Willis, Stettler Independent Management Ltd., Je 9-Jl 7, 1982; Pamela
        Webb, Stettler Independent Management Ltd., Jl 14, 1982+ Ed. by Lucy
        Barnes, Jl 14, 1982+

        AEP   or My 7, 1915-Ap 13, 1916; Ap 5, 1917-Je 24, 1925; Ja 13,
                1926+

BASSANO

57   *Bassano News.* Ap 1, 1910-Mr 11, 1914?//
        w. Political — Liberal

        Pub. by William Bleasdell Cameron, Ap 1, 1910-Ap 28, 1911; Leonard D.
        Nesbitt, My 5, 1911-Ap 11, 1912; J.R. Sharp, Ap 18, 1912-Oc 2, 1913; Harry
        G. Myser, Oc 19-Oc 23, 1913; John S. Brooks, Liberal, D 10, 1913-Mr 11,
        1914.
        Ref.: CAN 1914.

        AEP   or Ap 1, 1910-Mr 11, 1914

58   *Bassano Mail.* Oc 16? 1913-Ap 27, 1936//
        w.

        Pub. and ed. by J.R. Sharp, Oc 1913-F 19, 1914; L.M. Graham, F 26-Mr
        19, 1914; C.H.C. Ruffee, Mr 26-My 7, 1914; H.S. Cameron, My 11-Ag 13,
        1914; Bert J. Klebe, Ag 20-S 3, 1914; Rae Livingstone King, S 10, 1914-Je
        24, 1915; P.W. Stone, Je 30, 1915-My 24, 1917; E.G. Allen, My 31, 1917-Oc
        28, 1920; Leonard D. Nesbitt, N 1, 1920-Oc 31, 1926; Wallace J. Smith, N 1,
        1926-Ag 30, 1934; Clive B. Nesbitt and James L. Nesbitt, S 1, 1934-Ag 27,
        1936.
        Ref.: Correspondence with Publisher, Ja 3, 1985.

        AEP   or D 11, 1913; Ja 1, 1914-Ap 20, 1916; N 2, 1916-D 21, 1921; Ja
                13, 1927-Je 25, 1936

59   *Bassano Recorder.* Ja 14, 1937-Je 21, 1945//
        w.

        Suspended pub. D? 1942-N 11, 1943.

Pub. by Norman G. Cary, Ja 14, 1937-F 17, 1938; Floyd T. Cary, Mr 3, 1938-F 20, 1941; A. Kent Smalley, F 27-Jl 31, 1941; J.B. Robertson, Ag 7, 1941-D 1942; C.J. Flett, N 11, 1943-Je 21, 1945.

ACG   or Je 21, 1945
AEP   or Ja 14, 1937-N 13, 1941; Ja 8-N 19, 1942; N 11, 1943-Je 14, 1945

50   *Bassano Star.* 1946-1947?//
      w.?

Pub. and ed. by C.B. (Barney) Halpin, Jr. (Ref.: Black Diamond *Flare*, Oc 25, 1946; Correspondence with Publisher, *Brooks Bulletin*, Ja 3, 1985).

No issues located

51   *Bassano Herald.* N 23, 1955-1959?//
      w.

Pub. and ed. by Hugh Pearce.
Ref.: **CNLU**, p.2.

OONL   or N 23, 1955; Ja 4, Mr 15, 1956

52   *Bassano Times.* Ja 28, 1960-
      w.

Pub. by Irrigano Publishers Ltd., 1960-My 27, 1981; Mary Lou Brooks, Bassano Publishers, Je 1, 1981+ Ed. by John H. Bacon, 1960-D 15, 1965; Gordon N. Manning, 1960-Ap 30, 1975; Donald Cozzubbo, My 1, 1975-Je 9, 1976; Vic Toth, Je 16, 1976-My 27, 1981.

OONL   or Ja 28, Mr 2, 1960
AEP   or Ja 10, 1962+

BAWLF

53   *Bawlf Sun.* Ag 16, 1907-Oc 25, 1907?//
      w.

Superceded by *Bawlf Sun.* (64).
Pub. by B.A. Scovil.
Ref.: *Community Press*, Sedgewick, Ap 17, 1930.

AEP   or S 13-Oc 25, 1907

54   *Bawlf Sun.* Ja 2, 1908-Ap? 1930//
      w.

Superceded *Bawlf Sun* (63). Due to economic depression *Sedgewick Sentinel* (890.1) amalgamated Ap 17, 1930 with *Bawlf Sun* (64), *Daysland Press* (302), *Hardisty Mail* (608), *Killam News* (659), *Lougheed Express* (711) and *Strome Despatch* (941) to form *Community Press* (890.2), Sedgewick (Ref.: **SED** p.621).

Suspended pub. D 22, 1911-F 2, 1912 probably due to fire which destroyed building. Thereafter pub. in Killam (Ref.: *Bawlf Sun*, F 9, 1912).
Pub. and ed. by A.L. Eastly.
Ref.: **CAN** 1931.

AEP   or   Mr 5, 1908-D 22, 1911; F 2, 1912-Je 26, 1925; Ja 1, 1926-D 21, 1928

65   *Bawlf Banner.* Mr 20, 1947-N 30, 1949?//
w.

Pub. by Thomas W. Pue, Community Publications of Alberta, Edmonton.

AEP   or   Mr 20, 1947-N 30, 1949

BEAVERLODGE

66   *Advertiser.* D 6, 1956-
w.

Title varies: *Beaverlodge Advertiser.*
First regular issue appeared D 6, 1956. Prior to that written and mimeographed by Dr. McGill. Pub. by P.G. Harris, 1956-1959; Trevor Harris, 1959+ (Ref.: Correspondence with Publisher, N 28, 1984).

AEP   or   Ja 14, 1976-N 24, 1982

BEISEKER

67   *Recorder.* D 28, 1922-1924?//
w.

Pub. by The Recorder, 523 Centre St., Calgary (Ref.: **MK** 1922-1924).

No issues located

68   *Beiseker Times.* Mr? 1949-Ag 18, 1953//
w.

Pub. by Thomas W. Pue, Community Publications of Alberta and Sun Pub. Co. Ltd., Edmonton.

AEP   or   My 7, 1949-Ag 18, 1953

Five Village Weekly. N 6, 1975-D 30? 1980
See **ROCKY VIEW MUNICIPAL DISTRICT.** *Rocky View-Five Village Weekly* (862).

BELLEVUE

69   *Bellevue Times.* S 22, 1910-Je 28, 1918?//
w.

Same text as *Blairmore Times* (77) with minor variations concerning local news.
First issue, S 22, 1910, entitled *Bellevue Times and Frank Vindicator.*
Pub. and ed. by J.D.S. Barrett and W.J. Bartlett, Blairmore.
Ref.: **MK** 1911, 1913, 1917, 1918.

AEP   or   S 22, 1910-Je 28, 1918

BEVERLY

Incorporated as a village My 22, 1913, and as a town Ag 5, 1914.
Incorporated with Edmonton in 1961.
See **EDMONTON** for newspapers serving Beverly prior to incorporation:

Beverly Advertiser (373)
Beverly Page (440)
Olde Towne Crier (471)

BIG VALLEY

70   *Big Valley News.* N 9, 1916-Je 8, 1923?//
w.

Pub by News Pub. Co. Pub. by Henry Oke, N 9, 1916-Ag 1920; A.E. Birtwistle, S 1920-Je 1923.
Ref.: **MK** 1918-1923; **CAN** 1924.

AEP   or   N 9, 1916-Je 8, 1923

71   *Times.* 1923-1924//
w.

Pub. by Stewart Fullerton (Ref.: *Didsbury Pioneer* Mr 19, 1924; **MK** 1924; **CAN** 1925).

No issues located

72   *Journal.* Oc 15, 1924-Ag 30, 1934?//
w.

Pub. and ed. by W.J. Good.
Ref.: **MK** 1925-1934; **CAN** 1935.

AEP   or   Oc 15, 1924-Ag 30, 1934

BLACK DIAMOND

News. N 8, 1929-Oc 2, 1931
See **TURNER VALLEY.** *Tri-City Observer.* (975).

73   *Flare.* My 6, 1937-Oc 25, 1946//
w.

Continued by *Oilfields Flare,* Turner Valley (976).
Pub. by C.B. (Barney) Halpin, Jr. Ed. by Jack Lee, My 6, 1937-S 29, 1939.
Served the oilfields including "Little Chicago" and "Little New York".
Halpin went on to start the *Bassano Star* (60) when the *Flare* ceased pub.
Ref.: **SHE** p.92.

AEP   or   My 6, 1937-Oc 25, 1946

BLACKFALDS

74   *Blackfalds Mercury.* My 1903-? 1903//
w.

Pub. and ed. by Percy B. Gregson (Ref.: **MEE** p.161).

No issues located

BLACKIE

75   *Blackie Recorder.* 1921-?//
w.

Ref.: **CAN** 1922.

No issues located

BLAIRMORE

76   *Times.* 1903-1911?//
w.

Pub. and ed. by Harry J. Matheson (Ref.: **MK** 1905, 1907-1911;
Blairmore Graphic Ag 2, 1946).

No issues located

77.1
         Blairmore Enterprise and Frank Vindicator, N 25, 1909-S 22,
         1910/...
w.

77.2   *Blairmore Enterprise.* S 29, 1910-Jl 26, 1946//
w.

Succeeded by *Blairmore Graphic* (83) (Ref.: **COU** p.128)
Pub. and ed. by J.D.S. Barrett and J.A. McDonald, Foothills Job Print and
News. Co., N 25, 1909-F 24, 1910; W.J. Bartlett, Bartlett Pub. Co., Mr 3-Ag
11, 1910; W.J. Bartlett and J.D.S. Barrett, Ag 18, 1910-Jl 14, 1912; W.J.
Bartlett, Jl 11, 1912-Jl 26, 1946.

AEP   mf N 25, 1909-Jl 26, 1946

8   *Slovenské Slovo / Slovak Word.* My 1910-1911//
irreg. Slovak in Slov.

Pub. by Andrew Lukča and ed. by George Klesken (Ref.: **GEL**, p.118).
First Slovak newspaper in Canada (Ref.: **KIRS** p.288).
Ref.: **CNLC** p.270.

No issues located

9   *Pass Herald.* 1930-
w.

New series of voluming began in 1952; reverted back to original
sequence in 1977.
Est. and pub. by O.A. Botter, 1930-1952; Trevor H. Slopak, 1952-1977.
Sold to Gail Sygutek, pub., 1977+ Ed. by Slopak, 1977+ (Ref.: Publisher).

AEP   mf My 10, 1972-D, 1984
      or Ja, 1985+

0   *Hlas Národa / Voice of the Nation.* 1932-1934//
irreg. Slovak in Slov.

Pub. and ed. by George Klesken (Ref.: **KIRS** p.291).
Included supplement *Naša Mládež (Our Youth)* (Ref.: **CES 1** p.66).

No issues located

1   *Pass Daily Herald.* 1933-1934?//
d.

Mimeographed.
Pub. by Walter Tiberg (Ref.: **MK** 1934).

No issues located

2   *Slovenské Slovo / Slovak Word.* 1940//
irreg. Slovak in Slov.

Pub. and ed. by George Klesken. This was the third and last attempt at
publishing a Slovak newspaper in the Canadian west (Ref.: **KIRS** p.292).
Ref.: **CNLC** p.270

No issues located

3   *Blairmore Graphic.* Ag 2, 1946-1951?//
w.

Succeeded *Blairmore Enterprise* (77) (Ref.: **COU** p.127).
Pub. and ed. by J.R. McLeod.
Ref.: **COU** p.197; **CAN** 1952.

AEP   mf Ag 2, 1946-D 21, 1948

84.1   *Pass Promoter.* F 14, 1973-Ag 16, 1978/...
          w.

84.2   *Promoter.* Ag 23, 1978-Ag 20, 1980/...
          w.

84.3   *Pass Promoter.* Ag 27, 1980-
          w.

          Pub. and ed. by Richard Gillis, Promoter Press Ltd., 1973-Ag 5, 1981;
          Edward Moser, Crowsnest Communications Ltd., Ag 6, 1981+
              Ref.: CNLU, p.2.

          OONL   or   F 14, 1973
          AEP   mf Ja 7, 1976-1984
                     or   1985+

BON ACCORD

85   *Bon Accord Herald.* Jl 1, 1935-Ja 1, 1938//
          2m.

              Mimeographed.
              Pub. and ed. by 12-year-old Eddie Arrol.
              Ref.: *Edmonton Journal* Ja 2, 1937.

          ACG   photocopy Mr 29, 1936-Ja 1, 1938 (BB.4.B697)
          AEPAA   photocopy Oc 6, 1937 (67.298/11)

BONNYVILLE

86   *Bonnyville Nouvelle.* My 18, 1935-Jl 17, 1943?//
          w.

              Suspended pub. D 13, 1941-Ja 9, 1942.
              Pub. and ed. by John W. Johnston, My 16, 1935-Ag 10, 1940; Gertrude
              Johnston, Ag 17, 1940-Mr, 1942; Frank A. Lambert, Ap 4, 1942-Mr 13,
              1943; St. Paul Journal Ltd., St. Paul, Mr 20-Jl 17, 1943.

          AEP   or   Je 1, 1935-Jl 17, 1943

87.1   *Bonnyville Tribune.* My 30, 1947-Je 15, 1960/...
          w. Engl. (and Fr.)

87.2   *Tribune.* Je 22, 1960-My 30, 1962/...
          w.

87.3   *Bonnyville Tribune.* Je 9, 1962-F 29, 1964/...
          w.

57.4 *New Bonnyville Tribune.* Mr 7, 1964-Oc 19, 1968//
w.

Amalgamated with *Grand Centre Times* (579), and *Cold Lake Courier* (285) to form *Tribune,* Bonnyville (87.2), Je 22, 1960.
Pub. and ed. by Ovi and Denise Baril. Sold Je 1962 to Thomas W. Pue, Sun Pub. Co. Ltd., Edmonton.

AEP   mf My 30, 1947-Oc 19, 1968

58 *Bonnyville Newscope.* F 1964-Ap 1964//
w.

Pub. and ed. by L.H. Drouin (Ref.: Correspondence with Publisher, Ap 6, 1984).
Ref.: *Edmonton Journal,* My 2, 1964.

No issues located

59.1 *Bonnyville Nouvelle.* Mr 1, 1967-D 20, 1977/...
w.

59.2 *Bonnyville Nouvelle, Grand Centre Globe.* Ja 3, 1978-Mr 11, 1980/...
w.

59.3 *Bonnyville Nouvelle.* Mr 18, 1980-
w.

Pub. by Manfred Kronert. Ed. by Karl Mueller, Mr 1, 1967-Mr 31, 1978; Mansoor Ladha, My 23, 1978-Jl 8, 1980; Daniel Johns, Jl 15, 1980+
Pub. supplement *Grand Centre Globe* Ap 23, 1974-D 20, 1977.

AEP   or My 2, 1972+

BOW CITY

Bow City Star. S? 1913-? 1914//
See Supplement (1047)

BOW ISLAND

60 *Bow Island Review.* Je 25, 1910-1936?//
w.

Printed initially in Bow Island, then in Taber, Alta.
Pub. by W.P. Cotton, Je 25, 1910-D 20, 1918; Charles Avery, D 27, 1918-1936?
Ref.: **CAN** 1936.

AEP   or Je 25, 1910-Je 1, 1923

91   *Bow Island News.* Ag 31, 1954-1956//
      w.

      Ref.: **CNLU** p.3.

      OONL   or   Ag 31, D 14, 1954

92   *Graphic.* Jl? 1956-My 27, 1960//
      w.

      Superceded by *Graphic,* Bow Island (93).
      Pub. by Max Hamilton. Sold to *Medicine Hat News* (743), My 1960.

      AEP   or   Je 6, 1957-My 27, 1960

93   *Graphic* Je 9, 1960-My 3, 1962//
      w.

      Superceded *Graphic,* Bow Island (92).
      Pub. by *Medicine Hat News.* Ed. by Harold L. Gunderson.

      AEP   or   Je 9, 1960-My 3, 1962

      40-Mile County Commentator. Ag 18, 1971-
      See **FORTY MILE COUNTY.** *40-Mile County Commentator.* (563).

BOWDEN

94   *Bowden Reporter.* 1905?-Oc 1906?//
      w.

      Ref.: **CAN** 1906, 1907.

      No issues located.

95   *Bowden News.* Jl 30? 1909-Oc 24, 1912//
      w.

      Pub. by Fred L. Harris, News Pub. Co., Charles A. Hayden, ed. 1909-Jl 7,
      1910; F.H. Schooley, Jl 14, 1910-Ap 18, 1912; Leonard C. Newsom, Ap 25-
      Oc 24, 1912. Ed. by H.H. McKim, Jl 14, 1910-Ap 18, 1912.

      AEP   or   Ag 13, 1909-Oc 24, 1912

96   *Bowden Recorder.* 1920-?//
      w.

      Ref.: **CAN** 1921.

      No issues located

97   *Bowden Times.* Mr 12? 1923-1924?//
      w.

      Ed. by S.J. Clotworthy.

Ref.: CAN 1925

ABOM or Ap 12, 1923; [Oc 2, 1924]

8 *Bowden Booster.* F? 1937-Oc? 1938//
w.

Ed. by Lloyd Thompson.
Ref.: CAN 1938; CPP v47no11 N 1938.

ABOM or Mr 2, 1938-Mr 9, 1938

9 *Bowden Eye Opener.* Oc 6, 1976-
w.

Pub. by Ivan Raymond Warren and Alisdair F. Hamilton, Bowden Printers
Ltd. Ed. by Patricia Warren.
Ref.: *Advocate* Red Deer, F 20, 1980; *Calgary Herald* Je 24, 1980;
Bowden Eye Opener Oc 8, 1980.

AEP or Ja 24, Ag 22, 1979+

BOWNESS

Formerly a town, now a suburb of Calgary. Prior to 1942, the community
was called Critchley, then it took the name of Bowness and was incorporated
as a village in 1948. Four years later it became a town, but lost its identity in
the mid-1960s when it was incorporated into the city of Calgary. (Ref.:
Mardon, E.G. *Community Names of Alberta.* Lethbridge: University of
Lethbridge, 1973 p.39).
See **CALGARY** for papers serving Bowness prior to incorporation:

Beacon (189)
Bow Valley Advertiser (190)
Bowness Bulletin (1049.1)
Bowness News (1049.2)
Bowness Review (1050)

BOYLE

00.1 *Boyle Beacon.* 1949-N 16, 1968/...
w.

00.2 *Athabasca Sun.* N 23, 1968-Ja 18, 1969//
w.

Boyle Beacon absorbed by *Lac La Biche Herald* (662.2), My 11? 1963.
Continued as *Boyle Beacon* on Je 29, 1963.
Suspended pub. My 11?-Je 29, 1963.
Pub. by Thomas W. Pue, Sun Pub. Co. Ltd., Edmonton.
Alberta Golden Jubilee Edition, Ag 31, 1955.

AEP   or   Ja 16, 1952-Ja 18, 1969 (N 23, 1968-Ja 18, 1969 filed with
           Alberta Country Life (442)).

101   *Boyle Star.* Jl 4, 1970-My 14, 1977//
           w.

           Pub. by Thomas W. Pue., Sun Colorpress Ltd., Edmonton.

           OONL   or   Jl 4, 1970
           AEP   or   My 13, 1972-My 14, 1977

BRAGG CREEK

           Pioneer. S 3, 1980-My 26, 1982
           See **COCHRANE**. *Pioneer.* (282).

BRANT

102   *Brant Weekly.* 1917-1918?//
           w.

           Satellite of *Calgary Western Standard* (142.5).
           Pub. by Standard Newspaper Syndicate, Calgary (Ref.: **MK** 1918; **CAN**
           1920).

           No issues located

BROCKET

103   *Weasel Valley News.* 1982-1983?//
           m.?   Native (Pe)

           Pub. on Peigan Indian Reserve.
           Ref.: *Kainai News,* Stand Off, Je (no. 2), 1982:11.

           ACG   or   F 1983 (no. 13)

BROOKS

104   *Brooks Bulletin.* Ap 22, 1910-Je? 1910//
           w.

           Printed in Medicine Hat.
           Established by Brooks Board of Trade to attract homesteader and ranch
           trade. Ed. by E.O. (Bert) Coultis, a lumber company mgr. Seven issues were
           pub. and printed (Ref.: *Brooks Bulletin* N 3, 1960).
           Ref.: *Brooks Bulletin* Diamond Jubilee Edition, N 1971.

           No issues located

5.1 *Brooks Banner.* Ag 4, 1910-Je 1? 1912/...
w.

5.2 *Brooks Bulletin.* Je 8? 1912-
w.

Pub. by Calvin Goss, Ag 10, 1910-Je 1912; Leonard D. Nesbitt, Je 1912-Oc 31, 1920; J. Howard Nesbitt, N 1, 1920-Ap 25, 1929; Robert B. Williamson, My 1, 1929-Mr 31, 1935; Leonard Nesbitt, Ap 1, 1935-Ap 1969. Ed. by Clive B. Nesbitt, Ap 1, 1935-D 31, 1954; James L. Nesbitt, Sr., Ja 1, 1955-S 1981. Pub. by James L. Nesbitt, Sr., S. 1981+ Ed. by James L. Nesbitt, Jr., S 1981+

Alberta Golden Jubilee Edition, S 29, 1955; 50th Anniversary Issue, N 3, 1960; Diamond Jubilee Edition, N 1971.

AEUS or N 3, 1960
AEP mf Ag 4, 1910-D 1983
or 1984+

RUCE

6 *Bruce News.* Ag 2, 1911-1915?//
w.

Pub. by James Mewhort (Ref.: **MK** 1911, 1913; **CAN** 1916). Printed by *Holden Herald.*

AEP or Ag 2, 1911-Je 12, 1913

RUDERHEIM

7 *Bruderheim Review.* Mr 28? 1952-Ja 30, 1953//
w.

Pub. by Thomas W. Pue, Sun Pub. co. Ltd., Edmonton.

AEP or Ap 11, 1952-Ja 30, 1953

RULE

8 *B.D. Weekly.* Mr 31, 1922-Mr, 1923//
w.

Pub. and ed. by H.H. Lovat Dickson (Ref.: **Dick** I, **Dick** 2) Printed in Edmonton.

Title varied? *Brule District Weekly,* first issue Mr 31, 1922 (Ref.: **CPP** v22no4, Ap 1922).

In his autobiography *The ante-room*, Dickson calls it *Blue Diamond Weekly*, as his father managed that mine. Paper closed because Dickson was financed by the mine owners but supported unionization of workers.

No issues located

BUFFALO LAKE

109   *Buffalo Lake Wave.* 1895-?//
         ?

         Ref.: *Lacombe Globe* S 23, 1948.

         No issues located

BURDETT

110   *Burdett Tribune.* Mr 1910-1911?//
         w.

         Ed. by E.B. Warriner (Ref.: *Medicine Hat News* Mr 10, 1910:4).

         No issues located

111   *Burdett Times.* 1917-1918//
         w.

         Pub. by W.P. Cotton (Ref.: **MK** 1918).

         No issues located

112   *Burdett Review.* 1932-1935?//
         w.

         Pub. by Charles Avery (Ref.: **MK** 1932-1935; **CAN** 1935).

         No issues located

CALGARY

113.1   *Calgary Herald, Mining and Ranche Advocate and General Advertiser.* Ag 31, 1883-Mr 4, 1887/...
         w.

113.2   *Calgary Weekly Herald.* Mr 11, 1887-Mr 28, 1888/...
         w.

113.3   *Calgary Herald and Alberta Livestock Journal.* Ap 4, 1888-Jl 18, 1888/...
         w.

13.4 *Calgary Weekly Herald and Alberta Livestock Journal.* Jl 25, 1888-D 28, 1892/...
w.

13.5 *Calgary Weekly Herald.* Ja 4, 1893-Ag 30, 1893/...
w.

13.6 *Semi-Weekly Calgary Herald and Alberta Livestock Journal.* S 6, 1893-D 12, 1894/...
2w.

13.7 *Calgary Weekly Herald.* D 19, 1894-F 6, 1895/...
w.

13.8 *Weekly Herald.* F 13, 1895-Mr 7, 1918/...
w.

13.9 *Alberta Farmer and Calgary Weekly Herald.* Mr 14, 1918-S 29, 1932//
w.

Absorbed *Alberta Livestock Journal* Ap 4, 1888.
Pub. as Wednesday issue of d. ed. (115), F 12, 1890-Ag 30, 1893 and D 19, 1894-S 4, 1895.
Frequency varied: w. to Ag 30, 1893; 2w. S 6, 1893-D 12? 1894.
Began new voluming Ap 4, 1888; reverted back to original sequence S 12, 1888.
Pub. by Andrew M. Armour and Thomas B. Braden, Ap 31, 1883-N 26, 1884; Hugh St. Quentin Cayley, Herald Printing and Pub. Co., Jl 2, 1885-Ja 8, 1887; Alexander Lucas, Ja 10, 1887-S 30, 1888; Ernest J. Chambers, Herald Pub. Co. Ltd., Oc 1, 1888-N 27, 1889; John Livingston, D 4, 1889-Ag 31, 1892; Wesley F. Orr, G.E. Grogan, and John A. Reid, S 1, 1892-D 12, 1894; John J. Young and Charles A. Magrath, D 19, 1894-F 6, 1895; John J. Young, F 13, 1895-Ap 23, 1907; James Hossack Woods, Ap 24, 1907-S 29, 1932.
See also daily edition (115).
Ref.: **CNLU** p.3; **HAY; BRU; KES** p.114; **CRA** p. 272.

AEU mf Ag 31, 1883-D 31, 1890; Ja 4-My 31, 1893; Ja 7, 1897-My 30, 1907
AEPAA mf S 8-Oc 16, 1888; D 2, 1889-Ag 31, 1893; D 13, 1894-S 10, 1895
AEP or Jl 5, 1923-S 29, 1932

14 *Nor'-Wester.* Ap 22, 1884-My 14, 1885//
w. Political — Conservative

Pub. and printed by Warner and Company. Ed. by George B. Elliott.

Ref.: **CNLU**, p.5; **WAR** pp.125-126.

ACG   mf   Ap 29, 1884-Ap 16, 1885
MWP   or   Ap 22, 1884-My 14, 1885

115   *Calgary Herald.* Jl 2, 1885-
d.

Pub. am (*Morning Herald*) and pm editions My 7, 1906-Jl 10, 1907.
Title varies: *Calgary Daily Herald.* Jl 2, 1885-D 30? 1892; D 14, 1894-F
11, 1939.
Suspended pub. S 2, 1893-D 13, 1894.
Pub. by Hugh St. Quentin Cayley, Herald Printing and Pub. Co., Jl 2,
1885-Ja 8, 1887; Alexander Lucas, Ja 10, 1887-S 30, 1888; Ernest J.
Chambers, Herald Pub. Co. Ltd., Oc 1, 1888-N 27, 1889; John Livingston, D
4, 1889-Ag 31, 1892; Wesley F. Orr, G.E. Grogan, and John A. Reid, S 1,
1892-Ag 31, 1893; John J. Young and Charles A. Magrath, D 13, 1894-F 14,
1895; Young, F 15, 1895-Ap 23, 1907; James Hossack Woods, Ap 24, 1907-
D 31, 1935; O. Leigh Spencer, Ja 1, 1936-Ja 18, 1941; Peter C. Galbraith, Ja
20, 1941-D 13, 1946; John D. Southam, D 14, 1946-N 27, 1954; Basil Dean,
D 2, 1954-Ja 31, 1962; Frank Swanson, F 1, 1962-Jl 31, 1982; J. Patrick
O'Callaghan, Ag 3, 1982+. In Ja 1908, Southam Company (now Southam
Inc.) purchased a majority interest in Herald Pub. Co. Ltd.
5th Anniversary Edition, S 5, 1888; Alberta Golden Jubilee Edition, S 3,
1955; 75th Anniversary Edition, Ag 1, 1958; 85th Anniversary Edition, Ag
31, 1968; 100th Anniversary Edition, Ag 31, 1983.
See also weekly edition (113).
Ref.: **BRU**; **KES** p. 114; **CRA** p.272; **HAY**.

AEPAA   mf   S 8-Oc 16, 1888; D 2, 1889-Ag 31, 1893; D 13, 1894+

116.1   *Calgary Tribune and Bow River Advertiser.* S 16, 1885-D 17,
1886/...
w.

116.2   *Calgary Tribune.* D 24, 1886-F 5, 1895//
w.

Superceded by *Alberta Tribune.* w. ed., Calgary (123).
Pub. and ed. by Thomas B. Braden, T.B. Braden and Co., S 16, 1885-Oc
16, 1886; Braden and Baillie, Oc 22, 1886-Ap 24, 1889; Thomas B. Braden,
My 1, 1889-F 5, 1895.
See also d. ed. (117).

AEU   mf   S 16, 1885-N 21, 1894; Ja 8, 1895
ACG   or   S 16, 1885-F 5, 1895

117.1   *Calgary Tribune.* Oc 22, 1886-Jl 16, 1888/...
d.

117.2   *Evening Tribune.* Jl 17, 1888-N 29, 1888/...
d.

7.3 *Evening Tribune and Bow River Advertiser.* N 30, 1888-D 31, 1888/...
d.

7.4 *Calgary Tribune.* Ja 1889-S 6, 1893/...
d.

7.5 *Calgary Daily Tribune.* S 7, 1893-Ag 8, 1894/...
d.

7.6 *Calgary Tribune.* Ag 9, 1894-F 9, 1895//
d.

Superceded by *Alberta Tribune* d. ed. Calgary (122).
Pub. and ed. by Braden and Baillie, Oc 22, 1886-Ap 24, 1889; Thomas B. Braden, My 1, 1889-F 1895.
See also w. ed. (116).
Ref.: **CNLU**, p.5.

ACG   or   My 2, 1889
OONL   or   [Ap 4, 1887-D 31, 1888; Ja 2, 1890-N 21, 1894]; Ja 2-F 9, 1895

8 *Pioneer Post.* 1887-?
w.?

Ref.: *Banff Crag and Canyon* Ap 6, 1956.

No issues located

9 *Northwest Call.* Ap?-Je 1887//
? Labour

Pub. by Calgary Knights of Labor, Local Assembly #9787. Probably the first labour newspaper in Alberta (Ref.: **CARA 1** p.11). *Macleod Gazette,* Fort Macleod, Je 14, 1887 reported that "The Calgary Call ... announces its intention of suspending publication ... The editor of the *Call* says that the paper was issued for nine weeks."

No issues located

0 *Prairie Illustrated.* D 6, 1890-Ap 18, 1891//
w.

Started by John R. Innes (Ref.: **CPP** v9no12 D 1902).
Pub. by Thomas B. Braden, Ed. by Ernest Beaufort. *Macleod Gazette,* Ap 29, 1891, reported that this newspaper had ceased publication.

ACG   mf F 28, 1891
ACG   photocopy D 6, 1890-Ap 18, 1891

1 *Calgary Advance.* Oc 20? 1894//
?

First issue and suspension of this newspaper reported in *Calgary Tribune,*
Oc 31, 1894. Only one issue appears to have been published.

No issues located

122   *Alberta Tribune Daily Edition.* F 11, 1895-S 3, 1895//
         d.

         Superceded *Calgary Tribune* d. ed. (117).
         Tuesday issues entitled *Alberta Tribune Weekly Edition* (123.1).
         Pub. and ed. by J. Creagh and Co.
         See also w. ed (123).
         Ref.: **CNLU** p.3.

         OONL   or   [F 12-Ag 31, 1895]

123.1   *Alberta Tribune Weekly Edition.* F 13, 1895-D 16, 1899/...
         w.

123.2   *Alberta and the Alberta Tribune.* D 19, 1899-D 19, 1902/...
         2w.; w.

123.3   *Weekly Albertan.* D 26, 1902-D 29, 1920/...
         w.

123.4   *Western Farmer and Weekly Albertan.* Ja 5, 1921-My 26? 1927//
         w.

         Superceded *Calgary Tribune,* w. ed. (116).
         Merged with *Albertan,* (126) Calgary to form *Albertan and the Alberta
         Tribune,* D 19, 1899 (123.2).
         Title varied Oc 15-N 20, 1900: *Daily Albertan; Albertan; Semi-Weekly
         Albertan and the Alberta Tribune.*
         Frequency varied: w. F 13, 1895-D 16, 1899; 2w. D 19, 1899-Jl 25? 1902;
         w. Jl 30? 1902+. Pub. d. during federal election, Oc 15-N 7, 1900.
         To Ag 31, 1895 pub. as Tuesday issue of d. ed. To Ag 1895 used voluming
         of d. ed. except for first four issues. Adopted voluming of d. ed. D 27, 1905.
         Two pages were given over to *Western Independent,* Calgary (158) and
         pub. under the masthead of the Western Independent Pub. Co. Ltd., Jl 28?
         1920-Ja 25, 1922.
         Pub. and ed. by J. Creagh and Co., F 13-S 3, 1895; Francis H. Turnock,
         Alberta Tribune Pub. Co., S 10, 1895-Ap 25, 1896; William Leigh Bernard,
         My 2, 1896-D 16, 1899; Charles B. Halpin, D 19, 1899-Ag 18, 1900; Charles
         B. Halpin and Sam R. Hodson, Ag 25-S 1, 1900; Wilson and McCaffary, S 8,
         1900-Ja 4, 1902; W.M. Davidson, Ja 7, 1902-Oc 31, 1926; George M. Bell, N
         1, 1926-My 26? 1927.
         Ref.: **CNLU,** p.3.

         OONL   or   [F 13, 1895-D 16, 1899]

AEU	mf Ap 9, 1895-D 31, 1903; Ja 4, 1923-My 26, 1927 (on same reel as the *Morning Albertan*, Calgary)
ACG	mf Ja 8, 1904-Ja 4, 1906
AEP	or Jl 21, 1920-D 27, 1923

24   *Tiser.* My ? 1895-1896?//
w.

Pub. and ed. by A.C. Gibson, Gibson Printing Co. (Ref.: **HENW** 1895).

ACG   or Je 6, Jl 25, 1896

25   *Independent.* D ? 1898//
w.

Only one issue published?
Pub. by William Leigh Bernard (Ref.: **MK** 1899). Suspension of publication reported in *Medicine Hat News*, Ja 5, 1899.

No issues located

26   *Albertan.* N 28, 1899-D 15, 1899//
2w.

Merged with *Alberta Tribune Weekly Edition* (123.1), to form *Albertan and the Alberta Tribune*, (123.2) D 19, 1899.
Pub. and ed. by Charles B. Halpin, Alberta Printing Co.
Ref.: **CNLU** p.4.

OONL   or N 28, 1899
AEU   mf D 1, 1899

27.1   *Morning Albertan.* Ap 10, 1902-Mr 10, 1924/...
d. (am)

27.2   *Calgary Albertan.* Mr 11, 1924-Ja 18, 1936/...
d. (am; pm; am)

27.3   *Albertan.* Ja 20, 1936-F 15, 1980/...
d. (am)

27.4   *Calgary Albertan.* F 18, 1980-Ag 1, 1980//
d. (am)

First published with title *Morning Bulletin*.
Pub. am to My 15, 1934; pm My 16-D 31, 1934; am Ja 2, 1935-Ag 1, 1980.
Switched to tabloid format F 28, 1977.
Pub. by Albertan Pub. Co. Ltd. to Oc 1957; Albertan Division of FP Pub. (Western) Ltd. (Canadian Newspapers Co. Ltd.), Ja 12, 1980. Sold to Toronto Sun Pub. Corp., Je 5, 1980. Pub. by W.M. Davidson, Ap 10, 1902-

Oc 31, 1926. Purchased N 1, 1926 by George M. Bell and Charles E. Campbell who also shared with Bell the purchase of the *Edmonton Bulletin*. In a 1928 division of property, Campbell retained the *Bulletin* while Bell kept the *Albertan* Gordon Bell succeeded as pub. in Mr 1936, P.C. Galbraith was appointed to manage the paper, a position he held until 1940 when his duties were taken over by Harold Bell. In Ja 1936 an agreement for sale was arranged with the Social Credit party whereby stock was offered to the public. In My 1939, the agreement was cancelled as only one-sixth of the total purchase price of the *Albertan* had been paid through the sale of stock. G. Max Bell purchased the *Albertan* from the estate of George M. Bell in 1943 and remained pub. until Jl 19, 1972, succeeded by Bruce Rudd, Je 1973-Je 6, 1977, John A. Hamilton, Je 7, 1977-Oc 12, 1979; Donald R. Doram, Oc 14, 1979-Ag 1, 1980.

10th Anniversary Edition, F 28, 1912; 40th Anniversary Edition, Ap 2, 1942; 50th Anniversary Edition, Jl 26, 1952; Alberta Golden Jubilee Edition, S 6, 1955; 60th Anniversary Edition, S 27, 1962.

Ref.: **BOU 1** pp. 117-118; **CRA** pp. 285-293; **KES** p. 114.

ACG	or	My 8, 1902
AEU	mf	Ja 4, 1906-Ag 1, 1980

128   *Critic*. My 14, 1902-My 20, 1902//
           d. Political — General

Promotional newspaper published to support James Reilly, independent candidate for East Calgary in the 1902 election campaign for the Territorial Legislature.

ACG   or   My 14-My 20, 1902

129   *Bond of Brotherhood*. My 30, 1903-Je 18, 1904?//
           w. Labour

Subtitle: "A Weekly Journal devoted to the Organization and Education of the Worker."

Pub. by James Worsley and Alfred Palmer, My 30-S 26, 1903; Worsley, Oc 3-D 12, 1903; Worsley and Palmer, D 19, 1903-My 14, 1904; Palmer, My 31-Je 18, 1904. Ceased pub. sometime in Je 1904 due to "lack of funds, insufficient subscribers, opposition from employers and the departure of Worsley for England." (Ref.: **KLA** p. 268). Endorsed by Calgary Trades and Labor Council, Je 12, 1903-Mr 19, 1904.

AEPAA   mf   My 30, 1903-Je 18, 1904

130   *Bee*. Ag 8? 1903-D? 1903//
           w.

An illustrated weekly. Pub., Round-Up Pub. Co.; Herbert Lake, ed. Subscription list taken over by the magazine *Round-Up* pub. in Calgary, ca. Ja, 1904 (Ref.: **CPP** v13no1 Ja 1904).

ACG   or   Oc 24, 1903

Calgary Observer. 1904-1905?//
m. Prohibitionist

Pub. by Herald Pub. Co. Ltd. for Women's Christian Temperance Union
(W.C.T.U.) of Calgary. Ed. by Mrs. P.S. Woodhall; Mrs. W. Vicary, bus. mgr.

ACG   or   Pt. 1, no. 5, My 1, 1905
            mf   Pt. 1, no. 5, My 1, 1905

2.1   *Eye Opener.* Ja 1904-F 11, 1911/...
irreg.

2.2   *Calgary Eye Opener.* Ap 1911- Ag 18, 1923?//

Continued *Eye Opener,* High River (623).
Place of pub. varied: Port Arthur, Ont., 1909; Winnipeg, 1910-F? 1911.
Pub. and ed. by Robert Chambers Edwards until Jl 29, 1922. Edwards
died N 14, 1922 and a memorial issue was published N 25, 1922. Beginning
with N 25, 1922 a new series (v21no1) was pub. by R.C. Edwards Pub. Co.
owned by Katherine Edwards, and ed. by Alex Russell, N 25, 1922-Ag 1923.
A Minneapolis publishing house eventually bought the company and contin-
ued to use *Eye Opener* title on a small humour magazine.
Birthday issue, My 13, 1922; Memorial issue, N 25, 1922.
Ref.: **DEM; McE; NOL.**

AEU   mf   [Ja 2, 1904-N 25, 1922]
AEP   mf   [Ja 2, 1904-N 25, 1922]
ACG   mf   [Ja 2, 1904-N 25, 1922]
AEPAA   mf   [Ja 2, 1904-N 25, 1922]
ACG   or   [1904-Ag 18, 1923]

Alberta Clarion. Je 2, 1906-?//
See Supplement (1048)

3   *Chinook.* S 20, 1906-? 1907//
w.

First issue stated intention of pub. d. (a.m.); voluming of issues examined
indicates a w. publication schedule.
Pub. and ed. by M.T. McKay.
Ref.: **MK** 1907

ACG   or   S 20, N 1, 1906; Ag 2, 1907

Sunset News Bulletin. 1906-?//
See Supplement (1049)

4   *Prairie.* F? 1906-S? 1906//
w.

Pub. by Annie B. Merrill.
Ref.: **CPP** v16no3 Mr 1906; **HENC** 1907; **MK** 1907.

No issues located

135   *Town Topics.* Oc? 1906-1907?//
       w.

    Pub. and ed. by W.H. Footner to 1906 (Ref.: *Morning Albertan*, Calgary,
N 2, 1906; ed. by Annie B. Merrill, 1907. (Ref.: **CPP** v16no1 Ja 1907).

No issues located

136.1 *Daily News.* Mr 29? 1907-S 21, 1908/...
       d.

136.2 *Calgary Daily News.* S 22, 1908-N 25, 1910/...
       d.

136.3 *Calgary News Telegram.* N 26, 1910-Ap 12, 1918/...
       d.

136.4 *Calgary Canadian.* Ap 13, 1918-N 14, 1918//?
       d.

    Pub. by Daniel McGillicuddy, Daily News Publishing Ltd., Mr 1907-N
25, 1910; Jess Dorman, N 26, 1910-Je 29, 1912; G.M. Thompson and C.A.
Hayden, News-Telegram Pub. Ltd., Jl 1, 1912-Ap 12, 1918; Thompson and
Hayden, Alberta Newspapers Ltd., Ap 13-N 1918.
Prosperity Edition, Je 14, 1913.
Ref.: **CRA** pp.273, 279.

AEU	mf Mr 30-Oc 30, 1907; Ja 2-My 2, 1908; Jl 2, 1908-S 30, 1918
AEP	mf Ap 13-N 14, 1918

137   *Western Homestead.* 1908-?//
       w.

    J. Jones (Ref.: **CPP** v17no9 Oc 1907).
Ref.: **CAN** 1909.

No issues located

138   *Calgarian.* Mr 11? 1909-?//
       w.

    Printed and pub. by Star Printing Works, Calgary.

ACG   or   My 13, 1909

139   *Deutsch-Canadier.* Jl 15, 1909-D? 1914//
       w. German in Ger.

    Continued *Deutsch-Canadier*, Edmonton (355).

Pub. by Deutsch Canadier Pub. Co. Ltd., Jl 15, 1909-Ag 4, 1910; Deutsch Canadier Ltd., Ag 11, 1910-D? 1914. Ed. by Otto P. Woysch, Jl 15-D 16, 1909; F.W. Klein, D 23, 1909-Ap 28, 1910; Paul Walters, My 5, 1910-My 25, 1911; John Hensen, Je 1, 1911-My 21, 1914; Alfred Frank, My 28-D? 1914.
Ref.: CNLC p.114.

AEP or Jl 15, 1909-S 3, 1914

40 *Deutsch-Canadischer Farmer / German-Canadian Farmer.*
N 11, 1909- 1912?//
w.; m. Agriculture German in Ger.

Title varied: *Deutsche Canadishe Farmer* (Ref.: CNLC, p.116).
Frequency varied: w. N 11, 1910-Ja? 1911; M. F? 1911-1912 (Ref.: *Deutsch-Canadier* Ja 26, 1911:1).
Pub. by Deutsch-Canadier Pub. Co.; Josef Schuster, mgr. Ed. by A.V. Mielecki.
Ref.: CNLC, p.116.

AEP or N 11, 1909-D 29, 1910

41 *Calgary Optimist.* N 27, 1909-Ap 1910?//
w.

Pub. by Optimist Pub. Co. Ltd.; Jess Dorman, mnging ed. (Ref.: HENC 1911; MK 1911).

AEPAA mf N 27, 1909-F 10, 1910
ACG or Ap 23, 1910 (pp. 13-20)

42.1 *Provincial Standard.* Ap 22, 1911-Mr 9, 1912/...
w.

42.2 *Calgary Standard.* Mr 16, 1912-F 22? 1913/...
w.

42.3 *Western Standard.* Mr 20, 1913-Je 25? 1916/...
w.

42.4 *Calgary Sunday Standard.* Jl 2? 1916-Mr 11, 1917/...
w.

42.5 *Calgary Western Standard.* Mr 18, 1917-My 11, 1918/...
w.

42.6 *Canadian Western Standard.* My 18, 1918-N 9, 1918?//
w. Oil Industry

Editions: Pub. rural *Farm-Livestock Edition* and *Home Edition* (am and pm), S 8, 1917-Ag 1918.

Pub. by Standard Printing and Pub. Co. to F 1913; Western Standard Pub. Co., Mr 20-My 31, 1913; Press Pub. Co. Ltd., My 8-N 2, 1913; Western Standard Pub. Co., N 9, 1913-S 29, 1917; Standard Newspaper Syndicate, Oc 1917-1918. Ed. by J. Burt Malette, Ap 1911-Mr 2, 1912; H. Rosch Van Der Byll, Mr 9, 1912; Edward Emory, Mr 16-Ap 27, 1912; A.R. Schrag, My 4, 1912-F 1913; Bert Shepard White, Mr 1913-1918.

Included sections *"Developments in the Oil Field"*, and *"Discoveries in the Oil Field"*, My 23-Ag 15, 1914.

Souvenir edition pub. by Calgary Women's Press Club, Je 12, 1913 entitled *"Calgary, the Gateway to the Woman's West."*

ACG   or N 11, 1911; Ap 20, 1912; Ja 11, 1913; [Jl 30, 1916]; [Ag 20, 1916]

AEP   or Ja 6, 1912-F 22, 1913; Mr 20, 1913-Je 25, 1916; Ag 13, 1916-N 9, 1918

143   *Press.* 1912-1913?//
         w.

Pub. by Proverbs and Marshall (Ref.: **MK** 1913).

No issues located

144   *Alberta Federationist.* D 6? 1912-Je 20, 1913?//
         w. Labour

Official newspaper of Calgary Trades and Labor Council. Ed. by L.T. English.

"Annual Convention and Educational Number of Organized Labour for Alberta", Je 1913.

AEP   or Ja 10, 1913-Je 20, 1913

145   *Black Diamond Press.* 1913-1914?//
         w.? Oil Industry

Pub. by Coalinga Syndicate. Vernon Knowles, mnging ed.; B.J. Casey, bus. Mgr. "Contains the most authentic information and development notes on the Calgary oil fields." (Ref.: **HENC** 1914).

No issues located

146   *Scottish Standard.* 1913-1914?//
         ? Scottish

Pub. by Standard Pub. Co. Ltd., John C. Paterson, mgr. (Ref.: **HENC** 1914).

No issues located

147   *Natural Gas and Oil Record.* N 1, 1913-Oc 3, 1914?//
         w. Oil Industry

Pub. by J.L. Tucker, Gas and Oil Pub. Co. Included a directory of oil companies, stock quotes, maps, etc. "Devoted to the interests of the Alberta natural gas and oil fields." (Ref.: HENC 1914).

AEP   or   N 1, 1913-Oc 3, 1914

48   *Sunday Sun.* 1914//
w.

Ref.: CAN 1915.

No issues located

49   *Canadian Western Jewish Times.* Ap 1914-? 1914//
m.   Jewish

Abraham L. Barron, bus. mgr. (Ref.: HENC 1914).
Ref.: CES 2 p.134; CNLC p.198; GUT pp.179-181.

No issues located

50   *Alberta Oil Review.* 1915-1916?//
w.   Oil Industry

Title varied *Alberta Oil Review and Industrial Record* (Ref.: CAN 1918).
E.M. Robinson, ed.; H.E. Winser, bus. mgr. (Ref.: HENC 1916; CAN 1918).

No issues located

Fairplay. Je 1915-? 1918//
See Supplement (1050)

51   *Sentinel and Military News.* 1916-?//
w.   Military

Ref.: CAN 1917.

No issues located

52.1   *Nutcracker.* N 17, 1916-S 14? 1917/...
bw.   Political — Non-Partisan League

52.2   *Alberta Non-Partisan.* Oc 26? 1917-S 11, 1919//
bw.   Political — Non-Partisan League

Superceded by *Western Independent*, Calgary (158).
Pub. by Nutcracker Pub. Syndicate. Ed. by William Irvine.
Official organ of Non-Partisan League.
Ref.: WEI 5196, 5198

AEP   mf   N 17, 1916-Jl 7, 1919
AEP   or   N 23, 1917-S 11, 1919
AEU   mf   N 17, 1916-Jl 7, 1919

153.1   *Market Examiner.* My 18? 1917-D? 1922/...
         w. Agriculture

153.2   *Market Examiner and Western Farm Journal.* ? 1923-Ag 26,
         1954/...
         w. Agriculture

153.3   *Market Examiner.* S 2, 1954-My 26, 1955/...
         w. Agriculture

153.4   *Rocky View News and Market Examiner.* Ap 17, 1956-Ag 11, 1981//
         w. Agriculture

         Incorporated *Oilfields Flare,* (976). Turner Valley, Summer 1956.
         Amalgamated with *Calgary Rural Ad-Viser* (211) to form *Calgary Rural
         Week,* (218.1) Ag 1981.
         Subtitle 1956-Ag 1981: "Incorporating Oilfields Flare."
         Suspended pub. Je 1955-Mr 1956.
         New voluming began Ap 17, 1956 and continued to Ap 1961. On My 2,
         1961, voluming reverted back to original sequence (v45no2).
         Pub. by Examiner Press Co. Ltd., My 18? 1917-Ag 26, 1954; Hopkins
         Pub., S 2, 1954-My 26, 1955; North Hill News, Ap 18, 1956-Ag 11, 1981.
         Pub. by Roy Farran, Ap 18, 1956-Ja 25, 1972; D. Leif Erickson, F 1, 1972-
         Ag 11, 1981. Ed. by Everett D. Marshall and Jean A. Grant, My 18? 1917-D
         8, 1938; Marshall, Ja 2, 1941-S 1, 1949; Frank Gibbons, Ja 2, 1941-D 25,
         1952; Roy Farran, Je 25-D 17, 1953; Garth Hopkins, D 24, 1953-My 26,
         1955.
         Contract newspaper for Rocky View Municipal District, Ap 17, 1956-Ag
         11, 1981.

         ACG   or   [F 1, 1918-Ag 26, 1954]
         AEP   or   My 11, 1950-Ag 11, 1981

154   *Canadian Nation.* 1918?-1919?//
         w.?

         Ed. by D.M. LeBourdais (Ref.: **HENC** 1919).
         Radical paper (Ref.: **CPP** v28no3 Mr 1919)

         No issues located

155   *Alberta Veteran.* Mr 9, 1918-Ap 24, 1920?//
         w. Military Veterans

         Pub. by Alberta Veteran Pub. Co. Ed. by A. Russell, Mr 9-Mr 16, 1918;
         Hed. R. Atwill, Mr 23-28, 1918; Russell, Ap 6-Jl 20, 1918; Andrew David-
         son, Jl 27, 1918-Mr 29, 1919; E.M. Holliday, Ap 5-Ap 26, 1919; Russell, Jl
         18, 1919-Ap 24, 1920. Endorsed by Great War Veterans' Association and
         Great War Next-of-Kin Association.

         AEP   or   Mr 9, 1918-Ap 24, 1920

6   *Army and Navy News and Universal Weekly.* Jl 6? 1918-? 1919//
w. Veterans

Title varied: *Universal Weekly* (Ref.: **MK** 1919 memorandum dated Oc 2, 1919).
Pub. by Army and Navy News Co. Ed. by F. Hopwood. Official newspaper of Army and Navy Veterans in Canada (Inc.) (Ref.: **HENC** 1919; **MK** 1919, 1920).

ACG   or   Ja 25, 1919

57   *Calgary Strike Bulletin.* My 30, 1919-? 1919//
irreg. Labour

As occurred in Winnipeg, Man. during the General Strike of 1919, strike bulletins were published in Calgary and Edmonton. Pub. by authority of Central Strike Committee.
Ref.: **WEI** 5221

AEP   or   My 30, 1919 (with the *Edmonton Free Press* (384))
ACG   or   Je 2, 1919
MWPA   or   [My 31-Je 24, 1919] (RG4.A1/6)

58   *Western Independent.* Oc 1, 1919-Je 23, 1920//
w.; 2m. Political — United Farmers of Alberta

Superceded *Alberta Non-Partisan* Calgary (152.2).
Subtitle F 11-Je 23, 1920: "Organ of the United Farmers of Alberta."
Official organ of U.F.A. Political Association. Ed. by William Irvine. On Jl 5, 1920, a fire at the Western Print Works destroyed all material needed to print the last ed., making it impossible to complete the issue; it never again appeared as a separate paper. It was given the two middle pages of *Weekly Albertan,* Calgary from Jl-D 1920 at which time *Western Independent* was incorporated into the *Western Farmer and Weekly Albertan,* Calgary (123). (Ref.: **MARD** p.79).

AEP   or   Oc 1, 1919-Je 23, 1920
AEU   mf   Oc 1, 1919-Ap 14, 1920

59   *Searchlight.* N 14, 1919-Oc 22, 1920?//
w. Labour

Pub. by Searchlight Co. in the interests of workers in and around the coal mines of Alberta and southeastern British Columbia. No editor named. In an editorial on Ja 2, 1920:3, it was stated that *Searchlight* was not admitted to the Calgary Trades and Labor Council. Pub. for several months only (Ref.: **ELL** p.226).

AEPAA   mf   N 14, 1919-Oc 22, 1920

50.1   *U.F.A.* Mr 1, 1922-Ap 2, 1934/...
2m.; w.; m. Agriculture Political-United Farmers of Alberta

160.2   *United Farmer.* My 25, 1934-Mr 27, 1936//
              w. Agriculture Political-United Farmers of Alberta.

Superceded by *Western Farm Leader,* Calgary (181).
Frequency varied: 2m. Mr 1, 1922-F 15, 1932; m. Mr 1, 1932-Ap 2, 1934;
w. My 25, 1934-Mr 27, 1936. From 1924-1929 pub. w. during annual Spring
Session of the Alberta Legislature.
Official organ of United Farmers of Alberta, F 1, 1923-Mr 27, 1936; also
of Alberta Cooperative Marketing Pools, Ag 16, 1926-Mr 27, 1936, and
Alberta Cooperative Oil Pool, Ja 1, 1931-Mr 27, 1936. Ed. by W. Norman
Smith.

AEU   mf Mr 1, 1922-D 20, 1935
AEP   or Mr 1, 1922-Mr 27, 1936

161   *Liberty.* My 13, 1922-?//
              w. Political — General

Pub. by Liberty Press Ltd. A weekly review of political economy, political science and sociology.

ACG   or My 13, 1922

Westerner. Ja 12, 1923-Je 28, 1928//
See Supplement (1051)

162   *Alberta Sun.* 1925?-1927?//
              w.

Ed. by Wilber Horner; A.P. Van Buren, bus. mgr. (Ref.: **HENC** 1926;
MK 1928).

No issues located

163.1   *Alberta Oil Examiner.* F 20, 1926-D 31, 1926/...
              w. Oil Industry

163.2   *Western Oil Examiner.* Ja 8, 1927-F 9? 1929//
              w. Oil Industry

Superceded by *Western Examiner,* Calgary (165.1).
Format varied: magazine, F 20, 1926-F 11, 1928; tabloid, F 18, 1928-F 9,
1929.
Pub. and ed. by Jean A. Grant and Everett D. Marshall, F 20-My 1, 1926;
Marshall and D. Austin Lane, My 8, 1926-F 9, 1929.

ACG   or F 20, 1926-F 9, 1929

164.1   *Western Farmer.* D 10? 1928-1931?/...
              2m. Agriculture

164.2   *Western Stockman* 1932-?
              2m. Agriculture

Title change noted in **MK** 1932; **HENC** 1932.
Pub. by Western Farmer Ltd., a subsidiary of Albertan Pub. Co. Ltd. Ed.
by E.W. Brunsden; C.A. Weir, asst. ed. (Ref.: **HENC** 1931). Mgr. G.F. Gemeroy.

AEP   or   Ja 10-D 26, 1930

65.1   *Western Examiner.* Mr 2, 1929-S? 1949/...
w. Oil Industry

65.2   *Western Oil Examiner.* S ? 1949-Ap 1958//
w.; 2m.; m. Oil Industry

Superceded *Western Oil Examiner,* Calgary (163).
Frequency varied: w. Mr 2, 1929-Oc 15, 1955; 2m. N 1, 1955-Ag 15,
1957; m. S 1957-Ap 1958.
Format varied: newspaper, Mr 2, 1929-D 28, 1940; tabloid, Ja 4, 1941-S ?
1949; magazine, S ? 1949-Ap 1958.
Pub. by Market Examiner Press. Everett D. Marshall, mnging. ed. Mr 2-
Oc 5, 1929; D. Austin Lane, ed., Mr 2-Oc 5, 1929; Marshall, ed., Oc 12,
1929-S? 1949; Frank Gibbons, Ja 4, 1941-D 20, 1952; D.W. Brown, Ja 24,
1953-Oc 2, 1954; H. Gordon Spohn, D 18, 1954-Mr 5, 1955; James H. Gray,
Mr 12, 1955-Ap 1958.

ACG   or   [Mr 2, 1929-Ap 1958]
AEP   or   Mr 1, 1952-Ap 1958

Westerner. Je 12? 1923-Je 28, 1928//
See Supplement (1051)

66   *West-Ender.* Oc? 1929-1930?//
w.

Printed and pub. by F.H. Newnham, Commonwealth Press Ltd.

ACG   or   My 22, 1930

67   *Oil and Financial Review.* Oc 26, 1929-My 23, 1931?//
w. Business Oil Industry

Pub. by Oil and Financial Review Ltd. Ed. by D. Austin Lane.
Ref.: **MK** 1930, 1931; **HENC** 1930, 1931.

ACG   or   Oc 26, 1929-My 23, 1931

68   *Alberta Mercury.* Ja ? 1930-1931?//
w.

Pub. by Gordomer Pub. Ltd.; G.F. Gemeroy, mgr. (Ref.: **MK** 1931;
HENC 1931, 1932).

No issues located

Bridgeland and Riverside Echo. Je 13, 1930-?//
See Supplement (1052)

169   *Danskeren / Danish Review.* 1930-Je 11, 1934//
m. Danish in Dan

Title varied: 1930, *Den Danske Revy.*
Weyburn, Saskatchewan, paper pub. in Calgary by S.A. Hynd Litho Print
Ltd., 1933-1934.
Ref.: **MacD** p.134.

No issues located

170.1   *Western Miner.* S 18, 1930-S 8, 1931/...
irreg. Labour

170.2   *Canadian Miner.* Oc 12, 1931-Ap 24, 1933?//
2m.; irreg. Labour

Continued *Western Miner,* Lethbridge (700).
Edition: Western Edition.
Frequency varied: irreg. S 18, 1930-S 8, 1931; 2m. Oc 12, 1931-Mr 30,
1932; irreg. Ap 21, 1932-Ap 24, 1933.
Suspended pub. Jl-Ag 1930.
Issue of My 7, 1931 typewritten due to printers' ban of the newspaper.
Organ of Miners' Section, Workers' Unity League of Canada, S 18,
1930-S 8, 1931; Mine Workers' Union of Canada, Oc 12, 1931-Ap 24, 1933.
Pub. by Provisional Alberta District Executive Committee, Workers' Unity
League of Canada, Ap 27-S 8, 1931. Ed. by Murdock Clarke, Mr 12-S 10,
1932; Ralph Wootton, Oc 15, 1932-Ap 24, 1933.

ACG   mf S 18, 1930-Ap 24, 1933

171   *Free Lance.* Je 1? 1931-? 1931?//
2m.

Pub. by Ross Macdonald.

ACG   or Ag 15, 1931

Unemployed Bulletin. S 11? 1931-? 1932//
See Supplement (1053)

172   *Calgary Home News.* Ja 1932?-1933?//
w.

Ed. by C. Westergaard.

ACG   or F 17, 1933

173   *Spokesman.* Je 29? 1932-1933?//
w.

Official organ of Knights of Confederation.
Devoted to discussion of social problems, municipal, provincial, national
and international affairs. Pub. by Spokesman Newspaper Syndicate. Ed. by
Sigurd Nelson, 1932; W.D. Stovel, 1933.

ACG or Jl 13, 1932; Oc 14, 1933

4   *Political World.* 1934-1936?//
? Political — General

Roy H. Hilborn, mgr. (Ref.: **HENC** 1934, 1935, 1936).

No issues located

5.1   *Alberta Social Credit Chronicle.* Jl 20, 1934-Ja 17, 1936/...
w. Political — Social Credit

5.2   *Social Credit Supplement.* Ja 25, 1936-Ja 8, 1938//
w. Political — Social Credit

Became supplement to *Albertan*, Calgary (127), on Ja 25, 1936. On Ja 22,
1938 absorbed into *Magazine Section* of *Albertan* and entitled *Albertan
Magazine Section (with which is incorporated the Social Credit Chronicle).*
Pub. until Jl 16, 1938.
Subtitle Ja 25, 1936-Ja 8, 1938: "Formerly the *Alberta Social Credit
Chronicle.*"
Pub. by Charles K. Underwood and Frank Hollingworth, Jl 20, 1934-Ja
17, 1936. Ed. by Underwood, Jl 20, 1934-Ja 17, 1936.
Ref.: **IRV** pp.100-103.

AEP   or Jl 20, 1934-Ja 17, 1936
AEU   mf Ja 25, 1936-Jl 16, 1938 (on the same reel as the *Albertan,*
        Calgary)

6.1   *Social Justice Advocate.* S 1934-Oc 1934/...
m. Political — Social Credit

6.2   *Douglas Social Credit Advocate.* N 1934-Ag 1936//
m. Political — Social Credit

Official organ of Alberta Provincial Douglas Social Credit Association.
Printed by the Signal Pub. Co., Edson. No ed. named. Estab. by Gilbert
McGregor, with A.J. Logan and Sydney Cliffe.
Ref.: **IRV** p.85.

ACG   or S 1934
AEP   or [N 1934-Ag 1936]
AEPAA or Ja, My, Jl, N 1935 (74.173/590)

7.1   *Calgary Typo News.* Ja 15, 1935-Mr 1, 1935/...
w. Labour

177.2   *Typo News.* Mr 8, 1935-N 8, 1935?//
         w. Labour

    Pub. in the interest of locked-out printers of *Albertan* by Calgary Typo-
    graphical Union No. 449. No ed. named.
    Agreement to settle dispute signed with *Albertan*, F 1936. (Ref.: Calgary
    Printing Trades Union. Local No 1. *Papers*, 1935-1974. (ACG:M 2711)

    ACG   mf   Ja 15-Ag 16, 1935
                or   Oc 4-N 8, 1935

178   *Worker.* 1936-?//
         ? Labour

    Pub. by Worker Press Committee. Ed.? by Stanley Collier and Elsie
    Anderson (Ref.: HENC 1936).

    No issues located

179   *Western Canada Enquirer.* 1936-1938?//
         w.?

    Pub. by H.C. Fletcher and James Fry (Ref.: HENC 1937, 1938).

    No issues located

180   *Sports Guide.* 1936-1940?//
         ? Sport

    Ed. by William Phillips (Ref.: HENC 1936-1940).

    No issues located

181   *Western Farm Leader.* My 15, 1936-D 17, 1954//
         2m.   Agriculture   Political — United Farmers of Alberta

    Superceded *United Farmer*, Calgary (160).
    Absorbed by *Western Producer*, Saskatoon, Sask.
    Motto on banner: "Cooperation, Public Affairs, Social Progress."
    Pub. and ed. by W. Norman Smith.

    AEP   or   My 15, 1936-D 17, 1954
    AEPAA   or   My 15, Je 19, Jl 17, 1936; F 5 1943; Mr 16, 1945; D 20, 1946;
                          Ja 21, 1949; D 5, 19, 1952; N 20, 1953 (71.420/57 Box 4)

182   *Western Sentinel.* Mr 26? 1937-? 1937//
         w.

    Pub. by Sentinel Pub. Co. Ed. by Norman M. Plummer.

    ACG   or   Ap 30, 1937

183   *Commonsense (Social Credit).* Ap 2, 1937-?//
         w.   Political — Social Credit

    No pub. or ed. named.

AEPAA or Ap 16, 1937 (69.163/181 Box 2)
ACG or Ap 2, Ap 23-Je 4, 1937

4   *Rebel.* Ap 24, 1937-Ap 1, 1939//
m. Political — Conservative

Pub. by J.J. Zubick as an anti-Social Credit paper.
Ref.: **IRV** p.108

AEPAA mf Ap 24, 1937-Mr 1, 1938
ACG or Ap 24, 1937-Ap 1, 1939

Alberta Democrat. Oc 8, 1938-N 12, 1938//
See Supplement (1054)

5   *Calgary Sports Review.* 1942-?//
? Sport

Joseph McLeod, mgr. (Ref.: **HENC** 1942).

No issues located

6.1   *Call.* Mr 1, 1945-F 11, 1952/...
2m. Labour

6.2   *New Call.* F 27, 1952-Mr 26, 1952//?
2m. Labour

Official organ of Calgary Trades and Labor Council. Pub. by Public Relations Committee, Calgary Trades and Labor Council, Mr 1, 1945-S 20, 1950; "The Call" Committee of Calgary Trades and Labor Council, Oc 11, 1950-Mr 26, 1952. Ed. by George C. Kirke, Mr 1-D 1, 1945; Gordon C. Cushing, D 15, 1945-N 15, 1949; Harry B. Brogden, D 1, 1949-D 26, 1951; Kirke, F 11-Mr 26, 1952.
Pub. *Labor Day Annual.*

ACG mf Mr 1, 1945-Mr 26, 1952

7   *Calgary Citizen.* 1946?-1951?//
w.

Pub. and ed. by Burton W. Eagan, 1946-1948. Pub. by Cooke's Printing and Pub. and Ed. by Winston H. Cooke, 1949-1951 (Ref.: **HENC** 1947-1951).

No issues located

8   *Calgary News.* 1947?-1948?//
w.?

Pub. by John W.O. Stewart (Ref.: **HENC** 1948).

No issues located

Bowness Bulletin. D 15, 1948-Mr 16, 1951
See Supplement (1055.1)

Bowness News. Ap 2, 1951-F 15, 1952?//
See Supplement (1055.2)

189   *Beacon.* Ag 31? 1952-D 24, 1962?//
w.

Pub. by Prairie Pub. Ltd. Ed. by Donald W. Davies (Ref.: HENC 1953-
1956). Served areas of Bowness and Montgomery before amalgamation with
Calgary.
Ref.: CNLU p.3.

OONL   or   N 10, 1955; D 13, 1956
ACG   or   S 6, 1952-D 24, 1962

190   *Bow Valley Advertiser.* S 1953?-1959?//
w.

Pub. by Eric O. Burt, 1952-1955; Harvey J. Gilbert, 1956-1959. Pub. as
an advertising flyer, 1952-1953. Served the area of Bowness before amalgamation with Calgary (Ref.: HENC 1955-1959).

AEP   or   S 16-D 23, 1954

191.1   *North Hill News.* Mr 4, 1954-Ag 11, 1976/...
w.

191.2   *Calgary North Hill News.* Ag 18, 1976-Je 27, 1978/...
w.

191.3   *Calgary News.* Jl 4, 1978-Mr 4, 1981//
w.

Pub. by Roy Farran, North Hill News Ltd., Mr 4, 1954-Ja 27, 1972. Sold
F 1972 to J. and H. Investments Ltd. Pub. by D. Leif Erickson, F 1, 1972-Ag
13, 1980. Sold Ag 1, 1980 to Webb Offset Pub. Ltd., Toronto. Ed. by Graham
Smith, S 14, 1961-Mr 1981.

AEP   or   S 2-D 31, 1954; Oc 5, 1956-D 31, 1964; Ja 4, 1968-Mr 4,
1981

192   *South Calgary News.* My 14, 1957-Je? 1957//
w.

Pub. and ed. by Roy Farran, North Hill News Ltd.
Ref.: CNLU p.5.

OONL   or   My 14, Je 4, 1957

193   *Albertan's South Side Shopper.* My 30, 1957-? 1957//
w.

Pub. by *Albertan,* Calgary.
Ref.: CNLU p.4.

OONL   or   My 30, 1957

)4.1   *South Side Mirror.* 1960?-N 30? 1977/...
         w.

)4.2   *Mirror South Side.* D 7, 1977-Ap 16, 1980/...
         w.

)4.3   *South Side Mirror.* Ap 23, 1980-F 25, 1981/...
         w.

)4.4   *Calgary Mirror South Side Edition.* Mr 4, 1981-
         w.

         Pub. by *Albertan,* Calgary to Ag 1, 1980; *Calgary Sun,* Ag 3, 1980+.
         Doug B. Everett, mgr. to My 3, 1973; D. Ivan Mason, mgr., Mr 1974-F 13,
         1975; Bruce A. Omelchuk, mgr. and ed., F 20, 1975-Mr 25, 1980. Pub. by
         Donald R. Doram, Ap-Ag 6, 1980; J. Douglas Creighton, Ag 12-Ag 26,
         1980; Hartley Steward, S 3, 1981+. Ed. by G.L. Dempsey to F 28, 1974;
         Michael Shapcott, Ap-Ag 26, 1980; Greg Gilbertson, S 3, 1980-S 1, 1981;
         Harry Pegg, S 8, 1981+
             Ref.: **CNLU** p.5.

         OONL   or   Ap 26, 1962; Je 18, 1964
         AC   or   Oc 2, 1975+
         AEP   or   My 11, 1972-Ag 31, 1977; D 7, 1977+

95   *Gauntlet.* S 23, 1960-
         w. University

         Suspended during examination and vacation periods.
         Pub. by Gauntlet Pub. Society, an organ of students of University of Cal-
         gary.

         ACU   or   S 23, 1960+

         Sunday Calgarian. My 19, 1962-My 26? 1962//
         See Supplement (1053)

96   *Calgary Jewish News.* S 1962-
         m. Jewish

         Pub. 10 times a year.
         Pub. by Calgary Jewish Community Council. Eds. included Harry S.
         Shatz, Gary Kohn, Gil August, Douglas Wertheimer, Avrim Namak and
         Drew Staffenberg (Ref.: Correspondence with Publisher, N 26, 1984).
             Ref.: **CNLC** p.195.

         OONL   or   S, Oc, 1962
         ACUA   or   My 1968; F 1970; Ap 1972
         ACG   or   [1967-1970] Ja 1975-D 1981 [Ja 1982-D 1983]

197   *Praerie Nyt.* Ja 15, 1963-1965?//
        2m. Danish in Dan.

        Pub. by Danish Press Alberta-Social Club. Ed. by Otto Hermansen,
        1963-?
        Ref.: CNLC p. 77.

        AEPAA   or   Je 15, Je 30, 1963 (77.109 SE)
        OONL   or   Ja 15-N 30, 1963; Ja 15-N 15, 1964

        Bowness Review. My 16, 1963-N 14, 1963?//
        See Supplement (1054)

198   *Roundup.* 1968-
        w. Military

        Pub. by Canadian Forces Base Calgary. Printed by North Hill News Ltd.,
        Calgary. Eds. since 1975: J.H. Grey, Ja 29, 1975-Ag 4, 1977; R.S. Millar, Ag
        11, 1977-Ap 1978; S.M. Kierstead, Ap 1978-Je 28, 1979; G.H. Mather, Jl 5,
        1979-S 18, 1980; L. Gosselin, S 25-N 6, 1980; L. Haynes, N 20, 1980+ (Ref.:
        CARD 1983).

        ACG   or   Ja 29, 1975-D 17, 1981

199   *Panorama.* S 1968-My 1970?//
        m. Italian in Ital. (and Engl.)

        Ed. by G. Carozzi, C. Graighero, V. Panei, and G. Puco.
        Ref.: CNLC p.184.

        ACUA   or   My 1969
        OONL   or   S 1968-My 1970

200   *Mormoratore.* My 15, 1970-
        m. Italian in Ital.

        Pub. and ed. by Tony Baccari.
        Ref.: CNLC p.183; CNLU p.5.

        ACUA   or   My-S 1970
        OONL   or   1970-Mr 1975
        AECL   or   CM

201   *Wednesday Review.* Ap 14, 1971-? 1979//
        w.

        Superceded by *Calgary Sun* (212).
        Pub. by John T. Shapka, Ap 14, 1971-Jl 19, 1978; Eastbow Printing Ltd.,
        Jl 26, 1978-1979? Ed. by Gaylene Shapka, Ap 14, 1971-Jl 19, 1978; Gail
        Walt, Jl 26, 1978-1979? Served the communities of east Calgary.
        Ref.: CNLU p.5; HENC 1972-1980/81.

        OONL   or   Ap 14, 1971
        AC   or   Ap 12-N 22, 1978

02   *Italian News.* 1974?-1975?//
     ? Italian in Ital (and Engl.?)

      Ref.: **HENC** 1974, 1975.

      No issues located

03   *Sunday.* F 17, 1974-Je 23, 1974//
      w.

      Pub. by Michael E. Horsey, Sunday Pub. Ltd. Ed. by Bob Parkins. Nineteen issues pub. (Ref.: *Edmonton Journal* Ja 23, F 18, Je 29, 1974).
      Ref.: **CNLU**, p.5.

      OONL   or   F 17, 1974
      ACG   or   F 17, Ap 14, Je 23, 1974

04   *East City News.* Je 11, 1974-Oc 8, 1974//
      w.

      Incorporated *Calgary Shopper* (Ref.: **CNLU** p.4).

      OONL   or   Je 11, Oc 8, 1974

05.1   *North Side Mirror.* 1975-N 29? 1977/...
      w.

05.2   *Mirror North Side.* D 6, 1977-Ap 15, 1980/...
      w.

05.3   *North Side Mirror.* Ap 22, 1980-F 24, 1981/...
      w.

05.4   *Calgary Mirror North Side Edition.* Mr 3, 1981-
      w.

      Pub. by *Albertan,* Calgary to Ag 1, 1980; *Calgary Sun,* Ag 3, 1980+. Bruce A. Omelchuk, mgr., 1975-Mr 25, 1980. Pub. by Donald R. Doram, Ap-Ag 6, 1980; J. Douglas Creighton, Ag 12-Ag 26, 1980; Hartley Steward, S 3, 1981+ Ed. by Michael Shapcott, Ap-Ag 26, 1980; Greg Gilbertson, S 3, 1980-S 1, 1981; Harry Pegg, S 8, 1981+.
      Ref.: **CNLU** p.5.

      AEP   or   D 6, 1977+
      OONL   or   Mr 25, 1975

06   *Calgary Women's Newspaper.* F 1975-Ap/My 1981//
      m. Feminist

      Pub. by Calgary Status of Women Action Committee.
      Ref.: *Calgary Albertan.* Mr 24, 1980.

      AC   or   F 1975-Ap/My 1981

207 *Hrvatski Vjesnik Hrvatskog Društva Prijatelja Matice Hrvatske
     / Croatian Herald.* Ap 18, 1975-
     irreg. Croatian in Cro.

Continued magazine *Hrvatska Slaga.*
Pub. by Hrvatsko Društva Prijatelja Matice Hrvatske/Croatian Society of
Friends of Matica Hrvatska, a cultural and literary organization.
Ref.: CNLC p.67.

No issues located

208 *Dairy Contact.* Ap 1976-Mr 1982//
     m. Agriculture

Continued by *Dairy Contact,* Edmonton, (500).
Pub. by F. Rodney James, International Dairy Contact Ltd. Ed. by Brian
G. Kitchen. (Ref.: HENC 1977-1982).

AEAG or S, 1976-Mr 1982
OOAG or Ap 1976-Mr 1982
OONL or Ap 1976-Mr 1982

209 *World of Beef and Stockman's Recorder.* Ag 1976-
     m. Agriculture

Pub. by Sage Brush Ventures Ltd. as supplement to magazine *Limousin
Leader.* Harald L. Gunderson, pub.; ed. by Dorothea Schaab.
From Je/Jl 1984 in magazine format.

AC   or Jl 1980+
AEAG or 1Y+CY
OOAG or Ag 1976+

210 *Korean Dong-Baung News.* S 28, 1976-? 1976//
     ? Korean in Kor.

Pub. by Korean Dong-Baung News.
Ref.: CNLC p.225.

OONL or S 28, 1976

211 *Calgary Rural Ad-viser.* 1979-Ag 1981//
     2m. Agriculture

Amalgamated Ag 1981 with *Rocky View News,* Calgary (153.4), to form
Calgary Rural Week (218). (Ref.: *Calgary Rural Week,* Ag 19, 1981).
Pub. and ed. by Gary Kirker.

No issues located

212 *Calgary Sun.* Ja 10? 1979-Je 27, 1979?//
     w.

Superceded *Wednesday Review,* Calgary. (201).
Pub. by Calgary Sun, a division of Land West Pub. Ltd. Ed. by Mike
Matovich.

Ref.: **ALB** F 2, 1979:15.

AC   or   Ja 17-Je 27, 1979

3   *Seventeenth Avenue.* Fall 1979-D 1981//
5/yr

Superceded by *Calgary Avenues* (220).
Pub. and ed. by Pat Paterson, Avenue Advertising Ltd.
Ref.: *Calgary Albertan* Je 17, 1980:25.

AC   or   Fall 1979-D 1981

4   *Magyar Hírmondó / Calgary Hungarian Courier.* My 1980-
m. Hungarian in Hung. (and Engl.)

Pub. by Peter Beermann, Director of Communications and Cultural
Affairs, Hungarian Cultural Assoc. of Calgary. Ed. by Albert Seibert (Ref.:
Correspondence with Publisher, F 6, 1985).

AECL   or   CM

5   *Calgary Sun.* Ag 3, 1980-
d. (am)

Sunday ed. entitled *Sunday Sun.*
Pub. by Calgary Sun, a division of Toronto Sun Pub. Corp. Pub. by J.
Douglas Creighton, Ag 3-Ag 17, 1980; Hartley Steward, Ag 18, 1980+;
Lester Pyette, ed.-in-chief, Ag 3, 1980+

AEP   mf Ag 3, 1980+

6   *Jewish Star [Calgary Edition].* Ag 22/S 4, 1980-
bw. Jewish

Pub. by Jewish Star Newspaper Ltd. Ed. by Douglas Wertheimer (Ref.:
Correspondence with Publisher, Oc 9, 1984).
Ref.: *Calgary Herald* S 27, 1980.

AECL   or   CM
ACG   or   Ag 22/S 4, 1980+

7   *Canadian Chinese Times.* Je 13, 1981-
w. Chinese in Chi.

Pub. by North Hill News Ltd. Ed. by Jake Louie (Ref.: Editor).

No issues located

8.1   *Calgary Rural Week.* Ag 19, 1981-F 17, 1982/...
w. Agriculture

8.2   *Rural Week.* Mr 3, 1982-F 9, 1983//
w.; 2m. Agriculture

Superceded *Calgary Rural Ad-viser* (211).

Superceded by magazine *Alberta Rural Month.*
Frequency varied: w. Ag 19, 1981-Ja 6, 1982; 2m. Ja 20, 1982-F 9, 1983.
Pub. by North Hill News Ltd. Pub. and ed. by Peter D. Brouwer.

AEP   or   Ag 19, 1981-F 9, 1983

219   *Nyugati Magyarsàg / Hungarians of the West.* Ja? 1982-
m. Hungarian in Hung. (and Engl.)

Pub. by Corvin Pub. Ltd. Ed. by István Miklóssi.

AECL   or   CM

220   *Calgary Avenues.* Mr 1982-Jl 1982?//
q.

Superceded *Seventeenth Avenue,* Calgary (213).
Pub. and ed. by Pat Paterson.

ACG   or   Mr, Jl 1982

221   *Indochinese News.* Mr 18, 1982-
w. Chinese in Chi.

Pub. and ed. by Ben Fu Khuu, Indo Chinese News Ltd., Calgary.

AECL   or   CM
AC   or   2M+CM

222   *Opinion.* D? 1982-
m. Spanish in Span.

Subtitle: "The Spanish Newspaper of Alberta."
Pub. by Sociedad de Cultura y Comunicaciones Hispano americanas de
Alberta; directed by Eduardo de la Cruz.

AECL   or   CM

CALMAR

223   *Calmar Review.* 1975-?//
w.

Ref.: CAN 1976.

No issues located

CAMROSE

224   *Camrose Mail.* Jl 27, 1906-Ja? 1909//
w.

Camrose Mail and *Sedgwick Eagle* (889) issued together from Ja, 1908
(Ref.: CPP v18no2 F 1908).

"Captain T. Berville Thomas established the *Camrose Mail* on July 27, 1906, closing his plant three months after the establishing of the *Camrose Canadian*. The *Canadian* purchased the plant of the *Camrose Mail* on February 1, 1909, and the paper began publishing in Camrose." (Ref.: **DAL** p.63) Ref.: **CAN** 1909; **HENE** 1906, 1907.

No issues located

5   *Camrose Canadian.* D 3, 1908-
     w. Political — Liberal

Pub. by Camrose Canadian Ltd. Ed. by Hon. George P. Smith, Minister for Education, Liberal, D 3, 1908-D 29, 1921; Thomas H. Gray, Ja 5, 1922-D? 1927; Frederick John Slight, 1928-Ap 17, 1930; Mrs. Ida Slight, Ap 24, 1930-F 19, 1947; Rae Livingstone King, Kenneth Patrige, Fred A. King, F 26, 1947-My 30, 1951; R.L. King, Patrige, Charles A. MacLean, Je 1, 1951-1961; Patrige, MacLean and H. George Meyer, 1961-1974; MacLean 1974-Ap 1985; Bowes Pub. Ltd., Ap, 1985+.

Special Immigration issue, Ja 16, 1911; Alberta Golden Jubilee Edition, Je 22, 1955; Special Homecoming Edition, Jl 6, 1980.

Ref.: **HAMB** pp.53-55.

AEP   mf D 3, 1908-D 31, 1984
           or Ja 1973+

6   *Victoria Farmer.* S 11, 1922-My 16, 1924?//
     w. Political — United Farmers of Alberta

Pub. and ed. by Jacob Zantjer. Pub. was to relocate newspaper office after My 16, 1924 but may have discontinued pub. altogether.

Ref.: **CAN** 1924; **MK** 1922-1924.

ACG   or Ap 6, 1923
AEP   or Mr 2, 1923-My 16, 1924

7   *Camrose Booster.* N 25, 1952-
     w.

Pub. and ed. by William F. and Berdie Fowler, N 25, 1952-D 31, 1975; W. Blain Fowler and Berdie Fowler, Ja 1976+ (Ref.: Correspondence with Publisher, Je 29, 1984).

Ref.: **HAMB** pp.57-58

AEP   or Oc 31, 1978+

ANMORE

28   *Canmore Times.* F 25, 1931-F 1937?//
     bw.

Mimeographed.
Ed. by H.S. Young, 1931-1935; E. Deniston Garner, 1936-1937 (Ref.: **APP** p.117; *Calgary Herald* Oc 8, 1936).

ABA   or   [1931-1936]

229   *Three Sisters Clarion.* Ap? 1956-My? 1961//
       2m.

       Titles varied: *Clarion*
       Pub. by George Mandryk. Sold to Prairie Pub. Ltd., Bowness, ca. D 1957.
       Ed. by George Mandryk, Ap 1956-Ap 1958; Mrs. Grace A. Wright, Ap
       1958-Ap 1961.

       ACG   or   [My 3, 1957-My 11, 1961]

230   *Canmore Times.* 1966?-F 1970?//
       bw.

       No pub. or ed. information available.

       ABA   or   Ja 28-F 4, 1970

231   *Valley Views.* S 10, 1974-Je 6, 1975?//
       irreg.

       Issue of Oc 25, 1974 entitled *Bow Valley Views.*
       Mimeographed.
       Pub. through funds made available by Canmore Town Council. Ed. by
       Dave Sturdy.
       Ref.: CNLU p.6.

       OONL   or   S 10, Oc 25, 1974
       ABA   or   S 10, 1974-Je 6, 1975

232   *Canmore Miner.* F 5, 1975-Jl 27, 1983//
       w.

       Pub. by Canmore Miner Pub. Ltd. Ed. by T. Edward Fisher.

       ABA   or   F 5, 1975-N 4, 1981
       AEP   or   F 16, 1977-Jl 27, 1983

233   *Anthracite Chronicle.* Ja 23, 1976-Mr 1976//
       bm.?

       Pub. by Bow Corridor Cultural Improvement Society. Ed. by D.A.
       (Andy) Winfield.

       ABA   or   Ja 23-Mr 1976

234   *Hoodoo Highlander.* My 12, 1976-F 2, 1983//
       bw.

       Pub. and ed. by Patricia D. Parker.

       ABA   or   My 12, 1976-F 2, 1983

ARBON

5　　*Carbon Reporter.* 1911?-1913?//
w.

Pub. in Bowden by Bowden News (Ref.: **CAN** 1913; **MK** 1911).

No issues located

6　　*News.* 1912-?//
w.

Established by F.A. Wherry in 1912 (Ref.: **MK** 1913).

No issues located

7　　*Carbon News.* Ja 1, 1920-Oc 26, 1922.
w.

Pub. and ed. by Hubert Peters, 1920-F 10, 1921; Frank Peters, F 17, 1921-Je 15, 1922; Hubert Peters, Je 22-Oc 26, 1922 (Ref.: *Carbon Chronicle* F 4, 1932; **CAN** 1923).

AEP　　or　Ja 20-Ag 11, 1921; My 4-Oc 26, 1922

8.1　　*Carbon Chronicle.* 1922-Oc 27, 1927/...
w.

8.2　　*Chronicle.* N 3, 1927-S 5, 1929/...
w.

8.3　　*Carbon Chronicle.* S 12, 1929-S 1/8, 1960//
w.

Absorbed by *Sentinel,* Acme (3), S 16, 1960.
Suspended pub. Je 28-S 5? 1945.
Pub. by Edouard J. Rouleau, 1925-N 2, 1944; Clarence E. Wall, N 9, 1944-My 10, 1945; Rouleau, My 17-Je 28, 1945; Alvin V. Wallace, Oc 4, 1945-Mr 1948; W. Skerry, Didsbury, 1948-D 20, 1951; George Wheeler, Acme, Ja 10, 1952-S 1/8, 1960.
Pub. section for Swalwell, N 3, 1927-Ap 5, 1928.
Alberta Golden Jubilee Edition, S 1, 1955.

AEP　　or　Ja 6, 1927-Je 28, 1945; Oc 4, 1945-Mr 4, 1948; S 9, 1948-S 1/8, 1960

9　　*Village Press.* D 23, 1976-
w.

Pub. by Irricana Holdings Ltd. Pub. by Dennis Taylor and ed. by Geoff Taylor. Gladys Taylor ed.-in-chief. Serves communities of Carbon,

Carseland, Gleichen, Hussar, Rockyford, Rosebud, Sharples, Standard and Swalwell (Ref.: Correspondence with Publisher, D 19, 1984).

No issues located

CARDSTON

240.1   *Cardston Record.* Ag 6, 1898-S 1901/...
w.

240.2   *Alberta Star.* S 1901-Je 30, 1911/...
w.

240.3   *Cardston Globe.* Jl 12, 1911-Ap 28, 1921/...
w.

240.4   *Cardston Review.* My 19? 1921-1924/...
w.

240.5   *Cardston News.* 1924-S 1925//
w.

Superceded by *Cardston News* (241).
Pub. by Chauncey Edgar Snow, Ag 6, 1898-S 1901; leased to Norman W. McLeod, My, 1899-S, 1901; David Horton Elton, S 1901-Ag 1, 1908; Fred Burton, Ag 1, 1908-1911; T.B. Brandon, Mr 28-S 19, 1911; Fred Burton, Jl 12, 1911-D 1912; Fred Burton and W.S. Berryessa, Ja 9-Ap 24, 1913; Fred Burton and David C. Peterson, My 1, 1913-1920?; Fred Burton, My 19? 1921-S 1925.
Ref.: *Cardston News* S 9, 1926.

AEP   mf Ag 6, 1898-My 5, 1899; My 3, 1907-Je 30, 1911; Jl 12, 1911-D 28, 1922

241   *Cardston News.* S 17, 1925-My 7, 1964//
w.

Superceded *Cardston News* (240).
Superceded by *Cardston News* (242).
D.O. Wight, ed. and mnging. dir., Cardston News Pub. Co. Ltd., S 17, 1925-Je 9, 1936; Fred Burton, pub., Je 16, 1936-My 7, 1964. Sold My 1964 to Gordon F. West. New voluming begun Ag 12, 1964.

AEP   mf S 17, 1925-My 7, 1964

242   *Cardston News.* Ag 12, 1964-Jl 14, 1966?//
w.

Superceded *Cardston News* (241).
Pub. by Gordon F. West.

AEP   mf Ag 12, 1964-Jl 14, 1966

Cardston Unlimited. Mr 15, 1967-N 13, 1974//
w.

Pub. by Local Press. Ed. by Morris D. Shields and Logan McCarthy.

AEP   mf   Mr 15, 1967-N 13, 1974

Temple City Tribune. Jl 15, 1964-F 24, 1965?//
w.

Pub. by Morris D. Shields and David Curle, Local Press.

AEP   mf   Jl 15, 1964-F 24, 1965

Westwind News. Ap 16, 1975-D 19, 1979//
w.

Pub. by Logan McCarthy, Westwind Printing Ltd. Sold D 1979 to G.L.
(Bert) and Vonda Hancock, *Raymond Review.*

AEP   mf   Ap 16, 1975-D 19, 1979

Cardston Chronicle. Ja 15, 1980-
w.

Pub. and ed. by G.L. (Bert) Hancock, Ja 15-Oc 29, 1980 (Ref.: *Raymond
Review,* Oc 8, 1980). Sold N 1, 1980 to Nepñelokokkugia Holdings Ltd. and
pub. by Roy Sweet, and A.L. Treleaven, N 1, 1980-My 31, 1983; sold to
D.M.J.A.B. Printers, pub. Dan T. Barr, Je 1983+.

AEP   or   Ag 3, 1982+
ACG   or   Ja 15, 1980-Ag 1982; Jl 1, 1980, Cardston History Special
                Supplement

RLSTADT

Town of Carlstadt changed its name to Alderson Jl 1, 1915. See
ALDERSON for newspapers serving Carlstadt.

RMANGAY

Carmangay Sun. Mr 4, 1910-Ap 23, 1937//
w.

Pub. by A.E. Quayle, Mr 4, 1910-1920?; B.N. Woodhull, 1920; James
Mewhort, Oc 1920-1921; Louis A. Starck, 1921-Ap 23, 1937.
Ref.: *Calgary Herald* Ap 28, 1937.

AEP   or   Mr 4, 1910-S 5, 1918; Oc 22-D 24, 1920; Ja 11, 1929-Ap 23,
                1937

CARSELAND

248   *Carseland Recorder.* 1921?-N 1923?//
         w.

         Ref.: CAN 1922, 1923, 1924.

         No issues located

         Village Press. D 23, 1976-
         See **CARBON**. *Village Press.* (239).

CARSTAIRS

         Carstairs Reporter. Mr? 1903-?//
         See Supplement (1055).

249   *Carstairs Journal.* D 29, 1905-Je 28, 1923?//
         w.

         Pub. and ed. by L.E. Davis, D 29, 1905-N 10, 1911; William Lister, N 17,
         1911-N 20, 1914; Arthur S. Lorimer, N 27, 1914-Ag 8, 1919; C.C. Stuart, Ag
         15, 1919-Mr 11, 1920; Lorimer, Mr 18, 1920-1922; Henry Paul, 1922-1923.

         AEP   or   My 3, 1907-Je 28, 1923

250.1   *Carstairs News.* 1924-Ja 15, 1975/...
         w.

250.2   *Carstairs and District Community Press.* Ja 22, 1975-F 3, 1977/...
         w.

250.3   *Carstairs and District Community Press and Mountain View
         County News.* F 9, 1977-Ja 9, 1980/...
         w.

250.4   *Carstairs Community Press, Mountain View County News.*
         Ja 16, 1980-Jl 24, 1985//
         w.

         Pub. and ed. by R. Leslie Mills, 1924-Mr 31, 1966; Mrs. Vimy Currie, Ap
         7, 1966-Ag 26, 1970; Martin J. Neck, S 1, 1970-Jl 31, 1976; Joyce Dokter,
         Carstairs Community Press Ltd., Ag 1, 1976-Je 20, 1984; MHWH Pub. Inc.,
         Je 6, 1984-Jl 24, 1985; ed. by Andy McLeister.
         Became official newspaper for County of Mountain View F 9, 1977.
         Ref.: *Calgary Herald* F 14, 1978.

         AEP   or   Ja 8-Je 25, 1925; Ja 6, 1926-Jl 24, 1985

1   *Courier.* D 8, 1982-
     w.

Pub. by Irricana Holdings Ltd. Pub. by Dennis Taylor and ed. by Gladys
Taylor. Distributed to Carstairs, Crossfield, Cremona, Didsbury and Madden
(Ref.: Correspondence with Publisher, D 19, 1984).

No issues located

ASTOR

2   *Castor Advance.* N 26, 1909-
     w. Political — Liberal

Pub. by Advance Pub. Co. Ltd. Pub. and ed. by Frank H. Whiteside,
Liberal, N 26, 1909-S 21? 1911; W.F. Beamish, Oc 5, 1911-Ja 18, 1912;
Whiteside, Ja 25, 1912-Ap 24, 1913; George Broadley, Liberal, My 1, 1913-
Ap 30, 1914; Whiteside, My 7, 1914-S 21, 1916; Stanley A. Fawdrey, Oc 12,
1916-1926?; J.E. Hunt, 1926?-Ap 27, 1928; John H. Salton, My 4, 1928-D
24, 1947; Walter Mandick, Ja 1, 1948-My 29, 1958; Monte G. Keith, Je 1,
1958-D 22, 1965; Roy Ward Willis, Ja 1, 1966-Je 15, 1967; Roy W. Willis,
and R. Charles Willis, Je 22, 1967-Je 1973; Brian Higgins, Jl 19, 1973-Je
1977; Joseph Vincent Bain, Jl 21, 1977-My 11, 1978; Wendell Warman, Jl 1,
1978+.

Progress Number, Ap 24, 1913; Alberta Golden Jubilee Edition, Jl 14,
1955; 50th Jubilee Edition, Jl 7, 1960; School Reunion Issue 1908-1978, Jl 1,
1978.

AEP   or N 26, 1909-N 17, 1921; D 25, 1924; Ja 8-Je 25, 1925; Ja 6,
            1927+

Hoofprints. N 10, 1971-
See **STETTLER.** *Stettler Independent.* (923).

AYLEY

3   *Cayley Hustler.* D 17, 1909-N 19, 1913//
     m.; w.

Frequency varied: m. D 17, 1909-Ap 27, 1910; w. Ap 30, 1910-N 19,
1913.
Pub. and ed. by Rev. Frank Bushfield, D 17, 1909-D 14, 1910; A.
Nicholson, D 21, 1910-N 19, 1913.

AEP   or D 17, 1909-N 19, 1913

4   *Cayley Advertiser* 1914-?//
     w.?

Pub. by Harwood Duncan, Claresholm (Ref.: *Stavely Advertiser* masthead, Ap 9, 1914).

No issues located

CEREAL

255.1   *Acadia Review.* Jl 30? 1914-D 31? 1914/...
          w.

255.2   *Review.* Ja 7, 1915-1918?//
          w.

          Pub. and ed. by Leonard H. Horncastle.
          Ref.: **CAN** 1919.

          AEP   or   Ag 6, 1914-Oc 20, 1915

256   *Cereal Recorder.* 1920-Ag 28, 1947//
          w.

          Pub. by Ivan H. Holden, 1920-Ag 20, 1936; J.C. Cottrell, Ag 27, 1936-Ag
          28, 1947. Printed by *Strathmore Standard* (Ref.: **MK** 1922).

          AEP   or   Ja 7, 1926-Ag 28, 1947

CHAMPION

257   *Champion Spokesman* Ap 29, 1914-S 4, 1914?//
          w.

          Ref.: **GREG**, p.758.

          No issues located

258   *Champion Weekly.* 1917-1919?//
          w.

          Pub. by Standard Newspaper Syndicate, Calgary (Ref.: **MK** 1917; **CAN**
          1919).

          No issues located

259   *Champion News.* 1919-1920?//
          w.

          Pub. by Rev. F.T. Cook (Ref.: **MK** 1919, 1920).

          No issues located

260.1   *Champion Chronicle.* Je 1, 1919-N 13, 1941/...
          w.

260.2   *Chronicle.* N 20, 1941-Mr 25, 1943?//
          w.

Pub. by B.N. Woodhull, 1919?-D 1931; Mrs. Harvey Jopling, D 1931-Mr 1935; Louis A. Starck, Ap 4, 1935-My 13, 1937; C.A. Marshall, My 20, 1937-Ja 12, 1939; Gillivray S. McRae, Ja 19, 1939-Jl 31, 1941; Stanley Orris, Ag 1, 1941-1943.
Ref.: CNLU p.7.

AEP   or   Oc 21, 1920-My 5, 1921; Jl 2, 1925-Mr 25, 1943

AUVIN

Advance. Mr 7, 1912-S 12/19, 1912//
w.

Continued by *Great West Saturday Night Advance,* Edmonton (370).
Superceded by *Chauvin Gazette* (262).
Pub. by Great West Twentieth Century Pub. Co. Ed. by Mrs. Amy H. Keane.

AEP   or   Mr 7-S 12/19, 1912

Chauvin Gazette. S 13, 1912-S 12, 1913?//
w.

Superceded *Advance,* Chauvin (261).
Pub. by DeForrest Clyne.
Ref.: MK 1913; CAN 1914.

AEP   or   S 13, 1912-S 12, 1913

Chauvin Chronicle. Mr 26, 1914-D 29, 1948//
w.

Amalgamated with *Wainwright Star* (1007) to form *Star-Chronicle,* Wainwright (1009), Ja 19, 1949.
Pub. and ed. by Leonard D'Albertanson, Sr., 1914-1925; Leonard D'Albertanson, Jr., 1925-D 1948.
Pub. section *Edgerton Enterprise.* My 8, 1946-D 1948. Upon amalgamation with *Wainwright Star, Edgerton Enterprise* and *Chauvin Chronicle* were continued as sections.

AEP   or   Mr 26, 1914-D 22, 1920; Ja 6, 1926-D 29, 1948

Chauvin Chronicle. Ja 19, 1949-
See WAINWRIGHT. *Wainwright Star Chronicle* (1009.2).

INOOK

Chinook Advance. Ag 1, 1914-N 1, 1945//
w.

Suspended pub. Ap 15-Ag 19, S 9-Oc 21, 1920.
Pub. and ed. by Arthur Nicholson, 1914-Ap 1920; Robert Smith, Oc 21, 1920-S 29, 1927; Margaret C. Nicholson, Oc 1, 1927-N 1, 1945.

Ref.: **CNLU** p.7; *Albertan* Calgary, Oc 10, 1942; *Calgary Herald* Oc 10, 1942.

AEP   or   Ag 26, 1915-Mr 23, 1922; Ja 3, 1924-Je 25, 1925; Ja 6, 1927-N 1, 1945

CLAIRMONT

265   *Clairmont Independent.* Jl 20, 1916-Jl 18, 1918//
w.

Title varied: *Clairmont Independent and Lake Saskatoon Journal.*
Pub. and ed. by Gerald H. Heller, Jl 20, 1916-Ap 15, 1918 (Ref.: *Grande Prairie Herald* Jl 25, 1916); S.R. Tuffley, Ap 15-Jl 18, 1918.
Paper folded when Tuffley was arrested and placed in an internment camp for printing material detrimental to the efficient prosecution of the War. (Ref.: **CAM 2** p.118)

AEP   or   F 22-Jl 18, 1918

CLARESHOLM

266   *Claresholm Review.* 1904-Mr 16, 1916//
w. Political — Conservative Political — Liberal

Amalgamated Ap 7, 1916 with *Claresholm Advertiser* to form *Claresholm Review-Advertiser* (267).
Pub. and ed. by L.D. Shilling, 1904?-My 1907; A. Wylie, My 1907-Oc 30, 1908; J.D.S. Barrett, N 1908-F 5, 1909; T.W. Quayle, Conservative, F 12, 1909-My 1911; Harwood Duncan, Liberal, My 31, 1911-Ja 1914; L.G. Shortreed, Ja 26, 1914-Mr 16, 1916.

AEP   or   My 3-Oc 11, 1907; Mr 6, 1908-Mr 16, 1916

267.1   *Claresholm Advertiser.* Ap 15, 1914-Mr 30, 1916/...
w.

267.2   *Claresholm Review-Advertiser.* Ap 7, 1916-My 4, 1928//
w.

Amalgamated with *Claresholm Review* (266) Ap 7, 1916.
Absorbed by *Claresholm Local Press* (268), My 11, 1928.
Suspended pub. Ag 21-Oc 21, 1915.
Pub. and ed. by Harwood Duncan, Ap 15, 1914-Ag 21, 1915; Robert K. Peck and Ed V. Chambers, Oc 21-N 1915; Chambers, D 2, 1915-Mr 30, 1916; Peck and Chambers, Ap 7, 1916-S 13, 1918; F.H. Schooley, S 16, 1918-My 4, 1928.

AEP   or   Ap 15, 1914-D 31, 1920; My 6-Ag 26, 1921; Ja 2, 1925-My 4, 1928

8   *Claresholm Local Press.* Oc 8, 1926-
w.

Absorbed *Claresholm Review-Advertiser* (267) My 11, 1928.
Pub. and ed. by Rae Livingstone King, Oc 8, 1926-D 23, 1944; Gordon Neale, Ja 4, 1945-Ja 28, 1965; Eldon George (Andy) Anderson, F 1, 1965-Mr 30, 1978; Paul W. Rockley, Ap 1, 1978+.
Special issue to mark opening of No. 15 Service Flying Training School, Ag 14, 1941; Alberta Golden Jubilee Edition, S 8, 1955.

AEP   or   Oc 8, 1926+

9   *Footnotes and News.* N 1969-Oc 31, 1973//
bw.

Pub. by L. Walter Wiig, Walt's Shoe Store and Walt's Print Shop.
Ref.: **CNLU** p.7.

OONL   or   N 15, 1972

.IVE

0   *Clive News-Record.* Mr 4, 1914-Ja 30, 1918?//
w.

Pub. by Charles A. Roulston and Co., Mr 4, 1914-Mr 31, 1915; William Lister, Ap 5-S 29, 1915; John H. Salton, Oc 1, 1915-1918.
Ref.: **MK** 1917-1918, **CAN** 1919.

AEP   or   Mr 11, 1914-Ja 30, 1918

1   *Clive Review.* Mr? 1919-1921?//
w.

Title varied: *Clive Messenger.*
Pub. by P.E. Bachman (Ref.: **MK** 1919-1921; **CAN** 1922). Purchased by Henry Oke (Ref.: **CPP** v30no2 F 1921).

No issues located

.UNY

2   *Cluny Recorder.* 1921?-Oc 1924?//
w.

Ref.: **CAN** 1922-1925.

No issues located

.YDE

8   *Clyde Bulletin.* 1950-1952?//
w.

Pub. by Thomas W. Pue, Edmonton (Ref.: **AY** 1952; **CAN** 1953).

AEP   or   Ja 18-Jl 9, 1952

274   *Clyde Star.* 1972-1973?//
w.

Pub. by Thomas W. Pue, Sun Colorpress Ltd., Edmonton (Ref.: **AY** 1974; **CNLU** p.10).

OONL   or   My 27, Je 24, 1972

COALDALE

275   *Coaldale Times.* 1922?-1927?//
w.

Pub. as part of *Canadian Advocate*, Lethbridge (698). Same text as *Magrath Times* (716) (Ref.: **CAN** 1928; **MK** 1922-1925).

No issues located

276.1   *Coaldale Flyer.* 1950-N 21, 1958/...
w.

276.2   *Coaldale Flyer and the Lethbridge Northern News.* N 28, 1958-F
          13, 1959/...
w.

276.3   *Sunny South News.* F 20, 1959-F 13, 1974/...
w.

276.4   *County of Lethbridge Sunny South News.* F 20, 1974-
w.

Coaldale Flyer amalgamated with *Lethbridge Northern News*, Picture Butte, (812.2), N 28, 1958, to form *Coaldale Flyer and the Lethbridge Northern News*.
Est. and pub. by J.J. Loewen, 1950-F 25, 1967; J.B.R. (Bert) Staddon, Mr 1, 1960-S 29, 1971. Sold to and pub. by the Taber Times Ltd., 1967+ Ed. by B.J. (Bertrand) Staddon, Mr 1, 1960-Ja 17, 1963; Bill Schuurman, Oc 1, 1971-Mr 27, 1974; Barbara Duckworth, Ap 1, 1974-My 14, 1975; Kenneth M. Johansen, My 21-Ag 13, 1975; Colleen (Meaney) Valin, Ag 19, 1975+
Alberta Golden Jubilee Editions, Je 9, 17, 24, 1955.

AEP   or   Mr 21, 1958-Je 25, 1959; Ja 7, 1960+

277   *Neu-Kanadier.* D? 1954-1955//
w. German in Ger.

Place of pub. varied: Calgary (Ref.: **CNLC**, p.135).
Pub. by J.J. Loewen; ed. by Annie L. Hartwig.
Ref.: **ARN** p.228; **CNLC** p.135.

OONL   or   F 16, 1955

ALHURST

Coalhurst News. N 15? 1928-Oc 2, 1929//
w.

Pub. by F.H. Schooley.

AEP   or   F 27-Oc 2, 1929

CHRANE

Cochrane Advocate. Mr 11? 1909-S 8, 1927//
w.

Suspended pub. Oc 14, 1920-Mr 17, 1921; Oc 15, 1925-Je 9, 1927.
Pub. and ed. by James Mewhort, Mr 11?-Oc 2, 1909; Charles N. Austin,
Oc 9, 1909-Oc 12, 1911; Albert E. Strickland, Oc 26, 1911-My 8, 1913;
W.A. Mackenzie, My 15-S 11, 1913; Cochrane Advocate Co., S 18, 1913-Oc
7, 1915; F.C. Atkinson, Oc 14-Oc 21, 1915; Arthur Taylor, Oc-N 4, 1915;
Anthony C. Hathaway, N 11, 1915-Jl 18, 1918; R.J. Hawkey, Jl 25, 1918-Ag
7, 1919; Harold B. Willis, Ag 14, 1919-My 20, 1920; O.S. Love, My 20-Oc
14, 1920; C.C. Stuart, Mr 24, 1921-F 9, 1922; Hugh C. Farthing, Mr 16,
1922-Oc 8, 1925; Alwin Gissing, Je 16-S 8, 1927.
Ref.: **BRO** pp.140-141; **COCH** pp.175-176.

AEP   or   [Mr 10, 1910-Jl 20, 1917; Mr 21, 1918-Oc 15, 1925; Je 9-S8,
             1927]

Old Timer. Ap 1, 1943-Je 9, 1972?//
bw.

First issue entitled *Cochrane Old Timer.*
Mimeographed.
Pub. and ed. by J. Lessard, o.m.i., Ap 1, 1943-Ja 24, 1947; Bernice Reid, F
7, 1947-D? 1959; Bea Hammer and Maurine Williamson, Mr 4, 1960-Je 22,
1961; Bernice Reid, Jl 6, 1961-Jl 3, 1965; Dorothy Anderson, Jl 20, 1965-Je
9, 1972. First printed for servicemen overseas during WWII.
Ref.: *Albertan,* Calgary Ap 15, 1966:24; Correspondence with Bernice
Reid, N 14 1984.

ACOM   or   Ap 1, 1943-Je 9, 1972
ACG   or   Oc 14, 1943; S 29, 1944; Ag 31, 1966; [Ap 19, 1967-Oc 25,
             1967]

Cochrane Times. My 15, 1974-D 18, 1984//
bw.; w.

Frequency varied: bw. My 15, 1974-Ag 21, 1975; w. S 4, 1975-D 18, 1984.
Mimeographed to D 1977.
Pub. and ed. by Paula Barnhart, My 15, 1974-Je 7, 1975. Ed. by Donna Little, Je 21, 1975-1977. Sold to Mary P. Maxie, D 1, 1977. Maxie, pub. and ed., D 1, 1977-Ag 8, 1984; co-published with Andy Marshall, Ag 15-N 1984. Sold to Marshall, N 1984.
Cochrane's 75th Anniversary Edition, Ag 2, 1978.
Ref.: **CNLU** p.7.

OONL   or   My 15, 30, 1974
ACOM   or   My 30, 1974-D 18, 1984
AEP   or   Ja 4, 1978-D 18, 1984

282   *Pioneer.* S 3, 1980-My 26, 1982//
         2m.

         Pub. by Cochrane Times Ltd. Served Bragg Creek, Springbank, Priddis, and Redwood Meadows.

         AEP   or   S 3, 1980-My 26, 1982

283   *Town Crier.* Oc 8, 1980-Je 2, 1982//
         2m.

         Pub. by Cochrane Times Ltd. Served Cremona, Water Valley, Crossfield and Dogpound.

         AEP   or   Oc 8, 1980-Je 2, 1982

COLD LAKE

284   *Cold Lake Herald.* 1932-?//
         ?

         Ref.: **SKA** p.234.

         No issues located

285   *Cold Lake Courier.* 1959?-Je 1960//
         ? Military

         Amalgamated with *Grand Centre Times* (579) and *Bonnyville Tribune* Je 22, 1960 to form *Tribune,* Bonnyville (87.2) (Ref.: *Bonnyville Tribune,* Je 15, 1960).
         Pub. by RCAF Cold Lake (Ref.: **SKA** p.235).

         No issues located

286   *Cold Lake Sentinel.* Jl 15, 1959-? 1959//
         2m.

         Pub. by Chester Redel (Ref.: **SKA** p.235; **CNLU** p.8).

         OONL   or   Jl 15, 1959

7   *Canadian Forces Base Cold Lake Courier.* N 22, 1967-
     bw. Military

     Pub. by Canadian Forces Base Cold Lake, Medley. Ed. by O.G.
     Amesbury, N 22, 1967-F 21, 1969; T.J. McGale and A. Maskell, Mr 12-D
     1969; J. Eggenberger, Ja-My 6, 1970; A. Maskell, My 20-D 1970; J. Swal-
     low, Ja 1971-My 5, 1972; W.C. Stewart, My-Je 28, 1972; Gorm Jensen, Ag
     16, 1972-Ja 31, 1973; Al French, F 14-Oc 24, 1973; Bob Hardy, N 7, 1973-
     Ap 10, 1974; Howard Thibault, Ap 24, 1974-Ag 27, 1975; Brian Puttock, S
     10, 1975-Oc 20, 1976; Jack Limo, N 3, 1976-Ag 17, 1977; Bill Holland, S 7,
     1977-Mr 1, 1978; Bill McWilliams, Mr 15, 1978-Je 27, 1979; Rod Pederson,
     Jl 11-D 12, 1979; Clare Reilander, Ja 16, 1980+.
        Ref.: Correspondence with Publisher, Ap 11, 1984.

     AEP   or   My 3, 1972+

OLEMAN

8.1   *Coleman Miner.* Ap 10? 1908-S 10, 1909/...
       w.

8.2   *Coleman Miner and Carbondale Advocate.* S 17, 1909-D 9, 1910/...
       w.

8.3   *Coleman Miner.* D 16, 1910-My 26, 1911?//
       w.

       Pub. by Coleman Pub. Co. Ltd., H.S. French, ed. and mgr., Ap-Oc 16,
       1908; Foothills Job Print and News Co., Oc 23, 1908-Oc 14, 1910, J.D.S.
       Barrett, ed. and mgr., Oc 23, 1908-Ja 28, 1910; T.B. Brandon, ed., Ag 13,
       1909-F 24, 1911; Brandon and H.J. Wright, props., Oc 21, 1910-Mr 31, 1911;
       H.J. Wright, ed., Mr 3-Mr 31, 1911; H.J. Wright, pub. and ed., Ap 7-My 26,
       1911.
       Souvenir Edition [1909-1910]
       Seized by sherriff during 1911 strike (Ref.: COU p.122)

       AEP   mf   My 1, 1908-My 26, 1911
       AEPAA or   Souvenir Edition (971.234C677c)

9   *Coleman Bulletin.* Ap 1912-D 27, 1918?//
       w.

       Title varied: *Coleman Bulletin and Crow's Nest Pass Advertiser.*
       Pub. and ed. by W.F. Stanley, Ap 1912-Je? 1913; R.L. Norman, Jl 1913-D
       1918.
       Ref.: CAN 1919; MK 1913, 1917, 1918.

       AEP   mf   Ja 31, 1913-D 27, 1918

0.1   *Coleman Journal.* Ag? 1921-F 9, 1939/...
       w.

290.2   *Coleman Journal and Crows Nest Pass Advertiser.* F 16, 1939-D
           5, 1940/...

290.3   *Coleman Journal.* D 12, 1940-Oc 26, 1972/...
           w.; bw.

290.4   *Coleman Review.* N 1, 1972-D 18, 1974//
           w.; bw.

           Frequency varied: w. 1921-Je 1949; bw. Ja 16-D 23, 1952; w. Ja 14,
           1953-My 21, 1958; bw. Jl 9, 1958-S 12, 1973; w. S 26, 1973-Ag 14, 1974;
           bw. Ag 28-D 18, 1974.
           Suspended pub. Je 9? 1949-Ja 16, 1952; My 21-Jl 9, 1958; F 4-Oc 15,
           1970.
           Pub. by C. Dunning, 1921-1923; J.D.S. Barrett, 1923-1925; Ernest Frank
           Gare, 1925-Je 30, 1927; H.T. Halliwell, Jl 1, 1927-Ja 30, 1944; Thomas
           Holstead and Alex Balloch, lessees, F 1, 1944-D 31, 1948; Holstead and Lou
           Thomas, Ja 6-Je 1949; Holstead, Ja 16, 1952-F 4, 1970. Sold to Creston
           Review Ltd., Creston, B.C., Herbert F. Legg, pub., Oc 15, 1970-D 18, 1974.
           Continued as section *Coleman Review* in *Review Town and Country,* Ja 8,
           1975-Jl 12, 1978, and *Review Supplement,* Jl 26, 1978+, both supplements of
           Creston Review, B.C.
           Coleman's 50th Anniversary Edition, Je 30, 1953.

           AEP   mf Ag 27, 1925-Je 24, 1926; Ja 6, 1927-Je 9, 1949; Ja 16, 1952-D
                        18, 1974
           AEP   mf *Coleman Review* supplement, Ja 8, 1975-Ag 26, 1981

COLINTON

291   *Colinton Clipper.* 1951-D 21, 1955?//
           w.

           Pub. by Thomas W. Pue, Edmonton.
           Alberta Golden Jubilee Edition, Ag 31, 1955.
           Ref.: CAN 1956.

           AEP   or Ja 9, 1952-D 21, 1955

CONSORT

292.1   *Consort Enterprise.* D 12, 1912-Ag 10, 1922/...
           w.

292.2   *Enterprise (Consort and Monitor).* Ag 17, 1922-My 20, 1937/...
           w.

292.3   *Consort Enterprise.* My 27, 1937-
           w.

Amalgamated with *Monitor News* (763), Je 8, 1922.

Pub. and ed. by Henry Oke, D 12, 1912-N 27, 1914; Mabel DeWolfe, D 3, 1914-Ap 1921; Wilburn Alurd DeWolfe, Enterprise Pub. Co., F 24, 1916-D 1949; Charlie M. Scott, F 13, 1950-Oc 4, 1956; Arlos F. Tkach, Oc 18, 1956-Ap 4, 1957; Mary K. Readman, Ap 11, 1957+ Pub. by William J. Readman, S 9, 1965+.

Ref.: **DAL** p.68; *Consort Enterprise* D 7, 1972.

AEP   mf D 19, 1912-D 22, 1982
or   Ja 1983+

Hoofprints. N 10, 1971-
See **STETTLER**. *Stettler Independent* (923).

ORONATION

3   *Coronation Review.* S 27, 1911-
w.

Prospectus issue pub. by Grover Cleveland Duncan for Advance Pub. Co. Ltd., on S 27, 1911 entitled *News Review*.

Suspended pub. N 2, 1972-Ja 9, 1973.

Pub. and ed. by W.F. Beamish, N 1911-F 6, 1913; Edgar W. Harris, F 6, 1913-Ja 13, 1916; A.C. Harris, F 20-Mr 30, 1916; Frank H. Whiteside, Ap 6-S 21, 1916; Joseph A. Housiaux, Ap 6, 1916-Jl 12, 1917; W.A. McGillivray and Housiaux, Jl 19, 1917-1925?; McGillivray and Art Jensen, 1925?-My 21, 1942; Jensen, My 27, 1942-Oc 3, 1968; Howard Kroetsch, Oc 7, 1968-S 1, 1977. Ed. by Raymond E. Matthews, Oc 7, 1968-N 2, 1972. Pub. by Gordon Keith, S 8, 1977+.

25th Anniversary Number, S 24, 1936; Alberta Golden Jubilee Edition, S 1, 1955.

ACG   or   S 27, 1911
AEP   or   Jl 4, 1912-D 30, 1920; Ja 6, 1927+

Hoofprints. N 10, 1971-
See **STETTLER**. *Stettler Independent*, (923).

OUTTS

Coutts-Sweetgrass International Herald. Ja 26, 1911-?//
See Supplement (1056)

OWLEY

4   *Cowley Chronicle and Lundbreck Advertiser.* S 17? 1909-Ja 28, 1910//
w.

Pub. and ed. by W.J. Bartlett, Foothills Job Print and News Co.

AEP   mf D 3, 1909-Ja 28, 1910

CRAIGMYLE

295   *Craigmyle Gazette.* My 24, 1921-N 23, 1922//
           w.

           Pub. and ed. by Vin. C. Dunning, My 24-Jl 29, 1921; T.B. Malcolm, Ag
           4?-S 23, 1921; Victor W.R.B. Ball, S 29, 1921-N 23, 1922.

           AEP   or   My 24, 1921-N 23, 1922

CREMONA

           Town Crier. Oc 8, 1980-Je 2, 1982
           See **COCHRANE.** *Town Crier.* (283).

           Courier. D 8, 1982-
           See **CARSTAIRS.** *Courier.* (251).

CROSSFIELD

296   *Chronicle.* D 25? 1907-Jl 24, 1942//
           w.

           Title varied: *Crossfield Chronicle.*
           Pub. and ed. by James Mewhort, D 1907-Oc 30, 1909; E.M. Seager, D 3,
           1909-Ap 15, 1910; F.H. Schooley, Ap 29-Ag 19, 1910; Leonard C. Newsom,
           Ag 26, 1910-Mr 31, 1911; Anthony C. Hathaway, Ap 1, 1911- ?1912; Rev.
           A. Thorold-Eller,? 1912-Mr 27, 1913; Robert Whitfield, Ap 3, 1913-1928;
           Stanley A. Fawdrey, Mr-D 12, 1929; W.H. (Bill) Miller, D 19, 1929-Ja 30,
           1936; George Y. McLean, F 1, 1936-D 30, 1937; G.E. and C.E. Wall, Ja 6,
           1938-D 7, 1939; C.A. Marshall, D 14, 1939-Jl 31, 1941; Ivan (Bill) E. Ham-
           bly, Ag 7, 1941-Mr? 1942; J.B. Robertson and B. Strother, Je 12-Jl 24, 1942.

           AEP   or   Mr 4, 1908-Jl 4, 1912; F 20, 1913-D 29, 1921; Ja 1-Oc 8,
                      1925; F 21, 1929-Jl 24, 1942

297   *North American Collector.* 1908-?//
           m.

           Pub. by James Mewhort (Ref.: **MK** 1909).

           No issues located

298   *Crossfield Chronicle.* F 5, 1943-F 6, 1948//
           w.

Ed. by W.H. (Bill) Miller, F 5, 1943-D 1945, printed by *Olds Gazette*. Pub. by W.R. (Ronnie) Newsom and Neil K. Leatherdale, Ja 4, 1946-N 28, 1947; Roy Barnaby, D 5, 1947-F 6, 1948.

AEP   or   F 5, 1943-F 6, 1948

Crossfield Chronicle. F 13, 1948-D 31, 1948//
w.

Pub. by Harry May. Printed by *Olds Gazette*.

AEP   or   F 13-D 31, 1948

Crossfield Chronicle. Ap 24, 1949-Ag 18, 1953.
w.

Pub. by Thomas W. Pue, Community Publications of Alberta and Sun Pub. Co. Ltd., Edmonton.

AEP   or   Ap 24, 1949-Ag 18, 1953

Town Crier. Oc 8, 1980-Je 2, 1982
See **COCHRANE**. *Town Crier* (283).

Courier. D 8, 1982-
See **CARSTAIRS**. *Courier* (251).

ZAR

Czar Clipper. 1920-My 30, 1951?//
w.

Suspended pub. S 13, 1945-Ag 22, 1946.
Place of pub. varied: Provost, 1920-1921; Hughenden, 1921-1931; Hardisty, 1931-1945; Killam, 1946-1949; Edmonton, 1949-1951.
Pub. by G.W. Davidson, 1921-1923; H.W. Betts, 1923-S 13, 1946; Thomas W. Pue, Community Publications of Alberta, Ag 22, 1946-My 1951.
Ref.: CAN 1951.

AEP   or   Ja 7-Je 24, 1925; Ja 15, 1927-S 13, 1945; Ag 22, 1946-My 30, 1951

YSLAND

Daysland Press. My 26, 1907-F 13, 1930//
w.

Amalgamated with *Sedgewick Sentinel* (890.1) and *Killam News* (659) to form *Community Press*, Sedgewick (890.2) Ap 17, 1930.
Pub. and ed. by A.A.P. McDowell, 1907; Frederick John Slight, 1912; P.J. Murphy, 1922; A.L. Eastly, 1922-F 13, 1930.
Mid-Summer Special Edition, Je 25, 1908.

AEP or My 30-Oc 31, 1907; F 6, 1908-D 25, 1919; Ja 1, 1925-F 13, 1930

303   *Daysland Commercial.* My 21, 1930-Ap 23, 1931?//
w.

Pub. by John W. Johnston, My 21-D 31, 1930; G. and A. Storseth, Ja 7-Ap 23, 1931.

AEP or My 21, 1930-Ap 23, 1931

304   *Daysland Sun.* F 27, 1947-Ag 3, 1953//
w.

Pub. by Thomas W. Pue, Community Publications of Alberta and Sun Pub. Co. Ltd. Printed in Hardisty, Killam and Edmonton.

AEP or F 27, 1947-Ag 3, 1953

Enterprise. S 3, 1980-
See **ALLIANCE.** *Enterprise* (16.2)

DELBURNE

305   *Delburne Progress.* My 31, 1912-N 29, 1922?//
w.

Pub. by Progress Printing Press. Pub. successively by S. Arnold Gill, Milo B. Huffman, and W.R. Mott (Ref.: **MK** 1913-1922).
Pub. *Lousana Page* as supplement Mr?-N 1922. Only issue of N 22, 1922, no. 38, filmed.

AEPAA mf My 31, 1912-N 1, 1918; N 14, 1919; My 3-N 29, 1922

306   *Delburne News.* S 4? 1924-Mr 4, 1926?//
w.

Pub. by Mrs. A.T. Rowell (Ref.: **MK** 1925, 1926).

AEPAA mf Ja 1, 1925-Mr 4, 1926

307   *Delburne Observer.* 1927-1928?//
w.

Ref.: **CAN** 1928, 1929.

No issues located

308   *Delburne Independent.* Je 1, 1928-S 28, 1928?//
w.

Pub. by Melville Leathley.

AEPAA mf Je 8-S 28, 1928

9 *Delburne Times.* N 26? 1936-My 25, 1967?//
w.; 3m.; 2m.

Frequency varied: w. N 1936-Ap 10, 1958; 3m. Ap 19, 1958-Je 29, 1963; 2m. Jl 11, 1963-My 25, 1967.
Pub. by A.T. George.
Alberta Golden Jubilee Edition, Jl 14, 1955.

AEPAA mf Ja 7-Je 3, 1937; Ja 6, 1938-My 25, 1967

0 *Delburne and District Journal.* N2, 1967-Jl 1986//
bw.

Pub. and ed. by Aubrey and Audrey Stones.

AEP	or	My 4, 1972-Jl 1986
OONL	or	N 2, 1967; Ja 4, 1968

ELIA

1 *Hand Hills Echo.* 1916-1918?//
w.

Pub. by A.E. Snyder (Ref.: **MK** 1917, 1918; **CAN** 1919).

No issues located

2 *Delia Times.* Ja 30? 1919-D 22, 1960?//
w.

Pub. and ed. by Ernest Frank Gare, 1919-Ja 1923; pub. and ed., Joseph McKibbon, Ja 1923-D 22, 1960.

AEP or F 27-D 25, 1919; Ja 1, 1925-D 22, 1960

13 *Delia Times.* Ja 30, 1974-? 1974//
w.

Pub. by James Charles L'Herault.
Ref.: **CNLU** p.20.

OONL or Ja 30, 1974

EVON

14 *Devonian.* F 2, 1949-S 25, 1957//
w.

Absorbed by *Representative,* Leduc, (689) Oc 3, 1957.
Pub. and ed. by Fred Johns in Leduc.

AEP or F 2, 1949-S 25, 1957

315   *Devon Dispatch.* My 27, 1976-
        w.

        Pub. and ed. by Gary and Marlene Cavanagh, My 27, 1976-Je? 1979;
        Eugene Bourassa, Je? 1979-D 16, 1981; John Law, Ja 1, 1982-D 1985, pub.
        by Devon Printing and Pub. Ltd., Hugh Johnston, Uncle Hug Pub. Ltd., Ja
        1986+.

        AEP   or   Ap 16, 1980+

DIDSBURY

316   *Didsbury Courier.* 1903//
        w.?

        Pub. by Thomas Gaddes (Ref.: *Didsbury Pioneer* S 13, 1945).

        No issues located

317   *Didsbury Pioneer.* F 13, 1903-Ja 2, 1974//
        w.

        Amalgamated with *Didsbury Booster* (318.1), Ja 9, 1974, to form
        Didsbury Booster and Mountain View County News. (318.2).
        Pub. and ed. by G.E. Grow, F 13-Ag 21, 1903; A.J. Thomas, Ag 28,
        1903-Ap 1905; H.E. Osmond, Ap 1905-My 1925; W.P. Cotton, My 13,
        1925-My 31, 1928; W.C. Gooder and Edwin J.C. Gooder, Je 1, 1928-Oc 31,
        1944; Edouard J. Rouleau, N 1, 1944-Ap 30, 1952; James Currie, My 1,
        1952-My 14, 1965; Mrs. Vimy Currie, My 20, 1965-Oc 31, 1970; Martin J.
        Neck, S 1, 1970-N 30, 1972; Miller McCoy, D 1, 1972-Ja 2, 1974.
        Centennial Edition, S 6, 1967.

        ACG   or   S 6, 1967
        AEP   or   F 13, 1903-Ja 2, 1974

318.1   *Didsbury Booster.* My 2, 1961-Ja 2, 1974/...
        w.

318.2   *Didsbury Booster and Mountain View County News.* Ja 9, 1974-
        Jl 24, 1980/...
        w.

318.3   *Didsbury Pioneer and Mountain View County News.* Jl 30, 1980-
        Ap 23, 1986//
        w.

        Amalgamated with *Didsbury Pioneer* (317) on Ja 9, 1974 to form
        Didsbury Booster and Mountain View County News. (318.2).

Pub. and ed. by Miller McCoy, My 2, 1961-Mr 31, 1977; John Davis, Ap 1, 1977-Ap 23, 1986.
75th Anniversary issue of Didsbury newspaper, Jl 30, 1980.

AEP   or   My 2, 1961-Ap 23, 1986.

Courier. D 8, 1982-
See **CARSTAIRS**. *Courier* (251).

)GPOUND

Town Crier. Oc 8, 1980-Je 2, 1982
See **COCHRANE**. *Town Crier* (283).

)NALDA

● *Donalda Free Lance.* Ag? 1915-D 27, 1916?//
w.

Pub. and ed. by R.P. Brooks (Ref.: **MK** 1917; **CAN** 1917).

AEP   or   Oc 12-D 27, 1916

● *Donalda Recorder.* 1920-1921?//
w.

Ref.: **CAN** 1921.

ADOD   or   1 issue

◀ *Donalda Review.* Mr 1921-1927?//
w.

Pub. by Frederick John Slight (Ref.: **MK** 1922, 1925-1927; **CAN** 1922).

ADOD   or   Oc 21, 1921

:AYTON VALLEY

2 *Drayton Valley Tribune.* F 18, 1954-Je 13, 1958//
w.

Pub. by Thomas W. Pue, Sun Pub. Co. Ltd., Edmonton.
Alberta Golden Jubilee Edition, S 1, 1955.

AEP   mf F 18, 1954-Je 13, 1958

Drayton Valley Banner. Mr ? 1965-Ag ? 1965//
See Supplement (1057).

3 *Western Review.* S? 1965-
w.

Succeeded *Drayton Valley Banner* (1057).

Pub. by Western Review Ltd., S? 1965-F 29, 1976. Sold to H.M. Bowes, Lynard Pub. Ltd., Mr 1, 1976. Pub. by Ronald B. Smith, S? 1965-Je 21, 1972; Len Hogarth, Je 28, 1972-F 25, 1976; Gary MacDonald, Mr 1, 1976-Oc 16, 1980; Steven Dills, Oc 22, 1980-N 12, 1981; David Robb, N 18, 1981-S 1, 1982; Stuart Adams, Ag 25, 1982+.

AEP mf My 3, 1972-1984
    or 1985+

324 *Drayton Valley Booster.* 1977//
    w.

Advertiser published briefly by *Western Review* (323). (Information from Publisher, Ap 13, 1987).
Ref.: CAN 1978.

No issues located

DRUMHELLER

325.1 *Drumheller Review.* D 13, 1913-S 27, 1934/...
    w.

325.2 *New Review.* Oc 4, 1934-Jl 2, 1936/...
    w.

325.3 *Review.* Jl 9, 1936-S 17, 1936/...
    w.

325.4 *Drumheller Review.* S 24, 1936-Je 27, 1940?//
    w.

Pub. by Charles J. Porritt. Ed by Archibald F. Key, Oc 4, 1934-1936.

AEP or Ap 10-Je 26, 1914; Ja 4, 1918-D 31, 1920; F 10, 1928-Je 27, 1940

326 *Drumheller Standard.* 1917-Mr 1918//
    w.

Satellite of *Calgary Western Standard* (142.5). Pub. by Standard Newspaper Syndicate, Calgary, mgr. J. Linton.
Closure announced (Ref.: **CPP** v27no4 Ap 1918).
Ref.: **MK** 1918.

No issues located

327 *Drumheller Mail.* My 2, 1918-
    w.

Continued voluming of *Munson Mail* (775).

Printing plant of *Munson Mail* amalgamated with the job plant of E.C. Payne, Drumheller in Ap 1918.

Pub. by Grover Cleveland Duncan, My 2, 1918-Ja 30, 1947; A. Hector (Hap) Clarke and John G. Clarke, F 6, 1947-Je 2, 1954; Ossie Sheddy, Sam Robb, and John Anderson, Je 9, 1954-Jl 1972; Ossie Sheddy, Jl 19, 1972+ Ed. by Archibald F. Key, S 6, 1928-My 25, 1933.

Special edition Tosach 25th Anniversary, Oc 25, 1934. Jubilee Issue, Je 19, 1936; Alberta Golden Jubilee Edition, Ag 31, 1955.

Ref.: **DAL** p.70.

ACG or Oc 25, 1934, Je 19, 1936
AEP or My 2, 1918-D 25, 1919; Ja 1-Je 25, 1925; Ja 5, 1928+

28   *Daily Bulletin.* 1933-1936?//
d.

Mimeographed.
Pub. by G.H. Read (Ref.: *Drumheller Mail* Je 19, 1936).

No issues located

29   *Weekly Advertiser.* 1936-?//
w.

Mimeographed.
Pub. by James Hawkins (Ref.: *Drumheller Mail* Je 19, 1936).

No issues located

30   *Plaindealer.* Mr 12, 1936-Je 23, 1941?//
w.

Continued *Plaindealer,* Youngstown (1041).
Suspended pub. D 19, 1940-Je 23, 1941.
Pub. and ed. by Archibald F. Key.

AEP or Mr 12, 1936-D 19, 1940

31   *Daily Advertiser.* 1937-1942?//
d.

Mimeographed.
Pub. by William Danyluk (Ref.: **MK** 1940-1942).

No issues located

32.1   *Big Country News.* My 10, 1967-Ag 9, 1978/...
w.

32.2   *Drumheller Sun.* Ag 16, 1978-D 12, 1979//
w.

Pub. and ed. by Grace Bigford, 1967?-1975 (Ref.: *Edmonton Journal* My 10, 1967); Anthony Mayer, 1975-1978; Gerry and Trish Popplewell, Ag 1978-D 1979.

AEP   or   F 19, 1975-D 12, 1979

ECKVILLE

333   *Eckville Examiner.* Ja? 1949-
           w.

Pub. by J.C. (Jack) Gare, Ja 1949-My 23, 1950; Leslie D. Saul, My 30, 1950-Ja 16, 1954; Lawrence O. Mazza and Jack Gare, Ja 23, 1954-Mr 16, 1957; Jack A. and Olive Parry, Rimbey Record Ltd., Mr 23, 1957-S 1985; Record Publishing Ltd., R.C. Cooke Gen. Mgr., S 1985+.

AEP   or   Je 28, 1949+

EDGERTON

Edgerton Enterprise. My 8, 1946-D 1948
See **CHAUVIN.** *Chauvin Chronicle* (263).

Edgerton Enterprise. Ja 19, 1949-
See **WAINWRIGHT.** *Wainwright Star-Chronicle* (1009.2).

EDMONTON

334.1   *Bulletin.* D 6, 1880-F 14, 1881/...
           w.

334.2   *Edmonton Bulletin.* F 21, 1881-F 1, 1923//
           w.; 2w.

Frequency varied: w. D 6, 1880-Ap 30, 1892; 2w. My 2, 1892-F 1, 1923. Suspended pub. Ap 4-Oc 29, 1881.
Alexander Taylor and Frank Oliver, props., D 6, 1880-Ap 4, 1881; Oliver and Alexander Dunlop, props., Oc 29, 1881-My 3, 1884; Oliver, prop., My 10, 1884-Ag 11, 1898; Bulletin Pub. Co., pub., Ag 15, 1898-F 1, 1923.
Ref.: **CRA** pp. 283-297; **KES** p.31; **WAD.**
See also *Daily Edmonton Bulletin* (342).

AEU   mf   D 6, 1880-D 29, 1902

335   *Times.* Ag? 1893-Oc 1894//
           w.

Ed. and prop. J.B. Spurr, Ag 1893-ca My 1894; pub. and printed by William Park Evans ca. My-Oc, 1894. Suspension reported in *Calgary Tribune,* Oc 31, 1894.

ACG   or   Jl 5, 1894

.1 *South Edmonton News.* N 8, 1894-N 5? 1896/...
w.

.2 *Alberta Plaindealer.* N 12? 1896-Ap? 1900/...
w.; d.

.3 *Strathcona Plaindealer.* Ap? 1900-Ap 4, 1912/...
2w.

.4 *News-Plaindealer.* Ap 9, 1912-S 24, 1912/...
2w.

.5 *Edmonton News-Plaindealer.* S 27, 1912-Ag 29, 1913//
2w.

Superceded by *Edmonton News* (371) and *Alberta Illustrated News* (372).
Editions: McDonald and Skinner pub. two issues of a d. ed. My 2, 3, 1898.
Frequency varied: w. N 8, 1894-Ap 1900?; 2w. Ap 1900-Ag 29, 1913.
Pub. and ed. by R.P. Pettipiece, N 8, 1894-S 1, 1896; J. Hamilton
McDonald, S 3, 1896-S 30, 1897; McDonald and James D. Skinner, Oc 7,
1897-N 4, 1898; McDonald, N 11, 1898-Ja 30, 1912; Clarence H. Stout, F 1,
1912-F 7, 1913; A.M. McDonald ed. and R.A. Godson bus. mgr. My 17-Ag
29, 1913.
Ref.: **STO.**

AEU mf N 8, 1894-Mr 30, 1900; My 3-N 1, 1907; Mr 3, 1908-D 31,
1912
AEP mf Ja 3-Ag 29, 1913

7 *Edmonton Herald.* My 6, 1895-D? 1896//
2w.

Established by J.J. Young (Ref.: **CPP** v5no5 My 1895).
Pub. by Edmonton Herald Co. Ed. by William Short. Sold Ap 15, 1896 to
A. Johnson who had been mgr. since My 1895. *Edmonton Bulletin*, Ja 4,
1897, announced that *Edmonton Herald* was shipped to Revelstoke, B.C. on
Ja 1? 1897.
Chiefly a reprint of *Calgary Herald* (115).
Ref.: **CNLU** p.11.

OONL or My 6, 1895
ACG or N 9, 16, 23, 30, 1895

8 *Ouest canadien.* F 3, 1898-F 22, 1900//
w. Immigration French in Fr.

Subtitle: "Organe de la Société de la Colonisation d'Edmonton, Alberta."

Pub. by La Compagnie d'Imprimerie Canadienne d'Edmonton, F 3, 1898-Mr 21, 1899; Edmonton Printing Co. Ltd., Mr 28, 1899-F 22, 1900. Ed. by Frédéric-Edmond Villeneuve.
Ref.: **LAND** pp.6-7, 29.

AEAA   mf [F 3, 1898-F 22, 1900]
AEU   mf [F 3, 1898-F 22, 1900]

339   *Edmonton Post.* Ag 1899-Jl 16, 1902?//
       2w. Political — Conservative

       Initial issue reported in *Edmonton Bulletin* Ag 7, 1899. Pub. by Edmonton Post Printing Co. Ltd. Ed. by T.A. Gregg (Ref.: **HENW** 1900; **LO** 1901; **MK** 1901). Fell into bankruptcy in My 1902. Assets purchased by Richard Henry Secord and sold to John MacPherson and John W. Cunningham to establish *Edmonton Journal* (344).

       AEAA   or My 1, 1901
       ACGL   or Mr 12, Jl 16, 1902

340   *Alberta Sun.* S 1899-? 1900//
       w.; 2w.

       Originally entitled *Strathcolic*? (Ref.: **MacG** p.132).
       Pub. and ed. by Robert Chambers Edwards. Pub. in Leduc for a few months and then moved to Strathcona (now Edmonton) (Ref.: **DEM** p.10; **McE** p. 28; **HENW** 1900; **MK** 1901).

       ACGA   mf Ja 25, 1900

341   *Advertiser.* 1900//
       w.

       Pub. by James D. Skinner and Co. *Strathcona Plaindealer*, Ja 30, 1912, stated that *Advertiser* was conducted in Strathcona for about six months.
       Ref.: **HENW** 1900; **LO** 1901.

       No issues located

342.1 *Daily Edmonton Bulletin.* Ja 3, 1903-Ja 16, 1906/...
       d. (pm)

342.2 *Edmonton Daily Bulletin.* Ja 17, 1906-Ja 30, 1923//
       d. (pm)

       Pub. by Bulletin Pub. Co., Frank Oliver, president.
       See also *Bulletin* (334), weekly edition.

       AEU   mf Ja 3, 1903-S 30, 1911

343   *Alberta Herold.* Ap? 1903-Jl? 1915//
       w. Agriculture Political — Liberal German in Ger.

       Title varied: *Alberta Herold und Farmerfreund; Alberta Herold and Farmerfreund,* Ja 19, 1911-Je 13, 1912.

Pub. by Alberta Herold Pub. Co. Ltd. Ed. by Gustav Koermann, Ap? 1903-Mr 5, 1909; Carol Pohl, Mr 12-My 28, 1909; Koermann, Je 4, 1909-Jl 28, 1910; Heinrich Becker, Ag 4, 1910-D 31, 1914; A. von Hammerstein, Ja 7?-Jl? 1915.

Pub. single page devoted to agricultural items entitled *Farmerfreund: ein Ratgeber für Feld und Haus,* Oc 6, 1910-Oc 10, 1912. This page was neither numbered nor dated and pub. irreg. Issues of Oc 6, 20, 1910 were pub. as separate inserts, it was then printed as an integral part of the *Alberta Herold.*

Supported German cause in 1914. First the Alberta Legislature, then the Federal Parliament contemplated prosecution for treason or imposing censorship but paper ceased before any action was taken.

(Ref.: **BOU 2** pp.4-5).

AEPAA mf S 1, 1905-Jl 31, 1913; S 24, 1914-My 13, 1915
AEP mf F 7, 1908-Jl 31, 1913; S 24, 1914-My 13, 1915
or F 7, 1908-Jl 31, 1913; S 24, 1914-My 13, 1915

4.1 *Evening Journal.* N 11, 1903-F 28, 1907/...
d. (am and pm) and w.

4.2 *Edmonton Evening Journal.* Mr 1, 1907-F 18, 1909/...
d. (am and pm) and w.

4.3 *Evening Journal.* F 19, 1909-S 30, 1911/...
d. (am and pm) and w.

4.4 *Edmonton Journal.* Oc 2, 1911-
d. (am and pm) and w.

Editions: pub. both am *(Morning Journal)* and pm eds. Ag 13, 1906-S 11, 1911 and S 2, 1980+; pub. w. ed. Ag 3, 1908-F 6, 1913 *(Edmonton Weekly Journal).*

. Est. by John W. Cunningham, ed., John MacPherson, mgr. and Arthur Moore, Journal Co., pubs. F 5, 1905, partnership merged into a joint stock company known as Journal Co. Ltd. Ag 1, 1911 company reorganized under management of Canadian Newspapers Ltd. F 13, 1912, Southam Ltd. purchased a controlling interest. D 31, 1921 Edmonton Journal Ltd. became pub.; replaced by North Western Pub. Ltd. Oc 1, 1936. Assets sold to Southam Co. Ltd. D 31, 1941. *Edmonton Journal* currently operates as a division of Southam Inc. Pub.: Milton Robbins Jennings, Ap 1909-F 16, 1921; John Mills Imrie, Jl 6, 1921-Oc 1, 1941; Walter Augustus MacDonald, Ja 1, 1942-Ja 31, 1962; Basil Dean, F 1, 1962-D 1967; Ross Munro, Ja 1, 1968-Ja 2, 1976; J. Patrick O'Callaghan, Ja 3, 1976-Jl 31, 1982; William Newbigging, Ag 2, 1982+.

My 30, 1946-D 31, 1947 *Edmonton Journal* and *Edmonton Bulletin* pub. jointly as one newspaper by Alberta Free Press Ltd. and Southam Co. Ltd. during printers' strike.

10th Anniversary Edition, N 11, 1913; 50th Anniversary Edition, N 10, 1953; Alberta Golden Jubilee Edition, S 1, 1955; 75th Anniversary Edition, N 21, 1978.

Ref.: **BRU** pp. 134-141, 282-319; **CRA** p. 275; **GIL** p. 246-249; **KES** p.114; **STEW** pp. 157-169; Edmonton Journal Library files.

AEU   mf N 11, 1903+ (d. ed. only)

345   *Strathcona Chronicle.* 1904-1911?//
          w.; 2w.; w.

          Pub. 2w. 1908-1909.
          Pub. by Chronicle Co., Strathcona. Pub. and ed. by William Godson, 1904-1906; James Weir, 1907; Wright Beaumont and H. Jackman, 1907; H. Jackman, 1909-1911. Ed. by James Graham, 1908-1911? (Ref.: **HENE** 1905-1909; **MK** 1905, 1907, 1909, 1911; **CAN** 1911).
          See also daily edition. *Morning Chronicle* (350).

          AEP   mf S 11, 1908-Mr 5, 1909
          AEPAA or S 11, 1908-Mr 5, 1909

346   *Town Topics.* 1905-1919?//
          w.

          Title varied: *Edmonton Weekly Topics, Edmonton Town Topics, Edmonton Weekly Town Topics.*
          Suspended pub. D 1950-1908.
          Pub. by H.H. Hull Printing Co. Sold D 1905 to Saturday News Ltd. (Ref.: *Saturday News* D 23, 1905; **HENE** 1905). Continued pub. in 1908 by Joseph W. Adair, Edmonton Printing and Pub. Co. (Ref.: **HENE** 1908, 1911, 1914). Pub. by H.H. Hull Printing Co., 1915-1919.
          Christmas Number, 1905; Industrial and Investor's Number, 1913; Special Edition for Municipal Election, D 6, 1913.

          AEPAA or   D 10, 1914 (68.200/5)
                     or   [Oc 7, 1915-F 7, 1919] (65.124/429)
          AEP   mf Ap 21-D 29, 1917
          AEPAA or Christmas Number, 1905; Industrial and Investor's Number, 1913; Je 18, 1909; D 6, 11, 18, 1913

347   *Courrier de l'Ouest.* Oc 14, 1905-Ja 6, 1916//
          w. Political — Liberal French in Fr.

          Pub. by La Compagnie de Publication du Courrier de l'Ouest, Ltée., Oc 14-21, 1905; Courrier de l'Ouest Pub. Co. Ltd., Oc 28, 1905-Ja 6, 1916. Ed. by Raymond Brutinel and Alex Michelet, Oc 14, 1905-Jl 18, 1907; Michelet, Jl 25, 1907-Jl 31, 1913; François-Xavier Boileau, Ag 7, 1913-Ja 6, 1916.
          Ref.: **DEG 2; LAND** pp. 8-9, 30.

          AEPAA mf [Oc 14, 1905-Ja 6, 1916]
          AEP   mf [Oc 14, 1905-Ja 6, 1916]
          AEU   mf [Oc 14, 1905-Ja 6, 1916]

348   *Saturday News.* D 23, 1905-Jl 13, 1912?//
          w.

Pub. by Arthur Balmer Watt, D 23, 1905-S 29, 1906; Edmonton News
Pub. Co., Oc 6, 1906-N 6, 1909; Saturday News Ltd., N 13, 1909-Jl 1912;
Watt, mnging dir., N 13, 1909-Jl 1912.
Ref.: **HENE** 1908-1912.

AEPAA   or   My 21, S 3, 24, Oc 19, 29, D 10, 1910 (66.54/5-10)
           or   Je 25, Oc 8, N 12, D 3, 31, 1910 (65.124/432)
AEU   mf   D 23, 1905-Jl 13, 1912
AEP   mf   D 23, 1905-Jl 13, 1912

Edmonton Free Press. S? 1906-1907?//
See Supplement (1058).

Great West. F? 1907-Ja 20, 1909//
2m. Agriculture Labour

Absorbed by *Grain Growers Guide,* Winnipeg, Ja 1909.
Official organ of Canadian Society of Equity. Ed. by M.A. Strang (Ref.:
MK 1907). Became official organ of Trades and Labour Council, 1908 (Ref.:
EMB p.230).

ACG   or   Ap 1, 1907; Ja 20, 1909

Evening Chronicle. My 6, 1907-N 6, 1908?//
d.

Daily ed. of *Strathcona Chronicle* (345).
Pub. by Chronicle Co., Strathcona. Ed. by James Weir, 1907; James Graham, 1908. Wright Beaumont and H. Jackman, mgrs., 1907; H. Jackman,
mgr., Ag-N 1908.

AEP   mf   My 6-Oc 9, 1907; F 28-N 6, 1908

Clarion of Alberta. Ja 1908-? 1908//
w. Sport

An illustrated magazine newspaper mainly devoted to sports and pas-
times. Ed. by T.A. King Turner (Ref.: **HENE** 1908).

AEEA   or   F 8, 1908

West-Land. Ja 2, 1908-S 1913//
w.; bw.; m.; 2m.; m. Religious

Continued by *West-Land Magazine.*
Subtitles: "For the People of the West," Ja 2-N 19, 1908; "Righteousness
Exalteth a Nation", D 1908-S 1913.
Frequency varied: w. Ja 2-Je 4, 1908; bw. Je 18-N 19, 1908; m. D 1908-
Ap 1910; 2m. My 1, 1910-My 19, 1913; m. Je-S, 1913.
Format varied: newspaper, Ja 2-N 19, 1908; magazine, D 1908-S 1913.
Pub. prospectus issue on N 1, 1907.

Pub. by West-Land Pub. Co. Ed. by Aubrey Fullerton. Presbyterian newspaper.

AEP   or   Ja 2, 1908-S 1913

353.1   *Alberta Homestead.* Ja 8? 1908-Ap 19, 1911/...
          w. Agriculture

353.2   *Homestead.* Ap 26, 1911-N 28, 1913?//
          w. Agriculture

          Changed to magazine format Ag 1910.
          Official organ of Alberta Farmers' Association to Ag 1910. Pub. by
          Arthur Balmer Watt, News Pub. Co., to Ag 1910; Homestead Ltd., Ja 17,
          1912-N 28, 1913. Pub. and ed. by George B. Fraser, Ag 1910-My 8, 1912;
          Floyd H. Higgins, My 15, 1912-N 23, 1913.
          Special Edition to illustrate the Resources of the Province, Ap 15, 1908.

          AEP   or   F 12, 1908-N 28, 1913

354   *Kanadiiskaia Niva / Canadian Field.* S 1908-Ap 15, 1910//
          2m. Political — General Religious Russian Ukrainian in Ukr.

          Place of pub. moved to Edmonton from Winnipeg in the latter half of
          1909.
          Text in Ukrainian using Russian transliteration.
          Ed. by Rev. I. Arseny.
          Ref.: **BOM** p. 25; **LOV** p. 173; **MARU** p. 289.

          AEU   mf [S 1, 1908-Ap 2/15, 1910]

355   *Deutsch-Canadier.* N 12? 1908-Jl 8, 1909//
          w. German in Ger.

          Continued by *Deutsch-Canadier*, Calgary (139).
          Notice of change in place of pub. appears in Jl 8, 1909 issue.
          Pub. by Deutsch Canadier Pub. Co. Ltd.; Josef Schuster, mgr., Otto P.
          Woysch, ed.
          Ref.: **ARN** p.227; **CNLC** p. 114.

          AEP   or   F 18-Jl 8, 1909

356.1   *Edmonton Capital.* D 13, 1909-Ap 10, 1911/...
          d.

356.2   *Edmonton Daily Capital.* Ap 11, 1911-D 23, 1913/...
          d.

356.3   *Edmonton Capital.* D 24, 1913-N 19, 1914?//
          d.

          Pub. and ed. by Arthur Balmer Watt, D 13, 1909-N 5, 1910; William
          MacAdams, N 7, 1910-N 1914.

AEU   mf Ja 3, 1910-N 19, 1914
AEEA   or D 13, 1909

Canadai Magyar Farmer / Canadian Hungarian Farmer.
1910-1921//
w.; m.; 2m.; w. Agriculture Hungarian in Hung.

Superceded *Kanadai Mayarsag* (1905-1909) Winnipeg, and *Magyar Farmer*, Winnipeg which merged in 1910 to form *Canadai Magyar Farmer* (Ref.: **DRE** p.80).
Title varied: *Canada Magyar Farmer* (Ref.: **CNLC**, p.156).
Frequency varied: w. 1910-1914; m. 1915-1916; 2m. 1917; w. 1918-1921 (Ref.: **MK** 1911-1920).
Place of pub. varied: Winnipeg, 1910-1916; Crosswoods, Sask., 1917; Plunkett, Sask., 1918-1920; Edmonton, 1921.
Pub. by Canadian Pub. Co., Winnipeg, 1910-1912? (Ref.: **MK** 1911); Hungarian Pub. Co., Winnipeg, 1913?-1916 (Ref.: **MK** 1913, 1915); Hungarian Pub. Co., Crosswoods, Sask., 1917 (Ref.: **MK** 1917); Hungarian Press, Plunkett, Sask., 1918-1920 (Ref.: **MK** 1918-1920); Great Western Press Ltd., Edmonton, 1921 (Ref.: **HENE** 1921). Ed. by Kálmán and Lajos Kovácsi, 1910-1915 (Ref.: **DRE** pp.79-80); Father L.J. Schaffer, 1916-? (Ref.: **DRE** p.81); Stephen Kende, 1921 (Ref.: **HENE** 1921).

No issues located

8.1   *Edmonton Daily Bulletin.* My 2, 1910-N 8, 1915/...
       d. (am)

8.2   *Morning Bulletin.* N 9, 1915-Ja 28, 1924/...
       d. (am)

8.3   *Edmonton Bulletin.* Ja 29, 1924-Ja 20, 1951//
       d. (am; pm)

Suspended pub. Je 19-D 3, 1925 due to labour dispute with printers.
Became a pm newspaper D 3, 1925.
Pub. by Bulletin Pub. Co., Frank Oliver, pres., My 2, 1910-N 9, 1923. Oliver sold his financial interest in the company, N 1923. Company reorganized under George B. O'Connor as Edmonton Bulletin Ltd., Ja 30-D 29, 1924, and Edmonton Pub. Ltd., D 30, 1924-Je 19, 1925. Sold to Charles E. Campbell Oc 1925 and pub. by Alberta Free Press Ltd. Sold Ja 2, 1948 to Edmonton Bulletin Ltd. directed by G. Max Bell. Hal Straight was pub. and ed., Ja 2, 1948-Ja 20, 1951.
Pub. jointly with *Edmonton Journal* (344.4) as one newspaper, by Alberta Free Press Ltd. and Southam Co. Ltd. during printers' strike, My 30, 1946-D 31, 1947.
50th Anniversary Number, Jl 14, 1930; 60th Anniversary Number, Jl 10, 1940; 70th Anniversary Edition, D 30, 1950.
See also *Bulletin* (334) weekly edition.

AEU   mf Oc 2, 1911-Ja 20, 1957

359   *Gateway.* N 21, 1910-
        w.; w.; 2w.; 3w. University

        Frequency varies: m. N 21, 1910-? 1914, Mr 1922; w. N 1, 1915-My 4,
        1920, N 1, 1920-D 15, 1933, F 1-Mr 22, 1935, S 24, 1943-My 15, 1946, Oc
        27, 1950-My 18, 1954; 2w. Ja 2, 1934-Ja 29, 1935, Oc 11, 1935-My 17,
        1943, Oc 4, 1946-Oc 17, 1950; S 24, 1954-Mr 1968, Ja 12, 1971+; 3w. Oc
        2-Oc 11, 1920, Ap 10, 1968-Ja 8, 1971.
        Suspended pub. 1914-1915.
        Pub. from S to Ap only.
        Pub. by Alma Mater Society, University of Alberta, N 21, 1910-Ag 1912;
        Students' Union, Oc 1912+

        AEUA   or N 21, 1910+

360   *Alberta Deutsche Zeitung / Alberta German Newspaper.* D 8?
        1910-1913?//
        w. German in Ger.

        Suspended pub. Ag 17, 1911-Jl 16, 1912.
        Pub. by Alberta Deutsche Zeitung. Ed. by Gustav Koermann.
        Ref.: **ARN** p. 228; **CNLC** p.106.

        AEP   or Ja 12-Ag 10, 1911; Jl 23-D 19, 1912

361   *Financial News.* 1911-1913?//
        w. Business

        Pub. by Financial News (Ref.: **HENE** 1911; **MK** 1911, 1913).

        No issues located

362   *Ouest canadien.* Ja 7, 1911-Mr 1911?//
        2w. French in Fr.

        Pub. by Compagnie d'Imprimerie Nationale. Ed. by Wilfrid Gariépy.
        Probable cessation date Mr 1911 (Ref.: **DEG 1**, p.8).
        Ref.: **CLNU** p.13; **LAND** p.12, 32.

        OONL   or Ja 7, 1911

363   *Nova Hromada / New Society.* F 16, 1911-S 11, 1912//
        w. Political — Socialist Ukrainian in Ukr.

        Organ of Federation of Ukrainian Socialists in Canada. Ed. by Roman
        Kremar, F 16-Ag 25, 1911; Thomas Tomashevsky, S 1, 1911-? 1912; J.W.
        Semeniuk, 1912; Illa Kyriak, 1912.
        Ref.: **BOM** p.26; **MARU** p.272.

        AEU   mf [F 16, 1911-S 11, 1912]

364   *Kanadyiets / Canadian.* F 1? 1912-Oc 1, 1919?//
        2m.; w. Political — Liberal Ukrainian in Ukr.

        Amalgamated with *Ranak,* Winnipeg in late 1910-1920? (Ref.: **LOV**,
        p.173).

Subtitle: "Religious, Moral, Social, Scientific, Agricultural, Non-political, Canadian."
Frequency varied: 2m. F 1, 1912-early 1916; w. early 1916-Oc 1919?
Ed. by Michael Belagay.
Ref.: **BOM** p. 25; **MARU** p. 275.

AEU   mf [Jl 15, 1912-Oc 1, 1919]

.1   *Mirror.* Ag 23, 1912-N 9, 1912/...
      w. Political — General

.2   *Edmonton Saturday Mirror.* N 16, 1912-Ja 11, 1913?//
      w. Political — General

      Subtitle: "A journal of protest and conviction."
      Ed. by Gertrude Balmer Watt.

AEP   mf Ag 23, 1912-Ja 11, 1913
AEPAA or   N 2, 1912
ACG   or   Ag 30, 1912

      Moukari. 1913?-1915?//
      irreg. Political — Socialist   Finnish in Fin.

      Handwritten.
      Pub. by Finnish Socialist Organization of Edmonton. Ed. by O. Roslund, 1914?-F 1915; O. Nordström and Alex Pennanem, Mr 27, 1915; Pennanem, Alma Vijanen and Antti Braggee, Ap 30, 1915 (Ref.: **LIND** p.131; Correspondence with Archives of Ontario, N 29, 1984).

OTAR   mf [1913-1915]

      Novyny / News. Ja 7, 1913-Jl 15, 1915//
      w.; 2w.; 3w.; w.   Ukrainian in Ukr.

      Frequency varied: w. Ja 7-My 28, 1913; 2w. Je 6-Oc 17, 1913; 3w. Oc 23, 1913-Je 1915; w. Jl 1915.
      Organ of National Organization in America. Ed. by Roman Kremar, 1913-1915; Myroslaw Stechishin, 1914-1915.
      Ref.: **BOM** p.27; **MARU** pp.272-274.

AEU   mf [F 12, 1913-Jl 15, 1915]

      Rural Northwest and Edmonton Weekly Journal. F 13, 1913-Ag 10, 1916//
      w.

      Pub. by Canadian Newspapers Ltd. Ed. by Arthur Balmer Watt. Agricultural features combined in Saturday issue of *Edmonton Journal* (Ref.: **HENE** 1913, 1914; **CAN** 1916; Edmonton Journal Library files).

No issues located

369   *Russkyi Golos / Russian Voice.* Ap 4/17, 1913-Jl 3, 1916//
        w.   Russian   Ukrainian in Rus. and Ukr.

        In Russian, using a mixture of Russian and Ukrainian transliteration.
        Gazette for Russian people in Canada and the U.S.A. Pub. by Russian
        Pub. Co. Ltd. Ed. by Victor P. Hladyk, Ap 4/17-Jl 31, 1913; Wasyl Cherniak,
        F 5, 1914-Mr 6, 1916; P. Bozyk, My 8-Je 12, 1916; Cherniak, Je 19-Jl 3,
        1916.
        Ref.: **BOM** p.28; **MARU** pp.289-293.

        AEP   or   Ja 3-Mr 20, 1916
        AEP   mf   [Ap 4/17, 1913-Jl 3, 1916]
        AEU   mf   [Ap 4/17, 1913-Jl 3, 1916]

370   *Great West Saturday Night Advance.* My? 1913-? 1913//
        w.

        Continued voluming of *Advance*, Chauvin (261).
        Ed. by Mrs. Amy H. Keane. Pub. Great West Twentieth Century Pub. Co.
        Ref.: **CAN** 1914.

        ACG   or   Oc 18-25, 1913

371   *Edmonton News.* S 4, 1913-1919?//
        2w.

        Superceded *Edmonton News-Plaindealer* (336).
        Pub. by Edmonton News Pub. Co. and Plaindealer Co. Ed. by A.M.
        McDonald; R.A. Godson, mgr. (Ref.: **HENE** 1919).

        AEP   mf S 4-18, 1913
        AEPAA   or S 4-18, 1913

372   *Alberta Illustrated News.* S 6, 1913-1914?//
        w.

        Superceded *Edmonton News-Plaindealer* (336).
        Pub. by Edmonton News Pub. Co. Ed. by A.M. McDonald; R.A. Godson,
        mgr. (Ref.: **CAN** 1915; **HENE** 1914).

        AEP   or   Oc 11, D 13-23, 1913

373   *Beverly Advertiser.* 1914//
        w.

        Pub. by Arthur H. Coles and John W. Lightfoot at Edmonton Law
        Stationers Ltd.

        AEPAA   photocopy F 21, Mr 7, 1914 (76.121 SE)

374   *Progrès albertain.* F 26, 1914-Ag 19, 1915?//
        w.   Immigration   French in Fr.

        Continued *Progrès albertain*, Morinville (764.2).
        Subtitle: "Organe de la colonisation."

Pub. by Progressive Printing Co. Ltd. Ed. by Eugène Chartier. Probable last date of pub., Ag 19, 1915 (Ref.: **DEG 1** p.7).

Ref.: **LAND** p.13, 33.

AEPAA mf F 26, 1914-Ap 15, 1915
AEP mf F 26, 1914-Ap 15, 1915

Russian Life. 1915-1918?//
2m. Russian

Pub. by C.J. Sheremeta (Ref.: **CNLC** p.257; **MK** 1917).

No issues located

Western Weekly. Ja 22, 1915-Je 25, 1915?//
w.

Subtitle: "A Periodical of Independent Criticism on Matters Social and Political."

Pub. by Joseph W. Adair and Sylvester Tredway (Ref.: **HENE** 1915).

ACG or Ja 29, 1915
AEP mf Ja 22-Je 25, 1915

Statesman for Albertans. S 1/15, 1917-1918//
2m. Labour

Succeeded by *Statesman* (383).

Pub. by Statesman Pub. Syndicate, S 1-30, 1917; Edmonton Labor Representation League, Oc 1, 1917-1918? Ed. by W. Marshall, S 1, 1917-1918?

AEP mf S 1/15-N 1/15, 1917
AEPAA or S 1/15, 1917-1918

Union. N 15, 1917-Ap 18, 1929//
2m.; w. French in Fr.

Frequency varied: 2m. N 15, 1917-Oc 15, 1918; w. N 1, 1918-Ap 18, 1929.

Pub. by Imprimerie de l'Union, N 15, 1917-D 31, 1926?; Union Printing Ltd., Ja 6, 1927?-Ap 18, 1929. Ed. by Pierre Féguenne, N 14, 1918-Ja 9, 1919; J. LeCerf, Ja 16-Je 26, 1919; Anna Sindeff, Jl 10, 1919-192?; François-Xavier Boileau, 192?-Mr? 1924; Georges Bugnet, Ap? 1924-Ap 1928; Rodolphe Laplante, Je 28-Oc 18, 1928; Georges Bugnet, N 22, 1928-Ap 18, 1929.

Ref.: **LAND** pp.16-18, 35; **PAP** pp.124-125.

AEP or [N 15, 1917-D 11, 1919]; Ja 6, 1927-Ap 18, 1929

Novyny / News. D 18, 1917-Ja 28, 1922//
2w.; w. Ukrainian in Ukr.

Frequency varied: 2w. D 18, 1917-Oc 10, 1918; w. Ja 31, 1919-Ja 28, 1922.

Suspended pub. Oc 11, 1918-Ja 30, 1919.
Pub. by Commercial Printers, D 18, 1917-Jl 12, 1918; Ukrainian News
Pub. Co., Jl 31, 1918-Ja 28, 1922. Ed. by Roman Kremar.
Literary-informational newspaper for Ukrainian people of Canada.
Ref.: **BOM** p.27; **MARU** p.274.

AEU   mf [D 18, 1917-Ja 28, 1922]

380   *Great West Saturday Night.* Mr 30, 1918-? 1918//
           w.?

           Pub. by Great West Twentieth Century Pub. Co. Ed. by Amy H. Keane.

AEPAA or   Mr 30, 1918 (65.124/431)

381   *Soviet.* F 7, 1919-Ag 15, 1919?//
           w. Labour Political — Socialist

           Subtitle: "Devoted to the Interests of the Working Class."
           Pub. by Socialist Party of Canada, Edmonton Local No. 1. No ed. named.
           "It is interesting to note that, though the *Soviet* was datelined in Edmonton, it
           was actually printed in Fernie, B.C. and secretly shipped to the Alberta capi-
           tal to be distributed." (Ref.: **McC** p.476). Banned S 9, 1919 (Ref.: **WEI**
           5243).

AEPAA mf F 7-Ag 15, 1919

382   *One Big Union Bulletin.* Mr 25, 1919-Ap 25, 1919//
           irreg. Labour

           Pub. by One Big Union Provincial Executive Committee of Alberta. Ed.
           by Carl Berg (Ref.: **BER**, p.107). "Financed by voluntary contributions of
           the Trade Unionists of Alberta who believe in the principles of Industrial
           Unionism." (Ref.: Ap 4, 1919:2).
           Ag 12, 1919, another *O.B.U. Bulletin* began publishing in Winnipeg. It
           was designed to be the official publication of O.B.U. in western Canada
           (Ref.: **BER** p.107; **WEI** 5238).

AEPAA or   Ap 4, 25, 1919 (72.159)
MWPA or   Mr 25, 1919 (RG4/A1/6)
OOA   or   Ap 18, 1919 (MG 30.A47/4)
ACG   or   Ap 4, 1919

383   *Statesman.* Ap 4? 1919-1920?//
           w. Labour

           Succeeded *Statesman for Albertans* (377).
           Organ of Dominion Labor Party, Edmonton Branch, Ap 4?-Ag 29, 1919;
           Dominion Labor Party, Alberta Branch, S 5, 1919-1920? Pub. by S. Free-
           man, Ap 4? 1919-1920?
           Ref.: **WEI** 5244.

AEP   mf My 16-S 5, 1919

Edmonton Free Press. Ap 12, 1919-Ag 28, 1920//
w. Labour

Superceded by *Alberta Labor News,* Edmonton (386).
Official organ of Edmonton Trades and Labor Council, Ap 12, 1919-Ag
28, 1920. Pub. by Henry J. Roche, Ap 12-Ag 16, 1919; Edmonton Trades and
Labor Council, Ag 23, 1919-Ag 28, 1920. Ed. by Elmer E. Roper, Ag 23,
1919-Ag 28, 1920. As occurred in Winnipeg during the General Strike, a
strike bulletin was pub. in Edmonton appearing as *Special Strike Editions,*
no. 1 and 2, My 26-27, 1919 of *Edmonton Free Press,* pub. by Central Strike
Committee: "It is the purpose of the Strike Committee to issue the *Edmonton
Free Press* from time to time in order that all may be fully informed of what
is taking place in Organized Labor circles in respect to the strike in this city
and in other places." (Ref.: *Special Strike Edition* no. 1, My 26, 1919:2).

AEP   mf Ap 12, 1919-Ag 28, 1920
AEP   or *Special Strike Edition,* My 26, 27, 1919
AEPAA   or *Special Strike Edition,* My 26, 27, 1919; Je 2, 1919
         (66.169/1-4)

Edmonton Strike Bulletin. Je 2, 1919-Je 26? 1919//
irreg. Labour

Pub. by Strike Press Committee during the General Strike of 1919.
Opposed to the conservative stance of the *Edmonton Free Press* (384) which
also issued a strike bulletin.

AEPAA   or Je 2, 1919
AEP   or Je 14, 1919

.1   *Alberta Labor News.* S 4, 1920-Ja 18, 1936/...
       w. Labour

.2   *People's Weekly.* Ja 25, 1936-D 20, 1952//
       w.; bw.; m. Labour Political — C.C.F.

Superceded *Edmonton Free Press* (384).
Absorbed by *Commonwealth,* Regina, Sask., Ja 7, 1953.
Subtitle S 4, 1920-Ja 18, 1936: "Official Paper of Organized Labor in
Alberta."
Frequency varied: w. Ja 25, 1936-S 1, 1941; bw. S 13, 1941-D 23, 1944;
w. Ja 6, 1945-S 2, 1950; bw. S 16, 1950-S 1, 1951; m. Oc 27, 1951-D 20,
1952.
Official organ of Alberta Federation of Labor, S 4, 1920-D 23, 1944;
C.C.F. official organ, Ja 6, 1945-D 20, 1952. Ed. by Elmer E. Roper, S 4,
1920-D 23, 1944; William Irvine, assoc. ed. Ja 25, 1936-D 23, 1944. Pub.
board took over editorship Ja 6, 1945-S 2, 1950; no statement of editorial
responsibility appeared after this date.

AEP   or S 4-D 25, 1920; Ja 3, 1925-Je 1944; Ja 6, 1945-D 20, 1952;
         1937-1952
AEU   mf [S 16, 1944-D 20, 1952]

387   *Farmerske Slovo / Farmers' Word.* Mr 3, 1921-? 1921//
           w.   Agriculture   Ukrainian in Ukr.

           Pub. by Dmytro Prystash, Secty. of short-lived Ukrainian Farmers' Union
           of Alberta, ed. by Thomas Tomashevsky.
           Five issues published (Ref.: **MARU** p.125)
           Ref.: **BOM** p.24.

           AEU   mf Mr 10, 1921

388   *Western Catholic.* Je 23, 1921-Ag 25, 1965//
           w.   Religious

           Superceded by *Western Catholic Reporter,* Edmonton (453).
           Place of pub. varies: Wainwright, Ja 4-N 15, 1933.
           Official organ of Catholic Archdiocese of Edmonton, Ag 16, 1923-Ag 25,
           1965; Catholic Diocese of Calgary, F 22, 1933-Ag 25, 1965. Pub. by Great
           Western Press Ltd., Je 23, 1921-Jl 4, 1934; *Western Catholic* office, Jl 11,
           1934-Ag 25, 1965. Ed. by J.W. Heffernen, Je 23, 1921-My 6, 1926; James A.
           MacLellan, S 2, 1926-N 22, 1933; Robert W. Britton, Jl 25, 1934-S 28, 1949;
           A.D. O'Brien, Oc 5, 1949-My 17, 1961; Gregory A. Schiller, My 24-Oc 7,
           1961; J.A. MacLellan, Oc 21, 1961-Ag 4, 1965. Calgary eds.: M.L. Con-
           nolly, Ja 17, 1962-Je 26, 1963; Bryan McGill, Jl 3-S 18, 1963; E. Flanagan, S
           25, 1963-Oc 7, 1964.

           AEPAA mf Je 23, 1921-Ag 25, 1965

389   *Wedge.* Ag 20? 1921-? 1921//
           2m.   Labour

           Pub. by Wedge Co. Ed. by George L. Ritchie and P.F. Lawson.
           Ref.: **CARA 1** p.150.

           AEPAA or   S 3, 1921 (72.159/50)

390   *Western Illustrated News.* Oc 15, 1921-Oc 7, 1922//
           w.   Military Veterans

           Superceded magazine *Western Veteran.*
           Pub. by Western Veteran Pub. Co., Arthur H. Coles, mnging. dir., A.E.
           Nightingale, ed. Purpose was to "provide the West with its first and only pic-
           torial newspaper" along with coverage of "all matters of interest to veterans
           and their dependents" (Ref.: Oc 15, 1921:4).

           AEP   or   Oc 15, 1921-Oc 7, 1922

391   *Sports Review.* 1922-?//
           w.   Sport

           Pub. by Albert R. Keays. Ed. by Charles H. Bailey (Ref.: **HENE** 1922).

           No issues located

News Advertiser. 1922?-1923?//
w.

Pub. by Pioneer Press (Ref.: **HENE** 1922, 1923).

No issues located

Nash Postup / Our Progress. N 6, 1922-? 1929//
2m.; w.; 2m.   Ukrainian in Ukr.

Frequency varied: 2m. N 6, 1922-D 11, 1923; w. D 18, 1923-early 1928;
2m. early 1928-1929?
"Enlightenment and economic news for the Ukrainian people of Alberta."
Pub. by Canadian-Ukrainian Printing Co. Ed. by Thomas Tomashevsky, N 6,
1922-My 1925; T. Datskiv, Je 3, 1925-Ja 20, 1926; J.N Krett, Ja 27, 1926-Mr
23, 1927; Tomashevsky, Ap 1927-1929?
Ref.: **BOM** p.26; **MARU** p.485.

AEU   mf   [N 6, 1922-Ag 10, 1928]

International Labor News. 1923-1924?//
? Labour

Walter Long, prop. and mgr. (Ref.: **HENE** 1923, 1924).

No issues located

1   *Strathcona Booster.* 1923-1925/...
    2m.

2   *Strathcona Weekly News.* 1926-1939/...
    w.

3   *South Edmonton Weekly News.* 1940-1954?//
    w.

Printed at Excelsior Press. Pub. and ed. by Thomas S. Young, 1923-1939;
Bernard A. Langdon, 1940-1954 (Ref.: **HENE** 1925-1940, 1952-1954; **MK**
1926-1942).

AEUS   or   Mr 21, 1935 (Rutherford Pamphlet)
AEPAA   or   Mr 30, Ap 20, 1944; Ag 2, 1945; Ap 11, 25, Ag 8, 22, 1946

1   *Edmonton Weekly Journal.* Ja 31, 1923-Ja 24, 1924/...
    w.

2   *Edmonton Journal Farm Weekly.* Ja 30, 1924-Oc 29, 1924/...
    w.

396.3   *Edmonton Journal Farm Weekly and Alberta Farm Journal.*
          N 4, 1924-Mr 3, 1925/...
          w.

396.4   *Alberta Farm Journal and Edmonton Journal Weekly.*
          Mr 10, 1925-S 28, 1932//
          w.

          Pub. by Edmonton Journal Ltd. Ed. D.A. McCannell to 1927. Combined
          in Saturday issue of *Edmonton Journal*, Oc 1932 (Ref.: Edmonton Journal
          Library files).
          AEP   mf Ja 2-Je 25, 1924; Ja 6, 1925-S 28, 1932

397   *East-Ender.* F 8? 1923-1924?//
          w.

          Devoted to the interests of east Edmonton. Pub. by Henry Roche Printing
          Co. Ltd. (Ref.: **HENE** 1924).
          AEPAA   photocopy Je 21, 1923 (70.79)

398   *Glow Worm.* Ap 13, 1923-Jl 1, 1923//
          m.?

          Pub. by the Economic Pub. Co., to "shed light on social and economic
          subjects, labour interests, money and banking reform, an open forum for
          correspondents." Ed. by Ernest Brown.
          AEPAA or Ap 13, My 26, Jl 1, 1923 (65.124/430)

399   *Western News.* 1925-?//
          w.?

          Pub. by Western News Pub. Co. Ltd. No ed. named.
          ACG   or Oc 21, 1925

400   *Druh Naroda / People's Friend.* F 1926-S 23, 1930//
          m. Religious Russian Ukrainian in Ukr. and Rus.

          Gazette for Russian Orthodox people in Canada and U.S. Ed. by P.N.
          Samilo.
          Ref.: **BOM** p.24; **MARU** p.493.

          AEU   mf [Ap 1, 1926-S 23, 1930]
          AEP   mf [Ap 1, 1926-S 23, 1930]

401   *Town Topics.* Oc 1926?-1928//
          w.

          Pub. by Town Topics Pub. Co., Frank S. Wright, mgr. (Ref.: **HENE** 1927,
          1928).
          Devoted to city politics (Ref.: **CPP** v35no11 N 1926).

          No issues located

2.1 *Zakhidni Visti / Western News.* Ja 1928-D 30, 1931/...
m.; w.   Ukrainian in Ukr. and Engl.

2.2 *Ukrainski Visti / Ukrainian News.* Ja 6, 1932-
w.   Ukrainian in Ukr. and Engl.

Text in Ukr. and Engl. from 1981.
Frequency varied: m. Ja-Oc 1928; w. Oc 26, 1928+.
Organ of Ukrainian Catholics in Canada, D 13, 1929+ Pub. by Western News Co., Ja-S 1928; *Alberta Herald,* Oc 1928-S 27, 1929; Western News Pub. Oc 4, 1929-Jl 18, 1930; Ukrainian News Pub. Ltd., Jl 25, 1930+ Ed. by J.N. Krett, Ja-N 1928; V. Kysilevskyj, N 16, 1928-D 6, 1929; "The College", D 13, 1929-Oc 24, 1930; B. Dyky, Oc 31, 1930-196?; Dr. M. Sopulak, 1970?-1981; M. Chomiak, 1981-1982; M. Levitsky, Oc 1982+.
Ref.: **BOM** p.30; **MARU** p.486; **ISI** pp.31-33.

AEU   mf   N 2, 1938-D 23/30 1971

3 *Herold.* Ja 26, 1928-Ap 2? 1931//
w.   German in Ger.

Superceded by *Alberta Herold,* Edmonton (412).
Absorbed by *Courier,* Regina, Sask., Ap 8, 1931. Notice appeared in Ap 8, 1931, issue stating that *Herold* had ceased pub. because of financial problems; subscribers would receive *Courier* and H. Stuermer would be mgr. of Edmonton office.
Pub. by Herold Pub. Co. Ltd., Ja 26-Mr 29, 1928; Alberta Herold Ltd., Ap 5, 1928-Ja 10, 1929; Alberta Herald Ltd., Ja 17-S 19, 1929; North-West Pub., S 26, 1929-Jl 10, 1930; North-West Press Ltd., Jl 17, 1930-Ap 2? 1931. Ed. by a committee, Ja 26-S 13, 1928; Fritz Roth, S 20, 1928-Oc 31, 1929; Friedrich Meyer, N 7, 1929-Je 30, 1930; W.C. Boehnert, My 8, 1930-Mr 26, 1931.

AEP   or   F 2, 1928-Mr 26, 1931

4 *Survivance.* N 16, 1928-N 8, 1967//
w.   French in Fr.

Succeeded by *Franco-Albertain* (458.1).
Official organ of l'Association Canadienne Française de l'Alberta and Fédération Canadienne-Française de la Colombie, S 22, 1954-N 8, 1967. Pub. by Western Veteran Pub. Co., N 16, 1928-Ja 17, 1929; 'La Survivance' Printing Ltd., Ja 24, 1929-N 8, 1967. Ed. by Rodolphe Laplante, N 16, 1928-Oc 23, 1930; Maurice Lavallée, Ag 15, 1934-Ja 17, 1935; Jacques Sauriol, Ja 23-S 4, 1935; Denis-Alonzo Gobeil, o.m.i., S 11, 1935-Jl 27, 1938; Gérard Forcade, o.m.i., Ag 3, 1938-Mr 1, 1939; Paul-Emile Bréton, o.m.i., Mr 8, 1939-S 2, 1953; Jean Patoine, o.m.i., S 9, 1953-F 27, 1957; Hermann Morin, o.m.i., Mr 6-Ag 28, 1957; Patoine, S 4, 1957-Ag 5, 1964; Clément Tourigny, o.m.i., Ag 12, 1964-Ag 4; 1965; Jean-Maurice Olivier, Ag 11, 1965-N 8, 1967.
Alberta Golden Jubilee Edition, S 7, 1955.

Alberta Golden Jubilee Edition, S 7, 1955.
Ref.: **LAND** pp.19-21, 36-37.

AEPAA   mf   N 16, 1928-N 8, 1967
AEU   mf   N 16, 1928-N 8, 1967

405   *Union Laborer.* 1929-?//
m. Labour

Official organ of International Hod Carriers, Building and Common Laborers' Union of America, Edmonton Local No. 92. (Ref.: **ELL** p.229).

No issues located

406   *Novyi Krai / New Country.* Mr 1929-My 1929//
m. Immigration   Ukrainian in Ukr.

Organ of Ukrainian Immigration and Colonization Association in Edmonton.
Ref.: **BOM** p.27.

AEU   mf   Mr-My 1929

407   *Pravda Naroda / Truth of the People.* Mr 20, 1929-? 1929//
m. Ukrainian in Ukr.

Monthly Ruthenian [Russian] paper, ed. by Rev. A. Kizuin.
Ref.: **BOM** p.28.

AEU   mf   Mr 20, 1929

408   *Kirken og Hjemmet / Church and Home.* 1930-My 15, 1961//
m.; 2m.; m. Danish in Dan.

English ed. also pub.: *Church and Home / Kirken og Hjemmet* (Ref.:
CNLC p.77).
Frequency varied: no dates available.
Place of pub. varied: Edmonton, Calgary, Lacombe (Ref.: **CNLC** p.77);
Winnipeg (Ref.: **LOV**, p.152).
Pub. by United Danish Lutheran Church, 1930-1938; West Canada Dis-
trict of Danish and Lutheran Church, 1939-? (Ref.: **MK** 1932-1942). Ed. by
Christian Swendsen, 1930-? (Ref.: **KIRK** p.43).

OONL   or   [1954-1961]

409.1   *Vidrodzhennia / Renaissance.* F 1, 1930-S 1930/...
m. Prohibitionist   Ukrainian in Ukr.

409.2   *Albertiis' ka Zoria / Alberta Star.* Oc 1930-N 1930//
m. Prohibitionist   Ukrainian in Ukr.

Official organ of Ukrainian Temperance Society. Ed. by Thomas
Tomashevsky.

Ref.: **BOM** pp. 24, 30; **MARU** p. 487.

AEU   mf F 1-Oc 1930

Novyi Shliakh / New Pathway. Oc 30, 1930-My 30, 1933//
w. Political—General Ukrainian in Ukr.

Place of pub. moved to Saskatoon, Sask., Je 6, 1933 (v4no23).
Political and economic weekly, ed. by Michael Pohorecky.
Ref.: **BOM** p.27; **MARU** pp. 486-487, 633.

AEU   mf Oc 30, 1930-D 29, 1973

Deutsche Arbeiter Zeitung / German Labor News. N 1930-1931?//
m. Labour German in Ger. (and Engl.)

Subtitle: "Officielles Organ des Verbandes Deutschsprechender Arbeiter
fuer Alberta, Britisch Kolumbien und Saskatchewan."
Pub. by Association of German-Speaking Workers. Disbanded, Winter,
1931-1932 (Ref.: **GERW** p.118). Ed. by John Liebe.
Ref.: **CNLU** p.10.

OONL   or   Ja 1931

Alberta Herold / Alberta Herald. Oc 31, 1931-D? 1931//
w. German in Ger.

Superceded *Herold*, Edmonton (403).
Subtitle: "German Weekly."
Pub. and ed. by W.C. Boehnert (Ref.: *Edmonton Journal* Oc 22, 1931:14).
Ref.: **ARN** p. 228; **CNLC** p.106.

No issues located

Nor-East Ad-Viser. 1932?-?//
w.

Pub. and ed. by J.A. McLaren. Printed by Norwood Press.

AEPAA or   Mr 18, 1938 (69.163/248)

Spectator. N 5? 1932-1933?//
2w.

Pub. by Institute Press Ltd., Arthur H. Coles, mgr. dir., in the interests of
citizens and taxpayers of Edmonton.

ACG   or   N 8, 1932

Farmerskyi Holos / Farmers' Voice. D 10, 1932-Ap 6, 1934//
2m. Agriculture Labour Ukrainian in Ukr.

Devoted to farmers' and workers' interests. Ed. by Thomas Tomashevsky,
D 10, 1932-Oc 10, 1933; N. Syroidiw, Oc 25, 1933-Ap 6, 1934.
Ref.: **BOM** p.24; **MARU** p.485.

AEU   mf [D 10, 1932-Ap 6, 1934]

416.1   *Bear Lake Miner and Northern News.* Jl 1933-Ja 1935/...
               m.

> Subtitle: "A monthly devoted to Northern Development."
> Pub. by Publicity Bureau. Ed. by F.S. Wright.
> A magazine devoted primarily to northern mining development. Some-
> times cited as a newspaper.

416.2   *Nor' West Miner* F 1935-S/O 1950//
               m.

> Subtitle varies: A monthly devoted to Northern Development, incorporat-
> ing the Bear Lake Miner.
> Ed. by F.S. Wright.
> A magazine devoted primarily to northern mining development.

> **OOG**   or   D 1933-S/O 1950

417   *Ukrainska Gazeta / Ukrainian Gazette.* D 26, 1933-? 1934//
               m.   Political—Liberal   Ukrainian in Ukr. and Engl.

> "The only Ukrainian Liberal newspaper in Canada." Pub. by Ukrainian
> Gazette Pub. Co.
> Ref.: **BOM** p.29.

> **AEU**   mf   D 26, 1933-My 18, 1934

418   *Survivance des jeunes.* My 1934-194?//
               m.   French in Fr.

> Subtitle: "Organe de l'Avant-Garde."
> Pub. by Imprimerie 'La Survivance' Ltd. Ed. by Gérard Le Moyne
> (pseud. of Gérard Forcade)
> Ref.: **LAND** pp. 19-20, 38.

> **AEUSJ**   mf   [My 1934-Je 1940]
> **AEP**   or   D 1938, Ja 1939-Je 1940

419   *Weekly Tribune.* Ap 4, 1935-? 1935//
               w.

> Pub. by J. Meredith Scott.

> **ACG**   or   Ap 4, 1935

420   *Social Credit Gazette.* Jl? 1935-1936?//
               w.   Political — Social Credit

> New voluming began S? 1935.
> Format varied: mimeographed, Jl?-Ag 20, 1935.
> Pub. and ed. by Gilbert L. King.

> **AEPAA**   or   [Jl? 1935-Ja 17, 1936] (68.74; 72.232/24-25; 74.173/589;
>   82.153/17-32)
> **ACG**   or   Oc 25, N 8, N 22, D 6, 1935

21   *Today and Tomorrow.* D 23, 1935-Oc 5, 1944//
2m.; w. Political—Social Credit

Taken over by Social Credit Association of Canada, Oc 5, 1944 and absorbed by *Canadian Social Crediter,* Edmonton (428).
Frequency varied: 2m. D 23, 1935-F 7, 1936; w. F 24, 1936-Oc 5, 1944.
Pub. by Lucien Maynard, M.L.A., D 23, 1935-Je 10, 1943; Alberta Social Credit League, Je 17, 1943-Oc 5, 1944. Ed. by Maynard, D 23, 1935-Je 10, 1943; Rev. F.W. Williams, Je 17, 1943-Oc 5, 1944.

AEP   or   D 23, 1935-Oc 5, 1944

22   *Kupets / Merchant.* Ap 15, 1936-? 193?//
irreg. Business Ukrainian in Ukr. (and Engl.)

Organ of Independent Merchants of Alberta.
Ref.: **BOM** p. 26.

AEU   mf   Ap 15, 1936

23   *Suspilnyi Kredit / Social Credit.* F 18, 1937-? 1940//
2m. Political — Social Credit Ukrainian in Ukr.

"The only Ukrainian Social Credit paper in Canada" (Ref.: masthead).
Ed. by Anthony H. Hlynka. Pub. by Social Credit Publishers.
Ref.: **BOM** p.28; **MARU** p.487.

AEU   mf   [F 18, 1937-Mr 14, 1940]

24   *Alberta Herold.* S 15? 1937-1939?//
bw. German in Ger.

Subtitle: "German Bi-Weekly Published for the Edmonton District."
Ed. by Otto Tengermann. Printed by Union Printing Ltd. (Ref.: **ARN** p.228; **CES 3** p.68; **CNLC** p.106).

No issues located

25   *Edmonton Sports Record.* 1939-?//
? Sport

Ed. by Arthur Kramer (Ref.: **HENE** 1939).

No issues located

26   *Spotlight.* Ap 23, 1940-N 8, 1954?//
2m.; w.

Frequency varied: 2m. 1940-My 21, 1949; w. Je 4, 1949-N 8, 1954.
Est. and pub. by T.B. Windross, 1940-Mr 25, 1949; Thomas W. Pue, Sun Pub. Co. Ltd., Ap 1949-N 8, 1954 (Ref.: **CAN** 1955; *Edmonton Journal* Ag 23, 1940)

AEP   mf   Ja 25, 1949-N 8, 1954
ACG   or   F 13, 1942

427.1   *A.F.U. Bulletin.* Ja 1941-Ja 1949/...
m. Agriculture

427.2   *F.U.A. Bulletin.* F 1949/...
m. Agriculture

427.3   *Organized Farmer.* Mr 1949-Je 12, 1971//
m.; 2m.; w.; m. Agriculture

Superceded by magazine *Farm Trends.*
Frequency varied: m. Ja 1941-D 1962; 2m. Ja 5, 1963-Ja 17, 1964; w. Ja
24, 1964-Ja 24, 1966, except 2m. from Je-Ag; 2m. F 14, 1966-Mr 22, 1969;
m. Ap 12, 1969-Je 12, 1971.
Official organ of Alberta Farmers' Union (A.F.U.), Ja 1941-Ja 1949;
Farmers' Union of Alberta (F.U.A.), F 1949-Je 1971. Ed. by Henry Young,
Ja-N 1955; Arnold Platt, D 1955-D 1958; Ed Nelson, Ja 1959-D 6, 1963;
Paul Babey, Ja 17, 1964-Ja 18, 1965; Ken Nelson, F 1-Oc 4, 1965; Paul Ba-
bey, Oc 11, 1965-Mr 12, 1966; W.J. Plosz, Mr 26, 1966-Mr 1970; R.L. Tho-
mas, My 1970-Ja 1971.
Pub. supplement *Farm Business Trends,* Ja-Je 1971.
Alberta Golden Jubilee Edition, S 1955.

AEU   or [1955-1971]
AEPAA or N 1947 (75.188/82); S 1955 (75.188/83); [1956-1959]
(71.420/52)
ACG   or Ag 1941; Jl-Oc 1942; [Mr 1943-Oc 1947]; Oc 1962-F 1971
OOL   mf D 1947-Ja 1949

428   *Canadian Social Crediter.* Oc 12, 1944-N 24, 1949?//
w. Political — Social Credit

Superceded by *Canadian Social Crediter,* Edmonton (434).
Subtitle: "Incorporating *Today and Tomorrow*" (421)."
Official English language organ of Social Credit Association of Canada.
Ed. by John Patrick Gillese, Oc 12, 1944-Ja 1, 1948; Gordon E. Taylor, Ja 8-
S 2, 1948; S.C. Freeman, S 9, 1948-N 24, 1949.

AEP   or Oc 12, 1944-N 24, 1949
AEU   mf Oc 12, 1944-N 24, 1949

429   *News-Advertiser.* Mr 6? 1947-F 1948//
w. Labour

Pub. by Edmonton Typographical Union, No. 604, in the interests of the
locked-out printers of *Edmonton Bulletin* and *Edmonton Journal.* Pub.
approx. 50 issues (Ref.: **CPP** v57no3 Mr 1948).
Ref.: **CNLU**, p.13.

OONL or S 11, D 30, 1947
ACG   or Je 19, 1947

0   *Brivais Latvietis / Free Latvian.* Je 15, 1948-Ap 15/My 1, 1949//
     2m. Latvian in Lat.

     Merged with *Albalss,* Toronto, Ont. and *Kanadas Vestnesis,* Toronto, to form *Briva Balss,* Toronto, My 1, 1949.
     Pub. by K. Dobelis.
     Ref.: **CNLU** p.9.

     OONL   or Je 15, 1948-Ap 15/My 1, 1949

1   *Jasper Place Review.* 1949?-Mr 1951//
     w.

     Merged with *South Edmonton Sun* (432.1) and *North Edmonton Star* (435) to form *Edmonton Sun* (432.2), Ap 5, 1951 (Ref.: *Edmonton Sun* Ap 5, 1951).
     Pub. by Thomas W. Pue, Sun Pub. Co. Ltd.

     No issues located

2.1   *South Edmonton Sun.* S 8, 1949-Mr 29, 1951/...
     w.

2.2   *Edmonton Sun.* Ap 5, 1951-S 29, 1962/...
     w.; 2w.; 3w.; w.

32.3   *South Edmonton Sun.* Oc 6, 1962-Ja 18, 1969//
     w.

     Merged with *North Edmonton Star* (435) and *Jasper Place Review* (431) to form *Edmonton Sun* (432.2) Ap 5, 1951.
     Frequency varied: w. S 8, 1949-Ag 30, 1951; 2w. S 4-13, 1951; 3w. S 17-N 2, 1951; w. N 8, 1951-N 16, 1968.
     Pub. and ed. by Thomas W. Pue, Sun Colorpress Ltd.
     Published *Sherwood Park Sun* (894) as section, S 26, 1964-Ja 18, 1969?
     Alberta Golden Jubilee Edition, S 1, 1955.

     AEP   mf S 8, 1949-N 16, 1968

33   *Dzvin / Clarion.* 1950-1951?//
     irreg. Ukrainian in Ukr. (and Engl.?)

     Ref.: **BOM** p.37; **CES 1** p.86.

     No issues located

34.1   *Canadian Social Crediter.* Ja 5, 1950-Oc 1959/...
     bw.; m. Political — Social Credit

34.2   *Focus.* N 1959-
     m. Political — Social Credit

Superceded *Canadian Social Crediter,* Edmonton (428).

Subtitle: "The Canadian Social Crediter." Frequency varies: bw. Ja 5, 1950-Mr 9? 1955; m. Ap 1955-N 1962.

Place of pub. varies: Edmonton, Ja 5, 1950-N 1962; Ottawa, D 1962+

Format varies: newspaper, Ja 5, 1950-Mr 9? 1955; magazine, Ap 1955-Ag 1960; newspaper, S 1960+

Official organ of Social Credit Association of Canada. No ed. named Ja 5, 1950-D 1960. Ed. by J. Martin Hattersley, Ja 1961-N 1962.

AEU	mf Ja 5, 1950-Mr 9, 1955
AEP	or [Ja 5, 1950-1967]

435   *North Edmonton Star.* S 1950-Mr 1951//
        w.

Merged with *Jasper Place Review* (431) and *South Edmonton Sun* (432.1) to form *Edmonton Sun* (432.2) Ap 5, 1951.

Pub. by Thomas W. Pue, Sun Pub. Co. Ltd.

Ref.: **CNLU** p.13.

No issues located

436.1   *Jasper Place Citizen.* S 21, 1950-Ja 22, 1953/...
        w.

436.2   *Citizen.* Ja 29, 1953-F 28, 1957/...
        w.

436.3   *Suburban Times.* Mr 7, 1957-D 23, 1964?//
        w.

Pub. and ed. consecutively, by W.H. (Duke) DeCoursey, Russell Phillips and R.D. Butler. Butler sold business to Jasper Printing Ltd. Pub. and ed. by Jack Gorman and Al Wallace, 1952-Oc 3, 1953; Marion MacKay Robertson, Homes and Gardens Real Estate Ltd. and Creative Pub. Ltd., Oc 3, 1953-F 28, 1957; Suburban Times Pub. Co., Mr 7, 1957-D 1964. Ed. by William Copps, Mr 7-D 1957; J.F. Pain, Ja-Oc 10, 1958; W.H. Bourne, Oc 17, 1958-Ap 24, 1959; Donald H. McLeod, Jl 3, 1959-D 1964 (Ref.: **HENE** 1953-1964).

Ref.: **CPP** v59no11 N 1950.

AEP	or Ja 22, 1953-D 24, 1957
	mf Ja 8, 1958-D 23, 1964

437   *Banner.* Oc? 1950//
        w.?

A 16-page news sheet featuring city gossip and stressing civic issues, selling at 10 cents and carrying around 200 inches of advertising. Pub. by James P. Carleton for about 3 weeks (Ref.: **CPP** v59no11 N 1950).

No issues located

8 *News Bulletin.* F 8, 1951-Ag 26, 1951//
 w.

  Weekly supplement pub. by Thomas W. Pue, Sun Colorpress Ltd., Distributed with *South Edmonton Sun, Edmonton Sun* (432.2), *St. Albert Gazette (879)*, and *Redwater Review* (845).
  See *South Edmonton Sun* (432) for holdings.

9 *South East News.* 1953?-1954?//
 w.

  Pub. and ed. by Bernard A. Langdon (Ref.: **HENE** 1953, 1954).

No issues located

0 *Beverly Page.* Ag 1, 1953-
 2m.

  Pub. by Westweb Press, then Dalton Printing Co. Ltd. Ed. by Germaine Dalton, 1953-Oc 28, 1976; Marcel J. Dalton, N 15, 1976+
  Alberta Golden Jubilee Edition, S 15, 1955; 25th Anniversary Edition, D 20, 1978.
  Ref.: **CPP** v81no9 S 1972).

AEP or My 16, 1972-Jl 13, 1973; My 31, 1976+

1 *Holland Revue.* 1954-?//
 w. Dutch

  Pub. by G.N. Leenders (Ref.: **CPP** v63no7 Jl, 1954).

No issues located

2 *Alberta Country Life.* My 13, 1954-Ja 18, 1969//
 w.

  Pub. by Thomas W. Pue, Sun Pub. Co. Ltd., as supplement to all rural and urban newspapers pub. by the Company. Pub. as integral part of rural newspapers, N 16, 1968-Ja 18, 1969, rather than separate supplement.

AEP or My 13, 1954-Ja 18, 1969

3.1 *Biuletyn. Organizacji Polskich w Edmontonie /*
  Bulletin of Polish Association of Edmonton My 1956-N 1956/...
 2/yr. Polish in Pol. and Engl.

3.2 *Biuletyn. Kongresu Polonii Kanadyjskiej Okreg Alberta /*
  Bulletin of the Canadian Polish Congress. My 1957-
 2/yr. Polish in Pol. and Engl.

  Pub. by Polish Association of Edmonton, My-N 1956; Canadian Polish Congress, My 1957+ Ed. by Edward Henzel, N 1958-N 1969; T. Walkowski, N 1970+
  Ref.: **TUR** pp. 159-160; **CNLC** p.245.

OONL   or   1958-1970
AEPAA   or   My 1960-My 1971 (81.267)

444   *Edmonton News.* Oc 1, 1958-Je 25, 1959//
         w.

         Pub. by James E. Bowes; ed. by David M. Bowes. Pub. by Suburban Pub.
         Ltd.
         Ref.: **CNLU** p. 13.

         OONL   or   Oc 1, 1958
         AEP   mf   Oc 8, 1958-Je 25, 1959

445   *Scandinavian Centre News.* N 1, 1958-
         m. Danish Finnish Norwegian Swedish

         Pub. by Scandinavian Centre Cooperative Association Ltd. Ed. by Elsie
         Simmons, N 1, 1958-S 1, 1960; Eileen Peterson, Oc 1960-Oc 1965; Peggy
         Norgaard, N 1965-My 1968; Shirley Thorvaldson, Je 1968-Jl 1970; Gunnar
         Thorvaldson, Ag 1970-Mr 1971; Paul Karvonen, Ap 1971-F 1972; Leslie M.
         Morris, Mr 1972-F 1977; Eileen Peterson, Ap 1977+ (Ref.: Publisher's files).
         Ref.: **CNLC** p.77.

         OONL   or   N 1, 1958; Oc 1968; Ag 1970; N 1973-Jl 1974; S 1974+

         Progressive Student. 1959-1960?//
         See Supplement (1059)

446   *Alberta Jewish Chronicle.* 1960-
         irreg. Jewish

         Pub. and ed. by Herbert B. Hyman. Only one edition pub. for western
         Canada. First issues printed in Tofield (Ref.: Publisher).
         Ref.: **CNLU** p.26.

         ACG   or   Jl/Ag-N/D 1979; Ap 1980; Summer 1982-D 1983; Ag-S
                       1984; Ap, S 1985; Ap-S/Oc 1986
         OONL   or   May 1960

447   *Ukrainian Record.* Ja 1, 1960-Mr 1963//
         m.; irreg. Ukrainian

         Pub. irreg. after Je 1960.
         Ukrainian Catholic youth and education bulletin. Pub. by Ukrainian News
         Pub. Ltd. Ed. by R. Zaposocki, Ja 1, 1960-Mr/Ap 1961; Rev. A. Pawliuk,
         My 1961-Mr 1963.
         Ref.: **BOM** p.29.

         AEUCA   or   [Ja 1, 1960-Mr 1963]

Demonstrator. Mr 24, 1960//
See Supplement (1060)

Labor Advocate. Oc 1960-?//
See Supplement (1061)

48   *Edmonton Free Press.* Ag 16, 1961-F 7, 1962//
w.

Printed in Calgary by North Hill News Ltd.
Pub. in the interests of Edmontonians and free enterprise by J. (Wally)
Strang, Michael DeBranscoville, and William C. McCallum, consecutively.
Ref.: **CPP** Ag 1961:60, D 1961:104; Ja 1962:137; Mr 1962:63.

AEEA   or   Ag 16, S 6, 1961

Alberta Liberal. My 1961-F 1970//
See Supplement (1062)

49   *South Side Sun.* D 1? 1962-D 8, 1962?//
w.

Pub. by Thomas William Pue. May only have published a prospectus
issue.

AEP   or   D 8, 1962

50   *Alberta Labour.* N 1963-1979//
2m.; m.; bm.   Labour

Frequency varied: 2m. N 1963-Oc 1975; m. N 1975-Mr 1976; bm. Ap
1976-1979.
Voluming began with Ap/My 1976 issue.
Pub. in cooperation with the Labour Movement, N 1963-Mr/Ap 1975.
Pub. by Alberta Federation of Labour, My 1975-1978. Official publication of
Alberta Federation of Labour, Ap 1976-1978. Ed. by P. Quinlin, N 1963?-
Mr 1976; Warren Caragata, Ap 1976-1978; Jim Selby and Judy Samoil,
1978-1979?
12th Anniversary Issue, N 1975.

ACG   or   Oc 1973-N/D 1979
AEP   or   N/D 1973-v3no6, 1978

51   *Reporter.* Mr 18? 1964-? 1964//
w.

Pub. by L. Schotte for north-east Edmonton.
Ref.: **CNLU** p.13.

OONL   or   My 20, 1964

452   *Alberta Business Review.* Ap 15, 1965-? 1965//
          bm. Agriculture Business

          Pub. by AJC Publications in the interest of Alberta businessmen and
          farmers. Ed. by Graham Thomas. Possibly one issue only pub.

          ACG   or   Ap 15, 1965

453   *Western Catholic Reporter.* S 9, 1965-
          w. Religious

          Supercedes *Western Catholic,* Edmonton (388).
          Pub. by Western Catholic Reporter. Ed. by Doug Roche, S 9, 1965-S 3,
          1972; Victor Misutka, S 10, 1972-S 3, 1979; John Rasmussen, S 10, 1979-
          My 4, 1981; Glen Argan, My 11, 1981+

          AEPAA mf S 9, 1965-D 24, 1979
          AEU   or [1965+]

454   *Edmonton Gazette.* D 15, 1965-1966//
          w.?

          Pub. by Sturgeon Pub. Co. Ltd. Ed. by William J. Netelenbos.

          ACG   or   D 15, 1965

          Tory. F 8, 1966-?//
          See Supplement (1063)

455   *Messaggero Italiano.* F 12, 1966-F 19? 1966//
          w. Italian in Ital.

          Subtitle: "Settimanale Italiano."
          Ed. by Giancarlo Pasqualini (Ref.: *Edmonton Journal* F 17, 1966:39).
          Ref.: CNLU p.12.

          OONL   or   F 12, 19, 1966

456   *Mondo.* 1967?-Ag 1969?//
          m.; w.; 2m.; m. Italian in Ital.

          Subtitle: "L'unico giornale in lingua italiana nelle Praterie/The only
          Italian newspaper in the Prairie Provinces."
          Frequency varied: m. 1967?-Ag 1968; w. S 17, 1968-Ja 30, 1969; 2m. F
          11-25, 1969; m. Mr-Ag 1969 (Ref.: CNLU, p. 12).
          Place of pub. varied: Vancouver, B.C., D 5, 1968-Ag 1969 (Ref.: CNLU
          p.12).
          Pub. by Inter-Continental Travel Ltd. and Il Mondo Pub., 1967-1968?; Il
          Mondo Pub. and Broadcasting Co. Ltd., 1968-1969; Vittorio Coco, pub. and
          ed.
          Ref.: CNLU p.12.

          ACUA   or   My 20, 1968
          OONL   or   [Ja 31-Oc 8]-N 15, 1968-Mr 20, 1969

7 *Ryce Street Fysh Markete.* Oc 25, 1967-Je 6, 1968?//
2m. Underground Press

Pub. by Al Reynolds. Ed. by D.A. (Andy) Winfield. Member of the Underground Press Syndicate.
Ref.: *Edmonton Journal* Ja 17, 1968.

AEA or Oc 25, 1967-My 9, 1968; photocopy Je 6, 1968
BVAU mf Ap 25-Je 6, 1968

8.1 *Franco-albertain.* N 15, 1967-F 16, 1979/...
w. French in Fr.

8.2 *Franco.* F 23, 1979-
w. French in Fr.

Succeeded *Survivance* (404).
Subtitle: "Le seul journal de langue française de l'Alberta depuis 1928."
Official organ of l'Association Canadienne-française de l'Alberta, N 15, 1967-F 16, 1979. Pub. by 'La Survivance' Printing Ltd., N 15, 1967-Ag 6, 1975; Suncolor Press, Ag 13, 1975-Mr 2, 1977; North Hill News Ltd., Mr 9, 1977-F 16, 1979; Westweb Press, F 23, 1979+ Ed. by Jean-Maurice Olivier, N 15, 1967-Mr 18, 1970; Normand F. LeClerc, Mr 25-Oc 21, 1970; Olivier and Paul Denis, Oc 28, 1970-F 10, 1971; André Collin, F 17-Ag 11, 1971; Collin and Denis, Ag 18-Oc 29, 1971; Yvan Poulin, N 3, 1971-D 20, 1972; Guy Fournier, Ja 17-F 28, 1973; Arthur Gélinas, Mr 7-Ap 26, 1973; Jacinthe Perrault, My 2, 1973-My 15, 1974; Guy Lacombe, My 22, 1974-Oc 20, 1976; Gaétan Tremblay and Francine Gagné, Oc 27, 1976-Je 29, 1978; Maxim Jean-Louis, Jl 5, 1978-Jl 4, 1980; Sylvie Pollard-Kientzel, Jl 11, 1980-Jl 22, 1981; Paul Denis, Jl 29, 1981+
Ref.: **LAND** pp. 22-24, 39-41.

AEPAA mf N 15, 1967-F 27, 1981
AEUSJ mf N 15, 1967-D 22, 1982
       or F 23, 1979+
AEP   or [1970-1979]+

9 *Western Sports Weekly.* Mr 1, 1968-? 1968//
w. Sport

Pub. by Barry Whetstone and Bill Giles.

AEPAA or Mr 1, 1968 (68.53/1)

0 *Native People.* Jl 1968-D 3, 1982//
m.; w. Native in Engl. (and Cr.)

Frequency varied: m. Jl 1968-F 1972; w. Mr 2, 1972+
Pub. by Alberta Native Communications Society. Ed. by Doug Cuthand, My 1969-Jl 1971; Bill Lafferty, Ag-D 1971; George Lafleur, Ja 1972-Oc 17, 1975; Clint Buehler, D 5, 1975-Oc 15, 1976; David Anderson, Oc 29, 1976-

Je 23, 1977; Cecil Nepoose, Jl 15, 1977-F 10, 1978; Laurent Roy, F 17-D 29, 1978; Bert Crowfoot, Ja 28-My 23, 1980; Margie Lockhart, Je 6-20, 1980; Erica Denhoff, Je 27-S 26, 1980; Tim Buttle, N 3, 1980-N 6, 1981; Laurent Roy, N 13, 1981-D 3, 1982.
Ref.: **DANK** p.297.

AEU   or   Jl 1968-D 3, 1982

461   *Canada Goose.* Ag 23/S 5, 1968-Mr 21/Ap 3, 1969?//
bw. Underground Press

Pub. by Canada Goose Pub. Co. Ltd. Ed by Sam I. Agronin, M. Dale Phillips and Bernie Bloom. Associate member of Underground Press Syndicate; member of Liberation News Service.

BVAU   mf Ag 23, 1968-Ap 3, 1969

462   *Alberta Farm Life.* My 12, 1969-My 21, 1977?//
w. Agriculture

Pub. by Thomas W. Pue, Sun Colorpress Ltd. as a supplement to all weekly newspapers pub. by the Company. Continued as separate newspaper S 1977 (485).

AEP   or   Ja 8, 1972-My 14, 1977

463.1   *Edmonton Star and Alberta Farm Life.* My 12, 1969-F 6, 1971/...
w.

463.2   *Edmonton Star.* F 13, 1971-My 4, 1974//
w.

Pub. by Thomas W. Pue, Sun Colorpress Ltd.
Included *County of Two Hills Star* and *County of Lamont Star* as sections until 1969.
Ref.: **CNLU** p.14.

OONL   or   My 12, Jl 12, 1969
AEP   mf   S 20, 1969-My 4, 1974

464   *Telegram.* D 1, 1969-D 1975//
2m.; m.; bm.; irreg. Czechoslovakian Slovak in Czech (and Slov.)

Subtitle: "Western Canadian Bi-Weekly for Czechs and Slovaks."
Frequency varied: 2m. D 1, 1969-F 15, 1970; m. Mr 15-My 15, 1970; bm. Mr 1971-D 1973; irreg. Ja 1974-D 1975 (Ref.: **CNLU** p.15).
Suspended pub. Je 1970-F 1971; Je-S 1973; Ap-Jl 1974; Ja-Ap, Je-N 1975 (Ref.: **CNLU** p.15).
Pub. and ed. by Vladimir Valenta.
Ref.: **CNLU** p.15.

ACUA   or   D 15, 1969-My 15, 1973
OONL   or   D 1, 1969-My 15, 1970; Mr 1971-D 1975

55 *Messaggero delle Praterie / Prairies' Messenger.* D 26, 1969-
1977?//
m. Italian in Ital. (and Engl.)

Pub. by Prairies' Messenger's Printing and Pub. Ed. by Sergio Lanzieri
and Remo Bresciani, D 26, 1969-?; Melvin J. Beach, assoc. ed., 1975-1977
(Ref.: **HENE** 1975-1977).
Ref.: **CNLC** p.182.
OONL or [1969-1972]; [1977]
ACUA or D 26, 1969-Je 25, 1970

66 *Jornal Portugese.* 197?-1981?//
? Portuguese

Ed. by Marianna Ceia (Ref.: Telephone conversation with Alberto de
Carvalho, reporter with *Novo Mundo,* Toronto).

No issues located

Alberta Liberal. My ? 1970-? 1972//
See Supplement (1064)

67 *Examiner.* Ag 19? 1970-1971?//
w.

Pub. by L.L. Peltier and Dieter Rauh, PR Typography House Ltd. Ed. by
Clint Buehler.
Ref.: **CNLU** p.10.
OONL or S 30, 1970

68 *Source.* Oc 15, 1970-
2m.; irreg.; m. Arabic in Ara. and Engl.

Subtitle: "The Arab Voice in North America."
Frequency varied: 2m. Oc 15, 1970-Ag 15, 1973; irreg. S 15, 1973-D
1974; m. Ja 1975+ (Ref.: **CNLC**, p.39).
Place of pub. varies: Vancouver, B.C., 1970-1973; Edmonton, 1973-1978;
Ottawa, 1978+
Pub. by Canarab Holdings Ltd., Vancouver, Oc 15, 1970-Oc 15, 1973
(Ref.: **CES 3**); pub. in Edmonton by Source, N? 1973-Oc? 1978; in Ottawa
by the Source, N? 1978+ (Ref.: **CARD** Ja 1979). Ed. by Ahmad E. Murad.
Ref.: **CNLU** p.14; **ABU** p.153.

OONL or Oc 15, 1970-Ja 1971; F 15, 1972
ACUA or Ja 29-S 25, 1974

69 *Problysk.* Mr 1, 1971-Je 1, 1971//
irreg. Ukrainian in Ukr.

Only two issues pub. (Ref.: **CES 3** p.283).
Ref.: **BOM** p.37.

ACUCES sample issue

470   *Campus Lyfe.* Oc 29, 1971-Ap 6, 1972//
        m. University

        Pub. by Lyfe, a registered student organization of the University of
        Alberta. Ed. by Ralph Watzke.

        AEUA   or   Oc 29, 1971-Ap 6, 1972

471   *Olde Towne Crier.* N 1, 1971-1973//
        2m.

        Pub. and ed. by Germaine Dalton, Dalton Printing Co. Ltd., Beverly,
        (Ref.: *Beverly Page*, D 20, 1978; **CNLU** p.20).
        Ref.: **CPP** v89no9(S 1972)

        OONL   or   Ag 25, 1972

472   *Spokesman.* 1972-
        irreg.; m. Disabled

        Title varies: *Forum*, 1972; *AHCS News*, 1972-1976.
        Frequency varied: pub. irreg. during 1972.
        Format varies: newsletter to 1974; tabloid, 1974-N 1980; magazine, D
        1980+
        Est. as a newsletter for the handicapped in Alberta by university students
        on an Opportunities for Youth Program. Pub. by Alberta Handicapped Com-
        munications Society until Spring 1983. Presently pub. by Spokesman Publi-
        cations Society of Alberta. Ed. successively by Dwayne Jiry, Larry Pempeit
        to F? 1980; Herman Wierenga, Mr? 1980-1981; Colin F. Smith, 1981?-Mr
        1983; Dianne Worley, Ap 1984+; Bill Thompson, assoc. ed., N 1983+
        Ref.: *Edmonton Journal,* Mr 3, Ag 25, D 29, 1976; D 14, 1977; **ALB** My
        16, 1980:23.

        AEP   or   [My 1981-]
        AEML   or   Ja-D 1980; Ja-D 1982; Ap 1985+

473   *Western Livestock and Agricultural News.* Mr 1972-N 1982//
        m. Agriculture

        Continued *Edmonton Livestock Market News* (Ref.: **AGCL**).
        Superceded by *Western Beef Producers News*, Edmonton, 1983+
        Pub. and ed. by Doug Homersham, 1978-1982 (Ref.: **HENE** 1978-1982).

        AEAG   or   Ja-N 1982

        New Alberta Liberal. Ap 1972-1978?//
        See Supplement (1065)"

474   *Despertar.* Jl 1972-198?//
        m. Portuguese in Port.

Pub. by Associacão Luso-Canadiana de Edmonton (Ref.: Telephone conversation with Alberto de Carvalho, formerly reporter for *Despertar*, now with *Novo Mundo*, Toronto).
Ref.: **CNLC** p.249.

OONL or 1972-1973

On Our Way. Ag 1972-My? 1975//
bm. Feminist

Frequency varied: intended to be pub. monthly but issued bimonthly.
Pub. by a women's collective.
Ref.: *Canadian Newsletter of Research on Women* to My 1975; *Edmonton Journal*, Ag 15, 1972.

AEUS or Ag 1972
ACG or Mr 1973

Poundmaker. S 13, 1972-Ja 1975//
w. Underground Press University

Pub. by Harvey G. Thomgirt Publishing Society, an independent University of Alberta student society. The paper eventually disassociated itself from the University and became Edmonton's "alternative newspaper." Although pub. by a cooperative, two editors were named: Ron Yakimchuk to Ap 4, 1973, and Ross Harvey, My 24, 1973-Ja 1975.
Ref.: **ALB** N 11, 1974:4-6; My 26, 1975:2-3; Je 30, 1975:1.

AEUA or S 13, 1972-Ap 4, 1973; My 24, 1973-Ap 8/14, 1974

Portrait. My? 1973-Ag 6, 1975//
w. University

Pub. by Students' Union of University of Alberta during Spring and Summer session (My-Ag).

AEUA or My 9, 1974-Ag 6, 1975

Alberta Challenge. Je 1973-Oc 1973//
See Supplement (1066)

Prairie Star. Jl 1975-N/D 1977//
2m. Underground Press Political — Socialist

Format varied: Issue of N/D 1977 last in newspaper format; became quarterly magazine with Spring 1978 issue (v4no1).
Pub. by Prairie Star Press Graphix and Typesetting, a collective print shop. Billed as Edmonton's "alternative newspaper", which essentially replaced *Poundmaker* (476).
Ref.: **ALB** My 26, 1975:2-3.

AEP or Oc 6/19, 1975; Ag-N 1976; Ja-D 1977

479   *Business Reporter.* Oc 28, 1975-Mr 1977?//
           m. Business University

           Pub. by Commerce Association for Marketing Essential Literature,
           University of Alberta.

           AEUA   or   [Oc 28, 1975-Mr 1977]

480   *Kanadiyska Ukraina / Canadian Ukraine.* Ja 1976-D 1978//
           irreg. Ukrainian in Ukr.

           Pub. by L.U.L. Publications Ed. by Y. Slavutych.
           Ref.: **BOM** p.25.

           AEUCA or   Ja 1976-D 1978

481   *Summer Times.* Je 24, 1976-
           w. University

           Pub. by Students' Union, University of Alberta, during Spring and Sum-
           mer session, (My-Ag).

           AEUA   or   Je 24, 1976+

482   *Latin Report.* S 1976-Mr/Ap 1978//
           m. Spanish in Span. and Engl.

           Pub. by Latin Report Publications. Ed. by Sergio Martinez (Ref.: *Edmon-
           ton Journal,* Oc 13, 1976:48).
           Ref.: **CNLC** p.226.

           OONL   or   Oc 1976; [1977-Mr/Ap 1978]

           Commerce News. Oc 1976-
           See Supplement (1067)

483   *Lunch News.* Ap 18, 1977-Ag 30, 1977//
           d.

           Pub. by Collaborative Group. Ed. by Dwayne Hancock.
           Ref.: *Edmonton Journal* My 31, Ag 19, Ag 31, 1977.

           AEEA   or   Ap 19-Ag 19, 1977

484   *Strathcona Plaindealer.* S 1977-
           m.; q.

           Frequency varied: m. S-D 1977; q. 1978+
           Pub. by Old Strathcona Foundation Association. Contains news, opinions
           and items of historical interest.

           AEP   or   S 1977-Fall 1980

Alberta Farm Life. S 10? 1977-
w. Agriculture

Pub. by Thomas W. Pue, Sherwood Park Pub. Ltd., S 10, 1977-S 16, 1982.
Currently pub. by Keith Malcolm.

AEP   or   S 10, 1977+

Edmonton Examiner [South Editions]. Oc 20, 1977-
w.

Editions: South, Oc 20, 1977-Ap 30, 1980; Southeast — Zone 5, My 7,
1980+; Southwest — Zone 6, My 7, 1980+; Southwest — Zone 11, S 22,
1982+; Millwoods — Zone 7, Oc 7, 1981+
Title varies: *Edmonton Times,* Oc 1977-Oc 1978; *South Edmonton Times,*
N 1, 1978-Ag 29, 1979; *South Edmonton Times Examiner,* S 26-Oc 17, 1979.
Pub. by Ootes Press Ltd., Oc 20, 1977-Jl 18, 1979. Sold Jl 25, 1979 to
Pennysaver Publications, a division of London Free Press Printing Co. Ltd.
Ed. by David Holehouse, Oc 1977-Ag 16, 1978; Dan Allen, Ag 23, 1978-Jl
18, 1979; E. Ida Stanley, Jl 25-Oc 17, 1979; Don Wanagas, Oc 24, 1979-F
27, 1980; David Graham, Mr 5, 1980-Je 3, 1981; Dan Allen, Je 24, 1981+

AEEA   or   My 10-S 6, 1978
AEP   or   N 1, 1978+

Edmonton Examiner [West Editions]. N 9, 1977-
w.

Editions: West, N 9, 1977-F 11, 1981; West—Zone 1, F 18, 1981-Je 30,
1982; West Central—Zone 2, F 18, 1981-Je 30, 1982; West Central—Zone 1,
Jl 7, 1982+; Central—Zone 2, Jl 7, 1982+; West—Zone 9, Jl 7, 1982+
Title varies: *West Edmonton Examiner,* N 9, 1977-Ap 4, 1979; *Examiner,*
West Edmonton Edition, Ap 11-S 12, 1979.
Pub. by Randy Lennon, N 9, 1977-Mr 28, 1979 and Terry Clements, Ap
1-My 30, 1979 of Grove Pub. Ltd. Sold Je 1, 1979 to Pennysaver Publica-
tions, a division of London Free Press Printing Co. Ltd. Ed. by Deanna Dun,
Ap 4, 1979-My 21, 1980; David Graham, My 28, 1980-Je 3, 1981; Dan
Allen, Je 24, 1981+
Ref.: **ALB** Ag 18, 1978:3.

AEP   or   N 9, 1977+

Edmonton Sun. N 12, 1977-Ja 19? 1978//
w.

Subtitle: "Your Sunday Morning Star."
Pub. by John M. LeBel, Sunday Morning Sun Ltd. (Ref.: *Edmonton*
Journal, Ja 28, 1978).
Ref.: **ALB** Ja 23, 1978:20.

AEP   mf   N 12-D 25, 1977

Edmonton Sun. Ap 2, 1978-
d. (am)

Sunday ed. entitled *Sunday Sun.*
Pub. by Edmonton Sun, a division of Toronto Sun Pub. Corp. William J.
Bagshaw, pub., Ap 2, 1978-Ja 23, 1979; Ron Collister, ed., Ap 2, 1978-Ja 17,
1980; Donald Hunt, gen. mgr., Ja 24, 1979-S 2, 1980. Pub. by Elio Agostini,
Ag 6, 1979+; David Bailey, mnging. ed., Ja 18, 1979+
Ref.: **ALB** Ja 23, 1978:18-20; Mr 24, 1978:22; Ap 7, 1978:24-25; F 2,
1979:18.

AEU   mf Ap 2, 1978+
AEP   mf Ap 2, 1978+

Newscene. Ap 1978-My 1979//
See Supplement (1068)

490   *Edmonton Examiner [North Editions].* Ag 16, 1978-
w.

Editions: North, Ag 16, 1978-F 11, 1981; North—Zone 3, F 18, 1981+;
Northeast—Zone 4, F 18, 1981+; Castle Downs—Zone 8, F 10, 1982+;
North—Zone 10, S 22, 1982+
Title varies: *North Edmonton Examiner,* Ag 16, 1978-Ap 4, 1979;
Examiner North Edmonton Edition, Ap 11-S 12, 1979.
Pub. by Randy Lennon, Ag 16, 1978-Mr 28, 1979, and Terry Clements,
Ap 1-My 30, 1979, of Grove Pub. Ltd. Sold Je 1, 1979 to Pennysaver Publi-
cations, a division of London Free Press Printing Co. Ltd. Ed. by Gwen
Dambrofsky, Ag 16, 1978-My 21, 1980; David Graham, My 28, 1980-Je 3,
1981; Dan Allen, Je 24, 1981+

.**AEP**   or   Ag 16, 1978+

491.1   *Alberta Business.* Oc 20, 1978-Ag 28, 1981/...
w. Business

491.2   *Edmonton and Alberta Business.* S 5, 1981-F 5, 1982/...
3m. Business

491.3   *Edmonton Business.* F 19, 1982-Jl 29, 1982//
3m. Business

Frequency varied: w. Oc 20, 1978-Ag 28, 1981.
Suspended pub. Je 26-Ag 28, 1981 due to postal strike.
Division of Bowes Pub. Ltd. Pub. by James E. Bowes, Oc 20, 1978-Oc 19,
1979; Gerald A. Duncan, S 5, 1980-1981?; William R. Dempsey, 1981?-F 5,
1982. Ed. by Roy D. Cook, Oc 26, 1979-Je 10, 1982; Jim E. Watson, Je 21-Jl
29, 1982.
Ref.: **ALB** Oc 6, 1978:22.

AEP   or   Ja 12, 1978-Ag 28, 1981; Ja 8-Jl 29, 1982

492   *Noon News.* 1979//
d.

Eight page tabloid circulated to city lunch counters. Pub. by Walter Zicha (Ref.: *Edmonton Journal*, F 13, 1979).

No issues located

Nuovo Mondo. F 1979-
m. Italian in Ital. (and Engl.)

Subtitle: "Il Giornale Italiano del Canada meglio informato / Western Canada's Italian Newspaper.'"
Pub. by M.F. Siadi; ed. by R. Mattuli (Ref.: **CARD** Ja 1981).

AECL   or   CM
AE   or   6M

1   *Native Ensign.* S 1980-F? 1982/...
m. Native

2   *Nation's Ensign.* Mr 19, 1982-Oc 1983?//
m.; bw.; w. Native

Frequency varied: m. to Je? 1982; bw. to Mr 31, 1983; w. Ap 7-Oc 1983.
Suspended pub. Ag-Oc 1983.
Pub. by Alberta Society for the Preservation of Indian Identity, Ben Buffalo Rider, exec. dir. Ed. by Bert Crowfoot, 1980-1981; Stella Calahasen, 1981-Ag 6, 1982; Greg Harris, Ag 20-Oc 1982; Leanne McKay, N 1982; Evelyn Pratt, D 1982-My 12, 1983; Jim Ligerwood, My 19-Je 2, 1983; Angela Mah, Je 9-Oc 1983.

OONL   or   S 1980; Jl 1981
ACG   or   Oc 1980-Oc 1983
AEUB   or   S 1980; Jl 1981; N 15, 1982-Oc 1983

Jewish Star [Edmonton Edition]. D 1980-
m. Jewish

Pub. by Jewish Star Newspaper Ltd., Calgary. Ed. by Douglas Wertheimer (Ref.: Correspondence with Publisher, Oc 9, 1984).

AECL   or   CM

Korean Canadian Times. 1981-
?   Korean in Kor. (and Engl.)

Paul Kim, mgr. (Ref.: **HENE** 1981, 1982).

No issues located

Prairie Link. Ag 1981-
m. Asian

Subtitle: "Voice of South Asians."
Pub. by Prairie Link Communications Inc. Ed. by Gurcharan Singh Bhatia.
Ref.: Correspondence with Publisher, N 14, 1984.

AE   or   6M
AECL   or   CM

498   *Sonshine News.* D 1981-
        bw. Religious

> Est. by Rick Pearson (Ref.: *Red Deer Advocate* Jl 19, 1983).

No issues located

499   *English Express.* Mr 1982-
        m.

> Pub. by Alberta Advanced Education. Ed. by Bev Burke. A graded news-
> paper for adults learning to read English; designed to provide information
> about living in Alberta.
> Ref.: **ALB** Jl 7, 1978:22.

AEVC   or   Mr 1982+

500   *Dairy Contact.* Ap 1982-
        m. Agriculture

> Continued *Dairy Contact,* Calgary (208).
> Pub. and ed. by Allen F. Parr.

AEAG   or   1Y + CY
OOAG   or   Ap 1982+

501   *Diario.* Jl? 1982-
        m. Spanish in Span.

> Title varies: *Diario Hispano.*
> Subtitle: "Spanish Newspaper."
> Pub. by El Diario, César Ramirez, director. Ed. by Genaro Torres. Pub-
> lishing company est. Je 10, 1982.

AECL   or   CM

EDSON

502   *Edson Record.* 1910-?//
        w.?

> Pub. by Mr. Venn in Edson; printed in Edmonton (Ref.: *Edson News,* Mr
> 2, 1918).

No issues located

503.1   *Edson Leader.* F 17, 1911-Ja? 1914/...
        w.

503.2   *Western Leader.* Ja? 1914-Je 9? 1917/...
        w.

Edson Leader. Je 29, 1917?//
w.

Pub. by Edson Pub. Co. Ed. by James R. Andrews, F 17-Jl 7, 1911; W.X. Jones, Jl 14, 1911-1912?; W.C.R. Garrioch, My 23, 1912-D 11, 1913; L.J. Siljan, D 24, 1913-Ag 29, 1914; F.U. Laycock, S 5, 1914-Je 9, 1917.

AEP   mf F 17, 1911-Je 29, 1917

Western Star. Mr 13, 1913-Je 7, 1913/...
w.

Edson Critic. Je 14, 1913-N 5, 1913/...
w.; 2w.

Edson Semi-Weekly Critic. N 8, 1913-Ja 9, 1914?//
2w.

Became a semi-weeklly Jl 2, 1913.
Pub. and ed. by Arvie Quebar.

AEP   mf Mr 13, 1913-Ja 9, 1914

Edson Herald. Jl 6, 1917-D? 1917//
w.

Pub. by Edson Herald Pub. Co. Ed. by R.E. Johnston.

AEP   mf Jl 6-D 6, 1917

Edson News. Mr 2, 1918-Ag 31, 1918?//
irreg.

Pub. by Western Leader Pub. Co.

AEP   mf Mr 2, 1918-Ag 31, 1918

Edson Enterprise. Je 3, 1920-Jl 10, 1920?//
irreg.

Pub. by Three C's Print.

AEP   mf Je 3-Jl 10, 1920

District Call. Ap 14? 1921-My 25, 1922//
w.

Pub. and ed. by F.A. Briscoe.

AEP   mf My 26, 1921-My 25, 1922

Edson Headlight. N 30, 1922-1923?//
w.

Pub. by R.M. Whylock, Edson Headlight Pubs. (Ref.: **MK** 1922, 1923; **CPP** v32no1 Ja, 1923).

No issues located

510   *Edson Atom.* S? 1924-Oc 1924?//
         w.

         Written and pub. by R.M. Whylock at Mountefort Press, Edson.

         AEP   mf   Oc 20, 1924 (no.5)

511.1   *Edson-Jasper Signal.* F 24, 1928-Mr 17, 1943/...
         w.

511.2   *Western Signal.* Ag 1, 1946-F 25, 1960//
         w.

         Continued *Jasper Signal* (654); absorbed by *Edson Leader* (512) *Jasper Signal* was combined with a new Edson paper F 24, 1928 to form *Edson-Jasper Signal.*
         Suspended pub. in 1943; begun again Ag 1, 1946 as *Western Signal.*
         Pub. by Signal Pub. Co. and ptd. in Edmonton by Western Veteran Pub. Co. Pub. and ed. by J.L. Hollinshead, F 24-Je 22, 1928; Sydney H. Cliffe and Hollinshead, Je 28-D 20, 1928; Cliffe, Ja 3, 1929-D 19, 1957; G.H. (Nash) Mailhot, Ja 2, 1958-F 25, 1960.

         AEP   mf   F 24, 1928-F 25, 1943; Ag 1, 1946-F 25, 1960

512   *Edson Leader.* Ap 9, 1953-
         w.; 2w.

         Absorbed *Western Signal* (511.2)
         Frequency varies: w. Ap 9, 1953-Je 6, 1979; 2w. Je 9, 1979+
         Pub. by D. Marmaduke Caston, Edson Printers, Ap 9, 1953-Mr 22, 1967; Caston, Yellowhead Pub. Ltd., Mr 29, 1967+. Ed. by Carol R. Ahlf, Mr 29, 1967+
         Ref.: **CNLU** p. 16.

         OONL   or   Ap 9, My 21, 1953
         AEP   mf   N 11, 1954+

ELK POINT

513   *Elk Point Hunter.* Mr 11, 1961-Mr 2, 1963//
         w.

         Pub. by Thomas W. Pue, Sun Pub. Co. Ltd., Edmonton.

         AEP   or   Mr 11, 1961-Mr 2, 1963

514   *Elk Point Star.* 1972-1973//
         w.

Pub. by Thomas W. Pue, Sun Colorpress Ltd., Edmonton (Ref.: **AY** 1974).
Ref.: **CNLU** p. 10.

OONL or Je 17, 1972

Elk Point Reflections. Ap 10, 1979-Ja 8, 1980//
See Supplement (1069)

Elk Point Sentinel. S 26? 1979-1982//
w.

Pub. by Erik Nielsen, 1980?-1981; Ricksen Communications Ltd., 1981-1982 (Ref.: **CARD** 1981, 1982; **CAN** 1981, 1982; **DATA** 1982).

No issues located

Elk Point District News. Mr 17, 1982-
See **ST. PAUL** *St. Paul Journal.* (883.2).

ORA

Elnora Advance. Je? 1918-Jl 27, 1933//
w.

Incorporated with *Trochu Tribune* (973), Ag 11, 1933.
Pub. and printed by Tribune Pub. Co., Trochu. Ed. by William Cornelius Love Watson, Frank Peters, mgr. (Ref.: **CPP** v27no7 Jl, 1918).

AEP or Mr 19-D 31, 1920; Jl 24, 1924-Jl 27, 1933

Elnora Advance. Ag 11, 1933-D 24, 1970
See **TROCHU.** *Trochu Tribune* (973).

RESS

Empress Express. Je 6, 1913-Ag 27, 1936//
w.

Issue of Je 6, 1913 entitled *Express.*
Suspended pub. D 25? 1924-Mr 12, 1925 (11 issues).
Pub. by Alfred Hankin, Je 6, 1913-My 8, 1914; Hankin and C.E. Sexton, My 15, 1914-Ap 11, 1918; Hankin and E.S. Sexton, Ap 18, 1918-Ag 27, 1936. Ed. by J. McPhail Waggett, Jl 9, 1915-Ja 20, 1916.

AEP or Je 6, 1913-My 25, 1922; Mr 12, 1925-Ag 27, 1936

HANT

Enchant Weekly. 1917-1918?//
w.

Satellite of *Calgary Western Standard* (142.5).

Pub. by Standard Newspaper Syndicate, Calgary.
Ref.: **MK** 1918.

No issues located

ENTWISTLE

Peace River Pilot. Ja 20, 1910-F 12, 1910
See **PEACE RIVER** *Peace River Pilot* (862).

519   *Pembina Outlook and Entwistle News.* F 3, 1910-Oc 15, 1910?//
w. Immigration

Issue of F 3, 1910 entitled *Pembina Outlook.*
Originally pub. as a sister paper of *Peace River Pilot.* (800).
Pub. and ed. by Thomas D. Piche, F 3-Ap 1910; Arthur W. Arnup, ed., My
14-Oc 15, 1910; Pembina Outlook and Entwistle News Syndicate, props.,
My 10-Oc 15, 1910.

AEP   mf F 3-Oc 15, 1910

520   *Entwistle Enterprise.* F 10, 1912-F 8, 1913?//
w.

Pub. and ed. by Milo M. Oblinger. Sold to Arvie Quebar of *Western Star,*
Edson, F 1913 (Ref.: *Western Star* Mr 20, 1913; **CAN** 1914).

AEP   or F 10, 1912-F 8, 1913

ERSKINE

521   *Erskine Review.* N? 1912-Ap 28, 1921//
w.

Pub. by Fred J. Robertson, 1912-1917; Francis Cormack, 1917-D 26,
1919; Frederick John Slight, Ja 1, 1920-Ap 28, 1921 (Ref.: **MK** 1917-1921).

AEP   or Mr 16, 1917-Ap 21, 1921

522   *Erskine Times.* D 8? 1922-Ag 29, 1924//
w.

Pub. by W.J. Good (Ref.: **MK** 1922).

AEP   or Ja 12, 1923-Ag 29, 1924

EVANSBURG

Evansburg Pembina Herald. Ja 11-F 1, 1952.
See **PEMBINA MUNICIPAL DISTRICT** *Evansburg Pembina Herald*
(806.1).

Grand Trunk Poplar Press. Ag 1979.
w.

Place of pub. varies: Wildwood, Ag 1979-N 1982; Evansburg, N 1982+
Pub. by Wanda Cowley, W. and E. Cowley Pub. Ltd.

AEP or Ja 26, 1983+

RVIEW

Northern Review. Ap 10, 1923-My 20, 1924//
w.

Owned by Charles W. Frederick, Peace River; ptd. by R.N. Whillans,
Standard Press, Peace River; mg. and ed., Walter F. Gardener (Ref.: **CPP**
v32no4 Ap 1923).

AEP or Ap 10, 1923-My 20, 1924

Northern Review. Mr 8, 1929-D 26, 1933//
w.

Revival of *Northern Review* (524)
Suspended pub. F 28-Ap 2, 1931.
Pub. by Charles W. Frederick, Northern Newspapers Ltd., 1929-Ap 1931,
F-D 1933. Ed. by Walter F. Gardener, Mr 8, 1929-F 28, 1931. Pub. by James
Pennie, Review Pub. Co., Ap 3, 1931-Ja? 1933. Ed. by H.B. Matthews, F?-D
1933.
Ref.: **DAL** p.71.

AEP mf Mr 8, 1929-D 26, 1933

Fairview Post. Ap 18, 1940-D 1, 1953/...
w.

Post. D 3, 1953-
w.

Amalgamated D 1, 1953 with *Grimshaw Voyageur* (600), to form *Post.*
Amalgamated Jl 15, 1954 with *Battle River Herald,* Manning (721).
First issue, Ap 18, 1940, entitled *Post.*
Pub. and ed. by Elwyn Kelsey, Ap 18, 1940-My 29, 1952; Donald E. and
Iola Boyce, My 31, 1952-D 1, 1953; D.E. Boyce and John W. Hardie, North
Peace Pub. Co. Ltd., D 3, 1953-Ja 31, 1957; D.E. Boyce, F 1957-Ap 1960;
H.F. (Hec) MacLean, My 2, 1960-Oc 31, 1968; Bruce A. Gordon, Gordon
Printing Co. Ltd., N 1, 1968-N 13, 1975; Peter K. Schierbeck, Schierbeck
Printing and Pub. Ltd., N 13, 1975+
Alberta Golden Jubilee Edition, S 1, 1955.

AEP mf Ap 18, 1940-D 29, 1982
    or Ja 1983+

527   *Fairview This Week.* N 1, 1977-Mr 28, 1978//
        w.

        Pub. and ed. by Don Peterson and Dale Roberts, Craddock Publishing
        (Ref.: Correspondence with Fairview Public Library, Jl 25, 1984).
        Ref.: **NIC** p.41.

        No issues located

FALHER

        Courier, later *Smoky River News,* 1952-1963
            See **SMOKY RIVER MUNICIPAL DISTRICT** *Courier* (908.1) and
        Smoky River News (908.2)

528   *Falher News.* My 31, 1967-F 1969?//
        w. in Engl. (and Fr.)

        Superceded by *Falher News* (529.1).
        Title varied: *Courrier de Falher / Falher News*
        Pub. by D. Branigan, Manning Publishers, Manning. Ed. by F.G. (Gerry)
        Howis. Sold? to Reginald Burgar in 1969?
        Ref.: **CNLU** p.16.
        OONL   or   My 31, S 13, 1967; F 19, 1969

529.1   *Falher News.* 1969-Ap? 1972/...
        w.

529.2   *Smoky River Express.* My 3? 1972-Jl 4, 1973/...
        w.

529.3   *Express.* Jl 11, 1973-Oc 31, 1973/...
        w.

529.4   *Smoky River Express.* N 7, 1973-
        w.

        Superceded *Falher News* (528).
        Pub. in Falher for Smoky River District. Pub. by Reginald Burgar, 1969-Jl
        1972. Sold Jl 1, 1972 to Jeff Burgar, pub. and ed., Jl 1972+
        Included supplement *Northern Messenger* (622).

        AEP   or   My 3, 1972+

FORESTBURG

530   *Forestburg Advance.* Jl 29, 1916-1920?//
        w.

        Pub. by W. Frank Johnston, Jl 29, 1916-1919; ed. by F.H. Cramer, My 1,
        1918-Ja 31, 1919. Printed in Strome by *Strome Despatch* (Ref.: **MK** 1919;
        CAN 1921).

        AEP   or   Jl 29, 1916-D 26, 1919

Forestburg Home News. Ap 15? 1920-Oc 1922//
w.

Pub. and ed. by R.M. Whylock. Plant moved to Edson to publish *Headlight* (509).
Ref.: **MK** 1922.

AEP   or   Je 24, 1920-S 28, 1922

Forestburg Herald. S 1927-Mr 9, 1933//
w.

Pub. by Herbert Blauel, 1927?-My 18, 1928; John W. Johnston, My 25-N 16, 1928; J.D.S. Barrett, N 23, 1928-My 17, 1929; James Quinn, lessee, My 24, 1929-My 30, 1930; Barrett, Je 6, 1930-Je 18, 1931; H. Oxley, Je 25, 1931-Mr 1933. Printed by *Alliance Times,* My 25-N 16, 1928.
Included section entitled *Heisler News* Je 1, 1928-Jl 9, 1931.
Ref.: **MK** 1932; **CAN** 1933.

AEP   or   Mr 30, My 25, 1928-D 1, 1932

Forestburg Free Press. My 6, 1947-N 30, 1949?//
w.

Pub. by Thomas W. Pue, Community Publications of Alberta, Killam and Edmonton.

AEP   or   My 6, 1947-N 30, 1949

Enterprise. S 3, 1980-
See **ALLIANCE.** *Enterprise.* (16.2).

RT CHIPEWYAN

Moccasin Telegram. 1976-Ja 11, 1979?//
w.

Suspended Jl-Ag 1979.
Mimeographed.
Pub. at Bishop Piche School. Ed. by Maureen Clarke. Contained community news, advertisements and editorials.

AEUB   or   Ja 5, 1978-Ja 11, 1979

News. Oc 28, 1981-Oc 28, 1983?//
w.

Suspended during school vacations.
Mimeographed.
Pub. at Bishop Piche School by staff and students as a community service. Ed. by Gary Westhora.

AEUB   or   Oc 28, 1981-Oc 28, 1983

FORT MACLEOD

536.1   *Fort Macleod Gazette.* Jl 1, 1882-N 14? 1884/...
         2m.; 3m.; w.

536.2   *Macleod Gazette.* N 28, 1884-Je 28, 1887/...
         w.

536.3   *Macleod Gazette and Alberta Live Stock Record.* Jl 12, 1887-My
         25, 1894/...
         w.

536.4   *Gazette and Alberta Live Stock Record.* Jl 6, 1894-Je? 1907/...
         w.

536.5   *Macleod Gazette.* Je 13, 1907-Oc 31, 1907?//
         w. Political—Conservative

         Frequency varied: 2m. Jl 1-Jl 15, 1882; 3m. Jl 29, 1882-S 14, 1883; w. Oc
         9, 1883-Oc 31, 1907.
         Suspended pub. My 25-Jl 6, 1894.
         Pub. by C.E.D. Wood and E.T. Saunders, Jl 1, 1882-N 23, 1886; ed. by
         C.E.D. Wood, Jl 1, 1882-Jl 28, 1892, Jl 1, 1895-Je 30, 1903. Leased to R.
         Gordon Matthews, Ag 1, 1892-Ag 4, 1893. Pub. by Thomas and F. Clarke,
         Ag 25, 1893-My 25, 1894; Gazette Printing and Pub. Co. Ltd., Jl 6, 1894-Je
         28, 1895. Managed by George Scheer, Je 30, 1903-1905; George Grow,
         1905-1906; C.F. Harris, 1905-1906; H.S. French, 1906-Oc 1907.
         Ref.: **FORT** pp. 80-81; **CLAR.**

         AEP   mf Jl 1, 1882-Ap 26, 1906; Je 13-Oc 31, 1907

537   *Sentinel.* Jl 1894//
         w.

         Only one issue pub. by D.H. Murphy between Jl 19 and Jl 26, 1894 (Ref.:
         Edmonton Bulletin Jl 19, 26, 1894).

         No issues located

538.1   *Macleod Advance.* 1899-1907/...
         w.

538.2   *Advance and Southern Alberta Advertiser.* 1907-Je 2, 1909//
         w.

         Succeeded by *Macleod Advertiser* (540)
         Pub. by Thomas and F. Clarke, Clarke Bros. Ed. by Thomas Clarke.
         Ref.: **FORT** p.82.

         AEP   mf Ap 30, 1907-My 18, 1909

Weekly Chronicle. Ap 9, 1908-Je? 1908/...
w.

Macleod Chronicle. Jl? 1908-Je? 1909//
w.

   Pub. by R.W. Livingston.
   Ref.: **FORT** p.82.

AEP   mf Ap 23, 1908-F 25, 1909

Macleod Advertiser. My 25, 1909-S 11, 1913//
w.

   Succeeded *Advance and Southern Alberta Advertiser* (538.2).
   Absorbed by *Macleod Spectator* (542), S 18, 1913.
   Pub. by John E. Pember.
   Ref.: **FORT** p.82.

AEP   mf My 25, 1909-S 11, 1913

Buzzer, Mainly About Town. Oc 22, 1911-Ja 14, 1912?//
w.

   Printed on Advertiser Presses for Mssrs. Murdoch and McCormick.

AEP   mf Oc 22, 1911-Ja 14, 1912

Macleod Spectator. Ap 30, 1912-Oc 26, 1916//
w. Political—Conservative

   Absorbed *Macleod Advertiser* (540), S 18, 1913.
   Pub. by L.S. Gowe, Conservative, Ap 30, 1912-My 13, 1915; Herbert
Dennis, My 20-D 9, 1915; Charles K. Underwood, D 16, 1915-Oc 1916.
   Ref.: **FORT** p.82.

AEP   mf Ap 30, 1912-S 21, 1916

Macleod News. N 2, 1916-Je 1919/...
w.

Macleod Weekly News. Je 1919-Ap 15, 1920//
w.

   Absorbed by *Macleod Times* (544), Ap 21, 1920.
   Pub. by D.J. Grier, N 1916-Je 1919; Charles K. Underwood, N 1916-Je
1919; Underwood and J.H. Campbell, Jl 1919-1920.
   Ref.: **FORT** p.82.

AEP   mf N 9, 1916-Ap 15, 1920

544.1   *Macleod Times.* Mr 10, 1920-Ap 14, 1920/...
w.

544.2   *Macleod Times and Macleod Weekly News.* Ap 21, 1920-D 18,
1930//
w.

Absorbed *Macleod Weekly News* (543.2), Ap 21, 1920.
Pub. by Clara Jane Dillingham, Mr 10, 1920-Ag 30, 1923; D.J. Grier, S 6,
1923-Ja 7, 1926; Stephen Dillingham, Ja 14, 1926-Ag 7, 1930; Clara J.
Dillingham, Ja 30-D 18, 1930.
Pub. section entitled *Granum Times* 1928-1929.
Ref.: **FORT** p.82.

AEP   mf Mr 17, 1920-D 18, 1930

545   *Macleod Gazette.* Ja 8, 1931-
w.

Subtitle Ja 8-Mr 5, 1931: "With Which is Incorporated the *Macleod
Times"; Mr 12, 1931-F 1, 1934: "Successor to the *Macleod Times.*"
Est. by Ralph C. Jessup who took over *Macleod Times and Macleod
Weekly News* and renamed paper *Macleod Gazette.* Pub. by Ralph C. Jessup,
Ja 8, 1931-D 30, 1937, Ap 27, 1939-Je 20, 1940; Jessup and George Y.
McLean, Ja 6, 1938-Ap 20, 1939; H.T. Halliwell, lessee Je 27, 1940-Mr 31,
1961; Anna M. Jessup, Ap 6, 1961-Je 30, 1975. Ed. by Clifford L. Moses, Ap
6, 1961-Je 30, 1975. Pub. and ed. by Moses and J.H. (Jack) Murphy,
Macleod Gazette Ltd., Jl 1, 1975+
Diamond Jubilee Edition, Oc 18, 1934; Sixtieth Anniversary Issue, Je 25,
1942; Alberta Golden Jubilee Edition, S 1, 1955; Centennial Edition, Jl 1,
1982.

AEP   mf Ja 8, 1931-D 23, 1981
or Ja 1982+

546   *Macleod Argus.* D 13? 1939-Jl 17, 1940//?
w.

Mimeographed.
"The paper with a hundred eyes," managed by E. Jeanne Hunt.

ACG   or Ja 3-Jl 17, 1940

FORT McMURRAY

Northwest Review. Mr 5, 1939-?//
See Supplement (1070)

547   *McMurray Northlander.* 1949-1952//
w.

Continued by *McMurray Northlander* (549).
Ref.: **CNLU** p.12.

No issues located

Valhalla Star. 1941-?//
See Supplement (1071)

Northern Banner. Ap 2, 1959-Mr 2, 1965//
See Supplement (1072)

Fort McMurray Banner. Mr 9, 1965-1967//
w.

Pub. by Art Playford, Pembina News Advertiser Ltd. (Ref.: **CNLU**, p.17; *Edmonton Journal*, Mr 20, 1965).

OONL or Mr 9, 1965; F 9, 1966
AFMM or Ap 8, 1965

McMurray Northlander. Mr 5, 1966-N 1968?//
w.

Continued *McMurray Northlander* (547).
Pub. by Thomas W. Pue, Sun Pub. Co. Ltd. Printed in Edmonton.
Ref.: **CNLU** p.12.

OONL or Mr 5, 1966; Ap 20, 1968
AEP or Mr 12, 1966-Oc 19, 1968

Fort McMurray Northern Star. S 28, 1967-Je 1969//
2m.; w.

Pub. by Keith Randolph and Edward Romaine, Northern Star Pub. Co. Ltd.
Ref.: **CNLU** p.11.

OONL or S 28, 1967; Mr 2, 1968; Mr 1, 1969

Fort McMurray News Advertiser. Ap 9, 1968-My 26, 1970?//
See Supplement (1073)

Fort McMurray Sun. Oc 2? 1968-1969?//
See Supplement (1074)

McMurray Times. 1970?-1971?//
See Supplement (1075)

McMurray Courier. Je 10, 1970-N 28, 1975//
w.

Incorporated with *Fort McMurray Today* (552), D 5, 1975.
Mimeographed to Mr 10, 1971.

Pub. and ed. by Bernard C. and Frances K. Jean, Bernard Pub. Co., Je 10, 1970-S 11, 1974. Sold to Bowes Pub. Ltd., S 15, 1974. Pub. and ed. by Peter G. Duffy, S 18, 1974-N 28, 1975.

AEP   or   Je 10, 1970-Oc 17, 1975
AEUB   or   Jl 1, 1970; Oc 2, 1974-Oc 17, 1975
AEPAA mf   Oc 24-N 28, 1975 (on reel with *Fort McMurray Today*)

552   *Fort McMurray Today.* Oc 8, 1974-
           d.

Incorporated *McMurray Courier* (551), D 5, 1975.
Pub. by Bowes Pub. Ltd. Pub. by Peter G. Duffy, Oc 8, 1974-Jl 12, 1977; Graeme K. Connell, Jl 13, 1977-Ag 30, 1982; Donald J. Sinclair, gen mgr., Ag 31, 1982+. Ed. by Duffy, Jl 13, 1977-F 1, 1980; Ken Nelson, F 6, 1980-Ag 13, 1981; Howard Elliott, Ag 14, 1981+.
Special edition Celebrating City Status, S 2, 1980.

AEPAA mf   Oc 8, 1974-D 31, 1976+

553   *Fort McMurray Express.* Je 21, 1979-
           w.

Pub. by Irwin Huberman, Northstar Communications Ltd. Ed. by Dyane Harpe, Je 21, 1979-Oc 28, 1981; Steve Coop, N 4, 1981+ (Ref.: Correspondence with Publisher, Ap 11, 1984).
N 16-D 21, 1985 published weekend section.

AEP   or   Oc 21, 1981+

FORT SASKATCHEWAN

554   *Fort Saskatchewan News.* S ? 1899//
           w.?

Ref.: *Edmonton Bulletin*, Oc 2, 1899; **SMI** p.13.

No issues located

555   *Fort Saskatchewan Reporter.* My 7, 1903-D 30, 1909//
           w.

Pub. and ed. by W.J. Hunter, My 1903-D 1906; W.A. Pratten, Reporter Ltd., 1907-Mr 1908; John MacLaren, Ap-Ag 1908; John C. Macquarrie, S-D 3, 1908; John W. Johnston, D 10, 1908-D 30, 1909.
Ref.: **MK** 1905; **CAN** 1910; **REA** pp.550; **SMI** p.13.

ACG   or   Ja 2, 1907
AEP   mf   My 7, 1903; My 2, 1907-D 30, 1909

556   *Weekly Chronicle.* Ap 12, 1910-Je 21, 1911//
           w.

Pub. and ed. by John W. Johnston.

Ref.: **SMI** pp.13-14.

AEP   or   Ap 12, 1910-Je 21, 1911

Fort Saskatchewan Herald. Ap 6 1911-Oc 1911//
w.?

Pub. by Clara Jane Dillingham, ed. by Stephen Dillingham (Ref.: **SMI**
p.14; *Fort Saskatchewan Recorder,* N 16, 1911:1).
First issue, Ap 6 (Ref.: **CPP**, My 1911).

No issues located

Fort Saskatchewan Recorder. N 16, 1911-Oc 3, 1912?//
w.

Pub. and ed. by Joseph Burgess.

AEP   mf N 16, 1911-Oc 3, 1912

Conservator. Mr 27, 1913-Mr 22? 1922//
w.

Pub. and ed. by George O. Baetz, Mr 27, 1913-F 22, 1917; Mrs. G.O.
Baetz, Mr-My 1917; J.E. Buchanan, Je 7, 1917-1922? (Ref.: **CAN** 1922;
Record, Fort Saskatchewan, Ap 5, 1922).

AEP   or   Mr 27, 1913-D 30, 1920

.1   *Record.* Ap 5, 1922-Je 3, 1931/...
w.

.2   *Fort Saskatchewan Record.* Je 10, 1931-Ja 30, 1935/...
w.

.3   *Fort Record.* F 6, 1935-D 30, 1951/...
w.

.4   *Fort Saskatchewan Record.* Ja 9, 1952-Mr 23, 1960/...
w.

.5   *Record.* Mr 30, 1960-S 14, 1967/...
w.

.6   *Record and Lamont Gazette.* S 21, 1967-Mr 13, 1969/...
w.

.7   *Record.* Mr 20, 1969-N 15, 1978/...
w.

560.8   *Fort Record.* N 22, 1978-Ag 22, 1979/...
          w.

560.9   *Record.* Ag 29, 1979-
          w.

          Pub. by H. Oxley, Ap 5, 1922-Mr 26, 1930; Gordon Neale, Ap 2, 1930-S
          27, 1944; Bernard P. Knowles, Fort Record Ltd., Oc 4, 1944-Ag 30, 1962;
          Donald F. Hughes and Joseph J. Bell, Fort Record Ltd., S 1, 1962-S 8, 1965;
          John J. Bell, S 15, 1965-My 1, 1975; Jake J. Ootes, Ootes Press Ltd., My 8,
          1975-F 21, 1979; David Holehouse, gen. mgr., F 28, 1979-Ja 23, 1980; Terry
          Carroll, Ootes Press Ltd., Ja 30, 1980-My 6, 1981; Michael Lucas, Ootes
          Press Ltd., Ag 12, 1981-Jl 28, 1982; J.J. Ootes, Ag 1, 1982+. Sold to Bowes
          Pub. Ltd., D 1, 1982. Editors: D.S. Moore, Ja 7, 1971-My 1, 1975; Dawna
          Eagar, My 15-Je 26, 1975; Roger Young, Jl 3-Jl? 1975; David Holehouse,
          Ag? 1975-Jl 7, 1976; Norman Flaherty, Jl 4-S 15, 1976; Geoff Lee, S 22,
          1976-Ag 10, 1977; Kevin Mitchell, Ag 17-Ag 24, 1977; Mike Widmer, Ag
          31-Oc 5, 1977; Audrey Dorsch, D 21, 1977-Mr 22, 1978; Don Wanagas, Mr
          29-Je 14, 1978; Holehouse, Je 21-S 27, 1978; Tom Cusack, Oc 4, 1978-Jl 25,
          1979; Deborah Richmond, N 7, 1979-F 24, 1982; Bryant Avery, Mr 3,
          1982+.
          Alberta Golden Jubilee Edition, Ag 31, 1955.

          AEP   mf Ap 5, 1922-1984
                       or 1985+

561   *Fort Saskatchewan Star.* Mr 1, 1972-My 18, 1977//
          2m.; w.

          Frequency varied: 2m. to My 1974.
          Pub. by Thomas W. Pue, Sun Colorpress Ltd., Edmonton.
          Ref.: **CNLU** p.11.

          OONL   or Mr 1, 1972
          AEP   mf My 15, 1974-My 18, 1977

FORT VERMILION

562   *Northern Pioneer.* F 5, 1976-
          w.

          Pub. and ed. by M.T. and Ethel Mihaly, Mackenzie Highway News Ltd.
          (Ref.: Correspondence, High Level Library, Ag 8, 1984). Serves Fort
          Vermilion, La Crete, and Improvement District 23.
          Includes supplement *Mackenzie Highway Pictorial Review* (615).

          AEP   or Ag 9, 1978+

3   *40-Mile County Commentator.* Ag 18, 1971-
        w.

        Pub. and ed. by Oliver R. Hodge, Commentator Pub. Co. Ltd. Distributed
to ratepayers of Forty Mile County and Improvement District 1. Pub. in Bow
Island.
        Includes supplement *Cypress Courier* serving Improvement District 1 and
towns of Redcliff and Irvine. Pub. Mr 21, 1979+
        Ref.: CNLU p.3.

        OONL   or   Ag 18, 25, 1971
        AEP   or   My 3, 1972+

4   *Frank Sentinel.* Oc 25, 1901-1903//
        w.

        Pub. by Harry J. and Roderick Matheson, Matheson Bros. Moved to
Blairmore as *Times* (76) (Ref.: COU p.196, CNLU p.18).

        OONL   or   Oc 25, 1901
        ACG   or   My 2, 1903

5   *Drill.* 1904?-My 1905//
        w.?

        Succeeded by *Frank Paper* (566).
        Pub. by Charles E. Smitheringale (Ref.: HENW 1905).

        No issues located

6   *Frank Paper.* Je 1, 1905-N 11, 1909//
        w.

        Succeeded *Drill* (565).
        Pub. by C.E. Smitheringale who retired S 1905. Ed. by Mark Drumm, Je
1, 1905-S 23, 1909. Sold to Foothills Job Print and News Co., Coleman, S
23, 1909. Pub. and ed. by T.B. Brandon and J.D.S. Barrett, S 30-N 1909.
        Ref.: CAN 1911; COU p.196, CNLU p.18.

        OONL   or   Je 1, 1905
        ACG   or   My 17-31, 1906
        AEP   mf   [My 2, 1907-N 11, 1909]

7   *Frank Vindicator.* S 22, 1910-1915?//
        w.

        First issue entitled *Frank Vindicator and Blairmore Advertiser.*
        Pub. and ed. by W.J. Bartlett and J.D.S. Barrett, Blairmore (Ref.: CAN
1915).

Text identical to *Blairmore Enterprise* (77.2).

AEP   mf S 22, 1910-Ag 8, 1913

GADSBY

568   *Gadsby Gazette.* 1911?//
           w.

           Ref.: **MK** 1911.

           No issues located

           Gadsby Weekly Bulletin. Mr 6, 1913-N 20, 1913
           See **STETTLER.** *Stettler Independent.* (923).

569   *Gadsby Observer.* Mr 9, 1917-1918?//
           w.

           Pub. and ed. by Charles A. Roulston.
           Ref.: **MK** 1917, 1918; **CAN** 1919.

           AEP   or   Mr 9-S 7, 1917

570   *Gadsby Recorder.* 1920?-N 1922?//
           w.

           Ref.: **CAN** 1921, 1922, 1923.

           No issues located

GALAHAD

571   *Galahad Mail.* My 24, 1917-N 16, 1918?//
           w.

           Pub. and ed. by John W. Johnston.
           Ref.: **MK** 1918; **CAN** 1919.

           AEP   or   My 24, 1917-N 16, 1918

572   *Galahad Guardian.* D 1947-N 30, 1949?//
           w.

           Pub. by Thomas W. Pue, Community Publications of Alberta, Killam.

           AEP   or   D 25, 1948-N 30, 1949

           Enterprise. S 3, 1980-
           See **ALLIANCE.** *Enterprise.* (16.2).

IBBONS

73 *Gibbons Herald.* 1951-1952?//
w.

Ref.: **CAN** 1952; **AY** 1952.

No issues located

News. Mr 15, 1974-
See **THORHILD COUNTY.** *News.* (958).

LEICHEN

74 *Gleichen Echo.* D? 1903-1904//
w.?

Handwritten. Single copy posted.
Pub. by F. Corby. Included news, advertisements and features. (Ref.: *Calgary Herald* S 5, 1936:12).

ACG or Ja 14? 1904

75 *Gleichen Chronicle.* 1905?//
w.

No voluming.
Pub. and ed. by S.D. Milliken.

ACG or Oc 27, 1905

76.1 *Gleichen Call.* Mr 21? 1907-N 17, 1910/...
w.

76.2 *Bow Valley Call.* N 24, 1910-F 5, 1914/...
w.

76.3 *Gleichen Call.* F 12, 1914-Oc 3, 1956?//
w.

Title varied: first two issues entitled *Gleichen Newspaper* (Ref.: **GLE**, p.131).
Pub. and ed. by William Park Evans, Mr 1907-Ja 21, 1931; George Evans, F 4, 1931-Oc 1956.

AEP or My 2, 1907-D 29, 1920; Ja 7, 1925-Oc 3, 1956
ACG or Mr 21, 1907-Oc 3, 1956

Village Press. D 23, 1976-
See **CARBON.** *Village Press.* (239).

GLENDON

577   *Glendon Bulletin.* Je 4, 1952-Jl 28, 1955//
           w.

           Pub. by Thomas W. Pue, Sun Pub. Co. Ltd., Edmonton.

           AEP   or   Je 4, 1952-Jl 28, 1955

GLENWOOD

578   *Glenwood Gleanings.* Je 30, 1972-
           w.

           Pub. by Glenwood Senior Citizens Civic Group.

           ACG   or   D 10, 17, 1974 (BB.4 G558A)
           Publishers' files or Je 30, 1972+

GRAND CENTRE

579   *Grand Centre Times.* 1959?-Je 15, 1960//
           ?

           Amalgamated with *Bonnyville Tribune* (87.1) and *Cold Lake Courier*
           (285) to form *Tribune,* Bonnyville (87.2), Je 22, 1960.
           Pub. and ed. by C.C. (Chuck) Joly.
           Ref.: *Bonnyville Tribune* Je 15, 1960.

           No issues located

580   *Grand Centre Press.* Jl 14, 1962-N 16, 1968//
           w.

           Pub. by Thomas W. Pue, Sun Pub. Co. Ltd., Edmonton

           AEP   or   Jl 14, 1962-Oc 19, 1968

           Grand Centre Globe. Ap 23, 1974-D 20, 1977
           See **BONNYVILLE.** *Bonnyville Nouvelle* (89.1).

581.1   *Grand Centre-Cold Lake Sun.* Jl 5, 1977-Ag 8, 1978/...
           w.

581.2   *Grand Centre-Cold Lake-Bonnyville Sun.* Ag 15, 1978-
           w.

           Pub. and ed. by Jim Bentein, Bentein Press Ltd. Printed in Lloydminster
           and Edmonton. Owen Roberts appointed mng. ed. Je 29, 1982.

           AEP   or   Oc 18, 1977+

RANDE CACHE

2   *Grande Cache Star.* Ja 17, 1970-My 2, 1970//
     w.

     Pub. and ed. by Thomas W. Pue, Sun Colorpress Ltd., Edmonton.
     Ref.: **CNLU** p.11.

     OONL   or   Ja 24, Mr 28, 1970

3   *Grande Cache Mountaineer.* Ap 29, 1970-
     w.

     Pub. and ed. by Miriam Nelson, Ap 29, 1970-Ag 11, 1976; Noel H. Edey,
     Grande Cache Mountaineer Pub. Ltd., Ag 18, 1976-Oc 22, 1980; Lois M.E.
     Edey, pub., N 1980-Ag 27, 1986; Ed. by Noel H. Edey, Ag 16, 1976-Oc 22,
     1980; Lois M. Edey, N, 1980+.
     Ref.: Correspondence with Grande Cache Municipal Library, Jl 16, 1986;
     Correspondence with Publisher, Mr 1987; **CNLU**, p.18.

     OONL   or   Ap 29, 1970
     AEP   or   My 3, 1972+

RANDE PRAIRIE

4   *Grande Prairie Herald.* Mr 25, 1913-Ag 10, 1939//
     w.

     Amalgamated with *Northern Tribune,* Grande Prairie, (586.1), Ag 17,
     1939 to form *Herald-Tribune,* Grande Prairie. (586.2).
     Pub. and ed. by William C. Pratt, Herald Printing Co., Mr 25, 1913-Ag 10,
     1915; V.H. and Milo M. Oblinger lessees, Ag 17, 1915-1916. Sold to Charles
     Kitchen and George Duncan in 1916, who operated the paper until My 1,
     1927. Kitchen sold his half-interest to Charles W. Frederick in 1927 and
     Duncan his half-interest to Frederick in 1930. Plant destroyed by fire, Jl 25,
     1939 (**PUB**, Ag, 1939).
     Pioneer Historical Number, D 21, 1934.
     Ref.: *Herald-Tribune* Grande Prairie, Oc 5, 1950; **CAM 1** pp.39-51.

     AEP   mf   Mr 25, 1913-Ag 10, 1939

5   *Frontier Signal.* S 28, 1914-Ag 10, 1916?//
     w.

     Pub. and ed. by G.R. Wilson, Grande Prairie Pub. Co.

     AEP   mf   S 28, 1914-Ag 10, 1916

6.1 *Northern Tribune.* Je 30, 1932-Ag 10, 1939/...
     w.

586.2   *Herald-Tribune.* Ag 17, 1939-Mr 31? 1964/...
              w.; 2w.

586.3   *Daily Herald Tribune.* Ap 6, 1964-
              d.

              Amalgamated Ag 17, 1939 with *Grande Prairie Herald* (584) to form
              Herald-Tribune (586.2).
              Frequency varied: w. Ag 17, 1939-F 24, 1955; 2w. Mr 4, 1955-Mr 31?
              1964; d. Ap 6, 1964+
              Co-operatively owned by George Duncan, James Duncan, Arthur Jackson
              and J.B. Yule. Ed. by J.B. Yule, Ag 17, 1939-Mr 13, 1947; Gertrude Charters,
              Mr 27, 1947-Oc 18, 1950. Sold to Bowes Pub. Ltd. S 30, 1950. Ed. by Wil-
              liam H. Bowes and James E. Bowes, Oc 26, 1950-Jl 17, 1952; James E.
              Bowes, Jl 24, 1952-N 8, 1956; James G. English, N 9, 1956-Je 14, 1960;
              James E. Bowes, Je 17, 1960-D 1963. Pub. by James E. Bowes, Ap 6, 1964-Jl
              4, 1966; Kenneth Kirkpatrick, Jl 5, 1966-Ag 15, 1967; Gerald A. Duncan, Ag
              16, 1967-S 9, 1977; William R. Dempsey, S 12, 1977-Ag 28, 1980; Donald J.
              Sinclair, Ag 29, 1980-F 24, 1982; James L. Grasswick, Mr 15, 1982+. Ed. by
              Philip McLeod, Jl 2, 1969-Ag 13, 1970; Bill Scott, Ag 14, 1970+
                  Ref.: **CAM 1**, p.51.

              AEU   mf Je 30, 1932-Ag 10, 1939
              AEPAA mf Ap 6, 1964-D 31, 1976
              AEP   mf 1939-1978
                           or 1979+

587   *Herald-Tribune Rural Route.* Ap 12, 1972-
              w.

                  Title varies: *Rural Route*
                  Pub. by *Daily Herald Tribune.*
                  Ref.: **CNLU** p.18.

              OONL   or   S 19, 26, Oc 3-24, 1973

588.1   *Grande Prairie Booster.* Ap 15, 1972-My 27, 1981/...
              w.

588.2   *Grande Prairie This Week.* Je 3, 1981-
              w.

                  Pub. by R.D. (Bob) McFarlane and Brian Wilson, Focus Pub. Co. Ltd.,
              who purchased the paper from Meridian Printing Co. Ltd., Lloydminster, Ja
              1, 1976. Pub. by George Lanctot, Je 24, 1981+. Ed. by Graeme K. Connell
              to Je 29, 1977; E. Ida Stanley, Jl 6, 1977-Jl 12, 1978; Jack Brett, Ag 2, 1978-
              Mr 21, 1979; John Hart, Ap 18, 1979-Ap 30, 1980; Luba Dzubak, My 7,
              1980-My 20, 1981; Colin Lamont, Je 3, 1981-Mr 31, 1982.
                  Ref.: **CNLU** p.18.

              OONL   or   S 13, 1972

AEP   mf Ja 7, 1976-D 28, 1983
           or Ja 1984+

GRANUM

89   *Leavings Star.* 1905?//
    w.

    Pub. by Claresholm Pub. Co. (Ref.: **HENW** 1905).

    No issues located

90   *Granum Times.* Mr 2, 1908?//
    w.?

    No pub. or ed. named.

    ACG   or Mr 2, 1908

91   *Granum Press.* Jl 2, 1909-Ag 5, 1910//
    w.

    Pub. and ed. by John M. Millar.

    AEP   or Jl 2, 1909-Ag 5, 1910

92   *Granum News.* N 11? 1910-Oc 4, 1912?//
    w.

    Pub. by Fred J. Robertson, 1910-D 8, 1911; Harwood Duncan, D 15, 1911-Oc 1912. Managed and ed. by H. Lee Sammons, D 15, 1911-Ap 27, 1912. Printed by *Claresholm Review.*

    AEP   or F 10, 1911-Oc 4, 1912

93   *Granum Advertiser.* 1914//
    w.

    Pub. by Harwood Duncan, (Ref.: *Stavely Advertiser,* Ap 9, 1914:1). Plant moved to Claresholm to publish *Claresholm Advertiser* (267.1), Ap 15, 1914.

    No issues located

94.1   *Granum News.* Ap 6, 1917-Ap 5, 1918/...
    w.

94.2   *Granum Herald.* Ap 12, 1918-N 12, 1919//
    w.

    Printed in Claresholm, Ap 6, 1917-Mr 1918; Granum, Ap 5, 1918-N 12, 1919.
    Pub. by H.B. Tilden, Ap 6, 1917-Mr 1918; John H. Salton, Ap 12, 1918-N 12, 1919. Managed by Tilden, Ap 12-S 30, 1918.

AEP   or   Ap 6 1917-N 12, 1919

595   *Advertiser.* F 20, 1920-N 30, 1921?//
           w.

           Pub. and ed. by John H. Salton. Salton stated in N 30, 1921 issue that
           newspaper would be suspended for a month due to an extended trip to
           Winnipeg.
           Ref.: **MK** 1920, 1921.

           AEP   or   F 20, 1920-N 30, 1921

           Granum Times. 1928-1929
           See **FORT MACLEOD**. *Macleod Times and Macleod Weekly News.*
           (544.2).

GRASSY LAKE

596   *Grassy Lake News.* 1908-1909?//
           w.

           Title varied: *Grassy Lake Record,* same paper? Mr. Ashby, ed. (Informa-
           tion from Sir Alexander Galt Museum, Lethbridge).
           Pub. under auspices of Board of Trade (Ref.: **CPP** v18no7 Jl 1908).

           No issues located

597   *Outlaw.* 1910//
           w.?

           "Issued everytime the Ghost walks by the Outlaw Publishing Co." (Ref.:
           Issue, Mr 12, 1910:1). Ed. by Chedwy van Dusen. Printed by *Taber Free
           Press* (Ref.: *Taber Free Press* F 24, 1910; **MK** 1911. Both sources state Dr.
           Herbert Lake to be editor). An advertisement for the *Outlaw* appears in
           Medicine Hat News, Ja 27, 1910.

           ACG   or   Mr 12, 1910

598   *Grassy Lake Pilot.* Je? 1910-Je 30, 1911//
           w.

           Pub. by E.W. Schell, Je 1910-1911; J. Clark Knox, 1911.
           Ref.: **MK** 1911.

           AEP   or   Ap 21-Je 30, 1911

599   *Grassy Lake Gazette.* Jl 7, 1911-1917?//
           w.

           Pub. and ed. by J. Clark Knox (Ref.: **MK** 1913; **CAN** 1917); F.H. Cramer
           (Ref.: **CPP** v25no7 Jl 1916).

           AEP   or   Jl 7, 1911-Je 13, 1913; D 5, 1913

IMSHAW

Grimshaw Voyageur. Oc 2, 1952-N 28, 1953//
w.

Amalgamated with *Fairview Post* (526.1) D 1, 1953 to form *Post,* Fairview. (526.2).
Mimeographed to D 6, 1953.
Pub. and ed. by Allen and Shirley Ronaghan.

AEP   mf Oc 2, 1952-N 28, 1953

Grimshaw Spotlight. Ag 18, 1956-Ja 30, 1960//
w.

Pub. by Thomas W. Pue, Sun Pub. Co. Ltd. Printed in Edmonton.

AEP   mf Ag 18, 1956-Ja 30, 1960

Northerner. 1961-1962//
w.

Pub. and ed. by Jean Gentry and Carm B. Ellis. Suspended pub. in late 1962 and mailing list taken over by Fairview *Post* (526). Ran for 15 months (Ref.: **CPP** v72no1 Ja 1963).

AEP   mf My 10-My 31, 1962

Mile Zero News. Ja 31, 1979-
w.

Pub. by M.T. Mihaly, Mackenzie Highway News Ltd. Ed. by Mihaly, Ja 31, 1979-My 26, 1982; James Byard, Je 9, 1982+
Includes supplement *Mackenzie Highway Pictorial Review* (615).

AEP   mf Ja 31, 1979-D 21, 1983
             or Ja 1984+

OUARD

Grouard News. Ag 10, 1912-N 25, 1915//
w.

Pub. and ed. by R.S. Burns.

AEP   or Ag 10, 1912-N 25, 1915

NNA

.1   *Hanna Herald.* D 24, 1912-Oc 9, 1947/...
w.

.2   *Hanna Herald and East Central Alberta News.* Oc 16, 1947-
w.

Pub. by Herbert George McCrea, D 24, 1912-Jl 22, 1937; Lottie M.
(McCrea) Wall, McCrea Pub. Co., Ag 5, 1937-Jl 23, 1953; G.R. (Bob)
McCrea, Hanna Herald Pub., Jl 30, 1953-N 1, 1981; John T. Gorman, N 1,
1981+.
Alberta Golden Jubilee Edition, Ag 25, 1955; 50th Anniversary Issue, Ag
2, 1962.
Ref.: **DAL** p.74.

AEP   mf D 24, 1912-D 30, 1981
          or   Ja 1982+

606   *Hanna Leader.* 1913//
        w.

Probably error for *Hanna Herald* (605). Hanna and District Historical
Society states that only one local paper was published.
Ref.: **CAN** 1914.

No issues located

HARDISTY

607   *Hardisty Enterprise.* F 6, 1908-F 4, 1909//
        w. Political—Liberal

Pub. and ed. by Arthur H. Liversidge and J.G. Turgeon, F 6-Je 11, 1908;
Turgeon, Je 1908-F 4, 1909.

AEP   or   F 6, 1908-F 4, 1909

608   *Hardisty Mail.* Ag? 1910-1930?//
        w.

Due to economic depression, *Sedgewick Sentinel* (890.1), amalgamated
with *Bawlf Sun* (64), *Daysland Press* (302), *Hardisty Mail* (608), *Killam
News* (659), *Lougheed Express* (711) and *Strome Depatch* (941) to form
Community Press, Sedgewick (890.2), Ap 17, 1930 (Ref.: **SED** p.621).
Pub. and ed. by W.A. Skinner, 1910-N 27, 1913; John W. Haworth lessee
D 5, 1913-My 15, 1914; W.A. Skinner, My 22, 1914-S 10, 1915; H.W. Betts,
S 17, 1915-F 28, 1920; A.L. Eastly, Mr 4, 1920-1924? (Ref.: **CAN** 1924).

AEP   or   D 16, 1910; Ja 6, 1911-D 30, 1920

609   *Hardisty World.* Ap? 1924-D 19, 1952?//
        w.

Suspended pub. S 27, 1945-Ag 22, 1946.
Pub. and ed. by W.J. Whitehouse, Ap? 1924-Ja 15, 1925; James P. Dillon,
Ja 22, 1925-D 11, 1930; H.W. Betts, lessee, D 18, 1930-S 27, 1945, Thomas
W. Pue, Community Publications of Alberta, Edmonton, Ag 22, 1946-D 19,
1952.

AEP   or   Jl 3, 1924-Je 25, 1925; Ja 7, 1926-S 27, 1945; Ag 22, 1946-D
          19, 1952

ARTELL

> *News.* N 8, 1929-Oc 2,1931
> See **TURNER VALLEY.** *Tri-City Observer.* (975).

AY LAKES

0   *Hay Lakes Times.* 1925-1931?//
> w.

> Pub. by William Worton; ed. by J.W. Morrison.
> Established by A.J. Samis.
> Ref.: **CAN** 1931; **MK** 1926-1931.

AEP   or   D 16/27, 1927-My 10, 1929

1   *Hay Lakes Review.* 1946-N 24, 1949?//
> w.

> Pub. by Thomas W. Pue, Community Publications of Alberta, Killam and
> Edmonton.

AEP   or   Ja 24, 1947-N 24, 1949

:ISLER

> *Heisler News.* Je 1, 1928-Jl 9, 1931
> See **FORESTBURG.** *Forestburg Herald.* (532).

2   *Heisler Herald.* My 2? 1947-N 30, 1949?//
> w.

> Pub. by Thomas W. Pue, Community Publications of Alberta, Killam and
> Edmonton.

AEP   or   S 12, 1947-N 30, 1949

> *Enterprise.* S 3, 1980-
> See **ALLIANCE.** *Enterprise.* (16.2).

GH LEVEL

3   *Northern Echo.* Ja 8, 1969-? 1969//
> w.

> Title did not appear until F 5, 1969 (Ref.: *Northern Echo* Ja 8, 1969:2).
> Mimeographed.
> Pub. and ed. by Joe Fromhold (Ref.: Correspondence with Publisher,
> *Echo,* High Level, Jl 26, 1985).

Ref.: **CNLU** p. 19.

OONL   or   Ja 8, F 26, 1969

614   *Echo.* Ap 4, 1973-
w.

Title varies: *High Level Echo.*
Prospectus issue pub. Mr 8, 1973.
Pub. by M.T. Mihaly, Mackenzie Highway News Ltd. Ed. by J.W. (Bill)
Stevenson, 1977+
Includes supplement *Mackenzie Highway Pictorial Review* (615).
Ref.: Correspondence with High Level Library, Ag 8, 1984; *Echo*, Ap 2,
1980.

AEP   or   D 14, 1977+

615.1   *Mackenzie Highway Pictorial.* Ja 3, 1979-Jl 30, 1980/...
w.

615.2   *Mackenzie Highway Pictorial Review.* Ag 6, 1980-
w.

Supplement pub. by Mackenzie Highway News Ltd. Pub. by M.T.
Mihaly. Distributed as common section to *Mile Zero News,* Grimshaw
(603); *Banner Post,* Manning (722.2); *Echo,* High Level, (614); *Northern
Pioneer,* Fort Vermilion. (562).

AEP   or   Ja 3, 1979+ (with *Echo,* High Level)

HIGH PRAIRIE

616   *Northland Calling.* Ap? 1945-D? 1945//
w.

Founded by C.E. Gardiner in Grande Prairie (Ref.: *Northern Echo,* High
Prairie, Jl 1946).

No issues located

617   *Northern Echo.* Jl? 1945-Je 25, 1956?//
m.; 2m.

Frequency varied: m. Jl? 1945-Oc 1946; 2m. N 1946-Je 1956.
Suspended pub. Jl 1947 (2 issues) and F 14-Ap 11, 1955.
Format varied: magazine until N 1946, then changed to newspaper format
and issued 2m.
Pub. and ed. by C.E. Gardiner. Printed by Bulletin Printers Ltd.,
Edmonton, 1945-1950.

AEP   or   Mr 1946-Je 25, 1956
AHPD   or   Jl 1945-N 29, 1947; Ja 1948-D 25, 1950; F 27-Mr 5, 1951

8   *Northern Star.* Ja 20, 1955-My 16, 1958//
w.

Pub. and ed. by Thomas W. Pue, Sun Pub. Co. Ltd., Edmonton.
Alberta Golden Jubilee Edition, S 2, 1955.

AEP   or   Ja 27, 1955-My 16, 1958

9.1   *High Prairie Progress.* Jl 25, 1956-Je 4, 1958/...
w.

9.2   *Progress.* Je 11, 1958-Mr? 1959/...
w.

9.3   *High Prairie Progress.* Ap 10, 1959-My 11, 1963//
w.

Absorbed *Lesser Slave Lake Star* (899), F 27, 1960.
Absorbed by *Lac La Biche Herald* (662.1), Je 15, 1963.
Suspended pub. Mr?-Ap 10, 1959.
Pub. and ed. by A.F. Menzies, South Peace Pub. Co. Ltd., Jl 25, 1956-Mr
1959. Fire destroyed plant in Spirit River where newspaper was printed. Pub.
started again Ap 10, 1959 by Thomas W. Pue, Sun Pub. Co. Ltd., Edmonton.

AEP   or   Ag 1, 1956-D 17, 1958; Ap 10, 1959-My 11, 1963
AHPD   or   Jl 25, 1956, S 3, D 18, 1957 [1961-1963]

0   *South Peace News.* Mr 20, 1964-
w.

Pub. by South Peace News (High Prairie) Ltd. Pub. by Reginal Burgar to
Oc 18, 1972; ed. by Jeff Burgar. Sold to Jeff Burgar Jl 1, 1972, pub. and ed.,
Oc 25, 1972+
Included supplement *Northern Messenger* (622).

AEP   or   My 3, 1972+
AHPD   or   [1964-1966] 1967

4   *High Prairie Reporter.* F 27, 1974-Jl 23, 1975//
w.

Suspended pub. Ap 10-My 15, 1974.
Pub. and ed. by Bruce D. Thomas.
Ref.: **CNLU** p.19.

OONL   or   F 27, 1974
AEP   or   Mr 6, 1974-Jl 23, 1975

2   *Northern Messenger.* Je 11, 1974-S 4, 1974?//
w.

Supplement co-published by John Stillwell and Jeff Burgar. Distributed with *Smoky River Express*, Falher, (529.4); *Northland Free Press*, Slave Lake, (902); and *South Peace News*, High Prairie. (620).

AEP   or Je 11-Jl 24, 1974 (with *South Peace News*, High Prairie)
AEP   or Je 11-S 4, 1974 (with *Northland Free Press*, Slave Lake)

HIGH RIVER

623   *Eye Opener.* Mr 4, 1902-N 21? 1903//
         irreg.

         Contined by *Eye Opener*, Calgary. (132.1).
         Pub. and ed. by Robert Chambers Edwards who moved to Calgary in 1904 and continued publication there (Ref.: **DEM; McE**).

         AEU   mf Je 6, 1902-N 21, 1903
         ACG   or My 6-9, 1902; [Jl 18-N 21, 1903]

624   *Chinook.* 1904?-1905?//
         w.

         Pub. and ed. by John C. Brazier and J.E. Varley (Ref.: **HENW** 1905).

         No issues located

625.1   *High River Times.* D 7, 1905-D 4, 1975/...
         w.

625.2   *Times.* D 11, 1975-
         w.

         Subtitle: "Community Newspaper of the Foothills."
         Absorbed *Okotoks Review* (783.5), Jl 1970.
         Pub. and ed. by Charles A. Clarke, Sr., High River Times Co. Ltd., D 7, 1905-Ja 1949; Charles A. Clark, Jr., Ja 1949-Jl 1966; R.D. (Don) Tanner, Jl 1966-Mr 1, 1978. Sold Mr. 1, 1978 to William E.G. Holmes and Glenn Tanner, Holtan Pub. Ltd., pubs., Mr 1, 1978+.
         25th Anniversary Issue, D 4, 1930; Alberta Golden Jubilee Edition, Ag 18, 1955.
         Ref.: **CNLU** p.19; **KNU** pp.199-200.

         ACG   or D 4, 1930
         AEP   or Ja 7, 1971+

626   *Fort Spitzee Signal.* Mr 19, 1973-Oc 1974//
         w.

         Mimeographed.
         Pub. and ed. by Dennis Mercer (Ref.: *Calgary Herald*, Oc 9, 1974:85).
         Ref.: **CNLU** p.19.

         OONL   or Mr 19, 27, 1973.
         ACG   or Ap 3, Ag 14, 1973

NTON

7.1   *Hinton Herald.* Ag 18, 1955-Ag? 1969/...
        w.

7.2   *Hinton Herald Parklander.* Ag? 1969-Oc 16, 1974/...
        w.

7.3   *Herald Parklander.* Oc 23, 1974-S 8, 1976/...
        w.

7.4   *Parklander.* S 15, 1976-
        w.

        Ad-sheet *Parklander,* pub. by Charles and Evelyn West, combined with
        Hinton Herald Ag? 1969 to form *Hinton Herald Parklander.*
        Est. by Kenneth McCrimmon, pub., Ag 18, 1955-Je 1959. Sold to D.
        Marmaduke Caston, Edson, pub., Je 1959-1964. Ed. by Carol R. Ahlf, Je
        1959-1964 (Ref.: **CPP** v68no6 Je 1959). Sold 1964 to Al Clark, pub., 1964-
        1968? Sold to Fred Donovan, Jasper, pub., 1968?-Ag? 1969. Sold Ag? 1969
        to Charles and Evelyn West, pub., Ag? 1969-1971 (Ref.: **CPP** v78no10 Oc
        1969). Sold 1971 to Diane Erickson, Chinook Printing and Pub., pub., 1971-
        Ag 31, 1979. Sold S 1, 1979 to Bowes Pub. Ltd. Pub. by Wayne Jobb, S 1,
        1979+; ed. by Pat Jobb, S 1, 1979+

        AEP   or   My 17, 1972+

8   *News Advertiser Ad-Mart.* 1962-1964//
        w.

        Combined with *Hinton Herald* (627.1), in 1964.
        Pub. and ed. by Al Clark (Ref.: Publisher).

        No issues located

DADLEY

9   *North Country News.* 1920-1930?//
        irreg.

        Pub. by L.E. Brownlee on his own hand-built press now in the Glenbow
        Museum. Pub. intermittently during the 1920's and 1930's (Ref.: **SCH**
        p.156).

        No issues located

)   *North Country Times.* Ap 1950-? 1950//
        m.

        ACG   or   My 3, Jl 5, 1950

HOBBEMA

631   *Bear Hills Native Voice.* 1968?-D 1972?//
           m. Native (Cr)

           Pub. by Four Bands Enterprise, Hobbema. Ed. by Alfred Saddleback.
           Ref.: **CNLR** p.213; **CNLU** p.19.

           OONL   or   [D 1971-Je 1972]
           OORD   or   My/Je 1969

632   *Bear Hills Native Voice.* 1976-
           2w.; w. Native (Cr)

           Frequency varied: 2w. 1976-S 30, 1977; w. N 9, 1977+
           Pub. by Four Bands Enterprise. Ed. by Beryl Swampy, 1976?-S 30, 1977;
           Jack Art, N 9, 1977-Je 8, 1978; Mack Omeosoo, Ag 10, 1978-?; Murray
           Green, ?-N 4, 1982+

           ACG   or   Oc 15, 1977-Jl 17, 1980
           AEUB   or   N 4, 1982+

HOLDEN

633   *Holden Herald.* Ap 7, 1910-Mr 2, 1943//
           w.

           Suspended pub. Ja? 1930-Mr? 1932.
           Pub. and ed. by James Mewhort, Ap 7, 1910-F 20, 1913; C.N. Brisbin,
           Holden Herald Co., Mr 6, 1913-N 30, 1914; Robert Emond, Holden Herald
           Co., D 1, 1914-1930; J.D.S. Barrett, Mr? 1932-1943.

           AEP   or   Ap 7, 1910-Ag 5, 1920; F 10, 1921-Je 12, 1924; D 10-D 24,
                             1925; Ja 14-Ag 26, 1926; Ag 23, 1932-F 23, 1943

634   *Holden Herald.* Mr 21, 1944-N 16, 1968//
           w.

           Pub. by Clifford Foran and ed. by Grace L. Foran, Mr 21, 1944-Je 28,
           1960; Thomas W. Pue, Sun Pub. Co. Ltd., Edmonton, Jl 9, 1960-N 16, 1968.
           Alberta Golden Jubilee Edition, Ag 2, 1955.

           AEP   or   Mr 21, 1944-N 16, 1968

HORBURG

           Weekly News. 1920-1921?//
           See Supplement (1076)

HENDEN

Hughenden News. Ja 12, 1916-Jl 4, 1919//
w.

Superceded by *Ribstone Record,* Hughenden (636.1).
Pub. by H.W. Betts. Pub. by *Hardisty Mail,* with same text (Ref.: **MK** 1918).

AEP   or   Ja 12, 1916-Jl 4, 1919

Ribstone Record. Jl 11, 1919-S 24, 1920/...
w.

Hughenden Herald. Oc 29, 1920-D 26? 1920/...
w.

Hughenden Record. 1921-D 29, 1962?//
w.

Superceded *Hughenden News* (635), Jl 11, 1919. Absorbed *Amisk Advocate* (20), Mr 1921.
Suspended pub. S 13, 1945-Ag 22, 1946.
Place of pub. varied: Hughenden, 1919-1931; Hardisty, 1931-1945; Killam, 1946-1949; Edmonton, 1949-1951.
Pub. by H.W. Betts, Jl 11, 1919-S 24, 1920; Will D. MacKay, Provost, with George W. Davidson, mgr., Oc 29-D 1920; Betts, 1921-S 13, 1945; Thomas W. Pue, Community Publications of Alberta, Killam and Edmonton, Ag 22, 1946-D 1962.
Alberta Golden Jubilee Edition, Ag 31, 1955.
Ref.: **AY** 1963; **CAN** 1963.

AEP   or   Jl 11, 1919-S 24, 1920; Oc 29-D 26, 1920; Ja 6-D 25, 1926; Ja 7, 1928-S 13, 1945; Ag 22, 1946-D 29, 1962

SAR

Village Press. D 23, 1976-
See **CARBON.** *Village Press* (239).

LEY

Huxley New Era. S 25, 1915-? 1915//
w.

Pub. and ed. by L.C. Jesmore.

AEP   or   S 25-Oc 9, 1915

638   *Huxley Recorder.* 1920?-N 1922?//
            w.

>   Ed. by Mrs. Musberger. Printed in Trochu (Ref.: **ACAD** p.17; **CAN** 1921,
>   1922, 1923).

>   **No issues located**

HYTHE

639   *Hythe Headliner.* Oc 15, 1973-Oc 31, 1977//
            bw.

>   Pub. and ed. by Advisory Committee to Hythe and District Pioneer Home.
>   A senior citizen-sponsored newspaper which featured many full length arti-
>   cles on pioneers of the district.

>   **AEP**   or   Oc 15, 1973-Oc 31, 1977

INNISFAIL

640   *Innisfail Standard.* S 2, 1898-1899//
            w.

>   Pub. by F.M. Oldham (Ref.: **INN** p.170).
>   Ref.: **CNLU** p.20.

>   **OONL**   or   S 2, 1898

641   *Free Lance.* S 2, 1898-D ? 1901//
            w.

>   Superceded by *Free Lance*, Innisfail (642).
>   Ed. by Orville D. Fleming. "In August [1898], the Flemings had pur-
>   chased the press and equipment of the Wetaskiwin *Free Lance,* to which
>   R.C. 'Bob' Edwards of subsequent *Eye Opener* fame, was then a contributor.
>   Edwards continued to be a contributor and probably supervised publication
>   of the Innisfail *Free Lance* until the printing plant was set up in Innisfail,
>   which appears to have been in December 1898." (Ref.: **MEE** p.159). Sold to
>   George R. Westland D 1901.
>   Pub. simultaneously with Westaskiwin *Free Lance* (1018), S-N 1898.
>   Shared same voluming.
>   *Red Deer Gazette and Lacombe Advertiser* (832) pub. as supplement,
>   1898-1899 (Ref.: **MEE** p.139).

>   **ARDA**   photocopy Oc 6, 1898

642.1   *Free Lance.* Ja 2, 1902-Oc 16, 1902/...
            w.

642.2   *Innisfail Free Lance.* Oc 23, 1902-S 24? 1908//
            w.

Superceded *Free Lance,* Innisfail (641).
Absorbed by *Province,* Innisfail (643.1), Oc 1, 1908.
Pub. by George R. Westland, Ja 2, 1902-Jl 27, 1905; Frank F. Malcolm, Ag 3, 1905-Ap 4, 1907. Ed. by H.A. Malcolm, Ag 3, 1905-Ap 4, 1907; W.H. MacKay, Ap 9-Jl 11, 1907; J.A. McIntosh, Jl 25, 1907-S 1908.
Mr-Ag 1983 pub. twice weekly. (Ref.: **PUB** Ag, 1983)

AEPAA mf Ja 2, 1902-S 10, 1908

Province. Mr 1, 1906-N 17, 1927/...
w.

Innisfail Province. N 24, 1927-
w.

Absorbed *Free Lance,* Innisfail (642), Oc 1, 1908.
Subtitle Oc 1, 1908-Ja 2, 1936: "With Which is Incorporated the Innisfail Free Lance."
Pub. by S.P. Fream, Mr 1, 1906-Ja 17, 1907; Edward J. Fream, Ja 24, 1907-Mr 12, 1908; George R. Westland, Mr 19, 1908-1921; Rex B. Dillingham, 1921-Je 1, 1922; H.C. and Rex B. Dillingham, Je 8, 1922-F 22, 1923; Rex B. Dillingham and Art Jenson, Mr 8-Jl 5, 1923; Rex Dillingham, Jl 12, 1923-S 25, 1925; Ben A. Huckell, Oc 2, 1925-S 24, 1951; T. John Huckell, Oc 4, 1951-S 30, 1954; A. Hector (Hap) Clarke, Oc 1, 1954-F 24, 1976; Rod Stafford-Mayer, Col-Staff Holdings Ltd., Mr 1, 1976+
Alberta Golden Jubilee Edition, S 14, 1955.

ACG or Je 18, 1908
AEPAA mf Mr 1, 1906-F 6, 1908; Je 2-N 24, 1921; Ja 5, 1922-D 19, 1924
AEP or Ja 31, 1907-D 30, 1920; Jl 3, 1925+

Innisfail Independent. 1909-1911?//
w.

Pub. by Fred L. Harris, Bowden (Ref.: **INN** p.447; **MK** 1911).

No issues located

Innisfail Booster. Oc 1954-
w.

Est. and pub. by Leroy Humphrey, Oc 1954-1974. Purchased by Matt Lydon, pub., 1974-Oc 1979; purchased by Ray L. Brinson, pub., N 1979+. Free distribution newspaper (Ref.: Correspondence with Publisher, My 15, 1985).

No issues located

Innisfail Star. Ja 1977-F? 1977//
See Supplement (1077)

INNISFREE

Innisfree Times. My 12, 1927-Je 20, 1929
See **MANNVILLE.** *Mannville News and the Minburn and Innisfree Times.* (725.2).

646   *Innisfree Banner.* 1950-Ag 5, 1953?//
w.

Pub. by Thomas W. Pue, Sun Pub. Co. Ltd., Edmonton.
Ref.: **CAN** 1953.

AEP   or   Ja 11, 1952-Ag 5, 1953

IRMA

647.1   *Times.* F 9 ? 1917-Jl, 1922/...
w.

647.2   *Irma Times.* Ag 4, 1922-Ag 29, 1969//
w.

Amalgamated with *Viking News* to form *Viking News and Irma Times* (1000), S 3, 1969.
Subtitle Ag 4, 1922-My 31, 1929: Alberta Oil Gazette.
Suspended pub. Mr 27-My 15, 1925.
Pub. by H.G. Thunell, Viking, to Jl 1922; R.H. Thunell, Viking, Ag 4, 1922-Ag 29, 1969. Eds.: F.C. Watkinson, 1917-Ag 16, 1918; H.W. Love, D 24, 1918-1932; E.W. Carter, F 10, 1933-Ag 30, 1940; Winnifred Frances Reeves, later Mrs. Harvey Riley, S 6, 1940-Ja 6, 1967; Adelaide Dootson, Ja 13, 1967-D 22, 1969; Ella McRoberts, D 22, 1967-Ag 29, 1967.
Ref.: *Irma Times.* Ag 29, 1969.

AEP   mf [Ap 27, 1917-Ag 29, 1969]

648   *Irma Independent.* 1934-1935//
w.

Pub. by *Wainwright Record.* Ed. by R. Lobb (Ref.: **MK** 1935).

No issues located

IRRICANA

649   *Irricana Review.* 1911//
w.

Ref.: **CAN** 1912; **MK** 1911.

No issues located

Irricana Recorder. 1920//
w.

Ref.: **CAN** 1921.

No issues located

Five Village Weekly. N 6, 1975-D 30? 1980
See **ROCKY VIEW MUNICIPAL DISTRICT.** *Rocky View-Five Village Weekly.* (862.2).

NE

Irvine Index. N 14, 1912-Ap 10, 1913//
w.

Pub. and ed. by Calvin Goss.

AEP or N 14, 1912-Ap 10, 1913

Cypress Courier. Mr 21, 1979-
See **FORTY MILE COUNTY.** *40-Mile County Commentator.* (563).

Y

Wideawake. 1907?//
w.?

No pub. or ed. named.

ACG photocopy Mr 22, 1907

ROW

Jarrow Journal. Mr 16, 1911-1913?//
w.

Pub. and ed. by James Mewhort. Printed by *Holden Herald*.
Ref.: **MK** 1911; **CAN** 1913.

AEP or Mr 16, 1911-Mr 28, 1912

ER

Jasper Signal. Oc 6, 1927-F 16, 1928//
w.

Continued by *Edson-Jasper Signal*, Edson (511.1).
Pub. by J.L. Hollinshead.

AEP or Oc 6, 1927-F 16, 1928

655   *Totem Pole.* Summer 1947-F? 1948//
        w.

        Printed in Edmonton (Ref.: **CPP** v56no6 Je 1947).

        No issues located

656   *Jasper Totem.* 1955-Jl 5, 1967?//
        w.

        Pub. and ed. by Kenneth McCrimmon, Edson, 1955-1959; George
        Knight, ?-Jl 1967. Printed in Edson, 1955-1967.
        Ref.: **CNLU** p.20; **AY** 1968.

        OONL   or   Jl 24, 1957; Jl 5, 1967

657   *Jasper Booster.* F 13, 1963-
        2m.; w.

        Frequency varied: 2m. F 13, 1963-Jl 1969; w. Ag 7, 1969+
        Pub. by E.B. MacDonald to Je 1963; Ray Matthews, Jl 11, 1963-Ag 1965;
        Fred Donovan, Pyramid Press Ltd., S 15, 1965+. Ed. by Grant F. Rundle, My
        6, 1970+.
        Pub. as shopper to Ap 1969; tabloid with paid circulation, Ap 23, 1969+
        (Ref.: Correspondence with Publisher, Mr 14, 1985).

        AEP   or   My 12, 1976+

658   *Jasper Gateway.* S 29, 1965-S 1969//
        2m.; w.

        Frequency varied: 2m. to Oc 1967.
        Voluming began Oc 6, 1965.
        Pub. and ed. by Rev. Charles M.G. Bell, S 1965-F 1969; Roger and Toni
        Levett, F 26?-S 1969 (Ref.: **CPP** v78no3 Mr 1969).
        Ref.: **CNLU** p.20.

        OONL   or   S 29, 1965; Mr 10, 1966; F 26, 1969

JASPER PLACE

        Incorporated with Edmonton in 1962.
        See **EDMONTON** for newspapers serving Jasper Place prior to incor-
        poration:

            Jasper Place Citizen (436)
            Jasper Place Review (431)

HYRN

Five Village Weekly. N 6, 1975-D 30? 1980
　　See **ROCKY VIEW MUNICIPAL DISTRICT.** *Rocky View-Five
Village Weekly* (862.2).

MA

Five Village Weekly. N 6, 1975-D 30? 1980)
　　See **ROCKY VIEW MUNICIPAL DISTRICT.** *Rocky View-Five
Village Weekly* (862.2).

AM

Killam News. Oc 18, 1911-F 14, 1930//
w.

　　Due to economic depression, *Sedgewick Sentinel* (890.1) amalgamated
with *Bawlf Sun* (64), *Daysland Press* (302), *Hardisty Mail* (608), *Killam
News* (659), *Lougheed Express* (711) and *Strome Despatch* (941) to form
Community Press, Sedgewick (890.2) (Ref.: **SED** p.621).
　　Pub. and ed. by A.L. Eastly.
　　Ref.: **CNLU** p.20.

AEP　　or　Oc 18, 1911-1925; 1928-1930

Killam News. 1946-S 3, 1952//
w.

　　Pub. by Thomas W. Pue, Sun Pub. Co. Ltd., Edmonton.

AEP　　or　Ja 2, 1947-S 3, 1952

LA BICHE

Northern Herald. 1941-1948//
w.

　　Succeeded *Herald* of St. Catharine's Parish, pub. by Rev. Fr. McGrane
(Ref.: **PUB** v22no595 My 28, 1941).
　　Printed in Edmonton, 1947-1948.
　　Est. and pub. by Rev. Fr. Joseph E. McGrane. Sold in 1947 to A.
Christensen of Lac La Biche Bakery who ran the paper as a sideline and had
it printed in Edmonton (Ref.: **CPP** v57no11 N 1948; *Lac La Biche Herald,*
Oc 8, 1949).

No issues located

Lac La Biche Herald. Oc 9, 1948-N 16, 1968/...
w.

154   Historical Dir

662.2.   *Lac La Biche Sun.* N 23, 1968-Ja 18, 1969?//
w.

Absorbed *Boyle Beacon* (100.1), and *High Prairie Progress,* (619.3), My
11? 1963 (Ref.: *Lac La Biche Herald* Je 15, 1963).
Printed in Edmonton.
Pub. by Thomas W. Pue, Sun. Pub. Co. Ltd., Edmonton.
Alberta Golden Jubilee Edition, Ag 31, 1955.

AEP   or   Ja 1, 1949-D 21, 1968

663   *Lac La Biche Post.* Ja? 1968-
w.

Pub. by Ron E. Moore, Lac La Biche Post Ltd., 1968?-Jl 26, 1972. Ed. by
H. Gauthier, 1968?-Jl 26, 1972. Sold Ag 1, 1972 to J. Curt Svendsen, pub.
and ed., Ag 1, 1972-Ap 26, 1977. Sold to D and G. Communications Ltd.
My 1, 1977. Pub. by Duane Young, Jl 26, 1977+ and ed. by Gary Elaschuk,
My 3, 1977+

AEP   or   My 3, 1972+

664.1   *Lac La Biche Star.* D 5, 1970-F 23, 1974/...
w.

664.2   *Lac La Biche Herald.* Mr 9, 1974-My 21, 1977//
w.

Printed in Edmonton.
Pub. and ed. by Thomas W. Pue, Sun Colorpress Ltd., Edmonton.
Ref.: CNLU p.12.

OONL   or   D 5, 1970
AEP   or   My 13, 1972-My 21, 1977

LAC STE ANNE COUNTY

665.1   *Lac Ste Anne Chronicle.* Ja 16? 1936-N 16, 1968/...
w.

665.2   *Lac Ste Anne Sun.* N 23, 1968-Ja 18, 1969//
w.

Continued *Mayerthorpe Times* (733) on Ja 16? 1936.
Absorbed *Onoway Westerner* (793), Ag 14, 1953.
Suspended pub. Ja 10-Oc 10, 1946.
Place of pub. varied: Mayerthorpe, Ja 16? 1936-Mr 1937; Sangudo, Mr
25, 1937-My 1949; Edmonton, My 7, 1949-Ja 18, 1969.
Pub. by James D. Skinner, Ja 16, 1936-Ja 10, 1946; Elwood P. Hagen, les-
see, Oc 10, 1946-Mr 20, 1947; Skinner, Ap 17, 1947-Ap 28, 1949. Sold to
Thomas W. Pue, Community Publications of Alberta, Edmonton, My 1949.

Pue, pub., My 7, 1949-Ja 27, 1968; Sun Pub. Co. Ltd., Edmonton, F 3, 1968-Ja 18, 1969.
Alberta Golden Jubilee Edition, S 2, 1955.

AEP   or   Ja 16, 1936-Ja 10, 1946; Oc 17, 1946-D 31, 1966; Ja 6-D 21, 1968

Lac Ste Anne Advance. Ja 19, 1971//
w.

Pub. by Stony Plain *Reporter.* For financial reasons, only one issue pub. *Advance* continued as section of Stony Plain *Reporter* F 9-Ap 27, 1971. On My 14, 1971, title *Lac Ste Anne Advance* was changed to *Lac Ste Anne Reporter.* Ceased pub. as section of *Reporter* on D 19, 1972.
Ref.: **CNLU** p.25.

OONL   or   Ja 19, 1971

Lac Ste Anne Advance. F 9, 1971-Ap 27, 1971
See **STONY PLAIN.** *Reporter* (937).

Lac Ste Anne Reporter. My 4, 1971-D 19, 1972
See **STONY PLAIN.** *Reporter* (937).

Lac Ste Anne County Star. Oc 10, 1973-Mr 26, 1975
See **WHITECOURT.** *Whitecourt Star* (1033).

Lac Ste Anne Chronicle. F 2? 1974-My 14, 1977//
w.

Printed in Edmonton.
Pub. and ed. by Thomas W. Pue, Sun Colorpress Ltd., Edmonton, F 2? 1974-Ap? 1977; Colin Alexander, Sun Colorpress Ltd., Ap 23-My 14, 1977. Distributed to ratepayers of Lac Ste Anne County.

AEP   or   F 2, 1974-My 14, 1977

STE ANNE

1   *Echo de Ste-Anne.* ? 1895/...
m.   Native (Cr)   Cree, (Engl., Fr.)

Lithographed.
Signed by Z. Lizée, ptre., o.m.i.
Text in Cree syllabic, some English and French.
Only one issue published.

AEPAA   or   1895 (Oblate Archives. Lac Ste Anne/22)

2   *Echo de Ste-Anne.* Ja, 1897//
m.   Native (Cr)   Cree, (Engl., Fr.)

Lithographed.
Signed by Z. Lizée, ptre., o.m.i.

Text in Cree syllabic, some English and French.
Only one issue published.

AEPAA or Ja, 1897 (Oblate Archives. Lac Ste Anne/22)
AEUS photocopy Ja, 1897

Croix de Ste-Anne. Mr 1900-Ag 1905//
See Supplement (1078)

LACOMBE

669.1 *Advertiser and Central Alberta News.* 1898-Je 18, 1908/...
w. Political—Conservative

669.2 *Lacombe Advertiser and Central Alberta News.* Je 25, 1908-Ag 26,
1909//
w. Political—Conservative

Pub. and ed. by I.N. Burdick, 1898-1900; James D. Skinner, 1900-1905;
F.H. Schooley, Conservative, 1905-1909. Ed. by Alex Thomas, S 1902-F
1903 (Ref.: **MK** 1899, 1901, 1905; *Red Deer Echo* F 20, 1903).

AEP or My 2, 1907-Ag 26, 1909

Lacombe Weekly Press. 1899//
See Supplement (1079)

670.1 *Western Globe.* D 22, 1903-Ap 21, 1938/...
w. Political—Conservative

670.2 *Lacombe Globe.* Ap 28, 1938-
w.

Pub. and ed. by Charles B. Halpin, Sr., Conservative, D 22, 1903-S 30,
1935; Harry J. Ford, Oc 3, 1935-Ag 5, 1948; Herbert Campbell (Bert) Ford,
Ag 12, 1948-Ja 16, 1974; Allan L. (Butch) Treleaven, Ap 3, 1974+
Alberta Golden Jubilee Edition, Ag 11, 1955.
Ref.: **CNLU** p.20.

OONL or D 22, 1903
AEP or Ap 30-Oc 29, 1907; Ja 5, 1909-D 29, 1920; Jl 8-D 23, 1926;
Ja 5, 1928+

671 *Lacombe Guardian.* My 30, 1913-Ag 25, 1916//
w.

Pub. by F.H. Schooley.

AEP or My 30, 1913-Ag 25, 1916

Lacombe Municipal News. Ja ? 1946-1955?//
See Supplement (1080)

RETE

Northern Pioneer. F 5, 1976-
See **FORT VERMILION.** *Northern Pioneer* (562).

E LOUISE

Kicking Horse Chronicles. Mr 3, 1961-Mr 30, 1962//
w.

Pub. and ed. by Hilary McDowall with Joe Routledge.
Ref.: *Calgary Herald* Ap 28, 1973.

ACG or Mr 3, 1961-Mr 30, 1962
ABA or Mr 1961-Mr 1962

Kicking Horse News. Je 1962-Ap 1973//
irreg.

Mimeographed.
Pub. and ed. by Hilary McDowall "as often as events demand and time
permits."
Ref.: *Calgary Herald* Ap 28, 1973.

ACG or Je 1962-1970
ABA or Je 1962-Ap 1973

E SASKATOON

Lake Saskatoon Journal. Ap 13? 1917-Ap 15, 1918//
w.

Pub. and ed. by Gerald H. Heller and Frank Heller. Sold Ap 15, 1918 to
S.R. Tuffley.
See also *Clairmont Independent* (265).

AEP or Ap 20, 1917-Ap 15, 1918

EVIEW

Lakeview Wave. 1911//
w.

Pub. in Bowden by *Bowden News* (Ref.: **MK** 1911).

No issues located

ONT COUNTY

County of Lamont Star. 1969-Ag 2, 1975/...
w.

676.2   *Lamont County Star.* Ag 9, 1975-My 21, 1977//
w.

Printed in Edmonton.
Pub. by Thomas W. Pue, Sun Colorpress Ltd., Edmonton, 1969-Jl 24,
1976; Colin Alexander, Sun Colorpress Ltd., Ap 23,-My 21, 1977.
Ref.: **CNLU** p.10.

OONL   or   D 20-27, 1969; Ja 3, 1970
AEP   or   My 13, 1972-Mr 10, 1973; F 2, 1974-Ag 30, 1975; Ja 10,
                  1976-My 21, 1977

County of Lamont Star. My 12, 1969-Oc 11, 1969
See **EDMONTON.** *Edmonton Star* (463.2).

677   *Triangle.* Ag 17, 1977-
w.

Pub. by Judy A. and Robert D. Siebenforcher, Elk Island Triangle News
Ltd. Pub. on an acreage 7 miles south of Andrew, Ag 17, 1977-Ja 15, 1981.
Currently published in Lamont for the County (Ref.: Correspondence with
Publisher, D 3, 1984).

No issues located

LAMONT

678   *Lamont Weekly News.* My 10, 1907-Ag 2, 1907//
w.

Title varied? Same paper also entitled *Lamont Times*? (Ref.: **CAN** 1908).
Pub. by John W. Johnston, Fort Saskatchewan (Ref.: **HED** p.124).

No issues located

679   *Lamont Tribune.* Ap 1914-My 11, 1916//
w.

Pub. by A.E. Larkins. who left to enlist for military duty.

AEP   or   Ja 21, 1915-My 11, 1916

680   *Gazette.* S 19? 1918-1922?//
w. Political—Liberal

Pub. by J.E. Buchanan.
Continues to be published at *Conservator*, Fort Saskatchewan (Ref.: **CPP**
v31no3 Mr 1922).

AEP   or   S 26, 1918-D 25, 1920

681.1   *Tribune.* Je 1922-Ja 1, 1931/...
w.

2   *Lamont Tribune.* Ja 8, 1931-Je 26, 1941?//
w.

> Pub. by A.E. Larkins; 1939, leased to Walton Williams (Ref.: **PUB** v20no550 Jl 18, 1939).
> Ref.: **MK** 1941; **CA** 1942.
> Ceased recently (Ref.: **CPP** v50no9 S, 1941).

AEP   or   Ja 22-Je 25, 1925; Ja 5, 1928-Je 26, 1941

Lamont Banner. Jl 1946-Mr 15, 1951?//
w.; 2m.

> Frequency varied: w. Jl 1946-D? 1950; 2m. Ja 1-Mr 15, 1951.
> Pub. by E.G. Archer.

AEP   or   N 22, 1946; Je 26, S 17, 1947-Oc 21, 1948; D 5, D 15, 1949;
Ja 21-F 15, 1950; Ja 1-Mr 15, 1951

Lamont Journal. Ja 19, 1951-Ag 6, 1953//
w.

> Subscription list combined with that of *Mundare Star* (773), Ag 1953.
> Printed in Edmonton.
> Pub. by Thomas W. Pue, Sun Pub. Co. Ltd., Edmonton.

AEP   or   Ja 26, 1951-Ag 6, 1953

Lamont Bulletin. S 16, 1961-Ap 27, 1963//
w.

> Printed in Edmonton.
> Pub. by Thomas W. Pue, Sun Pub. Co. Ltd., Edmonton.
> Ref.: **CNLU** p.12.

OONL   or   S 16, 21, 1961
AEP   or   Oc 7, 1961-Ap 27, 1963

NGDON

Langdon Advance. 1911//
w.

> W.P. Evans, pub.
> Ref.: **MK** 1911.

No issues located

Langdon Leader. Oc 5? 1911-Oc 31, 1912//
w.

> Pub. by J.R. Sharp, 1911-Ap 5, 1912; Leonard D. Nesbitt, Ap 11-Oc 31, 1912.

AEP   or   Mr 7-Oc 31, 1912

LEAVINGS

>Name changed to Granum Oc 1, 1907.
>See **GRANUM** for newspapers serving Leavings.

LEDUC

>*Alberta Sun.* S 1899-1900
>See **EDMONTON** *Alberta Sun* (340)

687   *Leduc Record.* Je? 1903-Jl? 1904//
w.

>Pub. and ed. by William Godson.

ACG   or   Jl 2, 1904

688   *Enterprise.* S 1, 1904-D 27, 1906//?
w.

>Pub. by Arthur H. Liversidge, Liversidge Printing and Pub. Co., Leduc.
>Ref.: **LED** [p.15]; *Representative* Leduc, N 23, 1950; **CNLU**, p.20.

OONL   or   S 1, 1904
ACG   or   N 22, 29, D 13, 1906
AEPAA   or   D 27, 1906 (68.237/1)

689   *Representative.* F 22, 1907-
w.; 2w.

>Absorbed *Devonian,* Devon, (314), Oc 3, 1957. Absorbed *Western Messenger,* Thorsby (961), Ap 6, 1961.
>Frequency varied: w. F 22, 1907-S 30, 1980; 2w. Oc 2, 1980+
>Pub. and ed. by James A. Ker, F 22, 1907-D 4, 1909; A.R. Ennis, D 10, 1909-Ap 24, 1941; W.H. (Duke) DeCoursey, My 8, 1941-F 26, 1942; W.G. Hirst and G.T. Saunders, Mr 3, 1942-Ag 26, 1943; William I. Clark, S 1, 1943-D 20, 1945; Fred Johns, Ja 1, 1946-Mr 25, 1965; Howard M. Bowes, Lynard Pub. Ltd., Ap 1, 1965-Mr 8, 1972; Jack Gieg, Lynard Pub. Ltd., Ap 26, 1972+. Ed. by Jean Liebrecht, Ap 26-S 6, 1972; Don Reimer, Oc 2, 1974-Ag 16, 1978; Pat Bell, Ag 23, 1978+
>Pub. *Devonian* as section Oc 3, 1957-D 24, 1959.
>Alberta Golden Jubilee Edition, N 10, 1955.

AEP   mf   F 22, 1907-D 28, 1983
            or   Ja 1984+

690   *Northern Alberta Farmer.* Ap 1977-Oc 1977//
w. Agriculture

>Pub. by Howard M. Bowes, Lynard Pub. Ltd., Leduc (Ref.: *Alberta Farm Life,* Edmonton, N 19, 1977).

No issues located

Legal Record. S 4? 1948-Ag 13, 1953//
w.

Absorbed by *Morinville Journal* (765) Ag 20, 1953.
Printed in Edmonton.
Pub. by Thomas W. Pue, Community Publications of Alberta, Edmonton.

AEP or Ja 1, 1949-Ag 13, 1953

LIEVILLE

Western Star. My 30, 1979-
See Supplement (1081)

HBRIDGE

1 *Lethbridge News.* N 27, 1885-D 24, 1890/...
w.

2 *Semi-Weekly News.* Ja 6, 1891-N 4, 1891/...
2w.; w.

3 *Lethbridge News.* N 11, 1891-N 22, 1900/...
w.

4 *News and Alberta Irrigationist.* N 29, 1900-Mr 9, 1905/...
w.

5 *Lethbridge News and Southern Alberta Irrigationist.* Mr 16,
1905-My 25, 1905/...
w.

6 *Lethbridge News.* Je 2? 1905-N 2, 1906/...
2w.

7 *Southern Alberta News.* N 6, 1906-N 2? 1907/...
d. and w.

8 *Lethbridge News.* D 6? 1907-? 1910//
w.

Frequency varied: w. N 27, 1885-D 24, 1890; 2w. Ja 6-Je 30, 1891; w. Jl 8, 1891-My 18, 1905; 2w. Je 6, 1905-N 2, 1906; d. and w. N 6, 1906-N 2, 1907; w. D 6, 1907-1910.
Suspended pub. N 2?-D 6? 1907.
Pub. by C.E.D. Wood and E.T. Saunders, News Pub. Co., N 27, 1885-N 24, 1886; Saunders, D 1, 1886-Ag 19, 1891; N 25, 1891-N 28, 1905; Edward Hagell, D 1, 1905-1910. Ed. by James N. McDonald, Ja 6-Oc 28, 1891; T.W. Lett, N 4, 1891-Mr 2, 1892; K.H. Fessenden, D 1, 1905-N 2, 1907; J.L. Manwaring, D 1907-1910?
Ref.: **HAG 1; HAG 2; LON.**

AEPAA mf D 4, 1885-N 2, 1907 (only w. ed. filmed N 8-D 28, 1906)
AEP   or F 7-D 31, 1908

693   *Lethbridge Herald.* N 8, 1905-N 16, 1950//
           w.

Pub. by Fred E. Simpson and A.S. Bennett, N 8-D 20, 1905; Simpson and William A. Buchanan, D 27, 1905-N 1, 1906; Buchanan, N 8, 1906-N 1950. O.D. Austin, ed. and mgr., Mr 28-D 25, 1907.
Ref.: **FOOK** p.144.

AEU   mf N 8, 1905-Oc 28, 1908

694.1   *Lethbridge Daily Herald.* D 11, 1907-Je 19, 1926/...
           d.

694.2   *Lethbridge Herald.* Je 21, 1926-
           d.

Pub. and ed. by William Ashbury Buchanan, Daily Herald Printing Co. Ltd., D 11, 1907-Jl 9, 1954; Hugh P. Buchanan, pres. and ed., Lethbridge Herald Co. Ltd., Jl 19, 1954-Mr 31, 1956; H.G. Long, vice-pres. and pub., Jl 19, 1954-Mr 31, 1956. Pub. by Hugh P. Buchanan, Ap 1, 1956-Jl 25, 1959; Cleo W. Mowers, Mr 1, 1960-Ag 31, 1980; Donald R. Doram, S 1, 1980+. Sold to F.P. Pub. Ltd., Jl 25, 1959. Sold to Thomson Newspapers Ltd., Ja 12, 1980. Presently pub. by Canadian Newspapers Co. Ltd., a subsidiary of Thomson Newspapers.
Lethbridge Anniversary Edition, Je 26, 1926; Golden Jubilee Edition, Jl 11, 1935; 40th Anniversary Progress and Development Edition, D 11, 1947; Special Progress Edition, S 17, 1949; Alberta Golden Jubilee Edition, Je 25, 1955; Golden Anniversary and Progress Edition, Oc 5, 1957; Cardston Jubilee Edition, Je 23, 1962; 60th Anniversary and Progress Edition, D 11, 1967; Anniversary Edition, N 30, 1982.
Ref.: **GOL; FOOK; STEE.**

AEU   mf F 1, 1908-D 31, 1976
AEP   mf Ja 3, 1977+

695.1   *Lethbridge Daily News.* N 12, 1910-Je 1, 1912/...
           d.

5.2   *Morning News.* Je 3, 1912-Jl 31, 1913/...
       d.

5.3   *Lethbridge News Weekly.* Ag 1913-D 4, 1913//
       w.

       Frequency varied: d. N 12, 1910-Jl 31, 1913; w. Ag-D 1913.
       Pub. by L.S. Gowe, N 12, 1910-Mr 2, 1912 controlled by J.H. Woods.
       Sold to Southam Co. Ltd., Mr 1, 1912 and pub. by Canadian Newspapers
       Ltd. Ed. by John E. Wodell, Mr 2, 1912-D 1913?
          Ref.: **BRU** p.137; **DEW** p.140.

       AEP   mf N 14, 1910-D 31, 1912

6   *Southern Alberta Labor Bulletin.* 1908-1913?//
       2m. Labour

       Pub. by Trades and Labor Council of Lethbridge; J.M. Ritchie, mgr. (Ref.:
       MK 1911, 1913).

       AEP   or Mr 25, 1910-D 20, 1911

7   *Lethbridge Telegram.* D 3, 1914-Ja 2, 1919?//
       w.

       Backed by Conservatives (Ref.: **STEELE**).
       Edward Hagell, mgr., D 1914-Ja 1919; ed. by W.A.R. Cocq, Ap 8, 1915-
       Oc 31, 1918.

       AEPAA mf D 31, 1914-Ja 2, 1919
       ACG   or Oc 7, 1915

8   *Canadian Advocate.* 1918-1925?//
       w.

       Pub. by Canadian Advocate Pub. Co. (Ref.: **MK** 1919-1922; **CAN** 1925).
       J.B. Davies, ed. (Ref.: **WRI** 1920).

       No issues located

9   *Square Shooter.* D 15? 1922-1923?//
       2m.

       Pub. by Square Shooter Pub. Co., J.S. Kirkham and Assoc., eds.

       ACG   or F 15, 1923

0   *Western Miner.* F 20, 1930-S 8, 1931?//
       2m. Labour

       Continued by *Western Miner,* Calgary (170.1).
       Organ of Miners' Section, Workers' Unity League of Canada; James
       Sloan, secretary.
          Ref.: **WEI** 5355.

       ACG   mf F 20-Je 27, 1930

OOL   mf [F 20-S 8, 1931]

701   *Meliorist.* S 28, 1967-
         w. University

         Not pub. during examination and vaction periods.
         Pub. by the Meliorist Pub. Society, University of Lethbridge.

         ALUA or S 28, 1967+

         Chinook. Mr 16, 1972-Ag ? 1976//
         See Supplement (1082)

702   *Chinook Reporter.* 1978-1981?//
         w.

         Pub. by Jill E. Watson, ed. by Pat Byrne (Ref.: **AY** 1979-1982; **CAN**
         1980, 1981; **CARD** 1980).

         No issues located

LLOYDMINSTER

703.1   *Lloydminster Times.* Ap 23, 1905-D? 1906/...
         w.

703.2   *Lloydminster Times and District News.* Ja? 1907-N 26, 1914/...
         w.

703.3   *Lloydminster Times.* D 3, 1914-S 5, 1979/...
         w.

703.4   *Times Regional Weekly.* S 12, 1979-D 30, 1981/...
         w.

703.5   *Regional Times.* Ja 6, 1982-Mr 3, 1982/...
         w.

703.6   *Times Regional.* Mr 10, 1982-
         w.

         Pub. by a joint stock company, Lloydminster Printing and Pub. Co., Ap
         25, 1905-Ag 25, 1908. Joseph G. Willard ed. first issue and several mgrs. ran
         the paper until sold to Bertram Smith, prop. and ed., Ag 25, 1908-Mr 18,
         1909. Sold to Joseph G. Willard and J.A. Jacobs, props., Mr 25, 1909-Mr 16,
         1911. D.G. Tuckwell, prop., Mr 23, 1911-F 24, 1916; Willard and F.J.
         Stewart, props., Mr 2, 1916-Fall 1920; Willard, prop. and ed., Fall 1920-N 3,
         1938; Ellen Willard, prop. and E.J. Willard, ed., N 10, 1938-Mr 28, 1940;
         George F. Baynton, pub. and ed., Lloydminster Times Pub. Co., Ap 4, 1940-

1979; Fred W. Baynton, pub., Eastern Townships Pub. Co., S 1979-1980; Fred W. Baynton, pub., Sterling Newspapers Ltd., Vancouver, B.C., 1981+
Alberta Golden Jubilee Edition, Jl 20, 1955; Barr Colonists 60th Anniversary Issue, Jl 10, 17, 1963.
Ref.: **MacD** p.33.

AEU   mf My 2, 1905-D 25, 1906; Ap 30-Oc 29, 1907; Ja 28, 1908-D 25, 1919; Ja 6, 1921-N 2, 1922; Jl 2, 1925-D 31, 1942
AEP   or Ja 7, 1943-D 24, 1963; Ja 6, 1965-D 22, 1970; Ja 5, 1972+

4   *Lloydminster Review.* F 27? 1914-N 27, 1914?//
w.

Pub. and ed. by Walter John Huntingford; then J.P. Lyle (Ref.: **MacD** p.33).

AEP   or Mr 6-N 27, 1914

5   *Meridian Booster.* Jl 1959-
w.; 2w.

Title varies: *Booster.*
Frequency varies: w. Jl 1959-Ag 28, 1973; 2w. Ag 28, 1973+
Pub. by Meridian Printing Co. Ltd., 1959-1979; Meridian Printing (1979) Ltd., 1979+. Pub. by Byron H. Keebaugh, 1959-1982; Donald C. McDonald, 1982+. Ed. by Shirley M. Keebaugh, 1959-1967; Byron H. Keebaugh, 1967-Ag 1970; Donald L. Auty, Ag 1970-1972?; Helen Kearns, Ap 8-Jl 15, 1976; Donald J. Green, Ag 3-N 1976; Lillian Johnson, N 1976-Je 15, 1978; Jack Upshall, Je 20, 1978-My 1, 1980; Dave McCullough, My 1, 1980+
Barr Colony Diamond Jubilee Edition, Jl 18, 1963.
Ref.: **MacD** p.33.

SRA   mf D 22, 1959+

6   *Lloydminster Daily Times.* S 10, 1979-
d.

Pub. by Eastern Townships Pub. Co., 1979-1980; Sterling Newspapers Ltd., Vancouver, B.C., 1981+. Pub. by Fred W. Baynton and ed. by George F. Baynton.
Ref.: **MacD** p.33.

AEP   or 2M+CM

ODGEPOLE

7   *Log.* N 20? 1959-My 26, 1961 ?//
w.; 2m.

Suspended pub. Mr 18-S 16, 1960.
Mimeographed.
Pub. by Claude May.

AEPAA   or [N 20, 1959-My 26, 1961] (70.163)

LOMOND

708   *Lomond Press.* Ag 11? 1916-S 9, 1926//
        w.

        Pub. by Rae L. King. Pub. moved to Claresholm to start *Claresholm Local Press* (268).

        AEP   or   N3, 1916-D 31, 1920; Mr 24, My 12,-D 15, 1922; Ja 5-Jl 6,
                        1923; Ja 22, Mr 19, Ap 27, My 31, Je 18-Je 25, Jl 27, S 9, 1926

709   *Lomond Weekly.* 1917-1918?//
        w.

        Satellite of *Calgary Western Standard.* (142.5)
        Pub. by Standard Newspaper Syndicate, Calgary (Ref.: **MK** 1918).

        No issues located

710   *Lomond Press.* N 15, 1928//
        w.

        Prospectus issue pub. by B.N. Woodhull of *Champion Chronicle* (260).

        AEP   or   N 15, 1928

LOUGHEED

        Lougheed Leader. My 4, 1911-F 15, 1912
        See **SEDGEWICK**. *Community Press.* (890.2).

711   *Lougheed Express.* Ap 1912-1930?//
        w.

        Due to economic depression *Sedgewick Sentinel* (890.1) amalgamated
        with *Bawlf Sun* (64), *Daysland Press* (302), *Hardisty Mail* (608), *Killam
        News* (659), *Lougheed Express* (711), and *Strome Despatch* (941) to form
        Community Press, Sedgewick (890.2) in 1930 (Ref.: **SED** p.621).
        Pub. by A.L. Eastly.
        Ref.: **MK** 1922; **CAN** 1923.

        AEP   or   Jl 5, 1912-D 11, 1920

712   *Lougheed Journal.* Mr 1925-D 20, 1950?//
        w.

        Suspended pub. S 26, 1945-Ag 22? 1946.
        Printed in Hardisty and Edmonton.
        Pub. by James P. Dillon, 1925-Mr 26, 1931; H.W. Betts, Ap 2, 1931-S 26,
        1945; Thomas W. Pue, Community Publications of Alberta, 1946-1950.

)USANA

.3   *Lousana Observer.* 1922//
      w.

    Pub. by W.R. Mott (Ref.: **MK** 1922).

No issues located

    Lousana Page. Mr? 1922-N 1922
    See **DELBURNE.** *Delburne Progress* (305).

ACKLIN, SASKATCHEWAN

.4   *Macklin Times.* N 10, 1962-1963//
      w.

    Printed in Edmonton.
    Pub. by Thomas W. Pue, Sun Pub. Co. Ltd.
    Ref.: **CNLU**, p.12.; **MacD** p.14.

    OONL   or   N 10, 1962
    SRA   or   [few issues only]

ADDEN

    Courier. D 8, 1982-
    See **CARSTAIRS.** *Courier* (251).

AGRATH

.5   *Magrath Pioneer.* Je 1, 1906-My 15? 1915//
      w.

    Pub. by David Horton Elton, Je 1, 1906-Jl 28, 1908; Thomas W. Green, lessee, Ag 4, 1908-Oc 25, 1910; Elton, N 1, 1910-1912; J.J. Atherton, 1912-Je? 1913; Claude Fryer, Je? 1913-1915; J.M. Ritchie, 1915. (Ref.: *Magrath Pioneer,* My 1, 1907; **CAN** 1915).

    Ed. successively by D.H. Elton, T.W. Green, Robert Spoor, F.C. Spoor, W.J. Weston and C.M. Tonks (Ref.: **CPP** v12no1 Ja 1913).

    Completely destroyed by fire. (Ref.: **CPP** v14no5 My 1915).

    AEP   or   My 1, 1907-Oc 17, 1912; Ja 9, 1913-My 15, 1914

.6   *Magrath Times.* 1922-1923?//
      w.

    Pub. at Lethbridge as part of *Canadian Advocate* (698). Same text as *Coaldale Times* (Ref.: **MK** 1922; **CAN** 1921, 1923).

No issues located

717   *Magrath News.* 1929-Ap 17, 1933//
        w.

> Pub. by Cardston News Pub. Co. Ltd. and ed. by D.O. Wight. (Ref.: **MK**
> 1931, 1932).

ACG   or   Ag 7, 1929

718   *Garden City Times.* 1941-1949?//
        w.

> Printed in Lethbridge, 1948-1949.
> Pub. by H. Tilston-Jones (Ref.: **MK** 1942; **CAN** 1949). Ed.? by B.
> Bayley (Ref.: **CPP** v57no6 Je 1948).

No issues located

719   *Magrath Mirror.* Oc 1948-Je 14, 1951//?
        w.

> Pub. by Garden City Printers. Ed. by J.M. Sabey, 1948-My 10, 1951. Pub.
> by W.H. (Duke) DeCoursey, My 17-Je 1951.

AEP   or   Je 16, 1949-Je 14, 1951

720   *Garden City News.* Oc 18, 1951-D 20, 1951//?
        w.

> Pub. and ed. by Max Hamilton.

AEP   or   Oc 18-D 20, 1951

MANNING

721   *Battle River Herald.* D 22? 1949-Jl 8, 1954//
        w.

> Absorbed by *Post,* Fairview (526) Jl 15, 1954.
> Pub. and ed. by Duncan W. Dewar.

AEP   or   Ja 5, 1950-Jl 8, 1954

722.1   *Manning Banner Post.* D 29, 1966-Mr 29, 1978/...
        w.

722.2   *Banner Post.* Ap 5, 1978-
        w.

> Pub. and ed. by F.G. (Gerry) Howis, D 29, 1966-Mr 28, 1978 (Ref.:
> *Banner Post,* D 1, 1979). Sold to M.T. Mihaly, Mackenzie Highway News
> Ltd., Mr 29, 1978. Pub. by Mihaly, Mr 29, 1978+. Ed. by Herb Bryce, Ap
> 26, 1978-Mr 21, 1979; Eve Mihaly, Mr 24, 1979-Ja 30, 1980; Annis
> Kernaghan, Je 4, 1980-D 30, 1981; Eve Lees, Ja 6, 1982+

Includes supplement *Mackenzie Highway Pictorial Review* (615).

AEP   or   My 12, 1976+

ANNVILLE

3   *Mannville Telegram.* Jl 27, 1907-Ap 29, 1909//
        w.

        Briefly mgd. by J.A. Stewart; pub. and ed. by Arthur Wellesley Ebbett,
        Mannville Telegram Co. Ltd.
        First issue cited in **FIN**.

        AEP   or   D 17, 1908-Ap 29, 1909

4   *Mannville Empire.* Oc 20, 1910-1922?//
        w.   Political — Unionist

        Absorbed by *Link,* Vermilion (993) in 1922? (Ref.: **MK** 1923; **CAN**
        1924).
        Title varied: Oc 20, 1910-Oc 31, 1918: *Manville Empire.*
        Pub. and ed. by A.J.B. McLachlan, Unionist supporter, Oc 20, 1910-S 17,
        1914; W.A. Letson, Conservative, S 24, 1914-1922?

        AEP   or   Oc 20, 1910-D 16, 1915; Mr 18, 1917-D 25, 1919

5.1   *Mannville News.* Je 1923-My 12, 1927/...
        w.

5.2   *Mannville News and the Minburn and Innisfree Times.* My 19,
        1927-Je 20, 1929//
        w.

        Pub. and ed. by H.T. Taylor.
        Minburn and Innisfree Times pub. as section starting My 12, 1927.

        AEP   or   Oc 8, 1925-Je 20, 1929

6   *Mannville Mirror.* D 5, 1934-D 19, 1946//
        w.

        Pub. and ed. by W.J. Whitehouse.
        Ref.: *Mannville Mirror,* D 19 1946:1.

        AEP   or   Ja 3, 1935-D 19, 1946

7   *Manville [sic] Reporter.* 1935-1936?//
        w.

        Pub. by W.J. Whitehouse (Ref.: **MK** 1935, 1936).

        No issues located

8   *Mannville Review.* My 1948-1949?//
        w.

Pub. and ed. by R.L. Wright (Ref.: **CAN** 1950; **CPP** v57no7, Jl 1948).

No issues located

729   *Mannville Mirror.* 1949?-My 15, 1965//
        w.

        Combined with *Vegreville Mirror* (990) My 22, 1965 to become *County of Minburn Review* (758).
        Printed in Edmonton.
        Pub. by Thomas W. Pue, Sun Pub. Co. Ltd., Edmonton.
        Included supplement *Vegreville Mirror* (989).
        Alberta Golden Jubilee Edition, S 1, 1955.

        AEP   or Je 30, 1950-My 15, 1965

730   *Mannville Star.* Ap 3, 1971-Mr 24, 1973?//
        w.

        Printed in Edmonton.
        Pub. and ed. by Thomas W. Pue.
        Ref.: **AY** 1974; **CNLU** p.12.

        OONL   or Ap 3, 1971
        AEP   or My 13, 1972-Mr 24, 1973

731.1   *Mannville Reflections.* Jl 18, 1978-F 5, 1980/...
        w.

731.2   *Reflections.* F 12, 1980-F 1981/...
        w.

731.3   *Mannville Reflections.* F 1981-
        w.

        Absorbed *Elk Point Reflections*, (1069).
        Pub. and ed. by Ethel Schreyer and Heather Calder, Jl 18, 1978-S 1979; Schreyer, S 1979+ (Ref.: Correspondence with Publisher, Ag 8, 1984). Pub. for Mannville and Elk Point, F 12, 1980-F 1981.

        AEP   or Ap 21, 1982+

MANYBERRIES

732   *Manyberries Enterprise.* 1917-1919?//
        w.

        Pub. by Vin C. Dunning (Ref.: **CAN** 1919; **MK** 1918, 1919).

        No issues located

YERTHORPE

Mayerthorpe Times. S 3, 1931-D 27? 1935//
w. Political — Liberal

Continued by *Lac Ste Anne Chronicle,* Lac Ste Anne County (665).
Pub. and ed. by George H. Pearson, S 3, 1931-S 13, 1934 (Ref.:
Mayerthorpe Times Oc 17, 1935); F.M. Warnock, Liberal, S 15-N 9, 1934;
Kathleen E. Jones, S 15, 1934-Ag 29, 1935; James D. Skinner, N 15, 1934-
Oc 24, 1935.

AEP   or   Ja 18, 1934-D 27, 1935

Mayerthorpe Merchant. Jl 1939-1941?//
bw.

Mimeographed.
Ref.: **MK** 1940, 1941; **PUB** v20no554 (N 25, 1939); **CPP** v48no8 (Ag,
1939).

No issues located

Mayerthorpe Free Press. 1950?-D 1951?//
w.

Title varied? *Mayerthorpe Times,* pub. N.L. Daniels (Ref.: **CPP**, v59no1
Ja 1950).
Ref.: **CAN** 1951, 1952.

No issues located

Mayerthorpe Review. 1951-N 16, 1968//
w.

Printed in Edmonton.
Pub. by Thomas W. Pue, Sun Pub. Co. Ltd. on lease from D. Marmaduke
Caston, Edson.

AEP   or   Ja 20, 1956-N 16, 1968

.1   *Mayerthorpe-Lac Ste Anne Star.* 1970-Jl 8, 1972/...
w.

.2   *Mayerthorpe Star.* Jl 15, 1972-My 14, 1977//
w.

Title varied: *Lac Ste Anne and Mayerthorpe Star.*
Printed in Edmonton.
Pub. by Thomas W. Pue to 1972; Sun Colorpress Ltd., Jl 1972-My 1977.
Ref.: **CNLU** p.12.

OONL   or   Oc 24, 1970
AEP   or   My 13, 1972-My 14, 1977

738   *Freelancer.* Ap 5, 1978-
           w.

           Pub. by Edwin Cowley, W. and E. Pub. Ltd. Ed. by Wanda Cowley,
           1978-1984; Pub. by Howard M. Bowes, Lynard Publishers, ca Oc 1984+.

           AEP   or   Ap 5, 1978+

MEDICINE HAT

739.1   *Medicine Hat Times.* Oc 30, 1885-My 17, 1888/...
           w.

739.2   *Weekly Times.* My 23, 1888-Ag 10, 1888/...
           w.

739.3   *Medicine Hat Times.* Ag 18, 1888-F 22, 1894//
           w.

           Superceded by *Medicine Hat News,* w. ed. (741).
           Suspended pub. F 19-Mr 26, 1887.
           Pub. by Medicine Hat Pub. Co. Andrew M. Armour, ed. and prop., Oc 29?
           1885-Jl 8? 1886; B.J. McMahon, ed., Jl 15, 1886-F 19, 1887; D.G. Holt, ed.,
           My 28, 1887-Mr 16, 1889; J.K. Drinnan, ed. and prop., Mr 23, 1889-F 22,
           1894.
           Ref.: **MOR.**

           AEU   mf N 5, 1885-F 22, 1894

740   *Medicine Hat Daily Times.* My 7, 1888-Ag 10, 1888//
           d.

           Same voluming as *Medicine Hat Times,* w. ed. (739).
           Pub. by Medicine Hat Pub. Co. Ed. by D.G. Holt. See *Medicine Hat
           Times,* w. ed. (739).

           AMHM   or   My 25-Je 12, 1888

741   *Medicine Hat News.* Mr 8, 1894-Jl 7, 1910//
           w.

           Superceded *Medicine Hat Times* (739).
           Superceded by *Medicine Hat News* (744).
           Pub. by Medicine Hat Printing and Pub. Co. Ed. by A.M. Gordon to Ap
           1896; Fred G. Forster, ed. and mgr., Ap 1896-Jl 1910.
           Ref.: **GERS** pp.129-131.

           AEU   mf Mr 8, 1894-Jl 7, 1910
                       or Ap 1906-Jl 7, 1910

742.1   *Times.* S 1903-Oc 6, 1911/...
           w.

2.2   *Times Semi-Weekly.* Oc 10, 1911-N 1, 1912//
        2w.

> Superceded by *Morning Times,* Medicine Hat (746).
> Frequency varied: w. S 1903-Oc 6, 1911; 2w. Oc 10, 1911-N 1, 1912.
> Pub. by W.C. Harris, S 1903-1907; W. Lacey Amy, 1907-1910; Charles J.
> Wilson, ? 1910-N 1, 1910; Deighton R. Ware, N 8, 1910-Ag 25, 1911; G.E.
> Armour, Ag 29, 1911-N 1, 1912.
> Ref.: *Lethbridge Herald* D 11, 1947:27-29; **MK** 1905, 1907.

> **AEP**   mf Ap 30-N 5, 1907; Ja 11, 1910-N 1, 1911

3.1   *Medicine Hat Daily News.* Jl 11, 1910-Jl 29? 1910/...
        d.

3.2   *Medicine Hat News.* Ag 1? 1910-Je 28, 1941/...
        d.

3.3   *Medicine Hat Daily News.* Je 30, 1941-Mr 10, 1949/...
        d.

3.4   *Medicine Hat News.* Mr 11, 1949-N 6, 1971/...
        d.

3.5   *News.* N 8, 1971-Je 5, 1981/...
        d.

3.6   *Medicine Hat News.* Je 6, 1981-
        d.

> Pub. by Medicine Hat Printing and Pub. Co., Jl 11, 1910-Ja 7, 1911;
> Medicine Hat News Ltd., Ja 9, 1911-N 1948; Southam Inc., N 12, 1948+.
> Fred G. Forster, ed. and mgr., Jl 11, 1910-Ja 7, 1911; Alfred J.N. Terrill, ed.
> and mgr., Ja 9, 1911-Ag 3, 1940; T. Roy Osborne, pub., 1940-D 31, 1957;
> Fred McGuinness, pub., Ja 2, 1958-D 31, 1965; Ian Charles MacDonald,
> pub., Ja 3, 1966-My 31, 1981; Andrew Snaddon, pub., Je 1, 1981+
> Alberta Golden Jubilee Edition, S 3, 1955; Canada Centennial Edition, Je
> 29, 1967; Medicine Hat Centennial Edition, Mr 24, 1983; Medicine Hat
> News 100th Anniversary, F 28, 1985.
> Ref.: *Lethbridge Herald* D 11, 1949:27-29; **GERS** pp. 129-131; **BRU** pp.
> 378-383.

> **AEP**   mf Jl 11-D 30, 1910; Jl 2, 1914-D 31, 1915; Ja 3, 1977+
> **AEU**   mf [1910]; Ja 3, 1911-D 31, 1976

4.1   *Medicine Hat News.* Jl 14, 1910-Je 25, 1941/...
        w.

744.2   *Medicine Hat Weekly News.* Jl 3, 1941-1955?//
               w.

               Superceded *Medicine Hat News* (741).
               Same voluming as *Medicine Hat News*, d. ed. (743).

               AEU   mf Jl 14, 1910-D 27, 1917; Ja 8, 1920-D 31, 1947; Ja 12-D 28,
                            1949
               AMHM   or 1918-1929; 1944-1957

745   *Labor Day Bulletin.* S 2, 1912//
               ? Labour

               Probably only one issue pub. (Ref.: **GREG** p.760).

               WHL   or S 2, 1912

746   *Morning Times.* N 5, 1912-Ap 22, 1916//
               d. and w.

               Superceded *Times Semi-Weekly,* Medicine Hat (742).
               Also pub. w. ed. (748?)
               Pub. and ed. by G.E. Armour and C.F. Jamieson, N 5, 1912-Ag 15, 1913;
               Jamieson, Ag 16, 1913-N 14, 1914; J.B. Kenrick, N 16, 1914-Ap 22, 1916.
               Ref.: *Lethbridge Herald* D 11, 1947:27-29.

               AEP   mf N 5, 1912-Ap 22, 1916

747   *Medicine Hat Call.* D 1912-Jl 11, 1913//?
               d.

               Pub. by D. and A. Printing and Engraving Co. Ltd. Ed. by Arthur Harvey
               Smith, 1912-My 12, 1913; W.A. Clarke, My 13-Jl 1913.

               AEP   mf Ja 1-Jl 11, 1913

748   *Alberta Farmer.* Je 12? 1913-D 31, 1914//
               w. Agriculture

               Subtitle: "A Paper Devoted to the Interest of Farming in Alberta and
               Saskatchewan."
               Pub. by Alberta Farmer Pub. Co. Ed. by Ed L. Stone, Oc 16, 1913-F 19,
               1914; J.B. Kenrick, Mr 5, 1914-1916?
               Possibly weekly ed. of *Morning Times,* Medicine Hat (746) (Ref.: **MK**
               1915).
               Ceased D 31, 1914. (Ref.: *Medicine Hat Postmaster.* Memo to Postmaster
               General Oc 17, 1916. Photocopy, Medicine Hat Museum and Art Gallery).

               AEP   or Oc 16, 1913-D 31, 1914

749   *Western Union Printer.* Je? 1919-My 31, 1923?//
               m. Labour

               Pub. by Executive Officers of Western Canada Conference of Typographi-
               cal Unions. Ed. by Byron Webster (Bart) Bellamy.

               ACG   mf S 27, 1919-My 31, 1923

Medicine Hat Advertiser. 1939-1940//
bw?

Title varied? Same paper ? *Hat Air-Mail Weekly,* free distribution paper (Ref.: **PUB** v20no550 Jl 18, 1939).
Pub. by Oswald Everett (Ref.: **MK** 1940)

No issues located

Brüke. 1945-1946?//
irreg. German in Ger.

Pub. by German prisoners-of-war at Camp 132 in Medicine Hat. Pub. towards the end of WWII for internal circulation within the camp (Ref.: **ARN,** p.229).
Ref.: **CART.**

LC   or   N 24, 1945-Ja 26, 1946

Rattler. Je 19, 1969-Je 9, 1976//
w.

Title varied: *Prairie Rattler,* 1975-1976.
Pub. and ed. by Kit Farran, David May and Associates, Je 1969-Jl 1970; Richard Gillis, Jl-Oc 1970. Purchased by H. George Meyer and Walter W. Koyanagi, Taber Times Ltd., Oc 1970. Pub. by John Head, Jl 1972-Ap 1973. Purchased by Dinosaur Group, Drumheller, Jl 1973. Pub. by John Bell, 1973-1975; Ted Storch, Prairie Rattler Ltd., 1975-1976 (Ref.: Correspondence with Medicine Hat Museum and Art Gallery, Mr 12, 1985).

AEP   or   My 12-Je 2, 1976
AMHM   or   Je 19, 1969-Je 9, 1976

LK RIVER

1   *Milk River Review.* N 11, 1948-My 27, 1954/...
w.

2   *Review.* Je 17, 1954-Ag 21, 1958/...
w.

3   *County of Warner Review and Advertiser.* S 1, 1958-Mr 30, 1961/...
w.

4   *Milk River Review.* Je 1/8, 1961-N 16? 1961/...
w.

5   *North Lethbridge Breeze and Milk River Review.* N 23? 1961-D 14, 1961/...
w.

753.6   *Milk River Review Tourist and Recreation Guide.* Mr 29, 1962-Ap
26, 1962?//
2m.

County of Warner Review and Advertiser absorbed by *Chinook Belt
Advertiser,* Milk River (754), Ap 6, 1961 (Ref.: *County of Warner Review
and Advertiser,* Mr 30, 1961). Revived as *Milk River Review,* Je 1, 1961.
Frequency varied: w. N 11, 1948-N 16? 1961; 2m. N 23? 1961-Ap 26,
1962.
Suspended pub. Mr 30-Je 1/8, 1961; D 14, 1961-Mr 29, 1962.
Pub. by Donald W. Fretts, N. 11, 1948-Je 1960; L. Walter Wiig, Je 1960;
Stella and Ed Green, Jl 7, 1960-Ap 1962.

AEP   or   N 11, 1948-Ap 26, 1962

754   *Chinook Belt Advertiser.* N? 1960-Je? 1961?//
w.?

Absorbed *County of Warner Review and Advertiser* (753.3), Milk River,
Ap 6, 1961.
Pub. and ed. by Donald W. Fretts.
Ref.: *County of Warner Review and Advertiser* Mr 30, 1961.

No issues located

755   *Border County Recorder.* Jl 19, 1972-N 29, 1972//
w.

Continued *Raymond Recorder* (827).
Business moved to Milk River in order to serve a wider area. Pub. and ed.
by Bill Schuurman.

AEP   or   Jl 19, 1972-N 29, 1972

MILLET

756   *Packet.* Ag 13? 1909-Oc 7, 1910?//
w.

Pub. by H.B. Berryman.
Ref.: **MK** 1911; **CAN** 1911.

AEP   or   Ag 20, 1909-Oc 7, 1910

757   *Millet Bulletin.* Oc 10, 1946-Ag 24, 1949//
w.

Printed in Edmonton.
Pub. by Thomas W. Pue, Community Publications of Alberta, Edmonton.

AEP   or   Oc 10, 1946-Ag 24, 1949

◄NBURN COUNTY

8.1   *County of Minburn Review.* My 22, 1965-Je 12, 1965/...
        w.

8.2   *Minburn County Review.* Je 19, 1965-N 16, 1968/...
        w.

8.3   *Minburn Sun.* N 23, 1968-Ja 18, 1969//
        w.

        Printed in Edmonton.
        Pub. by Thomas W. Pue, Sun Pub. Co. Ltd. to Ja, 1968; George H. Stout,
        Sun Pub. Co. Ltd., F 3-Oc 5, 1968; Sun Pub. Co. Ltd., Oc 12, 1968-Ja 18,
        1969.
        Ref.: **CNLU** p.12.

        AEP   or   My 22, 1965-D 21, 1968

9   *Minburn County Star.* Mr 31, 1973-My 21, 1977//
        w.

        Pub. and printed in Edmonton.
        Pub. by Thomas W. Pue, Sun Colorpress Ltd.
        Ref.: **CNLU** p.12.

        OONL   or   Mr 31, 1973
        AEP   or   My 5, 1973-My 21, 1977

◄NBURN

        Minburn and Innisfree Times. My 12, 1927-Je 20, 1929
            See **MANNVILLE.** *Mannville News and the Minburn and Innisfree
        Times* (725.2).

◄RROR

        Reflector. Je 6, 1911-Ag 8, 1911?//
        w.

        Pub. and ed. by Charles W. Frederick.

        AEP   or   Je 6-Ag 8, 1911

        Mirror Journal. N 2, 1911-Ja 25, 1929?//
        w.

        Suspended pub. Je 30, 1916-Oc 23, 1919; S 24, 1924-My 3, 1928.

Pub. by W.J. Good and W.B. Ballantyne, N 2, 1911-F 4, 1915; John H. Salton, lessee F 12-Oc 1, 1915; Good, Oc 8, 1915-S 24, 1924; Melville Leathley, lessee My 3, 1928-Ja 25, 1929.

AEP   or   N 2, 1911-Je 30, 1916; Oc 23-D 25, 1919; My 4-D 27, 1922; Ja 4-S 24, 1924; My 3, 1928-Ja 25, 1929

762   *Mirror Mail.* D 1925-Je 16, 1927?//
w.

Pub. by J. Saywright.

AEP   or   Ap 14, 1926-Je 16, 1927

Mirror News Record. Oc 16, 1931-Ja 27, 1933; My 12-Ag 11, 1949
See **ALIX**. *Alix Free Press* (14).

MONITOR

763   *Monitor News.* D 1915-Je 29, 1922//
w.

Amalgamated with *Consort Enterprise* (292), Je 8, 1922. From Je 8-Je 29, 1922, *Consort Enterprise* and *Monitor News* pub. as separate sections of same newspaper.
Ed. by William H. Miller, D 1915-Mr 24, 1916; W.S. McCulloch, Ap 14, 1916-S 26, 1919; H.A. Warner, Oc 3, 1919-Ag 25, 1921; McCulloch, S 1, 1921-Je 1, 1922.

AEP   mf F 18, 1916-Je 29, 1922

MORINVILLE

764.1   *Progrès.* F 27, 1909-N 27, 1913/...
w. French in Fr.

764.2   *Progrès albertain.* D 4, 1913-F 19, 1914//
w. Immigration French in Fr.

Continued by *Progrès albertain*, Edmonton (374).
Subtitle F 27, 1909-N 27, 1913: "Organe des populations de la région de St. Albert"; D 4, 1913-F 19, 1914: "Organe de la colonisation."
Pub. by La Compagnie de Publication du Progrès Ltée., F 27, 1909-D 26, 1911; Progressive Printing Co. Ltd., Ja 2, 1912-F 19, 1914. Ed. by T.L. Girard and J.A. Nantel, Mr 27-Oc 21, 1909; Nantel, Oc 28, 1909-N 14, 1912; Eugène Chartier, N 21, 1912-F 19, 1914.
Ref.: **LAND** pp.10-11, 13.

AEPAA mf [Mr 6, 1909-F 19, 1914]
AEP   mf [Mr 6, 1909-F 19, 1914]

Morinville Journal. Je 16, 1948-My 27, 1961//
w.

Continued by *Sturgeon Journal*, Sturgeon Municipal District (943).
Absorbed *Legal Record* (691), and *St. Albert Gazette* (879), Ag 20, 1953.
Printed in Edmonton.
Pub. and ed. by Thomas W. Pue, Edmonton.
Alberta Golden Jubilee Edition, S 2, 1955.

AEP   or   Je 16, 1948-My 27, 1961

Morinville Star. 1969-D 1973/...
w.

Morinville Journal. Ja? 1974-My 14, 1977//
w.

Suspended pub. 1970 (Ref.: **CNLU** p.12).
Pub. in Edmonton.
Pub. by Thomas W. Pue, Sun Colorpress Ltd., Edmonton to Ap 16, 1977;
Colin Alexander, Sun Colorpress Ltd., Ap 23-My 14, 1977.

OONL   or   D 19, 1970
AEP   or   My 13, 1972-S 22, 1973; My 18, 1974-My 14, 1977

Morinville and Sturgeon Mirror. S 26, 1979-
w.

Title varies: *Morinville Mirror.*
Pub. and ed. by Gary and Marlene Cavanagh, S 26, 1979-Ag 1980 (Ref.:
Publisher); Mansoor Ladha, Morinville Mirror Pub. Ltd., Ag 1980+.

AEP   or   Jl 28, 1982+

¦LEY

Stoney Echo. Je? 1981-
m.   Native (St)

Pub. by Stoney Tribe. Ed. by Walt Chomyn.
Ref.: **CNLR** p.253; **DANK** p.399.

ACG   or   S/Oc 1981

¦RIN

Morrin Recorder. 1920?-N 1922?//
w.

Ref.: **CAN** 1921, 1922, 1923.

No issues located

770.1   *Morrin District News.* Oc 8, 1920-Ja 20, 1921/...
w.

770.2   *District News, Morrin News Section.* Ja 27, 1921-S 30, 1921//
w.

> Subtitle: "Morrin News Section".
> Continued by *District News,* Munson (778).
> Pub. by Charles A. Adsit.
> Printed back-to-back with *Munson District News,* Oc 8, 1920-Ja 20, 1921.
> From Ja 27-S 30, 1921, same text as *District News, Munson News Section.*
>
> **AEP**   or   Oc 8, 1920-S 30, 1921

MUNDARE

771   *Postup / Progress.* Jl 10, 1915-Jl ? 1917//
irreg. Agriculture Political — Liberal Ukrainian in Ukr.

> Founded by J.S. McCallum, Liberal M.L.A., who had a good knowledge of the Ukrainian language (Ref.: **MUN**, pp.41-42).
> Ed. by Dymtro Yaremko, Jl 10, 1915-early 1916; Myroslaw Stechishin, 1916; Thomas Tomashevsky, late 1916-1917. Pub. by Mundare Pub. Co.
> Became official organ of Ukrainian Farmers' Union of Alberta formed in Vegreville, Ja 22, 1917.
> Ref.: **BOM**, p.28; **MARU** pp.275-276.
>
> **AEU**   mf [Jl 10, 1915-Jl 26, 1917]

772   *Svitlo / Light.* My 1, 1938-D 1, 1949//
2m. Religious Ukrainian in Ukr.

> Place of pub. moved to Toronto, Ont., D 15, 1949.
> Pub. by Basilian Fathers Press. Ed. by M. Romanovich, My 1, 1938-Ag 1, 1943; A. Truch, Ag 15, 1943-1947; M. Bylyna, 1947-D 1, 1949.
> Illustrated supplement *Katolytski Kartyny / Ukrainian Catholic Pictorial* appeared from 1943-1948, with text in Ukr. and Engl. and motto "The saving of the Ukrainian nation through the Catholic Church."
> Ref.: **BOM** p.29; **ISI** pp.41-43; **MARU** p.644.
>
> **AEU**   mf [My 1, 1938-D 1970]

773   *Mundare Star.* Je 20, 1952-D 31, 1953
w.

> Pub. and printed in Edmonton.
> Pub. by Thomas W. Pue, Sun Pub. Co. Ltd.
>
> **AEP**   or Je 20, 1952-D 31, 1953

774   *Mundare Mirror.* 1958-Ap 1, 1961//
w.

Combined with supplement *Vegreville Mirror* (989) Ap 8, 1961.
Pub. and printed in Edmonton.
Pub. by Thomas W. Pue, Sun Pub. Co. Ltd.

AEP   or   Ja 2, 1959-Ap 1, 1961

NSON

Munson Mail. Ja 4, 1912-Ap 18, 1918//
w.

Suspended pub. Ag 27-N 19, 1914.
Amalgamated with *Drumheller Mail* (327), Ap 1918.
Pub. and ed. by Homer S. Mohr, Ja 4-F 29, 1912; Mohr and Grover
Cleveland Duncan, Mr 7, 1912-F 26, 1914; Duncan, Mr 19, 1914-Ap 18,
1918.

AEP   or   Ja 4, 1912-Ap 18, 1918

Munson Times. D 5? 1914-N 20, 1915?//
w.

Pub. by Munson Printing Co., owned by James D. Skinner. Ed. by J.P.
Lord, D 5? 1914-Ja 9, 1915; H.E. Cummer, Ja 16-N 20, 1915 when he
enlisted for military duty.
Ref.: **CAN** 1916.

AEP   or   Ja 2-N 20, 1915

Munson News. S 26? 1919-My 7, 1920//
w.

Superceded by *District News,* Munson (778).
Pub. and ed. by Charles A. Adsit. Pub. expanded area of distribution and
changed title to *District News* (778.1).

AEP   or   Ja 16-My 7, 1920

District News. My 13, 1920-S 23, 1920/...
w.

Munson District News. S 30, 1920-Ja 20, 1921/...
w.

District News, Munson News Section. Ja 27, 1921-S 30, 1921/...
w.

District News. Oc 15, 1921-N 4, 1921?//
w.

Superceded *Munson News* (777), My 13, 1920.
Continued *District News, Morrin News Section,* (770) on Oc 15, 1921.

Pub. by Charles A. Adsit.
Printed back-to-back with *Morrin District News,* Oc 8, 1920-Ja 20, 1921 (770.1). From Ja 27-S 30, 1921, same text as *District News, Morrin News Section* (770.2). Has suspended publication (Ref.: **CPP** v31no3 Mr 1922).
Ref.: **CAN** 1922.

AEP   or   My 13, 1920-N 4, 1921

MYRNAM

779   *Myrnam News.* S 1936-My 28, 1937//
         w.

         Pub. by William Halina (Ref.: *St. Paul Journal* Je 11, 1937).

         No issues located

NANTON

780   *Nanton News.* Je 25, 1903-
         w.   Political — Liberal

         Second issue published S 1, 1903.
         Pub. by Jno. M. Bender, Liberal, Je 25, 1903-My 18, 1905; Aaron Zenas Jessup and Dan Jones, Je 1, 1905-Ap 2, 1908; Aaron Jessup, Ap 2, 1908-Mr 29, 1938; Clyde Campbell Jessup, Mr 31, 1938-D 27, 1956; leased to O. Shoemaker for duration of war; H. George Meyer and Richard B. Hawk, Ja 3, 1957-1959; Hawk, 1959-F 24, 1977; Edward M. Maynard, Mr 1, 1977-N 22, 1979; Lynne Maynard, Nanton News Ltd., N 29, 1979-1986; George Meyer, 1986+.
         30th Anniversary Edition, Je 22, 1933; Alberta Golden Jubilee Edition, S 1, 1955; Jubilee Edition, Ag 8, 1957; 75th Anniversary Souvenir Edition, S 21, 1978.
         Ref.: *Calgary Herald,* Oc 21, 1978; **DAL** pp.79-80.

         ACG   or   Je 22, 1933; S 1, 1955; Ag 8, 1957
         AEP   mf   Je 25, 1903-D 21, 1979
                    or   Ja 1980+

NAPTHA

         News. N 8, 1929-Oc 2, 1931
         See **TURNER VALLEY.** *Tri-City Observer* (975).

NEW SAREPTA

781   *New Sarepta New Era.* Ja 31, 1948-N 24, 1949?//
         w.

         Pub. and printed in Killam and Edmonton.
         Pub. by Thomas W. Pue, Community Publications of Alberta.

         AEP   or   Ja 31, 1948-N 24, 1949

U

Nisku News. My 1981-S 30, 1986//
bw.

Pub. by Lynard Pub. Ltd. Compiled by *Representative*, Leduc. Ed. by Jim Morris, My-Oc 1981; Chris Woodall, Oc 1981-F 1982; Kevin Dooley, F 1982-D 1983; Pat Bell, Ja 1984-1986. (Ref.: Publisher).

No issues located

TOKS

Okotoks Times. F 9, 1901-Ja? 1903/...
w.

Western Star and Okotoks Times. Ja 10, 1903-D 19, 1903?/...
w.

Okotoks Review. Spring 1904-My 29, 1914/...
w.

Okotoks Review and Oilfields Record. Je 5, 1914-F 23, 1917/...
w.

Okotoks Review. Mr 2, 1917-Je 26, 1970//
w.

Absorbed by *High River Times* (625.2).
Masthead title D 12, 1903 issue: *Sentinel.*
Suspended pub. 1920-1924?; Oc 19-D 5, 1947.
Pub. and ed. by William E. McLeod and M. Hodgkin, 1901-Je? 1903 (Ref.: *Okotoks Review;* Mr 14, 1952); M. Hodgkin, Ag 1903-Spring 1904; Charles A. Clark, Sr. and Morice DeLong, Spring 1904-F 15, 1906; Sam R. Hodson, F 22, 1906-Oc 19, 1947; Clark, Sr., N 21? 1947-Ja 7, 1949; Charles A. Clark, Jr., Ja 14, 1949-Jl 8, 1966; R.D. (Don) Tanner, Jl 22, 1966-Je 26, 1970.
Ref.: **DAL** p.81.

AEPAA mf Ja 10-D 19, 1903
AEP or [My 3, 1907-1919, 1924, 1926-1970]
ACG or [F 28-D 12, 1903]

Okotoks Advance. D? 1908-1914?//
w.

Pub. and ed. by Frank D. Rogers.
Ref.: **CAN** 1914.

ACG   or   My 6, 1909
AEP   or   Ja 7, 1907-Ap 3, 1913

785   *Okotoks Observer.* Je 11, 1914-Ag 27, 1914?//
          w.

          Pub. by Observer Pub. Co. Ed. by H.A. Harding, Je 11-Ag 1914; Homer S.
          Mohr, Ag 20-Ag 27, 1914. Editorials signed "Wamba".
          Included section "Notes from the Oil Fields" (Dingman Well).

          AEP   or   Je 11-Ag 27, 1914

786   *Okotoks Weekly.* 1917-1918//
          w.

          Satellite of *Calgary Western Standard* (142.5).
          Pub. by Standard Newspaper Syndicate, Calgary (Ref.: **MK** 1918; **CAN**
          1919).

          No issues located

787   *Western Wheel.* Ag 3, 1976-
          w.

          Pub. and ed. by Stephen John Cook, Ag 3, 1976-F 22, 1978; Geoffrey and
          Monika Edmunds, Mr 1, 1978-Ap 14, 1983; Bruce Klippenstein, Ap 15,
          1983+

          AEP   or   Ag 3, 1976+

OLDS

788   *Olds Oracle.* Ag 16, 1900-Ja 3? 1904//
          w.

          Pub. and ed. by Adoniram J. Samis, apparently financed by A.J. Bush,
          Baptist clergyman and prominent businessman (Ref.: **JEN** p.16).
          OLDS p.57 gives starting date as 1896, all other sources indicate 1900.
          Destroyed by fire Ja 3, 1904.
          Ref.: **CPP** v13no1 Ja, 1904; **MK** 1901; **OLDS** pp.57, 249).

          ACG   mf N 21, 1902

789.1   *Olds Gazette.* Ja? 1904-Mr 17, 1960/...
          w.

789.2   *Olds Gazette and Mountain View News.* Mr 24, 1960-D 21, 1977/...
          w.

789.3   *Gazette.* Ja 4, 1978-
          w.

          Suspended pub. F 23-Je 27, 1919.

Pub. and ed. by Charles B. Halpin, Sr., Ja? 1904-?; J.E. Gooder and R.B. Campbell, 1904-1907; Tom L. Buckton Socialist, Jl 6, 1907-Ja 15, 1909. Hon. Duncan McLean Marshall, Liberal, acquired the buiness and est. Gazette Pub. Co. Ltd. in 1909. He operated the paper through a resident mgr. until 1923 (Donald Gillies and Frank C. Brower). Pub. by Brower, Walter C. Gooder and Daniel J. Greer, 1923-Ja 31, 1936; William H. Miller, F 1, 1936-D 27, 1945; Neil K. Leatherdale and W.R. (Ronnie) Newsom, Ja 1, 1946-Oc 18, 1956; Leatherdale, Leatherdale Pub. Ltd., Oc 1956+
    Alberta Golden Jubilee Edition, S 8, 1955.

ACG   mf [Mr 11, 1904-S 27, 1918]
AEP   or My 4, 1907-1919; 1925+
ABOM   or Mr 3, 1921

Olds News. 1935?-Ag 1944?//
m.

    Printed by Examiner Press, Calgary.
    Pub. by Wade Papers of Alberta.

ACG   or Ag 1944

Olds Moose-Paper. Je 20, 1961-? 1961//
w.

    Pub. by Moose McMillen.
    Ref.: CNLU p.22.

OONL   or Je 27, 1961

Olds Star. N 9, 1976-Je 28, 1977//
    See Supplement (1083).

Olds Optimist. S 19, 1982-
w.

    Pub. by John Davis, Davis Pub. Ltd., Didsbury. Ed. by Monica Dick and Francis DeJong (Ref.: Correspondence with Publisher, N 27, 1984).

No issues located

WAY

Onoway Westerner. Oc 1, 1949-Ag 14, 1953//
w.

    Continued *Westerner,* Sangudo (886.2).
    Absorbed by *Lac Ste Anne Chronicle,* Lac Ste Anne County (665), Ag 14, 1953.
    Pub. and printed in Edmonton.
    Pub. by Thomas W. Pue, Community Publications of Alberta.

AEP   or Oc 1, 1949-Ag 14, 1953

794.1   *Highway 43 Tribune.* Ag? 1978-Ag 29, 1979/...
2m.; w.

794.2   *Tribune.* S 5, 1979-Oc 1980/...
w.

794.3   *Onoway Tribune.* Oc 1980-Ap 1985//
w.

Frequency varied: 2m. Ag 1978-Mr 1, 1979; w. Mr 7, 1979+
Place of pub. varied: Whitecourt, Ag 1978-Mr 1, 1979; Onoway, Mr 7,
1979-Ap, 1985.
Pub. by BLB Publishing Ltd. and distributed bw. as shopper with
Whitecourt Star (1033). Sold to Pembina Pub. Ltd., Mr 1, 1979. Pub. by
Steven Dills, Mr 1, 1979-Jl 2, 1980; Barry Baniulis, Jl 15-Oc 1980. Sold to
Lynard Pub. Ltd., Oc 1, 1980. Pub. by Barry Heidecker, Oc 1, 1980-D 1981;
Steven Dills, Ja 5, 1982-S 1, 1984; H.M. Bowes, Lynard Publishers, S,
1984-Ap, 1985.
Ref.: Publisher's files; *Edmonton Journal* Mr 7, 1979; *Whitecourt Star* Oc
1, 1980.

No issues located

OYEN

795   *Oyen News.* F? 1914-Je 26, 1935?//
w.

Pub. and ed. by Charles L. Dunford.

AEP   or   Je 25, 1914-D 31, 1919; Jl 2, 1924-Je 26, 1935

796   *Telegram.* 1939-1940//
w.

Pub. by Oyen Printing Co. Pub. and ed. by Alvin V. Wallace (Ref.: **MK**
1940, 1941; **CAN** 1943).
Closed before the year's subscription had expired. (Ref.: Oyen and
District Historical Society).

ACOM   or   Ap 25, 1940

797   *Oyen Observer.* Jl 12? 1956-1957//
w.

Pub. and ed. by T.J. Adair, Adair and Co.
Ref.: CNLU, p.22.

OONL   or   Oc 27, 1956

798   *Oyen Echo.* 1960-
2m.; w.

Frequency varies: wm. 1960-Mr 25, 1974; w. Ap 1, 1974+.

Began as advertising sheet including local news. Mimeographed to Ja 28, 1974.

Pub. and ed. by David and Bunny Snideman, 1960-Ap, 1969; Helen Ball and Diana Walker, My 13, 1969-Ja, 1974; Ronald E. Holmes, Holmes Pub. Ltd., Medicine Hat, F 1, 1974+; Ed. by H. Ball and D. Walker, F, 1974+.

Ref.: CNLU p.22.

OONL   or   My 13, 1969;Ap 27, 1971
ACOM   or   [1964-Ap, 1969] My 13, 1969+
AEP   or   Ap 24, 1972+

KLAND COUNTY

Parkland County Examiner. D 7, 1977-Ja 18, 1978//
w.

Pub. by Grove Pub. Ltd., Randy Lennon, pub., Ian Kinsey, county reporter. Distributed to Parkland County ratepayers as a supplement to *Examiner*, Spruce Grove (913) to Ja 18, 1978, when it became an integrated section of the *Examiner*.

See also *Examiner*, Spruce Grove (913).

AEP   or   D 7, 1977-Ja 18, 1978

CE RIVER

Peace River Pilot. Ja 20, 1910-F 12, 1910//
w.   Immigration

Issue of Ja 20, 1910 entitled *Peace River Pilot and Entwistle News*.

Pub. and ed. by Thomas D. Piche, Entwistle, Alta.

Printed by Edmonton Printing and Pub. Co., Edmonton. Provided information on homesteading in the Peace River District. Only 2 issues appear to have been pub.

AEP   mf Ja 20-F 12, 1910

Peace River Standard and Farmers' Gazette. Je 22, 1917-D 14, 1922//?
w.

Succeeded by *Peace River Record* (802).

Pub. and ed. by Robert N. Whillans, Standard Press Ltd.

Ref.: CAN 1924; JOH.

AEP   mf Je 22, 1917-D 14, 1922

Peace River Record. Jl 23, 1914-My 22, 1924/...
w.

802.2   *Peace River Record and Northern Review.* My 29, 1924-D 31,
         1925/...
         w.

802.3   *Peace River Record.* Ja 7, 1926-Ag 31, 1939//
         w.

         Amalgamated with *Northern Gazette,* Peace River (803), S 8, 1939 to
         form *Record-Gazette,* Peace River (804).
             Pub. and ed. by Charles W. Frederick, Record Pub. Co., Jl 23, 1914-S 15,
         1920; John McLaren, lessee, S 16, 1920-Mr 30, 1921; Frederick, Ap 6,
         1921-Ag 31, 1939.
             Ref.: **JOH.**

         AEP   mf Jl 23, 1914-Ag 31, 1939

803   *Northern Gazette.* S 9, 1932-S 1, 1939//
         w.

         Amalgamated with *Peace River Record* (802), S 8, 1939 to form *Record-
         Gazette,* Peace River (804.1).
             Pub. and ed. by Ernest Edward Taylor.
             Ref.: **JOH.**

         AEP   mf S 9, 1932-S 1, 1939

804.1   *Peace River Record With Which is Amalgamated the Northern
         Gazette.* S 8, 1939-Ag 27, 1943/...
         w.

804.2   *Peace River Record-Gazette.* S 3, 1943-F 24, 1955/...
         w.

804.3   *Record-Gazette.* Mr 3, 1955-
         w.

         Continued *Peace River Record* (802) and *Northern Gazette* (803).
             Pub. and ed. by Garth D. Johnston and Ernest Edward Taylor, Record-
         Gazette Press Ltd., S 8, 1939-D 31, 1953. Sold to Bowes Pub. Ltd. Ja 1,
         1954. Ed. by David M. Bowes, Ja 1, 1954-Ag 30, 1956; Jean M. Holt, S 6,
         1956-Mr 31, 1960; Walter G. Nagel, S 6, 1956-Je 27, 1957; James L.
         Grasswick, D 1, 1960-Ap 28, 1965; E. Stan Parks, My 5, 1965-Ja 10, 1968;
         Gerald C. Scott, Ja 17, 1968-My 27, 1969; H.F. (Hec) MacLean, Je 3, 1970-
         D 31, 1981; Pearl Muir, Ja 6, 1981+
             Ref.: **JOH.**

         AEP   mf S 8, 1939-Ag 27, 1943
         AEP   or 1984+

805   *North Peace Pictorial.* Oc 1973-
         w.

Pub. in Grimshaw to 1982?
Pub. by David J. Nelson, Carcajon Graphics Ltd. Ed. by Dan Kyba.

No issues located

BINA MUNICIPAL DISTRICT

Evansburg Pembina Herald. Ja 11, 1952-F 1, 1952/...
w.

Pembina Herald. F 8, 1952-N 16, 1968//
w.

Suspended pub. Ap 27, 1963-Ag 21, 1965.
Pub. by Thomas W. Pue, Edmonton.
Alberta Golden Jubilee Edition, Ag 31, 1955.

AEP   or   Ja 18, 1952-Ag 27, 1963; Ag 21, 1965-N 16, 1968

Pembina News. F 2, 1956-1965//
w.

Continued by *Drayton Valley Banner* (1057).
Title varied: to 1961 as *Pembina News Advertiser.*
Pub. by Art Playford, Pembina News Advg. Ltd., Drayton Valley.
Ref.: **CNLU**, p.9; *Western Review*; Drayton Valley, S 8, 1982.

AEPAA   or   Jl 30, 1959 (86.125/650)
OONL   or   F 2, 1956; F 4, S 22, 1960

Pembina Star. N 28, 1970-Je 7, 1975/...
w.

Pembina Herald. Je 14, 1975-My 14, 1977//
w.

Pub. by Thomas W. Pue, Sun Colorpress Ltd., Edmonton.
Ref.: **CNLU** p.13.

OONL   or   N 28, 1970
AEP   or   My 13, 1972-My 14, 1977

HOLD

Penhold Reporter. D 1903-1904//
w.

Pub. by George and ed. by Orville D. Fleming (Ref.: **MK** 1905; **MEE**
p.161).

ARDA   or   [1904]

810   *Penhold Journal.* 1911-?//
           w.

               Ref.: **MK** 1911.

           No issues located

PICTURE BUTTE

811   *Northern Times.* My 2, 1940-Je 19, 1941//
           w.

               Title varied: *Picture Butte Northern Times.*
               Mimeographed.
               Pub. by J. Ross Anderson and David G. Wood, My 2-Ag 29, 1940;
               Anderson, S 5, 1940-Je 19, 1941. Ed. by Jean Blewett Anderson, My 2,
               1940-Je 19, 1941.

               AEP   or   Jl 11, 1940-Je 19, 1941

812.1   *Picture Butte Progress.* N 6? 1941-1954/...
           w.

812.2   *Lethbridge Northern News.* 1954-N 1958//
           w.

               Amalgamated with *Coaldale Flyer* N 28, 1958 to form *Coaldale Flyer
               and the Lethbridge Northern News* (276).
               Pub. and ed. by H. Tilston-Jones, 1941-1954. Sold to Sydney P. Johnson,
               1954, pub. and ed., 1954-N 1958. Sold N 1958 to J.J. Loewen (Ref.:
               Correspondence with Marie Sorgard, reporter and writer for Picture Butte
               and Lethbridge newspapers, Ap 26, 1985).
               Alberta Golden Jubilee Edition, S 1, 1955.

               AEP   or   [Ja 22, 1942-My 15, 1947]; S 1, 1955

PINCHER CITY

813   *Pincher City News.* 1908-1911?//
           w.

               Pub. by R.W. Morgan (Ref.: **MK** 1909, 1911).

           No issues located

PINCHER CREEK

814.1   *Rocky Mountain Echo.* Ag 15, 1900-Ag 3, 1906/...
           w.

4.2   *Pincher Creek Echo.* Ag 10, 1906-
        w.

        Pub. by E.T. Saunders, Ag 15, 1900-Je 22, 1911, R.L. Norman, Je 29,
        1911-Je 27, 1913; E.T. Saunders, Jl 25, 1913-Ja 9, 1920; Annie Helena
        (Derrett) Edwards, F 6, 1920-F 22, 1944; H.J. Hammond, prop., H.E.
        Diamond, ed. and mgr., Mr 1, 1944-D 27, 1951; Edouard J. Rouleau and
        Sons, Ja 3, 1952-My 28, 1959; E.L. Green, Je 1, 1959-D 21, 1960; Jim and
        Dave Rouleau, Ja 5, 1961-D 22, 1966; F.D. Rouleau, Ja 5, 1967+
            Diamond Jubilee Issue, Ag 17, 1960.
            Ref.: **MK** 1901; **DAL** pp.83-84.

        ACG   or Ag 15, 1900
        AEP   mf Jl 21-Oc 20, 1903; Mr 15, 1904-Jl 29, 1921; D 9, 1921-D 28,
                    1984
                or Ja 4, 1985-

5   *Round-Up.* D 13, 1902-D 20, 1902
        w.

        Pub. by Roderick Matheson; ed. by Herbert Lake.

        ACG   or D 13-D 20, 1902

PNOKA COUNTY

5   *Ponoka County News.* Oc 29, 1955-Je 4, 1976//
        m.

        Title varied: *County News.*
        Pub. by the Rimbey Record Ltd. Ed. by Jack Parry.
        Ref.: **CNLU** p.23.

        OONL   or My 26, 1956
        AEP   mf S 5, 1975-Je 4, 1976
        APFOM   or Oc 29, 1955-Je 4, 1976

NOKA

        Ponoka Herald. Ag 27, 1900-
        w.

        Est. by W.D. Pitcairn. Pub. and ed. by Eugene Rhian, 1902-1905; George
        Gordon, 1905-S 7, 1938; John F. Gordon, S 8, 1938-D 23, 1952; Pub. by the
        Ponoka Herald Ltd., 1953+. Keith Leonard, W. Ernie Jamison and Ken
        McLean, Ja 7, 1953-Jl 6, 1955; Jamison and McLean, Jl 26, 1955-Je 23,
        1964; McLean, Jl 1, 1964+.
            Alberta Golden Jubilee Edition, S 28, 1955.
            Ref.: **DAL** p.84.

        ACG   or S 28, 1955

AEPAA mf Ja 3-D 26, 1902; Ja 15-D 30, 1904; Ja 11-Ap 26, 1907; N 7-N
28, 1907; Ja 1-D 24, 1914; Ja 8, 1920-D 27, 1923
AEP   mf Ag 27, 1900-D 1984
or Ja 1985+

818   *Ponoka News and Advertiser.* N 15, 1949-
w.

Pub. by L. Harry Wright, 1949-1967; D.D. Wright, 1967+ (Ref.:
Correspondence with Publisher, Je 26, 1984).

No issues located

819   *Western Weekly Supplement.* My 17, 1962-Jl 25, 1968//
w.

Printed by *Albertan,* Calgary. A weekly tabloid supplement pub. by
United Pub. Ltd., Ernie Jamison, pres., Jack Kelly, mnging. ed. Editorial
offices were located in the Ponoka Herald Bldg. Distributed by 63 weekly
newspapers in British Columbia, Alberta, Saskatchewan, Manitoba,
Northwest Territories and Yukon.
Ref.: **CPP** v71no4 Ap 1962; v71no10 Oc 1962.

No issues located

POPLAR LAKE

820   *Saturday Blade.* 1903//
m.?

Handwritten.
Pub. by William M. Donley. Included local news and advertisements.

AEPAA   or   Je 20, 1903 (82.245 SE)

PRAIRIE GRANGE

See **ROCKY MOUNTAIN HOUSE.**

PRIDDIS

Pioneer. S 3, 1980-My 26, 1982
See **COCHRANE.** *Pioneer* (282).

PROVOST

821   *Provost Star.* Mr 18, 1910-Mr 30, 1917//
w.

Superceded by *Provost News* (822).
Est. by Schumacher and York in My 1910 (Ref.: **CNLU,** p.23; **DAL** p.85).
Pub. and ed. by C. Stafford Poulter, ?-Je 7, 1912; Phil Schumacher, Je

14, 1912-Oc 30, 1914; James G. Mackay, D 5, 1913-Mr 6, 1914; Frank J. Schumacher, N 6, 1914-Ja 29, 1915; N.A. Kilburn, N 6, 1914-Ja 29, 1915; Phil Schumacher, F 5, 1915-Mr 30, 1917.

AEP or Ap 21, 1911-Mr 30, 1917

Provost News. Ap 4, 1917-
w.

Suspended for almost eight months due to illness (Ref.: **PUB** v25no613, S/O 1943).
Superceded *Provost Star* (822).
Pub. by Provost Pub. Ltd., Ap 4, 1917-Mr 1, 1922. Ed. by C.A. Smith, Ap 4-D 19, 1917; A.A. Thoresen, D 26, 1917-My 8, 1918; Will D. Mackay, Jl 16, 1919-F 1, 1922; Frank J. Schumacher and John R. McLauchlin, F 8-Mr 1, 1922. Sold to Lindsay H. Meiklejohn, pub., Mr. 8, 1922-Oc 9, 1929; Stewart J. Fullerton, ed. and mgr., F 22, 1928-S 18, 1929. Sold to Edward Holmes and Son, pub., Oc 16, 1929-Oc 28, 1944. Pub. by George S. Holmes, N 1, 1945-Je 24, 1970; Holmes Pub. Ltd., Jl 1970+. Ed. by Ronald E. Holmes, Jl 1, 1970-Je 27, 1973; Richard C. Holmes, Jl 1, 1973+.

AEP or Ap 4, 1917+

DWAY

Radway Star. 1950?-D 1951?//
w.

Pub. and printed in Edmonton.
Pub. by Thomas W. Pue, Community Publications of Alberta, Edmonton.
Ref.: **AY** 1952; **CAN** 1951, 1952.

No issues located

YMOND

,1 *Chronicle.* Mr, 1903-Oc 1907/...
w.

,2 *Raymond Rustler.* Oc 1907-Je? 1911/...
w.

,3 *Raymond Leader.* Je 2, 1911-D? 1917/...
w.

,4 *Recorder.* 1917-S 15, 1922//
w. Political — Liberal

New paper appeared in March (Ref.: **CPP** v12no4 Ap 1903).
Pub. and ed. by R.O. Matheson, Mr 24, 1903-N 1905; Brigham S. Young, N 27, 1905-Ag 1907; David H. Elton, Ag 1907-Ag 1908; Fred Ford, Liberal,

S 3, 1908-Ap 1909; Otto L. Carr, My 7, 1909-Ja 1910; W.S. Berryessa, Mr 1910-Je 1914; Frank C. Steele, Je 5-Ap 1, 1917; David C. Peterson, 1916-1922. Eds: Frank C. Steele, Je 5, 1914-Ap 1, 1917; George H. Brewerton, Ap 6, 1917-1919; Steele, 1920-1921.

Plant destroyed by fire, S 1922 (Ref.: **CPP** v31no9 Oc 1922).

Ref.: **HIC** p.210; **CPP** v12no4 Ap 1903; **MK** 1918-1922.

AEP   or   Ap 19-Ag 2, 1907; Ja 29, 1909-My 26, 1911; Je 30, 1911-Jl 13, 1917

825.1   *Raymond Recorder.* Mr? 1923-D 7, 1928/...
w.

825.2   *Raymond-Magrath Recorder.* D 13, 1928-Ja 3, 1929/...
w.

825.3   *Raymond Recorder.* Ja 11, 1929-Jl 21, 1949?//
w.

Pub. and ed. by David C. Peterson, 1925-S 7, 1928; W.D. Mendenhall and Lee Brewerton S 14, 1928-Ap 12, 1929; S.I. May, Ap 19, 1929-D 1945; S.J. Weaver, Ja 1946-Jl 1949.

AEP   or   Jl 3, 1925-Jl 21, 1949

826.1   *New Raymond Recorder.* Mr 16, 1950-Mr 25, 1955/...
w.

826.2   *Raymond Recorder.* Ap 1, 1955-D 1956?//
w.

Pub. and ed. by Max Hamilton.
50th Anniversary of Raymond Issue, Je 28, 1951; Alberta Golden Jubilee Edition, Jl 8, 1955.
Ref.: **CNLU.** p.23.

AEP   or   Mr 16, 1950-My 11, 1956

827   *Raymond Recorder.* S 11, 1957-1972?//
w.

Continued by *Border County Recorder*, Milk River (755).
Printed in Coaldale.
Pub. and ed. by J.J. Loewen.
Ref.: **CAN** 1973; **CNLU** p.7.

OONL   or   S 11, D 18, 1957

828   *Raymond Review.* Je 7? 1965-
w.

Pub. and ed. by J.C. Adair, Je 1965-Ja 30, 1974 (Ref.: *Raymond Review*, Ja 30, 1974); Ray G. Johnson, F 1, 1974-Ja 8, 1975; Gilbert L. Hancock, Ja

15, 1975-Oc 29, 1980. Sold to Nephelokokkugia Holdings Ltd. and pub. by
A.J. Treleaven and Roy G. Sweet, N 1, 1980-1983; Marie Barr, DMJAB
Printers & Pub. Ltd., 1983+.

AEPAA   or   Ag 2, Ag 10, 1966
AEP   or   My 3, 1972+

ED DEER COUNTY

9   *Red Deer County News.* 1969-
          m.

          Not pub. in September.
          Pub. from the office of Sylvan Lake News.
          Ref.: **CNLU** p.26.

          OONL   or   Jl 3, 1970
          AEP   or   F 7, 1975+
          ARDA   or   1969+

0.1   *Advocate Shopper.* N 15, 1972-D 28? 1978/...
          w.

0.2   *Central Alberta Parkland News.* Ja 1, 1979-
          w.

          Pub. by Red Deer Advocate for Canwest Pub. Ltd. (Ref.: Correspondence
          with Publisher, F 14, 1985).

          AEP   or   D 1, 1982+

ED DEER

1   *Red Deer Review.* ? 1894-Ap 12, 1894//
          w.? Immigration

          Suspended publication Ap 12, 1894 (Ref.: **MEE**).
          Pub. by Saskatchewan Land and Homestead Co., mnging dir., J.T.
          Moore, to advertise land in the district. Red Deer Board of Trade paid the ex-
          press charges and looked after distribution. Ed. by D.H. Murphy (Ref.: **GAE**
          p.118; *Edmonton Bulletin* Jl 19, 1894).

          No issues located

2   *Red Deer Gazette and Lacombe Advertiser.* 1898-1899//
          w.

          Ed. by G.W. Green (Ref.: **MK** 1899).
          Pub. as supplement to *Free Lance,* Innisfail (641) (Ref.: **MEE**, p.159).

          No issues located

833   *Alberta Independent.* F 1898-Ja 1899//
          w.?

          Ref.: **MEE** p.158.

          No issues located

834.1   *Alberta Echo.* Ap 1, 1901-Ap 1903/...
          w.

834.2   *Alberta Advocate.* My 1, 1903-F 22, 1907/...
          w.

834.3   *Red Deer Advocate.* Mr 1, 1907-S 10, 1972/...
          w.; 2w.; d.

834.4   *Advocate.* S 11, 1972-
          d.

          Frequency varied: w. Ap 1, 1901-Jl 4, 1956; 2w. Jl 11, 1956-F 26, 1960; d.
          Mr 1, 1960+.
          Pub. by Orville D. Fleming and George Fleming, Ap 1, 1901-1902.
          Leased to O.A. Butterfield, Ag 1902-Ag 1903. Pub. and ed. by G.A. Love, Ja
          1-Je 1, 1904; O. Shoemaker and D.A. McLean, Jl 2-D 1904; Shoemaker and
          Co., Ja 1-Mr 31, 1905; John T. Moore, Advocate Pub. Co., Ap 1, 1905-N 23,
          1906; Francis Wright Galbraith, Red Deer Advocate Ltd., N 30, 1906-Mr 9,
          1934; Francis Philip Galbraith, Mr 10, 1934-My 15, 1970; Gordon J.
          Grierson, Jl 6, 1972+. Ed. by J.E. (Ted) Bower, F 28, 1970-Ap 11, 1979; R.
          Paul Willcocks, Oc 3, 1979+. Sold to the *Liverpool Daily Post and Echo,*
          U.K., Ja 1, 1958.
          Golden Jubilee Issue, Jl 18, 1934; Alberta Golden Jubilee Edition, Ag 3,
          1955.
          Ref.: **GAE**, p. 118; **GAL**, pp. 20-31; **MEE**, pp. 160-161.

          AEU   mf Ap 14, 1904-D 1976
          AEP   or 1907-1916; 1918-1920, 1923-1925, 1927-1929, 1948-1949, Ja
                   1985+
                   mf 1970-1974, Ja 3 1976-1984

835.1   *News.* Ja 1905-N 24, 1920/...
          w.

835.2   *Red Deer News.* D 1? 1920-My 5, 1926//
          w.

          Pub. by News Pub. Co. Pub. by G.A. Love and D.A. McLean, 1905-Jl 10,
          1906; Jno. A. Carswell, Jl 17, 1906-Ap 1, 1925; H.G. Scott, Ap 8, 1925-My
          5, 1926. Sold to the *Red Deer Advocate,* (834.3) My 1926.

          AEPAA mf Ja 23, 1906-Ja 13, 1926

AEP or Ap 16, 1907-D 28, 1921; Ja 3, 1923-My 5, 1926

6 *Optimist.* N 18, 1929-Ap? 1943//
bw.

Pub. and ed. by David C. Peterson, N 18, 1929-1931; Peterson and Ernest C. Fletcher, 1931-1933; Fletcher, 1933-1943 (Ref.: Ernest C. Fletcher).

ACG or [Jl 15, 1930-Ap 15, 1943]
ARDA or Je 29, N 16, D 15, 1938, Jl 5, 1939; Jl 16, 1941; N 5, N 12, 1942

M.D. Red Deer News. N ? 1945-S ? 1946//
See Supplement (1084)

7 *Red Deer Ad-Viser.* 1946-Ag 10, 1977//
w.; 2w.

Superceded by *Midweeker* (840), *Weekender* (839), and *Central Alberta Ad-Viser,* Red Deer (841).
Editions: Pub. a 2m. city edition and a w. rural edition *(Ad-Viser Rural Shop-a-Scope).*
Pub. by Les D. and David Rideout, Ad-Viser Pub.

AEP or F 20, 1976-Ag 10, 1977 (city ed. only)

8 *Civvy Street.* Ag 1, 1946-1948?//
? Veterans

Pub. at Graphic Arts School, Canadian Vocational Training Centre No. 8, Red Deer. Joe H. Ross, ed.-in-chief; A.A. (Bert) Frawley, ed.

ARDA or Ag 1, 1946

9 *Weekender.* Ag 12, 1977-S 7, 1979//
w.

Superceded *Red Deer Ad-Viser* (837).
Superceded by *Red Deer Shopper* (842).
Pub. by David Rideout, Ad-Viser Pub.

AEP or Ag 12, 1977-S 7, 1979

40 *Midweeker.* Ag 17? 1977-S 12, 1979//
w.

Superceded *Red Deer Ad-Viser* (837).
Superceded by *Red Deer Shopper* (842).
Pub. by David Rideout, Ad-Viser Pub.

AEP or Ag 17, 1977-S 14, 1979

41 *Central Alberta Ad-Viser.* Ag 17? 1977-
w.; 2w.

Superceded *Red Deer Ad-Viser,* rural ed. *(Ad-Viser Rural Shop-a-Scope)* (837).

Frequency varied: 2w. 1980?-1981? (Ref.: **CARD** 1979-1983).
Pub. by Ad-Viser Pub.

No issues located

842   *Red Deer Shopper.* S 14, 1979-
        2w.

        Superceded *Midweeker* (840), and *Weekender* (839), Red Deer.
        Pub. by David Rideout to S 5, 1980, and Keith Rideout, S 10, 1980+, Ad-
        Viser Pub.
        Ref.: **ALB** My 12, 1975:12.

        AEP   or   S 14, 1979-D 31, 1982

REDCLIFF

843   *Redcliff Review.* N 21, 1910-Je 6, 1940//?
        w.

        Suspended pub. S-D 1911; Ag 11-Oc 6, 1921.
        Pub. by A. Rollins McLeish, N 21, 1910-Ap 1911 (Ref.: *Redcliff Review;*
        Ja 5, 1933); C.W. White, Ap-Je 1911; L.R. Marion, Je-S 1911; W.H. Hatcher,
        Ja 5, 1912-Je 13, 1913; Hatcher and Hubbs, Je 20, 1913-Je 19, 1914;
        Hatcher, Je 26, 1914-Ag 11, 1921; Ed. L. Stone, Je 26, 1914-Ja 12, 1933;
        B.L. Stone, Ja 12, 1933-1940.

        AEP   mf Ja 28, 1911-Je 6, 1940
        AREM   or   N 21, 1910

844   *Redcliff Journal.* 1913//
        w.

        Title cited as *Redcliff Tribune* (Ref.: **MK** 1913; **CPP** v22no4 Ap 1913).
        Only two issues published?
        Pub. by D.M. Christian; ed. by R.S. Hodge.

        AREM   or   Ja 7, 14 1913

        Redcliff Review. Oc 6, 1976-? 1978//
        See Supplement (1085)

        Cypress Courier. Mr 21, 1979-
        See **FORTY MILE COUNTY.** *40-Mile County Commentator* (563).

REDWATER

845   *Redwater Review.* F 28, 1949-Mr 26, 1952?//
        w.

        Pub. by Thomas W. Pue, Community Publications of Alberta, Edmonton.

        AEP   or   F 28, 1949-Mr 26, 1952

46   *Redwater News.* F 28, 1950-Mr 1951//
         2w.

           Mimeographed.
           Pub. by Ed and Mary Arrol (Ref.: **CPP** v60no4 Ap 1951; *Edmonton Journal* N 18, 1950).

         No issues located

47   *Redwater News Daily Flashes.* Oc 1950-? 1950//
         d.

           Est. by William Bell and pub. by Redwater News (Ref.: *Edmonton Journal* N 18, 1950).

         No issues located

48.1   *Redwater News.* F 6, 1953-N 16, 1968/...
         w.

48.2   *Redwater Sun.* N 23, 1968-Ja 18, 1969//
         w.

           Pub. by Thomas A. Bruchal and ed. by Helen Gordon, 1953-Je 15, 1954.
           Sold to Thomas W. Pue, Sun Pub. Co. Ltd., Edmonton, Je 19, 1954.
           Alberta Golden Jubilee Edition, Ag 31, 1955.

         AEP   or   Mr 18, 1954-N 16, 1968
         ARDA   or   F 6, 1953

     Redwater Recorder. S 22, 1967-1969?
         See **THORHILD COUNTY.** *Thorhild County News* (956).

49   *Redwater Star.* D 19, 1970-Mr 10, 1973?//
         w.

           Pub. by Thomas W. Pue, Edmonton. Same text as *Thorhild Star* (959.2).
           Ref.: **CNLU** p.13.

         OONL   or   D 19, 1970
         AEP   or   My 13, 1972-Mr 10, 1973

0   *Redwater News.* F 11, 1972-Mr 8? 1974//
         w.

           Combined with *Thorhild News* (960), Mr 15, 1974 to form *News, Thorhild County* (958).
           Pub. by Westlock News Ltd. Ed. by John MacDonald.
           Ref.: **CNLU** p.27.

         OONL   or   F 11, 1972

     Tribune. Oc 28, 1981-
         w.

Pub. by Mansoor Ladha, M.M. Pub. Ltd.

AEP   or   Je 23, 1982+

REDWOOD MEADOWS

Pioneer. S 3, 1980-My 26, 1982
See **COCHRANE**. *Pioneer* (282).

RETLAW

852   *Retlaw Weekly.* 1917-1918?//
w.

Satellite of *Calgary Western Standard* (142.5). (Ref.: **CPP** v26no11 N
1917).
Pub. by Standard Newspaper Syndicate, Calgary. (Ref.: **MK** 1918).

No issues located

RIMBEY

The first paper published in Rimbey was a weekly news sheet published
every Saturday by a Mr. Thorpe, brother of the Thorpe of Thorpe and
Putland, general merchants. Title and duration unknown (Ref.: **SCH** p.151).

853   *Rimbey Pioneer.* 1919//
w.

Pub. by Charles B. (Barney) Halpin, Jr. (Ref.: **SCH** pp.151-155).
Presses wrecked by advocates of old site for the town (Ref.: **CPP** v29no5
My 1919).

No issues located

854   *Rimbey Advance.* F 17, 1921-N 30, 1922?//
w.

Pub. and ed. by Henry Oke, F 17, 1921-Ja 12, 1922; Elva Simmons, Ja
19-N 30, 1922.
Ref.: **CAN** 1923.

AEP   mf F 17, 1921-N 30, 1922

855.1   *Rimbey Record and Blindman Valley Advertiser.* Jl 17, 1930-F 14,
1936/...
w.

855.2   *Rimbey Record.* Ap 2, 1936-
w.

First issue Jl 17, 1930 (Ref.: **CPP** v39no8 Ag, 1930).
Suspended pub. F 14-Ap 2, 1936; Jl 1943-Ag 24, 1944.

Pub. and ed. by W.J. Good, Jl 1930-Oc 31, 1940; W.R. (Ronnie) Newsom lessee, N 7, 1940-N 11, 1941; Leonard C. Newsom, N 13, 1941-Jl 1943; Elsie Worton, Ag 24, 1944-Oc? 1945; Charles R. Worton, Oc? 1945-Je 25, 1958; Jack A. Parry, 1953-F 22, 1978; Olive and Jack A. Parry, Rimbey Record Ltd., Mr 1, 1978-S, 1985; Record Pub. Ltd., 1985+.

Alberta Golden Jubilee Edition, S 1, 1955.

AEP   or   Ja 1, 1932-My 2, 1946; My 1, 1957+

ROCKY MOUNTAIN HOUSE

56.1   *Rocky Mountain House Echo.* F 4, 1910-D? 1912/...
            m.; 2m.; w.

56.2   *Guide to Citizenship, Prosperity and Happiness.* D? 1912-F 23,
            1917//?
            w. Liberal

Frequency varied: m. F 4, 1910-D 1911; 2m. F 18, 1911-Oc 15, 1912; w. N 8, 1912-F 23, 1917.

Suspended pub. Oc 15-N 8, 1912.

Issue of F 4, 1910 stated pub. by Canadian Uncle Sam Amusement Club, Prairie Grange. Ed. by George T. Thomson, F 4, 1910-N 22, 1912; James D. Skinner, N 29, 1912-Mr 24, 1916; Thomas H. Fawcus, mgr., Mr 31, 1916-F 23, 1917.

Ref.: **FLE** pp.276-283; **GIS** pp.133-137.

AEU   mf F 4, 1910; F 18, 1911-F 23, 1917
AEP   or   Ja-F 23, 1917

57   *Mountaineer.* Mr 31, 1914-S 29, 1914//
            w.

Pub. and ed. by George T. Thomson. Est. as opposition paper to *Guide* (856). Pub. by James D. Skinner (Ref.: **GIS** pp.133-137).

AEU   mf Mr 31-S 29, 1914

58.1   *Rocky Mountain House Capital.* F? 1918-Ap 23, 1918/...
            w.

58.2   *Rocky Mountain Capital.* Ap 30, 1918-Ag? 1919/...
            w.

58.3   *Rocky Mountain House Capital.* S 4, 1919-D 1920//
            w.

Pub. and ed. by Charles A. Roulston.
Ref.: **GIS**, pp.133-137.

AEU   mf Ap 2-Oc 23, 1918

859   *Gazette.* Ja 15, 1921-S 6, 1923//
         w.

         Revival of *Capital* (858). (Ref.: **CPP** v30no4, Ap 1921).
         Pub. and ed. by T.B. Malcolm, Ja 15-D 29, 1921; Will I. Dyer and Chester
         E. Moffet, Ja 5-Oc 5, 1922; Norman T.J. Frost, lessee, Oc 7, 1922-S 6, 1923.
         Ref.: **GIS** pp.133-137.

         AEU   mf Ja 15, 1921-S 6, 1923
         AEP   mf Ja 15, 1921-S 6, 1923

860.1   *Mountaineer.* S 19, 1923-Ag 9, 1950/...
         w.

860.2   *Rocky Mountain House Mountaineer.* Ag 16, 1950-My 15, 1957/...
         w.

860.3   *Mountaineer.* My 23, 1957-D 15, 1960/...
         w.

860.4   *Rocky Mountain House Mountaineer.* Ja 5, 1961-Ja 3, 1963/...
         w.

860.5   *Mountaineer.* Ja 10, 1963-
         w.

         Pub. by Norman T.J. Frost, S 19, 1923-F 23, 1927; George H. Pearson,
         Mr 2-Ag 26, 1927; Ebenezer Beveridge, S 2, 1927-Ap 27, 1932; N. Frost,
         My 12, 1932-Ap 26, 1933; William H. Schierholtz, My 3, 1933-My 21,
         1947; J.C. (Jack) Gare and J.E. (Ted) Broughton, My 28, 1947-Ja 29, 1948;
         Broughton, F 1, 1948-Je 25, 1964; Gare, Jl 16, 1964-S 24, 1965; Lawrence
         O. Mazza, S 15, 1967+. Ed. by E.J. Jones, My 28, 1947-?; Grace Austin
         Schierholtz, and John Broughton, Mountaineer Printing and Pub. Co. Ltd., F
         1, 1948-Oc? 1963; John T. Bert, Je 25, 1964-S 13, 1967; Roland Pigeon, Ap
         7, 1976+.
         Jubilee Edition, Je 28, 1962.
         Ref.: **GIS**, pp.133-137.

         AEU   mf S 19, 1923-D 23, 1970
         AEP   or Ja 6, 1971+
                  mf S 19, 1923-D 23, 1970

ROCKYVIEW MUNICIPAL DISTRICT

861   *Rocky Weekly Press.* S 7, 1966-1967//
         w.

         Pub. by Monte G. Keith (Ref.: **AY** 1968).
         Ref.: **CNLU** p.24.

         OONL   or   S 7, 1966

2.1 *Five Village Weekly.* N 6, 1975-D 30? 1980/...
w.

2.2 *Rocky View-Five Village Weekly.* Ja 6? 1981-
w.

Pub. by Irricana Holdings Ltd. Pub. by Dennis Taylor and ed. by Gladys Taylor. To D 1980 served the communities of Acme, Beiseker, Irricana, Kathyrn and Keoma. Became official newspaper for Rocky View Municipal District Ja 1981 (Ref.: Correspondence with Publisher, Ja 10, 1985).

No issues located

Rocky View Times. S 26, 1979-
See **AIRDRIE**. *Rocky View Times* (10).

)CKYFORD

3 *Rockyford (Alta.) Weekly.* Ag? 1917-Ag 29, 1918?//
w.

Pub. and ed. by Leon Louis Plotkins.

AEP or Je 20, Ag 22, Ag 29, 1918

4 *Rockyford Reporter.* 1918?-1922?//
w.

Pub. and ed. by Leon Louis Plotkins (Ref.: **MK** 1920-1922; **CAN** 1923). Pub. in Calgary.

AEP or F 3, 1921

5 *Rockyford Budget.* 1921-1923//
w.

Cessation announced (Ref.: **CPP** v32no7 Jl 1923).
Pub. by W.C. Blount (Ref.: **MK** 1922, 1923).

No issues located

Rockyford Review. 1949-Je 21, 1957?//
w.

Pub. by Thomas W. Pue, Edmonton.
Alberta Golden Jubilee Edition, S 1, 1955.

AEP or Ja 4, 1952-Je 21, 1957

Village Press. D 23, 1976-
See **CARBON**. *Village Press* (239).

ROSALIND

867   *Rosalind Reporter.* Ja 23, 1948-N 30, 1949?//
        w.

        Pub. by Thomas W. Pue, Community Publications of Alberta, Killam and
        Edmonton.

        AEP   or   Ja 23, 1948-N 30, 1949

ROSEBUD

        Village Press. D 23, 1976-
        See **CARBON.** *Village Press* (239).

ROSEBUD CREEK

868   *Rosebud Recorder.* 1920?-Oc 1925?//
        w.

        Rosebud Record. C.A. Vigor, agt. (Ref.: **WRI** 1922).
        Ref.: **CAN** 1921-1926.

        No issues located

ROWLEY

869   *Rowley Recorder.* 1921?-Oc 1926?//
        w.

        Ref.: **CAN** 1922-1927.

        No issues located

RYCROFT

870   *Pisriverskyi Homin.* D 1956-?//
        m.? Ukrainian in Ukr.

        Ref.: **BOM** p.37; **CES1** p.109.

        ACUCES sample issue

871   *Signal.* My 14, 1980-
        w.

        Subtitle: "Serving the Central Peace".
        Pub. by Schierbeck Printing and Pub. Ltd. Pub. and ed. by Peter K.
        Schierbeck, My 14, 1980+ (Ref.: Correspondence with Publisher, N 28,
        1984).

        AEP   or   N 3, 1982+

YLEY

2   *Ryley Times.* N 1909-Mr 9, 1916//
w.

Pub. by L.H. Archer who enlisted for military duty and later re-established *Ryley Times* (873) in 1919.

AEP   or S 14, 1911-Mr 9, 1916

3   *Ryley Times.* D 4, 1919-Ja 17, 1924//
w.

New voluming begun D 21, 1921 (v3no1).
Pub. by L.H. Archer.

AEP   or D 4, 1919-Ja 17, 1924

4   *Ryley Times.* Je 5, 1924-Ap 9, 1925?//
w.

Pub. by Jacob Zantjer.
Ref.: **CAN** 1925.

AEP   or Je 5, 1924-Ap 9, 1925

5   *Temperance Advocate.* Mr 15, 1925?//
w. Prohibitionist

Ed. by Jacob Zantjer.

ACG   or Mr 15, 1925

Ryley Transcript. Mr 9, 1927-Mr 7, 1928
See **VEGREVILLE.** *Vegreville Observer* (987.2).

Ryley Times. Ag 22, 1946-Ag 1952
See **TOFIELD.** *Tofield Mercury* (969).

Ryley Times. Ag 28, 1952-Oc 19, 1967
See **TOFIELD.** *Mercury* (970.2).

. ALBERT

6   *North American News.* 1899//
w.

Pub. and ed. by J.A.H. Prevost (Ref.: *Edmonton Journal* Ja 10, 1958:4).

No issues located

7   *St. Alberta News.* Ap? 1912-D 4, 1914?//
w.

Suspended pub. Ap-D 4, 1914.

Pub. and ed. by Vera R. Hogan, Ap 1912-Ap 1914. Suspended; begun again on D 4, 1914 by Joseph P. Lafranchise. Possibly only one issue pub. after suspension (Ref.: *St. Albert News* D 4, 1914; *St. Albert Gazette* Je 17, 1961).

ACG   or   S 26, Oc 10, 31, 1913; D 4, 1914

878.1   *Etoile de St. Albert.* N 13, 1912-D 31, 1913/...
w. French in Fr. (and Engl.)

878.2   *Etoile de St. Albert / St. Albert Star.* Ja 7, 1914-Je ? 1914//
w. French in Fr. (and Engl.)

Pub. by L'Etoile de St. Albert. Ed. by Joseph P. Lafranchise and Albéric A. Ringuette, N 13, 1912-My 29, 1913; Lafranchise, Je 4, 1913-Je 1914. Probable cessation date Je 1914 (Ref.: **CANF** N 1916:10).
Ref.: **LAND** pp.14-15, 34.

AEPAA mf [N 13, 1912-Ap 29, 1914]
AEP   mf [N 13, 1912-Ap 29, 1914]

879   *St. Albert Gazette.* Ag 1949-Ag 13, 1953//
w.

Absorbed by *Morinville Journal* (765) Ag 20, 1953.
Pub. by Thomas W. Pue, Community Publications of Alberta, Edmonton.

AEP   mf Ja 1, 1949-Ag 13, 1953

880.1   *St. Albert Gazette.* Je 17, 1961-S 3, 1966/...
w.

880.2   *Gazette.* S 10, 1966-Ap 1, 1970/...
w.

880.3   *St. Albert and Sturgeon Gazette.* Ap 8, 1970-Mr 13, 1974/...
w.

880.4   *Gazette.* Mr 20, 1974-
w.

Title varies Mr 27-N 9, 1968: *St. Albert and Sturgeon Gazette, Sturgeon Gazette, Sturgeon and St. Albert Gazette, St. Albert-Sturgeon Gazette.*

Pub. by Sturgeon Pub. Co. Ltd., William J. Netelenbos, Sr., mgr., Je 17, 1961-S 3, 1966; W. Ernie Jamison, W.E.J. Pub. Ltd., S 10, 1966+. Ed. by D.W. (Duff) Jamison.

AEP   mf Je 17, 1961-D 23, 1986
           or Ja 1987+

881   *St. Albert Star.* Ja 25, 1972-Ap? 1973//
w.

Pub. by Sun Pub. Co. Ltd., Edmonton.
Ref.: **CNLU** p.13; **CAN** 1973; **AY** 1974.

OONL or Ja 25, Mr 21, 1972

Hub, St. Albert Edition. Ag 9, 1977-D 6, 1977
See **WESTLOCK.** *Hub* (1016).

PAUL

St. Paul Star. Oc 21? 1920-N 1, 1922?//
w. in Engl. (and Fr.)

Pub. by Star Pub. Co. Ed. by J.E. Buchanan; H.E. Diamond, mgr. Ptd. at
Conservator Office, Fort Saskatchewan until the coming of the railway (Ref.:
CPP v31no3 Mr, 1922).
Ref.: **CAN** 1924.

AEP mf N 11, 1920-Oc 2, 1922

1 *St. Paul Tribune.* S 4, 1925-Oc 2, 1925/...
w. Political — Conservative in Engl. (and Fr.)

AEP mf S 11, 1925

2 *St. Paul Journal.* Oc 9, 1925-
w. Political — Conservative in Engl. (and Fr.)

Suspended pub. Mr 1, 1934-Jl 9, 1935 due to disastrous fire.
Pub. and ed. by Gilbert La Rue, Conservative, S 4, 1925-N 28, 1929;
Ernest C. Fletcher, D 1, 1929-F 20, 1930; Gilbert La Rue, F 27, 1930-Oc 29,
1943; J.A. Thivièrge, N 5, 1943-Jl 20, 1945; George La Rue, Jl 25, 1945-D 2,
1949; L.H. Drouin, St. Paul Journal Ltd., D 9, 1949-Ja 1, 1985; D Drouin, St.
Paul Journal Ltd., Ja 1985+.
Pub. section *Elk Point District News*, Mr 17, 1982+. Pub. supplement *Two
Hills County Journal* (982).
Alberta Golden Jubilee Edition, Jl 7, 1955.

AEP mf S 11, 1925, Oc 9, 1925-D 28, 1983
or Ja 1984+

St. Paul Canadian. My 15, 1934-Jl 1935//
w.

Pub. by Stack and Williams, D.A. Stack, mgr., Walton Williams, ed. Est.
to replace *St. Paul Journal* (883.2) which was suspended due to a fire which
destroyed the office.

AEP mf My 15, 1934-Je 26, 1935

Independent Reformer. 1945//
w.

Pub. in the interests of economical, social and spiritual progress at St.
Paul. Ed. by H. Boyd Traxler.

AEP   mf Jl 25, Ag 1, 1945

SANGUDO

886.1   *Sangudo Star.* Je 12? 1947-Je 8 1948/...
            w.

886.2   *Westerner.* Jl 22, 1948-S 24, 1949//
            w.

            Continued by *Onoway Westerner* (793), Oc 1, 1949.
            Pub. by Elwood P. Hagen, Je 12, 1947-S 3, 1949; Thomas W. Pue, Com-
            munity Publications of Alberta, Edmonton, S 10-S 24, 1949.

            AEP   or   Je 19, 1947-S 24, 1949

887   *Sangudo Chronicle.* My 13? 1972-Mr? 1973//
            w.

            Pub. by T.W. Pue, Sun Colorpress Ltd., Edmonton.
            Ref.: **CNLU** p.14.

            OONL   or   My 27, Je 30, 1972

SCOTT'S COULEE

888   *Outlaw.* My 19, 1896-Je 30, 1896//
            w. Political — General

            Motto: "With Malice Towards All and Charity to None."
            Printed on Fort Macleod *Gazette* press.
            Pub. by Scott's Coulee Pub. Co. Ltd. Ed. by Capt. R. Gordon Matthews,
            Dr. G.A. Kennedy and John Black. Primarily a political rag which main-
            tained an independent policy during its short existence prior to the 1896
            federal election.
            Ref.: **FORT** pp.81-82.

            AEUS   photocopy My 19-Je 30, 1896
            ACG   or   My 19-Je 30, 1896

SEDGEWICK

889   *Sedgewick Eagle* S 6, 1907-1908?//
            w.

            Sedgwick Eagle and *Camrose Mail* (224) now issued together (Ref.: **CPP**
            v18no2 F 1908).

First issue appeared under title *Sedgewick Paper* with offer of $25 to any-one suggesting a name. Pub. by Capt. T. Berville Thomas of Mail Pub. Co., Camrose (REf.: **SED** p.606).

No issues located

0.1   *Sedgewick Sentinel.* Jl 16, 1908-D 19, 1929/...
w.

0.2   *Community Press.* Ap 17, 1930-
w.

Due to economic depression *Sedgewick Sentinel* amalgamated with *Bawlf Sun* (64), *Daysland Press* (302), *Hardisty Mail* (608), *Killam News* (659), *Lougheed Express* (711) and *Strome Despatch* to form *Community Press* (Ref.: **SED**, p.621).

Absorbed *Enterprise*, Alliance (16.2), S 3, 1980.

Pub. by A.J. Honey, Jl 16, 1908-Oc 28, 1915; A.L. Eastly, N 1, 1915-Mr 12, 1942; Arthur W. Eastly, Mr 19, 1942-S 1964; A.C. Eastly, S 24, 1964-Mr 20, 1968; A.W. Eastly, Mr 27, 1968-Oc 9, 1969; Monte G. Keith, Oc 16, 1969-Ap 1981; Rick Truss, My 1981+.

Pub. section *Lougheed Leader*, My 4, 1911-F 15, 1912. Pub. supplement *Enterprise* (16.2) for Daysland, Heisler, Forestburg and Galahad.

AEP   mf Jl 16, 1908-D 22, 1982
or Ja 1983+

Sedgewick Review. 1918//
w.

"In 1918, another newspaper appeared in Sedgewick, called the *Sedgewick Review*. This newspaper was published by W.C. Garrioch who had come to Sedgewick from Edmonton." (Ref.: **SED** p.621).

No issues located

XSMITH

Sexsmith Sentinel. S 1, 1949-Oc 6, 1954?//
w.

Suspended pub. on Oc 6, 1954 (Ref.: *Sexsmith Sentinel* Oc 6, 1954).

Pub. and ed. by A.F. Menzies and Malcolm Angus Menzies, South Peace Pub. Co. Ltd.

AEP   or Ap 5, 1951-Oc 6, 1954

ARPLES

Village Press. D 23, 1976-
See **CARBON**. *Village Press* (239).

SHERWOOD PARK

893   *Sherwood Park Herald.* F 1, 1963-Oc 11, 1968?//
m.; w.; irreg.; 2m.

Frequency varied: m. F 1, 1963-Mr 20, 1964; w. Ap 2, 1964-My 1, 1965;
2m. Ja 11-Oc 11, 1968; irreg. special issues, My 1, 1965-Ja 11, 1968.
Suspended pub. My 1, 1965-Ja 11, 1968; Mr 28-My 17, 1968.
Pub. by James B. McKenzie, Professional Printing Ltd.

AEP   mf F 1, 1963-My 1, 1965; N 6, 27, 1965; F 25, Ap 7, Ap 29,
          1966; S 28, N 2, 1967; Ja 11-Oc 11, 1968

894   *Sherwood Park Sun.* S 26, 1964-Ja 18, 1969?//
w.

Section of *South Edmonton Sun* (432).
Pub. by Thomas W. Pue, Sun Pub. Co. Ltd., Edmonton.
Ref.: **CNLU** p.14.

OONL   or S 26, 1964

895   *Sherwood Park Star.* Oc 31, 1969-My 18, 1977//
irreg.; w.

Suspended pub. Ap 18, 1970-? 1971.
Pub. by Thomas W. Pue, Sun Colorpress Ltd., 1969-Ap 1977; Colin
Alexander, Ap-My 1977. Ed. by Len Stahl, 1969-D 18, 1974; Barry
Schofield, D 31, 1974-F 26, 1975.
Ref.: **CNLU** p.14.

OONL   or Oc 31, 1969; Mr 9, 1972
AEP   mf Ja 30, 1974-S 10, 1975; Ja 7, 1976-My 18, 1977

896.1 *Sherwood Park News.* F 11, 1976-Ja 19, 1977/...
w.

896.2 *News, Sherwood Park.* Ja 26, 1977-D 13, 1978/...
w.

896.3 *Sherwood Park News.* D 20, 1978-
w.; 2w.

Superceded *County News,* Strathcona County (939.2).
Friday ed. entitled *Sherwood Park News Weekender,* Ag 17, 1979-My 23,
1980.
Frequency varies: w. F 1976-Ag 30, 1978; 2w. S 1, 1978+.
Pub. by Ootes Press Ltd., Fort Saskatchewan, F 1976-N 1982. Ed. by
David Holehouse, F 1976-S 14, 1977; Dan Allen, S 21, 1977-S 1, 1978; Don
Wanagas, S 1-Oc 11, 1978; Rob White, Oc 25, 1978-S 28, 1979. Pub. by Dan

Allen, Oc 3, 1979-My 6, 1981; Terry Carroll, My 13, 1981+. Ed. by Richard Jeffrey, Oc 3, 1979-Ap 29, 1981; Dana Weber, Je 3, 1981-My 14, 1982; Ken Whyte, My 19, 1982+. Sold to Bowes Pub. Ltd. D 1, 1982.

AEP mf Ja 5, 1977-Je 27, 1980
   or Je 30, 1980+

BALD

Sibbald Recorder. 1920//
w.

 Ref.: **CAN** 1921

No issues located

Sibbald Times. S 2, 1920-Ag 24, 1922?//
w.

 Pub. and ed. by Jacob Zantjer.
 Ref.: **MK** 1922.

AEP or S 2, 1920-Ag 24, 1922

VE LAKE

Lesser Slave Lake Star. Oc 31, 1958-F 13, 1960//
w.

 Absorbed by *High Prairie Progress* (619.3), F 27, 1960.
 Pub. and ed. by Thomas W. Pue, Sun Pub. Co. Ltd., Edmonton.

AEP or Oc 31, 1958-F 13, 1960

Slave Lake Centennial Press. Jl 1, 1967-D 29, 1970//
2m.

 Absorbed by *Athabasca Echo* (30.3), Ja 6, 1971.
 Est. by J. Gordon Delaney. Pub. by Athabasca Echo Printing Ltd. Ed. by Evelyn R. Rogers.

AEUB or Ja 15, 1968-D 29, 1970

Port of Slave Lake Oiler. Ja 13, 1970-Oc 25, 1972/...
w.

Lesser Slave Lake Scope. N 1, 1972-Oc 26, 1973/...
w.; 2w.

Scope. Oc 30, 1973-
2w.; w.

Frequency varied: w. Ja 13, 1970-Mr 1973; 2w. Mr 12-D 19, 1973; w. Ja 3, 1974+.

Est. as community service by John and Kay Stillwell and Bruce D. Thomas. Taken over as a full-time proposition by Thomas, Ja 1971. Thomas est. Port of Slave Lake Oiler Newspaper Ltd., N 1, 1972. Ed. by Thomas Ja 13, 1970+.

Pub. supplement entitled *Lesser Slave Lake Scope* Je 1-Oc 25, 1972. *Lesser Slave Lake Scope* and *Port of Slave Lake Oiler* combined N 1, 1972 under title *Lesser Slave Lake Scope.*

AEP   or   My 4, 1972+

902   *Northland Free Press.* S 27, 1972-N 4, 1975//
              w.

Title did not appear until Oc 18, 1972.
Pub. and co-ed. by John and Kay Stillwell, Northland Press.
Included supplement *Northern Messenger* (622).

AEP   or   S 27, 1972-N 4, 1975

903   *Lakeside Leader.* N 12, 1975-
              w.

·Pub. and ed. by Jerry Wallsten, N 12, 1975-Ja 15, 1981; Joy Kennedy, Ja 15-Je 24, 1981; Jeff Burgar, Lakeside Leader Ltd., Jl 1, 1981+.

AEP   or   N 12, 1975+
AEUB   or   N 12, 1975-F 11, 1976

SMOKY LAKE

904   *Holos Pravdy / Voice of Truth.* ? 1937-Ap 1960//
              w.; 2m.; m.   Ukrainian in Ukr.

Frequency varied: w. ? 1937-Oc 31, 1953; 2m. N 23-N 31, 1953; m. D 1953-Ap 1960.
Place of pub. varied: Smoky Lake, ? 1937-S 20, 1952; Edmonton, D 1, 1952-Ap 1960.
Ukrainian democratic paper ed. by Rev. Michael N. Cependa. Pub. by Voice of Truth Pub. Co., 1937-S 20, 1952; Economy Pub. and Printers, 1952-Ap 1960.
Ref.: **BOM** p.25; **MARU** p.497.

AEU   mf [Ap 19, 1941-Ap 1960]

905.1   *Smoky Lake Gazette.* 1948?-N 16, 1968/...
              w.

905.2   *Smoky Lake Sun.* N 23, 1968-Ja 18, 1969//
              w.

Pub. and ed. by Thomas W. Pue, Sun Pub. Co. Ltd., Edmonton.

Included supplement *Alberta Country Life* (442).
Alberta Golden Jubilee Edition, S 2, 1955.
Ref.: **CNLU**, p.14.

AEP   or   Ja 2, 1952-D 14, 1968

Smoky Lake Star. 1970?-Ag 24, 1974/...
w.

Smoky Lake Gazette. S 7, 1974-My 14, 1977//
w.

Title varied: e.g. *Smoky Lake County Star.*
Pub. by Thomas W. Pue, Sun Colorpress Ltd., Edmonton to Ap 16, 1977;
Colin Alexander, Sun Colorpress Ltd., Ap 23-My 14, 1977.
Ref.: **CNLU** p.14.

OONL   or   F 7, 1970
AEP   or   My 13, 1972-Ag 23, 1975; Ja 10, 1976-My 14, 1977

Smoky Lake Signal. My 3, 1978-
w.

Pub. and ed. by Lorne Taylor, Smoky Signal Press Ltd. (Ref.: Correspondence with Publisher, Ap 25, 1984).

AEP   or   Ja 23, 1980+

KY RIVER MUNICIPAL DISTRICT

Courier. S 15, 1952-My 25, 1953/...
w.

Smoky River News. Je 1, 1953-My 4, 1963//
w.

Est. by Maurice Charles Sullivan, S 1952. Ed. in Falher, pub. in
Edmonton. Sold to Thomas W. Pue, Community Publications of Alberta,
Edmonton, pub., N 29, 1952-My 4, 1963.
Alberta Golden Jubilee Edition, Ag 31, 1955.

AEP   or   N 29, 1952-My 4, 1963

Smoky River Express. My 3, 1972-
See **FALHER.** *Smoky River Express* (529.2).

IT RIVER

Spirit River Times. Je? 1916-1917?//
See Supplement (1086)

909   *Spirit River Echo.* Ag 15? 1917-Ap 8, 1921//
           w.

               Suspended pub. Ap 26-Jl 11, 1918; Ja 3-F 27, 1919.
               Pub. and ed. by G.A. Poole, Ag 15? 1917-Ap 19, 1918; G. Caruthers
               Findley, Jl 12-D 27, 1918; F.H. Cramer, F 28, 1919-Ap 8, 1921.

           AEP   or   S 26, 1917-Ap 8, 1921

910.1   *Spirit River Signal.* Ap 20, 1951-S 24, 1954/...
           w.

910.2   *Signal.* Oc 1, 1954-Mr 20, 1959/...
           w.

910.3   *Spirit River Signal.* Ap 10, 1959-Ap 3, 1965//
           w.

               Pub. by A.F. Menzies, South Peace Pub. Co. Ltd. Ed. by Helen Menzies,
               Ap 20, 1951-N 12, 1954; Malcolm Angus Menzies, N 12, 1954-Mr 20, 1959.
               Sold to Thomas W. Pue, Sun Pub. Co. Ltd., Edmonton, Ap 1, 1959.

           AEP   or   My 11, 1951-Ap 3, 1965

911   *Spirit River Bulletin.* S 1964-S 1969//
           m.

               Pub. and ed. by Peter James Weston (Ref.: Publisher).

           No issues located

SPRINGBANK

           Pioneer. S 3, 1980-My 26, 1982
           See **COCHRANE**. *Pioneer* (282).

SPRUCE GROVE

912   *Spruce Grove Star.* D 5, 1970-D 3, 1977//
           w.

               Pub. by Thomas W. Pue, Sun Colorpress Ltd., Edmonton to My 14, 1977;
               Sherwood Park Pub. Ltd., S?-D 1977.
               Ref.: CNLU p.14.

           OONL   or   D 5, 1970
           AEP   or   F 2, 1974-My 14, 1977

           Spruce Grove Sentinel. Ja 19, 1971-Ap 27, 1971
           See **STONY PLAIN**. *Reporter* (937).

Spruce Grove Reporter. My 4, 1971-D 19, 1972
See **STONY PLAIN.** *Reporter* (937).

Grove Examiner. Ap 2, 1974-Ap 4, 1979/...
w.

Examiner: Spruce Grove Edition. Ap 11, 1979-Jl 18, 1979/...
w.

Grove Examiner. Jl 25, 1979-D 30, 1980/...
w.

Examiner. Ja 7, 1981-
w.

Pub. by David C. Wilson, House of Print Ltd., Ap 2, 1974-Oc 12, 1976.
Sold to Grove Pub. Ltd. Oc 19, 1976. Pub. by Terry Clements, Oc 19, 1976-
Oc 5, 1977; Randy Lennon, Oc 12, 1977-F 21, 1979; Terry Clements, Ap 11,
1979-My 30, 1982. Sold Je 1, 1982 to Lynard Pub. Ltd. Pub. by Steven
Dills, Je 1, 1982+.

Pub. *Parkland County Examiner* (799) as supplement D 7, 1977-Ja 18,
1978; as integrated section, Ja 25, 1978+.

AEP or Ap 2, 1974+

ND OFF

Sun Dance Echo. F? 1964-Mr 1966?//
m. Native (Bl)

Pub. by Local Press, Cardston, for Blood Reserve, Stand Off. Ed. by Reggie Black Plume.

Ref.: **CNLR** p.252; **DANK** p.401.

ACG or Ap 1964-Mr 1966

Kainai News. F 15, 1968-
m.; 2m. Native (Bl)

Frequency varied: m. F 15, 1968-N 15, 1970; 2m. N 30, 1970+.

Pub. by Blood Indian Tribe, F 15, 1968-Oc 15, 1970; Indian News Media
Society, N 1970+. Ed. by Caen Bly, F 15, 1968-Jl 1, 1980; Jackie Red Crow,
Jl 2, 1980+.

Ref.: **DANK** p.236.

AEUB or Ja 15, 1970+
AEU or Ja 1976+

STANDARD

916   *Standard Enterprize.* 1920?-N 1921?//
           w.

                Ref.: **CAN** 1921, 1922.

           No issues located

917   *Standard Gazette.* 1921?-Oc 1926?//
           w.

                Pub. by Gazette Pub. Co.
                Ref.: **MK** 1922; **CAN** 1923-1927.

           No issues located

           Village Press. D 23, 1976-
                See **CARBON.** *Village Press* (239).

STARLAND MUNICIPAL DISTRICT

918   *Starland Reporter.* 1950-Ap 14, 1955//
           w.

                Pub. by Thomas W. Pue, Edmonton.

           AEP   or   Ja 4, 1952-Ap 14, 1955

STAVELY

919   *Stavely Gazette.* 1904-1905?//
           w.

                Pub. by Claresholm Pub. Co. (Ref.: **HENW** 1905).

           No issues located

920   *Stavely Standard.* Jl 1909-Ja 29, 1914?//
           w.

                Pub. and ed. by A. Nicholson.
                Ref.: **CAN** 1914.

           AEP   or   Ag 25, 1910-Ja 29, 1914

921   *Stavely Advertiser.* Ap 9, 1914-S 2, 1914?//
           w.

                Pub. by Harwood Duncan, Claresholm.

           AEP   or   Ap 9-S 2, 1914

Stavely Advertiser. Jl 14? 1916-Jl 30, 1965//
w.

Pub. and ed. by Robert K. Peck, Claresholm Review-Advertiser, Jl 1916-F 28, 1918; Leonard C. Newsom, Mr 1, 1918-S 18, 1925; J.D.S. Barrett, S 25, 1925-Ja 1, 1926; Wilson L. Kew, Ja 7, 1926-Ja 1942; Stanley Orris, Ja 9-Mr 20, 1942; Duane J. Walker, Mr 27, 1942-My 30, 1947; Gordon Neale, Claresholm Local Press, Je 6, 1947-Ja 29, 1965; Eldon George (Andy) Anderson, F 1-Jl 30, 1965.

Alberta Golden Jubilee Edition, S 23, 1955.

AEP   or   Jl 28, 1916-Jl 30, 1965

TTLER

Stettler Independent. Je 16, 1906-
w.

Official organ of Central Alberta Stock Grower's Association, S 24, 1907-My 25, 1916.

Pub. by William Godson, Je 16, 1906-Jl 14, 1908; Charles Lavelle Willis, Jl 15, 1908-My 10, 1956; Roy Ward Willis, My 11, 1956-Ja 3, 1973; R.W. Willis and Sons, Ja 10, 1973-Oc 5, 1977; R. Charles Willis, Oc 12, 1977+. Ed. by R.W. Willis, Ja 10, 1973+.

Pub. section *Gadsby Weekly Bulletin* Mr 6-N 20, 1913. Pub. supplement *Hoofprints* distributed in Castor, Coronation and Consort, N 10, 1971+.

Special Prosperity Issue, Oc 1913; Pioneer Edition, Je 18, 1931; Alberta Golden Jubilee Edition, Jl 28, 1955; 60th Anniversary Edition, Je 30, 1965; 75th Anniversary Edition, Je 24, 1981.

Ref.: **DAL** pp.92-93.

AEP   mf Je 23, 1906-D 30, 1981
         or Ja 1982+
ACG   or Je 18, 1931; Je 30, 1965

Stettler Gazette. 1909?-Oc 1911?//
w.

Ref.: **CAN** 1910, 1911, 1912.

No issues located

Citizen. D? 1909-1911?//
w.

Pub. and ed. by William Godson (Ref.: **MK** 1911; *Red Deer Advocate,* D 24, 1909).

No issues located

Actioneer. Oc 20, 1971-My 6, 1981/...
w.

926.2   *Voice of the Actioneer.* My 20, 1981-Ag 26, 1981//
              2m.

              Title varied: *Stettler Actioneer.*
              Frequency varied: w. Oc 20, 1971-Ap 29, 1981; 2m. My 6-Ag 26, 1981.
              New voluming started Ja 21, 1981 (v1no3).
              Pub. by Danny and Judy Gibson, then Stettler Actioneer Ltd.
              Ref.: **CNLU** p.25.

              OONL   or   Oc 20, 1971
              AEP   or   Ja 14-D 22, 1976
                          mf   Ja 5, 1977-Ag 26, 1981

STIRLING

927   *New Stirling Star.* Ap 21, 1910-Ag 24, 1910?//
              w.

              Pub. by Andrew E. Murdoch; ed. by David Horton Elton.

              AEP   or   Ap 21-Ag 24, 1910

STONY PLAIN MUNICIPAL DISTRICT

928   *Stony Plain Sun.* Ja 19, 1963-Ap 1, 1967//
              w.

              Pub. by Thomas W. Pue, Edmonton.

              AEP   mf   Ja 19, 1963-Ap 1, 1967

STONY PLAIN

929   *Gazette.* 1909-1910?//
              w.

              Ref.: **CAN** 1910.

              No issues located

930.1   *Stony Plain Advertiser and Lac Ste Anne Reporter.* D 9, 1909-Oc
              8, 1910/...
              w.

930.2   *Stony Plain Advertiser.* Oc 15, 1910-Ap 1, 1911//
              w.

              Superceded by *Stony Plain Advertiser* (931).
              Issue of D 9, 1909 entitled *Stony Plain Advertiser.*
              Pub. and ed. by F.H. Schooley, D 9, 1909-Ap? 1910; William Worton, Ap
              28, 1910-Ap 1, 1911.

Cessation announced. (Ref.: **CPP** v20no5 My, 1911).

AEP mf D 9, 1909-Ap 1, 1911

Stony Plain Advertiser. Oc 7, 1911-Ap 26? 1913//
w.

Superceded *Stony Plain Advertiser* (930.2).
Pub. and ed. by William Worton.

AEP mf Oc 7, 1911-Ap 26, 1913

Rural Weekly News and Rube's Farm Fun. 1912-1917?//
w. Agriculture Political — United Farmers of Alberta

A weekly newspaper published in the interest of the man on the land, to champion his cause, to teach co-operation among farmers and to preach the many truths advocated by the members of the U.F.A. (Ref.: Issue of Jl 24, 1915). Ed. by A.E. Bates.
Ref.: **CNLU** p.25.

AEP, ACG, AEPAA mf Jl 24, 1915; Ja 22, 1916

Stony Plain News. 1913?-Oc 23, 1914//
w. Political — Liberal

Title varied: *Aurora News* (Ref.: **CAN** 1915).
Ref.: *Mirror* Stony Plain, My 6, 1915; **CAN** 1914, 1915.

No issues located

Mirror. My 6, 1915-My 25, 1916//
w.

Pub. and ed. by W.H. Ashley.

AEP mf My 6, 1915-My 25, 1916

Stony Plain Herald. 1919-1920?//
w.

Pub. by S.H. Kettle (Ref.: **MK** 1919, 1920).

No issues located

Stony Plain Sun. Ag 5? 1920-Oc 27, 1938?//
w.

Pub. and ed. by Francis Cormack (Ref.: *Edmonton Journal* My 30, 1942; **CAN** 1940).

AEP mf Je 16, 1921-Oc 27, 1938

Stony Plain Reporter. Ap 6, 1945-Mr 8, 1967/...
w.

937.2   *Reporter.* Mr 15, 1967-
            w.

            Pub. by News of the North Pub. Ltd. and ed. by W.H. (Duke) DeCoursey,
            Ap 6, 1945-S 18, 1946; Gordon Smith, S 25, 1946-Ap 18, 1962; Walter
            Mandick, My 2, 1962-Mr 28, 1972. Sold Ap 1, 1972 to Lynard Pub. Ltd.
            Pub. by Arnie Larkins, Ap 1, 1972-Oc 26, 1976; Barbara Wright, N 2, 1976-
            N 11, 1981; Steven Dills, N 18, 1981+. Ed. by Stan Hilman, My 2-Ag 22,
            1972; Gary MacDonald, Oc 31, 1972-F 17, 1976; Wayne Rothe, F 24, 1976-
            Oc 31, 1978; Ursula Tillmann, D 12, 1978-Oc 31, 1979; John Morran, N 1,
            1979-My 6, 1981; Janice Leffler, My 13-Oc 14, 1981; Craig Spence, Oc 21,
            1981-Mr 24, 1982; Richard McGuire, Mr 31, 1982+.
            Pub. section *Spruce Grove Sentinel,* Ja 19-Ap 27, 1971; *Spruce Grove
            Reporter,* My 4, 1971-D 19, 1972; *Lac Ste Anne Advance,* F 9-Ap 27, 1971;
            Lac Ste Anne Reporter, My 4, 1971-D 19, 1972.
            Alberta Golden Jubilee Edition, Ap 3, 1955.

            AEP   mf   Ap 6, 1945-D 30, 1980
                         or   Ja 7, 1981+

STRATHCONA

Incorporated as a town Ap 29, 1899. Amalgamated with Edmonton in 1912.
See **EDMONTON** for newspapers serving Strathcona before amalgamation:

Advertiser (341)
Alberta Sun (340)
Evening Chronicle (350)
South Edmonton News (336)
Strathcona Chronicle (345)
Strathcona Plain Dealer (336.3)

STRATHCONA COUNTY

938   *Strathcona Wedge.* S 16, 1967-Jl? 1968//
            w.

            Pub. by W. Ernie Jamison, W.E.J. Pub. Ltd., St. Albert.
            Ref.: **CNLU** p.24.

            OONL   or   S 16, 1967

939.1   *Strathcona County News.* S 1969-Jl 30, 1975/...
            w.

939.2   *County News.* Ag 6, 1975-Ja 28, 1976//
            w.

            Superceded by *Sherwood Park News* (896).
            Pub. by John J. Bell and D.S. Moore, Fort Record Ltd., S 1969-Ap 25,
            1975; Jake J. Ootes, Ootes Press Ltd., My 8, 1975+.
            Ref.: **CNLU** p.24.

OONL   or   Oc 30, 1969; Ja 1, 22, 1970
AEP   mf   My 4, 1972-My 30, 1974; Ja 9, 1975-Ja 28, 1976

RATHMORE

1   *Strathmore and Bow Valley Standard.* Oc 2, 1909-Jl 31, 1929/...
     w.

2   *Strathmore Standard.* Ag 7, 1929-S 25, 1947/...
     w.

3   *Strathmore and Bow Valley Standard.* Oc 2, 1947-Mr 3, 1955/...
     w.

4   *Strathmore Standard.* Mr 10, 1955-
     w.

   William Park Evans, prop., Oc 2, 1909-Oc 1, 1910; John W. Mackenzie,
mgr., Oc 2, 1909-Oc 1, 1910; Mackenzie, pub. and ed., Oc 8, 1910-Ja 27,
1926; Andrew A. Moore, ed. F 1, 1926-N 29, 1933; Alberta M. Moore, pub.,
D 1, 1933-Mr 27, 1947; Charles A. MacLean, pub., Ap 3, 1947-Mr 29, 1951;
H.F. (Hec) MacLean, pub., Ap 1, 1951-Ja 31, 1957; Keith Bergh, pub., F 1,
1957-My 27, 1965; Keith D. Farran, pub., Je 1, 1965-Ap 27, 1977; Bob
Giles, pub., My 4, 1977+.
   Currently official newspaper for County of Wheatland. Provided free to
ratepayers.

AEPAA   mf   Oc 2, 1909-D 7, 1944; Ja 3, 1946-D 30, 1948
AEP   or   Ja 6, 1949+

ROME

   Strome Despatch. Oc 27? 1910-1929?//
   w.

   Pub. by Camrose Pub. Co., 1910-Ap 1912. Ed. by R.R. Elliot, 1910-Ap
27, 1911; Thomas G. Jenkyns, My 4-Oc 19, 1911; Bert J. Klebe. Oc 26,
1911-Ap 25, 1912; W. Frank Johnston, My 2, 1912-1929 (Ref.: MK 1929;
CAN 1930).

AEP   or   Ja 5, 1911-D 29, 1922; Jl 2, 1925-N 8, 1928

   Strome Star. Ja 23, 1947-Oc 25, 1950?//
   w.

   Pub. by Thomas W. Pue, Community Publications of Alberta, Killam and
Edmonton.
   Ref.: AY 1952.

AEP   or   Ja 23, 1947-Oc 25, 1950

STURGEON MUNICIPAL DISTRICT

943.1   *Sturgeon Journal.* Je 3, 1961-N 16, 1968/...
           w.

943.2   *Sturgeon Sun.* N 23, 1968-Ja 18, 1969//
           w.

           Continued *Morinville Journal* (765), Je 3, 1961.
           Pub. by Thomas W. Pue, Sun Pub. Co. Ltd., Edmonton.
           Included supplement *Alberta Country Life* (442).

           AEP   or   Je 3, 1961-D 14, 1968

           Sturgeon Gazette. Ap 8, 1970-Mr 13, 1974
           See **ST. ALBERT.** *Gazette* (880.4).

SUNDRE

944   *Sundre News-Advertiser.* Mr 1957-? 1957//
           2m.

           Ed. by Ed M. Vye. Printed by Olds Gazette.
           Ref.: **CNLU**, p.26.

           OONL   or   Jl 1, 1957

945.1   *Sundre Round Up.* F 4, 1960-Ap 25, 1973/...
           w.

945.2   *Sundre Round Up (1973).* My 2, 1973-S 20, 1978/...
           w.

945.3   *Sundre Round Up Publishing Ltd.* S 27, 1978-
           w.

           Pub. by Muriel Eskrick and Lorraine Coutts, F 4, 1960-1962; L.J.
           Rushka, 1962-Ap 25, 1973 (Ref.: *Sundre Round Up*, My 20, 1971); James H.
           Packer, My 1, 1973+. Ed. by R.W. (Bill) Scott, My 1, 1978+.

           AEP   or   Je 26, 1969+

SUNNYSLOPE

           Sunnyslope Sun. 1909-1914
           See **ACME.** *Acme News* (1).

ALWELL

Swalwell Recorder. 1920-1921?//
See Supplement (1087)

Chronicle, Swalwell Section. N 3, 1927-Ap 5, 1928
See **CARBON.** *Carbon Chronicle (238).*

Village Press. D 23, 1976-
See **CARBON.** *Village Press (239).*

AN HILLS

Swan Hills Grizzly. 1977//
w.

Pub. by Thomas W. Pue, Sun Colorpress Ltd., Edmonton (Ref.: **CARD** 1977, 1978).

No issues located

Grizzly Gazette. My 1977-
w.

Pub. by Barrhead Printers and Stationers Ltd. Pub. by Terry Clements, 1977-1982; Al Blackmere, 1982+. Ed. by Doris Fraser, Dave Orey, 1980-1982 (Ref.: **DATA** 1980-1983).

No issues located

VAN LAKE

Times. Mr 5? 1913-1914//
2m. in Engl. (and Fr.)

Pub. by Sylvan Lake Trading Company (Ref.: *Sylvan Lake World* F 1, 1923).

ARDA or Ap 1, 1913

Sylvan Lake World. S 19, 1922-My 21, 1926?//
w.

Pub. and ed. by Chester E. Moffet and K.A. Stockwell, S 19-Oc 3, 1922; Will D. MacKay lessee, Oc 10, 1922-Ap 31, 1925; W.M.C. Thomas, My 5, 1925-My 21, 1926.

ACU mf S 19, 1922-My 21, 1926

Advertiser. 1932-Ag 31? 1933//
w.

Pub. by Ernest C. Fletcher and David C. Peterson. Printed by Red Deer *Optimist.*

Issued in summer months only (Ref.: **MK** 1933).

No issues located

951.1   *Sylvan Lake News.* Oc 31, 1935-N 10, 1960/...
      w.

951.2   *Parkland Review and Sylvan Lake News.* N 17, 1960-Ag 24?
      1966/...
      w.

951.3   *Sylvan Lake News.* S 8, 1966-
      w.

      Pub. and ed. by Charles L. Dunford and C. Warren Dunford, Sylvan Press Ltd., Oc 31, 1935-S 3, 1964 (Ref.: *Sylvan Lake News*, N 1, 1973). Pub. by C.W. Dunford, S 10, 1964-Je 30, 1966; Monte G. Keith, Parkland Pub., Jl 1, 1966-Je 30, 1969; Jack A. and Olive Parry, Parry Pub. Ltd., Jl 1, 1969-Oc 31, 1980; Gary MacDonald, Sylvan Lake News Ltd., N 1, 1980+. Ed. by Harold Harrison, Jl 1, 1969-Ag 30, 1973; Barry Marshall, N 1-D 1973; Joyce Piller, Ja 1974-Jl 30, 1980.
      Alberta Golden Jubilee Edition, S 1, 1955.

      ACU   mf   Ja 2, 1936-D 22, 1953
      AEP   or   Ja 7, 1954+

TABER

952   *Taber Free Press.* F 21, 1907-Ag 25, 1910?//
      w.

      Suspended pub. D 9, 1909-F 3, 1910. Pub. and ed. by W.A.M. Bellwood, 1907-D 9, 1909; A.N. Mowat, lessee, F 3-Ag 1910 (Ref.: *Taber Times* Je 25, 1980; **CAN** 1911).

      AEP   mf   S 5, 1907-Ag 25, 1910

953   *Taber Advertiser.* Mr 31? 1910-Oc? 1911//
      w.

      Pub. by Ernest Cook, Advertiser Pub. Co. (Ref.: *Taber Times* Je 25, 1980; **TAB** p.86).

No issues located

954   *Taber Times.* My 13, 1911-
      w.

      Pub. Archie McLean and ed. by Colin G. Groff, My 13, 1911-Oc 2, 1919; W.P. Cotton, Oc 9, 1919-Oc 28, 1920; Thomas W. Green, N 4, 1920-S 29, 1927; Arthur H. Avery, Oc 6, 1927-Je 29, 1966; H. George Meyer, Jl 1, 1966-N 26, 1980; Walter W. Koyanagi and Meyer, D 3, 1980-Ja 1983; R. Schellenberg, Ja 1983+.

Special Anniversary Issue, Je 25, 1980.

AEP mf My 13, 1911-D 28, 1983
  or Ja 1984+

5 *Chinook Belt Advertiser.* D 1960-1961?//
  w.

No pub. or ed. named.

AEP mf Ap 5, 1961

ORHILD COUNTY

5 *Thorhild County News.* S 22, 1967-1969?//
  w.

Pub. by W. Ernie Jamison, WEJ Printing and Pub. Ltd., St. Albert.
Pub. *Redwater Recorder* as section.
Ref.: **CAN** 1969; **CNLU** p.27.

OONL or S 22, 1967

7 *Thorhild Star.* D 19, 1970-My 14, 1977//
  w.

Title varied: *Thorhild County Star.*
Pub. by Sun Colorpress Ltd., Edmonton.
Ref.: **CNLU** p.15.

OONL or D 19, 1970
AEP or F 2, 1974-My 7, 1977

8 *News.* Mr 15, 1974-D 3, 1986//
  w.

Continued *Thorhild News* (960) and *Redwater News* (850) which combined Mr 15, 1974.
Title varied: *Redwater-Thorhild News.*
Pub. by John MacDonald, Westlock News Ltd. Ed. by Judith Elizabeth Crewe, Jl 2, 1982-D 1986.

AEP or Mr 15, 1974+ (filed with Redwater newspapers).

ORHILD

1 *Thorhild Tribune.* Mr 19? 1949-N 16, 1968/...
  w.

2 *Thorhild Sun.* N 23, 1968-Ja 18, 1969//
  w.

Suspended pub. Ag 5, 1953-Ag 2, 1955.
Pub. by Thomas W. Pue, Community Publications of Alberta and Sun Pub. Co. Ltd., Edmonton.

Included supplement *Alberta Country Life* (442).
Alberta Golden Jubilee Edition, Ag 31, 1955.
Ref.: **CNLU**, p.15.

AEP   or   Mr 26, 1949-Ag 4, 1953; Ag 3, 1955-D 21, 1968

960   *Thorhild News.* Ap 28? 1972-Mr 8, 1974//
         w.

Title varied: *Redwater-Thorhild News.*
Combined with *Redwater News* (850) to form *News,* Thorhild County (958).
Pub. by Westlock News Ltd. Ed. by John MacDonald.

AEP   or   My 5, 1972-Mr 8, 1974

THORSBY

961   *Western Messenger.* 1937-Mr 30, 1961//
         w.

Absorbed by *Representative,* Leduc (689) Ap 6, 1961.
Pub. in Leduc by owners of *Representative* (Ref.: *Representative,* Leduc, Mr 30, 1961; **MK** 1938-1942; **CAN** 1961).

No issues located

962   *Thorsby Star.* D 5, 1970-Ap? 1973//
         w.

Pub. by Thomas W. Pue, Sun Pub. Co. Ltd., Edmonton.
Ref.: **CNLU** p.15; **CAN** 1972, 1973.

OONL   or   D 5, 1970

THREE HILLS

963   *Three Hills Herald.* 1911//
         w.

Pub. by *Bowden News,* Bowden (Ref.: **MK** 1911).

No issues located

964   *Three Hills Review.* Ja 7, 1915-Ag 13, 1915?//
         w.

Pub. by H.G. Knight, Three Hills Pub. Co.

AEP   or   Ja 7-Ag 13, 1915

965.1   *Three Hills Capital.* N 5, 1915-F 21, 1979/...
         w.

5.2 *Capital.* F 28, 1979-
w.

Pub. and ed. by Charles A. Roulston, N 5-D 31, 1915; J.J.R. Thompson, Ja 7-Je 16, 1916; T.W. Manning, Je 23, 1916-Ag 3, 1917; Charles H. Leathley, Ag 10, 1917-Oc 25, 1918; Hubert Peters, N 1, 1918-Mr 31, 1920?; C.H. Leathley, Ap 7, 1920-D 6, 1934; Gladys Leathley, D 13, 1934-Ag 29, 1935; Edouard J. Rouleau, S 1, 1935-Ap 30, 1936; John A. Strachan, My 1, 1936-Je? 1939; Melville Leathley, Je ? 1939-Jl 31, 1946; C.J. Davidson, Ag 1-N 27, 1946; B.N. Neutzling, D 4, 1946-F 1, 1956; R.V. (Bob) Dau, F 8, 1956-Ap 6, 1977; Betty Dau, Ap 13, 1977-D 31, 1979; Timothy J. Shearlaw, Ja 1, 1980+.
Presently serves Municipal District of Kneehill and provided free to ratepayers.
Ref.: **DAL**, p.94.

AEP   or   N 5, 1915-D 27, 1922; Ja 7, 1926-Jl 6, 1939; Ja 18, 1940+

Three Hills News. 1922?-Oc 1924?//
w.

Ref.: **CAN** 1923, 1924, 1925.

No issues located

FIELD

Tofield Standard. Ag 27? 1907-My 10, 1917//
w.

Title Varied: *Tofield Star,* Ag 27, 1907 by W.A. Pratten (Ref.: **PHI**, p.17).
Pub. and ed. by Robert N. Whillans, Standard Press Ltd. Ceased pub. when Whillans moved to Peace River to est. *Peace River Standard* (801).

AEP   mf Oc 1, 1907-My 10, 1917

Tofield Advertiser. Mr 29, 1917-Mr 14, 1918?//
w. Political — Liberal

Pub. and ed. by C.W. Barnes (Ref.: *Tofield Standard* Mr 29, 1917).

AEP   mf My 24, 1917-Mr 14, 1918

Tofield Mercury. Ag 28, 1918-Ag 14, 1952//
w.

Superceded by *Tofield Mercury* (970).
Title varied: *Mercury,* Jan 10-Ag 15, 1946.
Pub. and ed. by William Worton.
Pub. section entitled *Ryley Times,* Ag 22, 1946-Ag 1952.

AEP   mf Ag 28, 1918-Ag 14, 1952

970.1   *Tofield Mercury.* Ag 28, 1952-Ja 25, 1962/...
          w.

970.2   *Mercury.* F 1, 1962-
          w.

          Superceded *Tofield Mercury* (969).
          Pub. and ed. by Cliff Patterson, Ag 28, 1952-Ja 25, 1962. Sold to Camrose
          Canadian Ltd., Ja 25, 1962. Pub. by H. George Meyer, F 1, 1962-Je 23, 1966;
          Charles A. MacLean, Je 23, 1966+. Ed. by Ed Clinton, N 16, 1967+.
          Pub. section *Ryley Times,* Ag 28, 1952-Oc 19, 1967.
          Alberta Golden Jubilee Edition, Ag 25, 1955.

          AEP   mf Ag 28, 1952-D 1985
                       or Ja 1986+

TRAVERS

971   *Travers Weekly.* 1917-1918//
          w.

          Satellite of *Calgary Western Standard* (142.5) (Ref.: **CPP** v26no11 N
          1917).
          Pub. by Standard Newspaper Syndicate, Calgary. (Ref.: **MK** 1918; **CAN**
          1920).

          No issues located

TROCHU

972   *Trochu Times.* 1911-1913?//
          w.

          Pub. by *Bowden News,* Bowden (Ref.: **MK** 1911, 1913; **CAN** 1911).

          No issues located

973   *Trochu Tribune.* Mr 10, 1911-Je 16, 1977//
          w.

          Subtitle Ag 11, 1933-D 24, 1970: "With which is Incorporated the *Elnora
          Advance.*"
          Absorbed *Elnora Advance* (516), Ag 11, 1933.
          Pub. and ed. by A.K. MacMartin, Mr 10, 1911-Ag 23, 1912; Frank
          Thynne, Tribune Printing Co., Ag 30, 1912-Je 13, 1919; William Cornelius
          Love Watson, Je 27, 1919-N 9, 1934; W.A. Hamper, N 16? 1934-Oc 18,
          1935; Ernest Frank Gare, Oc 25, 1935-Mr 21, 1946; Sam C. Stuart, Ap 4,
          1946-Jl 31, 1947; Ralph F. Stuart, Ag 1, 1947-My 24, 1951; C.C. Stuart, My
          31, 1951-Mr 27, 1952; Ralph F. Stuart, Ap 3, 1952-Je 16, 1977.
          Last regular issue pub. Je 16, 1977; occasional issue pub. S 1, 1977.

Alberta Golden Jubilee Edition, S 8, 1955; 50th Anniversary Issue, Je 2, 1960; Trochu Golden Jubilee Issue, Je 22, 1961.

AEP or Mr 10, 1911-Je 16, 1977; S 1, 1977

4   *Trochu's Community Voice.* Oc 25? 1977-
w.

Pub. by Irricana Holdings Ltd. Pub. by Dennis Taylor and ed. by Gladys Taylor (Ref.: Correspondence with Publisher, Ja 10, 1985).

No issues located

JRNER VALLEY

5.1   *Valley Observer and Black Diamond, Naptha and Hartell News.*
N 8, 1929-Ja 10, 1930/...
w.

5.2   *Turner Valley Observer and Black Diamond, Naptha and Hartell News.* Ja 17, 1930-Ja 23, 1931/...
w.

5.3   *Tri-City Observer (Black Diamond, Hartell and Turner Valley).*
Ja 30, 1931-Oc 2, 1931//
w.

Pub. and ed. by Roy Milligan.

AEP or N 8, 1929-Oc 2, 1931

6   *Oilfield Flare.* 1947?-1956//
w.

Continued *Flare,* Black Diamond (73).
Incorporated in *Rocky View News and Market Examiner,* Calgary (153.4), Summer 1956.
Pub. and ed. by A. Burdett Horseman.

ACG or F 13, 1950; Je 22, 1956

7   *Turner Valley News.* F 1? 1957-?//
w.

Pub. by Prairie Pub. Ltd., Black Diamond. Ed. by Donald W. Davies and Ivan Peterson (Ref.: **SHE**, p. 93).

No issues located

8   *High Country Flare.* 1979?-1980//
bw.

Pub. by Kate Emmelkamp (Ref.: **CARD** Ja 1980).

No issues located

979   *Eagleview Post.* S 15, 1981-
           w. \

           Pub. and ed. by Douglas B. and Doris Lyon; Cathy Burwood and Lynne
           Andrews (Ref.: Correspondence with Publisher, N 27, 1984).

           ACG   or   S 15, 1981

TWO HILLS COUNTY

980.1   *Two Hills Reporter.* Ja? 1950-Je 3? 1950/...
           w.

980.2   *Eagle Review.* Je? 1950-Jl 6, 1963/...
           w.

980.3   *County of Two Hills Review.* Jl 13, 1963-Mr 30, 1968/...
           w.

980.4   *Two Hills Review.* Ap 6, 1968-N 16, 1968/...
           w.

980.5   *Two Hills Sun.* N 23, 1968-Ja 18, 1969?//
           w.

           Pub. and ed. by Thomas W. Pue, Community Publications of Alberta,
           Edmonton, 1950-N 16, 1968; Sun Pub. Co. Ltd., Edmonton, N 23-D 1968.
           Included supplement *Alberta Country Life* (442).
           Alberta Golden Jubilee Edition, S 1, 1955.

           AEP   or   Ap 15-Je 3, 1950; Oc 2, 1953-D 21, 1968

           County of Two Hills Star. My 12, 1969-Oc 11, 1969
           See **EDMONTON**. *Edmonton Star* (463).

981   *Two Hills County Star.* Ap 25, 1970-My 21, 1977//
           w.

           Title varied: *County of Two Hills Star.*
           Pub. by Thomas W. Pue, Sun Colorpress Ltd., Edmonton.
           Ref.: **CNLU** p.15.

           OONL   or   Ap 25, My 2, 1970
           AEP   or   My 13, 1972-My 21, 1977

2 *Two Hills County Journal.* Ja 9, 1974-
w.

 Supplement pub. by St. Paul Journal Ltd. and distributed with *St. Paul Journal* (883.2). Separate voluming.

 AEP mf Ja 9, 1974+ (with *St. Paul Journal*)

3 *Two Hills County Times.* 1980-1984//
w.

 Pub. and ed. by Carl H. Hohol (Ref.: AY 1984).

 No issues located

LLEYVIEW

4 *Valleyview Times.* Ag 8, 1956-D 22, 1962?//
w.

 Pub. by Thomas W. Pue, Edmonton.
 Ref.: AY 1963.

 AEP or Ag 8, 1956-D 22, 1962

5 *Valley Views.* D 19, 1963-
w.

 Pub. and ed. by Bernice P. Carmichael (Ref.: Correspondence with Publisher, Ap 19, 1984).

 AEP or My 3, 1972+

AUXHALL

6 *Vauxhall Advance.* Oc 26, 1978-
w.

 Pub. by H. George Meyer, Taber Times Ltd. Ed. by Shirley Forchuk, Oc 26, 1978-Je 12, 1980 (Ref.: *Vauxhall Advance*, Je 12, 1980); Heidi Lacey, Je 19, 1980-Ap 23, 1981; Rob Schellenberg, My 7, 1981-Ja, 1983; Frank McTighe, Ja 6-Je 1984; Barbara Glen, Je 1984-N 29, 1984.

 AEP or Ja 31, 1980+

EGREVILLE

7.1 *Vegreville Observer.* Mr 19, 1906-Mr 2, 1927/...
w.

7.2 *Vegreville Observer and Ryley Transcript.* Mr 9, 1927-Mr 7, 1928/...
w.

987.3   *Vegreville Observer.* Mr 14, 1928-
            w. Political — Liberal

   Pub. by W.W. Smith, Mr 19-Ap 16, 1906; Andrew Leslie Horton, Liberal,
   Ap 25, 1906-Je 14, 1958; Catherine Elizabeth Horton, Je 18, 1958-Jl 12,
   1962; Wilfred Laurier Horton, mnging ed., Mr 26, 1958-D 20, 1962; W.L.
   Horton, pub., Ja 3, 1963+.
   Pub. supplement *Ryley Transcript*, Mr 9, 1927-Mr 7, 1928.
   Alberta Golden Jubilee Edition, Ag 31, 1955; Jubilee Edition, Ap 4, 1956.

   AEP   mf Mr 19, 1906-D 21, 1983
              or   Ja 1984+

988.1   *News Advertiser.* 1950-My 25, 1977/...
            w.

988.2   *Vegreville News Advertiser Ltd.* Je 1, 1977-F 20, 1980/...
            w.

988.3   *Vegreville News Advertiser.* F 27, 1980-
            w.

   Pub. by Ed Chysowski, 1950-1962?; Herbert Schlamp, 1962-F 25, 1970;
   Daniel Beaudette, Mr 4, 1970+.

   AEP   mf Ja 5, 1966-D 27, 1983
              or   Ja 1984+

989   *Vegreville Mirror.* Ja 21, 1961-Ap 1, 1961//
            w.

   Combined with *Mundare Mirror* (774) Ap 8, 1961 and began new volum-
   ing.
   Superceded by *Vegreville Mirror* (990).
   Pub. as weekly supplement to *Mannville Mirror* (729), *Eagle Review*,
   Two Hills County (980.2), and *Mundare Mirror* (774). Pub. by Thomas W.
   Pue, Sun Pub. Co. Ltd., Edmonton.

   AEP   mf Ja 21-Ap 1, 1961

990   *Vegreville Mirror.* Ap 8, 1961-My 15, 1965//
            w.

   Superceded supplement *Vegreville Mirror* (989).
   Combined with *Mannville Mirror* (729), My 22, 1965 to form *County of
   Minburn Review* (758.1).
   Pub. by Thomas W. Pue, Sun Pub. Co. Ltd., Edmonton.

   AEP   mf Ap 8, 1961-My 15, 1965

VERMILION

91   *Vermilion Signal.* Mr 1, 1906-F 24, 1910?//
           w.

           Pub. and ed. by William Bleasdell Cameron, Vermilion Signal Pub. Co.
           After F 24, 1910, Cameron was succeeded by C.V. Caesar.
           Ref.: **CAN** 1912; **DAL** p.96.

           AEUS   or   Mr 1, 1906
           AEPAA   mf   [Mr 1, 1906-F 27, 1908]
           AEP   or   My 2, 1907-F 24, 1910

92.1   *Standard.* My 19, 1909-S 28, 1921/...
           w.

92.2   *Vermilion Standard.* Oc 5, 1921-S 3, 1975/...
           w.

92.3   *Standard.* S 10, 1975-
           w.

           Pub. and ed. by Sextus Ruthven Pringle Cooper, My 19, 1909-Ap 30,
           1953; Cooper Brothers (Vernon, Ashley, Douglas, Percy), My 7, 1953-My
           30, 1973; Hugh A. Stubbs, Je 1, 1973+. Ed. by Calvin Stubbs, Ja 31, 1979+.

           AEP   or   My 19, 1909-Ap 26, 1922; Ja 7, 1925+

93.1   *Link.* S? 1918-1922/...
           m.

93.2   *Link and Mannville Empire.* 1922-1923//
           m.; w. Agriculture Veterans

           Absorbed *Mannville Empire* (724), 1922.
           Frequency varied: m. S 1918-1922; w. 1923.
           Begun as monthly ed. by Harold A. Edwards. In 1921 pub. by Link Pub.
           Co. in the interests of veteran farmers (Ref.: **MK** 1921, 1922 1923).

           ACG   or   D 1918; Ap, Jl 1919; Ja 3, 1923

           Wild Rose Chronicle. Je 1978-N 1978//
           See Supplement (1088).

94   *Northeast News.* 1978-1979//
           w.?

           Succeeded *Wild Rose Chronicle* (1088).
           Pub. by Brent Lavallée and ed. by David Errington. (Ref.: *Edmonton
           Journal*, F 9, 1979).

           No issues located

VERMILION RIVER COUNTY

995   *Vermilion River News.* Ja 7, 1961-Ap 27, 1963?//
        w.

        Pub. and ed. by Thomas W. Pue, Edmonton.

        AEP   or   Ja 7, 1961-Ap 27, 1963

996   *Vermilion River County Star.* My 5, 1973-My 21, 1977//
        w.

        Pub. by Thomas W. Pue, Sun Colorpress Ltd., Edmonton.
        Ref.: **CNLU** p.15.

        OONL   or   My 5, 1973
        AEP   or   F 2, 1974-My 21, 1977

VETERAN

997   *Veteran Post.* 1933-1934//
        w.

        Pub. by H.D. Carrigan (Ref.: **MK** 1934).

        No issues located

998   *Veteran Eagle.* Ap 14, 1972-1973?//
        w.

        Mimeographed.
        Ed. by Danny Belair, Ap-Ag 1972; Betty Homan, S 1972-1973?
        Ref.: **CNLU** p.27.

        OONL   or   S 7, Oc 19, 1972

VIKING

999   *Viking Gazette.* Ap 28, 1910-1911//
        w.

        Pub. by W.L. Phillips (Ref.: **MK** 1911; **CAN** 1912).
        Plant and stock destroyed by fire, Ja, 1912 (Ref.: **VIK** p.39).

        AVIHS   or   Ap 28, 1910

1000.1 *Viking News.* My 15, 1913-Ag 27, 1969/...
        w.

1000.2 *Viking News and Irma Times.* S 3, 1969-Jl 31, 1974/...
        w.

00.3   *Viking News.* Ag 7, 1974-Jl 18, 1979//
w.

Amalgamated with *Irma Times* (647), S 3, 1969, to form *Viking News and Irma Times.*

Pub. by John W. Johnston, My 15, 1913-Je 4, 1914; Henry G. Thunell, Je 11, 1914-Ag 11, 1965; Robert Horton Thunell, Ag 19, 1965-My 1, 1974; D.C. Weeks, My 8, 1974-Jl 18, 1979. Sold to *Weekly Review,* Viking, Jl 1979.

AEP   mf My 15, 1913-My 31, 1922; F 20, 1924-Je 24, 1925; Ja 5, 1927-Jl 18, 1979

01   *Weekly Review.* F 14, 1978-
w.

Pub. by Lane Carrington, F 14, 1978-My 19, 1982; Dianne Clouston, My 26, 1982+. Ed. by P. Dickson Morris, F 14, 1978+.

AEP   mf   F 14, 1978-D 21, 1983
       or   Ja 1984+

LNA

)2   *Vilna Star.* Mr 28, 1951-Ag 5, 1953//
w.

Pub. by Thomas W. Pue, Edmonton.

AEP   or   Ap 11, 1951-Ag 5, 1953

3   *Vilna Bulletin.* Oc 6, 1955-Ap 27, 1963?//
w.

Pub. by Thomas W. Pue, Edmonton.

AEP   or   Oc 6, 1955-Ap 27, 1963

LCAN

4   *Vulcan Review.* My 19, 1912-1914?//
w.

Pub. by Frank D. Rogers and printed in Okotoks, Mr 19, 1912-1914? Ed. by T.R. Farrand, Mr 19-Ag 13, 1912; J.F. Anstett, Ag 20, 1912-1914? Ref.: **CNLU** p.27.

AEP   or   Mr 19, 1912-Ap 2, 1913

5   *Vulcan Advocate.* Ag 6, 1913-
w.

Pub. by Charles A. Clark, Sr., Ag 6, 1913-N 13, 1947; Clark and Robert C.R. Munro, N 13, 1947-Ja 14, 1949; Munro, 1950-Je 11, 1980; Peter M. Pickersgill, Vulcan Pub. (1979) Ltd., Je 11, 1980+. Ed. by R.W. Glover, Ag 6, 1913-My 7, 1919; F.D. McDonell, My 14-N 19, 1919; A.R. Ganoe, N 26, 1919-Mr 17, 1920; J. Duffield, Mr 24, 1920-Jl 20, 1921; Harry Nelson, Jl 1921-Ap 1929; Tom Whittingham, Ap 11, 1929-My 5, 1932; Charles A. Clark, Jr., My 1932-1933; R.D. McElroy, Ja 23-Ag 26, 1936; R.C.R. Munro, S 1, 1936-S 25, 1941; J. Lundy Findlay, Oc 1, 1941-Oc 7, 1943; Lola R. Bateman, Oc 14, 1943-Ap 19, 1945; Findlay, Ap 26, 1945-Ap 11, 1946; R.C.R. Munro, Je 6, 1946-N 13, 1947.

50th Anniversary Issue, Je 26, 1963.

Ref.: **DAL** p.98.

AEP   mf Ag 6, 1913-Je 1925; Ja 7, 1927-D 1985
            or Ja 1986+

WABAMUN

1006   *Mirror.* Oc 22, 1914-Ap 15, 1915//
         w.

Pub. by W.H. Ashley & Son. Pub. moved newspaper to Stony Plain, My 1915.

AEP   or Oc 22, 1914-Ap 15, 1915

WAINWRIGHT

1007   *Wainwright Star.* N 6, 1908-Ja 12, 1949//
         w.

Amalgamated with *Chauvin Chronicle* (263), Ja 19, 1949 to form *Star-Chronicle*, Wainwright (1009).

Owned by James Hossack Woods, 1908-S 30, 1910. Ed. by H.E. Cummer, N 1908-Ap 21, 1910; L.S. Gowe, Ap 28-S 29, 1910. Sold to Norman E. Cook, pub. and ed., Oc 1, 1910-N 25, 1914; Will T. Webb, D 2, 1914-Ap 26, 1916. Pub. by C.R. Morrison, 1916-Je 9, 1920. Walter John Huntingford bought plant in 1918 and co-pub. with Morrison until N 1921. Huntingford ed., My 1, 1916-Ja 17, 1945 except for brief periods in 1932 and 1933 when plant managed by W.H. Zook, Jl 1, 1932-N 16, 1933; John W. Johnston, Ja 1-Mr 15, 1933, and F.M. Warnock, Mr 22-N 15, 1933. Pub. by Walter Charles Huntingford, Ja 1945-Ja 12, 1949.

Special Board of Trade Edition, Je 9, 1910.

Ref.: **DAL** pp. 99-100; *Star-Chronicle* Ap 29, 1981.

AEP   or Jl 16, 1909-D 27, 1922; Jl 2-D 31, 1924; Ja 4, 1928-Ja 12, 1949

1008.1   *Wainwright Commercial.* Ap 19, 1933-Jl 26, 1933/...
         w.

8.2 *Wainwright Record.* Ag 2, 1933-D 12, 1934//?
w.

Pub. by John W. Johnston and W.H. Zook, Ap 19-Jl 26, 1933; Zook, Ag 2-N 22, 1933; E.H.L. Thomas, N 22, 1933-Ag 29, 1934; R. Lobb, S 5-D 1934.

AEP   or   Ap 19, 1933-D 12, 1934

)9.1 *Star-Chronicle.* Ja 19, 1949-S 21, 1949/...
w.

9.2 *Wainwright Star-Chronicle.* S 28, 1949-
w.

Superceded *Wainwright Star* (1007) and *Chauvin Chronicle* (263).
Pub. by Leonard D'Albertanson, Jr., Ja 19, 1949-Ja 1, 1970. Sold to Fred W. Stone, pub. and ed., Ja 1, 1970-Ap 29, 1981. Sold to M & K Pub. Ltd. My 4, 1981. Pub. by Monte G. Keith, My 4, 1981+ and ed. by Dave Mabell, My 4, 1981+.
Pub. sections entitled *Chauvin Chronicle* and *Edgerton Enterprise,* Ja 19, 1949+.
Ref.: **DAL** pp. 99-100; *Star-Chronicle* Ap 29, 1981.

AEP   or   Ja 19, 1949+

RNER COUNTY

County of Warner Review and Advertiser.
See **MILK RIVER.** *Milk River Review* (753).

RNER

0 *Warner Record.* My 12? 1910-Ag 25, 1916?//
w. Political — Liberal

Suspended pub. Oc 1914-Ja 15, 1915.
Ed. by F.E. Fairbanks, My 1910-N 7, 1912; L.D. Whitney, N 14, 1912-Ag 1916.
Ref.: **MK** 1911, 1913; **CAN** 1920.

AEP   or   Je 9, 1910-Oc 16, 1914; Ja 15, 1915-Ag 25, 1916

SKATENAU

1 *Witness.* D 4? 1930-Ap 12, 1934?//
w.

Pub. and ed. by Walton Williams.

AEP   or   Ja 1, 1931-Ap 12, 1934

1012   *Northern Post.* 1934-1935//
            w.

                Suspension announced (Ref.: **CPP** v44no9 S 1935).
                Pub. by H.D. Carrigan (Ref.: **CPP** v44no9 S 1935).

            No issues located

1013   *Booster.* 1937-1940//
            bw.

                Suspension announced (Ref.: **CPP** v49no11 Oc 1940).
                Pub. Leslie Phillips.
                Ref.: **MK** 1940

            No issues located

1014   *Waskatenau World.* Mr 19, 1949-D 22, 1962?//
            w.

                Suspended pub. Ag 19, 1953-Oc 6, 1955.
                Pub. and ed. by Thomas W. Pue, Community Publications of Alberta,
            Edmonton.
                Ref.: **AY** 1963.

            AEP   or   Ap 9, 1949-Ag 19, 1953; Oc 6, 1955-D 22, 1962

WATER VALLEY

            Town Crier. Oc 8, 1980-Je 2, 1982
                See **COCHRANE.** *Town Crier* (283).

WATERHOLE

            Waterhole became the village of Fairview Mr 28, 1929. See **FAIRVIEW**
            for newspapers having served Waterhole.

WATERWAYS

            Waterways amalgamated with Fort McMurray, May, 1947, to form village
            of McMurray, later town, now city of Fort McMurray.

WESTLOCK

1015.1   *Westlock Witness.* S 25, 1919-D 29, 1922/...
            w.

1015.2   *Witness.* Ja 5, 1923-D 19, 1929/...
            w.

5.3   *Westlock Witness.* D 23, 1929-Jl 28, 1949/...
         w.

5.4   *Witness.* Ag 18, 1949-Je 26, 1957/...
         w.

5.5   *Westlock News.* Jl 3, 1957-
         w.

         Pub. and ed. by Charles A. Roulston, S 1919-Mr 16, 1928; Robert Smith,
         Ap 5, 1928-Oc 31, 1945; H.E. Martin, N 1, 1945-My 26, 1954. Pub. by
         Martin Press Ltd., Je 2, 1954-Ap 30, 1956. Ed. by John MacDonald, Je 2,
         1954-Je 29, 1955; H.E. Martin, Jl 6, 1955-Ap 25, 1956. Sold My 1, 1956 to
         John MacDonald, Westlock News Ltd.
             Alberta Golden Jubilee Edition, Ag 10, 1955.
             Ref.: **DAL**, pp. 101-102.

         AEP   or   Ja 2, 1920-Je 19, 1925; Ja 6, 1928-F 29, 1940; F 14, 1946+

6   *Hub.* Ap 2, 1968-
         2m.; w.

         Frequency varies: 2m. Ap 2, 1968-Jl 27, 1971; w. Jl 27, 1971+.
             Pub. by George and Marie Greig, Ap 2-My 28, 1968; Kay Sulek, My 28,
         1968-My 15, 1982; Bob MacGregor, Hub Pub. Ltd., Ap 6, 1982+.
             Pub. *Hub, St. Albert Edition* as a supplement, Ag 9-D 6, 1977.
             Special Edition, 61 Years of Progress, Jl 1975.
             Ref.: Correspondence with Publisher, S 11, 1984.

         ACG   or   Jl 1975
         AEP   or   Mr 18, 1975+

TASKIWIN COUNTY

7   *Wetaskiwin County News.* Oc 24 ? 1966-D 1968?//
         w.

         Pub. by W. Ernie Jamison (Ref.: **CAN** 1968, 1969; **AY** 1969).
             Ref.: **CNLU** p. 27.

         AWCA   or   D 14, 1966
         OONL   or   D 9, 1968

TASKIWIN

8   *Free Lance.* D 2, 1897-N 18, 1898?//
         w.

         Pub. by Wetaskiwin Pub. Co. Ed. by Robert Chambers Edwards. John H.
         Walker, bus. mgr. Printed by *Strathcona Plaindealer,* Edmonton (Ref.: **REY**
         p. 65) or *Calgary Herald* (Ref.: **DEM** p. 9). Goodwill sold to George and
         Orville D. Fleming to begin *Free Lance,* Innisfail (641) in Ag 1898 (Ref.:
         MEE p. 159).

Same voluming as *Free Lance,* Innisfail, (641) S-N 18, 1898.

ACG   or   D 9, 1897
AEUS   or   Je 10, 1898
ACG   mf Ja 27, N 18, 1898

1019   *North Star.* Mr 15, 1900-? 1900//
          w.

          Pub. by William MacDonnell (Ref.: **REY** p. 143). Purchased by W.F.
          Treutner to publish as *News* (1020). (Ref.: **CPP** v9no10 Oc 1900).
          Ref.: **CNLU**, p.27.

          OONL   or   Mr 15, 1900
          ACG   or   My 24, 1900

1020   *Wetaskiwin News.* 1900//
          w. Political — Liberal

          Succeeded *North Star* (1019).
          Pub. by John H. Walker (Ref.: **MK** 1901; **REY** p.143).

          No issues located

1021   *Wetaskiwin Breeze.* Mr-Ap, 1901//
          w.

          Launched by Robert Chambers Edwards in Mr, 1901 (Ref.: *Weekly
          Herald,* Calgary, Mr 7, 1901). *Weekly Herald* (113.8) printed Edwards'
          columns from *Breeze* (Ref.: **DEM** p.11).
          Lasted till April (Ref.: **REY** pp.143-145).
          Ref.: **MK** 1901.

          No issues located

1022.1   *Wetaskiwin Times.* Mr 20, 1901-Ap 14, 1958/...
          w.

1022.2   *Times.* Ap 23, 1958-Ag 17, 1966/...
          w.

1022.3   *Wetaskiwin Times.* Ag 24, 1966-Ap 10, 1968/...
          w.

1022.4   *Times.* Ap 17, 1968-Ag 15, 1979/...
          w.

1022.5   *Wetaskiwin Times.* Ag 22, 1979-Jl 1983.
          w.

          Amalgamated with *News-Advertiser* (1022.5), Jl 1983 to form *Wetaskiwin
          Times Advertiser.*

Pub. and ed. by Victor Coleman French, Mr 21, 1901-Mr 20, 1941; Executors of the Estate of V.C. French, deceased, Mr 27, 1941-My 28, 1942; William Draayer, Je 4, 1942-1965; Kenneth Patrige and Charles A. MacLean, Wetaskiwin Pub. Ltd., 1965-1967; H.A. (Bert) Taylor, Wetaskiwin Times Ltd., Ja 1, 1968-Ap 1983; Bowes Pub. Ltd., Ap, 1983+.

Pub. as official newspaper for County of Wetaskiwin and distributed free to ratepayers.

Alberta Golden Jubilee Edition, Jl 20, 1955.

Ref.: **DAL** p.101.

AEPAA mf Mr 29, 1901-D 9, 1927; Ja 2, 1963-Je 24, 1981
AEP or Ap 11, 1907-D 30, 1920; Ja 5, 1928-D 28, 1960; Ja 3-D 26, 1962; Ja 6-D 29, 1965; Ja 10, 1968-D 30, 1970; Ja 5, 1972+

23 *Northwest Chronicle.* Je 5, 1904-Ag ? 1904//
w.

Succeeded by *Post* (1024).
Cessation announced (Ref.: **CPP** v13no9 S 1904).
Pub. by G.C. Inman (Ref.: **REY** p.146).
Ref.: **CNLU** p.27.

OONL or Je 5, 1904

24 *Post.* Ag 11? 1904-Ag 11, 1910//
w.

Succeeded *Northwest Chronicle* (1023).
Superceded by *Northern Albertan,* Wetaskiwin (1025).
Pub. and ed. by J. Young Byers, 1904-1907?; L.D. Von Iffland, 1907?-D 24, 1908; A.W. Keith, Ja 6, 1909-F 24, 1910; S.C. Andrews, Ja 6, 1909-Ag 11, 1910 (Ref.: **REY** p.146).

AEP or Ap 11, 1907-Ag 11, 1910

25.1 *Northern Albertan.* Ag 31, 1910-S 7, 1910/...
w.

25.2 *Central Albertan.* S 14, 1910-My 31, 1911?//
w. Immigration

Superceded *Post,* Wetaskiwin (1024).
William Chamberlain, pres. and mnging. ed., Ag 31, 1910-My 31, 1911; G.E. Rice, city ed., Ag 31-Oc 26, 1910; L.M. Graham, city ed., D 30, 1910-My 31, 1911.
Ref.: **CAN** 1912.

AEP or Ag 31, 1910-My 31, 1911

6.1 *Free Press.* Ag 16, 1911-Je 6, 1917/...
w.

1026.2   *Wetaskiwin Free Press.* Je 13, 1917-1941?//
         w. Political — Conservative

         Pub. and ed. by Arthur H. Liversidge, Conservative, Ag 16, 1911-Jl 31,
         1912; H.B. Berryman, Ag 1-D 25, 1912; Liversidge, Wetaskiwin Free Press
         Ltd., Ja 8, 1913-Ag 18, 1937; W.G. Atkinson with T.M. Brinsmead, S 1,
         1937-1941? (Ref.: **CPP** v66no9 S, 1937).
         Ref.: **DAL** p.101.

         AEP   or   Ag 16, 1911-D 25, 1920; Ja 3-Je 26, 1923; Jl 1, 1925-Oc 25,
                     1939

1027.1   *Journal.* D? 1911-Ap 4, 1912/...
         w.

1027.2   *Wetaskiwin Journal.* Ap 11, 1912-1914?//
         w.

         R.M. Angus, prop., Thomas G. Jenkyns, mnging. ed., D? 1911-Ja? 1912.
         Ref.: **CAN** 1914.

         AEP   or   Ja 4-Jl 18, 1912

1028   *New Age.* Oc 25, 1912-Mr 11, 1913?//
         2w. Political — Conservative

         F.A. Ambler, business mgr., Oc 25, 1912-Mr 11, 1913; G.E. Rice, ed.,
         Conservative, Oc 25-D 6, 1912; H.B. Berryman, ed., Ja 24-Mr 11, 1913.

         AEP   or   Oc 25, 1912-Mr 11, 1913

1029   *Wetaskiwin Alberta Tribunen.* ?-1914?//
         w. Swedish in Swed.

         Ref.: **GREG** p.761.

         No issues located

1030   *News Advertiser.* Ja 5, 1938-Jl 1983//
         w.

         Amalgamated with *Wetaskiwin Times* (1002.5) to form *Wetaskiwin Times
         Advertiser*, Jl 1983.
         Title varied: *Advertiser, Wetaskiwin News Advertiser (1971) Ltd.*
         Est. by Alex Barnhill. Barnhill family sold paper to Roger Vold, Vold
         Pub. Co., in 1971. Ed. by R.H. (Rick) Gross.
         Ref.: Correspondence with Publisher, Oc 12, 1984.

         No issues located

News-Record. Ag 27, 1914-Oc 25, 1917?//
w.; bw.

Frequency varied: w. Ag 27, 1914-Ag 5, 1916; bw. N 2, 1916-Oc 25, 1917.
Suspended pub. Ag 5-N 2, 1916.
Pub. by News-Record Pub. Co. Ltd. Ed. by C.D. McAlpine, Ag 27, 1914-Ag 5, 1916; J.S. Torgerson, N 2, 1916-Oc 25, 1917.
Ref.: **CAN** 1918.

AEP   or   Ag 27, 1914-Ag 5, 1916; N 2, 1916-Oc 25, 1917

Whitecourt Echo. 1959-Ja 18, 1969?//
w.

Pub. by Thomas W. Pue, Edmonton, until Ap 1963; Sun Pub. Co. Ltd., 1967-Ja 18, 1969.
Ref.: **CNLU** p.15.

AEP   or   Ja 2, 1960-Ap 27, 1963; Ja 7, 1967-Oc 12, 1968

Whitecourt Star. Je 8, 1962-
w.

Pub. by Doug Caston, Yellowhead Pub. Ltd., Je 1962-Ag 31, 1968; Ross Quinn, Whitecourt Pub. Ltd., S 1968-Ag 31, 1976. Sold S 1, 1976 to B.L.B. Pub. Ltd., Barry and Barbara Baniulis, pubs., S 1, 1976-S 24, 1980. Sold Oc 1, 1980 to H.M. Bowes, Lynard Pub. Ltd. Pub. by Barry Heidecker, Oc 1, 1980-Ap 28, 1982; Jim McCurdy, My 1, 1982+.
Pub. section *Lac Ste Anne County Star,* Oc 10, 1973-Mr 26, 1975.
Ref.: **CNLU** p.28.

OONL   or   Je 8, 1962; Mr 23, 1963
AEP   or   F 22, 1964-Ap 26, 1972; Ja 10, 1973-Mr 26, 1975; Ja 7, 1976+

Free Press. Oc 1982-Ja 1985//
w.

Pub. by Edwin Cowley, W. and E. Cowley Pub. Ltd. Ed. by Wanda Cowley. Sold Oc 1984, to Lynard Pub. Ltd., and became weekend ed. for distribution in Whitecourt, Blue Ridge and Fox Creek. Discontinued Ja, 1985 (Ref.: Edwin Cowley).

No issues located

Indian Advocate. N? 1897-1902?//
m.   Native (Cree)

Mimeographed to Ag? 1899.

Ed. by Rev. E.B. Glass, Whitefish Lake Methodist Mission. Contained news items of local interest and records of baptisms, marriages and deaths (Ref.: *Edmonton Bulletin* Ja 6, 1898; Ag 31, 1899).

AEPAA   or   Mr 1902 (83.284 UC 794/R1)

WILDWOOD

Plaindealer. 1949-1950?//
See Supplement (1089)

Grand Trunk Poplar Press. Ag 1979-
See **EVANSBURG.** *Grand Trunk Poplar Press* (523).

WILLINGDON

Willingdon Times. Ap? 1923-1938?//
See Supplement (1090)

1036   *Willingdon Review.* Ap 27? 1951-S 25, 1953//?
w.

Pub. by Thomas W. Pue, Community Publications of Alberta, Edmonton.
Ref.: **AY** 1952; **CAN** 1954.

AEP   or   Je 22, 1951-S 25, 1953

WIMBORNE

1037   *Valley News.* N 1945-D 23, 1953//
w.

Continued by *Valley News,* Acme (4).
Pub. by Mrs. Arend (Ref.: *Valley News* Acme, Ja 6, 1954). Sold to George
Wheeler, D 30, 1953; place of pub. moved to Acme.

AEP   or   Ap 9, 1948-D 23, 1953

WINFIELD

1038   *Winfield Gazette.* 1939-N 1954//
w.

Pub. by W.H. De Coursey, 1939-1942; W.A. Draayer, Wetaskiwin Pub.
Ltd., 1942-1946?; Fred Johns, Leduc Representative, 1946?-1954?
Ref.: **AY** 1952; **CAN** 1942-1955; **MK** 1941, 1942; **PUB** v20no550 Jl
1939, v27no650, My 1946.

No issues located

NNIFRED

9
Winnifred Record. 1911?-Oc 1912?//
w. Political — Liberal

Recently suspended publication, after a struggling existence of a little over a year (CPP D, 1912).
Ref.: CAN 1912, 1913.

No issues located

STOK

)
Ostoroha. N? 1912//
irreg. Ukrainian in Ukr.

Pub. by Dmytro Yaremko. Only 2 issues pub. (Ref.: CES 1 p.107; MARU p.289; BOM p.37).

No issues located

JNGSTOWN

Plaindealer. Ap 13, 1913-Ja 30, 1936//
w.

Continued by Plaindealer, Drumheller (330).
Pub. and ed. by Harold J. Cave, Ap 3, 1913-N 1, 1917; Edward G. Quick, N 1, 1917-Ja 30, 1936. Place of pub. moved to Drumheller, Mr 1936.

AEP   mf Ap 3, 1913-Ja 30, 1936

SUPPLEMENT

ARROWWOOD

1045   *Bow River News.* 1924-1927?//
        w.

      Pub. by Carroll Walker. Printed in Bassano.
      Ref.: **FUR** p.71.

No issues located

BARONS

1046   *Barons Beacon.* Oc 13, 1909-?//
        w?

      Ed. by Brainard and Piles.
      Ref.: Information from Alex Johnston, Sir Alexander Galt Museum, Lethbridge, March, 1987.

No issues located

BOW CITY

1047   *Bow City Star.* S? 1913-? 1914//
        irreg.

      Pub. and ed. by L.D. Nesbitt in Brooks. Published intermittently over several months and then discontinued.
      Ref.: **CPP** v13no10 Oc 1913; **RAI** p.74.

No issues located

CALGARY

1048   *Alberta Clarion.* Je 2, 1906-?//
        w. Labour

      Pub. by Western Canada Advertising Co. Organ of Calgary Trade Unions.
      Ref.: **CPP** v15no6 Je 1906.

1049   *Sunset News Bulletin.* 1906-?//
        d. Immigration

      Pub. by Canadian Western Immigration Assoc., C.N.R. and C.P. Editor-in-Chief, Mrs. Blake Coleman.

ACG   or   Je 1, 1906

Fairplay. Je 1915-? 1918//
2m.; w.

Ed. by D. Algar-Bailey.
Issue v6no10 (My 18, 1918) stated: published every Saturday, Vancouver, by Fairplay Pub. Co., Alberta distributing agent, Alexander News Stand. Notice: Fairplay is not a new journal. It first saw daylight in Calgary in June, 1915 and has been published regularly ever since. It has moved to Vancouver so that it can gain in circulation and to fight more powerfully for its ideal "Justice for all".

AEPAA or Ja 8, 1916; My 18, 1918 (71.115 OC)

Westerner. Je 12, 1923-Je 28, 1928//
2m. Business

Ed. by P.C. Potts; A.L. Elston, bus. mgr.
"Finance, economics, citizenship".

AEP or Je 12, 1923-Je 28, 1928

Bridgeland and Riverside Echo. Je 13, 1930-?//
w?

No publisher's statement.
Printed back-to-back with *North Hill Advocate.*

ACG or Je 20, 1930

North Hill Advocate. 1930. see *Bridgeland and Riverside Echo.* (1052).

Unemployed Bulletin. S 11? 1931-1932//
w. Labour.

Subtitle: Organ, National Unemployed Workers' Association, Calgary Branch.
Ref.: **WEI** 5370.

ACG or Oc 9, 23-30, D 5, 1931; Ja 25, 1932

Alberta Democrat. Oc 8, 1938-N 12, 1938//
w. Political — Social Credit

No publisher's statement.
A Social Credit paper.

AEPAA or Oc 8-N 5, N 12, 1938 (74/485)

Bowness Bulletin. D 15, 1948-Mr 16, 1951/...
2m.

Bowness News. Ap 2, 1951-F 15, 1952?//
2m.

Pub. and ptd. by Neeland Printing Services, Calgary. Ed. to D, 1951, by Dorothy Nielsen (Mrs. Charles V. Nielsen).

ACG   or   D 15, 1948-F 15, 1952

1053   *Sunday Calgarian.* My 19, 1962-My 26 1962//
        w.

Pub. by Roy Farran, North Hill News Ltd. Ed. by Graham Smith.

ACG   or   My 19-26, 1962

1054   *Bowness Review.* My 16, 1963-N 14, 1963?//
        w. 2m.

Pub. by B. Suchlandt.

ACG   or   My 16-N 14, 1963

CARSTAIRS

1055   *Carstairs Reporter.* Mr? 1903-?//
        w?

Ref.: **CPP** v12no4, Ap 1903.

No issues located

COUTTS

1056   *Coutts-Sweetgrass International Herald.* Ja 26, 1911-?//
        w?

Pub. by Floyd E. Fairbanks.
Ref.: Information from Alex Johnston, Sir Alexander Galt Museum, Lethbridge, March, 1987.

No issues located

DRAYTON VALLEY

1057   *Drayton Valley Banner.* Mr? 1965-Ag? 1965//
        w.

Succeeded *Pembina News* (807) and was succeeded by *Western Review* (323).
Pub. by Art Playford, News Advertiser Ltd.
Ref.: *Edmonton Journal*, Mr 20, 1965; **CPP** v74no4, Ap 1965.

No issues located

Edmonton Free Press. 5/ 1906-1907?//
w. Business

Sub-title: The people's popular weekly.
Ptd. by Free Press Pub. Co. Ltd. Real estate, industrial and commercial.
Ref.: **CPP** v15no10 Oc 1906; **HENE** 1907.

No issues located

Progressive Student. 1959-1960?//
2m. Political — C.C.F. University

Pub. by C.C.F. Campus Club, University of Alberta.

OOA or Ja, 1960 (MG 28.IV-1)

Demonstrator. Mr 24, 1960//
? University

"This copy of the U. of A. 'gag' paper was seized by campus officials and destroyed because of the comments made about Premier Manning". (ms. note on **ACG** copy).
No more published.

ACG or Mr 24, 1960

Labor Advocate. Oc, 1960-?//
m. Labour

Pub. by Alberta News Service Co. Ltd., V.W. Emmerson, Pres.

ACG or Oc, 1960

Alberta Liberal. My, 1961-F, 1970//
m. Political—Liberal

Succeeded by *Alberta Liberal* (1064).
Pub. by Liberal Association of Alberta. Ed. by Dr. John Donnachie.

ACG or Mr 1965; Ja 1966; D 1967-Ap 1968, S 1968-Mr 1969, Je, N-D 1969; F 1970

Tory. F 8, 1966-?//
? Political—Conservative University

Organ of the Alberta Progressive Conservative Student Federation, University of Alberta.

ACG or F 8, 1966

Alberta Liberal. My? 1970-1972//
bm. Political— Liberal

Succeeded *Alberta Liberal* (1062) and was succeeded by *New Alberta Liberal* (1065).

Published by the Liberal Party in Alberta as a special provincial edition of a national paper. Ed. by Robert Gillespie.

ACG   or   Je-N 1970; F-My, N 1971

1065   *New Alberta Liberal.* Ap 1972-1978?//
irreg. Political—Liberal

Succeeded *Alberta Liberal* (1064).
Pub. by Sun Colorpress Ltd. Ed. by Len Stahl, Ap 1972-?; Germaine Dalton for Liberal Party in Alberta.

ACG   or   [Ap 1972-Ja 1976] Ap 29, S 20-Oc 16, 1978
AEP   or   1975-1976

1066   *Alberta Challenge.* Je 1973-Oc 1973//
irreg. Political—Social Credit

Pub. by Alberta Social Credit League.

ACG   or   Je, 1973
AEP   or   Je-Oc, 1973
AEPAA   or   Oc, 1973 (82.153/29)

1067   *Commerce News.* Oc, 1976-
m. Business

Pub. by Terry Clements, Oc 1976-Ap 1979; Edmonton Chamber of Commerce, My 1979+.

AEP   or   Oc 1976+

1068   *Newscene.* Ap 1978-My 7 1979//
irreg. Political — Social Credit

Pub. by Alberta Social Credit Party. Ptd. by North Hill News (Edmonton Northern Ltd.).

AEPAA   or   Je-S 1978; Mr-My 1979 (82.153/32)

ELK POINT

1069   *Elk Point Reflections.* Ap 10, 1979-Ja 8, 1980//
w.

Absorbed by *Reflections*, Mannville (731.2).
Pub. by Heather Calder and Ethel Schreyer.
Ref.: Information from Mrs. I. Magnusson, Elk Point Historical Society, Ja 1987.

No issues located

T McMURRAY

Northwest Review. Mr 5, 1939-?//
w?

Ed. by H.A. Dalmer. Printed by La Survivance, Edmonton.

AFMM or Mr 15, 1939

Valhalla Star. ? 1941-?//
w?

Mimeographed. Pub. in Waterways.

AFMM or F 21, 28, Mr 9, 1941

Northern Banner. Ap 2, 1959-Mr 2, 1965//
w.

Succeeded by *Fort McMurray Banner* (548). Pub. by Art Playford.

AFMM or Ap 2, 1959

Fort McMurray News Advertiser. Ap 9, 1968-My 26, 1970?//
w.

Title varied: *Fort McMurray & News Advertiser.*
Pub. and ed. by Mrs. P.R. Switzer, Ap 1968-Je 1969; pub. and ed. by Clint Buehler, Jl 1, 1969-My 26, 1970.

AFMM or [Ap 9, 1968-My 26, 1970]

Fort McMurray Sun. Oc 2? 1968-1969?//
w.

Pub. and ed. by Deborah Pue, Sun Office, Fort McMurray.

AFMM or Ja 25, 1969

McMurray Times. 1970?-1971?//
w.

Subtitle: "Voice of Fort McMurray."
Title varied: *Fort McMurray Times.*
Pub. and ed. by Mrs. P.R. Switzer.

AFMM or [Ag 11, 1970-Ja 26, 1971]

BURG

Weekly News. 1920-1921?//
w.

Ed. by F.D. Watson.
Ref.: **WRI** 1920.

No issues located

LAC STE. ANNE

INNISFAIL

1077   *Innisfail Star.* Ja 1977-F 1977//
w.

Pub. by Neil Leatherdale.
Same text as *Olds Gazette* (789.2) with different banner title.
Lasted about three weeks. (Ref.: Information from R. Stafford-Mayer, Mr 16, 1987).

No issues located

LAC STE. ANNE

1078   *Croix de Ste. Anne /Ayamewatikum Manito Sakihagan.* Mr 1900-Ag 1905//
m.   Native (Cree) Cr. (Engl., Fr.)

Pub. and ed. by Rev. Z. Lizée, o.m.i.
In Cree syllabic, with occasional English and French.
From Jl 1902, in magazine format.
Succeeded by magazine *Petite Revue / Kitchitwa Miteh atchimomasinahigan / Cree Review,* Ag 1906-1979. Published by the Oblate Fathers at Sacred Heart Mission, Hobbema, to Ja 1912, thereafter successively at St. Paul, Le Goff, Hobbema and Lac La Biche.

AEPAA   or   My 1900-Ap 1905 (Oblate Archives) Lac La Biche/23-24
AEUS   or   Mr 1900-Ag 1905
AEGL   or   My 1901

LACOMBE

1079   *Lacombe Weekly Press.* 1899//
w.

Pub. by W.D. Pitcairn.
Ref.: **MEE** p.159.

No issues located

1080   *Lacombe Municipal News.* Ja? 1946-1955?//
m.

Pub. for Municipality by Harry Ford, Lacombe Globe.
Ref.: **CANC** My, 1973.

ACG   or   Jl-S 1949; S-Oc 1950; Ja, Ag-Oc 1952; F, My 1953; Ap-My, N 1954; Ja-F 1955

LIEVILLE

Western Star. My 30, 1979-
w.

Pub. and ed. by Danny and Judy Gibson.
Began as advertiser, with increasing local news content.
Ref.: Interview with Publishers, N, 1986.

No issues located

'HBRIDGE

Chinook. Mr 16, 1972-? 1976//
w.

Pub. by Lethbridge Herald.
Ref.: Information from Alex Johnston, Sir Alexander Galt Museum, Lethbridge, April 1987.

No issues located

S

Olds Star. N 9, 1976-Je 28, 1977//
w.

Pub. by Ivan Coles, Col-Staff Holdings for Bowden, Sundre, Trochu, Three Hills, Didsbury and Olds.
Ref.: **PUB** F, 1977.

No issues located

DEER

M.D. Red Deer News. N? 1945-S? 1946//
m.

Pub. by Municipal District of Red Deer No. 55. Ed. by Hugh Shipley.
Publication suspended (Ref.: **CPP** v55no9 Oc 1946).

ACG   or   Mr 1946

CLIFF

Redcliff Review. Oc 6, 1976-? 1978//
2m.

Pub. by Dave Broadfoot. Ed. by Pauline Sundby. Ptd. by Redcliff Publications.

AREM   or   N 21, 1976

SPIRIT RIVER

1086   *Spirit River Times.* Je? 1916-1917?//
          w.

              Ref.: **CPP** v25no7 Jl 1916.

          No issues located

SWALWELL

1087   *Swalwell Recorder.* 1920-1921?//
          w?

              E. Godfrey Allen, mgr.
              Ref.: **WRI** 1920

          No issues located

VERMILION

1088   *Wild Rose Chronicle.* Je 1978-N 1978//
          m.

              Succeeded by *Northeast News*, Vermilion (994).
              Pub. by Brent Lavallée.
              Ref.: Information from Mrs. I. Magnusson, Elk Point Historical Society,
          N, 1986.

          No issues located

WILDWOOD

1089   *Plaindealer.* 1949-1950?//
          2m.

              Pub. by N.L. Daniels.
              Ref.: **CPP** v59no1 Ja 1950.

          No issues located.

WILLINGDON

1090   *Willingdon Times.* Ap 23? 1937-1938?//
          w.

              Pub. by Sam Eaton.
              Ref.: **CPP** v46no4 Ap 1937.

          AEPAA   or   D 17, 1937 (75.74.1301)

Fugitive Titles

identified newspapers or periodicals, including titles which appear to have been
iounced but not published. These are not included in the Indexes.

us. Lethbridge. ca1969.

To be published in opposition to *Lethbridge Herald.*
Ref.: Alex Johnston, Sir Alexander Galt Museum, Lethbridge.

ureux. Edmonton. 1940.

Temperance. Dr. Joseph Boulanger.

der Times. Milk River. 1962.

ubs. Harvey Gilbert and William Dodge.
Ref.: *CPP* v71no12 D 1962.

Islander. Bow Island? 1963.

ubs. Harvey Gilbert and William Dodge.
Ref.: *CPP* v72no12 D 1963.

ige Booster. Lethbridge. 1963.

ubs. Harvey Gilbert and William Dodge.
Ref.: *CPP* v72no12 D 1963.

adian Freeman. Calgary. 1924.

o be a non-partisan political forum. Dr. Michael Clark to be the chief contributor.
ef.: *CPP* v33no7 Jl 1924.

ital. Medicine Hat. 1911.

.ef.: *CPP* v20no1 F 1911.

c. Lethbridge. ca1940.

ub. Robert Sage.
ef.: Sage's obituary, *Lethbridge Daily Herald,* N 8, 1920.

ader. Edmonton. 1935.

d. W.C. Boehnert.
ef.: *CPP* v44no5 My 1935.

Evening News. Calgary. 1918.

   To be published to support Moderation League, otherwise independent.
   Robb Sutherland, formerly of Nelson, B.C., pres., and gen. mgr.
   Ref.: *CPP* v28no4 Ap 1918.

Gibbons and Bon Accord Journal see Radway Journal.

Hillcrest Observer. Hillcrest. 1912.

   Ref.: Alex Johnston, Sir Alexander Galt Museum, Lethbridge.

Overland Mail. Daysland. 1906.

   To be established. B. Fuller of Summit, North Dakota, ed. and prop.
   Ref.: *CPP* v15no10 Oc 1906.

Radway Journal. St. Paul. 1928.

   G. La Rue to publish four-page paper, each page with different banner. *Radway Journal, Waskatenau Junior Farmer, Redwater Journal, Gibbons and Bon Accord Journal.*
   Ref.: *CPP* v37no1 Ja 1928.

Redwater Journal. see Radway Journal.

Ram's Horn. Calgary. 1906.

   T.A. Bagshaw, news staff, Calgary Herald to Ram's Horn. (Ref.: *CPP* v15no11 N
   1906).

Ram's Horn. Edmonton. 1914.
w.

   New weekend paper. A.G. Ridgeway, ed.
   Ref.: *CPP* v23no4 Ap 1914.

South Side. Edmonton. 1914.
w.

   Free to residents.
   Ref.: *CPP* v23no4 Ap 1914.

Town Topics. Fort Macleod. 1911.

   Ref.: Alex Johnston, Sir Alexander Galt Museum, Lethbridge.

Ukrainian Tribune and Review. Edmonton, 1939.

   To be published at Institute Press.
   Ref.: *CPP* v48no7 Jl 1939

xhall News. Vauxhall. 1962.

Pub. by Harvey Gilbert and William Dodge.
Ref.: *CPP* v71no12 D 1962.

katenau Junior Farmer. See *Radway Journal.*

tern Canadian Oil News. Calgary. 1949.

Projected. W.H. De Coursey ed. and pub.
Not mentioned in De Coursey's autobiography.
Ref.: *CPP* v58no12 D 1949.

Fugitive Titles Listed by Place

Bow Island	*Bow Islander.*	1963
Calgary	*Canadian Freeman.*	1924
	Evening News.	1918
	Ram's Horn.	1906
	Western Canadian Oil News.	1949
Daysland	*Overland Mail.*	1906
Edmonton	*Bieureux.*	1940
	Crusader.	1935
	Ram's Horn.	1914
	South Side.	1914
	Ukrainian Tribune and Review.	1939
Fort Macleod	*Town Topics.*	1911
Hillcrest	*Hillcrest Observer.*	1912
Lethbridge	*Argus.*	ca1969
	Bridge Booster.	1963
	Critic.	ca1940
Medicine Hat	*Capital.*	1911
Milk River	*Border Times.*	
St. Paul	*Radway Journal.*	1928
Vauxhall	*Vauxhall News.*	1962

Indexes

Biographical Index 261
Chronological Index of Daily Newspapers 461
Chronological Index of Newspapers Other Than Dailies 462
Ethnic Index 489
Subject Index 495
Title Index 503

Biographical Index

Sources cited in this index are listed in the *Bibliography* In addition, newspapers cited frequently have been coded as follows:

AC *Albertan*, Calgary; CH *Calgary Herald; EJ Edmonton Journal; LH Lethbridge Herald*

Achenbach, Jim
Pub.
Banff Summit News 45

Adair, James Chester
Pub.
Came to Raymond from Eatonia, Sask. (**HIC** p.336)
Raymond Review 828

Adair, Joseph W. (Joe)
Pub; printer; ed.
b. Glasgow, 1877; d. Edmonton?, N 1 1960.
Learned printing trade in Glasgow; 1899, came to Canada; worked on newspapers in Toronto and Winnipeg; 1906, came to Edmonton to work on *Edmonton Bulletin*; 1911, founded linotyping business which he operated until 1946; served on Edmonton City Council. (EJ N 2 1960)
Town Topics, Edmonton 346
Western Weekly, Edmonton 376

Adair, T.J.
Pub.; ed.
Oyen Observer 797

Adams, Stuart
Pub.
Western Review, Drayton Valley 323

Adsit, Charles A.
Pub.
District News, Munson 778
Morrin District News 770
Munson News 777

Agostini, Elio
Pub.
b. ca. 1943
Member of the Thomson organization since 1977; formerly pub. of Mississauga *News*, Oakville *Beaver*, Brampton *Guardian*, Barrie *Examiner*, Kamloops *Daily Sentinel*; 1984, V.P., Marketing, Houston *Post*, Tex. (EJ Jl 25 1979; PUB Ap 1984).
Edmonton Sun 489

Agronin, Sam I.
Pub.; ed.; businessman
Canada Goose, Edmonton 461

Ahlf, Carol R.
Ed.
Edson Leader 512
Hinton Herald 627

Alberta. Alberta Advanced Education
English Express, Edmonton 499

Alberta C.C.F. Party
People's Weekly, Edmonton 386

Alberta Cooperative Marketing Pools
United Farmer, Calgary 160

Alberta Cooperative Oil Pool
United Farmers, Calgary 160

Alberta Farmers' Association
Alberta Homestead, Edmonton 353

Alberta Farmers' Union
A.F.U. Bulletin, Edmonton 427

Alberta Federation of Labour
Alberta Labor News, Edmonton 386
Alberta Labour, Edmonton 450

Alberta Handicapped Communications Society
Spokesman, Edmonton 472

Alberta Native Communications Society
Native People, Edmonton 460

Alberta Progressive Conservative Student Federation
Tory, Edmonton 1063

Alberta Provincial Douglas Social Credit Association
Social Justice Advocate, Calgary 176

Alberta Social Credit League
Alberta Challenge, Edmonton 1066
Today and Tomorrow, Edmonton 421

Alberta Social Credit Party
Newscene, Edmonton 1068

Alberta Society for the Preservation of Indian Identity
National Ensign, Edmonton 494

Albertanson, Leonard d'
See **D'Albertanson**, Leonard

Albertanson, Leonard d', Sr.
See **D'Albertanson**, Leonard, Sr.

Alexander, Colin
Pub.; prop.; businessman
b. England, ca. 1940
Bus. mgr. *Time and Tide* (Eng.); founder Frobisher Trading Co., Frobisher
Bay, N.W.T.; pub. *News of the North*, Yellowknife. (EJ N 10 1967; EJ
undated clipping).
Lac Ste. Anne Chronicle 667
Lamont County Star 676
Morinville Journal 766
Sherwood Park Star 895
Smoky Lake Gazette 906

Algar-Bailey, D.
Ed.
Formerly of Lethbridge and Carmangay; moved to Vancouver.
(**CPP** v.14 no.9, S 1915).
Fairplay, Calgary 1050

Allen, Dan
Ed.; pub.
Edmonton Examiner [North editions] 490
Edmonton Examiner [South editions] 486
Edmonton Examiner [West editions] 487

Allen, E. Godfrey
Pub.
Bassano Mail 58
Swalwell Recorder 1087

Allnutt, Alexander John (Alex J.)
Prop.; electrical engineer
b. Scotland, ca. 1889; d. Victoria, B.C., Ag 31, 1966.
1924, arrived Alliance, where was inspector of telephones; 1937, Dir., Public Relations, Alberta Press Bureau of Information; 1939-1945, served in
army; 1945, became electrical surveyor with B.C. Hydro, Victoria.
(**ALC** p.259; **CPP** v.46 no.11, N 1937)
Alliance Times 16

Ambler, F.A.
Pub.
New Age, Wetaskiwin 1028

Amy, William Lacey
Prop.; ed.; author
d.1962.
"Prolific Canadian writer of fiction; early in the century was proprietor
and editor of the *Medicine Hat Times*; used the pseudonym Luke Allan
for his Western Canadian stories..." **(PEEL)**
Times Medicine Hat 742

Anderson, David
Ed.
Native People, Edmonton 460

Anderson, Dorothy
Pub.; ed.
Old Timer, Cochrane 280

Anderson, Eldon George (Andy)
Pub.; printer
b. Arnprior, Ont., Oc 22, 1923
Worked on several Ontario newspapers; linotype operator for Ottawa
Citizen for 19 years; active in provincial and community affairs **(WWAI**
1974)
Claresholm Local Press 268
Stavely Advertiser 922

Anderson, Elsie
Ed.
Worker, Calgary 178

Anderson, J. Ross
Pub.
Husband of Jean Blewett Anderson (q.v.)
Northern Times, Picture Butte 811

Anderson, Jean Blewett
Ed.
Wife of J. Ross Anderson (q.v.)
Northern Times, Picture Butte 811

Anderson, John
Pub.
b. ca. 1907; d. Drumheller, 1962.
Drumheller Mail 327

Andrews, James R.
Ed.
Edson Leader 503

Andrews, Lynne
Pub.; journalist
b. Vulcan, Jl 27, 1953
Eagleview Post, Turner Valley 979
Vulcan Advocate 1005

Andrews, Silas Colin (Si)
Pub.; printer
b. Ontario; d. 1936.
Printer's apprentice, Clinton, Ont.; moved to Alix, 1911 **(PAR** p.93-4;
GLEA p.52)
Alix Free Press 14
Bashaw Record 55
Post, Wetaskiwin 1024

Angus, Robert M.
Prop.
1892, arrived in West; active in Wetaskiwin community. **(REY)**
Post, Wetaskiwin, 1024

Anstett, J.F.
Ed.
Vulcan Review 1004

Archer, E. Gordon (Gordon)
Printer; businessman; farmer
b. Lamont, 1910; d. Banff, 1955.
Job printer; owned trucking business; 1954, moved to Fairview, thence to
Banff. **(STA** p.173)
Lamont Banner 682

Archer, Leslie Herbert
Pub.; printer
b. Detroit, Mich., 1888; d. Tacoma? Wash., 1962.
1903, moved to Wetaskiwin where was printer's apprentice; then journeyman on several Alberta newspapers; in service, World War I; 1945, moved
to Tacoma, Wash. where mg ed., Tacoma *Labor Advocate*; 1952, retired.
(ROY p.181-2)
Ryley Times 872-873

Arend, Nina L.
Ed.
Formerly published stamp collector's magazine distributed to 22 coun-
tries. **(CWNA** v.27 no.650, My 1946)
Valley News, Wimborne 1037

Argan, Glen
Ed.; journalist; teacher
b. Winnipeg, Man., ca. 1953
Reporter, Red Deer *Advocate*, for 3 years; lecturer in philosophy and logic, Campion College and Luther College, Regina. (*Western Catholic Reporter* My 4 1981)
Western Catholic Reporter, Edmonton 453

Armour, Andrew M.
Ed.; prop.; pub.; printer
Came from Barrie, Ont., where was printer. (CH Ag 31 1968; **HAY** pp.50-2)
Calgary Herald, Mining and Ranche Advocate and General Advertiser 113
Medicine Hat Times 739

Armour, George E.
Pub.; ed.
Morning Times, Medicine Hat 746
Times, Medicine Hat 742

Armstrong, George W.
Pub.
Possibly same as George W. Armstrong, b. Mt. Forest, Ont., Mr 10 1879; printer, Lucknow, Ont., *Sentinel* 1892; to British Columbia, 1897; 1912, ed. and pub. Salmon Arm *Observer*. (**WW** 1912)
Bashaw Star 56

Arnup, Arthur W.
Pub.
d. Victoria, B.C., 1946.
1906, came to Canada; homesteaded, Evansburg district; operated store and was J.P. in Entwistle; later worked in the mine; retired to Victoria, 1925. (**PEM** v.1 p.557)
Pembina Outlook & Entwistle News 519

Arrol, Ed (Eddie)
Pub.; journalist; teacher; photographer
b. Copeland, Sask., ca. 1922, d. Calgary, N 28 1985.
Son of United Church minister, Bon Accord; served in RCAF, World War II; 1967, photographer in Calgary. (**CHU** p.61; EJ N 30 1985)
Bon Accord Herald 85
Redwater News 846

Arseny, Chahovetz
Ed.; Eastern Orthodox clergyman
Russian Orthodox abbot, came to Canada 1908; built up Russian Orthodox Church; founded Brotherhood of the Holy Trinity; left Canada 1910.

(**MARU** p.288-9)
Kanadiiskaia Niva, Edmonton 354

Art, Jack
Ed.
Bear Hills Native Voice, Hobbema 632

Ashby, Mr.
Ed.
Grassy Lake News 596

Ashley, W.H.
Pub.
Publishing firm, W.H. Ashley and Son; for many yrs, pub. of Boissevain
Globe, Man.; (**STON** p.38; **CPP** v.24 no.5, My 1915)
Mirror, Stony Plain 934
Mirror, Wabamun 1006

Atherton, J.J.
Prop.; printer
Calgary printer. (**CPP** v.26 no.3 Mr 1917)
Magrath Pioneer 715

Atkinson, F.C.
Prop.; ed.
Cochrane Advocate 279

Atkinson, William G.
Pub.
Printer on *Camrose Canadian* for 8 yrs before buying *Wetaskiwin Free Press*. (**CPP** v.46 no.9, S 1937)
Wetaskiwin Free Press 1026

Atwill, Hed. R.
Ed.
Alberta Veteran, Calgary 155

August, Gil
Ed.
Calgary Jewish News 196

Austin, Charles N. (Daddy)
Pub.
Came to Cochrane district early 1900s; 1909, sold homestead. (**COCH** p.192)
Cochrane Advocate 279

Austin, O.D.
Ed.
Lethbridge Herald 693

Auty, Donald L.
Ed.
Meridian Booster, Lloydminster 705

Avery, Arthur H.
Pub.
Son of Charles Avery (q.v.); 1942, enlisted in army; retired 1966; later,
mayor of Taber. (**THO** p.343; **CWNA** v.22 no.590, Ja 23 1942)
Taber Times 954

Avery, Charles
Pub.; Railway timekeeper
b. Brixton, Eng., ca. 1868; d. England, 1937.
CPR timekeeper for construction crews; bought newspaper and printing
business; returned to England. (**THO** p.342-3)
Bow Island Review 90
Burdett Review 112

Aylesworth, Nellie
Mgr; ed.
Wife of F.C. Aylesworth.
Olds Gazette 789

Babey, Paul
Ed.
Pres., United Farmers of Alberta (EJ D 6 1966)
Organized Farmer, Edmonton 427

Baccari, Tony
Ed.; pub.
Mormatore, Calgary 200

Bachman, P.E.
Pub.
Clive Review 271

Bacon, John H.
Pub.
Bassano Times 62

Baetz, George O.
Pub.
d. F 1917.
Conservator, Fort Saskatchewan 559

Bagshaw, W.J. (Bill)
Pub.; mgr; journalist
b. Medicine Hat, N 10, 1932

Formerly, mgr of several radio stations; later, Pres., The Focal Group Ltd.
(Questionnaire)
Edmonton Sun 488, 489

Bailey, Charles H.
Ed.
Sports Review, Edmonton 391

Bailey, D. Algar-
See **Algar-Bailey,** D.

Bailey, David
Ed.
Edmonton Sun 489

Baillie, W.
Pub., ed.
Calgary Tribune and Bow River Advertiser 116

Bain, Joseph Vincent (Joe)
Pub.; businessman
d. Castor, May 15, 1978.
Grew up in Castor; operated Bain's Household Furnishings, then became
owner of local pool hall. (*Castor Advance* My 18 1978)
Castor Advance 252

Ball, Helen
Pub.; ed.
Oyen Echo 798

Ball, Victor W.R.B.
Mgr; ed.; printer
Ran printing establishment in Banff with W.H. Kidner (q.v.); after 1928
operated Advance Printing, Drumheller; was in Langley, B.C., for 5
months. (*Crag and Canyon* F 27 1942; **CWNA** v.22 no.594, Ap 25 1942)
Banff Mercury 43
Crag and Canyon, Banff 38
Craigmyle Gazette 295

Ballantyne, W.B.
Pub.
Mirror Journal 761

Balloch, Alex
Pub.
Coleman Journal 290

Baniulis, Barbara
Pub.
Onoway Tribune 794
Whitecourt Star 1033

Baniulis, Barry
Pub.
Onoway Tribune 794
Whitecourt Star 1033

Baril, Denise
Pub.; ed.
Bonnyville Tribune 87

Baril, Ovi
Pub.; ed.
Bonnyville Tribune 87

Barnaby, Roy
Prop.; ed.
Crossfield Chronicle 298

Barnes, George W. (Barney)
Pub.; ed.; railway worker
b. Henley-on-Thames, Eng., Ag 1893; d. Calgary, N 6, 1973.
1912, came to Saskatchewan; served in Canadian forces during 1st World
War; worked for CPR in Banff for many years. (*Banff Crag and Canyon*
N 14 1973)
Crag and Canyon, Banff 38
Tofield Advertiser 968

Barnhart, Paula
Pub.; ed.
Cochrane Times 281

Barnhill, Alexander (Alex or Barney)
Pub.
b. Wetaskiwin, Je 7, 1907; d. Wetaskiwin, Ja 13, 1970.
Father kept livery stable in Wetaskiwin; worked with Canadian Bank of
Commerce and Dept. of Agriculture. (**REY** p.134-5; Wetaskiwin City
Archives)
News Advertiser, Wetaskiwin 1030

Barr, Dan W.T.
Pub.
b. Ottawa, Ont., Ap 27 1943
Cardston Chronicle 246
Raymond Review 828

Barr, Marie A.
Pub.
b. Grande Prairie, Ap 9 1947
Cardston Chronicle 246
Raymond Review 828

Barrett, J.D.S.
Pub.; ed.; printer
Probably from Newfoundland; brother of A.L. Barrett of *Western Star*,
Curling, Nfld.; associated with W.J. Bartlett (q.v.) also of Curling, Nfld.,
in Foothills Job Print. Co., later Bartlett and Barrett, newspaper publishers
and printers, Blairmore; 1924, joined A.L. Barrett; ca. Jl 1929, moved to
Coast for health reasons. (**CROW** p.194; **CPP** v.19 no.2, F 1910, v.33 no.10,
Oc 1924, v.38 no.7, Jl 1929)
Bellevue Times 69
Blairmore Enterprise and Frank Vindicator 77
Claresholm Review 266
Coleman Journal 290
Coleman Miner 288
Forestburg Herald 532
Frank Paper 566
Frank Vindicator 567
Holden Herald 633
Stavely Advertiser 922

Bartlett, Walter James
Pub.
b. Curling, Nfld, My 11 1880; d. My 15 1946.
1904, associated with *Western Star*, Curling, Nfld.;
1907, came to Coleman and entered partnership with T.B. Brandon (q.v.);
1909-10, established business with J.D.S. Barrett (q.v.), Bartlett and
Barrett, newspaper publishers and job printers, Blairmore. (CH My 16
1946; **COU** p.197; **CROW** p.194)
Bellevue Times 69
Blairmore Enterprise 77
Cowley Chronicle and Lundbreck Advertiser 294
Frank Vindicator 567

Bateman Mrs. C.N.
Ed.
Wife of Rev. C.N. Bateman, Padre of Royal Canadian Legion, Barrhead
Branch, and Rector of St. Mary Abbot's Anglican Church. (**BARR** p.84,
159)
Barrhead News 51

Bateman, Lola R.
Ed.
1904, came from Utah with family to Snake Creek; assistant to J. Lundy
Findlay (q.v.) of *Vulcan Advocate*; ed. when Findlay in Air Force 1943-

45; later, married Findlay. (**VUL** p.35, 288-90)
Vulcan Advocate 1005

Bates, Arthur Elmer
Ed.; farmer
d. Oc 30, 1917
Known as "Hobo Bard". Homesteaded in the Holborn district before moving to Stony Plain; contributed poetry and letters to earlier papers and published the *Inga Imp* for a short time; had a printing press on the homestead; enlisted in the Armed Forces in 1915 and was killed in action. (**STON** p.38)
Rural Weekly News & Rube's Farm Fun, Stony Plain 932

Bayley, B.
Ed.
Garden City Times Magrath 718

Baynton, Frederick Willard (Fred)
Pub.
b. Lloydminster, Oc 16 1942
Son of George Franklin Baynton (q.v.); grandson of Joseph G. Willard (q.v.) (Questionnaire)
Lloydminster Daily Times 706
Lloydminster Times 703

Baynton, George Franklin (G.F.)
Pub.; ed.; teacher
b. Arkona, Ont., Mr 13 1912; d. Ja 5 1983.
Son-in-law of Joseph G. Willard (q.v.); formerly high school principal, Woodfibre, B.C. (Questionnaire)
Lloydminster Daily Times 706
Lloydminster Times 703

Beach, Melvin J.
Mgr.
Messaggero delle Praterie, Edmonton 465

Beamish, William F.
Pub.; ed.
Castor Advance 252
Coronation Review 293

Beaudette, David (Frenchy)
Pub.
b. Vegreville, Mr 1 1948
News Advertiser, Vegreville 988

Beaufort, Ernest
Ed.
Prairie Illustrated, Calgary 120

Beaumont, Wright
Mgr.
Evening Chronicle, Edmonton 350
Strathcona Chronicle, Edmonton 345

Becker, Heinrich
Ed.; writer
Issued pamphlet, Mr 1914, *The Truth About Canada* intended to aid organized German immigration to West. (**CANA** v.14, 1914, p.663)
Alberta Herold, Edmonton 343

Beerman, Peter
Pub.
Magyar Hirmondo , Calgary 214

Belagay, Michael
Ed.
On Board of National Trading Co.
Kanadyiets, Edmonton 364

Belair, Danny
Ed.
Veteran Eagle 998

Bell, Charles M. G.
Pub.; ed.; clergyman
Jasper Gateway 658

Bell, George Maxwell (Max)
Pub.; prop.; businessman; horsebreeder and racer
b. Regina, Sask., 1912; d. Montreal, Que., Jl 19 1972.
Son of George Melrose Bell (q.v.); began in newspapers on *Albertan* at time of father's death; became millionaire newspaper and racehorse owner by investing in oil; mid-1960s sold oil interests and concentrated on newspaper operation; Chrmn of Board, FP Publications Ltd; Pres., Sun Pub. Co. Ltd.; dir., CP Rail. (EJ Jl 20 1972; **CAWW** 1970)
Albertan, Calgary 127
Edmonton Bulletin 358

Bell, George Melrose
Pub.; entrepreneur
b. Manitoba, ca. 1885; d. Mr 19 1936.
Brother of Gordon Bell (q.v.) and Harold Bell (q.v.); in his 20s, was assistant postmaster of Regina, Sask.; made fortune in insurance and became wealthy newspaper owner, but at time of death his last remaining newspaper, was in pawn to bankers. (EJ Jl 20 1972)

Calgary Albertan 127
Western Farmer and Weekly Albertan Calgary 123

Bell, Gordon
Pub.
Brother of George Melrose Bell (q.v.) and Harold Bell (q.v.)
Albertan, Calgary 127

Bell, Harold A.
Pub.
d. Oc 22 1976.
Brother of George Melrose Bell (q.v.) and Gordon Bell (q.v.); entered
newspaper business in Vancouver and was founder and bus. mgr,
Vancouver *News-Herald*. (AC Oc 25 1976)
Albertan, Calgary 127

Bell, John
Pub.; ed.
Rattler, Medicine Hat 752

Bell, John J.
Pub.
County News, Strathcona County 939
Record, Fort Saskatchewan 560

Bell, Joseph J. (Joe)
Pub.
b. Dublin, Ireland, F 7 1930; d. Fort Saskatchewan, N 11 1983.
Published *Lamont Municipal and School Gazette*, with Bernard Porritt
Knowles (q.v.)
Record, Fort Saskatchewan 560

Bell, William Alexander (Pat)
Ed.; pub.
b. Coronation, Ag 31 1955
Nisku News 782
Representative, Leduc 689

Bell, William H.
Ed.
Redwater News Daily Flashes 847

Bellamy, Byron Webster (Bart)
Pub.; ed.
Worked on Huntsville, Ont., *Forester*; on mechanical staff, *Wetaskiwin
Times*, for 15 yrs; mg dir. on death of V.C. French (q.v.) (**CWNA** v.21 no.
580, Je 30 1941, v.22 no. 597, Je 20, 1942,; **CPP** v.51 no.8, Ag 1942)
Athabasca Echo 30
Western Union Printer, Medicine Hat 749
Wetaskiwin Times 1022

Bellwood, W. A. M.
Pub.
Taber Free Press 952

Bender, John M.
Pub.
b.ca. 1872; d. Vancouver, My 1933.
After he had sold the *Nanton News* he moved to Vancouver and worked on the Vancouver *Province* for 20 years. (**NAN** p.140)
Nanton News 780

Bennett, A. S.
Pub.
Formerly of Oil Springs *Chronicle*, Ont., came to Alberta to edit newspaper and manage printing shop in Medicine Hat. (**CPP** v.12 no.8, Ag 1903)
Lethbridge Herald 693

Benoit, E. P.
Ed.; clergyman
b. Calgary, N 28 1918
Minister of Church of Christ, Nanton, 1958 on. (**WWA1** 1968)
Nanton News 780

Bentein, James G. (Jim)
Pub; ed.; journalist
b. Sarnia, Ont., S 13 1946
Reporter on many newspapers in Ontario and Alberta, including the *Edmonton Journal*. (Questionnaire)
Grand Centre-Cold Lake-Bonnyville Sun, Grand Centre 581

Berg, Carl Emil
Ed.; labour leader
b. Stockholm, Sweden, 1888; d. Edmonton, Ap 28 1958.
1904 emigrated to U. S., and to Canada in 1906; worked in construction for CPR, homesteaded near Wetaskiwin; moved to Edmonton to work for Crown Paving Co.; by 1910 was active union leader; 1929, Pres., Edmonton Trades and Labour Council for over 10 years; 1944, Vice-Pres., Alberta Federation of Labour; labour leader and representative at national and international level; active in civic politics. (**CARA** 1 p.64; EJ Ap 29 1958)
One Big Union Bulletin, Edmonton 382

Bergh, Keith
Pub.
Strathmore Standard 940

Bernard, William Leigh
Pub.; lawyer

b. Ireland? Ja 1 1845; d. Calgary, My 19 1911.
1880-83, edited Thom's *Statistics of the United Kingdom*; legal ed., *Irish Ecclesiastical Gazette*; enrolled as advocate for Northwest Territories, 1888, and was lawyer in Calgary. (*Calgary News Telegram* My 20 1911)
Alberta Tribune Weekly Edition, Calgary 123
Independent, Calgary 125

Berryessa, W. S.
Pub.
Cardston Globe 240
Raymond Leader 824

Berryman, H. B.
Pub.; ed.
New Age, Wetaskiwin 1028
Packet, Millet 756
Wetaskiwin Free Press 1026

Bert, John T.
Ed.
Mountaineer, Rocky Mountain House 860

Betts, Mrs. G. E.
Prop.
d. D 1941.
Amisk Advocate 20
Czar Clipper 301
Hughenden Record 636

Betts, H. W.
Pub.
Amisk Advocate 20
Czar Clipper 301
Hardisty Mail 608
Hardisty World 609
Hughenden News 635
Hughenden Record 636
Lougheed Journal 712

Beveridge, Ebenezer
Pub.
Mountaineer, Rocky Mountain House 860

Bhatia, Gurcharan Singh
Ed.; pub.
b. Kashmir State, India, Ag 2 1931
Prairie Link, Edmonton 497

Bigford, Grace
Pub.; ed.
Big Country News, Drumheller 332

Birch, H. J.
Agent; teacher
Gadsby Recorder 570

Birtwistle, A. E.
Pub.
Big Valley News 70

Black, John
Ed.
b. Ontario
Lived in Montana before moving to Fort Macleod; storekeeper, Fort Macleod. (**FORT** p.60, 82, 95)
Outlaw, Scotts Coulee 888

Black Plume, Reggie
Ed.
Sun Dance Echo, Stand Off 914

Blackmere, Al
Pub.
With Barrhead Printers and Stationers, 1978-83. (**PUB** Ja 1983)
Barrhead Leader 52
Grizzly Gazette, Swan Hills 947

Blauel, Herbert
Pub.
Forestburg Herald 532

Bloom, Bernie
Ed.
Canada Goose, Edmonton 461

Blount, W. C.
Pub.
Rockyford Budget 865

Blow, E. A.
Pub.; ed.
Athabasca Times 27

Bly, Caen
Ed.
Kainai News, Stand Off 915

Boehnert, W. C.
Ed.; pub.
Alberta Herold, Edmonton 412
Herold, Edmonton 403

Boileau, François-Xavier
Ed.
Dir. and agent-gen., Société de colonisation, 1906-7; Mayor, Brosseau-Duvernay, 1909; Pres., Duvernay Creamery Assoc., 1912; 1913, moved to Edmonton; Vice-Pres., Société Saint-Jean-Baptiste, Edmonton.
(**DEG** 1 p. 13-14)
Courrier de l'Ouest, Edmonton 347
Union, Edmonton 378

Boorne, W. Hanson
Ed.; photographer; landscape artist.
Photographer and landscape artist in Calgary in 1880s. (**PEEL**)
Rocky Mountain Echoes, Banff 36

Boswell, Pat
Pub.
Husband of Stephanie Boswell (q.v.)
Banff Crag and Canyon 38

Boswell, Stephanie
Pub.
Wife of Pat Boswell (q.v.)
Banff Crag and Canyon 38

Bourassa, Eugene
Pub.
Devon Dispatch 315

Bourdais, Donat Marc le
See **Le Bourdais**, Donat Marc

Bourne, W. H.
Ed.
Suburban Times, Edmonton 436

Bow Valley Cultural Improvement Society
Anthracite Chronicle, Canmore 233

Bower, J. E. (Ted)
Ed.; journalist
12 years with *Edmonton Journal* news and editorial departments before returning to Red Deer *Advocate* Ja 1, 1963. (**EJ** undated clipping)
Advocate, Red Deer 834

Bowes, David M.
Ed.
Edmonton News 444
Record-Gazette, Peace River 804

Bowes, Howard M.
Pub.
b. Moose Jaw, Sask., Ja 14, 1931
Pres., Lynard Pub. Ltd.
Examiner, Spruce Grove 913
Freelancer, Mayerthorpe 738
Grand Trunk Poplar Press, Evansburg 523
Nisku News 782
Onoway Tribune 794
Reporter, Stony Plain 937
Representative, Leduc 689
Western Review, Drayton Valley 323
Whitecourt Star 1033

Bowes, James E.
Pub.; ed; journalist
b. Ingersoll, Ont.
First newspaper experience with Regina *Leader-Post*; later worked for *Sentinel-Review*, Woodstock, Ont., London *Free Press*, and Montreal *Standard*; during War staff writer with *The Maple Leaf*, in Europe; after War formed Bowes Publishers Ltd., with William Bowes (q.v.). (*Daily Herald Tribune* Ap 26 1966)
Alberta Business, Edmonton 491
Edmonton News 444
Herald-Tribune, Grande Prairie 586

Bowes, William H.
Pub.
Formed Bowes Publishers Ltd. with James E. Bowes (q.v.) after War.
Herald-Tribune, Grande Prairie 586

Boyce, Donald E.
Pub.
Husband of Iola Boyce (q.v.)
Fairview Post 526

Boyce, Iola
Pub.
Wife of Donald E. Boyce (q.v)
Fairview Post 526

Bozyk, Pantelemon
Ed.; pub.; Eastern Orthodox clergyman; writer
b. 1879; d. 1944.

1900, came to Canada from Bukovina; member Russian Orthodox Church; after 1st World War abandoned tsarophilism and became Ukrainian Greek Orthodox priest; moved to Winnipeg ca. 1920 where was active in church work and publishing; poet and novelist. (PEEL)
Russkyi Golos, Edmonton 369

Brabyn, E. J.
Ed.
Crag and Canyon, Banff 38

Braden, Thomas B. (Tom)
Pub; printer; businessman
b. Millbrook, Ont.; d. Ag 18, 1904.
Learned trade as printer in Peterborough; in insurance and real estate business in Calgary. (CH Ag 18 1904, J1 8 1950)
Calgary Herald 113, 115
Calgary Tribune and Bow River Advertiser 116
Prairie Illustrated, Calgary 120

Braggee, Antti
Ed.
Moukari, Edmonton 366

Brainard
Ed.
Barons Beacon 1046

Brandon, T. B.
Pub.; prop.; ed.
In partnership with Walter James Bartlett (q.v.) under name Foothills Job Print. Co.; 1911, left firm to go to Cardston.
Alberta Star, Cardston 240
Coleman Miner 288
Frank Paper 566

Brainigan, D.
Pub.
Falher News 528

Brazier, John C.
Pub.
Chinook, High River 624

Bresciano, Remo
Ed.
Messaggero delle Praterie, Edmonton 465

Breton, Paul-Emile, o.m.i.
Ed.; historian; Catholic clergyman
b. Quebec, 1902; d. 1972.

Author of several historical and biographical works. **(PEEL; STRATHERN)**
Survivance, Edmonton 404

Brett, Jack
Pub.
Grande Prairie This Week 588

Brewerton, Lee Gray
Pub.
1906, came from Salt Lake City with family; prop., Raymond Theatre; active in community **(HIC** p.366-7)
Raymond Leader 824

Brice, Edward
Pub.; ed.; lawyer
d. Winnipeg, Man., D 17 1979.
1906, came to Alberta; 1909, called to bar; practised in Edmonton. **(WW** 1917/18)
Barrhead News 51

Brinsmead, Thomas McMaster
Printer; pub.
b. Toronto, Ag 16 1886; d. Edmonton, Ja 7 1977.
Began newspaper work in Toronto at age 14; learned printing trade; worked with father, T. H. Brinsmead in Ont. and Sask.; retired 1957, thereafter free-lance newspaper work until complete retirement at age of 88. (Questionnaire; interview with widow)
Bashaw Star 56

Brinson Ray L.
Pub.; ed
Innisfail Booster 645

Brisbin, Charles Nelson
Pub.; teacher; farmer
b. Harriston, Ont., 1879; d. 1921.
Ca. 1900 moved with family to Holden area; high school teacher; farmed during First World War. **(HEM** p.242)
Holden Herald 633

Briscoe, Frank A.
Pub.
Later, pub. weekly in Armstrong, B. C. until retirement on west coast, 1943. **(CWNA** v.25 no.614, N 1943)
District Call, Edson 508
Bassano Recorder 59

Britton, Robert V.
Ed.; clergyman

1927, came to Edmonton from Toronto; ordained 1932; originated radio show, *Catholic Truth Broadcasts*; provincial dir., Catholic Women's League Canada; parish priest; retired 1957. (EJ Mr 14 1957)
Western Catholic, Edmonton 388

Broadfoot, Dave
Pub.
Redcliff Review 1085

Broadley, George
Pub.
Castor Advance 252

Brogden, Harry B.
Ed.
Call, Calgary 186

Brooks, Johns
Pub.
Bassano News 57

Brooks, Mary Lou
Pub.
Bassano Times 62

Brooks, R. P.
Pub.; clergyman
Served as United Church minister in Donalda, 1923-7. (DON p.65)
Donalda Free Lance 319

Broughton, J. E. (Ted)
Pub.
Came from Creelman, Sask.; in service in World War II. (CPP v.56 no.5, My 1947)
Mountaineer, Rocky Mountain House 860

Brouwer, Peter D. (PB)
Pub.; ed.
b. Leiden, Netherlands, Ap 29 1935
Calgary Rural Week 218
North Hill News, Calgary 191

Brower, Frank C.
Prop.; printer
b. ca. 1878
Printer by trade, newspaper career began in Baxter, Iowa, 1892; 1904, came from Baxter to join parents on ranch in Olds district; 1957, wrote autobiography. (OLDS p.59)
Olds Gazette 789

Brown, C.
Prop.
Of Calgary. (**CPP** v.32 no.1, Ja 1923)
Carmangay Sun 247

Brown, D. W.
Ed.
Western Oil Examiner, Calgary 165

Brown, Ernest
Mgr; ed.; photographer.
b. Middlesborough, Eng., 1877; d. Edmonton, 1951.
1904, arrived Edmonton; business collapsed 1914; ran unsuccessfully
1921 provincial election; spent 8 yrs in Vegreville photographing,
cataloguing his collection, and writing *Birth of the West*; returned to
Edmonton 1929 and operated Pioneer Days Museum 1933-39, exhibiting
his artifacts and photographs; 1947, province purchased collection.
(**CANE** v.1, p.242)
Glow Worm, Edmonton 398

Brownlee, Leroy
Pub.; printer; miller
Came from U. S.; worked on steamers on Arrow Lakes, B. C.;
homesteaded, Springdale; 1920s, operated wood-sawing and feed-
grinding operation; later, printed manuals on sawing, shingling,
blacksmithing, *National Hobby and Trades* magazine, and a matrimonial
magazine; retired in Grande Prairie. (**TRIB** p. 213-5)
North Country News, Hoadley 629
North Country Times, Hoadley 630

Bruce, Reginald Wyndham
Pub.; ed.
Formerly with Winnipeg *Saturday Post* and Prince Albert *Herald.*
(**CPP** v.22 no.2, F 1913)
Athabasca Times 27

Bruchal, Thomas A.
Pub.
Redwater News 848

Brunsden, Edwin William (Ted)
Ed.; agriculturalist; journalist; politician
b. Tunbridge Wells, Eng., D 10 1896; d. Calgary, S 28 1976.
Served in infantry in World War I; 1927, graduated in agriculture from
University of Alberta; associate-ed., Nor'_West_Farmer, Winnipeg; exec.
secy, Alberta Federation of Agriculture; gen. mgr, Eastern Irrigation
District, Brooks; freelance writer; 1958-62, Progressive Conservative MP
for Medicine Hat. (**WWC** 1973; *Brooks Bulletin* F 7 1973; CH S 30 1976)
Western Farmer, Calgary 164

Brutinel, Raymond
Ed.
Courrier de l'Ouest, Edmonton 347

Bryce, Herb
Ed.
Banner Post, Manning 722

Buchan, John
Pub.; mgr
b. Coburg, Ont.
Lived in England for 11 yrs. **(PUB** Je 1985)
Record-Gazette, Peace River 804

Buchanan, Hugh P.
Pub.; writer
Son of William Ashbury Buchanan (q.v.); left Lethbridge Ag 1967 for
Palm Springs, Calif.; became Hollywood writer. (LH Ag 16 1968)
Lethbridge Herald 694

Buchanan, J. E.
Pub.; ed.
Conservator, Fort Saskatchewan 559
Gazette, Lamont 680
St. Paul Star 882

Buchanan, William Ashbury
Pub.; ed.; politician
b. Fraserville, Ont., Jl 2 1876; d. Jl 11 1954.
Father of Hugh P. Buchanan (q.v.); early newspaper work in Ontario.,
ending as mg. ed. and dir., St. Thomas Times-Journal; came to Lethbridge
1905; 1907, organized Legislature library; Liberal MLA, 1909, Minister
Without Portfolio, resigned 3 mths later; 1911 and 1917 elected Liberal
MP for Medicine Hat; retired from House of Commons 1921; mbr of Sen-
ate from 1925 until death. **(WWC** 1952; **STEE; BYR** p.20)
Lethbridge Herald 693

Buckton, Thomas L. (Tom)
Prop.; ed.; school teacher; farmer; engineer
Family came from Durham County, B. C.; 1898, came to Alberta, taught
school and farmed; 1909, retired from homesteading, had grist mill with
brother Harry; 1915, engineer with electric light plant in Olds. **(OLD**
p.238-40)
Olds Gazette 789

Buehler, Clint
Ed.; pub.; song-writer, broadcaster
1977, became Pres., Global Village Publications; 1980, Dir., United Way
Public Relations. (Unidentified newspaper clipping)
Examiner, Edmonton 467

Fort McMurray News Advertiser 1073
Native People, Edmonton 460

Buffalo Rider, Ben
Dir.
Nations Ensign, Edmonton 494

Bugnet, Georges Charles Jules
Ed.; writer; botanist
b. Chalon-sur-Saone, France, F 23 1879; d. St. Albert, Ja 11 1981.
1905, came to Rich Valley, northwest of Edmonton; published 6 novels and book of poetry; known internationally for hybridization of roses; founder and Pres., Association canadienne-francaise de l'Alberta. (PEEL; CANE v.1 p.238)
Union, Edmonton 378

Burde, Richard John
Ed.; pub.; politician.
d. Port Alberni, B. C., D 17 1954.
1898, news ed., Vancouver Province; editorial positions on Winnipeg *Telegram*, Victoria *Colonist*, Nanaimo *Free Press*; 1907, established Port Alberni *News*; mayor, Nanaimo, 5 yrs; Independent MLA, B. C. Legislature, 1919-1928. (CH D 20 1954)
Crag and Canyon, Banff 38

Burdick, Isaac Newton
Pub.; ed.
b. ca. 1844
1898-1902, overseer of Lacombe; 1900, elected dir. of forerunner of Central Alberta Agricultural Society; school trustee, Blackfalds School District. (LACO p.560)
Advertiser and Central Alberta News, Lacombe 669

Buren, Abram P. Van
see **Van Buren**, Abram P.

Burgar, Jeff
Pub.
Falher News 529
Lakeside Leader, Slave Lake 903
Northern Messenger, High Prairie 622

Burgar, Reginald
Pub.
Falher News 529

Burgess, Joseph
Pub.
Fort Saskatchewan Recorder 558

Burke, Bev
Ed.
English Express, Edmonton 499

Burns, Roy S.
Pub.; ed.; mgr
With *Edmonton Bulletin* before going to Grouard; left *Edmonton Journal* to go to Bashaw; moved to B. C. coast after sold *Bashaw Star*. (**CPP** v.21 no.9, S 1912, v.27 no.5, My 1918)
Bashaw Star 56
Grouard News 604

Burt, Eric O.
Pub.; ed.
Bow Valley Advertiser, Calgary 190

Burton, Fred
Pub.
b. Portage La Prairie, Man., O 19 1866; d. Je 19 1977.
Apprenticed to David Horton Elton (q.v.) as printer's devil; lived in Magrath; 1964, retired. (**CARDS** p.266)
Alberta Star, Cardston 240
Cardston News 241

Burwood, Catherine (Cathy)
Pub.; graphics and camera-room technician
b. Vulcan, My 15 1953
Eagleview Post, Turner Valley 979
Vulcan Advocate 1005

Bushfield, Frank
Ed.; clergyman
First resident Methodist Church minister, Cayley, 1909-1912. (**WHI** p.116)
Cayley Hustler 253

Butler, Richard D. (Dick)
Pub.
b. Edmonton, ca. 1921; d. 1958.
Moved to Jasper Place in 1945, after having lived in northern Alberta and British Columbia; in Army Signal Corps during War; elected Jasper Place Town Council; shot and killed by madman. (City of Edmonton Archives Reference files)
Jasper Place Citizen, Edmonton 436

Butterfield, O. A.
Prop.; printer
Came from Iowa, Ap 1900, to Lacombe; Ag 1903 departed for Seattle, returned to Lacombe 1904. (**MEE** p.160)
Lacombe Advertiser 669
Red Deer Advocate 834

Fort Saskatchewan Reporter office, 1904. Item 555. (Provincial Archives of Alberta Photograph. E. Brown Collection B3097).

Le Progrès Building, Morinviille, 1911. Item 764. (Provincial Archives of Alberta Photograph A3739).

Eugène Chartier and Adelard Baril in Progrès Albertain office, Edmonton, 1914. Item 374. (Provincial Archives of Alberta Photograph A6669).

Edmonton Capital Editorial office, 1913. Item 356. (Glenbow Archives Photograph NC-6-239).

Calgary Herald Newsboys, c. 1913. Item 113. (Glenbow Archives Photograph NB-42-31).

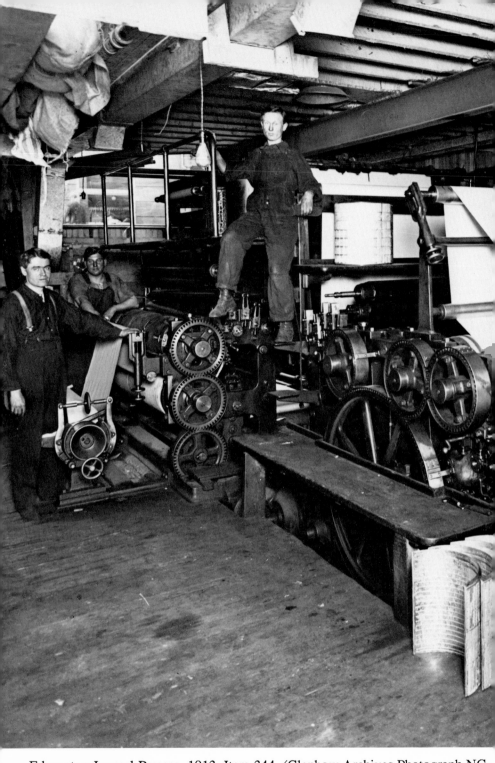

Edmonton Journal Presses, 1913. Item 344. (Glenbow Archives Photograph NC-6-242).

onton Capital Composing Room, 1913. Item 356. (Glenbow Archives Photo-
1 NC-6-242).

onton Journal Composing Room, 1910. Item 344. (Glenbow Archives Photo-
1 NA-1328-61627).

Vendor with doll selling Edmonton Journal, 1920. Item 344. (Glenbow Arch Photograph NC-6-5582).

National Park Life office with Charles B. (Charley) Halpin, publisher, in the d way, Banff, 1888. Item 35. (Glenbow Archives Photograph NA-529-27).

ville Examiner Building, 1951. Item 333. (Provincial Archives of Alberta ograph A8818).

icine Hat News Press Room, 1956. Item 743. (Provincial Archives of Alberta ograph A8522).

Drumheller Mail Staff Members, 1956. Item 327. (Provincial Archives of Alb⟩
Photograph A8528).

Olds Gazette Building, 1967. Item
789. (Provincial Archives of Alberta
Photograph PA 3822).

Innisfail Province Building, 1967.
Item 643. (Provincial Archives of
Alberta Collection PA 4071).

Buttle, Tim
Ed.
Native People, Edmonton 460

Byard, James
Ed.
Mile Zero News, Grimshaw 603

Byers, Ike
Tramp printer
Banff National Park Gazette 37

Byers, J. Young
Ed.; stockman; businessman
b. Newcastle-on-Tyne, Eng.
Ca. 1892, came to Canada; engaged in stock-raising, Dried Meat Lake;
1899, moved to Wetaskiwin; accountant, then store mgr; had B. M. Angus
implement warehouse, two opera houses; founder of village 10m. from
Wetaskiwin. (*Manitoba Free Press* My 28 1904)
Post, Wetaskiwin 1024

Bylyna, M.
Ed.; clergyman
Svitlo, Mundare 772

Byrne, Pat
Ed.
Chinook Reporter, Lethridge 702

C. C. F.
See **Co-operative Commonwealth Federation**

Caesar, Charles Vivian
Pub.; ed.
Vermilion Standard 992

Calahasen, Stella
Ed.
Nations Ensign, Edmonton 494

Calder, Heather
Pub.
Elk Point Reflections 1069
Mannville Reflections 731

Calgary Jewish Community Council
Calgary Jewish News 196

Calgary Status of Women Action Committee
Calgary Women's Newspaper 206

Calgary Trades and Labor Council
Alberta Clarion, Calgary 1048
Alberta Federationist, Calgary 144
Call, Calgary 186

Calgary Typographical Union No. 449
Calgary Typo News 177

Calgary Women's Press Club
Western Standard, Calgary 142

Cameron, H. S.
Pub.
Bassano Mail 58

Cameron, William Bleasdell
Pub.; public servant; ed.; journalist
b. Trenton, Ont., Jl 28 1862; d. Meadow Lake, Sask., Mr 3 1951.
1881, arrived in West; survivor of Frog Lake massacre, 1885; in service of
the Hudson's Bay Co. and the Dominion Govt.; lived in U. S. A. for a
time, where he edited *Forest and Stream*; "discovered" Charles M.
Russell, cowboy artist; contributed many stories of Indian life and fur
trade to magazines. **(PEEL)**
Bassano News 57
Vermilion Signal 991

Campbell, Charles Edwin
Pub.
b. Des Moines, Iowa, My 16 1885
Dir., Vancouver *Sun*, 1912-23; owner, Vancouver *World*, 1920-23; ini-
tiated and owned Vancouver *Daily Star* for 3 mths in 1923; established
and owned Regina *Daily Star*, 1928-33. **(WWC 1949)**
Edmonton Bulletin 358

Campbell, J. H.
Pub.
Macleod Weekly News, Fort Macleod 543

Campbell, R. Bowman
Ed.
Olds Gazette 789

Campbell, Robert Eldon
Teacher; mountain guide; politician
b. Montague, Ont., Ag 15 1851
Taught school in Banff; chief guide with CPR in Rocky Mountains;
organizer and charter mbr of Canadian Alpine Club; elected Independent
MLA, 1913 and 1917; Captain, World War I; published autobiography, *I*

Would Do It Again: Reminiscences of the Rockies (1959) (**AL; CAMP**)
Rocky Mountain Courier, Banff 40

Canadian Polish Congress
Biuletyn. Kongresu Polonii Kanadyjskiej Okreg Alberta, Edmonton 443

Canadian Society of Equity
Great West, Edmonton 349

Canadian Uncle Sam Amusement Club
Rocky Mountain House Echo 856

Canadian Western Immigration Association
Sunset News Bulletin, Calgary 1049

Caragata, Warren
Ed.; labour historian
Author of *Alberta Labour: A Heritage Untold* (1979)
Alberta Labour, Edmonton 450

Carleton, James P.
Pub.; ed.
Banner, Edmonton 437

Carmichael, Bernice Phoebe
Pub.; ed.
b. Traynor, Sask., Mr 22 1920
Valley Views, Valleyview 985

Carozzi, G.
Ed.
Panorama, Calgary 199

Carr, Otto L.
Pub.
Raymond Rustler 824

Carrigan, Harry D.
Ed.; pub.
Became Sec. Treas., Post-war Construction Committee; later with Alberta
Dept. of Economic Affairs.
Northern Post, Waskatenau 1012
Veteran Post 997

Carrington, Lane
Pub.
Weekly Review, Viking 1001

Carroll, Terry Bruce
Pub.; journalist; farmer; sod farm mgr

b. West Lorne, Ont., N 29 1950
Record, Fort Saskatchewan 560
Sherwood Park News 896

Carswell, John Alfred
Prop.; ed.; farmer
b. Oshawa, Ont., Je 7 1856; d. Red Deer, N 13 1936.
Worked on newspapers in Ont., and owned Oshawa *Vindicator* 1881-
1891; moved to Red Deer 1891; 1893, Justice of Peace; 1914-15, Mayor,
Red Deer. (**ARDA; WW** 1912; **BLU** v.2 p.75)
News, Red Deer 835

Cartier, Eugene William (Gene)
Ed.; farmer
d. Ja 1977.
Native of Debut, N. S., came west in fall 1910, first to Saskatchewan for a
yr, then to Medicine Hat where worked as labourer; moved to Irma,
homesteaded; 1915, enlisted in World War I; winter 1919-20, gave up
farming; Sec-Treas., Town Council, 1932 on; 1946, moved to Wainwright.
(**IRMA** p.457)
Irma Times 647

Cary, Floyd T.
Pub.
Son of Norman G. Cary (q.v.)
Bassano Recorder 59
Bow Valley Resource, Arrowwood 24

Cary, Norman G.
Pub.; ed.
b. Oak Lake, Man.; d. F 1938.
Bassano Recorder 59
Bow Valley Resource, Arrowwood 24

Caston, Douglas Marmaduke
Pub.; politician
b. Macklin, Sask., S 3 1917
Served in air force during World War II; with R. E. Gardner, owned Edson
Printers; Progressive Conservative MP for Jasper-Edson, 1967-8; ran as
Independent Conservative for Rocky Mountain 1968 but was defeated;
Pres., Yellowhead Publishers and Central Web Offset Ltd. (**BYR** p.22;
CPP v.59 no.12, D 1950)
Edson Leader 512
Hinton Herald 627

Catholic Archdiocese of Edmonton
Western Catholic, Edmonton 388
Western Catholic Reporter, Edmonton 453

Catholic Diocese of Calgary
Western Catholic, Edmonton 388

Cavanagh, Gary
Pub.; ed.
Husband of Marlene Cavanagh (q.v.)
Devon Dispatch 315
Morinville and Sturgeon Mirror, Morinville 767

Cavanagh, Marlene
Pub.; ed.
Wife of Gary Cavanagh (q.v.)
Devon Dispatch 315
Morinville and Sturgeon Mirror, Morinville 767

Cave, Harold J.
Pub.; ed.
Plaindealer, Youngstown 1041

Cayley, Hugh St. Quentin
Lawyer; ed.; pub.; politician
b. Toronto, Ont., N 19 1857; d. Vancouver, B. C., Ap 13 1934.
Practised law, Silver City; Conservative mbr, Legislative Council, Northwest Territories, 1886-1894; Premier, 1893; Senior Judge of County Court; moved to Vancouver 1897; retired 1933. (CH Ap 13 1934)
Calgary Herald 115

Ceia, Marianna
Ed.
Journal Portugese, Edmonton 466

Central Alberta Stock Growers' Association
Stettler Independent 923

Central Strike Committee (Calgary)
Calgary Strike Bulletin 157

Central Strike Committee (Edmonton)
Edmonton Free Press 384

Cependa, Michael
Ed.; clergyman
b. ca. 1899; d. Arizona, 1980.
1936, to Smoky Lake; priest at Ewand and Pakan churches; left Smoky Lake 1962(?). (**OUR** p.346)
Holos Pravdy, Smoky Lake 904

Chabot, Ernest (Ernie)
Pub.

Worked for Alex. J. Allnutt (q.v.) in Edmonton. (**CPP** v.48 no.9, S 1939)
Alliance Times 16

Chamberlain, William
Mgr; ed.
Central Albertan, Wetaskiwin 1025

Chambers, Edward Vincent (Ed)
Pub.; printer
b. Orillia, Ont., Ag 18 1866; d. Lacombe, Ap 19 1941.
Began newspaper career in Ontario; went to British Columbia, 1890 and
founded several newspapers there before coming to Claresholm; printer
for CNR in Edmonton; thence to Alix. (Questionnaire; **CPP** v.44 no.11, N
1935)
Mirror News-Record 14
Claresholm Advertiser 267

Chambers, Ernest John
Pub.; journalist; author
b. Pentridge, Eng., Ap 16 1862; d. Ottawa, Ont., My 11 1925.
Came to Canada, 1870; active in journalism, Montreal, from 1880; 1888-
9, ed. *Calgary Herald*; civil servant in Ottawa, 1904-25; best known in
Montreal as a writer, in connection with municipal journalism, historical
and military literature; published many articles. (**MACM; WW** 1917/18)
Calgary Daily Herald 115
Calgary Herald and Alberta Livestock Journal 113

Chambers, F. Velma
Pub.
Wife of Ed V. Chambers (q.v.)
Alix Free Press 14

Charters, Gertrude
Ed.
Herald-Tribune, Grande Prairie 586

Chartier, Eugene
Ed.
Progrès, Morinville 764
Progrès albertain, Edmonton 374

Cherniak, Wasyl
Ed.; pub.
From Chechy, Ukraine; "rabid Russophile"; made fortune in gold in
Alaska; Chrmn, Russian Pub. Co. (**MARU** p. 289-90)
Russkyi Golos, Edmonton 369

Chernin, Lynn
Ed.
Parklander, Hinton 627

Cheyne, Donna
Ed.
b. Nanaimo, B. C., Ja 2 1957
Vauxhall Advance 986

Chomiak, M.
Ed.
Ukrainian News, Edmonton 402

Chomyn, Walt
Ed.
Stoney Echo, Morley 768

Christensen, A.
Pub.
Northern Herald, Lac La Biche 661

Christian, D. M.
Pub.
Formerly on editorial staff, *Toronto Globe*. (**CPP** v.22 no.4, Ap 1913)
Redcliff Journal 844

Chysowski, Ed
Pub.
News Advertiser, Vegreville 988

Clark, Alan Leslie (Al)
Pub.; businessman
b. Jasper Park, N 7 1927
Hinton Herald 627
News Advertiser Ad-Mart, Hinton 628

Clark, Charles A. (Sr.)
Pub.; prop.; ed.
b. Kincardine, Ont., Mr 27 1870; d. 1949
1890-99, worked on Kincardine *Review*; served in Boer War; 1903-4, horse-ranching in Alberta. (**VUL** p.35; **WW** 1912; **AC** D 7 1945; **CH** My 12 1982)
High River Times 625
Okotoks Review 783
Vulcan Advocate 1005

Clark, Charles A. (Jr.)
Pub.; ed.
b. High River, Ag 6 1910; d. High River, My 10 1982.
High River Times 625
Okotoks Review 783
Vulcan Advocate 1005

Clark, William I.
Pub.

Of Edmonton when bought *Representative* (**CWNA** v.25 no.613, S/Oc 1943)
Crag and Canyon, Banff 38
Representative, Leduc 689

Clarke, Arthur Howard (Hap)
Pub.; journalist
b. Fort Macleod, N 25 1910
Brother of John Graham Clark (q.v.); reporter on Canadian Army *Maple Leaf* newspaper during and after War; retired 1976, became freelance journalist and published local Chamber of Commerce newsletter. (Questionnaire)
Drumheller Mail 327
Innisfail Province 643

Clarke, F.
Pub.
Brother of Thomas Clarke (q.v.)
Gazette and Alberta Live Stock Record, Fort Macleod 536
Macleod Advance, Fort Macleod 538

Clarke, John Graham
Pub; printer
b. Olds, Mr 23 1917
Brother of Arthur Clarke (q.v.)
Drumheller Mail 327

Clarke, Maureen
Ed.
Moccasin Telegram, Fort Chipewyan 534

Clarke, Murdock
Ed.
Canadian Miner, Calgary 170

Clarke, Thomas
Pub; policeman
Brother of F. Clarke (q.v.); North West Mounted Policeman. (**FORT** p.80-1)
Gazette and Alberta Live Stock Record, Fort Macleod 536
Macleod Advance, Fort Macleod 538

Clarke, W. A.
Ed.
Medicine Hat Call 747

Clements, Terry
Pub.
Barrhead Leader 52
Commerce News, Edmonton 1067
Edmonton Examiner [North editions] 490

Edmonton Examiner [West editions] 487
Examiner, Spruce Grove 913
Grizzly Gazette, Swan Hills 947

Clerc, Normand F. Le
See **Le Clerc**, Normand F.

Cliffe, Sydney H.
Pub.; ed.
d. D 28 1958.
Douglas Social Credit Advocate, Calgary 176
Edson-Jasper Signal, Edson 511

Clinton, Ed
Ed.
Mercury, Tofield 970

Clotworthy, S. J.
Ed.; druggist
Bowden Times 97

Clouston, Diann
Pub.
Weekly Review, Viking 1001

Clyne, DeForrest
Pub.
Chauvin Gazette 262

Coach, Ken
Ed.
Previously worked on *News of the North*, Yellowknife.
Athabasca Call 32

Coco, Vittorio
Pub.; ed.
Mondo, Edmonton 456

Cocq, W. A. R.
Ed.
When *Lethbridge Telegram* suspended publication, went to *Lethbridge Herald* where Buchanan made a place for the "bookish Etonian, "No War" Cocq" retired to Deep Cove, B. C. (STEE p.49-50; CPP v.50 no.9, S 1941)
Lethbridge Telegram 697

Coleman, Mrs. Blake
Ed.
Sunset News Bulletin, Calgary 1049

Coles, Arthur H.
Pub.; printer
Beverly Advertiser, Edmonton 373
Spectator, Edmonton 414
Western Illustrated News, Edmonton 390

Coles, Ivan
Pub.
Olds Star 1083

Collier, Stanley
Ed.
Western Ilustrated News, Edmonton 390
Worker, Calgary 178

Collin, André
Ed.
Franco-albertain, Edmonton 458

Collister, Ron
Ed.; broadcaster; journalist
b. Liverpool, Eng., ca. 1930
Worked on Toronto *Telegram* before joining CBC; 1975, columnist for
Toronto *Sun*; 1978, came to Edmonton to help launching of *Edmonton
Sun*; 1980, joined *Edmonton Journal* as ed. at large. (EJ Ja 18 1980)
Edmonton Sun 489

**Commerce Association for Marketing Essential Literature,
University of Alberta**
Business Reporter, Edmonton 479

Connell, Graeme K.
Pub.; journalist; photographer
1968, Information Officer, New Zealand Antarctic Research program;
came to Canada and was news ed., *Daily Herald Tribune*, Grande Prairie;
1971, edited Whitehorse *Star*. (Whitehorse Star S 30 1971)
Fort McMurray Today 552
Grande Prairie Booster 588

Connolly, M. L.
Ed.
Western Catholic, Edmonton 388

Conquest, Charles H.
Pub.
Son of William Conquest (q.v.); worked with father on *Athabasca Echo*;
joined army 1941. (**CWNA** v.21 no.577, My 27 1941)
Athabasca Echo 30

Conquest, William
Pub.
b. Hitchin, Eng.; d. My 16 1942.
Founded North London *Chronicle* and Woods Green *Journal*; pub. Kerrobert *Citizen*, Kindersley *Clarion* and *Magyard Farmer* in Saskatchewan before coming to Alberta; homesteaded briefly nr Coronation; worked on *Killam News*. (**CWNA** v.22 no.595, My 28 1942)
Athabasca Echo 30

Cook, Ernest (Ernie)
Pub.
b. Manitoulin Island, Ont.
1909, moved to Taber; 1913, to Grouard; homesteaded nr Spirit River and was in lumber business; 1919, moved to Conjuring Creek, Leduc district, on wife's family farm; 1947, to Edmonton; on CCF executive. (EJ F 15 1973)
Taber Advertiser 953

Cook, Fred T.
Pub.; clergyman
United Church Minister in Champion, 1918-19. (**CLE** p.115)
Champion News 259

Cook, Norman E.
Pub.; teacher; farmer; politician
b. Woodstock, Ont., D 9 1888; d. Olds, Ag 5 1950.
Taught school, Woodstock; 1910, came to Calgary and worked for John Deere and Massey-Harris; 1918, farming in Olds district; 1936, moved to Eagle Valley; 1948, established farm at Bergen; Social Credit MLA, elected 1940, 1944, 1948. (**ALI**; EJ Ag 8 1950; Olds Gazette Ag 10 1950)
Wainwright Star 1007

Cook, Roy D.
Ed.
Alberta Business, Edmonton 491

Cook, Stephen John
Ed.; pub.
Western Wheel, Okotoks 787

Cooke, Winston H.
Ed.
Calgary Citizen 187

Coop, Steve
Ed.
Fort McMurray Express 553

Cooper, Ashley Horace Cholwel
Pub.; ed.; teacher; politician

b. Baldur, Man., F 6 1905; d. 1982.
Son of Sextus Ruthven Pringle Cooper (q.v.); brother of Douglas, Percy and Vernon Cooper (all q.v.); teacher, 1924-29, Vermilion; elected Social Credit MLA, 1959-71 elections inclusively; Deputy Speaker 1964-68; active in community. (**ALI; CANP** 1975; **PUB** D 1982)
Vermilion Standard 992

Cooper, Douglas
Pub.; ed.
Son of Sextus Ruthven Pringle Cooper (all q.v.); brother of Ashley, Percy and Vernon Cooper (all q.v.)
Vermilion Standard 992

Cooper, Percy
Pub.; ed.
Son of Sextus Ruthven Pringle Cooper (q.v.); brother of Ashley, Douglas and Vernon Cooper (all q.v.)
Vermilion Standard 992

Cooper, Sextus Ruthven Pringle
Ed.; pub.
b. Holland Landing, Ont., Mr 24 1873; d. Vermilion, 1964.
1878, moved to Baldur, Man., founded Baldur *Gazette*; 1907, sold paper and moved to Vermilion where homesteaded, initially; financially interested in *Vermilion Signal*. (EJ My 11 1954; **VER** p.34-5; *Vermilion Standard* Mr 28 1957)
Standard, Vermilion 992

Cooper, Vernon
Pub.; ed.
Son of Sextus Ruthven Pringle Cooper (q.v.); brother of Ashley, Douglas and Percy Cooper (all q.v.)
Vermilion Standard 992

Co-operative Commonwealth Federation
People's Weekly, Edmonton 386

Copps, William
Ed.
Suburban Times, Edmonton 436

Corby, Frank
Pub.
Gleichen Echo 574

Cormack, Francis
Pub.
d. ca. 1940.
Formerly of Toronto, Ont. (**CPP** v.31 no.3, Mr 1922)

Erskine Review 521
Stony Plain Sun 936

Cotton, William Percy
Ed.; pub.
b. Canterbury, Eng.; d. Vancouver, B. C.
Learned printing trade on Fleet Street; 1903, came to Canada and ran
News, Maple Creek, Sask., 1906-9; moved to Victoria, B. C., 1928. (**CPP**
v.37 no.8, Ag 1928; **THO** p.433)
Bow Island Review 90
Burdett Times 111
Didsbury Pioneer 317
Taber Times 954

Cottrell, J. C.
Pub.; politician; businessman
b. Iowa; d. Cereal, S 30 1949.
In Iowa House of Representatives; came to Cereal, 1910; in real estate
and insurance; built first hotel in Cereal. (**CER** v.1 p.24)
Cereal Recorder 256

Coultis, E. O. (Bert)
Ed.; businessman
Came to Brooks from Ontario; ran a lumberyard; moved to Steveville
where homesteaded and ran Steveville store; later, moved to Wardlaw.
(**DEL** p.59-61)
Brooks Bulletin 104

Cousins, William
Prop.; businessman
Medicine Hat Times 739

Coutts, Lorraine
Ed.; pub.
Sundre Round Up 945

Cowell, John Robert
Ed.; politician; businessman
b. Liverpool, Eng., Mr 6 1849; d. Victoria, B. C., Ap 14 1923.
Served 20 yrs in House of Keys, Isle of Man, as elected member; 1902,
came to Canada; 1905, bought Shoemaker and Co., printers, Red Deer;
Clerk of Alberta Legislature, 1905-23. (**ARDA**; **CPP** v.14 no.5, My 1905)
Red Deer Advocate 834

Cowley, Edwin (Ed)
Pub.
Husband of Wanda Cowley (q.v.)
Free Press, Whitecourt 1034
Freelancer, Mayerthorpe 738
Grand Trunk Poplar Press, Evansburg 523

Cowley, Wanda
Pub.
Wife of Edwin Cowley (q.v.)
Free Press, Whitecourt 1034
Freelancer, Mayerthorpe 738
Grand Trunk Poplar Press, Evansburg 523

Cozzubbo, Donald
Ed.
Bassano Times 62

Cramer, F. H.
Pub., ed.
Forestburg Advance 530
Grassy Lake Gazette 599
Spirit River Echo 909

Creagh, J.
Ed.
Alberta Tribune Daily Edition, Calgary 122
Alberta Tribune Weekly Edition, Calgary 123

Creighton, J. Douglas
Pub.
Pub. of Toronto *Sun.*
Calgary Mirror North Side Edition 205
Calgary Mirror South Side Edition 194
Calgary Sun 215

Crewe, Judith Elizabeth
Ed.; journalist; teacher
b. Calgary, Je 11 1948
News, Thorhild County 958

Croatian Society of Friends of Matica Hrvatska
Hrvatski Vjesnik Hrvatskog Drustva Prijatelja Matice Hrvatske, Calgary
207

Crowfoot, Bert
Ed.
Nations Ensign, Edmonton 494

Cruz, Eduardo de la
Ed.
Native People, Edmonton 460
Opinion, Calgary 222

Cummer, H. E.
Ed.; printer
Sept. 1909, appointed assistant fire chief, Munson; 1916, left to enlist.
(**MUNS** p.212; **GILT** p.32)
Munson Times 776
Wainwright Star 1007

Cunningham, John W.
Ed.
Edmonton Post 339
Evening Journal 344

Curle, David
Pub.
Temple City Tribune, Cardston 244

Currie, James
Ed.; pub.
d. My 14 1967
Husband of Vimy Currie (q.v.); apprenticed printer *Olds Gazette*; also
worked on *Lacombe Globe*; saw service in World War II; worked on *Calgary Herald* and *Albertan*. (**CANW** Je 1965)
Didsbury Pioneer 317

Currie, Vimy
Pub.; ed.
Wife of James Currie (q.v.)
Carstairs News 250
Didsbury Pioneer 317

Cusack, Tom
Ed.
Record, Fort Saskatchewan 560

Cushing, Gordon C.
Ed.
Call, Calgary 186

Cuthand, Doug
Ed.
Native People, Edmonton 460

D'Albertanson, Leonard, Sr. (Len)
Pub.
b. Pimlico, London, Eng., F 17 1879; d. S 2 1925.
Learned printing trade in Great Britain; came to Canada 1906; 1906-14,
homesteaded in Lloydminster district. (**CHA** p.108-11; Questionnaire)
Chauvin Chronicle 263

D'Albertanson, Leonard (Leon)
Pub.
b. Erith, London, Eng., Ag 28 1904
Son of Leonard D'Albertanson, Sr. (q.v.); came to Canada with parents, 1906; active in community, church and newspaper organizations; 1955, published *The Story of Alberta Division, Canadian Weekly Newspapers Association*; on Senate, University of Alberta. (Questionnaire)
Chauvin Chronicle 263
Wainwright Star-Chronicle 1009

Dalmer, H. A.
Ed.
Northwest Review, Fort McMurray 1070

Dalton, Germaine
Ed.; pub.; teacher
b. Roberval, Que.; d. Edmonton, Ag 8 1984.
Wife of Joseph Dalton; came to Alberta early '30s; teacher, Joussard district; moved to Edmonton, 1942; keenly interested in politics. (EJ Ag 10 1984)
Beverly Page, Edmonton 440
New Alberta Liberal, Edmonton 1065
Olde Towne Crier, Edmonton 471

Dalton, Marcel J.
Ed.
Son of Germaine Dalton. (q.v.)
Beverly Page, Edmonton 440

Dambrofsky, Gwen
Ed.
Edmonton Examiner [North Editions] 490

Daniels, Norman L.
Pub.
Mayerthorpe Times 735
Plaindealer, Wildwood 1089

Danish and Lutheran Church, West Canada District
Kirken og Hjemmet, Edmonton 408

Danish Press Social Club
Praerie Nyt, Calgary 197

Danyluk, William
Pub.
Daily Advertiser, Drumheller 331

Datskiv, T.
Ed.
Nash Postup, Edmonton 393

Dau, Betty
Pub.; ed.
Three Hills Capital 965

Dau, R.V. (Bob)
Pub.; ed.
Three Hills Capital 965

Davidson, Andrew
Ed.
Alberta Veteran, Calgary 155

Davidson, C. J.
Pub.; ed.
Three Hills Capital 965

Davidson, Geo. W.
Ed.; mgr; prop.
Was with D. MacKay (q.v.) on *Provost News* (**CPP** v.30 no.6, Je 1921)
Czar Clipper 301
Hughenden Herald 636

Davidson, William McCartney
Pub.; politician; journalist
b. Wellington, Ont., N. 12 1872; d. Victoria, B. C., Mr 23 1942.
Began newspaper career as parliamentary correspondent for Toronto *Star*;
ed., London, Ont., *News*; 1902, moved to Calgary; twice elected MLA, in
1917 as Liberal and in 1923 as Independent Liberal; 1930, moved to
Victoria, B.C.; wrote column for *Calgary Albertan*. (EJ Mr 24 1942;
PEEL)
Albertan and Alberta Tribune 123

Davies, Donald William
Pub.; ed.
Co-owner, Prairie Publications Ltd.
Beacon, Calgary 189
Turner Valley News 977

Davies, J. B.
Ed.
Canadian Advocate, Lethbridge 698
Magrath Times 716

Davis, John
Ed.; pub.
From Orangeville, Ont. **(PUB** Je 1977)
Didsbury Booster and Mountain View County News 318
Olds Optimist 792

Davis, L. E.
Ed.; printer
Carstairs Journal 249

Dean, Basil
Pub.; journalist; ed.
b. Newbury, Eng., N 12 1915; d. Toronto, Ont., D 16 1968.
1936-38, reporter, *Daily Herald*, London, Ont.; 1938-41, Hamilton *Spectator*; in RCAF and press officer during War; 1945-49, Southam News Service correspondent, London, Eng.; associate-ed., *Calgary Herald*, 1949-54; Vice-Pres. and dir., Southam Press Ltd. (EJ D 18 1968)
Calgary Herald 115
Edmonton Journal 344

DeBranscoville, Michael
Pub.
Edmonton Free Press 448

DeCoursey, P.
Pub.
Jasper Place Citizen 436

DeCoursey, Wellington Harris (Duke)
Pub.
b. Choteau, Mont., 1913
Family moved to Alberta 1919; in print office, *Rimbey Record*, 1930 on; worked for Edmonton Job Print Co., then on *Sylan Lake News* in late 1935; served with air force 1941-5; 1945, established *News of the North*, Yellowknife, N.W.T.; 1955, worked for *Northern Mail*, The Pas, Man.; 1958, in Dauphin, Man., at Parkview Publishing, and at Thompson, Man., published Thompson *Citizen* for 10 yrs; 1969, moved to Squamish, B. C. (DEC)
Magrath Mirror 719
Representative, Leduc 689
Stony Plain Reporter 937
Western Messenger, Thorsby 961
Winfield Gazette 1038

DeJong, Francis
Ed.
Olds Optimist 792

De la Cruz, Eduardo
See **Cruz**, Eduardo de la

Delaney, J. Gordon
Prop.
Slave Lake Centennial Press 900

DeLong, Maurice (Morice)
Ed.
Okotoks Review 783

Dempsey, G. L.
Ed.
Calgary Mirror South Side Edition 194

Dempsey, William R.
Pub.
Edmonton and Alberta Business 491

Denhoff, Erica
Ed.
Native People, Edmonton 460

Denis, Paul
Ed.
Franco-albertain, Edmonton 458

Dennis, Herbert
Pub.
Macleod Spectator 542

Derbyll, H. Rosch Van
See **Van Derbyll**, H. Rosch

Dewar, Duncan W.
Pub.; prop.; journalist
b. Peace River; d. ca. S 10 1975.
Retired to Fairview and freelanced with northern newspapers. (*Daily Herald-Tribune* S 10 1975; **NIC** p.40)
Battle River Herald, Manning 721
Fairview Post 526

De Wolfe, Mabel
Pub.; ed.
Sister of Wilburn De Wolfe (q.v.); retired upon her marriage in 1921 (married name Mattoon). (**SMI** p.40,90)
Consort Enterprise 292

De Wolfe, Wilburn Alurd
Pub.; ed.; engineer
b. Osborne, Ont., Jl 18 1882; d. Edmonton, Ja 9 1950.

Qualified as steam engineer; homesteaded, 1909, but practised as engineer; active in community; Social Credit candidate. (**DAL** p.61, 68; **SMI** p.4-5, 90)
Consort Enterprise 292
Enterprise, Alliance 16

Diamond, H. E.
Ed.; mgr
Pincher Creek Echo 814
St. Paul Star 882

Dick, Monica
Ed.
With QCTV (**PUB** F 1983)
Olds Optimist 792

Dickson, Horatio Henry Lovat (Rache; Lovat)
Ed.; pub.; author
b. Australia, 1902; d. Toronto, Ont., Ja 3 1987.
Came to Canada 1917; attended University of Alberta, 1923-27; returned to England where he became a publisher and novelist; retired to Toronto. (**PEEL**)
B. D. Weekly, Brule 108

Dillingham, Clara Jane (nee Bayne)
Pub.
Wife of Stephen Dillingham (q.v.).
Fort Saskatchewan Herald 557
Macleod Times and Macleod Weekly News, Fort Macleod 544

Dillingham, H. C.
Pub.
d. San Francisco, Calif., Ap 13 1927.
Brother of Stephen Dillingham (q.v.)
Province, Innisfail 643

Dillingham, Rex B.
Pub.
Province, Innisfail 643

Dillingham, Stephen
Pub.; ed.
b. Lindsay, Ont., Je 1 1872
Brother of H. C. Dillingham (q.v.) and husband of Clara Jane Dillingham (q.v.); became printer on Brandon *Times*; 1898, established Brandon *Independent*, published it for 2 yrs; was foreman on various U. S. papers; 1907, moved to Saskatchewan where he worked on various papers. (**BLU** v.2, p.27-8)
Crag and Canyon, Banff 38

Fort Saskatchewan Herald 557
Macleod Times and Macleod Weekly News, Fort Macleod 544

Dillon, James P.
Pub.; printer; Catholic clergyman
b. Peterborough, Ont., ca. 1888; d. Coronation, 1951.
Worked on papers in North Dakota and Ontario; after disposing of *Hardisty World* entered Roman Catholic seminary. (**CPP** v.60 no.4, Ap 1951)
Hardisty World 609
Lougheed Journal 712

Dills, Steven
Pub.
b. Hamilton, Ont., D 31 1955
Third-generation newspaper publisher. (Questionnaire)
Examiner, Spruce Grove 913
Onoway Tribune 794
Reporter, Stony Plain 937
Western Review, Drayton Valley 323

Dobelis, K.
Pub.
Brivais Latvietis, Edmonton 430

Dokter, Joyce
Ed.; pub.
b. Holland, ca. 1938
Emigrated to Canada at age 18. (**PUB** Jl/Ag 1984)
Carstairs and District Community Press 250

Dolman, Richard J.
Ed.
High River Times 625

Dolphin, Francis (Frank)
Ed.
Western Catholic, Edmonton 388

Dominion Labor Party
Statesman, Edmonton 383

Donley, Wm. M.
Pub.
Saturday Blade, Poplar Lake 820

Donnachie, John
Ed.
Alberta Liberal, Edmonton 1062

Donovan, Fredrick Timothy (Fred)
Pub.
b. Dodsland, Sask.
Jasper Booster 657

Dooley, Kevin
Ed.
Nisku News 782

Dootson, Adelaide (nee Elliott)
Ed.
From Wainwright (?) married William (Bill) Dootson, an Irma farmer, in
1933; sold farm ca.1966. **(IRMA** p.509-10)
Irma Times 647

Doram, Donald R.
Pub.
Albertan, Calgary 123
Calgary Albertan 127
Calgary Mirror North Side Edition 205
Calgary Mirror South Side Edition 194

Dorman, Jess
Pub.; mg. ed.
Worked first on newspaper in Washington State; practised law in
Spokane; journalist in San Francisco; mining in Nevada; on staff *Calgary
Herald;* later went to live in San Francisco. **(CPP** v.21 no.7, Jl 1912)
Calgary News Telegram 136
Calgary Optimist 141

Dorsch, Audrey
Ed.
Record, Fort Saskatchewan 560

Draayer, William
Pub.
b. Swift Current, Sask.
Worked on newspapers in Saskatchewan after finishing school; came to
Alberta early 1940s. **(REY** p.306-7)
Wetaskiwin Times 1022

Drinan, John Keith
Ed.; prop.; teacher; rancher; businessman
d. Medicine Hat, N 4 1942.
From Georgian Bay, Ont., came to teach school in Medicine Hat; had
served as boatman on Nile in Wolsey's campaign; farmed in Medicine
Hat area. (AC N 4 1982; **CPP** v.44 no.6 Je, 1935)
Medicine Hat Times 739

Drouin, Darrell
Pub.
Succeeded father Lucien Drouin (q.v.)
St. Paul Journal 883

Drouin, Lucien Henri (Drew; L. H.)
Ed.; pub.
b. St. Paul, D 18 1919
Bonnyville Newscope 88
St. Paul Journal 883
Two Hills County Journal 982

Drumm, Mark
Pub.
Retired to California. (**COU** p.126)
Frank Paper 566

Duckworth, Barbara
Ed.
County of Lethbridge Sunny South News, Coaldale 276

Duffield, J.
Ed.
Vulcan Advocate 1005

Duffy, Peter G.
Pub.; ed.
Fort McMurray Today 552
McMurray Courier, Fort McMurray 551

Dun, Deanna
Ed.
Edmonton Examiner [West Editions] 487

Duncan, Eugene Sydney (Sid)
Ed.
b. Rock Springs, Wyo., 1882; d. Banff, Mr 22 1938.
Father was newspaper publisher in Wyoming; cowboy in Idaho; 1903, threshing crew cook, Magrath; thereafter worked on newspapers Lethbridge, Edmonton, Nanaimo, Kamloops, Hanna, then Banff; called "second Bob Edwards" for original thinking and independent opinions. (CH Mr 22, 23, 24 1938)
Crag and Canyon, Banff 38

Duncan, George
Prop.
Brother of James Duncan (q.v.)
Grande Prairie Herald 584
Northern Tribune, Grande Prairie 586

Duncan, Gerald A.
Pub.
b. Ladysmith, B. C.
Son of James Duncan (q.v.); came to Grande Prairie 1928 as child. (*Daily Herald Tribune* Ap 26 1966)
Alberta Business, Edmonton 491
Daily Herald Tribune, Grande Prairie 586

Duncan, Grover Cleveland
Prop.; mgr; printer; ed.
b. Kansas City, Mo., Ja 6 1885; d. Drumheller, F 1 1972.
1905, learned printing trade, Sherwood, N. D.; 1907, came to Alberta and homesteaded at Halkirk; worked on *Edmonton Journal*; 1911, was in Castor, Coronation; 1918, moved to Drumheller; assistant agent for CPR, Pincher Creek Station; retired 1947. (CH Oc 12 1960; **DRUM** p.180; **MUNS** p.36)
Coronation Review 293
Drumheller Mail 327
Munson Mail 775

Duncan, Harwood
Pub.
Formerly of Hillsdale, Ont. (**CPP** v.20 no.8, Ag 1911)
Barons Enterprise 48
Cayley Advertiser 254
Claresholm Advertiser 267
Claresholm Review 266
Granum Advertiser 593
Granum News 592
Stavely Advertiser 921

Duncan, James
Prop.
b. Lossiemouth, Scotland, 1900; d. Nanaimo, B. C., ca. My 25 1970.
Brother of George Duncan (q.v.); came to Canada 1906; went to Grande Prairie as pressman; retired to Nanaimo, 1950. (Glenbow newspaper clipping)
Northern Tribune, Grande Prairie 586

Duncan, K. D.
Ed.; mgr
Barons Enterprise 48

Duncan, N. L.
Ed.
Son of Eugene Sydney Duncan (q.v.)
Crag and Canyon, Banff 38

Dunford, Charles L.
Pub.; draftsman

b. Newcastle-on-Tyne, Eng., 1884; d. Mr 30 1964.
Came to Canada, 1905; worked as architectural draftsman in various cities; 1911-1913, edited News, Alsask, Sask.; 1914, moved to Oyen; served during World War I; 1935, moved to Sylan Lake. (**JAR** p.284; CH Mr 31 1964; **REF** p.187-8)
Oyen News 795
Sylvan Lake News 951

Dunford, Charles Warren
Pub.
Son of Charles L. Dunford (q.v.); 1966, Town Mgr, Stettler. (**REF** p.187-8)
Sylvan Lake News 951

Dunlop, Alexander
Pub.
Edmonton Bulletin 334

Dunning, C.
Pub.
Coleman Journal 290

Dunning, G. A.
Pub.
Wife of Vincent C. Dunning? (q.v.)
Barons Globe 50

Dunning, Vincent C.
Ed.; pub.
From Robsart, Sask.; family came to Barons about 1918; 1923, moved to Ladner, B. C., where Mrs. Dunning published Ladner *Optimist*. (**BARO** p.232)
Barons Globe 50
Craigmyle Gazette 295
Manyberries Enterprise 732

Dusen, Chedwy Van
See **Van Dusen**, Chedwy

Dyer, Will I.
Pub.
Gazette, Rocky Mountain House 859

Dyky, B.
Ed.
Ukrainian News, Edmonton 402

Eagan, Burton W.
Pub.; ed.
Calgary Citizen 187

Eagar, Dawna
Ed.
Record, Fort Saskatchewan 560

Eastly, Arthur Clayton (Ace)
Pub.
b. F 10 1936
Son of Arthur W. Eastly (q.v); left newspaper business to become engineer in oil industry. (**SED** p.271-4)
Community Press, Sedgewick 890

Eastly, Arthur Le Grande
Pub.
b. Bon Homme County, Dakota Territory, Ja 27 1879; d. Ap 9 1944.
Learned printing trade in Dakota; 1905, moved to Wetaskiwin where worked in printing office of *Times*. (**SED** p.269-71)
Bawlf Sun 64
Daysland Press 302
Hardisty Mail 608
Killam News 659
Lougheed Express 711
Sedgewick Sentinel 890

Eastly, Arthur William (Art)
Pub.
b. Bawlf, Ag 28 1908; d. Sedgewick, F 8 1982.
Son of Arthur Le Grande Eastly (q.v.); active in community; retired 1969.
(**SED** p.271-4; **PUB** Mr 1982)
Community Press, Sedgewick 890

Eaton, Sam
Pub.
Willingdon Times 1090

Ebbett, Arthur Wellesley
Pub.
Mannville Telegram 723

Edey, Lois Mary Eunice (née Lummis)
Pub.; teacher
b. Valleyfield, Que., Ja 7 1929; d. Ag 27 1986.
Wife of Noel Harold Edey (q.v.); taught school in Quebec and Ontario for 20 yrs. (Questionnaire)
Grande Cache Mountaineer 583

Edey, Noel Dalton
Pub.; ed.; journalist
b. Ajax, Ont., S 28 1959.
Son of Lois Edey (q.v.) and Noel Harold Edey (q.v.); reporter on *Grande*

Cache Mountaineer 1977-80. (Questionnaire)
Grande Cache Mountaineer 583

Edey, Noel Harold
Pub.; journalist
b. Aylmer, Que., N 29 1926; d. Oc 31 1980.
Husband of Lois Edey (q.v.); served in navy; worked on Montreal *Star*
and various Ontario newspapers; 1975, moved to Grande Cache. (Questionnaire; **PUB** N 1980)
Grande Cache Mountaineer 583

Edmonton Chamber of Commerce
Commerce News, Edmonton 1067

Edmonton Labor Representation League
Statesman for Albertans, Edmonton 377

Edmonton Trades and Labor Council
Edmonton Free Press 384
Great West, Edmonton 349

Edmonton Typographical Union
News-Advertiser, Edmonton 429

Edmunds, Geoffrey
Ed.; pub.
Husband of Monika Edmunds (q.v)
Western Wheel, Okotoks 787

Edmunds, Monika
Ed.; pub.
Wife of Geoffrey Edmunds (q.v.)
Western Wheel, Okotoks 787

Edwards, Annie Helena
Pub.
Wife of Frank Thomas Edwards (q.v.); formerly, Mrs. A. H. Derrett.
(LH Mr 14 1959)
Pincher Creek Echo 814

Edwards, Frank Thomas
Pub.; ed.
b. Hounslow, Eng., 1884; d. Victoria, B. C., Mr 11 1959.
1900, came to Canada; in army during War; managed creamery in Pincher
Creek; F 1926, married Mrs. A. H. Derrett (Annie Helena Edwards, q.v.)
(LH Mr 14 1959)
Pincher Creek Echo 814

Edwards, Harold A.
Ed.; pub.; clergyman
Anglican clergyman.
Link, Vermilion 993

Edwards, Robert Chambers (Eye-Opener Bob)
Pub.
b. Edinburgh, Scotland, S 12 1864; d. Calgary, N 14 1922.
Emigrated to Western Canada 1894; in newspapers in Alberta until 1909,
when went to Eastern Canada, returning to Calgary, 1911; won election as
Independent MLA 1921, but died after only one sitting. (CANE v.1
p.552)
Alberta Sun, Edmonton 340
Calgary Eye Opener 132
Eye Opener, High River 623
Free Lance, Wetaskiwin 1018
Wesaskiwin Breeze 1021

Elaschuk, Gary (Flash)
Ed.
b. Elk Point, Ap 27 1951
Lac La Biche Post 663

Eller, A. Thorold-
see **Thorold-Eller, A.**

Elliot, R. R.
Ed.
Strome Despatch 941

Elliott, George B.
Ed.
Nor'-Wester, Calgary 114

Elliott, Howard
Ed.
Fort McMurray Today 552

Ellis, Carin
Pub.; ed.
Northerner, Grimshaw 602

Ellison, A. E.
Pub.; ed.
Joined RCAF, World War II. (CWNA v.21 no.576, Ap 26 1941)
Big Valley News 70

Elston, A. L.
Ed.
Westerner, Calgary 1051

Elton, David Horton (Dave)
Pub.; ed.; lawyer
b. Worcester, Eng., Ja 12 1877; d. Calgary, Ag 13 1963.
Emigrated with mother to Salt Lake City 1890; served 5 yrs' apprentice-ship as stonecutter and 3 yrs as Latter-Day Saints missionary in the Southern States, during which he edited *Southern Star*, Chattanooga, Tenn.; returned to Salt Lake City, 1901, and later in same yr emigrated to Alberta, settling at Cardston; helped organise Alberta and Eastern British Columbia Press Association; 1908, moved to Lethbridge where studied law and was admitted to the bar, 1913; later, Mayor of Lethbridge; mbr of High Council of LDS Church; wrote poetry. (**HIC** p.408; **CAWW** 1955; **BLU** v.2 p.120, 123-4
Alberta Star, Cardston 240
Magrath Pioneer 715
New Stirling Star, Stirling 927
Raymond Rustler 824

Emmelkamp, Kate
Pub.
High Country Flare, Turner Valley 978

Emmerson, V. W.
Pub.
Labor Advocate, Edmonton 1061

Emond, Robert (Bob)
Pub.
b. Selkirk, Scotland, 1887; d. Je 1974.
Apprenticed to watchmaker-jeweller before emigrating to Calgary 1907; came to Holden, 1909; operated optometry business, 1909-1915; active in community; moved to Edmonton, 1943; continued in newspaper printing until retirement at age 79. (**HEM** p.298)
Holden Herald 633

Emory, Edward
Ed.
Calgary Standard 142

English, H. A.
Pub?
Operated lumber yard; 1919, took over operation of post office; town councillor. (**WILK** p.126, 173)
Airdrie Recorder 6

English, James G. (Jim)
Ed.

Worked on *Peace River Gazette* ca.1953 and Dawson, B.C., *Star* ca.1956; resigned from *Herald-Tribune* to enter public relations business in eastern Canada. (**CWNA** v.42 no.812, Ag 1960)
Herald-Tribune, Grande Prairie 586

English, L. T.
Ed.
Alberta Federationist, Calgary 144

Ennis, Albert Russell
Pub.
b. Hamilton, Ont., D 22 1881; d. ca. Ap 24 1941.
Was ed. in Hamilton; 1909, came to Alberta. (**WW** 1912)
Representative, Leduc 689

Erickson, Diane
Pub.
Hinton Herald Parklander 627

Erickson, Donald Leif
Pub.; accountant
b. Calgary, D 16 1935
Accountant, own company in Calgary; 1971, Chrmn, Alberta Universities Commission; resigned to become newspaper pub. (**WWA** 1 1974)
North Hill News, Calgary 191
Rocky View News and Market Examiner, Calgary 153

Errington, David
Pub.; ed.
Northeast News, Vermilion 944

Eskrick, Muriel
Ed.; pub.
Sundre Round-up 945

Evans, George William
Pub.; ed.; businessman
b. Toronto Ont., 1890; d. F 25 1958.
Son of William Park Evans (q.v.); opened first funeral home in Gleichen, in conjunction with furniture store. (**GLEI** p.131, 194)
Gleichen Call 576.

Evans, William Park (Park)
Pub.; ed.
b. Durham, Ont., Je 27 1869; d. ca. F 4 1931.
Printer's devil on Chesley, Ont., *Enterprise*; 1892, managed Moosomin, Sask., *Courier*; published *Outcrop*, Wilmer, B. C.; 1907, moved to Gleichen; chrmn, Gleichen's first village council. (**GLEI** p.131, 193-4)
Gleichen Call 576
Langdon Advance 685

Strathmore and Bow Valley Standard 940
Times, Edmonton 335

Everett, Doug B.
Mgr
Calgary Mirror South Side Edition 194

Everett, Oswald
Pub.; prop.
Prop., Brock, Sask., *News*, 1929-1940. (**CWNA** v.20 no.550, Jl 18 1939)
Medicine Hat Advertiser 750

Fairbanks, Floyd E.
Pub.; ed.; businessman
1909, came from North Dakota; in real estate business; 1912, left for Nelson, B. C., and later went to Oregon. (**WARN** p.96)
Coutts-Sweetgrass International Herald, Coutts 1056
Warner Record 1010

Farmers' Combined Irriagation Committee
Farmers Tribune, Alderson 13

Farmers' Union of Alberta
F. U. A. Bulletin, Edmonton 427

Farran, Keith D.
Pub.
Brother of Roy Farran (q.v.)
Strathmore Standard 940

Farran, Kit
Pub.; ed.
Rattler, Medicine Hat 752

Farran, Roy Alexander St. Thomas
Pub.; ed.; author; politician; farmer; journalist
b. Kingswinford, Eng., Ja 1921
Brother of Keith D. Farran (q.v.); retired from British Army 1948; alderman, Calgary, 1961-71; Progressive Conservative MLA 1971-9; Minister of Telephones and Utilities, 1973-5; Solicitor-Gen., 1975-9; columnist, *Calgary Herald*. (**ALI; WWAB** 85/86)
Market Examiner and Western Farm Journal, Calgary 153
North Hill News, Calgary 191
South Calgary News 192
Strathmore Standard 940
Sunday Calgarian 1053

Farrand, T. R.
Ed.
Vulcan Review 1004

Farthing, Hugh Cragg
Prop.; ed.; lawyer; politician
b. Woodstock, Ont., Jl 18 1892; d. Calgary, Je 8 1968.
Served in World War I; 1919, called to Ontario bar; 1922, to Alberta bar; elected Conservative MLA, 1930; K. C., 1935; active in Canadian Legion, Red Cross and Anglican Church; 1954, appointed to Alberta Supreme Court.
(ALI) *Cochrane Advocate* 279

Fawcus, Thomas H.
Mgr
Linotype operator on Red Deer *News*. **(CPP** v.26 no.11, N 1917)
Guide to Citizenship, Prosperity and Happiness, Rocky Mountain House 856

Fawdrey, Stanley A.
Pub., ed.
Moved to Vancouver. **(DAL** p.66)
Castor Advance 252
Chronicle, Crossfield 296

Federation Canadienne-Francaise de la Colombie
Survivance, Edmonton 404

Federation of Ukrainian Socialists in Canada
Nova Hromada 363

Fèguenne, Pierre
Ed.
Union, Edmonton 378

Fessenden, K. H.
Ed.
b. Bolton, Que., Jl 15 1868
To West, 1887; editorial writer on Winnipeg *Tribune* and Winnipeg *Telegram*, 1892 on. **(WW** 1912)
Lethbridge News 692

Findlay, J. Lundy
Ed.
Formerly with Trochu and Three Hills newspapers; Served in Air Force 1943-5; married Lola R. Bateman (q.v.) **(VUL** p.35, 290; **CWNA** v.22 no.586, Oc 30 1941)
Vulcan Advocate 1005

Findlay, William
Pub.
Hot Springs Record, Banff 34

Findley, G. Caruthers
Pub.
Spirit River Echo 909

Finnish Socialist Organization of America
Moukari, Edmonton 366

Fisher, T. Bernard
Ed.
Canmore Miner 232

Flaherty, Norman
Ed.
Record, Fort Saskatchewan 560

Flanagan, E.
Ed.
Western Catholic, Edmonton 388

Fleming, George
Pub.
b. St. Mary's, Ont., Mr 1854; d. Vancouver, B. C., D 11 1926.
1889, visited Penhold; 1890, homesteaded and was store owner; 1910, moved to Vancouver where employed as checker on wharves. **(ARDA)**
Alberta Echo, Red Deer 834

Fleming, Orville D.
Ed.; pub.; businessman
b. Essex, Ont., 1880; d. Passchendaele, Belgium, Oc 1917.
Son of George Fleming (q.v.); homesteaded, Red Deer area, and operated real estate and insurance business; 1907, moved to Vancouver; enlisted in First World War; killed in action, Passchendaele. **(MEE, p.162)**
Advocate, Red Deer 834
Free Lance, Innisfail 642
Penhold Reporter 809

Fletcher, C. P.
Prop.
In charge CPR plant, Calgary for 2 yrs; with various country newspapers in British Columbia., before buying *St. Paul Journal*. **(CPP** v.38 no.12, D 1929)
St. Paul Journal 883

Fletcher, Ernest C.
Pub.
Advertiser, Sylan Lake 950
Optimist, Red Deer 836
St. Paul Journal 883

Fletcher, H. C.
Pub.
Post Office clerk. (**HENC**)
Western Canada Enquirer, Calgary 179

Flett, C. J.
Pub.
Bassano Recorder 59

Footner, William Hulbert
Pub.; ed.; author
b. 1879; d. 1944.
A native of Hamilton, Ont., came to Alberta 1905-6; had been connected
with some of best New York papers and with large pub. house; later,
returned to New York, employed at Doubleday and Page, pubs.; novelist
and mystery writer. (**CPP** v.15 no.2, F 1906; **PEEL**)
Climber, Banff 39
Town Topics, Calgary 135

Foran, Clifford
Pub.
Holden Herald 634

Foran, Grace L. (née Lake)
Ed.
Arrived Holden with family early 1900s from Iowa; married Archie Foran who
came from Ontario with Trader's Bank. (**HEM** p.467)
Holden Herald 634

Forcade, Gerard, o. m. i.
Ed.; Catholic clergyman
b. ca. 1900; d. Ja 1964.
Survivance, Edmonton 404
Survivance des Jeunes, Edmonton 418

Forchuk, Shirley
Ed.
Vauxhall Advance 986

Ford, Fred
Pub.
Formerly of Western Stationery Co., Lethbridge. (**CPP** v.17 no.9, S 1908)
Raymond Rustler, 824

Ford, Harry J.
Pub.
d. Ag 11, 1948.

From Regina, Sask.; came to Lacombe with family, 1935. (**CPP** v.44
no.11, N 1935)
Lacombe Globe 670
Lacombe Municipal News 1080

Ford, Herbert Campbell (Bert)
Pub.
d. 1974.
Son of Harry J. Ford (q.v.) and brother of Thomas H. Ford (q.v.); with
RCAF, World War II. (**CPP** v.49 no.8, Ag 1940)
Lacombe Globe 670

Ford, Thomas H. (Tom)
Pub.
b. Calgary, Mr 22 1922; d. F 19 1968.
Son of Harry J. Ford (q.v.) and brother of Herbert Campbell Ford (q.v.);
came to Lacombe with parents, 1935. (**CANC** Mr 1968)
Lacombe Globe 670

Forster, Frederick George
Pub.; ed.; mgr; rancher
b. Toronto, Ont., Ja 5 1870; d. Banff, F 1929.
Printer's devil, Listowel, Ont., 1884; 1888, came to Alberta; 1903, pur-
chased Maple Creek *Signal*; appointed Chief License Inspector for
Alberta. (**CPP** v.20 no.12, D 1911; **GERS** p.130; EJ F 15 1929; F 14
1970)
Medicine Hat News 741

Fournier, Guy
Ed.
Franco-albertain, Edmonton 458

Fowler, Berdie
Ed.
Wife of William F. Fowler (q.v.)
Camrose Booster 227

Fowler, W. Blain
Pub.
Son of Berdie Fowler (q.v.) and William F. Fowler (q.v.)
Camrose Booster 227

Fowler, William F. (Bill)
Pub.
Husband of Berdie Fowler (q.v.)
Camrose Booster 227

Frank, Alfred
Ed.
Deutsch-Canadier, Calgary 139

Fraser, Doris
Ed.
Grizzly Gazette, Swan Hills 947

Fraser, George B.
Ed.
Alberta Homestead, Edmonton 353

Frawley, A. A. (Bert)
Ed.
Civvy Street, Red Deer 838

Fream, Edward John
Pub.; public servant
d. 1950.
Brother of S. P. Fream (q.v.); 1889, came from Gloucester, Eng.; first Secretary, United Farmers of Alberta; Secretary, Alberta Co-op Elevator Co.; 1922, Alberta govt. dir. for Relief of Drought Areas; 1925, Commissioner, Public Utility Board; 1925-6, Commissioner, Debt Adjustment Board. (**INN** p.74, 135; EJ My 11 1950)
Innisfail Province 643

Fream, S. P.
Pub.
Brother of Edward John Fream (q.v.); 1889, came from Gloucester, Eng.; ca. 1907, moved to Maritimes. (**INN** p.74, 135; EJ My 11 1950)
Innisfail Province 643

Frederick, Charles William
Pub.; postmaster; businessman; printer
b. Glencoe, Ont.; d. San Diego, Calif., ca. 1963.
Worked on Elgin, Ont., *Sun*; worked on papers in Leduc and Edmonton; 1918? postmaster, Peace River, also mayor; 1939, moved to U. S. and worked in real estate; with U. S. Army Engineers at Fort Huachuca during World War II; printer in San Diego, Calf. (**CPP** v.32 no.4, Ap 1923; **PEA** p. 378-9)
Alix Free Press 14
Northern Review, Fairview 525
Peace River Record 802
Reflector, Mirror 760

Freeman, S.
Pub.
Statesman, Edmonton 383

Freeman, S. C.
Ed.
Canadian Social Crediter, Edmonton 428

French, H. S.
Ed.
Prop., Colwater *Planet*, Ont. (**CPP** v.22 no.8, Ag 1913)
Coleman Miner 288
Macleod Gazette, Fort Macleod 536
Northern News, Athabasca 26

French, Victor Coleman
Pub.
b. Oshawa, Ont., Je 27 1875; d. Wetaskiwin, Mr 24 1941.
Printer in Ontario; came to Alberta late 1890s. (Glenbow clipping file)
Wetaskiwin Times 1022

Fretts, Donald W.
Pub.; ed.
Came originally from Medicine Hat; in navy for 4 yrs during Second
World War. (**CAMP** p.87)
Chinook Belt Advertiser, Milk River 754
Milk River Review 753

Fromhold, Joe
Pub.; ed.; teacher
Was with chartered bank ca. 1964-67; 1967, "went bush"; 1980, taught
native crafts and culture at Alberta Vocational Centre, Lac La Biche. (EJ
F 7 1980)
Northern Echo, High Level 613

Frost, Norman T. J.
Pub.; ed.
Moved to Toronto. (**DAL** p.89)
Crag and Canyon, Banff 38
Gazette, Rocky Mountain House 859
Mountaineer, Rocky Mountain House 860

Fry, James
Pub.
Western Canada Enquirer, Calgary 179

Fryer, Claude
Pub.
Magrath Pioneer 715

Fullerton, Aubrey
Ed.
West-Land, Edmonton 352

Fullerton, Stewart J.
Ed.; mgr; printer

With RCMP; resigned to return to printing *Provost News* (**CPP** v.37 no.5,
My 1928)
Provost News 822
Times, Big Valley 71

Gaddes, Thomas
Pub.
Didsbury Courier 316

Gagn´e´', Francine
Ed.
Franco-albertain, Edmonton 458

Galbraith, Francis Philip (Philip)
Pub.; journalist; civil servant; businessman
b. Guelph, Ont., D 14 1896; d. Red Deer, My 16 1970.
Son of Francis Wright Galbraith (q.v.); served in World War I; on staff
Red Deer Advocate 1920 on; spent 8 yrs in U. K. between Wars; prom-
inent in Red Deer community and newspaper associations; 1959, Hon.
LLD, University of Alberta; Chancellor, University of Alberta, 1964-70.
(*Folio* My 21 1970)
Red Deer Advocate 834

Galbraith, Francis Wright
Businessman; prop.; ed.
b. Guelph, Ont., D 24 1862; d. Red Deer, Mr 9 1934.
Apprenticed to tinsmith; 1884 worked on Guelph *Mercury*, becoming ed.
and part-owner 1898-1905; 1906, moved west for wife's health, settling
in Red Deer 1907; Red Deer City Councillor, 1909, 1926; 1913, Mayor.
(**ARDA**; Glenbow clipping file; *Folio* My 21 1970)
Red Deer Advocate 834

Galbraith, Peter C.
Pub.; mgr; ed.
b. Charlo, N. B., 1889; d. Ja 25, 1954.
Came west early in life; served in France in First World War; in newspa-
per work in Saskatoon, Regina, Winnipeg, becoming mg. ed. Winnipeg
Tribune; 1929, pub., *Northern Mail*, The Pas, Man.; dir., The Canadian
Press; dir., Canadian Newspapers Association. (AC undated clipping; CH
F 10 1940)
Albertan, Calgary 127
Calgary Herald 115

Ganoe, A. R.
Ed.
Vulcan Advocate 1005

Gardener, Walter Frederick
Printer; ed.; mgr
b. London, Eng., 1881

1913, came to Saskatoon; 1919, to Peace River; printer of *Northern Review*, Fairview, and *Northern Gazette*, Peace River. (EJ N 12 1960)
Northern Review, Fairview 525

Gardiner, C. E.
Pub.
Northern Echo, High Prairie 617

Gare, Ernest Frank (Ernie)
Ed.; pub.
d. Calgary, Ap 29 1948.
Came from England to St. Catharine's, Ont., at age 4; Worked on St. Catharine's Expositor, then Brandon *Sun*; started newspapers in Kindersley and Alsask, Sask.; retired to Calgary, 1946. (EJ Ap 29 1948; **TRO** p.228)
Coleman Journal 290
Delia Times 312
Trochu Tribune 973

Gare, J. C. (Jack)
Pub.
Son of Ernest Frank Gare (q.v.)
Eckville Examiner 333
Mountaineer, Rocky Mountain House 860

Gariepy, Wilfrid
Ed.; lawyer; politician
b. Montreal, Que., Mr 14 1877; d. Three Rivers, Que., Ja 13 1960.
Lawyer in Quebec; in Alberta 1904-20s, first in military, then in law; Liberal MLA 1913-21, for Beaver River; Minister of Municipal Affairs, 1913-8; 1918-21, Provincial Sec.; 1921, returned to Quebec; elected Liberal-Labour MP for Three Rivers, 1935 and 1945. (EJ Ja 14 1960; **WWC** 1952)
Ouest canadien, Edmonton 362

Garner, E. Deniston
Ed.
Canmore Times 228

Garrioch, W. C. R.
Pub.; ed.
d. 1957.
Formerly of Willingdon and Central Saskatchewan. (**PUB** Je 30 1939)
Barrhead Leader 52
Edson Leader 503
Sedgewick Review 891

Gauthier, H.
Ed.
Lac La Biche Post 663

Geisinger, James
Pub.; ed.
Advocate, Athabasca 33
Leader, Barrhead 52

Gelinas, Arthur
Ed.
Franco-albertain, Edmonton 458

Gemeroy, Gordon F.
Mgr
Came west from Ontario in 1915; taught school for several years; 1921, advertising mgr for *Agricultural Alberta*; 1922, advertising mgr for *Farm and Ranch Review*; 1922-28, worked on *Saskatchewan Farmer*, Regina. (**CCP** v.37 no.4, Ap 1928)
Alberta Mercury, Calgary 168
Western Farmer, Calgary 164

Gentry, Jean
Pub.; ed.
Northerner, Grimshaw 602

George, Arthur Thomas
Ed.; pub.
b. Walsall, Eng., N 27 1904; d. Oc 4 1967.
Came to Canada 1905, to Roland, Man.; printer for CPR; 1936, moved to Alberta; retired due to ill health. (*Red Deer Advocate* Oc 11 1967; **LEW**, p.124)
Delburne Times 309

Gibbons, Frank
Ed.
Market Examiner and Western Farm Journal, Calgary 153
Western Examiner, Calgary 165

Gibson, A. C.
Pub.; ed.
Tiser, Calgary 124

Gibson, Danny
Pub.
Husband of Judy Gibson (q.v.); worked on *Red Deer Advocate* before becoming advertising entrepreneur. (Interview)
Actioneer, Stettler 926
Western Star, Leslieville 1081

Gibson, Judy
Pub.
Wife of Danny Gibson (q.v.)

Actioneer, Stettler 926
Western Star, Leslieville 1081

Gieg, John Harold (Jack)
Pub.
b. Regina, Sask., Ja 4 1935
Representative, Leduc 689

Gilbert, Harvey J.
Pub.; ed.
Bow Valley Advertiser, Calgary 190

Gilbertson, Greg
Ed.
Calgary Mirror North Side Edition 205
Calgary Mirror South Side Edition 194

Giles, Bill
Pub.
Western Sports Weekly, Edmonton 459

Giles, Bob
Pub.
From Lachine, Que.; 3rd generation weekly newspaperman. (**PUB** Je 1977)
Strathmore Standard 940

Gill, Sidney Arnold
Pub.; printer
b. Port Hope, Ont., Ja 17 1882; d. N 16 1964.
Went West for health; on editorial staff of *Stettler Independent*; Sec.
Treas. of Delburne village, 1913-1919; 1921, moved to Calgary where
was composing room proof-reader on *Morning Albertan* for 39 yrs. (AC
N 18 1964; **LEW** p.457)
Alix Free Press 14
Delburne Progress 305

Gillese, John Patrick
Ed.
Canadian Social Crediter, Edmonton 428
Western Catholic, Edmonton 388

Gillespie, Robert
Ed.
Alberta Liberal, Edmonton 1064

Gillies, Donald
Mgr
ca.1918, had farm 4 miles nth of Olds. (**OLDS** p.136)
Olds Gazette 789

Gillis, Richard
Pub.; ed.
Pass Promoter, Blairmore 84
Rattler, Medicine Hat 752

Girard, T. L.
Ed.
Progrès, Morinville 764

Gissing, Alwin
Prop.; ed.
Nephew of English novelist, George Gissing; went to Brisco, B. C.
(**COCH** p. 219; undated obit. of brother Roland Gissing)
Cochrane Advocate 279

Glass, E. B.
Ed.; clergyman
Indian Advocate, Whitefish Lake 1035

Glen, Barbara J. (Barb)
Ed.; journalist, photographer
b. Edmonton, Ap 2 1961
County of Lethbridge Sunny South News, Coaldale 276

Glenwood Senior Citizens Civic Group
Glenwood Gleanings 578

Glover, Randall W.
Ed.
Later engaged in musical activities in Calgary; moved to Vancouver,
ca.1926.
(**CPP** v.35 no.7, Jl 1926)
Vulcan Advocate 1005

Gobeil, Denis-Alonzo, o. m. i.
Ed.; Catholic clergyman
Survivance, Edmonton 404

Godson, Reginald Arthur
Pub.; mgr; printer; businessman
b. Muskoka, Ont., S 4 1882; d. Jl 17 1961.
Became printer in Ontario; 1911, moved to Fort Macleod and, in 1912, to
Edmonton where he became a prominent businessman, active in sports,
community and fraternal organizations. (*Edmonton Bulletin* N 4 1937;
Sears Craftsman v.2 no.5
Alberta Illustrated News, Edmonton 372
Edmonton News 371
Edmonton News-Plaindealer 336

Godson, William
Pub.
Native of Australia; later returned there. (**CLA** p.94; **PUB** Ag 1981)
Citizen, Stettler 925
Leduc Record 687
Stettler Independent 923
Strathcona Chronicle, Edmonton 345

Good, W. J. (Billy)
Pub.
1918, enlisted; 1940, joined army; after service, lived in Vancouver.
(**CPP** v.49 no.11, N 1940; **RIM** p.33; **LAM** p.389)
Erskine Times 522
Journal, Big Valley 72
Mirror Journal 761

Gooder, Edwin J. C.
Pub.; ed.
Son of Walter C. Gooder (q.v.)
Didsbury Pioneer 317

Gooder, John E. (Jack)
Pub.
Brother of Walter C. Gooder (q.v.); 1901, came to Olds, joining *Olds
Oracle* staff; retired to B. C. coast. (**CWNA** v.41 no.779, Jl 1957; **OLD**
p.266)
Olds Gazette 789

Gooder, Walter C.
Pub.; ed.
Brother of John E. Gooder (q.v.); mortician and motor ambulance opera-
tor in Olds; active in musical circles. (**OLDS**) *Didsbury Pioneer* 317 *Olds
Gazette* 789

Gordon, A. M. Ed. *Medicine Hat News* 741

Gordon, Bruce A. Pub.
Apprenticed on *Spirit River Signal*; spent 10 yrs with Menzies printers
before moving to Fairview *Post*.
(**CANC** D 1968)
Post, Fairview 526

Gordon, George (Scotty)
Pub.; postmaster
d. 1949.
Native of Aberdeenshire, Scotland; apprenticed printer on Inverness
Northern Chronicle, came to Ponoka, 1905, with family; Postmaster for
26 yrs. (**PON** p. 58-9; **CPP** v.24 no.12, D 1915; **EJ** S 28 1965)
Ponoka Herald 817

Gordon, Helen
Ed.
Redwater Sun 848

Gordon, John Fraser
Pub.; banker; businessman
b. Inverness, Scotland, ca. 1899; d. S 26 1965.
Son of George Gordon (q.v.); came to Ponoka, 1905; served overseas in
World War I; with Canadian Imperial Bank of Commerce throughout
Alberta, returning to Ponoka in 1938; in RCAF during World War II;
1953, entered insurance business. (EJ S 28 1965; **PON** p. 58-59)
Ponoka Herald 817

Gorman, John Thomas (Jack)
Pub.; ed.; printer; writer; public affairs director
b. Camrose, Je 24 1929
1947-1957, was printer; 1964, Public Relations Officer for Flying Tiger
Line, California; 1969, returned to Calgary where became columnist for
Herald; has written many articles; Public Affairs Dir. for Canadian
Petroleum Assoc. (Questionnaire)
Banff Summit News 45
Hanna Herald and East Central Alberta News, Hanna 605
Jasper Place Citizen, Edmonton 436

Goss, Calvin
Pub.
Came from U. S. (**DAL** p.62)
Alderson News 12
Brooks Bulletin 105
Irvine Index 651

Gowe, L. S.
Pub.; ed.
Formerly city ed., *Sun*, St. John, Nfld. (**CPP** v.19 no.12, D 1910)
Lethbridge Daily News 695
Macleod Spectator 542
Wainwright Star 1007

Graham, David
Ed.
Edmonton Examiner [North Editions] 490
Edmonton Examiner [South Editions] 486
Edmonton Examiner [West editions] 487

Graham, James
Ed.
Evening Chronicle, Edmonton 350
Strathcona Chronicle, Edmonton 345

Graham, L. M.
Ed.; pub.
Bassano Mail 58
Central Albertan, Wetaskiwin 1025

Graighero, C.
Ed.
Panorama, Calgary 199

Grant, Jean A.
Ed.; pub.
b. Stratford, Ont.; d. Calgary, D 9 1938.
Taught school Saskatchewan and Alberta; 1st woman ed. *Calgary Daily Herald*, ca. 1910; married Everett D. Marshall (q.v.). (*Western Examiner* D 10 1938)
Alberta Oil Examiner, Calgary 163
Market Examiner, Calgary 153

Grasswick, James L.
Ed.
Record-Gazette, Peace River 804

Gray, James Henry
Ed.; author
b. Whitemouth, Man., Ag 31 1906
Clerical work and on relief, 1922-33; reporter, ed. writer and Ottawa correspondent, Winnipeg *Free Press*, 1935-47; Public Relations Mgr, Home Oil Co., 1958-64; author 10 books on Prairies history; many awards and honorary degrees. (**CAWW** 1986)
Western Oil Examiner, Calgary 165

Gray, Thomas H.
Ed.
b. New Westminster, B. C., Ag 6 1888
Worked on newspapers in British Columbia; associated with *Edmonton Bulletin*
for 7 yrs; 1918, moved to Camrose; 1927, retired to New Westminster. (**BLU** v.3, p.414-5, **CPP** v.36 no.2, F 1927; **DAL** p.64)
Camrose Canadian 225

Great War Next-of-Kin Association
Alberta Veteran, Calgary 155

Great War Veterans' Association
Alberta Veteran, Calgary 155

Green, Donald J.
Ed.
Meridian Booster, Lloydminster 705

Green, E. L.
Prop.
Of Lethbridge; no previous newspaper experience. (**CWNA** v.41 no.799,
Jl. 1979)
Pincher Creek Echo 814

Green, Ed
Pub.
Husband of Stella Green (q.v.)
County of Warner Review and Advertiser, Milk River 753

Green, George Wellington
Ed.; lawyer; judge
b. Athens, Ont., Je 5 1862; d. Athabasca, Jl 14 1936.
Admitted to Ontario bar 1888; 1893, came to Red Deer; 1907, barrister in
Alberta; 1916, admitted to bench. (CH Jl 15 1936; **CAWW** 1936)
Red Deer Gazette 832

Green, Murray
Ed.
Bear Hills Native Voice, Hobbema 632

Green, Stella
Pub.
Wife of Ed Green (q.v.)
County of Warner Review and Advertiser, Milk River 753

Green, Thomas W.
Pub.; ed.; printer
Printer with various sthrn Alberta newspapers; wounded in World War I;
later, established plant at Powell River, B. C. (**THO** p.343; **CPP** v.25
no.6, Je 1916)
Magrath Pioneer 715
Taber Times 954

Greer, Daniel J.
Prop.
Lost leg in an accident and became night operator, Alberta Government
Telephones. (**OLDS** p.199)
Olds Gazette 789

Gregg, T. A.
Ed.; pub.
Edmonton Post 339

Gregson, Percy B.
Pub.
Weed Inspector; secy to Blindman and Blackfalds School District from
inception; practised law; later returned to England. (**MEE** p.191; **LACO**

p.576)
Blackfalds Mercury 74

Greig, George E.
Pub.; printer
b. Didsbury
Husband of Marie Greig (q.v.); family moved to Trochu where began printing career; later, Calgary, Innisfail and Wetaskiwin; 1965, founded firm, Greig Print and Stationery Ltd. **(EIG** p.488)
Hub, Westlock 1016

Greig, Marie
Pub.
Wife of George E. Greig (q.v.)
Hub, Westlock 1016

Grier, David Johnson (Dave)
Pub.; policeman; farmer
b. Griersville, Ont., Ja 15 1857
1877, became North West Mounted Policeman; 1880, upon discharge went to Fort Macleod where farmed, homesteaded, and was in Indian dept. of government; defeated as provincial conservative candidate for Macleod, 1905; Mayor for 11 yrs during 1901-18; built Empire Hotel and Union Bank building in Macleod. **(BLU** v.2 p. 252-3; **FORT** p.23, 40, 82, 101)
Macleod Times and Macleod Weekly News, Fort Macleod 544
Macleod Weekly News, Fort Macleod 543

Grierson, Gordon J.
Pub.
Advocate, Red Deer 834

Groarke, John
Ed.
Rocky View Times 10
Rocky View Times and Airdrie Echo 8

Groff, Colin Gemmell
Pub.; ed.; printer; journalist
b. Selkirk, Man., Mr 14 1885; d. Toronto, Ont., Ag 10 1959.
Printer in Dundas and Winnipeg for several yrs; reporter on *Edmonton Journal* and *Capital*; ed. on *Lethbridge Herald* and *Calgary Herald*; Government Publicity Chief for the United Farmers of Alberta; on colonization staff, CNR; 1935, moved to Nova Scotia Dept. of Agriculture; 1942, on Wartime Prices and Trade Board; 1944, Secretary, Canadian Federation of Agriculture; 1955, retired; did freelance writing on agricultural topics. **(WW** 1912; EJ Ag 11 1959)
Taber Times 954

Grogan, George Edward
Pub.; journalist
b. England, ca. 1856; d. Calgary, D 19 1939.
1975, came to Canada; in NWMP, 1886; 1910, moved to Victoria; returned to Calgary ca. 1939. (AC D 21 1939)
Calgary Herald 115
Calgary Weekly Herald and Alberta Livestock Journal 113

Gross, R. H. (Rick)
Ed.
News Advertiser, Wetaskiwin 1030

Grow, G. E.
Ed.; pub.
Originally from Nebraska. (**JEN** p.80)
Didsbury Pioneer 317

Grow, George
Mgr.
Gazette and Alberta Live Stock Record, Fort Macleod 536

Gunderson, Harold (Gundy)
Pub.; journalist
b. Maple Creek, Sask., Je 18 1929
Graphic, Bow Island 93
World of Beef and Stockman's Recorder, Calgary 209

Hagell, Edward G. (Ed)
Pub.; mgr; printer
b. Maidstone, Eng., ca. 1861; d. Vancouver, B. C., ca. Ap 1953.
Printer; 1889, came to Canada; farmed in MacLean, Sask.; worked on Regina
Leader, Oc 1890; continued in printing business in Alberta until 1921,
when moved to British Columbia; in newspaper and printing business in
Fraser Valley; 1924-1942, with Vancouver *Province*; retired, 1942. (**CPP**
v.62 no.5, My 1953; **HAG** 1; LH D 31 1986)
Lethbridge News 692
Lethbridge Telegram 697

Hagen, Elwood P.
Pub.
Lac Ste Anne Chronicle 665
Sangudo Star 886

Halina, William
Pub.
Myrnam News 779

Halliwell, Herbert Thomas (Tom)
Ed.; printer; prop.; pub.
b. London, Eng., Jl 1 1881; d. Fort Macleod, ca. S 10 1970.

Served in Boer War; emigrated to Oxbow, Sask., where was farm worker; prop., *Observer*, Estevan, Sask., 1913-24, and ed., *Review*, Weyburn, Sask., 1926-42; Pres., Canadian Weekly Newspapers Association; shared award from Columbia University for combatting Social Credit Press Gag, 1937. (**COU** p.128; *Fort Macleod Gazette* S 10 1970)
Coleman Journal 290
Macleod Gazette, Fort Macleod 545

Halpin, Charles Bernard, Sr.
Pub.; prop.
b. London, Ont., S 5 1864; d. Calgary, Mr 4 1955.
Farmed; store clerk in Winnipeg; became connected with CPR and arrived Calgary on first train, 1884; 1884-7, in Calgary where entered newspaper circles; published *Manitoba Liberal* at Portage La Prairie for 13 yrs, then returned to Calgary for 3 yrs, thence to Lacombe; retired from *Globe* to become printing instructor at trade school. (**BLU** v.3, p.232-3; **CPP** v.4 no.5, My 1895, v.60 no.4, Ap 1951; **OLDS** p.55-6)
Albertan, Calgary 126
Albertan and Alberta Tribune, Calgary 123
Olds Gazette 789
Western Globe, Lacombe 670

Halpin, Charles Bernard (Barney)
Ed.; pub.
b. 1899; d. 1977.
Son of Charles Bernard Halpin Sr. (q.v.); left school early in World War I to help father; wrote book of poems, *Pulpit-Pounding Bill*, skit on Aberhart regime. (**RIM** p.157; **SHE** p.92)
Bassano Star 60
Flare, Black Diamond 73
Rimbey Pioneer 853

Hambly, Ivan E. (Bill)
Ed; pub.
Came from Abbotsford, B. C.; with British Columbia newspapers 12 yrs. (**CWNA** v.22 no.584, Ag 27 1941)
Chronicle, Crossfield 296

Hamilton, John A.
Pub.
Albertan, Calgary 127

Hamilton, Max
Pub.
Garden City News, Magrath 720
Graphic, Bow Island 93
Raymond Recorder 826

Hammer, Bea
Pub.
Old Timer, Cochrane 280

Hammerstein, Count Alfred Von.
Ed.
b. Germany; d. Edmonton, D 20 1941.
Came to New York ca.1890; 1897, to Edmonton; active in oil business in
Fort McMurray, in partnership with John Gillespie; probably involved
with salt plant, Fort McMurray. (*Edmonton Bulletin* D 22 1941; COM
p.12-17)
Alberta Herold, Edmonton 343

ammond, Henry J.
Prop.; farmer
Pincher Creek Echo 814

Hamper, W. A.
Ed.
Son-in-law of William Cornelius Love Watson (q.v.) (**TRO** p.73)
Trochu Tribune 973

Hancock, Dwayne
Ed.
b. Santa Ana, Calif.
Came to Edmonton ca.1973 to do animation films for CITV. (EJ Ag 19
1977)
Lunch News, Edmonton 483

Hancock, G. L. (Bert)
Pub.
Cardston Chronicle 246
Raymond Review 828

Hankin, Alfred
Pub.
Empress Express 517

Hansch, G. J.
Prop.
Winnifred Record 1039

Hardie, John William
Pub.
Post, Fairview 526

Harding, H. A.
Ed.
Enlisted in 1st World War. (**CEN** p.8)
Okotoks Observer 785

Harpe, Dyane
Ed.
Fort McMurray Express 553

Harris, A. C.
Pub.; ed.
Coronation Review 293

Harris, Edgar W.
Ed.
b. ca.1883; d. Ja 12 1916.
In Vancouver, ca.1909-1911; moved to Coronation 1911. (**CPP** v.25 no.2, F 1916)
Coronation Review 293
Pincher Creek Echo 814

Harris, Fred L.
Pub.
Bowden News 95
Innisfail Independent 644

Harris, Greg
Ed.
Nations Ensign, Edmonton 494

Harris, Peter Gambell
Pub.; ed.; clergyman
b. England, N 22 1903; d. Cobble Hill, B. C., Jan 1968.
1959, returned to University to study for Anglican ministry; ordained, 1961, and took over parish Fort McMurray-Waterways; 1964, went to Cobble Hill, Vancouver Island. (Questionnaire)
Advertiser, Beaverlodge 66

Harris, Trevor Peter Gambell
Ed.; pub.; pressman; journalist
b. England, My 8 1933
Advertiser, Beaverlodge 66

Harris, W.C.
Pub.
On editorial staff *Canadian Thresherman,* Winnipeg, before moving to Medicine Hat. (**CPP** v.13 no.6, Je 1904)
Times Medicine Hat 742

Harrison, Harold
Ed.
Sylvan Lake News 951

Hart, John
Ed.
Grande Prairie Booster 588

Hartwig, Annie L.
Ed.
Neu-Kanadier, Coaldale 277

Harvey, A.L.
Ed.
1923, on Council, Airdrie; left Airdrie 1925. (**WILK** p.173, 182)
Airdrie Recorder, 6

Harvey, Ross (Harry Foont)
Journalist; ed; legislature executive assistant; legislature researcher
b. Vancouver, B.C., Ap 25 1952
Associated with student newspapers; wrote music; executive assistant to
New Democratic Party leader, Grant Notley, and caucus; dir. of research,
New Democrat Official Opposition. (Questionnaire)
Poundmaker, Edmonton, 476

Hatcher, W.H.
Pub.
d. 1920
Formerly of Minneapolis Minn.; American veteran of Philippines war.
(**CPP** v.2l no.5, May 1912; **HALL** p.25)
Redcliff Review 843

Hathaway, Anthony C.
Prop.; ed.; pub.
Chronicle, Crossfield 296
Cochrane Advocate 279

Hattersley, John Martin (Martin)
Ed.; lawyer; writer; politician
b. Swinton, Eng., N 10 1932
Emigrated to Canada 1956; called to Alberta bar 1957; National Pres.,
Social Credit League of Canada, 1973-78, National Leader, 1980-83; Social Credit candidate in 1979 provincial, and 1972 and 1974 federal, elections; published *Human Rights—The New Political Direction* and *Mone-
tary Reform for Canada* 1980. (**CAWW** 1986)
Focus: The Canadian Social Crediter, Edmonton 434

Hawk, Richard B. (Dick)
Pub.
b. Calgary
First apprenticed to *Nanton News*, D 1945; senior in print shop from 1949.
(**CWNA** v.38 no.771, Ja 1957)
Nanton News 780

Hawkey, R. J.
Ed.; prop.
Cochrane Advocate 279

Hawkins, James
Pub.
Weekly Advertiser, Drumheller 329

Haworth, John W.
Pub.
Hardisty Mail 608

Hayden, Charles A. (Charlie)
Ed.
b. Port Hope, Ont., Je 9 1877; d. Vernon, B. C., 1957.
Reporter, Ottawa *Citizen*, 1899-1904, when joined Ottawa *Journal* Press Gallery; 1904-08, editorial staff, Montreal *Herald*; went from staff, *Calgary Herald* to farm magazine in British Columbia. (**WW** 1917/18; **BRU** p.195; **CPP** v.3 no.5, My 1894)
Bowden News 95
Calgary News Telegram 136

Head, John
Pub.
Rattler, Medicine Hat 752

Heffernan, Jeremiah W. (Jerry)
Ed.; lawyer; politician
b. Picton, Ont., Ja 4 1884; d. S 21 1969.
Practised law, Toronto; from 1912, in Edmonton; prosecuting attorney then crown prosecutor for Alberta, 1914-1919; 1921, K.C.; 1921-6, Liberal MLA; Pres., West Edmonton Liberal Association for 5 yrs. (**CAWW** 1967; **BLU** v.2 p.56-57)
Western Catholic, Edmonton 388

Heidecker, Barry
Pub.
Onoway Tribune 794
Whitecourt Star 1033

Heller, Frank
Pub.
Lake Saskatoon Journal 674

Heller, Gerald H.
Pub.; ed.
Clairmont Independent 265
Lake Saskatoon Journal 674

Hensen, John
Ed.
Deutsch-Canadier, Calgary 139

Henzel, Edward
Ed.; electrical engineer; civil servant
b. Poland, Mr 23 1906
Officer in Polish army, imprisoned by Russians 1939; escaped, 1940, and
was imprisoned by Germans 1940-45, when joined Second Corps in Italy;
1946-50, teacher, Polish Resettlement Corps, Millom, Eng.; 1950, came
to Canada; worked for Alberta Transportation until retirement in 1971;
prominent in Polish community, nationally and locally. (Questionnaire)
Biuletyn. Kongresu Polonii Kanadyjskiej Okreg Alberta, Edmonton 443

Herault, James Charles L'
See **L'Herault**, James Charles

Herbert, Gary
Pub.
Carstairs Community Press, Mountain View County News 250

Hermansen, Otto
Ed.
Praerie Nyt, Calgary 197

Hermanson, C.
Ed.
Barons Globe 50

Higgins, Brian
Pub.
Castor Advance 252

Higgins, Floyd H.
Ed.
Alberta Homestead, Edmonton 353

Hilborn, Roy H.
Mgr
Political World, Calgary 174

Hildebrandt, Herb
Pub.
Banff Summit News 45

Hilman, Stan
Ed.
Reporter, Stony Plain 937

Hirst, W. G.
Pub.
Formerly with Hamly Press, Edmonton. (**CPP** v.51 no.3, Mr 1942)
Representative, Leduc 689

Hladyk, Victor P.
Ed.
Edited Russophile papers in U.S.; 1913, came to Canada to publish
Russian Voice; "notorious Russophile and Ukrainophobe"; 1914, went to
Winnipeg to publish *Russian People*; towards end World War I, left for
England and Europe. (**MARU** p.289-294)
Russkyi Golos, Edmonton 369

Hlynka, Authony H.
Ed.; politician
b. Western Ukraine, My 28 1907; d. 1957.
Came to Canada at age 3; became second Ukrainian MP, elected 1940
and 1945 as Social Credit candidate for Vegreville; leader in Ukrainian
community; as MP, opposed forced repatriation of displaced persons,
especially Ukrainian refugees. (**MARU** p.419, 439-440; **BYR** p.34)
Suspil' nyi Kredit, Edmonton 423

Hodge, Oliver R.
Pub.; clergyman
United Church minister in Burdett and Bow Island for six years; ter-
minated ministry, 1977 (**PUB** Je 1977)
40-Mile County Commentator 563

Hodge, Richard S.
Ed.
"(A) native of England and an early employee of the Redcliff Brick and
Coal Company"; on 1st town council. (**HALL** p.52)
Redcliff Journal 844

Hodgkin, M.
Prop.
Okotoks Times 783

Hodson, Samuel R. (Sam)
Prop.; ed.; pub.
b. Dublin County, Ireland; d. High River, S 5 1961.
Emigrated, with family, to Calgary, 1892; printer's devil, *Calgary
Tribune*, then shop foreman, *Calgary Herald*; 1906, moved to Okotoks;
active for many yrs in town govt., church and fraternal organizations;
1947, retired. (**CEN** p.8, 293-4)
Albertan and Alberta Tribune, Calgary 123
Okotoks Review 783

Hogan, Vera (née Rheaume)
Pub.; ed.

Wife of Mike Hogan.
St. Albert News 877

Hogarth, Leonard
Pub.
Western Review, Drayton Valley 323

Hohol, Carl M.
Pub.; ed.
b. ca. 1948
Rhino Party candidate, 1980 federal election. (EJ F 16 1980)
Two Hills County Times 983

Holden, Ivan Herman
Pub.
b. Des Moines, Idaho; d. Calgary, Oc 3 1942.
1912, moved to Cereal; was town barber for many yrs; retired to Calgary.
(AC Oc 3 1942; **CER** v.1 p.44)
Cereal Recorder 256

Holehouse, David
Ed.; mgr; journalist
b. Derbyshire, Eng., Ap 30 1953
On editorial staff, *Edmonton Journal*. (Questionnaire)
Edmonton Examiner [South Editions] 486
Record, Fort Saskatchewan 560
Sherwood Park News 896

Holliday, E. M.
Ed.
Alberta Veteran, Calgary 155

Hollingworth, Frank
Pub.
Alberta Social Credit Chronicle, Calgary 175

Hollinshead, John Lester
Pub; ed.; teacher
b. Falmouth, Mich.; d. Edmonton, ca. Ja 29 1970.
1906, moved to Stettler district where taught school; 1931, with federal
food and drug administration until retirement, 1953; veteran of both
World Wars. (EJ Ja 29 1970)
Edson-Jasper Signal, Edson 511
Jasper Signal 654

Holmes, Edward
Pub.; printer
b. Bradford, Eng., ca.1878; d. Oc 28 1944.
At age 11 was in composing room, Bradford *Telegram*; later, Bradford
Daily Argus as reporter and printer; 1900, came to Canada; homesteaded

Assiniboia district, Sask., spending winter months working on Saskatchewan newspapers; bought Carlyle *Herald*; 1922, founded Dauphin *Progress*; city ed., *Manitoba Free Press*, 1924-28; ardent aviator. (**EAR** p.19-20; **CPP** v.38 no.11, N 1929; unidentified clipping Oc 31 1944)
Provost News 822

Holmes, George Sloan (Pudge)
Ed.; pub.
b. Carlyle, Sask.; Ap 1914; d. Medicine Hat, Mr 2 1987.
Son of Edward Holmes (q.v.); served in Navy during World War II; Pres., Alberta Weekly Newspaper Association, 1957-58; served 2 terms as Mayor, Provost; active in ham radio operation and scouting; left Provost 1970 to expand family printing business in Medicine Hat; active in amateur aviation and computers. (EJ Mr 4 1987; Questionnaire)
Provost News 822

Holmes, Richard C. (Rick)
Ed.
b. Provost, Alta., Ag 1951
Son of George Sloan Holmes (q.v.); 1979, established Macklin *Mirror*, Sask.; active in community. (Questionnaire)
Provost News 822

Holmes, Ronald Edward (Ron)
Pub.; ed.
b. Provost, F 11 1947
Son of George Sloan Holmes (q.v.); 1973, moved to Medicine Hat to assist father in family printing business; active in community. (Questionnaire)
Oyen Echo 798
Provost News 822

Holmes, William E. G. (Bill)
Pub.; mgr; ed.
b. High River, S 26 1941
High River Times 625

Holstead, Thomas
Pub.
b. England, Je 11 1898; d. Ag 30 1970.
In Army 1917-19. (*Pincher Creek Echo* S 10 1970)
Coleman Journal 290

Holt, D. G.
Ed.
Went to Santa Monica, in newspaper business there. (**MOR**)
Medicine Hat Times 739

Holt, Jean M.
Ed.
Record-Gazette, Peace River 804

Homan, Betty
Ed.
Veteran Eagle 998

Homersham, Doug
Pub.; ed.
Western Livestock and Agricultural News, Edmonton 473

Honey, A. J.
Pub.
Came from England, 1908. (**SED** p.620)
Sedgewick Sentinel 890

Hopkins, Garth
Ed.
Market Examiner and Western Farm Journal, Calgary 153

Hopwood, F.
Ed.
Army and Navy News and Universal Weekly, Calgary 156

Horncastle, Leonard H.
Pub.
Review, Cereal 255

Horner, Wilber
Pub.; ed.
Alberta Sun, Calgary 162

Hornsby, Ed. P.
Pub.; ed.
Barrhead Leader 52
Bulletin, Barrhead 53

Horseman, A. Burdett
Pub.; ed.
Oilfields Flare, Turner Valley 976

Horsey, Michael E. (Mike)
Pub.
Edited *Ubyssey* 1964; 1965, worked on Vancouver *Sun*, and joined public
relations firm where founded *Ski Trails*; 1969, exec. assistant to Rod
Sykes; 2 yrs later, founded own public relations firm, Calgary. (Edmonton
Journal clipping files)
Sunday, Calgary 203

Horton, Andrew Leslie
Pub.; teacher; journalist
b. Frome, Ont., Mr 25 1875; d. Je 14 1958.
Taught in Carberry, Man. for 10 yrs, and gave it up because of increasing deafness; wrote for Winnipeg *Free Press*; farmed and published Carberry *News*; 1906, came to Vegreville. (**WW** 1912; **VEG** p.552-5)
Vegreville Observer 987

Horton, Catherine Elizabeth
Pub.
Wife of Andrew Leslie Horton (q.v.)
Vegreville Observer 987

Horton, Wilfred Laurier
Mg. ed.; pub.
Son of Andrew Leslie Horton (q.v.)
Vegreville Observer 987

Housiaux, Joseph A.
Ed.; pub.; printer
b. England; d. 1959.
Came to New York from France where worked on newspaper; printer in New York; 1914, partner to Edgar W. Hams (q.v.) (**COR** p.247-8)
Coronation Review 293

Howis, F. G. (Gerry)
Pub.; ed.
Falher News 528
Manning Banner Post 722

Hubbs, W.
Pub.
1914, went to New York to join family. (**CPP** v.23 no.10, Oc 1914)
Redcliff Review 843

Huberman, Irwin
Pub.
b. Montreal, Je 30 1953
Fort McMurray Express 553

Huckell, Benjamin Arthur
Pub.
b. Ottawa, Je 3 1874; d. Innisfail, S 24 1951.
Worked on father's paper, Carberry *Express*, then went west for Toronto Type Foundry, 1912; 1914, in real estate; 1937, won Pulitzer Prize; established Benjamin Huckell Memorial Trophy for best front page in weeklies with 1,000-2,000 circulation. (AC S 25 1951; **INN** p.185-6)
Innisfail Province 643

Huckell, Thomas John
Pub.
b. Carberry, Man.; d. Calgary, N 4 1960.
Son of Benjamin A. Huckell (q.v.); 1911, moved to Innisfail; moved to
Calgary 1955; printing salesman, John D. McAra Print. Co. (INN p.74;
CWNA v.43 no. 816, D 1960)
Innisfail Province 643

Huffman, Milo Bert
Pub.
b. Kamela, Ore., Ag 2 1900; d. Ag 18 1979.
1940-47, in Canadian Army. (CH Ag 20 1979)
Delburne Progress 305

Hughes, Donald F.
Pub.
Record, Fort Saskatchewan 560

Hull, Hugh Henry
Pub.; printer.
b. Ont.; d. Edmonton, Oc 20 1933.
Came to Battleford and taught printing at Indian mission school; own
printing firm, H. H. Hull Print. Co.; full-time worker Alberta Prohibition
Association. (EJ Oc 21 1933)
Town Topics, Edmonton 346

Humphrey, Leroy
Pub.
Innisfail Booster 645

Hungarian Cultural Association of Edmonton
Magyar Hirmondo, Calgary 214

Hunt, Donald
Gen. mgr
Edmonton Sun 489

Hunt, E. Jeanne
Mgr
Macleod Argus, Fort Macleod 546

Hunt, J. E.
Pub.
Castor Advance 252

Hunter, W. J.
Pub.
Formerly with *Edmonton Bulletin* for 10 yrs. (*Edmonton Bulletin* Ap 7 1903)
Fort Saskatchewan Reporter 555

Huntingford, Walter Charles
Pub.
Son of Walter John Huntingford (q.v.)
Wainwright Star 1007

Huntingford, Walter John
Pub., ed.
b. Wales, 1867; d. Ja 1945.
Served with British forces in Boer War; came to Canada ca.1901; was in newspaper printing in Manitoba and Saskatchewan (Biggar, Elstow and Lloydminster); ca.1916, moved to Edmonton; 1918 to Wainwright; active in community, on Town Council and Board of Trade; Pres., Alberta Press Association, 1922. (**GILT** p.137-9; *Strathmore Standard* Oc 25 1922)
Lloydminster Review 704
Wainwright Star 1007

Hyman, Herbert B.
Pub.; ed.
Alberta Jewish Chronicle, Edmonton 446

Hynd, Samuel A.
Pub.
b. London, Ont.; d. Calgary, Ja 8 1949
With London Print. and Litho; on *Farmers Advocate*, Winnipeg; mgr, Herald-Western Co. Ltd., Calgary; printer-owner, S. A. Hynd Litho-Print Ltd. (**CPP** v.58 no.2, F 1949)
Danskeren, Calgary 169

Hythe and District Pioneer Home
Hythe Headliner 639

Iffland, L. D. von
Pub.
Post, Wetaskiwin 1024

Imrie, John Mills
Pub.
b. Toronto, Ont., O 21 1883; d. Je 18 1942.
Apprentice printer, 1897-1902; mg. dir., Imrie Print. Co. Ltd.; 1913-18?, Mgr, Canadian Press Association Inc.; 1919-20, Mgr, Canadian Daily Newspapers Assn Inc.; 1921, came to Edmonton; 1929, became dir., Southam Pub. Co. Ltd. (**CAWW** 1938; EJ Je 19 1942)
Edmonton Journal, 344

Independent Merchants of Alberta
Kupets, Edmonton 422

Inman, G. C.
Pub.
Northwest Chronicle, Wetaskiwin 1023

Innes, John R.
Ed.; journalist; artist
b. England; d. Vancouver, B. C.
Ranched nr Calgary for some yrs; cartoonist, *Calgary Herald*; on staff
Westminster *Ledger* and drew for *Hornet*; moved to Toronto; contributed
series on Boer war to *Mail and Empire*. (**CPP** v.3 no.6, Je 1894, v.9 no.10,
Oc 1900)
Mountain Echoes, Banff 35
Prairie Illustrated, Calgary 120

International Hod Carriers, Building & Common Laborers'
Union of America,
Edmonton Local no. 92
Union Laborer, Edmonton 405

Irvine, William
Ed.; clergyman; journalist; politician
b. Gletness, Scotland, Ap 19 1885; d. Edmonton, Oc 26 1962.
Came to Canada ca.1902; Presbyterian Minister at Emo, Ont., 1913-5,
acquitted in ecclesiastical courts of charge of heresy 1914; Unitarian minister at Calgary 1915-19; author of several pamphlets and plays; after World
War I homesteaded in Bentley district, and became successful farmer; active
in CCF for many yrs, he was elected as Labour MP in 1921 and for UFA in
1926, 1930, 1945; was provincial and federal candidate but was defeated
several times in same period. (**BYR** p.36-7; **PEEL**)
Nutcracker, Calgary 152
People's Weekly, Edmonton 386
Western Independent, Calgary 158

Jackman, H.
Mgr
Evening Chronicle, Edmonton 350
Strathcona Chronicle, Edmonton 345

Jackson, Arthur
Prop.
Northern Tribune, Grande Prairie 586

Jacobs, J. A.
Prop.
Lloydminster Times and District News 703

James, F. Rodney
Pub.
Dairy Contact, Calgary 208

Jamieson, C. F.
Pub.; ed.
Lawyer in Calgary.
Morning Times, Medicine Hat 746

Jamison, Donald William (Duff)
Journalist; ed.; pub.
b. Montreal, Que., My 6 1952
Gazette, St. Albert 880

Jamison, William Ernest (Ernie)
Pub.; politician
b. Edmonton, F 27 1924
Served in RCAF as pilot; Pres., Alberta Weekly Newspapers 1961-62; elected Progressive Conservative MLA 1971 and 1975. **(AL)**
Gazette, St. Albert 880
Ponoka Herald 817
Strathcona Wedge, Strathcona County 938
Thorhild County News 956
Western Weekly Supplement Ponoka 819

Jean, Bernard C.
Pub.
Husband of Frances K. Jean (q.v.); moved to Fort McMurray 1967, and started stationery store. (*Edmonton Journal* clipping files)
McMurray Courier, Fort McMurray 551

Jean, Frances K.
Ed.
Wife of Bernard C. Jean (q.v.)
McMurray Courier, Fort McMurray 551

Jean-Louis, Maxim
Ed.
b. Haiti
Franco-albertain, Edmonton 458

Jeffrey, Richard
Ed.
Sherwood Park News 896

Jenkyns, Thomas G.
Mgr; ed.; pub.
Banff Advocate and Rocky Mountains Park District Recorder 41
Rocky Mountain Courier, Banff 40, 42
Strome Despatch 941
Wetaskiwin Journal 1027

Jennings, Milton Robbins
Pub.; journalist
b. Warsaw, N. Y., Mr 4 1874; d. Victoria, B. C., F 16 1921.
Reporter in Rochester and Buffalo, N. Y., 1890-95; 1895, worked on Montreal *Herald*; 1897, advertising mgr, Washington, D.C. *Times*; fought in Spanish-American War; 1898, to Toronto *Mail and Empire* and, later, to *Telegram*; engaged in mining enterprises in Cobalt country and in Nevada;

1909, came to Edmonton. (EJ F 16 1921)
Evening Journal 344

Jensen, Marion
Ed.
Carstairs and District Community Press and Mountain View County News 250

Jenson, Arthur (Art)
Pub.; printer
b. England, ca. 1900; d. Mr 22 1981.
Coronation Review 293
Province, Innisfail 643

Jesmore, L. C.
Pub.
Huxley New Era 637

Jessup, Aaron Zenas (A.Z.; Jess)
Ed.; pub.
b. Fort Scott, Kan., N 28 1861; d. Nanton, Mr 29 1938.
In Oregon Militia, Bannock Indian outbreak, 1878; worked in country print-
ing shops Oregon, Washington, Idaho; 1888, went to Seattle and worked on
daily papers Seattle and Spokane; 1899, bought and published Mount Vernon
Argus; 1905, came to Nanton; active in community, on Town Council, was
Mayor 1917-18. (EJ Mr 31 1938; **CPP** v.47 no.5, My 1938; **NAN** p.406)
Nanton News 780

Jessup, Anna M.
Pub.
b. Taber
Wife of Ralph C. Jessup (q.v.) (NAN p.406-7)
Macleod Gazette, Fort Macleod 545

Jessup, Clyde Campbell
Pub.
d. 1961.
Son of A. Z. Jessup (q.v.); served in World War II; Mayor, Nanton, 1945- 46.
(NAN p.406-7)
Nanton News 780

Jessup, Ralph C.
Pub.
d. 1943.
Son of A. Z. Jessup (q.v.); served in both World Wars. (NAN p.406-7)
Macleod Gazette, Fort Macleod 545

Jiry, Dwayne
Ed.
Spokesman, Edmonton 472

Jobb, Pat
Ed.
Wife of Wayne Jobb (q.v.)
Parklander, Hinton 627
Sherwood Park News 896

Jobb, Wayne
Pub.
Husband of Pat Jobb (q.v.)
Parklander, Hinton 627
Sherwood Park News 896

Johansen, Kenneth M.
Ed.
County of Lethbridge Sunny South News, Coaldale 276

Johns, Daniel Brian (Dan)
Ed.
b. Sault Ste. Marie, Ont., Mr 11 1952
Bonnyville Nouvelle 89

Johns, Frederick (Fred)
Pub.; printer
b. Neyland, Wales, My 14 1905; d. Leduc, Mr 5 1975.
Came to Lloydminster at age 7; worked on newspapers in Saskatchewan, Alberta and U. S. A.; 1932 started *Herschel Herald* in Dodsland, Sask.; served overseas during War; 1946, moved to Leduc. (Unidentified newspaper clipping Mr 8 1975)
Devonian, Devon 314
Representative, Leduc 689
Western Messenger, Thorsby 961
Winfield Gazette 1038

Johnson, Arthur (Art)
Mgr; pub.
b. Kinlough, Ont., Ap 22 1865.
Worked on several western newspapers, then moved to Revelstoke, 1896, to establish publishing business. (WW 1912)
Edmonton Herald 337

Johnson, Lillian
Ed.
Meridian Booster, Lloydminster 705

Johnson, R. G. (Ray)
Pub.
Raymond Review 828

Johnson, Sydney P.
Pub.
Lethbridge Northern News, Picture Butte 812

Johnston, Dave
Pub.
Nephew of Dorothy D. Wright (q.v.)
Ponoka News and Advertiser 818

Johnston, Garth Dunham
Pub.; ed.
1923, started working as printer's devil for *Peace River Record*; ed. in 1930s; moved to Douglas, Ariz., after sold *Record Gazette*, and worked on Douglas *Dispatch*; resigned 1966 to become publicity dir. for Cochise College. (**PEA** p.214,379)
Peace River Record-Gazette 804

Johnston, Gertrude
Pub.
Wife of John W. Johnston (q.v.)
Bonnyville Nouvelle 86

Johnston, John William
Pub.; printer
b. Attica, Ind., ca. 1870; d. Bonnyville, Ag 10 1940.
Husband of Gertrude Johnston (q.v.); brakeman on railroad, North Dakota; lost fingers in accident and went into printing; came to Canada 1907; during Depression operated travelling job plant in Alberta. (**CWNA** v.21 no.568, Ag 27 1940; *Edmonton Bulletin* Ag 21 1940)
Alliance Times 16
Bonnyville Nouvelle 86
Daysland Commercial 303
Forestburg Herald 532
Fort Saskatchewan Reporter 555
Galahad Mail 571
Lamont Weekly News 678
Viking News 1000
Wainwright Record 1008
Wainwright Star 1007
Weekly Chronicle, Fort Saskatchewan 556

Johnston, R. E.
Ed.
Edson Herald 505

Johnston, W. Frank
Pub.; ed.
Homesteaded north of Daysland, 1906; moved to B. C. and worked in miners' camps. (**LANT** p.236-7)
Forestburg Advance 530
Strome Despatch 941

Joly, C. O. (Chuck)
Pub.; ed.
Grand Centre Times 579

Jones, Dan C.
Pub.
From Coulee City, Wash.; returned to Washington State, 1908. (**NAN** p.140)
Nanton News 780

Jones, E. J.
Ed.
Mountaineer, Rocky Mountain House 860

Jones, H. Tilston-
see **Tilston-Jones**, H.

Jones, J.
Pub?
From Harmsworth, Eng.
Western Homestead, Calgary 137

Jones, Kathleen E.
Pub.
Mayerthorpe Times 733

Jones, W. X.
Ed.
Edson Leader 503

Jopling, Mrs. Harvey (née Woodhull)
Pub.
Daughter of B. N. Woodhull (q.v.)
Chronicle, Champion 260

Karvonen, Paul
Ed.
Scandinavian Centre News, Edmonton 445

Kaye-Kysilewsky, Vladimir J.
See **Kysilevskj**, W.

Keane, Amy H.
Pub.; ed.; author
Author of *The Gambler's Wife* and *Stories of the West*. (**CPP** v.21 no.12, D 1912)
Advance, Chauvin 261
Great West Saturday Night, Edmonton 380
Great West Saturday Night Advance, Edmonton 370

Kearns, Helen
Ed.
Meridian Booster, Lloydminster 705

Keays, Albert R.
Pub.
Sports Review, Edmonton 391

Kee, Charles L.
Pub.
Alix-Mirror Free Press 14

Keebaugh, Byron H.
Pub.; ed.
b. Holbein, Sask., Ag 17 1932
Meridian Booster, Lloydminster 705

Keebaugh, Shirley M.
Ed.
b. Kelvington, Sask., Je 7 1928
Meridian Booster, Lloydminster 705

Keith, A. W.
Pub.
Post, Wetaskiwin 1024

Keith, Gordon Alexander
Pub.
b. Rimbey, S 21 1955
Coronation Review 293

Keith, Gordon Monte (Monte)
Pub.; printer
b. Regina, Sask., Je 13 1933
Castor Advance 252
Community Press, Sedgewick 890
Enterprise, Alliance 16
Rocky Weekly Press, Rocky Mountain House 861

Sylvan Lake News 951
Wainwright Star-Chronicle 1009

Kelly, Jack
Ed.
Western Weekly Supplement, Ponoka 819

Kelsey, Elwyn
Pub.
Fairview Post 526

Kemp, Rev.
Prop.; clergyman
Chronicle, Crossfield 296

Kende, Stephen
Ed.
Canadai Magyar Farmer, Edmonton 357

Kennedy, George Allan
Ed.; physician and surgeon
b. Dundas, Ont., Ap 16 1858; d. Winnipeg.
Came to Northwest Territories, 1878; surgeon, NWMP 1878-87; practising physician, 1887 on; surgeon, CPR, 1897 on; Pres., Northwest Medical Council for 2 yrs; Pres., Council of College of Physicians and Surgeons of Alberta, 1907; mbr of Senate, Univ. of Alberta, for 2 yrs; appointed Governor of same, 1911; prominent in Fort Macleod community. (**FORT**; WW 1912)
Outlaw, Scotts Coulee 888

Kennedy, Joy
Pub.
Lakeside Leader, Slave Lake 903

Kenrick, J. B.
Pub.; ed.
Alberta Farmer, Medicine Hat 748
Morning Times, Medicine Hat 746

Ker, James A.
Pub.; printer
Apprenticed Mount Forest *Representative*; 1909, went to Kinistino, Sask., to start another *Representative*. (**PUB** Mr 1982)
Representative, Leduc 689

Kernaghan, Annis
Ed.
Banner Post, Manning 722

Ketchum, Herbert S.
Pub.
Alderson News 12
Farmers Tribune, Alderson 13

Kettle, S. H.
Pub.
Stony Plain Herald 935

Kew, Wilson L.
Pub.

b. Kamloops, ca. 1900; d. Vancouver, 1949.
Came to Stavely ca.1925; accomplished musician; during War, joined
Canadian Legion War Services, Inc., and left Stavely; 1944, moved to
Vancouver. (BUT p.274-5)
Stavely Advertiser 922

Key, Archibald Frederick
Pub.; ed.; fine art, museum consultant; author; broadcaster
b. Huddersfield, Eng., Jan 19 1894
Newspaper ed. and pub. until 1941; since 1930s, prominent in arts, holding
many offices and receiving various awards; broadcast regular classical
record radio program, 1953-59; wrote books, poetry, a play, articles; 1946-
64, founding mbr and Dir., Calgary Allied Arts Centre. (CAWW 1982)
Drumheller Mail 327
Plaindealer, Drumheller 330
Review, Drumheller 325

Khuu, Ben Fu
Ed.; pub.
Indo Chinese News, Calgary 221

Kidner, William H. (Billy)
Pub.; ed.; teacher; printer
b. Bristol, Eng., 1868; d. Calgary, F 27 1943.
Learnt printing trade with Bristol *Mercury*; came to Canada 1903; taught
printing Calgary pre-vocational school, 1913-27?; ran printing establishment
in Banff with Victor W.R.B. Ball (q.v.); 1929, returned to Calgary and
worked on *Calgary Herald*; retired 1930. (*Crag and Canyon* Mr 5 1943)
Crag and Canyon, Banff 38
Banff Mercury 43

Kientzel, Sylvie Pollard-
See Pollard-Kientzel, Sylvie

Kilburn, Nicholas Alexander
Pub.; ed.
b. Bishop Auckland, Eng., 1875; d. 1931.
Came to Canada with Barr Colonists; homesteaded—failed; 1917, moved to
Edmonton, where was in business with W. L. Wilkin and George Hunt.
(EAR p.22)
Provost Star 821

Kim, Paul
Mgr
Korean Canadian Times, Edmonton 496

King, Don R.
Ed.
High River Times 625

King, Fred Anderson
Pub.; ed.; investment executive
b. Lomond, My 1 1922
Son of Rae Livingstone King (q.v.)
Camrose Canadian 225

King, Gilbert L.
Pub.; ed.
Social Credit Gazette, Edmonton 420

King, Rae Livingstone
Printer
b. Tillsonburg, Ont.; d. Ag 19 1959.
Bassano Mail 58
Camrose Canadian 225
Claresholm Local Press 268
Lomond Press 708

Kiriak, Illya
Ed.; author; teacher
b. Ukraine, 1888; d. 1957.
Came to Canada 1906; poet; wrote novel, *Sons of the Soil*; school teacher;
dir. of Michael Hrushevsky Institute, Edmonton, 1940-42. (**PEEL; MARU** p.
502-3)
Nova Hromada, Edmonton 363

Kirke, George C.
Ed.
Call, Calgary 186

Kirker, Gary
Pub.; ed.
Calgary Rural Ad-Viser 211

Kirkham, James Stanley
Ed.; barrister; hotelier
b. Alberta, ca. 1889; d. My 13 1941.
Square Shooter, Lethbridge 699

Kirkpatrick, Kenneth
Ed.
b. Brandon, Man.
1949, moved to Grande Prairie. (*Daily Herald Tribune* Ap 26 1966)
Daily Herald Tribune, Grande Prairie 586

Kitchen, Brian G.
Ed.
Dairy Contact, Calgary 208

Kitchen, Charles Steven (Charlie)
Prop.

d. Dawson Creek, B. C., ca. D 1959.
After having worked on *Grande Prairie Herald* moved to Dawson Creek and
produced own paper. (**CAM** 2 p.293, 315; **CPP** v.68 no.12, D 1959)
Grande Prairie Herald 584

Kizuin, A., Rev.
Ed.; clergyman
Pravda Naroda, Edmonton 407

Klebe, Bert J.
Ed.; pub.
Mechanical foreman with *Strome Despatch* since its inception. (**CPP** v.20
no.12, D 1911)
Bassano Mail 58
Strome Despatch 941

Klein, F. W.
Ed.
Deutsch Canadier, Calgary 139

Klesken, George
Ed.
Hlas Naroda, Blairmore 80
Slovenske Slovo, Blairmore 78, 82

Klippenstein, Robert Bruce (Bruce)
Pub.
b. Manitoba, N 19 1943
Western Wheel, Okotoks 787

Knight, George
Pub.; ed.
Jasper Totem 656

Knight, H. G.
Pub.
Three Hills Review 964

Knights of Confederation
Spokesman, Calgary 173

Knights of Labour. Local #9787, Calgary.
Northwest Call, Calgary 119

Knoch, Marilynn
Ed.
High River Times 625

Knowles, Bernard Porritt (Ben)
Pub.; printer

b. Oakengates, Eng., Ja 18 1903; d. Fort Saskatchewan, S 5 1977.
Served apprenticeship with Esdale Press; in composing room, *Edmonton Bulletin*, for 17 yrs; published *Lamont Municipal and School Gazette* with Joseph J. Bell (q.v.) (**CWNA** v.25 no.629, Oc/N 1944)
Fort Record, Fort Saskatchewan 560

Knowles, Vernon
Mg ed.; businessman; journalist
b. Nottingham, Eng., S 16 1890
Ed., mgr, mg. ed. many newspapers in Toronto, Winnipeg, Saskatoon, Calgary, Vancouver, and Miami, Fla.; 1936, Public Relations Advisor, Canadian Bankers Assoc. (**CAWW** 1949)
Black Diamond Press, Calgary 145

Knox, J. Clark
Pub.; ed.
Of Weyburn, Sask. (**CPP** v.20 no.5, My 1911)
Grassy Lake Gazette 599
Grassy Lake Pilot 598

Koermann, Gustav
Pub.; ed.
Rumoured to be Mr. Koermann of Winnipeg *Nordwestern*. (**CPP** v.12 no.4, Ap 1903)
Alberta Deutsche Zeitung, Edmonton 360
Alberta Herold, Edmonton 343

Kohn, Gary
Ed.
Calgary Jewish News 196

Kovacsi, Kalman
Ed.
Canadai Magyar Farmer, Edmonton 357

Kovacsi, Lajos
Ed.
Canadai Magyar Farmer, Edmonton 357

Koyanagi, Walter Wataru
Pub.; mg. ed.
b. Sea Island, B. C., S 12 1920
On staff Medicine Hat *Rattler* for 20 yrs. (**CANW** D 1969)
Rattler, Medicine Hat 752
Sunny South News, Coaldale 276
Taber Times 954
Vauxhall Advance 986

Kramer, Arthur
Ed.
Edmonton Sports Record 425

Krankenhagen, Wilhelm
Ed.; mgr
b. Hanover, Ger., Mr 5 1885
Served in German Army, 1903-4; 1904, came to Alberta; mgr, Alberta
Herold Pub. Co.; later, moved to U.S.A. (**ENT**; WW 1912)
Alberta Herold, Edmonton 343

Kremar, Roman
Ed.
b. Halychyna Province, Austria (now Ukraine) F 5 1886; d. Ja 13 1953.
Born Michael Solodukha; qualified as lawyer in Lvov; fled country after selling land to Ukrainian peasants following 1902 peasant strike in Halychyna,
changing name to Roman Kremar; arrived Edmonton 1910; timekeeper on
Grand Trunk Pacific Railway near Edson, then returned to work as lawyer;
involved in Ukrainian social democratic circles; later, involved more gen-
erally with Ukrainian interests, and fought for same all his life; N 1918,
appointed ed. *Canadian Rutherian* in Winnipeg; first on *Canadian Novyny*
then *New Pathway*; wrote novel *Beyond Good and Evil*. (**UKR** v.2 p.166-71)
Nova Hromada, Edmonton 363
Novyny, Edmonton 369

Krett, James N.
Ed.; pub.
b. 1883; d. 1964.
Established Ruthenian Press, Winnipeg, 1908; published books, pamphlets,
and illustrated magazine *Khata* (Home), 6 issues only; in close association
with contemporary Ukrainian writers. (**MARU** p.280, 307, 310)
Nash Postup, Edmonton 393
Ukrainian News, Edmonton 402

Kroetsch, Howard
Pub.
Coronation Review 293

Kronert, Manfred
Pub.
Bonnyville Nouvelle 89

Kyba, Dan
Ed.
North Peace Pictorial, Peace River 805

Kyriak, Illa
See **Kiriak**, Illya

Kysilvskyj, W. (a.k.a. **Kaye-Kysilewsky** or **Kaye**)
Ed.; writer; historian; professor
b. 1896; d. 1975.
Author of *Early Ukrainian Settlement in Canada 1895 - 1900*, and *Slavic
Groups in Canada*; historian and professor, Dept. of Slavic Studies,

University of Ottawa; Liaison Officer for ethnic groups, Canadian Citizenship Branch; compiled *Dictionary of Ukrainian Canadian Biography.* (**MARU** p.661, 710)
Ukrainian News, Edmonton 402

Lacey, Heidi
Ed.
Vauxhall Advance 986

Lacombe, Guy
Ed.; public servant; teacher
b. Sherbrooke, Que.
Ottawa-based civil servant; came to Alberta ca. 1950; teacher of French literature, Collège Universitaire St. Jean; resigned from editorship of *Franco-albertain* 1976 to join *Le Droit.* (EJ Jl 30 1976)
Franco-albertain, Edmonton 458

La Cruz, Eduardo de
See **Cruz**, Eduardo de la

Ladha, Mansoor
Pub.
b. Zanzibar, Tanzania, Mr 3 1943
Formerly with newspapers in Dar es Salaam and Nairobi. (Questionnaire)
Bonnyville Nouvelle, Grand Centre Globe, Bonnyville 89
Morinville and Sturgeon Mirror 767
Tribune, Redwater 851

Lafferty, Bill
Ed.
On Northwest Territories Council, 1976. (**EJ** Oc 20 1976)
Native People, Edmonton 460

Lafleur, George
Ed.
Native People, Edmonton 460

Lafranchise, Joseph P.
Ed.
Etoile de St. Albert 878
St. Albert News 877

Lake, Herbert
Ed.; dentist
Bee, Calgary 130
Outlaw, Grassy Lake 597
Round-Up, Pincher Creek 815

Lambert, Frank A.
Pub.
Bonnyville Nouvelle 86

Lamont, Colin
Ed.
Grande Prairie This Week 588

Lane, Daniel Austin
Lawyer; ed.
b. Gainsborough Township, Ont.; d. Ja 20 1966.
Graduated from Queen's University in journalism, then in law from
Cambridge University; with Toronto *Star* for some yrs, then telegram ed.,
Calgary *Albertan*; in British Army during 1st World War and RCAF during
2nd. (AC Ja 22 1966; CH Ja 22 1976)
Oil and Financial Review, Calgary 167
Western Examiner, Calgary 165
Western Oil Examiner, Calgary 163

Langdon, Bernard A.
Pub.; ed.
South East News, Edmonton 439
South Edmonton Weekly News 395

Lanzieri, Sergio
Ed.
Messaggero delle Praterie, Edmonton 465

Laplante, Rudolphe
Ed.
Survivance, Edmonton 404
Union, Edmonton 378

Larkins, Arnold (Arnie)
Pub.
Son of E. A. Larkins (q.v.)
Reporter, Stony Plain 937

Larkins, Arthur Evans (Art; Pop)
Pub.
b. Iowa; d. Barrhead, ca. Ap 1960
Came to Canada 1910; farmed in Lamont area; served in World War I,
1915-8; 1941, moved to Barrhead; strong supporter of community sports.
(**HED** p.28, 124; unidentified newspaper clipping Ap 23 1960)
Barrhead Leader 52
Lamont Tribune 679, 681

Larkins, E. A. (Ed.)
Pub., ed
b. Mundare, Sask., 1921

Son of Arthur Evans Larkins (q.v.); retired in 1969.
Barrhead Leader 52

La Rue, George
Pub.
d. Ja 15 1946.
Moved to California following disastrous fire, 1934. (**CPP** v.43 no.9, S 1934)
St. Paul Journal 883

La Rue, Gilbert
Pub.
Moved to California, 1934. (**CPP** v.43 no.9, S, 1934)
St. Paul Tribune 883

Lavallée, Brent
Pub.
Northeast News, Vermilion 944
Wild Rose Chronicle, Vermilion 1088

Lavallée, Maurice
Ed.
Moved from Quebec to Edmonton 1927 to teach French immersion class;
worked for Dept. of Education Correspondence School Branch 1934-62;
founded Edmonton's first French book store; Pres., Assoc. of Bilingual
Educators, for 18 yrs; French separate school in Edmonton named after him.
(EJ Ja 7 1985)
Survivance, Edmonton 404

Law, John
Pub.
Devon Dispatch 315

Lawson, P. F.
Ed.
Searchlight, Calgary 159
Wedge, Edmonton 389

Laycock, F. U.
Ed.
Edson Leader 503

Leatherdale, Neil K.
Pub.; ed.
b. Winnipeg, 1918
Came to Alberta with RCAF; after discharge joined father-in-law, W.H.
Miller (q.v.), on *Olds Gazette*. (**OLDS**)
Crossfield Chronicle 298
Innisfail Star 1077
Olds Gazette 789

Leathley, Charles H.
Pub.; ed.
b. Leeds, Eng., 1873; d. D 12 1934.
1903, to Saskatoon with Barr colonists; 1905, prop. and ed. *Hanley Herald*,
Davidson, Sask.; operated newspapers Kelowna, Prince George; moved to
Three Hills 1917. (Glenbow Library clipping file)
Bashaw Star 56
Three Hills Capital 965

Leathley, Gladys
Pub.; ed.
Daughter of Charles H. Leathley (q.v.)
Three Hills Capital 965

Leathley, Melville
Pub.; ed.
Son of Charles H. Leathley (q.v.)
Bashaw Star 56
Delburne Independent 308
Mirror Journal 761
Three Hills Capital 965

LeBel, John M.
Pub.
Educational publisher's representative; children's book pub.
(Questionnaire; EJ N 24 1973)
Edmonton Sun 488

Le Bourdais, Donat Marc
Ed.; journalist; salesman
b. Clinton, B. C., Ap 25 1887
Since 1921 has written articles on wide variety subjects; 1921-25, freelance
journalist in Ottawa and New York; returned to Toronto to continue writing;
ed., *Mental Health*, 1927-33. (**CAWW** 1961)
Canadian Nation, Calgary 154

Lecerf, J.
Ed.
Union, Edmonton 378

Le Clerc, Normand F.
Ed.
Franco-albertain, Edmonton 458

Lee, Geoff
Ed.
Record, Fort Saskatchewan 560

Lee, Jack
Ed.

Veteran of World War I; enlisted in World War II. (**CPP** v.48 no.9, S 1939)
Flare, Black Diamond 73

Leender, G. N.
Pub.
Holland Revue, Edmonton 441

Lees, Eve
Ed.
Banner Post, Manning 722

Leffler, Janice
Ed.
Reporter, Stony Plain, 937

Legg, Herbert F.
Pub.; ed.
Worked on *Calgary Herald*; edited *Creston Review*, B. C. (CH Oc 21 1970)
Coleman Review 290

Lemoyne, Gerard, pseud.
See **Forcade**, Gerard

Lennon, Randall Joseph (Randy)
Pub.; ed.; journalist; policeman
b. Edmonton, S 19 1956
Co-owner, Grove Pub. Ltd.; since 1979, police constable. (Questionnaire)
Edmonton Examiner [North Editions] 490
Edmonton Examiner [West Editions] 487
Grove Examiner, Spruce Grove 913
Parkland County Examiner 799

Leonard, Keith
Pub.
Associate-ed., *Canadian Printer and Publisher*; worked for MacLaren
Advertising Co., Montreal. (**CPP** v.62 no.4, Ap 1953)
Ponoka Herald 817

Le Riche, Tim
Ed.
Later, with Meadowlake, Sask., *Northwestern Sun*. (**PUB** Jl/Ag 1984)
Grande Centre-Cold Lake-Bonnyville Sun, Grand Centre 581

Leska, Frank S.
Ed.
Was employee of *Crag and Canyon* for some yrs before becoming ed.
(**CWNA** v.21 no.568, Ap 27 1940)
Crag and Canyon, Banff 38

Lessard, Jean, o.m.i.
Pub.; ed; Catholic clergyman
b. St. Paul, N 14 1911; d. Edmonton, Ap 24 1966.
Active in Indian education. (*Survivance* Ap 27 1966)
Old Timer, Cochrane 280

Lethbridge Trades and Labor Council
Southern Alberta Labor Bulletin, Lethbridge 696

Letson, William A. (Billy)
Pub.
b. Queen's County, N. S., 1847
Journalism career began 1862; worked on several provincial newspapers and
in Parliamentary Print. Off., Ottawa; arrived Chailey district ca.1907 from
Nova Scotia; homesteaded; moved to Mannville; later returned to Nova
Scotia. (**CPP** v.31 no.5, My 1922; **MANN**, p.540)
Mannville Empire 724

Lett, T. W.
Ed.
Lethbridge News 692

Levett, Roger
Pub.; ed.
With wife, Toni Levett (q.v.), experienced in Ontario and Alberta newpapers
and radio. (**CPP** v.78 no.3, Mr 1969)
Jasper Gateway 658

Levett, Toni
Pub.; ed.
Wife of Roger Levett (q.v.)
Jasper Gateway 658

Levytsky, Myron
Ed.
b. 1913
Graduate, Cracow Academy of Arts; graphic artist. (**MARU** p.673)
Ukrainian News, Edmonton 402

L'Herault, James Charles
Pub.
Delia Times 313

Liberal Association of Alberta
Alberta Liberal, Edmonton 1062

Liberal Party in Alberta
Alberta Liberal, Edmonton 1064
New Alberta Liberal, Edmonton 1065

Liebe, John
Ed.
Deutsche Arbeiter Zeitung, Edmonton 411

Liebrecht, Jean
Ed.
Representative, Leduc 689

Ligerwood, Jim
Ed.
Nation's Ensign, Edmonton 494

Lightfoot, John W.
Pub.
Beverly Advertiser, Edmonton 373

Lilley, Evelyn
Ed.
Crossfield Chronicle 300

Linton, J.
Ed.
Formerly with *Calgary Herald*. (**CPP** v.27 no.4, Ap 1918)
Drumheller Standard 326

Lipsett, Robert W.
Pub.
Connected with Winnipeg newspapers for over 10 yrs; with *Calgary Herald*
2 yrs; moved to Banff, 1914. (*Banff Crag and Canyon* Ap 18 1914)
Rocky Mountain Courier, Banff 40

Lister, William
Ed.; pub.
Carstairs Journal 249
Clive News-Record 270

Little, Donna
Ed.
Cochrane Times 281

Liversidge, Arthur Henry
Pub.
b. Liverpool, Eng.; d. Ap 30 1942.
Had printing business, Owen Sound, Ont.; 1892, on Winnipeg *Free Press*;
with other papers, including *Edmonton Journal*. (Glenbow clipping file)
Enterprise, Leduc 688
Hardisty Enterprise 607
Wetaskiwin Free Press 1026

Livingston, John
Pub.
From Toronto *Empire*; later returned to Montreal. (CH Ag 31 1963)
Calgary Daily Herald 115
Calgary Weekly Herald and Alberta Livestock Journal 113

Livingston, R.W.
Pub.
Macleod Chronicle 539

Lizée, Zéphiron, o.m.i.
Pub.; ed.
b. Montreal, Que., Je 18 1856; d. Edmonton, Ja 28 1928.
Croix de Ste.-Anne, Lac Ste-Anne 1078
Echo de Ste-Anne, Lac Ste-Anne 668

Lobb, R.
Ed.; pub.
Irma Independent 648
Wainwright Record 1008

Lockart, Margie
Ed.
Native People, Edmonton 460

Loewen, Jacob J.
Pub.; ed.
b. Russia
1929, went to Germany as refugee; 1930, to Canada, where farmed in
Saskatchewan; 1934, moved to Coaldale; 1939, printed religious tracts for
German prisoner-of-war camps; 1940, had own job printing business. (CH
S 22 1956)
Coaldale Flyer 276
Lethbridge Northern News, Picture Butte 812
Neu-Kanadier, Coaldale 277
Raymond Recorder 827

Long, Walter
Prop.
International Labor News, Edmonton 394

Lord, J. P.
Mgr
Munson Times 776

Lorimer, Arthur S.
Ed.; pub.
Carstairs Journal 249

Louie, Jake
Ed.
Canadian Chinese Times, Calgary 217

Louis, Maxim Jean-
See **Jean-Louis,** Maxim

Love, George Albert
Pub.; business; clergyman
b. Bay of Quinte area, Que.; d. Redlands, Ont.
1885, ordained Methodist minister; 1897, had sawmill in Red Deer; 1903, Mayor of Red Deer; 1925, ordained priest in Liberal Catholic Church of St. Francis. **(MEE** p.162-3)
Alberta Advocate, Red Deer 834
News, Red Deer 835

Love, Harry W.
Ed.
1909, homesteaded Sunnybrae School District; moved to Irma; 1932, moved to Edmonton. **(TIM** p.17)
Irma Times 647

Love, O. S.
Ed.; prop.
Cochrane Advocate 279

Lucas, Alexander
Pub.; ed.
Calgary Herald 115
Calgary Weekly Herald 113

Lucas, Michael
Pub.
Record, Fort Saskatchewan 560

Lukca, Andrew
Pub.
Slovenske Slovo, Blairmore 78

Luxton, Norman Kenny (Mr. Banff)
Pub.
b. Winnipeg, Man., N 2 1876; d. Banff, Oc 23 1962.
Son of William Fisher Luxton, founder of Manitoba *Free Press*; worked on Press after school, typesetting; when 16 yrs old apprenticed as clerk to Indian agent at Rat Portage, Kenora; worked on *Herald*, Calgary, and Vancouver *News Advertiser*; in Banff ran trading post, Sign of the Goat, and private museum that became the Luxton Museum; owned King Edward Hotel. (CH Oc 24 1962; Glenbow clipping file)
Crag and Canyon, Banff 38

Lydon, Matt
Pub.
Innisfail Booster 645

Lyle, John Percival
Pub.; ed.; businessman
b. Barnstaple, Eng., Jl 14 1878
Insurance agent, London, Eng., 1897; in Boer War; came to Canada 1903;
estab. own business 1905; Mayor of Lloydminster, 1910. (**WW** 1912)
Lloydminster Review 704

Lyon, Doris
Pub.
Wife of Douglas B. Lyon (q.v.)
Eagleview Post, Turner Valley 979

Lyon, Douglas B.
Pub.
Husband of Doris Lyon (q.v.)
Eagleview Post, Turner Valley 979

Mabell, Dave
Ed.
Wainwright Star-Chronicle 1009

MacAdams, William
Pub.; ed.
b. Sarnia, Ont.
Sporting ed., Vancouver *World*; founded Sandon, B. C., *Paystreak*; imprisoned in British Columbia for contempt of court, 1902; upon release,
appointed mg. ed., *Edmonton Bulletin*. (**MOR**)
Edmonton Capital 356

Macdonald, E. B.
Pub.
Jasper Booster 657

MacDonald, Gary Alexander
Pub.
b. Winnipeg, Man., Oc 10, 1945
Reporter, Stony Plain 937
Sylvan Lake News 951
Western Review, Drayton Valley 323

MacDonald, Ian Charles
Pub.
b. Edmonton, ca. 1919
Reporter, *Edmonton Journal*; 1940, joined RCAF; returned to newspaper
after War. (EJ N 26 1969)
Medicine Hat News 743

MacDonald, John
Pub.
News, Thorhild County 958
Redwater News 850
Witness, Westlock 1015

MacDonald, Ross
Pub.
Free Lance, Calgary 171

MacDonald, Walter Augustus
Pub.
In 1920s and 1930s worked on Vancouver *World*, Vancouver *Sun*, *Farm and Home*, and Vancouver *Province*; 1937, bus. mgr *Edmonton Journal*. (EJ Ja 31 1962)
Edmonton Journal 344

MacDonnell, William
Pub.
North Star, Wetaskiwin 1019

MacGregor, Robert W.
Pub.
Athabasca Echo 30

MacGregor, Bob
Pub.
Hub, Westlock 1016

MacKay, James G.
Pub.
Provost Star 821

MacKay, W. H.
Ed.
Innisfail Free Lance 642

Mackay, Will D.
Pub.
Served overseas World War I. (CPP v.28, no.1, Ja 1919)
Alderson News 12
Hughenden Record 636
Provost News 822
Sylvan Lake World 949

Mackenzie, John W.
Mgr; pub.; ed.; printer
b. Rothesay, Scotland, F 1 1887
Son of a newspaper man; 1909, emigrated and came to Calgary, where

worked on *Albertan* for 3 mths; moved to Strathmore; commercial
printer; enlisted during First World War; Pres., Alberta Press Association.
(**BLU** v.2, p.111-3)
Strathmore and Bow Valley Standard 940

MacLaren, John
Ed.
Fort Saskatchewan Record 555
Peace River Record 802

MacLean, Charles A. (Chuck)
Pub.; ed.
Grandson of Andrew A. Moore (q.v.); brother of H. F. MacLean (q.v.)
(**CPP** v.56 no.6, Je 1947)
Camrose Canadian 225
Mercury, Tofield 970
Strathmore and Bow Valley Standard 940
Wetaskiwin Times 1022

MacLean, H. F. (Hec)
Ed; pub.
d. Peace River, F 6 1983.
Grandson of Andrew A. Moore (q.v.); brother of Charles A. MacLean
(q.v.); former sports writer on *Albertan* and *Calgary Herald*; after sale
Strathmore Standard spent 2 yrs on *Calgary Herald* wire service; 1959,
went to Dawson Creek. (**PUB** Mr 1983; **CANW** D 1968)
Post, Fairview 526
Record-Gazette, Peace River 804
Strathmore and Bow Valley Standard 940

MacLellan, James Alexander, Monsignor
Ed.; Catholic clergyman
b. Nova Scotia; d. Edmonton, Ja 21 1981.
Ordained in Edmonton, 1925; for 6 yrs after ordination ran Great Western
Press. (**EJ** Ja 23 1981
Western Catholic, Edmonton 388

MacLeod, Norman W.
Printer
From Salt Lake City, Utah; nephew of Col. Macleod, RCMP; published
Picturesque Cardston and Environments (1900) (**BAT** p.137)
Cardston Record 240

MacMartin, A. K.
Ed.
Trochu Tribune 973

MacPherson, John
Mgr; prop.
b. Ayr, Ont.; d. Vancouver, B. C., Ja 9 1956.

Produced weekly newspapers for some yrs; owned paper Portage La Prairie; after sold *Edmonton Journal* worked with Canadian National Railways in land purchasing dept. (EJ Ja 10 1956)
Evening Journal, Edmonton 344

Macquarrie, J. C.
Pub.
Fort Saskatchewan Reporter 555
Northern News, Athabasca 26

Magrath, Charles Alexander
Pub.; public servant; politician; author
b. North Augusta, Ont., Ap 22 1860; d. Victoria, B. C., Oc 30 1949. Dominion topographical surveyor, North West Territories, 1878-85; Mgr, Canadian North West Irrigation Co., 1885-1906; mbr, War Trade Board, World War I; Chrmn, Ontario Hydro Electric Power Commission, 1925-31; 1st Mayor of Lethbridge, 1891; sat for Lethbridge in Territorial Assembly, 1891-1902; Conservative MP for Medicine Hat 1908-11; on International Joint Commission 1911-14, and Canadian Chrmn of same, 1914-36; 1927, elected Fellow, Royal Society of Canada; author of *Canadian Growth and Some Problems Affecting It* (1910) and *The Galts: Father and Son, Pioneers in the Development of Southern Alberta* (1935). (**BYR** p.43-4; **CAWW** 1948; **MACM**)
Calgary Daily Herald 115
Calgary Weekly Herald 113

Mah, Angela
Ed.
Nation's Ensign, Edmonton 494

Mailhot, G. H. (Nash)
Pub.
Continued to operate *Western Signal* plant as job printing establishment. (**CPP** v.69 no.5, My 1960)
Western Signal, Edson 511

Malcolm, Frank F.
Pub.
Brother of Harry A. Malcolm (q.v.)
Innisfail Free Lance 642

Malcolm, Harry A.
Ed.; teacher
b. Scotland, Ont., Mr 31 1860; d. Ja 1946.
Brother of Frank F. Malcolm (q.v.); 1891, arrived Innisfail, homesteaded in Aberdeen distrivt, taught school for one yr; worked in Innisfail land office for 12 yrs. (**INN** p.247)
Innisfail Free Lance 642

Malcolm, Keith
Pub.
Alberta Farm Life, Edmonton 485

Malcolm, Thomas B.
Pub.
1926 owned and edited *Gazette*, Verwood, Sask. (**CPP** v.28 no.1, Ja 1919)
Craigmyle Gazette 295
Gazette, Rocky Mountain House 859

Malette, J. Burt
Ed.
Provincial Standard, Calgary 142

Mandick, Walter
Pub.
Castor Advance 259
Stony Plain Reporter 937

Mandryk, George
Pub.; ed.; theatre manager; public servant
b. Hairy Hill, Oc 22 1923
(Questionnaire)
Clarion, Canmore 229

Manning, Gordon N.
Pub.
Bassano Times 62

Manning, T. W.
Pub.; ed.
Three Hills Capital 965

Manwaring, J. L.
Ed.
Lethbridge News 692

Marion, L. R. (Joe Bush)
Pub.
Formerly on editorial staff, Medicine Hat. (**CPP** v.20 no.8, Ag 1911)
Redcliff Review 843

Marshall (of **Proverbs and Marshall**)
Printer
Press, Calgary 143

Marshall, Andrew Paul (Andy)
Pub.; ed.; journalist
b. England
1966, came to Calgary and was reporter for *Herald* and *Albertan*; 1972,

exec. assistant to Rod Sykes. (Interview)
Airdrie and District Echo 8
Cochrane Times 281
Rockyview Times, Airdrie 9, 10

Marshall, Barry
Ed.
Barrhead Leader 52

Marshall, C. A.
Ed.; pub.
Chronicle, Champion 260
Chronicle, Crossfield 296

Marshall, Duncan McLean
Ed.; mgr; journalist; pub.; agriculturalist; politician
b. Ellerslie Township, Ont., S24 1872; d. Ja 18 1946.
School teacher in Ontario 1890-94; owned newspapers in Ontario before
coming west to become manager *Edmonton Bulletin*; farmed at Olds and
was Conservative MLA for Olds, 1909-21, and Minister of Agriculture;
Pres. Gazette Pub. Co. Ltd. for 14 yrs. thereafter prominent in agriculture
and agricultural industry; Minister of Agriculture for Ontario, 1934-38;
appointed to Senate in 1938. (**CAWW** 1938; **CANP** 1946)
Edmonton Bulletin 334
Olds Gazette 789

Marshall, Everett D.
Ed.; printer
b. Megantic County, Ont., D 19 1875; d. Calgary Ag 24 1949.
Husband of Jean Grant (q.v.); 1888, was carrier boy for Journal; became
linotype operator; 1917, founded Market Press with Jean Grant; 1923,
purchased Avenue Press. (CH Ag 25 1949)
Alberta Oil Examiner Calgary 163
Market Examiner Calgary 153
Western Examiner, Calgary 165

Marshall, W.
Ed.
Statesman for Albertans, Edmonton 377

Martin, Henry Ernest (Hal, Harry)
Pub.
With Sudbury *Star* and papers in Victoria, Saskatoon, Guelph and Miami;
city ed., *Albertan*; in forces World War II; 1954, ed., Alberta Dept. of
Economic Affairs publications. (**CPP** v.54 no.11, N 1945; v.65, no.5, My
1956)
Witness, Westlock 1015

Martinez, Sergio
Ed.

b. Chile, ca. 1946
Worked on daily newspaper in Chile; fled Chile after Sept. 1973 coup;
worked with Argentinian news agency for 2 yrs; came to Edmonton 1976.
(EJ Oc 13 1976)
Latin Report, Edmonton 482

Mason, D. Ivan
Mgr
Calgary Mirror South Side Edition 194

Matheson, Harry J.
Pub.; ed.
Brother of Roderick Matheson (q.v.)
Frank Sentinel 564
Times, Blairmore 76

Matheson, Roderick
Pub.
Brother of Harry J. Matheson, (q.v.)
Frank Sentinel 564
Round-Up, Pincher Creek 815

Matovich, Mike
Ed.
Calgary Sun 212

Matthews, H. B.
Ed.
Northern Review, Fairview 525

Matthews, R. Gordon, Capt.
Mgr; pub.
Macleod Gazette and Alberta Live Stock Record, Fort Macleod 536
Outlaw, Scotts Coulee 888

Matthews, Randolph Ellison (Randy)
Ed.; pub.
b. Prince Edward Island, D 20 1916; d. Vancouver, B. C., S 17 1961.
Came with family to Wilkie, Sask., where worked after school on Wilkie
Press; apprenticed to *Consort Enterprise* in charge of Alliance Press.
(ALC p.442)
Enterprise, Alliance 16

Matthews, Ray
Pub.
Jasper Booster 657

Matthews, Raymond E.
Pub.; ed.

Coronation Review 293
Enterprise, Alliance 16

Matthews, Vera
Pub.
Enterprise, Alliance 16

Mattuli, R.
Ed.
b. Fiume, Italy, Ap 17 1927
Nuovo Mondo, Edmonton 493

Maxie, Mary P.
Pub.
Cochrane Times 281

May, Claude
Pub.
Log, Lodgepole 707

May, David Campbell
Pub.; ed.
b. Glasgow, Scotland, Mr 27 1945
In publishing in Dundee, Scotland; came to Canada to work on Calgary
Albertan; 3 yrs on Victoria *Times*; worked on *Edmonton Journal*;
freelance journalist; S 1986, in Public Affairs, University of Alberta.
(Questionnaire; interview)
Rattler, Medicine Hat 752

May, Harry
Ed.; pub.; farmer
b. Hereford, Eng.
Served in 1st World War; farmed Crossfield area; 1944, sold farm and
moved into Crossfield; Sec.-Treas., Crossfield Village. (**CRO** p.143)
Crossfield Chronicle 298

May, Sterling Ibey
Pub.; ed.
b. Cardston, 1896; d. Mr 19 1963.
Mayor of Raymond for several yrs; in Stake Mission work, temple
officiator; founded Local Press. (**HIC** p.542; **LH** Mr 21 1963)
Raymond Recorder 825

Mayer, Anthony
Pub.; ed.
Big Country News, Drumheller 332

Mayer, Rodney John Matthew Stafford-
See **Stafford-Mayer**, Rodney John Matthew

Maynard, Edward M. (Ed.)
Pub.; electrical engineer
Husband of Lynne Maynard (q.v.); originally from Ontario.
Nanton News 780

Maynard, Joseph Lucien Paul (Lucien)
Pub.; ed.; politician; barrister
Elected Social Credit MLA 1935 through 1955 elections; Minister of Municipal Affairs, 1937-43; Attorney-General 1943-55; appointed provincial judge 1971; active in establishing *La Survivance*; Pres., Association canadienne-française de l'Alberta, and of Radio Edmonton Ltée. (EJ Oc 16 1958; CH D 10 1985; AL)
Today and Tomorrow, Edmonton 421

Maynard, Lynne
Pub.
Wife of Edward M. Maynard (q.v.)
Nanton News 780

Mazza, Lawrence O.
Pub.
b. Kerrobert, Sask., Je 23 1935
Formerly plant superintendent, Kyle Printers. (**CPP** v.75 no.11, N 1966)
Eckville Examiner 333
Mountaineer, Rocky Mountain House 860

McAlpine, Charles D.
Pub.
News-Record, Whitecourt 1031

McCaffary, John
Pub.; printer; oilman
b. ca. 1872; d. Calgary, Jl 17 1939.
Came West with survey party early '90s and resided in Calgary from 1896; 1904-31, assistant sheriff; retired 1931 and involved himself in oil business; Pres., Madison Oil Co. (CH Jl 17 1939)
Albertan and Alberta Tribune, Calgary 123

McCaig, J. C. (Billy)
Ed.
On Barrhead Council 1927; 1927-37, Sec.-Treas., Barrhead Village.
(**BAR** p.34, 35)
Barrhead News 51

McCallum, J. C.
Prop.
Postup, Mundare 771

McCallum, William C.
Pub.
Edmonton Free Press 448

McCarthy, Logan
Ed.; pub.
Cardston Unlimited 243
Westwind News, Cardston 245

McCormick, Mr.
Prop.
Buzzer, Fort Macleod 541

McCoy, Miller
Ed.; pub.
Didsbury Booster 318

McCrea, George Robert (Bob)
Pub.
b. Hanna, S 7 1916; d. Hanna, My 31 1982.
Son of Herbert George McCrea (q.v.)
Hanna Herald and East Central Alberta News 605

McCrea, Herbert George
Pub.
b. Peterborough, Ont., Jl 18 1892; d. Hanna, Jl 27 1937.
Married Lottie Wall (q.v.); came West to Saskatchewan ca.
1910; on mining survey gang in Rockies 1911; joined *Langdon Leader.*
(CH Je 3 1982)
Hanna Herald 605

McCrimmon, Kenneth
Pub.; ed.
Moved to Edmonton after sale of *Hinton Herald.* (**CPP** v.68 no.1, Ja 1959)
Hinton Herald 627
Jasper Totem 656

McCullough, Dave
Ed.
Meridian Booster, Lloydminster 705

McCulloch, W. S.
Ed.
Former well-known Hamiltonian. (**CPP** v.25 no.9, S 1916)
Monitor News 763

McCurdy, James Frederick (Jim)
Pub.; journalist; cartoonist
b. Sylvan Lake, F 28 1937
Whitecourt Star 1033

McCusker, William B. (Bill)
Pub.; ed.

b. Regina, Sask,. S 20 1917
Previously sports ed., Trail *Daily Times*, ed. Powell River *News*, Comox
Free Press, prop. Campbell River *Courier*. (Questionnaire; CWNA v.41
no.780, D 1957)
Banff Crag and Canyon 38

McCutcheon, Harry
Ed.
Alberta Democrat, Calgary 1054

McDonald, Archibald M.
Pub.; ed.; clergyman
Formerly pastor, Fort Rouge Baptist Church; appointed Superintendent of
Neglected Children, 1915; mgr, Pioneer Press. (**CPP** v.22 no.4, Ap 1913,
v.24 no.7, Jl 1915, v.37, no.4, Ap 1928)
Alberta Illustrated News, Edmonton 372
Edmonton News 371
Edmonton News-Plaindealer 336

McDonald, Donald C.
Pub.
Meridian Booster, Lloydminster 705

McDonald, J. A.
Pub.
Blairmore Enterprise 77

McDonald, James Hamilton
Pub.
d. Je 20 1936
Son of Rev. Archibald McDonald (q.v.); operated Pioneer Press for 24 yrs.
(EJ Je 22 1936)
South Edmonton News 336

McDonald, James N.
Ed.
Lethbridge News 692

McDonell, F. D.
Ed.
Vulcan Advocate 1005

McDowall, Jean Hilary Mary (Hilary) (née Adams)
Pub.; ed.
b. Luton, Eng., Je 6 1920; d. Kelowna, B. C., Ja 5 1983.
Worked in intelligence unit during World War II; lecturer in Italian
literature, London University; Jl 1951, came with husband to Lake Louise
to develop ski resort; Lake Louise correspondent of *Calgary Herald*;
1973, moved to Kaslo, B. C. (*Banff Crag and Canyon* Mr 23 1983)
Kicking Horse Chronicles, Lake Louise 672
Kicking Horse News, Lake Louise 673

McDowell, Asa Amos Phillip
Pub.
b. Tillsonburg, Ont., Je 18 1866
Ed., Cass City *Enterprise*, Mich.; came to Alberta 1906; worked for
Edmonton Bulletin and *Camrose Mail*, 1906-7; moved to Daysland, 1907.
(**WW** 1914)
Daysland Press 302

McElroy, Robert Duncan
Ed.; printer
Former resident of Blackie; 1936, moved to Vancouver. (**VUL** p.35)
Vulcan Advocate 1005

McFarlane, Robert David
Pub.
Grande Prairie Booster 588

McGill, Dr.
Pub.
Advertiser, Beaverlodge 66

McGill, Bryan
Ed.
Western Catholic, Edmonton 388

McGillicuddy, Daniel
Pub.
On Goderich, Ont., *Signal* for many yrs. (**CPP** v.3 no.1, Ja 1894)
Daily News Calgary 136

McGillivray, W. A.
Pub.
In Texas for health reasons for some yrs ca.1928. (**CPP** v.39 no.8, Ag
1930)
Castor Advance 252
Coronation Review 293

McGrane, Joseph E.
Pub.; printer; clergyman
Printer and newsman before ordination; 1940, moved to Lac La Biche
parish; Pres., Canadian Legion; Commanding officer, Lac La Biche sea
cadets; built and operated movie-house to finance parish; moved to
Edmonton 1960. (**WWA1** 1968)
Northern Herald, Lac La Biche 661

McGregor, Gilbert
Pub.
Social Justice Advocate, Calgary 176

McGuinness, Fred
Pub.
Medicine Hat News 743

McGuire, Richard
Ed.
Later, published *Input* newspaper for Commodore computer users. (**PUB** D/Ja 1985)
Reporter, Stony Plain 937

McIntosh, J. A.
Ed.
Innisfail Free Lance 642

McKay, Leanne
Ed.
Nation's Ensign, Edmonton 494

McKay, M. T.
Ed.
Chinook, Calgary 133

McKenzie, James B. (Jim)
Pub.
Sherwood Park Herald 893

McKenzie, W. A.
Prop.; ed.
Cochrane Advocate 279

McKibbon, Joseph
Pub.; ed.
d. Ap 1968.
Lived on premises of *Delia Times* until his death. (**DELI** p.19-20)
Delia Times 312

McKim, H. H.
Ed.
Bowden News 95

McLachlan, A. J. B. (Biz)
Pub.
d. 1944.
Worked on newspapers in Asquith, Sask. and on Regina *Leader-Post*; 1906, moved to Mannville, homesteading in Forest Hills district; after sold paper ran grocery store; active in community sports; Mayor at time of death. (**MANN** p.612-3)
Mannville Empire 724

McLaren, J. A.
Pub.; ed.
Nor-East Ad-Viser, Edmonton 413

McLauchlin, John R.
Pub.
Provost News 822

McLean, Archie
Pub.
Taber Times 954

McLean, D. A.
Pub.
Originally from Brandon, Man. (**MEE** p.161-2)
Alberta Advocate, Red Deer 834

McLean, George Y.
Ed.; mgr; pub.
Chronicle, Crossfield 296
Macleod Gazette, Fort Macleod 545

McLean, Ken W.
Pub.
Ponoka Herald 817

McLeish, Archibald Rollins
Pub.
b. Kilmalcolm, Scotland; d. 1916.
A Scotsman, who had worked on an Edinburgh daily and wrote in a style
similar to R. C. Edwards (q.v.) (**HALL** p.24-25)
Redcliff Review 843

McLeister, Andy
Ed.
Carstairs Community Press, Mountain View County News 250

McLeod, Donald H.
Ed.
Suburban Times, Edmonton 436

McLeod, G. W.
Pub.
Recorder, Altario 19

McLeod J. R.
Pub.
Blairmore Graphic 83

McLeod, Joseph
Mgr
Calgary Sports Review 185

McLeod, Philip
Ed.
Daily Herald Tribune, Grande Prairie 586

McLeod, William E.
Ed.; prop.
Okotoks Times 783

McMahon, B. J.
Ed.
Medicine Hat Times 739

McMillen, Moose
Ed.
Olds Moose-Paper 791

McNeil, Holly
Ed.
Times, High River 625

McRae, Gillivray S.
Pub.
Champion Chronicle 260

McRoberts, Sarah Ella (Ella) (née Currie)
Ed.
b. West Cape, PEI, 1896
1916, came West to teach school; married Irma farmer, Alexander Robb McRoberts, Fall 1916; farmed until latter died in 1943. (**IRMA** p.766)
Irma Times 647

McTighe, Frank
Ed.; journalist
On *Calgary Herald* 2 yrs; sports ed., *Taber Times*; sports ed., *High River Times*. (**PUB** F 1983, Jl/Ag 1984, Mr 1985)
County of Lethbridge Sunny South News, Coaldale 276
Vauxhall Advance 986

Meiklejohn, Lindsay H.
Pub.
Left *Provost News* to devote time to Edalta Oil Co. (**CPP** v.38 no.11, N 1929)
Provost News 822

Meliorist Pub. Society
Meliorist, Lethbridge 701

Mendenhall, W. Deal
Printer
Installed 1st linotype in Raymond with Lee Brewerton; worked on father's farms with 2 brothers in Raymond and Magrath districts. (**HIC** p.211, 554)
Raymond-Magrath Recorder, Raymond 825

Menzies, Arthur F.
Pub.; printer
Printer in Saskatchewan; came 1938 to run McDonald Grain Elevator Co. elevator; 1949, returned to printing business; Mayor, 1950-54; active in community. (**WAG0** p.643-4)
Sexsmith Sentinel 892

Menzies, Malcolm Angus
Pub.; printer
Son of Arthur F. Menzies (q.v.); prop., Menzies Printers, Grande Prairie. (**WAGO** p.643-4)
Sexsmith Sentinel 892

Mercer, Dennis
Pub.
Fort-Spitzee Signal, High River 626

Merrill, Annie B.
Pub.
Formerly contributed to Toronto papers; ed-in-charge, Calgary *Town Topics*. (**CPP** v.16 no.1, Ja 1907)
Prairie, Calgary 134

Mewburn, Thomas C. (Tom)
Ed.
d. Vancouver, B. C., Mr 1 1962.
Of Kelowna, B. C., at time of death. (*Banff Crag and Canyon* Mr 14 1962)
Crag and Canyon, Banff 38

Mewhort, James
Pub.; ed.; prop.
b. Edinburgh, Scotland, N 27 1875
On *Scottish Leader*, Edinburgh; evangelist in England for 5 yrs; came to Alberta 1905; on staff *High River Times* for 2 yrs. (**WW** 1912)
Airdrie News 5
Barons Globe 50
Bruce News 106
Carmangay Sun 247
Chronicle, Crossfield 296
Cochrane Advocate 279
Holden Herald 633
Jarrow Journal 653
North American Collector, Crossfield 297

Meyer, Friedrich
Ed.
Herold, Edmonton 403

Meyer, Henry George (George)
Printer; pub.; journalist; ed.
b. Medicine Hat, F 26 1929
Went to Nanton with parents, 1939; started apprenticing as printer on *Nanton News* 1948; worked on various newspapers in Alberta and Swift Current, Sask.; Mayor of Taber 1980-83 and 1986. (Questionnaire)
Camrose Canadian 225
Mercury, Tofield 970
Nanton News 780
Rattler, Medicine Hat 752
Vauxhall Advance 986

Michaud, Jan
Ed.
Barrhead Leader 52

Michelet, Alex
Ed.
Courrier de l'Ouest, Edmonton 347

Mielecki, A. V.
Ed.
Deutsch Canadischer Farmer, Calgary 140

Mihaly, Ethel
Pub.
Northern Pioneer, Fort Vermilion 562

Mihaly, Eve
Ed.
Banner Post, Manning 722

Milhaly, M. T.
Pub.
Banner Post, Manning 722
Echo, High Level 614
Mackenzie Highway Pictorial Review, High Level 615
Mile Zero News, Grimshaw 603
Northern Pioneer, Fort Vermilion 562

Miklossi, Istvan
Ed.
Nyugati Magyarsa'g, Calgary 219

Millar, John M.
Pub.; ed.

Granum Press 591
Northern News, Athabasca 26

Miller, William Henry
Ed.; mgr; pub.
b. Maple Creek, Sask., ca.1891; d. Olds, Je 23 1963.
For many yrs, foreman *Vegreville Observer* shop; retired 1945. (**CWNA** v.21 no.572, D 10 1940, v.45 no.848, Ag 1963)
Chronicle, Crossfield 296
Monitor News 763
Olds Gazette 789

Milligan, Roy
Pub.
Tri-City Observer, Turner Valley 975

Milliken, S. D.
Pub.; ed.
Gleichen Chronicle 575

Mills, George
Bus. mgr; farmer; politician
b. Oxford, Ont., Ja 17 1876
On Lambton County Council, 1896-98; Municipal Council, Edson; Mayor, ca. 1916, for one term; elected in 1920 as Liberal MLA for Athabasca, re-elected as Independent Liberal in 1921 and 1926. (**CANP** 1921; **ATH** p.198, 200, 209; **ALI**)
Athabasca Herald 28

Mills, R. Leslie
Ed.; prop; pub.
Carstairs News 250

Mine Workers' Union of Canada
Canadian Miner, Calgary 170

Misutka, Victor
Ed.
b. Czechoslovakia, ca 1927
Worked on B. C. newspapers in Castlegar, Trail and Penticton; Winnipeg *Free Press*; night ed., *Edmonton Journal*. (EJ N 11 1972)
Western Catholic Reporter, Edmonton 453

Mitchell, Kevin
Ed.
Record, Fort Saskatchewan 560

Moffet, Chester E. (Chet)
Pub.; journalist; advertising mgr.
b. Spencer, Neb.; d. Edmonton, F 26 1962.

Served RCAF in both wars; worked on various newspapers in Alberta,
Saskatchewan, South Dakota and Vancouver, B. C.; 1924, advertising mgr,
T. Eaton Co. until retired in 1959. (EJ F 27 1962)
Gazette, Rocky Mountain House 859
Sylvan Lake World 949

Mohr, Homer S.
Ed.; prop.
Formerly of Stettler; homesteaded south of Delia. (**CPP** v.21 no.2, F
1912; **MUNS** p.36)
Munson Mail 775
Okotoks Observer 785

Moore, Alberta M.
Pub.
b. ca.1881; d. Calgary, 1965.
Wife of Andrew A. Moore (q.v.); retired 1947. (**CPP** v.74, no.1, Ja 1965)
Strathmore Standard 940

Moore, Andrew A.
Pub.
d. N. 29 1933.
Husband of Alberta M. Moore; formerly, Calgary newsman. (**CPP** v.35
no.2, F 1926)
Strathmore Standard 940

Moore, Arthur
Printer
Evening Journal, Edmonton 344

Moore, D. S.
Ed.
Record, Fort Saskatchewan 560

Moore, John Thomas (McClintock Moore)
Pub.; promoter; businessman
b. Markham, Ont., Jl 3 1844; d. Toronto, Ont., Je 5 1917.
1933, Mgr-in-chief, Colonization Co; alderman, Toronto, 1884; mg. dir.
Saskatchewan Land and Homestead Co., 1886; elected, 1905, as MLA for
Red Deer; Pres., Alberta Central Railway, 1911; wrote pamphlet, *The
Settler's Guide to Homesteads in the Canadian Northwest*; established
Western General Electric Co; noted rose fancier, termed Rose King of
Canada, residence Moore Park, Toronto. (**MOR; ARDA; MEER**)
Alberta Advocate, Red Deer 834

Moore, Ron E.
Pub.
Lac La Biche Post 663

Morgan, Brian
Ed.
Scree, Banff 47

Morgan, R. W.
Pub.
Pincher City News 813

Morin, Hermann, o.m.i.
Ed.; Catholic clergyman
Survivance, Edmonton 404

Morran, John
Ed.
Reporter, Stony Plain 937

Morris, Jim
Ed.
Nisku News 782

Morris, Leslie M.
Ed.
Scandinavian Centre News, Edmonton 445

Morris, P. Dickson
Ed.
Weekly Review, Viking 1001

Morrison, C. R.
Pub.
Wainwright Star 1007

Morrison, J. W.
Ed.
Hay Lakes Times 610

Moser, Edward Henry (Ted)
Pub.; ed.
b. Pincher Creek, Ja 23 1932
General reporter and on editorial staff several western newspapers; 1965-
81 held editorial positions on *Globe and Mail*. (EJ N 3 1978; **PUB** S
1981; Questionnaire)
Pass Promoter, Blairmore 84

Moses, Clifford L.
Ed.; pub.
Joined *Macleod Gazette* in 1937. (**PUB** Ja 1976)
Macleod Gazette, Fort Macleod 545

Mott, Wallace R.
Pub.
Delburne Progress 305
Lousana Observer 713

Mowat, A. N.
Pub.; ed.
Pincher Creek Echo 814
Taber Free Press 952

Mowers, Cleo W.
Pub.
b. Sibbald
Student minister, but quit cloth; ed., University of Saskatchewan's *Sheaf*;
worked on *Star-Phoenix*, *Free Press Weekly*, Winnipeg, and associate ed.,
Calgary Albertan, 1944-48. (LH Ag 30 1980)
Lethbridge Herald 694

Moxhay, F. W.
Pub.; ed.; clergyman; printer
Anglican minister; ca.1909, sent to establish mission at Lake Saskatoon;
used printing press for missionary work among natives. (**GREG** p.164-5)
Northern Light, Athabasca 25

Mueller, Karl
Ed.
Bonnyville Nouvelle 89

Muir, Pearl
Ed.
Record-Gazette, Peace River 804

Mundy, J. C.
Pub.
Bashaw Record 55

Munro, Robert C. R.
Pub.
Came to Vulcan with parents 1926; worked after school at *Advocate* and
in printing office, High River; enlisted in 1941, served overseas. (**VUL**
p.35)
Vulcan Advocate 1005

Munro, Robert Ross (Ross)
Pub.; journalist
b. Ottawa, Ont., S 6 1913
Reporter and ed. with Canadian Press, Toronto, Ottawa, Winnipeg,
Montreal, New York and Washington D. C.; joined Southam Newpapers
1948; with Vancouver Province 1951, ed.-in-chief 1955, assistant pub.,
1957; pub., Winnipeg *Tribune* 1959-65, *Canadian Magazine* 1965-68, and

Gazette, Montreal, 1976-79; Pres., Canadian Press 1974-76., 1978-79.
(CAWW 1986; EJ F 29 1968)
Edmonton Journal 344

Murad, Ahmad Eed
Ed.
Source, Edmonton 468

Murdoch, Walpole
Prop.
With *Pilot Mound Sentinel* ca. 1896; ed., *Western Prairie*, Cypress River,
Man.; 1901, bought *Star*, Hartney, Man., which he sold D 1910. (**CPP**, v.6
no.12, D 1897, v.10 no.5, My 1901, v.20 no.1, Ja 1911)
Buzzer, Fort Macleod 541

Murdoch, Andrew E.
Prop.
New Stirling Star 927

Murphy, D. H.
Pub.
Came from Donaldson, Minn., F 1894; in Ja 1899 was ed. and pub. of
paper in Dedham, Iowa. (**MEER**)
Red Deer Review 831
Sentinel, Fort Macleod 537

Murphy, J. H. (Jack)
Pub.
Macleod Gazette, Fort Macleod 545

Murphy, P. J.
Pub.
Daysland Press 302

Musberger, Mrs.
Ed.
Wife of Huxley butcher. (**ACAD** p.17)
Huxley Recorder 638

Myser, Harry G.
Pub.
Bassano News 57

Nagel, Walter G.
Ed.; journalist
b. Grande Prairie
Joined *Herald Tribune* staff in 1955 after high school graduation; later
worked on editorial staff of other northern newspapers. (Unidentified
newspaper clipping)
Record-Gazette, Peace River 804

Namak, Avrim
Ed.
Calgary Jewish News 196

Nantel, J. A.
Ed.
Progrès, Morinville 764

National Organization in America
Novyny, Edmonton 367

National Unemployed Workers' Association. Calgary Branch.
Unemployed Bulletin, Calgary 1053

Neale, Gordon
Pub.; printer
b. Ottawa
Printer's devil with Elmer Roper (q.v.) on *Alberta Labour News*; 1929,
finished apprenticeship; 1970, moved to Edmonton (**CL** p.380)
Claresholm Local Press 268
Record, Fort Saskatchewan 560
Stavely Advertiser 922

Neck, Martin J.
Ed.; pub.
Carstairs News 250
Didsbury Pioneer 317

Nelson, David J.
Pub.; ed.
North Peace Pictorial, Peace River 805

Nelson, Ed.
Ed.
d. D 9 1969.
Of Brightview; Pres., Farmers' Union of Alberta for 5 yrs. (**EJ** ca. D 9
1969)
Organized Farmer, Edmonton 427

Nelson, Harry
Ed.
b. Ontario, D 15 1871
1905, moved to High River to work on newpaper; retired, 1929. (**BLU** v.2
p.463-4; **VUL** p.35)
Vulcan Advocate 1005

Nelson, Ken
Ed.
Fort McMurray Today 552

Nelson, Miriam
Pub.
Grande Cache Mountaineer 583

Nelson, Sigurd
Ed.
Spokesman, Calgary 173

Nepoose, Cecil
Ed.
Native People, Edmonton 460

Nesbitt, Clive Bertram
Pub.; ed.
b. Brooks, Jl 7 1913; d. Calgary, Ag 23 1981.
Eldest son of Leonard D. Nesbitt (q.v.); 1955, moved to British Columbia to work on various newspapers; storekeeper, Chilliwack, B. C.; 1973, retired to Calgary. (*Brooks Bulletin* S 2 1981)
Bassano Mail 58
Brooks Bulletin 105

Nesbitt, J. Howard
Pub.
1929, went to Ontario to continue in printing. (**CPP** v.38. no.7, Jl 1929)
Brooks Bulletin 105

Nesbitt, James L., Sr. (Jim)
Ed.; pub.
Son of Leonard D. Nesbitt (q.v.)
Bassano Mail 58
Brooks Bulletin 105

Nesbitt, James L., Jr. (Jamie)
Ed.; journalist
b. Calgary, Ap 4 1952
Son of James L. Nesbitt, sr (q.v.)
Brooks Bulletin 105

Nesbitt, Leonard D.
Pub.; journalist; ed.
b. Lisburne, Ireland, F 29 1888; d. Calgary, My 1969.
1890, family emigrated to Lindsay, Ont.; reporter in Ontario; moved to Calgary 1910 as sports ed. for *Albertan*, then general reporter for *Herald*; 1926-55, superintendent of publicity for Alberta Wheat Pool, writing many pamphlets and books, broadcasting, editing *Wheat Pool Budget*; 1962, published *Tides in the West*. (**PEEL**; CH S 30 1936)
Bassano Mail 58
Bassano News 57
Bow City Star 1047

Brooks Bulletin 105
Langdon Leader 686

Nesbitt, Robert Lee (Lee)
Pub.; printer
b. Calgary, My 1 1917; d. Sardis, B. C., S 17 1971.
Son of Leonard D. Nesbitt (q.v.);started as printer on *Bassano Mail*, 1936;
worked for *High River Times* and *News of the North*, Yellowknife, N. W.
T.; served with RCAF in World War II; worked on *Albertan*, Calgary;
1971, moved to Sardis where was in business with brother Clive (q.v.)
(CH S 20 1971; unidentified newspaper clipping S 23 1971)
Brooks Bulletin 105

Netelenbos, William J.
Pub.
Edmonton Gazette 454
St. Albert Gazette 880

Neutzling, B. N.
Pub.; ed.
Three Hills Capital 965

Newbigging, William
Pub.
b. Toronto, F 3 1939
Junior reporter, *Edmonton Journal*, 1957; city ed., 1965; news ed., 1967;
assistant to pub., 1971; worked on Ottawa *Citizen*, 1973-81, becoming
vice-pres. and pub., 1978-81. **(WWC 1986)**
Edmonton Journal 344

Newman, Mr.
Ed.
Formerly railroad conductor.
(*Crag and Canyon* D14, 1923, F 19 1958)
Hot Springs Record, Banff 34

Newnham, F. H.
Pub.
West-Ender, Calgary 166

Newsom, Leonard C.
Ed.; pub.
Was on *Acme News* staff 1911. **(CPP** v.20 no.5, My 1911)
Bowden News 95
Chronicle, Crossfield 296
Crag and Canyon, Banff 38
Rimby Record 855
Stavely Advertiser 922

Newsom, W.R. (Ronnie)
Pub.; ed.
b. Banff
Son of Leonard C. Newsom (q.v.); 1936, moved to Olds where worked for 4 years for William Henry Miller (q.v.); enlisted in World War II; ran newspaper office at Heritage Park, Calgary. (**OLDS** p.169; *Weekend Magazine* Ja 13 1973)
Bashaw Star 56
Crossfield Chronicle 298
Olds Gazette 789
Rimbey Record 855

Nicholson, Arthur N.
Pub.; printer; ed.
Left for northern Ontario. (**CPP** v.22 no.2, F 1913)
Cayley Hustler 253
Stavely Standard 920

Nicholson, Arthur
Pub.
d. 1920.
Chinook Advance 264

Nicholson, Margaret C.
Pub.
d. ca. Ja 1948.
Wife of Arthur Nicholson (q.v.)
Chinook Advance 264

Nicol, A.M.
Pub.; ed.
Athabasca Times 27
Northern News, Athabasca 26

Nielsen, Dorothy
Ed.
Wife of Charles V. Nielsen
Bowness Bulletin, Calgary 1055

Nielsen, Erik
Pub.
Elk Point Sentinel 515

Nightingale, A.E.
Ed.
Western Illustrated News, Edmonton 390

Nisbet, Gina
Ed.
Leader, Barrhead 52

Non-Partisan League
Nutcracker, Calgary 152

Nordstrom, O.
Ed.
Moukari, Edmonton 366

Norgaard, Peggy
Ed.
Scandinavian Centre News, Edmonton 445

Norman, R.L.
Pub.; ed.
Coleman Bulletin 289
Pincher Creek Echo 814

Oblinger, Milo M.
Pub.
Brother of V.H. Oblinger (q.v.)
Entwistle Enterprise 520

Oblinger, V.H.[
Pub.
Brother of Milo M. Oblinger (q.v.)
Grande Prairie Herald 584

O'Brien, A.D.
Ed.
Western Catholic, Edmonton 388

O'Callaghan, J(eremiah) Patrick
Pub.; journalist
b. Mallow, Ire., Oc 8 1925
Reporter and ed. of several English newspapers; came to Canada, 1959;
1959-68, mg. ed. and assistant-pub., *Red Deer Advocate*; assistant to pub,
Edmonton Journal, 1968-9; exec. ed., Southam News Service, Ottawa,
1969-71; exec. assistant, Southam Press, 1971-2; pub., Windsor *Star*
1972-6. (**WWC** 1986)
Calgary Herald 115
Edmonton Journal 344

O'Connor, George Bligh
Pub.; lawyer
b. Walkerton, Ont., My 16 1883; d. Ja 13 1957.
1905, moved to Alberta and called to Alberta bar; K.C., 1913; 1920, Pres.,
Edmonton Bar Association; 1941, appointed Justice, Supreme Court;
1944, Chrmn, Wartime Labour Relations Board; 1948-53, Chrmn, Canada
Labour Relations Board; 1950, appointed Chief Justice of Alberta.

(WWC 1952)
Edmonton Bulletin 358

OKE, Henry
Pub.
Went to British Columbia for health, 1922. (**CPP** v.31 no.3, Mr 1922)
Big Valley News 70
Consort Enterprise 292
Rimbey Advance 854

Old Strathcona Foundation Association
Strathcona Plaindealer, Edmonton 484

Oldham, Frederick Mountford
Pub.; lawyer; rancher
b. Melton Mowbray, Eng., Mr 29 1863; d. Ap 2 1926.
Practised law in England before emigrating to Canada, where worked on
cattle ranch in sthrn Alberta; 1896, moved to Innisfail where practised
law until his death; Mayor of Innisfail, 1922-26. (Glenbow Library clipping files)
Innisfail Standard 640

Oldring, Robert C. (Bob)
Pub.
b. Pine Lake, Mr 5, 1912
Alix Free Press Mirror News Record 14

Oldring, Velma F.
Pub.
b. Maple Creek, Sask., Ap 29 1915
Daughter of F.V. Richards (q.v.)
Alix Free Press Mirror News Record 14

Oliver, Frank
Pub.; politician
b. Peel County, Ont., S 14 1853; d. Ottawa, Ont., Mr 31 1933.
Mbr, North-West Council 1883-5 for Edmonton; elected to Legislative
Assembly of North-West Territories in 1888 and 1894; sat in House of
Commons as Liberal 1896-1917, and was Minister of the Interior and
Superintendent General of Indian Affairs, 1905-11. (**CANE** v.2 p.1317)
Bulletin, Edmonton 334

Olivier, Jean-Maurice
Ed.
Franco-albertain, Edmonton 458
Survivance, Edmonton 404

Omelchuk, Bruce A.
Mgr

Calgary Mirror North Side Edition 205
Calgary Mirror South Side Edition 194

Omeosoo, Mack
Ed.
Bear Hills Native Voice, Hobbema 632

One Big Union Provincial Executive Committee of Alberta
One Big Union Bulletin, Edmonton 382

Ootes, Jake J.
Pub.
b. Holland
Emigrated to Renfrew, Ont., with parents, 1952; writer and photographer, Renfrew *Mercury*; exec. assistant and information dir. to Commissioner for the Northwest Territories for 10 yrs. (**EJ** undated clipping)
County News, Strathcona County 939
Edmonton Examiner [South Editions] 486
Record, Fort Saskatchewan 560
Sherwood Park News 896

Orey, Dave
Ed.
Grizzly Gazette, Swan Hills 947

Orr, Wesley Fletcher
Ed.; pub.; mgr; entrepreneur
b. La Chute, Que., Mr 3 1831; d. Calgary, ca. F 19 1898.
After various business ventures in Ontario and the U.S., settled in Calgary, 1886; 1894, 1st Mayor; active in land and railway development including Alberta Southern Railway Co. (**FORA** p.289-307)
Calgary Herald 115
Calgary Weekly Herald and Alberta Livestock Journal 113

Orris, Stanley
Pub.
Chronicle, Champion 260
Stavely Advertiser 922

Osborne, T. Roy
Pub.
Joined *Medicine Hat News* 1912 as circulation, then gen, mgr. (**GERS** p.131)
Medicine Hat News 743

Osmond, H.E.
Ed.; pub.
1904, came to Innisfail from London, Ont.; 1925, moved to Spokane and later died there. (**KIN** p.145-6) *Didsbury Pioneer* 317

Oxley, Herbert Pub.; ed.
Returned to central British Columbia after sale of *Record*. (**CWNA** v.25
no.629, Oc/N 1944)
Athabasca Herald 29
Forestburg Herald 532
Record, Fort Saskatchewan 560

Packer, James H.
Ed.; mgr; prop.
Sundre Round Up 945

Pain, J.F.
Ed.
Suburban Times, Edmonton 436

Palmer, Alfred
Pub.
Bond of Brotherhood, Calgary 129

Panei, V.
Ed.
Panorama, Calgary 199

Parker, Patricia D.
Pub.; ed.
Hoodoo Highlander, Canmore 234

Parker, R.A.
Ed.
Winnifred Record 1039

Parkins, Robert (Bob)
Ed.
b. ca. 1942
With Canadian Press several yrs.; joined *Calgary Herald*, 1971; returned
to *Herald* in 1977 as national ed. and night news ed.; 1980, senior ed.,
news service, Southam News; 1981, Ottawa ed., *Calgary Herald*. (CH S 1
1981)
Sunday, Calgary 203

Parks, E. Stan
Ed.
Record-Gazette, Peace River 804

Parr, Allen F. (3Al)
Ed.; pub.
b. Onaway, Mich., N. 13 1942
Dairy Contact, Edmonton 500

Parry, John Albert (Jack)
Pub.
Husband of Olive Louise Parry (q.v.)
Eckville Examiner 333
Ponoka County News 816
Rimbey Record 855
Sylvan Lake News 951

Parry, Olive Louise
Pub.; ed.
b. Gadsby, Ap 13, 1917; d. Ja 13 1975.
Wife of John Albert Parry (q.v.).
Eckville Examiner 333
Rimbey Record 855
Sylvan Lake News 951

Pasqualini, Giancarlo
Ed.
Messaggero Italiano, Edmonton 455

Paterson, John C.
Mgr.
Scottish Standard, Calgary 146

Paterson, Pat
Pub.; ed.
Calgary Avenues 220
Seventeenth Avenue, Calgary 213

Patoine, Jean, o.m.i.
Ed.; Catholic clergyman
b. ca. 1911; d. S 25 1972
Pioneer of Ste-Anne parish; 1944-53, priest of parish St.-Joachim; Dir.,
Franco-albertain; Sec.-Gen., Assoc. canadienne des franco-albertains,
1953-72. (*Franco-albertain* S 27 1972)
Survivance, Edmonton 404

Patrige, Kenneth (Ken)
Pub.
b. Wisconsin, ca. 1909; d. Ag 4 1976.
Moved with parents to Canada 1908, settling in sthrn Saskatchewan; early
30s, district correspondent for Regina *Leader-Post*; staff photographer
with Saskatchewan Bureau of Publications, 1935 until joined RAF during
War; helped publish Air Force newspaper out of *Claresholm Weekly
Press*, where continued to work until 1947, when moved to Camrose;
Pres. of both Alberta and Canadian Weekly Newspaper Assocs. (EJ Ag 16
1976).
Camrose Canadian 225
Times, Wetaskiwin 1022

Patterson, Cliff
Pub.
Mercury, Tofield 970

Paul, Henry
Ed.; Pub.
Carstairs Journal 249

Pawliuk, A., Rev.
Ed.
Ukrainian Record, Edmonton 447

Pearce, Hugh
Pub.; ed.
Bassano Herald 61

Pearson, George H.
Pub.
1927-31, prop., *Lanigan News*, Guernsey, Sask. (**CPP** v.36 no.10, Oc 1927)
Mayerthorpe Times 733
Mountaineer, Rocky Mountain House 860

Pearson, Rick
Prop.
Sonshine News, Edmonton 498

Peck, Robert Key
Pub.; missionary
b. England, ca. 1872; d. Edmonton, D 19 1958.
Methodist missionary, ordained Winnipeg 1898; 1904, posted to
Claresholm; resigned from church to farm; Secretary, United Farmers of
Alberta, 1910; 1921, moved to Edmonton; 1933, ordained Presbyterian
minister; moved to Rocky Mountain House. (AC D 29 1958).
Claresholm Advertiser 267
Stavely Advertiser 922

Pegg, Harry
Ed.
Calgary Mirror North Side Edition 205
Calgary Mirror South Side Edition 194

Peltier, J.L.L.
Pub.; ed.
Examiner, Edmonton 467

Pember, John E.
Pub.
Formerly of Boston; retired, 1913. (**CPP** v.18 no.8, Ag 1909, v.22 no. 10,
Oc 1913)
Macleod Advertiser, Fort Macleod 540

Pempeit, Larry
Ed.
Spokesman, Edmonton 472

Pennanem, Alex
Ed.
Moukari, Edmonton 366

Pennie, James
Ed.
Northern Review, Fairview 525

Perrault, Jacinthe
Ed.
Franco-albertain, Edmonton 458

Perry, Thomas
Pub; ed.
b. Sudbury, Ont., D 5 1967
With Sudbury *Star* 1978-9, and *Daily Miner and News*, Kenora, 1979-85.
(Questionnaire)
Record-Gazette, Peace River 804

Peters, Frank
Pub.; mgr
Carbon News 237
Elnora Advance 516

Peters, Hubert
Pub.; ed.
Three Hills Capital 965
Carbon News 237

Peterson, David C.
Pub.
1922, working for *Taber Times*; 1930, to post on *Grande Prairie Herald*.
(CPP v.31 no.9, S 1922, v.39, no.7, Jl 1930).
Advertiser, Sylvan Lake 950
Cardston Globe 240
Optimist, Red Deer 836
Raymond Review 824

Peterson, Don
Pub.
Fairview This Week 527

Peterson, Eileen
Ed.
Scandinavian Centre News, Edmonton 445

Peterson, Ivan
Ed.
Turner Valley News 977

Pettipiece, Richard Parmater (Parm)
Pub.; labour leader
b. ca. 1876; d. 1960.
Son of Ontario Orangeman; went west in early 90s; founded *Lardeau Eagle*, Ferguson, B.C., radical journal popular in mining camps; with Vancouver Trades and Labour Council, edited its organ, *British Columbia Federationist*; 1903-34, printer with Vancouver *Province*. (**CPP** v.69 no.2. F 1960; *Edmonton Bulletin* Ag 1 1940).
South Edmonton News 336

Phillips, Leslie
Pub.
Moved to Saskatchewan paper. (**CPP** v.49 no.10, Oc 1940)
Booster, Waskatenau 1013

Phillips, M. Dale
Ed.; journalist
b. Vulcan, Ja 9 1943
1966-68, Recreation Planner, City of Edmonton; 1968, apprenticed with *Georgia Strait*, Vancouver; in broadcasting and films, 1969 to present. (Questionnaire)
Canada Goose, Edmonton 461

Phillips, Russell
Pub.
Jasper Place Citizen, Edmonton 436

Phillips, W.L.
Pub.
Viking Gazette 999

Phillips, William
Ed.
Sports Guide, Calgary 180

Piche, Thomas D.
Pub.; prop.
Established Peace River Bureau, 1910, to promote settlement.
Peace River Pilot 800
Pembina Outlook and Entwistle News, Entwistle 519

Pickersgill, Peter Michael
Pub.; ed.
b. South Moore, Eng., Ap 8 1927
Apprentice printer 1946-52, *High River Times*; 1952-57, in composing room *Calgary Herald*. (Questionnaire)
Vulcan Advocate 1005

Pigeon, Roland R. (Rollie)
Ed.; journalist
b. St. Paul, Jl 30 1947
Mountaineer, Rocky Mountain House 860

Piles
Ed.
Barons Beacon 1046

Piller, Joyce
Ed.
Sylvan Lake News 951

Pitcairn, W.D.
Pub.; ed.
Lacombe Weekly Press 1079
Ponoka Herald 817

Platt, Arnold
Ed.; agricultural scientist
b. Innisfree
Developed Rescue Wheat, 1944, at federal Dept. of Agriculture Research
Station, Swift Current; in charge of cereal breeding program, Dominion
Experimental Station, Lethbridge, until 1951; 1951, became mg.dir., farm
on Blood Indian Reserve; mbr, Royal Commission on Transportation,
1960; on executive, United Farmers of Alberta, for 11 yrs; admitted to
Alberta Agricultural Hall of Fame, 1972; hon LLD and on Board of
Governors University of Alberta; mbr of Senate, University of Calgary.
(EJ Ap 19 1951, F 6 1960, Oc 7 1972, Ja 15 1973)
Organized Farmer, Edmonton 427

Playford, Art
Pub.
Drayton Valley Banner 1057
Fort McMurray Banner 548
Northern Banner, Fort McMurray 1072
Pembina News 807

Plosz, W.J.
Ed.
Organized Farmer, Edmonton 427

Plotkins, Leon Louis
Ed.; businessman; public servant
b. Paris, France, ca. 1894; d. Jl 21 1974.
1910, came to Canada; in army during war until 1917; 1918, Postmaster,
Rockyford, and also worked in pharmacy; 1919, Registrar, Alberta Dept.
of Health; established Rockyford Realty and Investment Co. Ltd.; moved
to Calgary, 1928, to enter business there. (**WHE** p.353-4)

Rockyford Reporter 864
Rockyford (Alta.) Weekly 863

Plummer, Norman Montague
Ed.; author; public servant; lawyer
b. Swindon, Eng., S 5 1882
1901, qualified as auctioneer, surveyor and valuer; 1907, emigrated to
Edmonton; in govt. service, Grouard and Calgary; 1914, Anglican Church
deacon; 1918-19, in army; returned to Calgary to study law; admitted to
bar, 1922; 1923, opened law practice; published novels, *The Good, The
Long Arm.* (**BLU** v.2 p.60-3; CH Ap 29 1944)
Western Sentinel, Calgary 182

Pohl, Carl
Ed.; mgr.
Alberta Herold, Edmonton 343
Deutsch-Canadier, Calgary 139

Pohorecky, Michael
Ed.
Novyi Shliakh, Edmonton 410

Polish Association of Edmonton
Biuletyn. Organizacji Polskich w Edmontonie, Edmonton 443

Pollard-Kientzel, Sylvie
Ed.
Franco, Edmonton 1979

Poole, G.A.
Pub.
Spirit River Echo 909

Popplewell, Gerry
Pub.; ed.
Drumheller Sun 332

Popplewell, Trish
Pub.; ed.
Drumheller Sun 332

Porritt, Charles J.
Pub.; printer
b. Lancashire, Eng., O 22 1877
Printer in England; 1913, came to Canada, worked on *Golden Star*,
Golden, B.C.; moved to Calgary where worked on several papers; moved
to Drumheller. (**BLU** v.3 p.404-5; **DRUM** p.341).
Drumheller Review 325

Potts, P.C.
Ed.
Westerner, Calgary 1051

Poulin, Yvan
Ed.
Franco-albertain, Edmonton 458

Poulter, C. Stafford
Pub.
Provost Star 821

Pratt, Evelyn
Ed.
Nation's Ensign, Edmonton 494

Pratt, William C. (Bill; Will)
Ed.; pub.; businessman
b. Kemptville, Ont., Mr 16 1881; d. Grande Prairie, D 7 1943.
Learned printing trade in Ontario; ran poolroom Edmonton; followed
Alaska Gold Rush; opened poolroom Stewart, B.C.; moved to Grande
Prairie; started oil agency and operated wholesale business and flower
warehouse; freelance writer for *Herald-Tribune* and trade magazines.
(*Grande Prairie Herald Tribune* D 16 1943; EJ undated clipping)
Grande Prairie Herald 584

Pratten, W.A.
Pub.
Fort Saskatchewan Reporter 555
Tofield Standard 967

Prevost, J.A.H.
Pub.
North American News, St. Albert 876

Priestley, Norman Flaxman
Mg. dir.; agriculturalist
b. Huddersfield, Eng., Jl 18 1884; d. Calgary, O 4 1958.
Apprentice stone-cutter; came to Canada with family 1904; homesteaded
at Onoway; student minister; enlisted, World War I; Methodist minister,
Wainwright; association with UFA developed into executive positions,
eventually gen. mgr of United Farmers of Alberta Co-operative Ltd.,
1940-51; wrote *Summer Fever and Other Verses* (1945); at time of death
was engaged in writing history of farmers' movement in Alberta.
(*Western Producer* Oc 9 1958; *Edmonton Bulletin* Ja 23 1931; **PEEL**)
U.F.A., Calgary 160

Progressive Conservative Student Federation, University of Alberta
Tory, Edmonton 1065

Proverbs, Percy, J.
Printer
(HENC 1928)
Press, Calgary 143

Prystash, Dmytro
Pub.
Secretary of short-lived Ukrainian Farmers' Union. (**MAKU** p.94, 96, 100)
Farmerske Slovo, Edmonton 387

Puco, G.
Ed.
Panorama, Calgary 199

Pue, Deborah (née Chawner)
Pub.
b. Winnipeg
Wife of Thomas William Pue (q.v.); office stenographer and bookkeeper,
Central Press; retired 1977. (**CPP** v.58 no.8, Ag 1949; EJ S 22 1982)
Fort McMurray Sun 1074

Pue, Thomas William
Pub.
b. Brandon, Man., 1915; d. S 16 1982.
Husband of Deborah Pue (q.v.); sold newspapers at age 11; 3 yrs later,
boy organizer for *Liberty Magazine*; at 18, organized Brandon News Co.,
magazine distribution business; travelled for McFadyen Publications and
Toronto *Star* in their distribution; circulation mgr, Brandon *Daily Sun*
and, in 1944, *Edmonton Bulletin*; retired 1977. (**CPP** v.58 no.8, Ag 1949;
EJ, S 22 1982)
Alberta Country Life, Edmonton 442
Alberta Farm Life, Edmonton 462
Athabasca Advance 31
Athabasca Sun, Boyle 100
Barrhead Star 54
Beiseker Times 68
Boyle Star 101
Bruderheim Review 107
Clyde Bulletin 273
Clyde Star 274
Colinton Clipper 291
County of Milburn Review 758
Crossfield Chronicle 300
Czar Clipper 301
Daysland Sun 304
Drayton Valley Tribune 322
Edmonton Star 463
Elk Point Hunter 513
Elk Point Star 514
Forestburg Free Press 533

Fort Saskatchewan Star 561
Glendon Bulletin 577
Grand Centre Press 580
Grande Cache Star 582
Grimshaw Spotlight 601
Hardisty World 609
Hay Lakes Review 611
Heisler Herald 612
High Prairie Progress 619
Holden Herald 634
Hughenden Record 636
Innisfree Banner 646
Jasper Place Review, Edmonton 431
Killam News 660
Lac La Biche Sun 662
Lac Ste-Anne Chronicle 667
Lac Ste-Anne Sun 665
Lamont Bulletin 684
Lamont County Star 676
Lamont Journal 683
Legal Record 691
Lesser Slave Lake Star 899
Lougheed Journal 712
Macklin Times 714
Mannville Mirror 729
Mannville Star 730
Mayerthorpe Review 736
Mayerthorpe-Lac Ste-Anne Star 737
McMurray Northlander 549
Millet Bulletin 757
Minburn County Star 759
Minburn Sun 758
Morinville Star 766
Mundare Mirror 774
Mundare Star 773
New Sarepta New Era 781
News Bulletin, Edmonton 438
North Edmonton Star 435
Northern Star, High Prairie 618
Onoway Westerner 793
Pembina Star 808
Radway Star 823
Redwater Review 845
Redwater Star 849
Redwater Sun 848
Rockyford Review 866
Rosalind Reporter 867
Sangudo Chronicle 887
Sherwood Park Star 895
Sherwood Park Sun 894

Smoky Lake Gazette 905
Smoky Lake Star 906
Smoky River News 908
South Edmonton Sun 432
South Side Sun, Edmonton 449
Spirit River Signal 910
Spotlight, Edmonton 426
Spruce Grove Star 912
St. Albert Gazette 879
Starland Reporter 918
Stony Plain Sun 928
Strome Star 942
Sturgeon Journal 943
Swan Hills Grizzly 946
Thorhild Tribune 959
Two Hills County Star 981
Two Hills Review 980
Valleyview Times 984
Vegreville Mirror 989
Vermilion River News 995
Vilna Bulletin 1003
Vilna Star 1002
Waskatenau World 1014
Westerner, Sangudo 886
Whitecourt Echo 1032
Willingdon Review 1036

Pyette, Lester
Ed.
Calgary Sun 215

Quayle, Albert Ernest (Quayley)
Pub.; printer
b. Paisley, Ont.
Brother of Thomas W. Quayle (q.v.); Printer on Toronto *Daily Star*; moved to Calgary, 1920; worked at Western Print. and Lithographing Co.; died in home for aged and infirm printers Colorado. (**CWNA** v.20 no542, Ja 27 1939; **HAT** p.35)
Carmangay Sun 247

Quayle, Thomas W.
Pub.
b. Liverpool, Eng., S 8 1868
Brother of Albert Ernest Quayle (q.v.); came with parents to Paisley, Ont.; worked on Ottawa *Free Press*; later managed Ottawa *Citizen* and Calgary *Daily News*; left for Ottawa 1907, as private secretary to Hon. A.L. Sifton; news ed., *Lethbridge Herald*, 1911-13. (**CPP** v.16 no.2, F 1907, v.27 no.4, Ap 1918; **CWNA** v.20 no.542, Ja 27 1939; **MOR**)
Claresholm Review 266

Quebar, Arvie
Pub.
Western Star, Edson 504

Quick, Edward Gordon
Prop.; printer
b. Jersey, Channel Is., Jl 16 1885; d. Weyburn, Sask., My 22 1965.
Printer's apprentice in England, 1899-1905; 1905, emigrated to
Winnipeg; 1906, came to Regina where worked in several printing shops
and newspapers; 1910, homesteaded near Youngstown, working for
Calgary printing firms during winters; active in community affairs; 1936,
moved to Weyburn, Sask., where purchased Weyburn *Review*; retired ca.
1959. (**CWNA** v.63 no.825, S 1961; **YOU** p.134)
Plaindealer, Youngstown 1041

Quinn, George Ross (Ross)
Pub.
Whitecourt Star 1033

Quinn, J.
Printer
Died a suicide. (**RIM** p.33)
Rimbey Record 855

Quinn, James
Printer
Owned *Record*, Rocanville, Sask., 1928-34. (**CPP** v.38 no.7, Jl 1929)
Forestburg Herald 532

Ramire, Cesar
Dir.
Diario, Edmonton 501

Randolph, Keith
Pub.
Fort McMurray Northern Star 550

Rasmussen, John
Ed.
Western Catholic Reporter, Edmonton 453

Rauh, Dieter
Pub.
Examiner, Edmonton 467

Read, G.H.
Pub.
Daily Bulletin, Drumheller 328

Readman, Mary K.
Ed.
Wife of William J. Readman (q.v.)
Consort Enterprise 292

Readman, William J.
Pub.
Husband of Mary K. Readman (q.v.)
Consort Enterprise 292

Red Crow, Jackie
Ed.
Kainai News, Stand-Off 915

Redel, Chester
Pub.; ed.
Cold Lake Sentinel 286

Reeves, Winnifred Frances (Winnie)
Ed.
From Mannville district, was housekeeper and beginning ed. when married Harry Riley, Oc 1949. (**IRMA**, p.865-6)
Irma Times 647

Reid, Bernice
Pub.; ed.
Old Timer, Cochrane 280

Reid, John Alexander
Pub.; ed.; public servant
b. Liverpool, Eng., Mr 4 1862; d. Regina, Sask., N 23 1928.
Arrived Canada 1883; 1883, with NWMP in Riel Rebellion; 1884-9, in Dominion Government service; 1892, ed. Regina *Leader*; Clerk of the Executive Council, North West Territories; 1905, Deputy Provincial Treasurer and Govt Printer of Saskatchewan; financial commissioner; 1913, Agent General for Alberta in London. (Glenbow clipping file; **WW** 1912).
Calgary Herald 115
Calgary Weekly Herald and Alberta Livestock Journal 113

Reilly, James
Pub.
Critic, Calgary 128

Reimer, Don
Ed.
Representative, Leduc 689

Rhian, Eugene
Pub.
Ponoka Herald 817

Rice, G.E.
Ed.
Alix Free Press 14
Central Albertan, Wetaskiwin 1025
New Age, Wetaskiwin 1028

Richards, Florence Vera (Vera)
Pub.
b. Nanaimo, B.C., Ja 18 1894
Daughter of Edward Vincent Chambers (q.v.), worked in newspaper
offices most of her life, initially for her father. (Questionnaire)
Alix Free Press Mirror News-Record 14

Riche, Tim Le
See **Le Riche**, Tim

Richmond, Deborah
Ed.
Record, Fort Saskatchewan 560

Rideout, David
Pub.
b. Red Deer, Jl 4 1948
Midweeker, Red Deer 840
Red Deer Ad-Viser 837
Red Deer Shopper 842
Weekender, Red Deer 839

Rideout, Keith
Pub.
b. Red Deer, Jl 6 1953
Central Alberta Ad-viser, Red Deer 841
Red Deer Shopper 842

Rideout, Les D.
Pub.
Red Deer Ad-viser 837

Riley, Mrs. H.
See **Reeves**, Winnifred Frances

Ringuette, Alberic A.
Ed.
Etoile de St. Albert 878

Ritchie, George L.
Ed.
Wedge, Edmonton 389

Ritchie, J.M.
Mgr
1908, Mgr, Trades and Labour Council. (*Lethbridge News* undated clipping)
Magrath Pioneer 715
Southern Alberta Labor Bulletin, Lethbridge 696

Robb, David
Pub.
Western Review, Drayton Valley 323

Roberts, Dale
Ed.
Fairview This Week 527

Roberts, Owen
Mg ed.
1984, went to work for *Alberta Report*. (**PUB** Jl/Ag 1984)
Grande Centre-Cold Lake-Bonnyville Sun, Grand Centre 581

Robertson, Fred J.
Pub.
Erskine Review 521
Granum News 592

Robertson, J.B.
Pub.
Bassano Recorder 59
Chronicle, Crossfield 296

Robertson, Marion MacKay
Ed.
Citizen, Edmonton 436

Robinson, E.M.
Ed.
Alberta Oil Review, Calgary 150

Roche, Douglas James (Doug)
Journalist; ed.; statesman
b. Montreal, Je 14 1929
Journalist and ed., various Ontario and Quebec newspapers, 1949-65; elected Progressive Conservative MP, 1972, 1974, and 1980; Pres., United Nations Association in Canada, 1984; Leader, Canadian delegation to the Disarmament Committee, United Nations; many offices held in international and national organizations; winner of many awards;

author of political and Catholic publications. **(CAWW** 1986)
Western Catholic Reporter, Edmonton 453

Roche, Henry Joseph
Pub.; printer
East-Ender, Edmonton 397
Edmonton Free Press 384

Rockley, Paul W.
Pub.; printer
b. Calgary, Je 22, 1945
Printer; 10 yrs with Albertan Job Press Ltd. and 2 yrs with Davis and
Henderson, Toronto. **(PUB** Ap 1978;)
Claresholm Local Press 268

Rogers, Evelyn R.
Pub.; ed.
d. 1986.
Began working with *Wetaskiwin Times*; active in community. (*Athabasca
Echo* My 13 1986)
Athabasca Echo 30
Slave Lake Centennial Press 900

Rogers, Frank D.
Ed.; prop.; pub.
Okotoks Advance 784
Vulcan Review 1004

Romaine, Edward
Pub.
Fort McMurray Northern Star 550

Romanovich, A., Rev.
Ed.
Svitlo, Mundare 772

Ronaghan, Allen (Al)
Pub.; ed; teacher
b. Islay, Mr 10, 1923
Husband of Shirley Ronaghan (q.v.)
Grimshaw Voyageur 600

Ronaghan, Shirley
Pub.; ed.; teacher
b. Lakesend, Jl 16, 1926
Wife of Allen Ronaghan (q.v.)
Grimshaw Voyageur 600

Roper, Elmer Ernest
Ed.; printer; labour leader; politician

b. Igonish, N.S., Je 4 1893
1907, apprentice printer; 1911, in pressmen's union; active in labour
movement, heading Calgary Trades and Labour Council for a time; with
Henry Roche Print. Co. ca 1921-36; after several defeats in provincial and
federal elections, elected MLA (C.C.F.) in 1942 by-election, 1944, 1948,
1952, defeated 1955; 1959, Hon. LLD, University of Alberta; Mayor of
Edmonton, 1959-63, when retired to Victoria; Governor, Canadian Junior
Chamber of Commerce. (CARA p.72; EJ Oc 10 1979; CANP 1952; ALI)
Alberta Labor News, Edmonton 386
Edmonton Free Press 384

Roslund, O.
Ed.
Moukari, Edmonton 366

Ross, Joe H.
Ed.
Civvy Street, Red Deer 838

Roth, Fritz
Ed.
Herold, Edmonton 403

Rothe, Wayne
Ed.
Reporter, Stony Plain 937

Rouleau, Edouard J.
Pub.; ed.
b. Rosthern, Sask., ca. 1908; d. Pincher Creek, Jl 31 1962.
Learnt trade from father, F. S. Rouleau, of Kaslow, B. C.; retired ca. Jl
1959 due to ill-health. (CWNA v.41 no.799, Jl 1959, v.64 no.837, S 1962)
Carbon Chronicle 238
Didsbury Pioneer 317
Pincher Creek Echo 814
Three Hills Capital 965

Rouleau, David
Pub.
Son of Edouard J. Rouleau (q.v.)
Pincher Creek Echo 814

Rouleau, F. D.
Pub.
Son of Edouard J. Rouleau (q.v.)
Pincher Creek Echo 814

Rouleau, James
Pub.
Son of Edouard J. Rouleau (q.v.)
Pincher Creek Echo 814

Roulston, Charles A.
Pub.; ed.
Bashaw Star 56
Clive News-Record 270
Gadsby Observer 569
Rocky Mountain House Capital 858
Three Hills Capital 965
Westlock Witness 1015

Routledge, Joe
Pub.
Kicking Horse Chronicles, Lake Louise 672

Rowell, Ethel
Pub.
Married to Archie T. Rowell; moved from Red Deer to Delburne 1912;
1927, moved to Calgary. (**LEW** p. 483-4)
Delburne News 306

Roy, Laurent Clement
Ed.
b. Ile-a-la-Crosse, Sask., Jl 19 1943
Chief Executive Officer, Native Outreach Association of Alberta; has
spent 12 yrs in native communications area. (Questionnaire)
Native People, Edmonton 460

Rudd, Bruce L.
Pub.; mgr
Previously with Ottawa *Journal*, FP Publications in Winnipeg; gen. mgr,
Lethbridge Herald. (EJ My 30 1973)
Albertan, Calgary 127

Rue, George La
See **La Rue**, George

Ruffee, C. H. C.
Pub.
Bassano Mail 58

Rumball, Herbert H. (Herb)
Ed.; farmer; businessman
b. Turkey
Father in diplomatic service; lived in U. S.; proof-reader, *Edmonton
Bulletin*; farmed; had Massey-Harris and car agency; in real estate
business. (**BARR** p.400)
Barrhead News 51

Rundle, Grant
Ed.
Jasper Booster 657

Rushka, L. J.
Pub.; ed.; mgr
Sundre Round Up 945

Russell, Alexander (Sandy)
Mg ed.
With editorial staff *Calgary Herald*; Captain, World War I, invalided
home from France. (**CPP** v.28 no.8, Ag 1919)
Albertan Veteran, Calgary 155

Russell, Mrs. Alexander
Ed.; mg. ed.
Alberta Veteran, Calgary 155

Rutherford, Phil
Pub.; ed.
Barrhead Leader 52

Sabey, J. M.
Ed.
Magrath Mirror 719

Saddleback, Alfred
Ed.
Bear Hills Native Voice, Hobbema 631

Salton, John H.
Pub.
Previously in Winnipeg for 8 yrs. (**CPP** v.37 no.5, My 1928)
Advertiser, Granum, 595
Castor Advance 252
Clive News-Record 270
Granum Herald 594
Mirror Journal 761

Samilo, P. N
Ed.
Druh Naroda, Edmonton 400

Samis, Adoniram J.
Pub.; ed.
Son of Rev. James Samis, Baptist Minister, who founded churches in Olds
and Innisfree; moved to Calgary, where became alderman and city
commissioner; later moved to California. (**OLDS** p.35, 57; **SAM** p.163-5)
Hay Lakes Times 610
Olds Oracle 788

Sammons, H. Lee
Mgr; ed.
Granum News 592

Samoil, Judy
Ed.
Alberta Labour, Edmonton 450

Sanburn, Richard Louis (Dick)
Ed.; journalist
b. Victoria, B. C., S 25 1912; d. Calgary, Oc 15 1982.
Reporter in Saskatchewan, Winnipeg; war correspondent, Southam
Newspapers, 1943-45, and chief of its London Bureau, 1949-51; mbr of
Parliamentary Press Gallery, Ottawa, 1945-49. (CH Ag 26 1976; Oc 16
1982; **WWA1** 1968)
Calgary Herald 115

Sands, Jim
Ed.
High River Times 625

Saul, Leslie D.
Pub.
Former Manitoba ed. (**CPP** v.58 no.11, N 1949)
Eckville Examiner 333

Saunders, E. T.
Pub.
d. California, Ja 9 1920.
With NWMP; son-in-law of John Keen who set up sawmill at Mountain
Mill 1877; later, purchased Fairview Ranch. (**PRA** p. 568-9) *Guide to
Citizenship, Prosperity and Happiness*, Rocky Mountain House 856
Lethbridge News 692
Macleod Gazette 536
Pincher Creek Echo 814

Saunders, G. T.
Pub.
Representative, Leduc 689

Sauriol, Jacques
Ed.
Survivance, Edmonton 404

Saywright, J.
Pub.
Mirror Mail 762

Scandinavian Centre Cooperative Association Ltd.
Scandinavian Centre News, Edmonton 445

Schaab, Dorothea
Ed.
World of Beef and Stockman's Recorder, Calgary 209

Schaffer, L. J.
Ed.
Canadai Magyar Farmer, Edmonton 357

Schatz, Harry S.
Ed.
Calgary Jewish News 196

Scheer, George
Mgr.
Gazette and Alberta Live Stock Record, Fort Macleod 536

Schell, E. W.
Pub.
Grassy Lake Pilot 598

Schellenberg, Rob
Ed.
b. Beechy, Sask., Ap 25 1959
Vauxhall Advance 986

Schierbeck, Peter Kenning
Pub.
b. Lachine, Que., Ja 22 1944
Post, Fairview 526
Signal, Rycroft 871

Schierholtz, Grace Austin (née Yeoward)
Ed.; teacher
b. Moosomin, Sask.; d. Mr 1 1966.
Wife of William H. Schierholtz (q.v.); became teacher; transmitted weather forecasts with Chief Walking Eagle. (EJ Mr 2 1966,; **FLE** p.629)
Mountaineer, Rocky Mountain House 860

Schierholtz, William H.
Pub.; printer
b. Kitchener, Ont.; d. Osoyoos, B.C., Ag 15 1947.
Moved to Osoyoos for health reasons. (EJ Mr 2 1966)
Mountaineer, Rocky Mountain House 860

Schiller, Gregory A.
Ed.
b. Edmonton
Joined *Western Catholic* 1949 as office-mgr; established General Church Supplies, 1964. (EJ Oc 10 1964)
Western Catholic, Edmonton 388

Schlamp, Herbert
Pub.
News Advertiser, Vegreville 988

Schmidt, Paul
Mg. dir.
Alberta Herold, Edmonton 343

Schofield, Barry
Ed.
Sherwood Park Star 895

Schooley, Charles H.
Pub.
Acme News 1
Telegram-Tribune, Acme 2

Schooley, Frank H.
Ed.; pub.
Acme News 1
Bowden News 95
Chronicle, Crossfield 296
Claresholm Review-Advertiser 267
Coalhurst News 278
Lacombe Advertiser and Central Alberta News 669
Lacombe Guardian 671
Stony Plain Advertiser 930

Schooley, Harold H.
Pub.
Acme News 1
Telegram-Tribune, Acme 2

Schotte, L.
Pub.; ed.
Reporter, Edmonton 451

Schrag, Astor R.
Ed.; clergyman; journalist
b. Brantford, Ont., ca. 1882; d. N 2 1978.
Congregational Church pastor Alton, Ont., Yarmouth, N. S., and First
Congregational Church, Calgary; free-lance journalist. (AC Ap 29 1912; CH
N 4 1978)
Calgary Standard 142

Schreyer, Ethel
Pub.
Elk Point Reflections 1069
Mannville Reflections 731

Schroeder, Elmer
Pub.
Bashaw Star 56

Schumacher, Frank J.
Pub.
Provost News 822
Provost-Star 821

Schumacher, Phil
Pub.
Provost Star 821

Schuster, Josef
Mgr
Deutsch-Canadischer Farmer, Calgary 140

Schuurman, Bill
Pub.
Border County Recorder, Milk River 755
County of Lethbridge Sunny South News, Coaldale 276

Scott, Bill
Ed.
Daily Herald Tribune, Grande Prairie 586

Scott, Charlie M.
Pub.
Theatre-owner. (**CPP** v.59 no.5, My 1950)
Consort Enterprise 292

Scott, Gerald C.
Ed.
Recorder-Gazette, Peace River 804

Scott, H. G.
Pub.; lawyer
b. Scotland
1910, came to Canada; lawyer and magistrate in Alberta; served in both
World Wars; moved to Vancouver.
Red Deer News 835

Scott, J. Meredith
Pub.
Weekly Tribune, Edmonton 419

Scott, R. W. (Bill)
Pub.
Sundre Round Up 945

Scovil, Barclay Allaire
Pub.
b. Fredericton, N. B., ca. 1867; d. Calgary, ca. Oc 6 1950.
Guide and cook with Dominion survey teams in Yukon and Northwest Territories; assistant Indian agent in Grouard; 1905, moved to Edmonton and
lived there for some yrs before moving to Calgary. (EJ Oc 6 1950)
Bawlf Sun 63

Seabury, J. A.
Ed.
Formerly of *New York Herald*. (**CPP** v.28 no.12, D 1919)
Altario Arrow 18

Seager, E. M.
Ed.; pub.
Chronicle, Crossfield 296

Secord, Richard Henry
Prop.; businessman
b. Burford, Ont., Jl 19 1860; d. Ja 12 1935.
Went to Edmonton at age 20; teacher until D 1885; in business as gen. merchant with John McDougall (McDougall and Secord); started own store in
fur trade, Athabasca Landing, 1888; returned to Edmonton 1891; in fur trade
partnership with McDougall; 1902, elected to Territorial Assembly; sold
mercantile business 1909 and established new McDougall and Secord in
finance, real estate, and insurance. (**LEO**)
Edmonton Post 339

Segrave, Charles Christopher
Pub.; printer
b. nr Dublin, Ireland, D 1869; d. Calgary, My 29 1970.
Came to Canada 1887; worked in Vancouver; 1895, learned printing and
worked on newspapers in British Columbia; typesetter on Calgary *Eye
Opener*; 1934, moved to Vancouver and retired; 1949, returned to Calgary.
(CH Je 2 1970)
Sentinel, Acme 3

Seibert, Albert
Ed.
Magyar Hirmondo, Calgary 214

Selby, Jim
Ed.
Alberta Labour, Edmonton 450

Semeniuk, J. W.
Ed.
Nova Hromada, Edmonton 363

Sexton, C. E.
Pub.
Empress Express 517

Sexton, E. S.
Pub.
Empress Express 517

Shapcott, Michael
Ed.
Calgary Mirror North Side Edition 205
Calgary Mirror South Side Edition 194

Shapka, Gaylene
Ed.
Wednesday Review, Calgary 201

Shapka, John T.
Pub.
Wednesday Review, Calgary 201

Sharp, James R.
Pub.; journalist; businessman
d. Vimy, France.
English reporter; reporter on *Calgary Herald*; in real estate business in Calgary with W. B. Cameron (q.v.); died on active service. (CH S 30 1936)
Bassano Mail 58
Bassano News 57
Langdon Leader 686

Shearlaw, Timothy J.
Pub.
Capital, Three Hills 965

Sheddy, Osborne (Ossie)
Pub.; journalist
b. Wardlow, S 20 1922
Drumheller Mail 327

Sheremeta, C. J.
Pub.
Russian Life, Edmonton 375

Shields, Morris D.
Pub.
Cardston Unlimited 243
Temple City Tribune, Cardston 244

Shilling, L. D.
Pub.
Claresholm Review 266

Shipley, Hugh
Ed.
M. D. Red Deer News 1084

Shoemaker, O.
Pub.; printer
Came from Fernie, B. C.; on exec. first Albertan Press Assoc, formed Ja 27
1905; left for Vancouver, 1905; in Nanton during World War II. (**MEE**
p.161)
Alberta Advocate, Red Deer 834
Nanton News 780

Short, William
Ed.; lawyer
b. nr Elora, Ont., Ja 11 1866
1889, came to Calgary; 1894, called to bar; Mayor of Edmonton 1902-04;
practised in Edmonton; 1907, K.C.; Pres., Board of Trade of Edmonton;
(**BLU** v.2 p.176-7)
Edmonton Herald 337

Shortreed, L. G. (Shorty)
Pub.
Left Claresholm for Toronto. (**CL** p.432)
Claresholm Review 266

Siadi, M. F.
Pub.
Nuovo Mondo, Edmonton 493

Siebenforcher, Judith A.
Pub.
b. Mundare, Ap 20 1944
Triangle, Lamont County 677

Siebenforcher, Robert D. (Bob)
Pub.
b. Spokane, Wash., Oc 12 1948
Triangle, Lamont County 677

Siljan. L. J.
Ed.
Edson Leader 503

Simmons, Elsie
Ed.
Scandinavian Centre News, Edmonton 445

Simmons, Elva
Pub.
Rimbey Advance 854

Simpson, Fred E.
Ed.; pub.
Lethbridge Herald 693

Sinclair, Denny
Ed.
Carstairs Journal 249

Sinclair, Donald J. (Don)
Pub.
b. Lafleche, Sask., Je 25 1944
Worked on Saskatchewan and Alberta newspapers in sales and plant management; owned newspapers in Ontario and British Columbia. (Questionnaire)
Daily Herald Tribune, Grande Prairie 586
Fort McMurray Today 552
Parklander, Hinton 627
Record-Gazette, Peace River 804

Sindeff, Anna
Ed.
Union, Edmonton 378

Skerry, W.
Pub.
Carbon Chronicle 238

Skinner, James D.
Pub.; printer; prop.
b. Kimbur, Ont., ca. 1875; d. Oc 18 1965.
Started in printing business with *Calgary Tribune*; before 1900 had worked in print shops and newspapers in various parts of the prairies; Mayor of Rocky Mountain House, Gadsby, Sangudo; 1960, retired to Edmonton, running a small print shop until he died. (EJ Oc 19 1965)
Advertiser, Edmonton 341
Advertiser and Central Alberta News, Lacombe 669
Alberta Plaindealer, Edmonton 336
Guide to Citizenship, Prosperity and Happiness, Rocky Mountain House 856
Lac Ste Anne Chronicle 665
Mayerthorpe Times 733
Munson Times 776

Skinner, William A.
Pub.; prop.
d. Simcoe, Ont., ca. Je 14 1940.
Came to Hardisty 1910; 1915, went to Simcoe, Ont., where he operated Simcoe Job Press until death. (*Edmonton Bulletin* Je 14 1940)
Hardisty Mail 608

Slavutych, Yar
Ed.; poet; professor
b. Hryhory Zhuchenko in Ukraine; 1949, emigrated to U. S. A.; 1960, moved to Edmonton and taught at University of Alberta until retired, 1981. (EJ Jl 11 1981)
Kanadiyska Ukraina, Edmonton 480

Slight, Frederick John
Ed.; pub.
b. England, Oc 31 1889; d. Camrose, Ap 21 1930.
Came to Canada 1910; went to Vancouver for one yr; located in Didsbury where worked for a yr on *Didsbury Pioneer*; lived in Daysland for 6 mths; served in World War I; active in community. (**DON** p.18; **BLU** v.3 p.367-8)
Camrose Canadian 225
Daysland Press 302
Donalda Review 321
Erskine Review 521

Slight, Ida Dee (née Henry)
Ed.
d. Mr 14 1948.
Wife of Frederick John Slight (q.v.)
Camrose Canadian 225

Sloan, James
Secretary
Western Miner, Lethbridge 700

Smalley, A. Kent
Pub.
Bassano Recorder 59

Smith, Arthur Harvey
Ed.
Owned *Listowel Banner*, Ont. (**CPP** v.22 no.1, Ja 1913)
Medicine Hat Call 747

Smith, Bertram
Pub.; ed.
Lloydminster Times and District News 703

Smith, C. A.
Ed.
Provost News 822

Smith, Colin F.
Ed.
Spokesman, Edmonton 472

Smith, George Peter
Ed.; politician
b. Middlesex County, Ont., Ag 26 1873; d. Dundas, Ont., N 9 1942.
Taught school; moved to Alberta 1901; gen. merchant, Duhamel Trading;
moved to Camrose 1904; elected Liberal MLA 1909, 1913, 1917; Minister of Education, 1918-21; mg. dir. Round Hill Collieries; gen. mgr F. F.
Dailey Corp., Hamilton, Ont. (EJ N 30 1942; **AL**)
Camrose Canadian 225

Smith, Gordon William
Pub.
b. Orillia, Ont.; d. Ap 18 1981.
Came to Youngstown as child; worked 8 yrs on Youngstown *Plain Dealer*
and 6 yrs on *Drumheller Review*; kept family gen. store, Breton; 1931-
1941, operated power plant, Calmar; 1941, with Dept. of National Defense, Winnipeg; joined Bulletin Printers, Kelowna; retired 1977. (**PUB**
Je 1981)
Stony Plain Reporter 937

Smith, Graham
Ed.
North Hill News, Calgary 191
Sunday Calgarian 1053

Smith, Hugh
Pub.
Castor Advance 252

Smith, Robert
Pub.; clergyman
b. Northallerton, Eng.; d. Elk Point, F 12 1951.
Came to Canada 1910; ed. several Saskatchewan weeklies; worked on papers in Oyen and Chinook; worked in Edmonton before moving to Westlock; United Church pastor, Elk Point, until death. (EJ F 14 1951; PUB
v.32 no.709, Mr 1951)
Chinook Advance 264
Witness, Westlock 1015

Smith, Ronald Birnie
Pub.
Later worked in public relations for United Farmers of Alberta.
Western Review, Drayton Valley 323

Smith, W. Norman
Ed.; pub.
U. F. A., Calgary 160
Western Farm Leader, Calgary 181

Smith, W. W.
Pub.
Vegreville Observer 987

Smith, Wallace J. (Wally)
Pub.; orchardist
b. Toronto, Ont., Ag 9 1899; d. Penticton, B. C., N 25 1982.
1934, moved to Oliver, B. C., where published a tabloid paper and contributed articles to several newspapers. (Brooks Bulletin N 12 1970, D 22 1982)
Bassano Mail 58

Smitheringale, Charles E.
Pub.
Drill, Frank 565

Snaddon, Andrew William
Pub.; ed.; mg ed.
b. Winnipeg, Man., Ap 28 1921
Edited *Ubyssey* at University of British Columbia, 1942; joined navy; reporter, *Calgary Herald*, 1945-51; Chief, London Bureau, Southam News Services 1951-3; writer, Southam Bureau, Ottawa Press Gallery, 1953-4; ed., *Calgary Herald*, 1954-62; ed., *Edmonton Journal*, 1962-81; in broadcasting and private radio. (**CA WW** 1986)
Medicine Hat News 743

Snideman, Dave
Pub.; businessman
Operated Bill Cross Men's Shop. (**JAR** p.284)
Oyen Echo 798

Snideman, Mrs. Dave
Pub.
Oyen Echo 798

Snow, Chauncey Edgar
Pub.: businessman; author; banker
b. Brigham City, Utah, Jl 8 1870
1890, drugstore owner for one yr; opened shorthand and typewriting school; 1895, published novel, *Sister Gratia*; 1895, came to Cardston; opened mercantile business; 1899, became banker. (**BLU** v.2 p.475-7)
Cardston Record 240

Snuggs, John
Pub.
b. London, Eng., ca. 1922; d. ca. N 1971.
Came to Canada with RAF, World War II; 1949-67, with *Albertan*. (**CANW** N 1971)
South Side Mirror, Calgary 194

Synder, Annie E.
Pub.

Well-known reader and entertainer. (**CPP** v.26 no.3, Mr 1917)
Hand Hills Echo, Delia 311

Social Credit Association
Canadian Social Crediter, Edmonton 428, 434

Socialist Party of Canada
Soviet, Edmonton 381

Sociedad de Cultura y Communicaciones Hispano Americanas de Alberta
Opinion, Calgary 222

Societe de la Colonisation de'Edmonton
Ouest Canadien, Edmonton 338

Sopulak, Dr. M.
Ed.
Ukrainian News, Edmonton 402

Southam, John D.
Pub.
b. Ottawa, Ont., Ap 12 1909; d. Calgary, N 27 1954.
With Royal Bank of Canada, 1928-9; 1930-2, with Ottawa *Citizen*; Pres.,
Calgary Broadcasting Co., Radio Stn CFAC; Dir., Canadian Newspapers
Assoc. (**CAWW** 1952)
Calgary Herald 115

Spence, Craig
Ed.
Reporter, Stony Plain 937

Spencer, O. Leigh
Pub.; conservationist; farmer; journalist
b. Toronto, 1883 or 4; d. Saltspring Island, B. C., N 23 1965.
Came West with family at age 5; worked for Crowsnest Pass Coal Co.;
1907, joined *Calgary Herald*, advancing through several depts. over yrs;
1940, went to Vancouver as assistant to pub. of the *Province*; 1946, pub.
the *Province*; 1947, retired. (Two unidentified news clippings)
Calgary Herald 115

Spiller, Lin
Ed.
d. West Vancouver, B. C., S 16 1969.
Formerly with *High River Times*. (**CPP** v.55 no.4, Ap 1946)
Crag and Canyon, Banff 38

Spohn, H. Gordon
Ed.
Western Oil Examiner, Calgary 165

Spoor, F. C.
Ed.
Magrath Pioneer 715

Spoor, Robert
Ed.
Magrath Pioneer 715

Spurr, J. B.
Ed.; prop.
Times, Edmonton 335

Stack, D. A.
Pub.
St. Paul Canadian 884

Staddon, Bertrand J.
Ed.
Son of Joseph Bertrand R. Staddon (q.v.)
Sunny South News, Coaldale 276

Staddon, Joseph Bertrand R. (Bert)
Pub.; printer
b. England, ca. 1892; d. May 1970
Apprenticed as printer in England; stationed in Halifax during World War
II; emigrated to Lethbridge, 1956; worked on *Pincher Creek Echo*; active
in community. (**COA** p.870)
Sunny South News, Coaldale 276

Staffenberg, Drew
Ed.
Calgary Jewish News 196

Stafford-Mayer, Rodney John Matthew (Rod)
Pub.; journalist; broadcaster
b. Durban, South Africa, Ja 2 1949
Active in Innisfail community; 1983-5, Pres., Western Regional Newspa-
pers. (Questionnaire)
Innisfail Province 643

Stahl, Len
Ed.
New Alberta Liberal, Edmonton 1065.
Sherwood Park Star 895

Stanley, E. Ida
Ed.
Edmonton Examiner [South Editions] 486
Grande Prairie Booster 588

Stanley, W. F.
Ed.; pub.
Coleman Bulletin 289
Crag and Canyon, Banff 38

Stack, Louis A.
Pub.; farmer; implement dealer
b. Otterey, Eng., 1879
1901, came to Canada, to Ontario; 1904, moved to Carmangay, where farmed; 1919, moved to town and became implement dealer; later, ran newspaper in Coquitlam, B. C., and *Semiahmoa Sun*, White Rock, B. C. (**HAT** p.367)
Carmangay Sun 247
Champion Chronicle 260

Stead, Percy B.
Ed.
Crag and Canyon, Banff 38

Stechishin, Myroslav
Ed.; writer; Ukrainian leader
b. 1883; d. 1947.
Leader of organized Ukrainianism in Canada; involved in organization of Ukrainian teachers and Ukrainian labour; worked on *Red Banner*; 1909, organized monthly *The Working People*; made translations and wrote original stories dwelling on social injustices; during World War I broke with socialist circles; 1916, joined Ukrainian Diplomatic Mission, Washington, D.C.; after the War, edited *Ukrainian Voice*. (**MARU**)
Novyny, Edmonton 367
Postup, Mundare 771

Steele, Charles Franklin (Frank)
Pub.; journalist; author
Local reporter; 1910, assisted Westran with *Progressive Magrath*; one of first to attend Knight Academy, Raymond; 1917, went on mission to southern states of U. S. A.; spent yr at Valparaiso University; 1920, began as reporter for *Lethbridge Daily Herald* and was assoc. ed. when retired, 1961; author of several books, including *Prairie Editor: The Life and Times of Buchanan of Lethbridge* (1961) (**HIC** p.210, 638-9; **MAG** p.179-80)
Raymond Leader 824

Stephen, Kathy
Ed.
Northern Echo, High Level 613

Stevenson, J. W. (Bill)
Ed.
Echo, High Level 614

Steward, Hartley
Pub.; journalist
Calgary Mirror North Side Edition 205
Calgary Mirror South Side Edition 194
Calgary Sun 215

Stewart, Mr.
Ed.
CPR agent in Andrew. (**AND** p.47)
Carstairs Journal 249

Stewart, F. J.
Prop.
Lloydminster Times 703

Stewart, J. A.
Pub.
Went to Alberta County, N. B.
Manville Telegram 723

Stewart, John W. O.
Pub.
Calgary News 188

Stewart, S.
Pub.; ed.
Weekly Advance, Andrew 21

Stillwell, John
Pub.
Husband of Kay Stillwell (q.v.)
Northern Messenger, High Prairie 622
Northland Free Press, Slave Lake 902
Scope, Slave Lake 901

Stillwell, Kay
Pub.
Wife of John Stillwell (q.v.)
Northern Messenger, High Prairie 622
Northland Free Press, Slave Lake 902
Scope, Slave Lake 901

Stockwell, K.A.
Mgr
Sylvan Lake World 949

Stone, Bertha Luella
Pub.
b. Walkerton, Ont., Mr 6 1883
Wife of Edward L. Stone (q.v.); 1912, moved to Medicine Hat, then

Redcliff; taught school for 40 yrs. (*Medicine Hat* News Mr 28 1980)
Redcliff Review 843

Stone, Edward L. (Ed.)
Ed.
b. Perth, Ont., Mr 29 1876; d. Ag 1943.
Husband of Bertha Luella Stone (q.v.); 1901, published Hamiota *Echo*,
Manitoba; 1913, bus. mgr, *Medicine Hat Daily Times*; retired ca. 1939,
due to ill health. (**CWNA** v. 25 no. 613, S/Oc 1943; **HALL** p.25)
Alberta Farmer, Medicine Hat 748
Medicine Hat Daily Times 740
Redcliff Review 843

Stone, Fred W. (Stoney)
Ed.; pub.
b. Edgerton, Oc 2 1935
Began working at *Wainwright Star-Chronicle* 1954. (Questionnaire)
Wainwright Star-Chronicle 1009

Stone, P. W.
Ed.; pub.
Bassano Mail 58
Crag and Canyon, Banff 38
Rocky Mountain Courier, Banff 40

Stones, Aubrey
Pub.
b. Lousana
Husband of Audrey Stones (q.v.)
Delburne and District Journal 310

Stones, Audrey
Pub.
Wife of Aubrey Stones (q.v.)
Delburne and District Journal 310

Storch, Ted
Pub.
Rattler, Medicine Hat 752

Storseth, A.
Pub.
Daysland Commercial 303

Storseth, G.
Pub.
Daysland Commercial 303

Stout, Clarence H.
Pub.; broadcaster; businessman

b. Tremont Prairie, Ill., N 9 1882; d. Leduc, D 1 1974.
1895, came to Leduc to homestead; left *Plaindealer* for real estate business; ed., *Edmonton Bulletin*; associated with *Calgary Herald, Albertan*, CFCN radio; published autobiography, *Backtrack On Old Trails* (1973). (AC D 2 1974; **CPP** v.22 no.2, F 1913; **STO**)
Edmonton News-Plaindealer 336

Stout, George H.
Pub.; journalist
b. Edmonton, ca. 1916
Reporter and ed., *Albertan*; 1941, joined *Edmonton Journal*; served in World War II; 1945 on, ed., *Edmonton Journal*; 1963, bought Tweed *News*, Ont. (**CPP** v.72 no.10, Oc 1963; EJ Ap 23 1962)
Minburn County Review 758

Stovel, William David (Bill)
Ed.; journalist
b. Stratford, Ont., 1900; d. Victoria, B. C., Ja 1 1976.
Moved to Calgary as child; freelance journalist; worked on *Albertan* and various Ontario and Saskatchewan newspapers; joined *Edmonton Bulletin*; 1951, returned to *Albertan*. (EJ Ja 5 1976)
Spokesman, Calgary 173

Strachan, John A.
Pub.; ed.
Three Hills Capital 969

Straight, Hal
Pub.; ed.; journalist
Formerly journalist in Vancouver, B. C. (*Edmonton Bulletin* Ja 29 1948)
Edmonton Bulletin 358

Strang, J. Wally
Pub.
Edmonton Free Press 448

Strang, M. A.
Ed.
Great West, Edmonton 349

Strickland, Albert E.
Pub.
Cochrane Advocate 279

Strother, B.
Ed.
Chronicle, Crossfield 296

Stuart, Charles Clifford
Ed.; prop.; pub.

b. Derbyshire, Eng Jl 6, 1884; d. Trochu, F 25 1958.
Learned printing trade in England; 1909, came to Canada; spent 45 yrs on
Alberta and Saskatchewan weeklies. (**CWNA** v.41 no.784, Ap 1958)
Alderson News 1
Carstairs Journal 249
Cochrane Advocate 279
Trochu Tribune 973

Stuart, Ralph Frederick
Ed.
b. Imperial, Sask., Mr 23, 1929
Later Supervisor of Environmental Services, St. Mary's Health Care Centre, Trochu. (Questionnaire) *Trochu Tribune* 973

Stuart, Sam Charles Ed. b. Blairmore, Alta., Ja 8 1921 Worked on *Blaine
Lake Echo* in early 1940s. (Questionnaire) *Trochu Tribune* 973

Stubbs, Calvin Ed. *Standard*, Vermilion 992

Stubbs, Hugh A. Pub.; ed.
Worked on Flin Flon *Daily Miner*, and other papers in Manitoba and
Saskatchewan; joined *Vermilion Standard* as printer, 1963. (**PUB** S 1984)
Vermilion Standard 992

Sturdy, Dave
Ed.
Valley Views, Canmore 231

Suchlandt, B.
Pub.
Bowness Review, Calgary 1054

Sulek, Kay
Pub.
Hub, Westlock 1016

Sullivan, Maurice Charles
Pub.
d. 1976.
Courier, Smoky River M. D. 908

Sundby, Pauline
Ed.
Redcliff Review 1085

Svendsen, J. Curt
Pub.; ed.
Lac La Biche Post 663

Swampy, Beryl
Ed.
Bear Hills Native Voice, Hobbema 632

Swanson, Frank
Pub.
Calgary Herald 115

Sweet, Roy G.
Pub.
Cardston Chronicle 246
Raymond Review 828

Swendsen, Christian
Ed.
Kirken og Hjemmet, Edmonton 408

Switzer, Mrs. P. R.
Pub; ed.
Fort McMurray News Advertiser 1073
McMurray Times, Fort McMurray 1075

Syroidiw, N.
Ed.
Farmers' kyi Holos, Edmonton 415

Tanner, Glenn
Mgr; prop.
High River Times 625

Tanner, R. D. (Don)
Ed.; pub.
Began Moosomin, Sask., *World Spectator*; with Esterhazy, Sask., *Miner* for 4 yrs; 1960, shop steward, *High River Times*. (**PUB** S 1976)
High River Times 625
Okotoks Review 783

Tarr, F. M.
Pub.
Recorder, Altario 19

Taylor, Alexander
Pub.
b. Ottawa; d. F 12 1916.
Came to Edmonton 1877 to build telegraph line; started Edmonton telephone system; 1890s, postmaster and clerk of Supreme Court; promoter and organizer of Edmonton Electric Co.; Alex Taylor Road and School are named after him. (**CAS** p. 118-121)
Bulletin, Edmonton 334

Taylor, Arthur
Pub.
Cochrane Advocate 279

Taylor, Dennis
Pub.
Son of Gladys Taylor (q.v.)
Courier, Carstairs 251
Rocky View-Five Village Weekly, Rocky View M. D. 862
Trochu's Community Voice 974
Village Press, Carbon 239

Taylor, Ernest Edward
Pub.
b. Middle Musquodoboit, N. S.; d. Peace River, ca. N 8 1965.
In RAF during World War I; 1920, moved to Peace River. (EJ N 8 1965)
Northern Gazette, Peace River 803
*Peace River Record with which is Amalgamated
The Northern Gazette*, Peace River 804

Taylor, Geoff
Ed.
Village Press, Carbon 239

Taylor, Gladys
Ed.
From Manitoba; moved to Ontario after War, living in Toronto, then
Sherbrooke and Thetford Mines, Que.; wrote two novels; published mobile
home magazine in Calgary for 8 yrs.; 1975, moved to Irricana. (**OUR** p.
890-1).
Courier, Carstairs 251
Rocky View-Five Village Weekly, Rocky View M.D. 862
Trochu's Community Voice 974
Village Press, Carbon 239

Taylor, Gordon Edward
Ed.; politician; teacher; businessman
b. Calgary, Je 20 1910
1930s, taught school; in R.C.A. during World War II; 1946, real estate and
insurance business, Drumheller; elected Progressive Conservative MLA in
1940-71 elections, and as Independent in 1975; elected Progressive Conservative MP in 1979, 1980, 1984. (**ALI; CANP** 1986).
Canadian Social Crediter, Edmonton 428

Taylor, H.A. (Bert)
Pub.
Times, Wetaskiwin 1022

Taylor, H.T.
Pub.

Later, on *Vegreville Observer* (**CPP** v.38 no.6, Je 1929).
Mannville News and the Minburn and Innisfree Times, Mannville 725

Taylor, Lorne
Pub.
b. Toronto
Son of Gladys Taylor (q.v.); worked on mother's mobile home magazine for
8 yrs.; moved to Irricana, 1975; 1978, moved to Smoky Lake. (**OUR** p. 890-
1).
Smoky Lake Signal 901

Tengermann, Otto
Ed.
Alberta Herold, Edmonton 424

Tennant, John Charles (Jack)
Prop.; pub.; journalist
b. Arrow River, Man., D 23 1935
Newspaper and television reporter, Brandon, Man., 1962-8; 1968-71, ed.,
Kamloops *Sentinel*; 1971-7, gen. mgr of hockey in Calgary and Kamloops;
1977, appointed city ed., Calgary *Albertan*. (**WWA2** 1978).
Airdrie and District Echo, Airdrie 8
Rocky View Times, Airdrie 10

Terrell, Alfred J.N.
Ed.; prop.
b. Hamilton, Ont., 1869
Began work with Grand Trunk Railroad Co.; worked on newspaper in
Cumberland, Md, for 2 yrs; worked on newspapers in Ontario; 1904, came to
Medicine Hat; active in community. (**BLU** v.2 p.90-1).
Medicine Hat News 744

Thivièrge, J.A.
Pub.
St. Paul Journal 883

Thomas, A.J.
Ed.; pub.
Didsbury Pioneer 317

Thomas, Alex
Ed.
Advertiser and Central Alberta News, Lacombe 669

Thomas, Bruce D.
Pub.; ed.
b. Philadelphia, Pa.
Recreation dir. for Town of Slave Lake until 1971. (**EJ** undated clipping)
High Prairie Reporter 621
Scope, Slave Lake 901

Thomas, E.H.L.
Pub.
Wainwright Record 1008

Thomas, Graham
Ed.
Alberta Business Review, Edmonton 452

Thomas, Lou
Pub.
Coleman Journal 290

Thomas, T. Berville
Pub.; ed.
English captain. (**CPP** v.15 no.10, Oc 1906)
Camrose Mail 224
Sedgewick Paper 889

Thomas, R.L.
Ed.
Organized Farmer, Edmonton 427

Thompson, Bill
Ed.; journalist
b. Edmonton, N 7 1963
Spokesman, Edmonton 472

Thompson, Claude James (Jim)
Pub.; printer
b. Lacombe, N 4 1924
Alix Free Press 14

Thompson, George Marshall
Pub.
From Windsor, Ont.; 1906-12, owned Saskatoon *Capital*. (**CPP** v.21 no.6, Je
1912, v.26 no.9, S 1917)
Calgary News Telegram 136

Thompson, J.J.R.
Pub.; ed.
Three Hills Capital 965

Thompson, Lloyd
Pub.; teacher; airman; insurance underwriter
b. Somerville, Mass., Ag 13 1908
Bowden Booster 98

Thoms, W.M.C.
Pub.
Sylvan Lake World 949

Thomson, George T.
Ed.; pub.
b. Caledon, Ont.; d. Vancouver, ca. 1949.
Came West ca. 1897. (**GIS** p.130-3; **CPP** v.58 no.8, Ag 1949)
Mountaineer, Rocky Mountain House 857
Rocky Mountain House Echo 856

Thoreson, A.A.
Pub.
Worked on *Viking News* and *Wainwright Star*. (**CPP** v.27 no.3, Mr 1918)
Provost News 822

Thornton, R.H.
Pub.
Alderson News 12

Thorold-Eller, A.
Ed.; pub.; clergyman
Chronicle, Crossfield 296

Thorvaldson, Gunnar
Ed.
Scandinavian Centre News, Edmonton 445

Thorvaldson, Shirley
Ed.
Scandinavian Centre News, Edmonton 445

Thunell, Henry G.
Printer; pub.
d. Ag 11 1965.
1913, came from Minneapolis, Minn.; 1914, printer to John William
Johnston (q.v.); Mayor of Viking, 1925-37. (**DAL** pp.97-98; **LET** p.7-8, 13)
Times, Irma 647
Viking News 1000

Thunell, Robert Horton
Pub.
Son of Henry G. Thunell (q.v.)
Viking News 1000

Thynne, Frank
Ed.
d. St. Paul, Minn., 1926.
Gymnastics instructor in England; 1911, came to Canada; 1912, operated
rooming-house in Trochu; 1919, moved to St. Paul, Minn. (**TRO** p.393)
Trochu Tribune 973

Tiberg, Walter
Pub.
Pass Daily Herald, Blairmore 81

Tilden, Harry Breck
Pub.; mgr; grocer
b. Lebanon, N.H., ca. 1876; d. Willow Creek, Je 27 1959.
As child, moved to California; went to the Klondike in 1898; 1903, home-
steaded near Claresholm; grocer in Claresholm and Granum. (*Claresholm
Local Press* Jl 2 1959)
Granum News 594

Tillmann, Ursula
Ed.
Reporter, Stony Plain 937

Tilston-Jones, H.
Pub.
Garden City Times, Magrath 718

Tkach, Arlos F.
Ed.
Consort Enterprise 292

Tomashevsky, Thomas
Ed.; pub.
b. Stetsera, Galicia, My 15 1884; d. ca. F 4 1969.
At 13, secretary to district court; 1900, family emigrated to Canada; 1904,
worked in Lethbridge coal mines; organized Ukrainian Social Democratic
Party of Canada, with which he split 1911-12; publications included
Harapnyk/The Whip, a satirical journal published in 18 issues in Andrew,
1921-22. (**ANDR** p.68, EJ F 4 1969)
Albertiis' ka Zoria, Edmonton 409
District Press, Andrew 22
Farmerske Slovo, Edmonton 387
Farmerskyi Holos, Edmonton 415
Nash Postup, Edmonton 393
Nova Hromada, Edmonton 363
Postup, Mundare 771

Tonks, C.M.
Ed.
Magrath Pioneer 715

Torgerson, J.S.
Pub.
News-Record, Whitecourt 1031

Torres, Genaro
Ed.
Diario, Edmonton 501

Toth, Vic
Pub.
Bassano Times 62

Tourigny, Clement, o.m.i.
Ed.; Catholic clergyman
Survivance, Edmonton 404

Trades and Labor Council of Calgary
See **Calgary Trades and Labor Council**

Trades and Labor Council of Edmonton
See **Edmonton Trades and Labor Council**

Trades and Labor Council of Lethbridge
See **Lethbridge Trades and Labor Council**

Traxler, H. Boyd
Ed.
Independent Reformer, St. Paul 885

Tredway, Sylvester
Prop.; businessman
d. San Luis Obispo, Calif., D 15 1942.
Worked on *Edmonton Capital*; in contracting, with father, Yellowknife,
N.W.T.; owned coal mine, with father and brother, Dodds; 1939, retired to
San Luis Obispo, Calif. (EJ D 18 1942)
Western Weekly, Edmonton 376

Treleaven, Allan Lorne (Butch)
Pub.; mg. ed.; journalist
b. Wetaskiwin, S 18 1945
Cardston Chronicle 246
Lacombe Globe 670
Raymond Review 828

Tremblay, Gaetan
Ed.
Franco-albertain, Edmonton 458

Trentner, W.F.
Prop.
North Star, Wetaskiwin 1019

Truch, A.
Ed.; clergyman
Svitlo, Mundare 772

Truss, Richard George (Rick)
Pub.
b. Killam, Ap 29 1952
Community Press, Sedgewick 890

Truss, Robert F.
Ed.
Athabasca Herald 28
Northern News, Athabasca 26

Tucker, J.L.
Pub.
Natural Gas and Oil Record, Calgary 147

Tuckwell, David Grieve
Prop.
b. Chesham, Eng., Ja 8 1865
Worked with London pub. for several yrs; with Bathurst *Daily Free Press*, N.S.W., Australia, 10 yrs.; editorial staff, Manitoba *Free Press*, *Western Sportsman*, *Morning Herald*, Fort William, Ont.; prop., Rainy River *Gazette*, Ont.; ed., Yorkton *Times*, Sask. (**WW** 1912)
Lloydminster Times and District News, Lloydminster 703

Tuffley, S.R.
Pub.; ed.
Clairmont Independent 265
Lake Saskatoon Journal 674

Turgeon, James Gray
Pub.; financial agent; senator
b. Bathurst, N.B., O 7 1879; d. Vancouver, B.C., F 14 1964.
Moved to Alberta 1907; elected Liberal MLA, 1913, 1917; elected Liberal MP, 1935, 1940; appointed to Senate, 1947. (**CANP** 1944; **CAWW** 1961)
Hardisty Enterprise 607

Turnbull, Fred
Printer; pub.
b. Stratford, Ont., Sept. 1889; d. Red Deer, Ag 9 1979.
Persuaded by Francis Wright Galbraith (q.v.) to give up Toronto position and take over printing of *Advocate*; Mayor of Red Deer; prominent in community. (**EJ** Ag 11 1979)
Red Deer Advocate 834

Turnock, Francis H.
Pub.; ed.
Alberta Tribune Daily Edition, Calgary 122
Alberta Tribune Weekly Edition, Calgary 123

U.F.A.
See **United Farmers of Alberta**

Ukrainian Catholics in Canada
Ukrainski Visti, Edmonton 402

Ukrainian Farmers' Union of Alberta
Formed in Vegreville, Ja 22 1917.
Farmske Slovo, Edmonton 387
Postup, Mundare 771

Ukrainian Immigration and Colonization Association in Edmonton
Novyi Krai, Edmonton 406

Ukrainian Temperance Society
Albertiis'ka Zoria, Edmonton 409

Underwood, Charles K.
Pub.
Alberta Social Credit Chronicle, Calgary 175
Macleod Spectator, Fort Macleod 542

Union of Canadian Ukrainian Farmers
See **Ukrainian Farmers' Union of Alberta**

United Danish Lutheran Church
Kirken og Hjemmet, Edmonton 408

United Farmers of Alberta
U.F.A., Calgary 160

University of Alberta
See also **Commerce Association for Marketing Essential Literature**

University of Alberta. C.C.F. Campus Club
Progressive Student, Edmonton 1059

University of Alberta. Progressive Conservative Student Federation
Tory, Edmonton 1063

University of Alberta. Students' Union
Gateway, Edmonton 359
Portrait, Edmonton 477
Summer Times, Edmonton 481

University of Lethbridge
See **Meliorist Pub. Society**

Upshall, Jack
Ed.
Meridian Booster, Lloydminster 705

Valenta, Vladimir
Pub.
Telegram, Edmonton 464

Valin, Colleen (née Meaney)
Ed.
County of Lethbridge Sunny South News, Coaldale 276

Van Buren, Abram P.
Mgr
b. Morden, Man.; d. Calgary, F 2 1973.
Came West after 1900 to Fort Macleod district and, in 1907, to Calgary. (AC F 5 1973)
Alberta Sun, Calgary 162

Van Derbyll, H. Rosch
Ed.
Calgary Standard 142

Van Dusen, Chedwy
Ed.
Outlaw, Grassy Lake 597

Varley, James Edward
Ed.; lawyer
b. Huddersfield, Eng., 1871; d. Calgary, Oc 1 1957.
1886, came to Canada; called to bar in Toronto, 1893; 1893, joined Canadian militia; 1904, came West to High River where practised law for 4 yrs; 1908, moved to Calgary and practised there. (CH Oc 3 1957)
Chinook, High River 624

Velker, Ellis T.
Ed.
Beiseker Times 68

Velker, N.J.
Ed.
Beiseker Times 68

Venn, Mr.
Pub.
Edson Record 502

Vicary, Mrs. W.
Bus. mgr
Calgary Observer 131

Vijanen, Alma
Ed.
Moukari, Edmonton 366

Villeneuve, Frédéric-Edmond
Ed.; lawyer; librarian
b. Montreal, Mr 6 1867; d. Montreal, Ap 3 1915.
Admitted to Quebec bar, 1891; practised law, St. Albert; 1898, mbr of
Legislature, Northwest Territories; 1902, returned to Montreal; 1909-15,
Conservateur de la bibliothèque, Montreal. (**DEG** 2 p.125)
Ouest-canadien, Edmonton 338

Vold, Roger
Pub.
News Advertiser, Wetaskiwin 1030

Von Hammerstein, Count Alfred
see **Hammerstein**, Count Alfred von

Von Iffland, L.D.
see **Iffland**, L.D. von

Vye, Ed M.
Ed.
Sundre News-Advertiser 944

Waggett, J. McPhail
Ed.
Empress Express 517

Walker, Carroll
Ed.; pub.
Came with family from Cameron, Mo. (Questionnaire)
Bow River News, Arrowwood 1045

Walker, Diana
Pub.; ed.
Oyen Echo 798

Walker, Duane J.
Pub.; ed.
Came to Stavely from Duluth, Minn., 1905; worked for Wilson Kew (q.v.)
before becoming ed.; later, for Gordon Neale (q.v.). (**BUT** p.79, 410-11)
Stavely Advertiser 922

Walker, John H.
Pub.; pharmacist; public servant
d. 1910.
Chemist for 12 yrs in Liverpool, Eng.; 1889, came to Calgary; 1893, came to
Wetaskiwin when railway went through; 1902-10, Inland Revenue collector.
(Questionnaire)
Free Lance, Wetaskiwin 1018
Wetaskiwin News 1020

Walkowski, Tadeusz
Ed.
b. Poland, 1898; d. Edmonton, Ja 5 1983.
During World War II was in Polish army; 1955, in *Edmonton Journal* circulation dept.; retired 1963. (EJ Ja 6 1983)
Biuletyn. Kongresu Polonii Kanadyjskiej Okreg Alberta, Edmonton 443

Wall, Clarence E.
Pub.
Carbon Chronicle 238

Wall, G.E.
Ed.; pub.
Chronicle, Crossfield 296

Wall, Lottie May (née Stanley)
Pub.
b. Duluth, Minn.; d. Calgary, Je 20 1975.
Wife of Herbert George McCrea (q.v.); 1912, moved to Hanna; active in community, especially theatre; later, married William Ernest Wall, railway engineer. (*Brooks Bulletin* Jl 2 1975)
Hanna Herald 605

Wallace, Al
Pub.
Jasper Place Citizen, Edmonton 436

Wallace, Alvin V.
Pub.
Later, worked on Calgary *Albertan*; moved to Creston, B.C., and worked as printer on *Review*. (**CWNA** v.22 no.586, Oc 30 1941; Oyen and District Historical Society Ja 1987)
Carbon Chronicle 238
Telegram, Oyen 796

Wallsten, Jerry
Pub.
Lakeside Leader, Slave Lake 903

Walt, Gail
Ed.
Wednesday Review, Calgary 201

Wanagas, Don
Ed.; journalist
Later, columnist on *Edmonton Sun*.
Edmonton Examiner [South Editions] 490
Record, Fort Saskatchewan 560
Sherwood Park News 896

Ware, Deighton Ray
Pub.; ed.; teacher; journalist; public servant
b. Brighton, Ont., S 28 1887
Came to Alberta 1906; taught school, Camrose; school principal, Medicine Hat, 1907-9; reporter, *Lethbridge Herald*, 1909-10; customs collector, Medicine Hat area. (**WW** 1912; **CPP** v.21 no.5, My 1912)
Times, Medicine Hat 742

Warman, Wendell
Pub.
Castor Advance 252

Warner, H.A.
Ed.
Monitor News 763

Warnock, F.M.
Pub.; mgr
Mayerthorpe Times 733
Wainwright Star 1007

Warren, Ivan R.
Pub.
b. ca. 1929
Apprentice printer in Regina at 17; worked on newspaper presses, British
Columbia; with *Olds Gazette* 23 yrs. (**ANDE** p.377)
Bowden Eye Opener 99

Warriner, E.B.
Ed.
Burdett Tribune 110

Watkinson, F.W.
Ed.
Irma Times 647

Watson, F.D.
Ed.
Weekly News, Horburg 1076

Watson, Jill E.
Pub.
Chinook Reporter, Lethbridge 702

Watson, Jim E.
Ed.
Edmonton Business 491

Watson, William Cornelius Love
Ed.
b. Huntingdon, Eng., 1870; d. Trochu, N 9 1934.

With *Western Daily Press*, Bristol, Eng., and *Pall Mall Gazette*, London; 1911, emigrated to Canada; with *Calgary Daily Herald*. (*Trochu Tribune* N 16 1934)
Elnora Advance 516
Trochu Tribune 973

Watt, Arthur Balmer
Ed.; pub.
b. Brantford, Ont., 1876; d. Edmonton, Jl 1 1964.
Husband of Gertrude Balmer Watt (q.v.); with newspapers in Ontario; came to Edmonton 1905; 1912, ed. with *Edmonton Journal* until retirement, 1945.
(**PEEL**; EJ Jl 4 1964)
Edmonton Capital 356
Homestead, Edmonton 353
Rural Northwest and Edmonton Weekly Journal, Edmonton 368
Saturday News, Edmonton 348

Watt, Frederick
Prop.
Northern News, Athabasca 26

Watt, Gertrude Balmer (née Hogg)
Ed.; journalist
b. Guelph, Ont., S 1879; d. Edmonton, Je 12 1963.
Wife of Arthur Balmer Watt (q.v.); came to Edmonton 1905; women's ed., *Sentinel-Review*, Woodstock, Ont.; women's ed. and columnist, Edmonton *Saturday News*; published *A Woman in the West* (1907) and *Town and Trail* (1908); active in civic affairs. (**AC** Je 18 1963; **EJ** undated clipping).
Edmonton Saturday Mirror 365

Watzke, Ralph
Ed.
Campus Lyfe, Edmonton 470

Weaver, S.J.
Pub.
Raymond Recorder 825

Webb, Will T.
Pub.
Wainwright Star 1007

Weber, Dana
Ed.
Sherwood Park News 896

Webster, Joyce E. (née Nelson)
Pub.

b. Coronation, N 23 1953
Coronation Review 293

Weeks, D.C.
Pub.
Viking News 1000

Weir, C.A.
Ed.
Western Farmer, Calgary 164

Weir, James
Pub.; ed.; farmer; politician
b. Ag 5 1863, Elginfield, Ont.
Edited papers Hamilton and Windsor, Ont., and Saskatoon, Sask.; active
in U.F.A.; elected Independent Farmer MLA, 1917. (**ALI**)
Evening Chronicle, Edmonton 350
Strathcona Chronicle, Edmonton 345

Wertheimer, Douglas
Ed.
Calgary Jewish News 196
Jewish Star [Calgary Edition] 216
Jewish Star [Edmonton Edition] 495

West, Charles
Pub.
Hinton Herald Parklander 627

West, Evelyn
Pub.
Hinton Herald Parklander 627

West, Gordon F.
Pub.; ed.
Cardston News 242

Westergaard, C.
Ed.
Calgary Home News 172

Western Canadian Conference of Typographical Unions
Western Union Printer, Medicine Hat 749

Westhora, Gary
Ed.
News, Fort Chipewyan 535

Westland, George R.
Pub.

1923, purchased *Express*, Beamsville, Ont. (**CPP** v.32 no.7, Jl 1923)
Innisfail Free Lance 642
Province, Innisfail 643

Weston, Peter James
Ed.; pub.
b. Oshawa, Ont., S 18 1937
Worked on Spirit River *Signal*, 1955-6; 1956-64, with Canadian Superior
Oil; ambulance operator, Spirit River. (**WWA1** 1968).
Spirit River Bulletin 911

Weston, W.J.
Ed.
Magrath Pioneer 715

Wheeler, Arthur
Pub.; ed.; businessman
b. Brentwood, Ont., My 21 1884; d. Acme, S 18 1956
Worked with father as woodsman; 1904, moved to Crossfield with family;
19085, moved to Acme; homesteaded and opened store; 1919, ran
insurance agency, sold and serviced radios, audited; postmaster; active in
civic affairs. (**ACME** p.469-70)
Acme Sentinel 3

Wheeler, George
Pub.
Son of Arthur Wheeler (q.v.)
Worked on *Acme Sentinel* 1934 until served with RCAF during War;
resumed duties afterwards. (**ACME** p.469-70)
Acme Sentinel 3
Carbon Chronicle 238

Whetstone, Barry
Pub.
Western Sports Weekly, Edmonton 459

Whillans, Robert N.
Prop.; pub.
d. 1925.
1917, came to Peace River; ca. 1924, moved to Denver, Colo., for health
reasons. (**CPP** v.33 no.1, Ja 1924; **PEA** p.231)
Peace River Standard and Farmers Gazette, Peace River 801
Tofield Standard 967

White, Bert Shepard
Ed.
Western Standard, Calgary 142

White, Charles W.
Pub.

Ran boarding house in Redcliff; gas superintendent and town foreman, ca.
1911-12; later, moved to California. (**HALL** p.17, 22, 27)
Redcliff Review 843

White, Rob
Ed.
Sherwood Park News 896

Whitehouse, W. J.
Pub.
Hardisty World 609
Mannville Mirror 726
Manville [sic] Reporter 727

Whiteside, Frank H.
Pub.; ed.; farmer; politician
b. Ottawa, Ont., Jl 1874; d. Coronation, S 29 1916.
Left New Brunswick 1892; worked in lumber camp, British Columbia;
moved to Innisfail; 1905, homesteaded at Botha; moved to Castor; home-
stead inspector, Castor, for 2 yrs; elected Liberal MLA, 1917. (**ALI**;
Questionnaire)
Castor Advance 252
Coronation Review 293

Whitfield, James H. (Harry)
Printer
Son of Robert Whitfield (q.v.); arrived in Canada 1910; printed *Crossfield
Chronicle* for Rev. Kemp (q.v.) and then for father. (**CRO** p.234-7)
Chronicle, Crossfield 296

Whitfield, Robert
Prop.; ed.; pub.; printer
d. 1929.
From Lancashire, Eng.; arrived 1910; worked for Charles N. Austin (q.v.)
on *Cochrane Advocate*; 1913, moved to Crossfield and took over printing
office; 1914, postmaster. (**CRO** p.235-7; **COCH** p.609)
Chronicle, Crossfield 296
Cochrane Advocate 279

Whitney, Lyle Dudley
Prop.
b. Keithsburg, Ill., 1889; d. Foremost, 1958.
Family moved to North Dakota then to homestead at Lucky Strike; 1913,
moved to Warner. (**WAG** p.892)
Warner Record 1010

Whittingham, Tom
Ed.
Left 1932 to edit Cranbrook paper. (**VUL** p.35)
Vulcan Advocate 1005

Whylock. R. M.
Pub.
Edson Atom 510
Edson Headlight 509
Forestburg Home News 531

Whyte, Dr.
Prop., physician
Assistant to Dr. Brett at the Banff Sanitarium. (**CWNA** v.38 no.774, Ap 1957)
Banff National Park Gazette 37

Whyte, Ken
Ed.
Sherwood Park News 896

Widmer, Mike
Ed.
Record, Fort Saskatchewan 560

Wierenga, Herman
Ed.
Spokesman, Edmonton 472

Wight, David Osborn
Pub.; farmer; teacher
b. Cardston, S 27 1891
Cardston News 241
Magrath News 717

Wiig, L. Walter
Pub.; businessman
b. Ellsworth, N. D., F 24 1913
County of Warner Review and Advertiser, Milk River 753
Footnotes and News, Claresholm 269

Willard, E. J.
Ed.
Son of Joseph G. Willard (q.v.)
Lloydminster Times 703

Willard, Ellen
Prop.
Wife of Joseph G. Willard (q.v.)
Lloydminster Times 703

Willard, Joseph G.
Pub.
d. N 1938.
Lloydminster Times and District News, Lloydminster 703

Willcocks, R. Paul
Ed.
Advocate, Red Deer 834

Williams, F. W.
Ed.; clergyman; teacher;
b. Cardiff, Wales, 1897
Apprenticed to solicitor's office before joining army in 1914; 1919, came
to Edmonton; taught school briefly; 1924, entered ministry. (*Today and
Tomorrow* Je 17 1943)
Today and Tomorrow, Edmonton 421

Williams, Walton
Ed.; pub.
Lamont Tribune 681
St. Paul Canadian 884
Witness, Waskatenau 1011

Williamson, Doug
Ed.
Two Hills County Journal 982

Williamson, Maurine
Pub.
Old-Timer, Cochrane 280

Williamson, Robert B.
Pub.; businessman
(**CPP** v.38 no.7, Jl 1929)
Bashaw Star 56

Willis, Charles Lavalle (Charlie)
Pub.; ed.; teacher
b. Seaforth, Ont., Je 10 1882; d. Stettler, My 10 1956.
Taught school for 3 yrs in Manitoba and Saskatchewan; 1905, ed. of
Manitoba weekly; active in community and church. (**BLU** v.2 p.115-6;
CH My 11 1956; **CLA** p.95)
Stettler Independent 923

Willis, Harold B.
Ed.; prop.
Cochrane Advocate 279

Willis, R. Charles (Charles)
Pub.
Castor Advance 252
Stettler Independent 923

Willis, Roy Ward
Pub.; ed.
Son of Charles Lavalle Willis (q.v.)
Castor Advance 252
Stettler Independent 923

Wilson (of **Wilson** and **McCaffary**)
Pub.
Albertan and Alberta Tribune, Calgary 123

Wilson, Brian
Pub.
Grande Prairie Booster 588

Wilson, Charles J.
Pub.; ed.
Times, Medicine Hat 742

Wilson, David C.
Pub.
Grove Examiner, Spruce Grove 913

Wilson, G. R.
Pub.
Frontier Signal, Grande Prairie 585

Windross, Thomas Beswick
Pub.; journalist
b. England
Came to Canada to study for ministry; did church work in Newfoundland; ordained in Evangelistic Association of New England; journalist in Ottawa; 1928, came to Calgary; 1929, began work on *Edmonton Journal*; spent 20 yrs in Ottawa Press Gallery. (**EJ** Ap 3 1963)
Spotlight, Edmonton 426

Winfield, D. A. (Andy)
Ed.
Anthracite Chronicle, Canmore 233
Ryce Street Fysh Markete, Edmonton 457

Winser, H. E.
Bus. mgr
Alberta Oil Review, Calgary 150

Wodell, John E.
Pub.; ed.
b. Watford, Eng.
Moved to Hamilton, Ont. with parents; journeyman printer; reporter, mg. ed., *Hamilton Spectator*; 1913-45, with *Calgary Herald*. (**BRU**; p.29, 40,

137 **CH D** 31 1945)
Morning News, Lethbridge 695

Wolfe, Mabel De
See **De Wolfe**, Mabel

Wolfe, Wilburn Alurd De
See **De Wolfe**, Wilburn Alurd

Wolters, Paul
Ed.
Deutsch Canadier, Calgary 139

Wowmen's Christian Temperance Union
Calgary Observer 131

Wood, Charles Edward Dudley
Pub.; lawyer; insurance agent
b. Washington, D. C., O 16 1856; d. Estevan, Sask., Mr 1925.
Joined NWMP and came to Fort Macleod, 1880; called to bar, North West
Territories; 1896, practised law and was insurance agent, Fort Macleod;
1903, moved to Regina Sask.; Deputy Attorney-General, Northwest Terri-
tories, 1904-6; resumed law practice 1906. (**MOR**; **WW** 1912; **FORT**)
Fort Macleod Gazette 536
Lethbridge News 692

Wood, David G.
Pub.
Northern Times, Picture Butte 811

Woodhall, Chris
Ed.
Nisku News 782

Woodhall, Elizabeth (née Maddocks)
Ed.
Wife of Polycarp Spurgeon Woodall, Pres., Western Foundry and Metal Co.
Calgary Observer, 131

Woodhull, Benjamin Nelson
Pub.; printer
b. Lambeth, Ont., 1868; d. D 28 1931.
Family moved to Brandon, Man., 1882; became printer; published Hol-
land *Observer*, Man., La Fleche *Advocate*, Sask., Alameda *Dispatch*,
Sask. (**AC D** 31, 1931)
Carmangay Sun 247
Champion Chronicle 260
Lomond Press 710

Woods, James Hossack (Bert)
Prop.; pub.; journalist; businessman

b. Quebec, Que., Jl 12 1867; d. Calgary
Reporter, *Mail and Empire*, Toronto; news ed., Montreal and Toronto
Heralds; bus. mgr, Toronto *News*; 1900-7, partner, Woods-Norris
Advertising Agency, Toronto; held many offices; wrote short stories, pol-
itical and economic articles for Canadian newspapers. (**CAWW** 1938; **EJ**
My 21 1941)
Calgary Herald 115
Lethbridge Daily News (695)
Wainwright Star 1007
Weekly Herald, Calgary 113

Wootton, Ralph
Ed.
Canadian Miner, Calgary 170

Worker Press Committee
Worker, Calgary 176

Workers' Unity League of Canada. Miners' Section.
Western Miner, Calgary 170
Western Miner, Lethbridge 700

Workers' Unity League of Canada. Provincial Alberta District Executive
Committee.
Western Miner, Calgary 170

Worley, Dianne (Di)
Ed.; teacher
b. Edmonton
Spokesman, Edmonton 472

Worsley, James
Pub.
Bond of Brotherhood, Calgary 129

Worton, Charles Richard (Charlie)
Pub.
b. Tofield, ca. 1921; d. Calgary, Ap 19 1963.
Apprenticed to *Tofield Mercury*, owned by father, William Worton (q.v.);
came to Rimbey following naval service; 1958, moved to Calgary for
health reasons; employed *North Hills News* and *Calgary Herald* as linotype operator; active in community, church and newspaper organizations.
(**CWNA** v.46 no.845, My 1963)
Rimbey Record 855

Worton, Elsie (née Grinde)
Pub.
Wife of Charles Richard Worton (q.v.); 1958, moved to Calgary. (**CWNA** v.46
no.845, My 1963)
Rimbey Record 855

Worton, William
Pub.
d. 1951.
Barrhead News 51
Hay Lakes Times 610
Stony Plain Advertiser 930
Tofield Mercury 969

Woysh, Otto P.
Ed.
Deutsch Canadier, Calgary 139
Deutsch Canadier, Edmonton 355

Wright, Barbara
Pub.
Reporter, Stony Plain 937

Wright, Dorothy D.
Pub.
d. 1986.
Wife of L. Harry Wright (q.v.)
Ponoka News and Advertiser 818

Wright, Frank S.
Mgr; ed.
b. St. Albans, Eng.; d. Edmonton, N 9 1950.
Came to Canada, 1899; enlisted in NWMP and served 5 yrs in Yukon;
1921, came to Edmonton; ed., *Good Roads Magazine*; interested in civic
affairs; organized road expeditions and made canoe trips. (**EJ** N 13 1950)
Bear Lake Miner and Northern News, Edmonton 416
Town Topics, Edmonton 401

Wright, Grace A.
Ed.
Clarion, Canmore 229

Wright, H. J.
Pub.; ed.
Coleman Miner 288

Wright, L. Harry
Pub.
d. Oc 7 1967.
Ponoka News and Advertiser 818

Wright, R. L.
Pub.; ed.
Mannville Review 728

Wylie, A.
Pub.
Claresholm Review 266

Yakimchuk, Ron
Ed.
Poundmaker, Edmonton 476

Yaremko, Dmytro
Pub.; ed.
Emigrated from Ukraine; follower of Abbot Arseny (q.v.); assistant to Illya Kiriak (q.v.) on *Nova Hromada*. (**MARU** p.289)
Ostoraha, Wostok 1040
Postup, Mundare 771

York, W. O.
Prop.; physician
d. Edmonton, F 28 1953.
Native of Belfont, Ark.; 1906, came from Harrison, Ark., as doctor to Stettler settlers; 1907, homesteaded near Czar; CPR doctor; 1909, moved to Provost; opened drugstore; retired, 1946, to Edmonton. (**EJ** Mr 3 1953; **EAR** p. 50-51)
Provost Star 821

Young, Brigham Spence
Pub.
Came to Raymond from Salt Lake City 1904; Mayor for 3 terms; active in Mormon church; moved to Lethbridge. (**HIC** p.210, 697)
Chronicle, Raymond 824

Young, Duane
Pub.
b. Elk Point, Ja 16 1947
Lac La Biche Post 663

Young, H. S.
Ed.
Canmore Times 228

Young, Henry
Ed.
Organized Farmer, Edmonton 427

Young, John Jackson
Pub.; politican
b. Newark, Eng., 1868; d. Vancouver B. C., Je 26 1923.
Came to Canadian West 1884; engaged in journalism from 1885; successively edited Regina *Leader*, Moosomin *Spectator*, and *Calgary Daily Herald*; 1902-5, Mgr., Territorial Assembly; Pres., Western Canadian

Press Association and Alberta Press Association; moved to Spokane, Wash., to become orchardist; retired to Vancouver, B.C. (**CH** S 6 1958; **CAWW** 1912)
Calgary Herald 115
Calgary Weekly Herald 113

Young, Roger
Ed.
Record, Fort Saskatchewan 560

Young, Thomas S.
Pub.
d. White Rock, B. C., 1954.
Strathcona Weekly News, Edmonton 395

Yule, James B.
Prop.; ed.
Northern Tribune, Grande Prairie 586

Zantjer, Jacob
Pub.
Ryley Times 874
Sibbald Times 898
Temperance Advocate, Ryley 873
Victoria Farmer, Camrose 226

Zapisocki, R.
Ed.
Ukrainian Record, Edmonton 447

Zicha, Walter
Pub.; ed.
Noon News, Edmonton 492

Zook, W. H.
Pub.; clergyman
Baptist minister at Provost (**CPP** v.41 no.8, Ag 1932)
Hardisty World, 609
Wainwright Record 1008
Wainwright Star 1007

Zubick, J. J.
Pub.
Conservative, vehemently anti-Social Credit. (**IRV** p.108)
Rebel, Calgary 184

Chronological Index of Daily Newspapers

Dates	Place	Title	Item
1885-	Calgary	Calgary Herald	115
1886-1895	Calgary	Calgary Tribune	117
1888	Medicine Hat	Medicine Hat Daily Times	740
1895	Calgary	Alberta Tribune Daily Edition	122
1902-1980	Calgary	Calgary Albertan	127
1902	Calgary	Critic	128
1903-1923	Edmonton	Daily Edmonton Bulletin	342
1903-	Edmonton	Edmonton Journal	344
1906	Calgary	Sunset News Bulletin	1049
1906-1907	Lethbridge	Southern Alberta News	692
1907-1918	Calgary	Daily News	136
1907-1908	Edmonton	Evening Chronicle	350
1907-	Lethbridge	Lethbridge Herald	694
1909-1914	Edmonton	Edmonton Capital	356
1910-1951	Edmonton	Edmonton Bulletin	358
1910-1913	Lethbridge	Lethbridge Daily News	695
1910-	Medicine Hat	Medicine Hat News	743
1912-1913	Medicine Hat	Medicine Hat Call	747
1912-1916	Medicine Hat	Morning Times	746
1933-1934	Blairmore	Pass Daily Herald	81
1933-1936	Drumheller	Daily Bulletin	328
1937-1942	Drumheller	Daily Advertiser	331
1950	Redwater	Redwater News Daily Flashes	847
1960-	Red Deer	Advocate	834
1964-	Grande Prairie	Daily Herald Tribune	586
1974-	Fort McMurray	Fort McMurray Today	552
1977	Edmonton	Lunch News	483
1978-	Edmonton	Edmonton Sun	489
1979	Edmonton	Noon News	492
1979-	Lloydminster	Lloydminster Daily Times	706
1980-	Calgary	Calgary Sun	215

Chronological Index of Newspapers other than Dailies

Dates	Place	Title	Item
1880-1923	Edmonton	Bulletin (w. ed.)	334
1882-1907	Fort Macleod	Fort Macleod Gazette	536
1883-1932	Calgary	Calgary Herald (w. ed.)	113
1884-1885	Calgary	Nor'-Wester	114
1885-1895	Calgary	Calgary Tribune (w. ed.)	116
1885-1910	Lethbridge	Lethbridge News	692
1885-1894	Medicine Hat	Medicine Hat Times	739
1887	Banff	Hot Springs Record	34
1887	Calgary	Northwest Call	119
1887	Calgary	Pioneer Post	118
1888-1889	Banff	National Park Life	35
1890-1891	Calgary	Prairie Illustrated	120
1893	Banff	Banff Echoes	36
1893-1894	Edmonton	Times	335
1894	Calgary	Calgary Advance	121
1894-1913	Edmonton	South Edmonton News	336
1894	Fort Macleod	Sentinel	537
1894-1910	Medicine Hat	Medicine Hat News	741
1894	Red Deer	Red Deer Review	831
1895	Buffalo Lake	Buffalo Lake Wave	109
1895-1927	Calgary	Alberta Tribune Weekly Edition	123
1895-1896	Calgary	Tiser	124
1895	Lac Ste Anne	Echo de Ste-Anne	668.1
1896	Edmonton	Edmonton Herald	337
1896	Scott's Coulee	Outlaw	888
1897	Lac Ste Anne	Echo de Ste-Anne	668.2
1897-1898	Wetaskiwin	Free Lance	1018
1897-1902	Whitefish Lake	Indian Advocate	1035
1898	Calgary	Independent	125
1898-1925	Cardston	Cardston Record	240
1898-1900	Edmonton	Ouest canadien	338
1898-1901	Innisfail	Free Lance	641
1898-1899	Innisfail	Innisfail Standard	640
1898-1909	Lacombe	Advertiser and Central Alberta News	669
1898-1899	Red Deer	Alberta Independent	833
1898-1899	Red Deer	Red Deer Gazette	832
1899	Calgary	Albertan	126
1899-1900	Edmonton	Alberta Sun	340
1899-1902	Edmonton	Edmonton Post	339
1899-1909	Fort Macleod	Macleod Advance	538
1899	Fort Saskatchewan	Fort Saskatchewan News	554
1899	Lacombe	Lacombe Weekly Press	1079
1899	St. Albert	North American News	876
1900	Banff	National Park Gazette	37

Chronological Index of Newspapers other than Dailies

Dates	Place	Title	Item
1900-	Banff	Crag and Canyon	38
1900	Edmonton	Advertiser	341
1900-1905	Lac Ste. Anne	Auamewatikum Manito Sakihajan	1079
1900-1905	Lac Ste. Anne	Croix de Ste. Anne	1079
1900-1904	Olds	Olds Oracle	788
1900-	Pincher Creek	Rocky Mountain Echo	814
1900-	Ponoka	Ponoka Herald	817
1900	Wetaskiwin	North Star	1019
1900	Wetaskiwin	Wetaskiwin News	1020
1901-1903	Frank	Frank Sentinel	564
1901-1970	Okotoks	Okotoks Times	783
1901-	Red Deer	Alberta Echo	834
1901	Wetaskiwin	Wetaskiwin Breeze	1021
1901-1983	Wetaskiwin	Wetaskiwin Times	1022
1902-1903	High River	Eye Opener	623
1902-1908	Innisfail	Free Lance	642
1902	Pincher Creek	Round-up	815
1903	Blackfalds	Blackfalds Mercury	74
1903-1911	Blairmore	Times	76
1903	Calgary	Bee	130
1903-1904	Calgary	Bond of Brotherhood	129
1903	Carstairs	Carstairs Reporter	1055
1903	Didsbury	Didsbury Courier	316
1903-1974	Didsbury	Didsbury Pioneer	317
1903-1915	Edmonton	Alberta Herold	343
1903-1909	Fort Saskatchewan	Fort Saskatchewan Reporter	555
1903-1904	Gleichen	Gleichen Echo	574
1903-	Lacombe	Western Globe	670
1903-1904	Leduc	Leduc Record	687
1903-1912	Medicine Hat	Times	742
1903-	Nanton	Nanton News	780
1903-1904	Penhold	Penhold Reporter	809
1903	Poplar Lake	Saturday Blade	820
1903-1922	Raymond	Chronicle	824
1904-1905	Calgary	Calgary Observer	131
1904-1923	Calgary	Eye Opener	132
1904-1916	Claresholm	Claresholm Review	266
1904-1911	Edmonton	Strathcona Chronicle	345
1904-1905	Frank	Drill	565
1904-1905	High River	Chinook	624
1904-1906	Leduc	Enterprise	688
1904-	Olds	Olds Gazette	789
1904-1905	Stavely	Stavely Gazette	919
1904	Wetaskiwin	Northwest Chronicle	1023

Chronological Index of Newspapers other than Dailies

Dates	Place	Title	Item
1904-1910	Wetaskiwin	Post	1024
1905-1906	Bowden	Bowden Reporter	94
1905-1923	Carstairs	Carstairs Journal	249
1905-1916	Edmonton	Courrier de l'Ouest	347
1905-1912	Edmonton	Saturday News	348
1905-1919	Edmonton	Town Topics	346
1905-1909	Frank	Frank Paper	566
1905	Gleichen	Gleichen Chronicle	575
1905	Granum	Leavings Star	589
1905-	High River	High River Times	625
1905-1950	Lethbridge	Lethbridge Herald	693
1905-	Lloydminster	Lloydminster Times	703
1905-1926	Red Deer	News	835
1906	Banff	Climber	39
1906	Calgary	Alberta Clarion	1048
1906-1907	Calgary	Chinook	133
1906	Calgary	Prairie	134
1906-1907	Calgary	Town Topics	135
1906-1909	Camrose	Camrose Mail	224
1906	Edmonton	Edmonton Free Press	1058
1906-	Innisfail	Province	643
1906-1915	Magrath	Magrath Pioneer	715
1906-	Stettler	Stettler Independent	923
1906-	Vegreville	Vegreville Observer	987
1906-1910	Vermilion	Vermilion Signal	991
1907	Bawlf	Bawlf Sun	63
1907-1942	Crossfield	Chronicle	296
1907-1930	Daysland	Daysland Press	302
1907-1909	Edmonton	Great West	349
1907-1956	Gleichen	Gleichen Call	576
1907	Islay	Wideawake	652
1907	Lamont	Lamont Weekly News	678
1907-	Leduc	Representative	689
1907-1909	Mannville	Mannville Telegram	723
1907-1908	Sedgewick	Sedgewick Eagle	889
1907-1910	Taber	Taber Free Press	952
1907-1917	Tofield	Tofield Standard	967
1908-1911	Airdrie	Airdrie News	5
1908	Athabasca	Northern Light	25
1908-1930	Bawlf	Bawlf Sun	64
1908	Calgary	Western Homestead	137
1908-	Camrose	Camrose Canadian	225
1908-1911	Coleman	Coleman Miner	288
1908	Crossfield	North American Collector	297

Chronological Index of Newspapers other than Dailies

Dates	Place	Title	Item
1908-1913	Edmonton	Alberta Homestead	353
1908-1910	Edmonton	Canadian Field	354
1908	Edmonton	Clarion of Alberta	351
1908-1909	Edmonton	Deutsch-Canadier	355
1908-1910	Edmonton	Kanadiiskaia Niva	354
1908-1913	Edmonton	West-Land	352
1908-1909	Fort Macleod	Weekly Chronicle	539
1908	Granum	Granum Times	590
1908-1909	Grassy Lake	Grassy Lake News	596
1908-1909	Hardisty	Hardisty Enterprise	607
1908-1913	Lethbridge	Southern Alberta Labor Bulletin	696
1908-1914	Okotoks	Okotoks Advance	784
1908-1911	Pincher City	Pincher City News	813
1908-	Sedgewick	Sedgewick Sentinel	890
1908-1949	Wainwright	Wainwright Star	1007
1909-1914	Acme	Acme News	1
1909-1953	Alix	Alix Free Press	14
1909-1916	Athabasca	Northern News	26
1909	Barons	Barons Beacon	1046
1909-1946	Blairmore	Blairmore Enterprise	77
1909-1912	Bowden	Bowden News	95
1909	Calgary	Calgarian	138
1909-1910	Calgary	Calgary Optimist	141
1909-1914	Calgary	Deutsch-Canadier	139
1909-1912	Calgary	Deutsch-Canadischer Farmer	140
1909-1912	Calgary	German-Canadian Farmer	140
1909-	Castor	Castor Advance	252
1909-1913	Cayley	Cayley Hustler	253
1909-1927	Cochrane	Cochrane Advocate	279
1909-1910	Cowley	Cowley Chronicle	294
1909-1913	Fort Macleod	Macleod Advertiser	540
1909-1910	Granum	Granum Press	591
1909-1911	Innisfail	Innisfail Independent	644
1909-1910	Millet	Packet	756
1909-1914	Morinville	Progrès	764
1909-1916	Ryley	Ryley Times	872
1909-1914	Stavely	Stavely Standard	920
1909-1914	Stavely	Stavely Standard	920
1909-1911	Stettler	Citizen	925
1909-1911	Stettler	Stettler Gazette	924
1909-1910	Stony Plain	Gazette	929
1909-1911	Stony Plain	Stony Plain Advertiser	930
1909-	Strathmore	Strathmore and Bow Valley Standard	940
1909-	Vermilion	Standard	992

Chronological Index of Newspapers other than Dailies

Dates	Place	Title	Item
1910-1914	Bassano	Bassano News	57
1910-1918	Bellevue	Bellevue Times	69
1910-1911	Blairmore	Slovak Word	78
1910-1911	Blairmore	Slovenske Slovo	78
1910-1936	Bow Island	Bow Island Review	90
1910-	Brooks	Brooks Banner	105
1910	Brooks	Brooks Bulletin	104
1910-1911	Burdett	Burdett Tribune	110
1910-1937	Carmangay	Carmangay Sun	247
1910-1913	Edmonton	Alberta Deutsche Zeitung	360
1910-1913	Edmonton	Alberta German Newspaper	360
1910-1921	Edmonton	Canadai Magyar Farmer	357
1910-1921	Edmonton	Canadian Hungarian Farmer	357
1910-	Edmonton	Gateway	359
1910	Edson	Edson Record	502
1910	Entwistle	Pembina Outlook & Entwistle News	519
1910-1911	Fort Saskatchewan	Weekly Chronicle	556
1910-1915	Frank	Frank Vindicator	567
1910-1912	Granum	Granum News	592
1910-1911	Grassy Lake	Grassy Lake Pilot	598
1910	Grassy Lake	Outlaw	597
1910-1930	Hardisty	Hardisty Mail	608
1910-1943	Holden	Holden Herald	633
1910-1922	Mannville	Mannville Empire	724
1910-	Medicine Hat	Medicine Hat Daily News	743
1910-1955	Medicine Hat	Medicine Hat News (w. ed.)	744
1910	Peace River	Peace River Pilot	800
1910-1917	Provost	Provost Star	821
1910-1940	Redcliff	Redcliff Review	843
1910-1917	Rocky Mountain House	Rocky Mountain House Echo	856
1910	Stirling	New Stirling Star	927
1910-1929	Strome	Strome Despatch	941
1910	Taber	Taber Advertiser	953
1910-1911	Viking	Viking Gazette	999
1910-1916	Warner	Warner Record	1010
1910-1911	Wetaskiwin	Northern Albertan	1025
1911-1918	Alderson	Carlstadt Progress	12
1911	Alderson	Times-Reporter	11
1911-1912	Barons	Barons Enterprise	48
1911-1913	Bashaw	Bashaw Record	55
1911-1915	Bruce	Bruce News	106
1911-1918	Calgary	Provincial Standard	142
1911-1913	Carbon	Carbon Reporter	235
1911-	Coronation	Coronation Review	293

Chronological Index of Newspapers other than Dailies

Dates	Place	Title	Item
1911	Coutts	Coutts - Sweetgrass International Herald	1056
1911-1913	Edmonton	Financial News	361
1911-1912	Edmonton	Hova Hromada	363
1911-1912	Edmonton	New Society	363
1911	Edmonton	Ouest canadien	362
1911-1917	Edson	Edson Leader	503
1911-1912	Fort Macleod	Buzzer, Mainly About Town	541
1911	Fort Saskatchewan	Fort Saskatchewan Herald	557
1911-1912	Fort Saskatchewan	Fort Saskatchewan Recorder	558
1911	Gadsby	Gadsby Gazette	568
1911-1917	Grassy Lake	Grassy Lake Gazette	599
1911	Irricana	Irricana Review	649
1911-1930	Killam	Killam News	659
1911	Lakeview	Lakeview Wave	675
1911	Langdon	Langdon Advance	685
1911-1912	Langdon	Langdon Leader	686
1911-1929	Mirror	Mirror Journal	761
1911	Mirror	Reflector	760
1911	Penhold	Penhold Journal	810
1911-1913	Stony Plain	Stony Plain Advertiser	931
1911-	Taber	Taber Times	954
1911	Three Hills	Three Hills Herald	963
1911-1913	Trochu	Trochu Times	972
1911-1977	Trochu	Trochu Tribune	973
1911-1941	Wetaskiwin	Free Press	1026
1911-1914	Wetaskiwin	Journal	1027
1911-1912	Winnifred	Winnifred Record	1039
1912-1913	Calgary	Alberta Federationist	144
1912-1913	Calgary	Press	143
1912	Carbon	News	236
1912	Chauvin	Advance	261
1912-1913	Chauvin	Chauvin Gazette	262
1912-1918	Coleman	Coleman Bulletin	289
1912-	Consort	Consort Enterprise	292
1912-1922	Delburne	Delburne Progress	305
1912-1919	Edmonton	Canadian	364
1912-1919	Edmonton	Kanadyiets	364
1912-1913	Edmonton	Mirror	365
1912-1913	Entwistle	Entwistle Enterprise	520
1912-1921	Erskine	Erskine Review	521
1912-1916	Fort Macleod	Macleod Spectator	542
1912-1915	Grouard	Grouard News	604
1912-	Hanna	Hanna Herald	605

Chronological Index of Newspapers other than Dailies

Dates	Place	Title	Item
1912-1913	Irvine	Irvine Index	651
1912-1930	Lougheed	Lougheed Express	711
1912	Medicine Hat	Labor Day Bulletin	745
1912-1913	Medicine Hat	Medicine Hat Call	747
1912-1916	Medicine Hat	Morning Times	746
1912-1918	Munson	Munson Mail	775
1912-1914	St. Albert	Etoile de St. Albert	878
1912-1914	St. Albert	St. Albert News	877
1912-1917	Stony Plain	Rural Weekly News and Rube's Farm Fun	932
1912-1914	Vulcan	Vulcan Review	1004
1912-1913	Wetaskiwin	New Age	1028
1912	Wostok	Ostoroha	1040
1913-1915	Athabasca	Athabasca Times	27
1913-1936	Bassano	Bassano Mail	58
1913-1914	Bow City	Bow City Star	1047
1913-1914	Calgary	Black Diamond Press	145
1913-1914	Calgary	Natural Gas and Oil Record	147
1913-1914	Calgary	Scottish Standard	146
1913-1940	Drumheller	Drumheller Review	325
1913-1914	Edmonton	Alberta Illustrated News	372
1913-1919	Edmonton	Edmonton News	371
1913	Edmonton	Great West Saturday Night Advance	370
1913-1015	Edmonton	Moukari	366
1913-1915	Edmonton	News	367
1913-1915	Edmonton	Novyny	367
1913-1916	Edmonton	Rural Northwest & Edmonton Weekly Journal	368
1913-1916	Edmonton	Russian Voice	369
1913-1916	Edmonton	Russkyi Golos	369
1913-1914	Edson	Western Star	504
1913-1936	Empress	Empress Express	517
1913-1922	Fort Saskatchewan	Conservator	559
1913-1939	Grande Prairie	Grande Prairie Herald	584
1913	Hanna	Hanna Leader	606
1913-1916	Lacombe	Lacombe Guardian	671
1913-1914	Medicine Hat	Alberta Farmer	748
1913	Redcliff	Redcliff Journal	844
1913-1914	Stony Plain	Stony Plain News	933
1913-1914	Sylvan Lake	Times	948
1913-1979	Viking	Viking News	1000
1913-	Vulcan	Vulcan Advocate	1005
1913-1936	Youngstown	Plaindealer	1041
1914-1973	Acme	Acme Sentinel	3

Chronological Index of Newspapers other than Dailies

Dates	Place	Title	Item
1914	Acme	Telegram-Tribune	2
1914	Alderson	Farmers Tribune	13
1914-1918	Banff	Rocky Mountain Courier	40
1914	Calgary	Canadian Western Jewish Times	149
1914	Calgary	Sunday Sun	148
1914	Cayley	Cayley Advertiser	254
1914-1918	Cereal	Acadia Review	255
1914	Champion	Champion Spokesman	257
1914-1948	Chauvin	Chauvin Chronicle	263
1914-1945	Chinook	Chinook Advance	264
1914-1928	Claresholm	Claresholm Advertiser	264
1914-1918	Clive	Clive News-Record	270
1914	Edmonton	Beverly Advertiser	373
1914-1915	Edmonton	Progrès albertain	374
1914-1916	Grande Prairie	Frontier Signal	585
1914	Granum	Granum Advertiser	593
1914-1916	Lamont	Lamont Tribune	679
1914-1919	Lethbridge	Lethbridge Telegram	697
1914	Lloydminster	Lloydminster Review	704
1914-1915	Munson	Munson Times	776
1914	Okotoks	Okotoks Observer	785
1914-1935	Oyen	Oyen News	795
1914-1939	Peace River	Peace River Record	802
1914	Rocky Mountain House	Mountainee	857
1914	Stavely	Stavely Advertiser	921
1914-1915	Wabamun	Mirror	1006
1914-?	Wetaskiwin	Wetaskiwin Alberta Tribunen	1029
1914-1917	Whitecourt	News-Record	1031
1915-	Bashaw	Bashaw Star	56
1915-1916	Calgary	Alberta Oil Review	150
1915-1918	Calgary	Fairplay	1050
1915-1916	Donalda	Donalda Free Lance	319
1915-1918	Edmonton	Russian Life	375
1915	Edmonton	Western Weekly	376
1915	Huxley	Huxley New Era	637
1915-1922	Monitor	Monitor News	763
1915-1917	Mundare	Postup	771
1915-1917	Mundare	Progress	771
1915-1916	Stony Plain	Mirror	934
1915-	Three Hills	Three Hills Capital	965
1915-	Three Hills	Three Hills Review	964
1916-	Alliance	Alliance Times	16
1916-1919	Athabasca	Athabasca Herald	28
1916-1923	Big Valley	Big Valley News	70

Chronological Index of Newspapers other than Dailies

Dates	Place	Title	Item
1916-1919	Calgary	Nutcracker	152
1916	Calgary	Sentinel and Military News	151
1916-1918	Clairmont	Clairmont Independent	265
1916-1918	Delia	Hand Hills Echo	311
1916-1920	Forestburg	Forestburg Advance	530
1916-1920	Fort Macleod	Macleod News	543
1916-1919	Hughenden	Hughenden News	635
1916-1926	Lomond	Lomond Press	708
1916-1917	Spirit River	Spirit River Times	1086
1916-1965	Stavely	Stavely Advertiser	922
1917-1918	Brant	Brant Weekly	102
1917-1918	Burdett	Burdett Times	111
1917-1981	Calgary	Market Examiner	153
1917-1919	Champion	Champion Weekly	258
1917-1918	Drumheller	Drumheller Standard	326
1917-1922	Edmonton	News	379
1917-1922	Edmonton	Novyny	379
1917-1918	Edmonton	Statesman for Albertans	377
1917-1929	Edmonton	Union	378
1917	Edson	Edson Herald	505
1917-1918	Enchant	Enchant Weekly	518
1917-1918	Gadsby	Gadsby Observer	569
1917-1918	Galahad	Galahad Mail	571
1917-1919	Granum	Granum News	594
1917-1969	Irma	Irma Times	647
1917-1918	Lake Saskatoon	Lake Saskatoon Journal	674
1917-1918	Lomond	Lomond Weekly	709
1917-1919	Manyberries	Manyberries Enterprise	732
1917-1918	Okotoks	Okotoks Weekly	786
1917-1922	Peace River	Peace River Standard & Farmer's Gazette	801
1917-	Provost	Provost News	822
1917-1918	Retlaw	Retlaw Weekly	852
1917-1918	Rockyford	Rockyford (Alta.) Weekly	863
1917-1921	Spirit River	Spirit River Echo	909
1917-1918	Tofield	Tofield Advertiser	968
1917-1918	Travers	Travers Weekly	971
1918-1922	Banff	Banff Advocate	41
1918-	Barons	Barons Weekly	49
1918-1919	Calgary	Okotoks Weekly	786
1918-1919	Calgary	Army and Navy News and Universal Weekly	156

Chronological Index of Newspapers other than Dailies

Dates	Place	Title	Item
1918-1919	Calgary	Canadian Nation	154
1918-	Drumheller	Drumheller Mail	327
1918	Edmonton	Great West Saturday Night	380
1918	Edson	Edson News	506
1918-1933	Elnora	Elnora Advance	516
1918-1922	Lamont	Gazette	680
1918-1925	Lethbridge	Canadian Advocate	698
1918-1920	Rocky Mountain House	Rocky Mountain House Capital	858
1918-1922	Rockyford	Rockyford Reporter	864
1918	Sedgewick	Sedgewick Review	891
1918-1952	Tofield	Tofield Mercury	969
1918-1923	Vermilion	Link	993
1919	Altario	Arrow	18
1919-1921	Barons	Barons Globe	50
1919	Calgary	Calgary Strike Bulletin	157
1919-1920	Calgary	Searchlight	159
1919-1920	Calgary	Western Independent	158
1919-1943	Champion	Champion Chronicle	260
1919-1920	Champion	Champion News	259
1919-1921	Clive	Clive Review	271
1919-1960	Delia	Delia Times	312
1919-1920	Edmonton	Edmonton Free Press	384
1919	Edmonton	Edmonton Strike Bulletin	385
1919	Edmonton	One Big Union Bulletin	382
1919	Edmonton	Soviet	381
1919-1920	Edmonton	Statesman	383
1919-1962	Hughenden	Ribstone Record	636
1919-1923	Medicine Hat	Western Union Printer	749
1919-1920	Munson	Munson News	777
1919	Rimbey	Rimbey Pioneer	853
1919-1924	Ryley	Ryley Times	873
1919-1920	Stony Plain	Stony Plain Herald	935
1919-	Westlock	Westlock Witness	1015
1920	Alliance	Argus	17
1920-1921	Athabasca	Athabasca Herald	29
1920	Bowden	Bowden Recorder	96
1920-1922	Carbon	Carbon News	237
1920-1947	Cereal	Cereal Recorder	256
1920-1951	Czar	Czar Clipper	301
1920-1921	Donalda	Donalda Recorder	320
1920-1952	Edmonton	Alberta Labor News	386
1920	Edson	Edson Enterprise	507
1920-1922	Forestburg	Forestburg Home News	531
1920-1930	Fort Macleod	Macleod Times	544

Chronological Index of Newspapers other than Dailies

Dates	Place	Title	Item
1920-1922	Gadsby	Gadsby Recorder	570
1920-1921	Granum	Advertiser	595
1920-1930	Hoadley	North Country News	629
1920-1921	Horburg	Weekly News	1076
1920-1922	Huxley	Huxley Recorder	638
1920	Irricana	Irricana Recorder	650
1920-1921	Morrin	Morrin District News	770
1920-1922	Morrin	Morrin Recorder	769
1920-1921	Munson	District News	778
1920-1925	Rosebud Creek	Rosebud Recorder	868
1920	Sibbald	Sibbald Recorder	897
1920-1922	Sibbald	Sibbald Times	898
1920-1922	St. Paul	St. Paul Star	882
1920-1921	Standard	Standard Enterprize	916
1920-1938	Stony Plain	Stony Plain Sun	936
1920-1921	Swalwell	Swalwell Recorder	1087
1921-1926	Airdrie	Airdrie Recorder	6
1921-1923	Altario	Recorder	19
1921-1951	Amisk	Amisk Advocate	20
1921	Blackie	Blackie Recorder	75
1921-1923	Carseland	Carseland Recorder	248
1921-1924	Cluny	Cluny Recorder	272
1921-1974	Coleman	Coleman Journal	290
1921-1922	Craigmyle	Craigmyle Gazette	295
1921-1927	Donalda	Donalda Review	321
1921	Edmonton	Farmers' Word	387
1921	Edmonton	Farmerske Slovo	387
1921	Edmonton	Wedge	389
1921-1965	Edmonton	Western Catholic	388
1921-1922	Edmonton	Western Illustrated News	390
1921-1922	Edson	District Call	508
1921-1922	Rimbey	Rimbey Advance	854
1921-1923	Rocky Mountain House	Gazette	859
1921-1923	Rockyford	Rockyford Budget	865
1921-1926	Rowley	Rowley Recorder	869
1921-1926	Standard	Standard Gazette	917
1922	Banff	Rocky Mountain Courier	42
1922-1924	Beiseker	Recorder	67
1922-1923	Brule	B.D. Weekly	108
1922-?	Calgary	Liberty	161
1922-1936	Calgary	U.F.A.	160
1922-1924	Camrose	Victoria Farmer	226
1922-1960	Carbon	Carbon Chronicle	238
1922-1927	Coaldale	Coaldale Times	275

Chronological Index of Newspapers other than Dailies

Dates	Place	Title	Item
1922-1929	Edmonton	Nash Postup	393
1922-1923	Edmonton	News Advertiser	392
1922-1929	Edmonton	Our Progress	393
1922	Edmonton	Sports Review	391
1922-1923	Edson	Edson Headlight	509
1922-1924	Erskine	Erskine Times	522
1922-	Fort Saskatchewan	Record	560
1922-1941	Lamont	Tribune	681
1922-1923	Lethbridge	Square Shooter	699
1922	Lousana	Lousana Observer	713
1922-1923	Magrath	Magrath Times	716
1922-1926	Sylvan Lake	Sylvan Lake World	949
1922-1924	Three Hills	Three Hills News	966
1923-1924	Big Valley	Times	71
1923-1928	Calgary	Westerner	1051
1923-1924	Bowden	Bowden Times	97
1923-1924	Edmonton	East-Ender	397
1923-1932	Edmonton	Edmonton Weekly Journal	396
1923	Edmonton	Glow Worm	398
1923-1924	Edmonton	International Labor News	394
1923-1954	Edmonton	Strathcona Booster	395
1923-1924	Fairview	Northern Review	524
1923-1929	Mannville	Mannville News	725
1923-1949	Raymond	Raymond Recorder	825
1923-	Rocky Mountain House	Mountaineer	860
1924-1927	Arrowwood	Bow River News	1045
1924-1934	Big Valley	Journal	72
1924-1985	Carstairs	Carstairs News	250
1924-1926	Delburne	Delburne News	306
1924	Edson	Edson Atom	510
1924-1952	Hardisty	Hardisty World	609
1924-1925	Ryley	Ryley Times	874
1925-1927	Calgary	Alberta Sun	162
1925-1964	Cardston	Cardston News	241
1925	Edmonton	Western News	399
1925-1931	Hay Lakes	Hay Lakes Times	610
1925-1950	Lougheed	Lougheed Journal	712
1925-1927	Mirror	Mirror Mail	762
1925	Ryley	Temperance Advocate	875
1925-	St. Paul	St. Paul Tribune	883
1926-1929	Calgary	Alberta Oil Examiner	163
1926-	Claresholm	Claresholm Local Press	268
1926-1930	Edmonton	Druh Naroda	400
1926-1930	Edmonton	People's Friend	400

Chronological Index of Newspapers other than Dailies

Dates	Place	Title	Item
1926-1928	Edmonton	Town Topics	401
1927-1931	Barrhead	Barrhead News	51
1927-1928	Delburne	Delburne Observer	307
1927-1933	Forestburg	Forestburg Herald	532
1927-1928	Jasper	Jasper Signal	654
1928-1986	Athabasca	Athabasca Echo	30
1928	Banff	Banff Mercury	43
1928-1932	Calgary	Western Farmer	164
1928-1929	Coalhurst	Coalhurst News	278
1928	Delburne	Delburne Independent	308
1928-1931	Edmonton	Herold	403
1928-1967	Edmonton	Survivance	404
1928-	Edmonton	Western News	402
1928-	Edmonton	Zakhidni Visti	402
1928-1960	Edson	Edson-Jasper Signal	511
1928	Lomond	Lomond Press	710
1929-1951	Banff	Banff News	44
1929-1931	Calgary	Oil and Financial Review	167
1929-1930	Calgary	West-Ender	166
1929-1958	Calgary	Western Examiner	165
1929	Edmonton	New Country	406
1929	Edmonton	Novyi Krai	406
1929	Edmonton	Pravda Naroda	407
1929	Edmonton	Truth of the People	407
1929-?	Edmonton	Union Laborer	405
1929-1933	Fairview	Northern Review	525
1929-1933	Magrath	Magrath News	717
1929-1943	Red Deer	Optimist	836
1929-1931	Turner Valley	Valley Observer	975
1930-	Blairmore	Pass Herald	79
1930-1931	Calgary	Alberta Mercury	168
1930	Calgary	Bridgeland and Riverside Echo	1052
1930-1934	Calgary	Danish Review	169
1930-1934	Calgary	Danskeren	169
1930-1933	Calgary	Western Miner	170
1930-1931	Daysland	Daysland Commercial	303
1930-1961	Edmonton	Church and Home	408
1930-1931	Edmonton	Deutsche Arbeiter Zeitung	411
1930-1931	Edmonton	German Labor News	411
1930-1961	Edmonton	Kirken og Hjemmet	408
1930-1933	Edmonton	New Pathway	410
1930-1933	Edmonton	Novyi Shliakh	410
1930	Edmonton	Renaissance	409
1930	Edmonton	Vidrodzhennia	409

Chronological Index of Newspapers other than Dailies

Dates	Place	Title	Item
1930-1931	Lethbridge	Western Miner	700
1930-	Rimbey	Rimbey Record	855
1930-1934	Waskatenau	Witness	1011
1931	Andrew	Weekly Advance	21
1931-1936	Arrowwood	Bow Valley Resource	24
1931	Calgary	Free Lance	171
1931-1932	Calgary	Unemployed Bulletin	1053
1931-1937	Canmore	Canmore Times	228
1931	Edmonton	Alberta Herold	412
1931-	Edmonton	Alberta Herald	412
1931-	Fort Macleod	Macleod Gazette	545
1931-1935	Mayerthorpe	Mayerthorpe Times	733
1932-	Barrhead	Barrhead Leader	52
1932-1934	Blairmore	Hlas Naroda	80
1932-1934	Blairmore	Voice of the Nation	80
1932-1935	Burdett	Burdett Review	112
1932-1933	Calgary	Calgary Home News	172
1932-1933	Calgary	Spokesman	173
1932	Cold Lake	Cold Lake Herald	284
1932-1934	Edmonton	Farmers' Voice	415
1932-1934	Edmonton	Farmerskyi Holos	415
1932-?	Edmonton	Nor-East Ad-Viser	413
1932-1933	Edmonton	Spectator	414
1932-	Grande Prairie	Northern Tribune	586
1932-1939	Peace River	Northern Gazette	803
1932-1933	Sylvan Lake	Advertiser	950
1933-1935	Edmonton	Bear Lake Miner	416
1933-1934	Edmonton	Ukrainian Gazette	417
1933-1934	Edmonton	Ukrainska Gazeta	417
1933-1934	Veteran	Veteran Post	997
1933-1934	Wainwright	Wainwright Commercial	1008
1934-1938	Calgary	Alberta Social Credit Chronicle	175
1934-1936	Calgary	Political World	174
1934-1936	Calgary	Social Justice Advocate	176
1934-194?	Edmonton	Survivance des Jeunes	418
1934-1935	Irma	Irma Independent	648
1934-1946	Mannville	Mannville Mirror	726
1934-1935	St. Paul	St. Paul Canadian	884
1934-1935	Waskatenau	Northern Post	1012
1935-1946	Andrew	District Press	22
1935-1938	Bon Accord	Bon Accord Herald	85
1935-1943	Bonnyville	Bonnyville Nouvelle	86
1935	Calgary	Calgary Typo News	177
1935-1939	Edmonton	Nor'West Miner	416

Chronological Index of Newspapers other than Dailies

Dates	Place	Title	Item
1935-1936	Edmonton	Social Credit Gazette	420
1935-1944	Edmonton	Today and Tomorrow	421
1935	Edmonton	Weekly Tribune	419
1935-1936	Mannville	Manville [sic] Reporter	727
1935-1944	Olds	Olds News	790
1935-	Sylvan Lake	Sylvan Lake News	951
1936-1940	Calgary	Sports Guide	180
1936-1938	Calgary	Western Canada Enquirer	179
1936-1954	Calgary	Western Farm Leader	181
1936	Calgary	Worker	178
1936-1967	Delburne	Delburne Times	309
1936-1941	Drumheller	Plaindealer	330
1936	Drumheller	Weekly Advertiser	329
1936-193?	Edmonton	Kupets	422
1936-193?	Edmonton	Merchant	422
1936-1969	Lac Ste Anne County	Lac Ste Anne Chronicle	665
1936-1937	Myrnam	Myrnam News	779
1937-1945	Bassano	Bassano Recorder	59
1937-1946	Black Diamond	Flare	73
1937-1938	Bowden	Bowden Booster	98
1937-?	Calgary	Commonsense	183
1937-1939	Calgary	Rebel	184
1937	Calgary	Western Sentinel	182
1937-1942	Drumheller	Daily Advertiser	331
1937-1939	Edmonton	Alberta Herold	424
1937-1940	Edmonton	Suspilnyi	423
1937-1960	Smoky Lake	Holos Pravdy	904
1937-1960	Smoky Lake	Voice of Truth	904
1937-1961	Thorsby	Western Messenger	961
1937-1940	Waskatenau	Booster	1013
1937	Willingdon	Willingdon Times	1090
1938	Calgary	Alberta Democrat	1054
1938-1949	Mundare	Light	772
1938-1949	Mundare	Svitlo	772
1938-1983	Wetaskiwin	News Advertiser	1030
1939	Edmonton	Edmonton Sports Record	425
1939-1940	Fort Macleod	Macleod Argus	546
1939-1940	Fort McMurray	Northwest Review	1070
1939-1941	Mayerthorpe	Mayerthorpe Merchant	734
1939-1940	Medicine Hat	Medicine Hat Advertiser	750
1939-1940	Oyen	Telegram	796
1939-	Peace River	Peace River Record-Gazette	804
1939-1954	Winfield	Winfield Gazette	1038
1940	Blairmore	Slovak Word	82

Chronological Index of Newspapers other than Dailies

Dates	Place	Title	Item
1940	Blairmore	Slovenske Slovo	82
1940-1954	Edmonton	Spotlight	426
1940-	Fairview	Fairview Post	526
1940-1941	Picture Butte	Northern Times	811
1941-1971	Edmonton	A.F.U. Bulletin	427
1941	Fort McMurray	Valhalla Star	1071
1941-1948	Lac La Biche	Northern Herald	661
1941-1949	Magrath	Garden City Times	718
1941-1958	Picture Butte	Picture Butte Progress	812
1942	Calgary	Calgary Sports Review	185
1943-1972	Cochrane	Old Timer	280
1943-1948	Crossfield	Crossfield Chronicle	298
1944-1949	Edmonton	Canadian Social Crediter	428
1944-1968	Holden	Holden Herald	634
1945-1952	Calgary	Call	186
1945-1956	High Prairie	Northern Echo	617
1945	High Prairie	Northland Calling	616
1945-1946	Medicine Hat	Brüke	751
1945-1946	Red Deer	Red Deer News	1084
1945	St. Paul	Independent Reformer	885
1945-	Stony Plain	Stony Plain Reporter	937
1945-1953	Wimborne	Valley News	1037
1946-1947	Bassano	Bassano Star	60
1946-1951	Blairmore	Blairmore Graphic	83
1946-1951	Calgary	Calgary Citizen	187
1946-1949	Hay Lakes	Hay Lakes Review	611
1946-1952	Killam	Killam News	660
1946-1955	Lacombe	Lacombe Municipal News	1080
1946-1951	Lamont	Lamont Banner	682
1946-1949	Millet	Millet Bulletin	757
1946-1948	Red Deer	Civvy Street	838
1946-1977	Red Deer	Red Deer Ad-Viser	837
1947-1949	Bawlf	Bawlf Banner	65
1947-1968	Bonnyville	Bonnyville Tribune	87
1947-1948	Calgary	Calgary News	188
1947-1953	Daysland	Daysland Sun	304
1947-1948	Edmonton	News-Advertiser	429
1947-1949	Forestburg	Forestburg Free Press	533
1947-1949	Galahad	Galahad Guardian	572
1947-1949	Heisler	Heisler Herald	612
1947-1948	Jasper	Totem Pole	655
1947-1949	Sangudo	Sangudo Star	886
1947-1950	Strome	Strome Star	942
1947-1956	Turner Valley	Oilfields Flare	976

Chronological Index of Newspapers other than Dailies

Dates	Place	Title	Item
1948-1951	Calgary	Bowness Bulletin	1055
1948	Crossfield	Crossfield Chronicle	299
1948-1949	Edmonton	Brivais Latvietis	430
1948-1949	Edmonton	Free Latvian	430
1948-1969	Lac La Biche	Lac La Biche Herald	662
1948-1953	Legal	Legal Record	691
1948-1951	Magrath	Magrath Mirror	719
1948-1949	Mannville	Mannville Review	728
1948-1962	Milk River	Milk River Review	753
1948-1961	Morinville	Morinville Journal	765
1948-1949	New Sarepta	New Sarepta New Era	781
1948-1949	Rosalind	Rosalind Reporter	867
1948-1969	Smoky Lake	Smoky Lake Gazette	905
1949-1953	Beiseker	Beiseker Times	68
1949-1969	Boyle	Boyle Beacon	100
1949-1953	Crossfield	Crossfield Chronicle	300
1949-1957	Devon	Devonian	314
1949-	Eckville	Eckville Examiner	333
1949-1951	Edmonton	Jasper Place Review	431
1949-1969	Edmonton	South Edmonton Sun	432
1949-1952	Fort McMurray	McMurray Northlander	547
1949-1954	Manning	Battle River Herald	721
1949-1965	Mannville	Mannville Mirror	729
1949-1953	Onoway	Onoway Westerner	793
1949-	Ponoka	Ponoka News and Advertiser	818
1949-1952	Redwater	Redwater Review	845
1949-1957	Rockyford	Rockyford Review	866
1949-1954	Sexsmith	Sexsmith Sentinel	892
1949-1953	St. Albert	St. Albert Gazette	879
1949-1969	Thorhild	Thorhild Tribune	959
1949-	Wainwright	Star-Chronicle	1009
1949-1962	Waskatenau	Waskatenau World	1014
1949-1950	Wildwood	Plaindealer	1089
1950-1952	Clyde	Clyde Bulletin	273
1950-	Coaldale	Coaldale Flyer	276
1950	Edmonton	Banner	437
1950-	Edmonton	Canadian Social Crediter	434
1950-1951	Edmonton	Clarion	433
1950-1951	Edmonton	Dzvin	433
1950-1964	Edmonton	Jasper Place Citizen	436
1950-1951	Edmonton	North Edmonton Star	435
1950	Hoadley	North Country Times	630
1950-1953	Innisfree	Innisfree Banner	646
1950-1951	Mayerthorpe	Mayerthorpe Free Press	735

Chronological Index of Newspapers other than Dailies

Dates	Place	Title	Item
1950-1951	Radway	Radway Star	823
1950-1956	Raymond	New Raymond Recorder	826
1950-1951	Redwater	Redwater News	846
1950	Redwater	Redwater News Daily Flashes	847
1950-1955	Starland M.D.	Starland Reporter	918
1950-1969	Two Hills County	Two Hills Reporter	980
1950-	Vegreville	News Advertiser	988
1951-1953	Andrew	Andrew Advocate	23
1951-1952	Calgary	Bowness News	1055
1951-1955	Colinton	Colinton Clipper	291
1951	Edmonton	News Bulletin	438
1951-1952	Gibbons	Gibbons Herald	573
1951-1953	Lamont	Lamont Journal	683
1951	Magrath	Garden City News	720
1951-1968	Mayerthorpe	Mayerthorpe Review	736
1951-1965	Spirit River	Spirit River Signal	910
1951-1953	Vilna	Vilna Star	1002
1951-1953	Willingdon	Willingdon Review	1036
1952-1953	Bruderheim	Bruderheim Review	107
1952-1962	Calgary	Beacon	189
1952-	Camrose	Camrose Booster	227
1952-1955	Glendon	Glendon Bulletin	577
1952-1953	Grimshaw	Grimshaw Voyageur	600
1952-1953	Mundare	Mundare Star	773
1952-1968	Pembina M.D.	Evansburg Pembina Herald	806
1952-1963	Smoky River M.D.	Courier	908
1952-	Tofield	Tofield Mercury	970
1953-1955	Acme	Valley News	4
1953-1959	Calgary	Bow Valley Advertiser	190
1953-	Edmonton	Beverly Page	440
1953-1954	Edmonton	South East News	439
1953-	Edson	Edson Leader	512
1953-1969	Redwater	Redwater News	848
1954-1956	Bow Island	Bow Island News	91
1954-1981	Calgary	North Hill News	191
1954-1955	Coaldale	Neu-Kanadier	277
1954-1958	Drayton Valley	Drayton Valley Tribune	322
1954-1969	Edmonton	Alberta Country Life	442
1954-?	Edmonton	Holland Revue	441
1954-	Innisfail	Innisfail Booster	645
1955-1959	Bassano	Bassano Herald	61
1955-1961	Canmore	Three Sisters Clarion	229
1955-1958	High Prairie	Northern Star	618
1955-	Hinton	Hinton Herald	627

Chronological Index of Newspapers other than Dailies

Dates	Place	Title	Item
1955-1967	Jasper	Jasper Totem	656
1955-1976	Ponoka County	Ponoka County News	816
1955-1963	Vilna	Vilna Bulletin	1003
1956-1957	Athabasca	Athabasca Advance	31
1956-	Beaverlodge	Advertiser	66
1956-1960	Bow Island	Graphic	92
1956-	Edmonton	Biuletyn. Organizacji Polskich	443
1956	Edmonton	Bulletin of Polish Association	443
1956-1960	Grimshaw	Grimshaw Spotlight	601
1956-1963	High Prairie	High Prairie Progress	619
1956-1957	Oyen	Oyen Observer	797
1956-1965	Pembina M.D.	Pembina News	807
1956-?	Rycroft	Pisriverskyi Homin	870
1956-1962	Valleyview	Valleyview Times	984
1957-1959	Alix	Alix Promoter	15
1957	Calgary	Albertan's South Side Shopper	193
1957	Calgary	South Calgary News	192
1957-1972	Raymond	Raymond Recorder	827
1957	Sundre	Sundre News-Advertiser	944
1957-?	Turner Valley	Turner Valley News	977
1958-1959	Edmonton	Edmonton News	444
1958-	Edmonton	Scandinavian Centre News	445
1958-1961	Mundare	Mundare Mirror	774
1958-1960	Slave Lake	Lesser Slave Lake Star	899
1959-1960	Cold Lake	Cold Lake Courier	285
1959	Cold Lake	Cold Lake Sentinel	286
1959-1960	Edmonton	Progressive Student	1059
1959-1965	Fort McMurray	Northern Banner	1072
1959-1960	Grand Centre	Grand Centre Times	579
1959-	Lloydminster	Meridian Booster	705
1959-1961	Lodgepole	Log	707
1959-1969	Whitecourt	Whitecourt Echo	1032
1960-	Bassano	Bassano Times	62
1960-1962	Bow Island	Graphic	93
1960-	Calgary	Gauntlet	195
1960-	Calgary	South Side Mirror	194
1960-	Edmonton	Alberta Jewish Chronicle	446
1960-	Edmonton	Demonstrator	1060
1960	Edmonton	Labor Advocate	1061
1960-1963	Edmonton	Ukrainian Record	447
1960-1961	Milk River	Chinook Belt Advertiser	754
1960-	Oyen	Oyen Echo	798
1960-	Sundre	Sundre Round Up Publishing Ltd.	945
1960-1961	Taber	Chinook Belt Advertiser	955

Chronological Index of Newspapers other than Dailies

Dates	Place	Title	Item
1961-1964	Barrhead	Bulletin	53
1961-1986	Didsbury	Didsbury Booster	318
1961-1970	Edmonton	Alberta Liberal	1062
1961-1962	Edmonton	Edmonton Free Press	448
1961-1963	Elk Point	Elk Point Hunter	513
1961-1962	Grimshaw	Northerner	602
1961-1962	Lake Louise	Kicking Horse Chronicles	672
1961-1963	Lamont	Lamont Bulletin	684
1961	Olds	Olds Moose-Paper	791
1961-	St. Albert	St. Albert Gazette	880
1961-1969	Sturgeon M.D.	Sturgeon Journal	943
1961-1965	Vegreville	Vegreville Mirror	990
1961	Vegreville	Vegreville Mirror	989
1961-1963	Vermilion River Cty.	Vermilion River News	995
1962-	Calgary	Calgary Jewish News	196
1962	Calgary	Sunday Calgarian	1053
1962	Edmonton	South Side Sun	449
1962-1968	Grand Centre	Grand Centre Press	580
1962-1964	Hinton	News Advertiser Ad-Mart	628
1962-1973	Lake Louise	Kicking Horse News	673
1962-1963	Macklin	Macklin Times	714
1962-1968	Ponoka	Western Weekly Supplement	819
1962-	Whitecourt	Whitecourt Star	1033
1963	Calgary	Bowness Review	1054
1963-1965	Calgary	Praerie Nyt	197
1963-1979	Edmonton	Alberta Labour	450
1963-	Jasper	Jasper Booster	657
1963-1968	Sherwood Park	Sherwood Park Herald	893
1963-1967	Stony Plain M.D.	Stony Plain Sun	928
1963-	Valleyview	Valley View	985
1964	Bonnyville	Bonnyville Newscope	88
1964-1966	Cardston	Cardston News	242
1964-1965	Cardston	Temple City Tribune	244
1964	Edmonton	Reporter	451
1964-	High Prairie	South Peace News	620
1964-1969	Sherwood Park	Sherwood Park Sun	894
1964-1969	Spirit River	Spirit River Bulletin	911
1964-1966	Stand Off	Sun Dance Echo	914
1965	Drayton Valley	Drayton Valley Banner	1057
1965-	Drayton Valley	Western Review	323
1965	Edmonton	Alberta Business Review	452
1965-1966	Edmonton	Edmonton Gazette	454
1965-	Edmonton	Western Catholic Reporter	453
1965-1967	Fort McMurray	Fort McMurray Banner	548

Chronological Index of Newspapers other than Dailies

Dates	Place	Title	Item
1965-1969	Jasper	Jasper Gateway	658
1965-1969	Minburn County	County of Minburn Review	758
1965-	Raymond	Raymond Review	828
1966-1970	Canmore	Canmore Times	230
1966	Edmonton	Messaggero Italiano	455
1966	Edmonton	Tory	1063
1966-1968	Fort McMurray	McMurray Northlander	549
1966-	Manning	Manning Banner Post	722
1966-1967	Rocky Mountain House	Rocky Weekly Press	861
1967-1970	Banff	Banff Summit News	45
1967-	Bonnyville	Bonnyville Nouvelle	89
1967-1974	Cardston	Cardston Unlimited	243
1967-	Cold Lake	Canadian Forces Base Cold Lake Courier	287
1967-1986	Delburne	Delburne and District Journal	310
1967-1979	Drumheller	Big Country News	332
1967-	Edmonton	Franco-albertain	458
1967-1969	Edmonton	Mondo	456
1967-1968	Edmonton	Ryce Street Fysh Markete	457
1967-1969	Falher	Falher News	528
1967-1969	Fort McMurray	Fort McMurray Northern Star	550
1967-	Lethbridge	Meliorist	701
1967-1970	Slave Lake	Slave Lake Centennial Press	900
1967-1968	Strathcona County	Strathcona Wedge	938
1967-1969	Thorhild County	Thorhild County News	956
1967-1968	Wetaskiwin County	Wetaskiwin County News	1017
1968	Banff	Mountain Merchandiser	46
1968-1970	Calgary	Panorama	199
1968-	Calgary	Roundup	198
1968-1969	Edmonton	Canada Goose	461
1968-1982	Edmonton	Native People	460
1968	Edmonton	Western Sports Weekly	459
1968-1970	Fort McMurray	Fort McMurray News Advertiser	1073
1968-1969	Fort McMurray	Fort McMurray Sun	1074
1968-1972	Hobbema	Bear Hills Native Voice	631
1968-	Lac La Biche	Lac La Biche Post	663
1968-	Stand Off	Kainai News	915
1968-	Westlock	Hub	1016
1969-1973	Claresholm	Footnotes and News	269
1969-1977	Edmonton	Alberta Farm Life	462
1969-1974	Edmonton	Edmonton Star and Alberta Farm Life	463
1969-1977	Edmonton	Messaggero delle Praterie	465
1969-1977	Edmonton	Prairies' Messenger	465
1969-1975	Edmonton	Telegram	464

Chronological Index of Newspapers other than Dailies

Dates	Place	Title	Item
1969-	Falher	Falher News	529
1969	High Level	Northern Echo	613
1969-1977	Lamont County	County of Lamont Star	676
1969-1976	Medicine Hat	Rattler	752
1969-1977	Morinville	Morinville Star	766
1969-	Red Deer	Red Deer County News	829
1969-1977	Sherwood Park	Sherwood Park Star	895
1969-1976	Strathcona County	Strathcona County News	939
1970-1977	Boyle	Boyle Star	101
1970-	Calgary	Mormoratore	200
1970-1972	Edmonton	Alberta Liberal	1064
1970-1971	Edmonton	Examiner	467
1970-	Edmonton	Source	468
1970-1975	Fort McMurray	McMurray Courier	551
1970-1971	Fort McMurray	McMurray Times	1075
1970-	Grande Cache	Grande Cache Mountaineer	583
1970	Grande Cache	Grande Cache Star	582
1970-1977	Lac La Biche	Lac La Biche Star	664
1970-1977	Mayerthorpe	Mayerthorpe-Lac Ste Anne Star	737
1970-1977	Pembina M.D.	Pembina Star	808
1970-1973	Redwater	Redwater Star	849
1970-	Slave Lake	Port of Slave Lake Oiler	901
1970-1977	Smoky Lake	Smoky Lake Star	906
1970-1977	Spruce Grove	Spruce Grove Star	912
1970-1977	Thorhild County	Thorhild Star	957
1970-1973	Thorsby	Thorsby Star	962
1970-1977	Two Hills County	Two Hills County Star	981
1971	Banff	Scree	47
1971-1977	Barrhead	Barrhead Star	54
1971-1979	Calgary	Wednesday Review	201
1971-1972	Edmonton	Campus Lyfe	470
1971-1973	Edmonton	Olde Towne Crier	471
1971	Edmonton	Problysk	469
1971-	Forty Mile County	40-Mile County Commentator	563
1971	Lac Ste Anne County	Lac Ste Anne Advance	666
1971-1973	Mannville	Mannville Star	730
1971-1981	Stettler	Actioneer	926
1972-1974	Airdrie	Tri-Neighbour Press	7
1972-1973	Clyde	Clyde Star	274
1972-198?	Edmonton	Despertar	474
1972-1978	Edmonton	New Alberta Liberal	1065
1972-1975	Edmonton	On Our Way	475
1972-1975	Edmonton	Poundmaker	476
1972-	Edmonton	Spokesman	472

Chronological Index of Newspapers other than Dailies

Dates	Place	Title	Item
1972-1982	Edmonton	Western Livestock & Agricultural News	473
1972-1973	Elk Point	Elk Point Star	514
1972-1977	Fort Saskatchewan	Fort Saskatchewan Star	561
1972-	Glenwood	Glenwood Gleanings	578
1972-	Grande Prairie	Grande Prairie Booster	588
1972-	Grande Prairie	Herald-Tribune Rural Route	587
1972-1976	Lethbridge	Chinook	1082
1972	Milk River	Border County Recorder	755
1972-	Red Deer County	Advocate Shopper	830
1972-1974	Redwater	Redwater News	850
1972-1973	Sangudo	Sangudo Chronicle	887
1972-1975	Slave Lake	Northland Free Press	902
1972-1973	St. Albert	St. Albert Star	881
1972-1974	Thorhild	Thorhild News	960
1972-1973	Veteran	Veteran Eagle	998
1973-	Blairmore	Pass Promoter	84
1973	Edmonton	Alberta Challenge	1066
1973-1975	Edmonton	Portrait	477
1973-	High Level	Echo	614
1973-1974	High River	Fort Spitzee Signal	626
1973-1977	Hythe	Hythe Headliner	639
1973-1977	Minburn County	Minburn County Star	759
1973-	Peace River	North Peace Pictorial	805
1973-1977	Vermilion River Cty.	Vermilion River County Star	996
1974	Calgary	East City News	204
1974-1975	Calgary	Italian News	202
1974	Calgary	Sunday	203
1974-1975	Canmore	Valley Views	231
1974-1984	Cochrane	Cochrane Times	281
1974	Delia	Delia Times	313
1974-1975	High Prairie	High Prairie Reporter	621
1974	High Prairie	Northern Messenger	622
1974-1977	Lac Ste Anne County	Lac Ste Anne Chronicle	667
1974-	Spruce Grove	Grove Examiner	913
1974-	Thorhild County	News	958
1974-	Two Hills County	Two Hills County Journal	982
1975-	Airdrie	Airdrie and District Echo	8
1975-1977	Athabasca	Athabasca Call	32
1975-1981	Calgary	Calgary Women's Newspaper	206
1975-	Calgary	Croatian Herald	207
1975-	Calgary	Hrvatski Vjesnik Hrvatskog	207
1975-	Calgary	North Side Mirror	205
1975	Calmar	Calmar Review	223

Chronological Index of Newspapers other than Dailies

Dates	Place	Title	Item
1975-1983	Canmore	Canmore Miner	232
1975-1979	Cardston	Westwind News	245
1975-1977	Edmonton	Business Reporter	479
1975-1977	Edmonton	Prairie Star	478
1975-	Rocky View M.D.	Five Village Weekly	862
1975-	Slave Lake	Lakeside Leader	903
1976-	Bowden	Bowden Eye Opener	99
1976-1982	Calgary	Dairy Contact	208
1976	Calgary	Korean Dong-Baung News	210
1976-	Calgary	World of Beef	209
1976	Canmore	Anthracite Chronicle	233
1976-1983	Canmore	Hoodoo Highlander	234
1976-	Carbon	Village Press	239
1976-	Devon	Devon Dispatch	315
1976-1978	Edmonton	Canadian Ukraine	480
1976-	Edmonton	Commerce News	1067
1976-1978	Edmonton	Kanadiyska Ukraina	480
1976-1978	Edmonton	Latin Report	482
1976-	Edmonton	Summer Times	481
1976-1979	Fort Chipewyan	Moccasin Telegram	534
1976-	Fort Vermilion	Northern Pioneer	562
1976-	Hobbema	Bear Hills Native Voice	632
1976-	Okotoks	Western Wheel	787
1976-1977	Olds	Olds Star	1083
1976-1978	Redcliff	Redcliff Review	1085
1976-	Sherwood Park	Sherwood Park News	896
1977	Airdrie	Rocky View Times	9
1977	Drayton Valley	Drayton Valley Booster	324
1977-	Edmonton	Alberta Farm Life	485
1977-	Edmonton	Edmonton Examiner [South Editions]	486
1977-	Edmonton	Edmonton Examiner [West Editions]	487
1977-1978	Edmonton	Edmonton Sun	488
1977-	Edmonton	Strathcona Plaindealer	484
1977-1978	Fairview	Fairview This Week	527
1977-	Grand Centre	Grand Centre-Cold Lake Sun	581
1977	Innisfail	Innisfail Star	1077
1977-	Lamont County	Triangle	677
1977	Leduc	Northern Alberta Farmer	690
1977-1978	Parkland County	Parkland County Examiner	799
1977-	Red Deer	Central Alberta Ad-Viser	841
1977-1979	Red Deer	Midweeker	840
1977-1979	Red Deer	Weekender	839
1977-	Swan Hills	Grizzly Gazette	947
1977	Swan Hills	Swan Hills Grizzly	946

Chronological Index of Newspapers other than Dailies

Dates	Place	Title	Item
1977-	Trochu	Trochu's Community Voice	974
1978-1982	Edmonton	Alberta Business	491
1978-	Edmonton	Edmonton Examiner [North Editions]	490
1978-1979	Edmonton	Newscene	1068
1978-1981	Lethbridge	Chinook Reporter	702
1978-	Mannville	Mannville Reflections	731
1978-	Mayerthorpe	Freelancer	738
1978-1985	Onoway	Highway 43 Tribune	794
1978-	Smoky Lake	Smoky Lake Signal	907
1978-	Vauxhall	Vauxhall Advance	986
1978-1979	Vermilion	Northeast News	994
1978	Vermilion	Wild Rose Chronicle	1088
1978-	Viking	Weekly Review	1001
1979-	Airdrie	Rocky View Times	10
1979-1981	Calgary	Calgary Rural Ad-viser	211
1979	Calgary	Calgary Sun	212
1979-1981	Calgary	Seventeenth Avenue	213
1979-	Edmonton	Nuovo Mondo	493
1979-1980	Elk Point	Elk Point Reflections	1069
1979-1982	Elk Point	Elk Point Sentinel	515
1979-	Evansburg	Grand Trunk Poplar Press	523
1979-	Fort McMurray	Fort McMurray Express	553
1979-	Grimshaw	Mile Zero News	603
1979-	High Level	Mackenzie Highway Pictorial	615
1979-	Leslieville	Western Star	1081
1979-	Morinville	Morinville and Sturgeon Mirror	767
1979-	Red Deer	Red Deer Shopper	842
1979-1980	Turner Valley	High Country Flare	978
197?-1981	Edmonton	Jornal Portugese	466
1980-	Calgary	Calgary Hungarian Courier	214
1980-	Calgary	Calgary Sun	215
1980-	Calgary	Jewish Star [Calgary Edition]	216
1980-	Calgary	Magyar Hirmondo	214
1980-	Cardston	Cardston Chronicle	246
1980-1982	Cochrane	Pioneer	282
1980-1982	Cochrane	Town Crier	283
1980-	Edmonton	Jewish Star [Edmonton Edition]	495
1980-1983	Edmonton	Native Ensign	494
1980-	Rycroft	Signal	871
1980-1984	Two Hills County	Two Hills County Times	983
1981-1983	Calgary	Calgary Rural Week	218
1981-	Calgary	Canadian Chinese Times	217
1981-	Edmonton	Korean Canadian Times	496
1981-	Edmonton	Prairie Link	497

Chronological Index of Newspapers other than Dailies

Dates	Place	Title	Item
1981-	Edmonton	Sonshine News	498
1981-1983	Fort Chipewyan	News	535
1981-	Morley	Stoney Echo	768
1981-1986	Nisku	Nisku News	782
1981-	Redwater	Tribune	851
1981-	Turner Valley	Eagleview Post	979
1982-	Athabasca	Advocate	33
1982-1983	Brocket	Weasel Valley News	103
1982	Calgary	Calgary Avenues	220
1982-	Calgary	Hungarians of the West	219
1982-	Calgary	Indo Chinese News	221
1982-	Calgary	Nyugati Magyarsa'g	219
1982-	Calgary	Opinion	222
1982-	Carstairs	Courier	251
1982-	Edmonton	Dairy Contact	500
1982-	Edmonton	Diario	501
1982-	Edmonton	English Express	499
1982-	Olds	Olds Optimist	792
1982-1985	Whitecourt	Free Press	1034

Ethnic Index

Title	Place	Dates	Item
Arabic			
Source	Edmonton	1970-	468
Asian			
Prairie Link	Edmonton	1981-	497
Chinese			
Canadian Chinese Times	Calgary	1981-	217
Indochinese News	Calgary	1982-	221
Croatian			
Croatian Herald	Calgary	1975-	207
Hrvatski Vjesnik Hrvatskog Drustva Prijatelja Matice Hrvatske	Calgary	1975	207
Czechoslovakian			
Telegram	Edmonton	1969-1975	464
Danish			
Church and Home	Edmonton	1930-1961	408
Danish Review	Calgary	1930-1933	169
Danskeren	Calgary	1930-1933	169
Kirken og Hjemmet	Edmonton	1930-1961	408
Praerie Nyt	Calgary	1963-1965	197
Scandinavian Centre News	Edmonton	1958-	445
Dutch			
Holland Revue	Edmonton	1954	441
Finnish			
Moukari	Edmonton	1913-1915	366
Scandinavian Centre News	Edmonton	1958-	445

Ethnic Index

Title	Place	Dates	Item
French			
Courrier de l'Ouest	Edmonton	1905-1916	347
Etoile de St. Albert	St. Albert	1912-1914	878
Franco	Edmonton	1979-	458
Franco-albertain	Edmonton	1967-1979	458
Ouest canadien	Edmonton	1898-1900	338
Ouest canadien	Edmonton	1911	362
Progrès	Morinville	1909-1913	764
Progrès albertain	Edmonton	1914-1915	374
Progrès albertain	Morinville	1913-1914	764
St. Albert Star	St. Albert	1914	878
Survivance	Edmonton	1928-1967	404
Survivance des Jeunes	Edmonton	1934-194?	418
Union	Edmonton	1917-1929	378
German			
Alberta Deutsche Zeitung	Edmonton	1910-1913	360
Alberta German Newspaper	Edmonton	1910-1913	360
Alberta Herald	Edmonton	1931	412
Alberta Herold	Edmonton	1903-1915	343
Alberta Herold	Edmonton	1931	412
Alberta Herold	Edmonton	1937-1939	424
Brüke	Medicine Hat	1945-1946	751
Deutsch-Canadier	Calgary	1909-1914	139
Deutsch-Canadier	Edmonton	1908-1909	355
Deutsch-Canadischer Farmer	Calgary	1909-1912	140
Deutsche Arbeiter Zeitung	Edmonton	1930-1931	411
German-Canadian Farmer	Calgary	1909-1912	140
German Labor News	Edmonton	1930-1931	411
Herold	Edmonton	1928-1931	403
Neu-Kanadier	Coaldale	1954-1955	277
Hungarian			
Calgary Hungarian Courier	Calgary	1980-	214
Canada Magyar Farmer	Edmonton	1910-1921	357
Canadai Magyar Farmer	Edmonton	1910-1921	357
Canadian Hungarian Farmer	Edmonton	1910-1921	357
Hungarians of the West	Calgary	1982-	219
Magyar Hirmondo	Calgary	1980-	214
Nyugati Magyarsa'g	Calgary	1982-	219

Ethnic Index

Title	Place	Dates	Item

Italian

Italian News	Calgary	1974-1975	202
Messaggero delle Praterie	Edmonton	1969-1977	465
Messaggero Italiano	Edmonton	1966	455
Mondo	Edmonton	1967-1969	455
Mormoratore	Calgary	1970-	200
Nuovo Mondo	Edmonton	1979-	493
Panorama	Calgary	1968-1970	199
Prairies' Messenger	Edmonton	1969-1977	465

Jewish

Alberta Jewish Chronicle	Edmonton	1960-	446
Calgary Jewish News	Calgary	1962-	196
Canadian Western Jewish Times	Calgary	1914	149
Jewish Star [Calgary Edition]	Calgary	1980-	216
Jewish Star [Edmonton Edition]	Edmonton	1980-	495

Korean

Korean Canadian Times	Edmonton	1981-	496
Korean Dong-Baung News	Calgary	1976	210

Latvian

Brivais Latvietis	Edmonton	1948-1949	430
Free Latvian	Edmonton	1948-1949	430

Native

Bear Hills Native Voice (Cree)	Hobbema	1968-1972	631
Bear Hills Native Voice (Cree)	Hobbema	1976-	632
Croix de Ste. Anne	Lac Ste. Anne	1900-1905	1078
Echo de Ste-Anne (Cree)	Lac Ste. Anne	1895-1897	668
Indian Advocate (Cree)	Whitefish Lake	1897-1902	1035
Kainai News (Blood)	Stand Off	1968-	915
Nation's Ensign	Edmonton	1982-1983	494
Native Ensign	Edmonton	1980-1982	494
Native People	Edmonton	1968-1982	460
Stoney Echo (Stoney)	Morley	1981-	768

Ethnic Index

Title	Place	Dates	Item
Sun Dance Echo (Blood)	Stand Off	1964-1966	914
Weasel Valley News (Peigan)	Brocket	1982-1983	103

Norwegian

Scandinavian Centre News	Edmonton	1958-	445

Polish

Biuletyn. Kongresu Polonii Kanadyjskiej Okreg Alberta	Edmonton	1957-	443
Biuletyn. Organizacji Polskich w Edmontonie	Edmonton	1956	443
Bulletin of Polish Association of Edmonton	Edmonton	1956	443
Bulletin of the Canadian Polish Congress	Edmonton	1957-	443

Portuguese

Despertar	Edmonton	1972-198?	474
Jornal Portugese	Edmonton	197?-1981	466

Russian

Canadian Field	Edmonton	1908-1910	354
Druh Naroda	Edmonton	1926-1930	400
Kanadiiskaia Niva	Edmonton	1908-1910	354
People's Friend	Edmonton	1926-1930	400
Russian Life	Edmonton	1915-1918	375
Russian Voice	Edmonton	1913-1916	369
Russkyi Golos	Edmonton	1913-1916	369

Scottish

Scottish Standard	Calgary	1913-1914	146

Slovak

Hlas Naroda	Blairmore	1932-1934	80
Slovak Word	Blairmore	1910-1911	78
Slovak Word	Blairmore	1940	82
Slovenske Slovo	Blairmore	1910-1911	78
Slovenske Slovo	Blairmore	1940	82

Ethnic Index

Title	Place	Dates	Item
Telegram	Edmonton	1969-1975	464
Voice of the Nation	Blairmore	1932-1934	80

Spanish

Diario	Edmonton	1982-	501
Latin Report	Edmonton	1976-1978	482
Opinion	Calgary	1982-	222

Swedish

Scandinavian Centre News	Edmonton	1958-	445
Wetaskiwin Alberta Tribunen	Wetaskiwin	1914	1029

Ukrainian

Alberta Star	Edmonton	1930	409
Albertiis'ka Zoria	Edmonton	1930	409
Canadian	Edmonton	1912-1919	364
Canadian Field	Edmonton	1908-1910	354
Canadian Ukraine	Edmonton	1976-1978	480
Clarion	Edmonton	1950-1951	433
Druh Naroda	Edmonton	1926-1930	400
Dzvin	Edmonton	1950-1951	433
Farmers' Voice	Edmonton	1932-1934	415
Farmers' Word	Edmonton	1921	387
Farmerske Slovo	Edmonton	1921	387
Farmerskyi Holos	Edmonton	1932-1934	415
Holos Pravdy	Smoky Lake	1937-1960	904
Kanadiiskaia Niva	Edmonton	1908-1910	354
Kanadiyska Ukraina	Edmonton	1976-1978	480
Kanadyiets	Edmonton	1912-1919	364
Kupets	Edmonton	1936	422
Light	Mundare	1938-1949	772
Merchant	Edmonton	1936	422
Nash Postup	Edmonton	1922-1929	393
New Country	Edmonton	1929	406
New Pathway	Edmonton	1930-1933	410
New Society	Edmonton	1911-1912	363
News	Edmonton	1913-1915	367
News	Edmonton	1917-1922	379
Nova Hromada	Edmonton	1911-1912	363

Ethnic Index

Title	Place	Dates	Item
Novyi Krai	Edmonton	1919	406
Novyi Shliakh	Edmonton	1930-1933	410
Novyny	Edmonton	1913-1915	367
Novyny	Edmonton	1917-1922	379
Ostoroha	Wostok	1912	1040
Our Progress	Edmonton	1922-1929	393
People's Friend	Edmonton	1926-1930	400
Pisriverskyi Homin	Rycroft	1956-?	870
Postup	Mundare	1915-1917	771
Pravda Naroda	Edmonton	1929	407
Problysk	Edmonton	1971	469
Progress	Mundare	1915-1917	771
Renaissance	Edmonton	1930	409
Russian Voice	Edmonton	1913-1916	369
Russkyi Golos	Edmonton	1913-1916	369
Social Credit	Edmonton	1937-1940	423
Suspilnyi Kredit	Edmonton	1937-1940	423
Svitlo	Mundare	1938-1949	772
Truth of the People	Edmonton	1929	407
Ukrainian Gazette	Edmonton	1933-1934	417
Ukrainian News	Edmonton	1932-	402
Ukrainian Record	Edmonton	1960-1963	447
Ukrainska Gazeta	Edmonton	1933-1934	417
Ukrainski Visti	Edmonton	1932-	402
Vidrodzhennia	Edmonton	1930	409
Voice of Truth	Smoky Lake	1937-1960	904
Western News	Edmonton	1928-1931	402
Zakhidni Visti	Edmonton	1928-1931	402

Title	Place	Dates	Item

Agriculture

Title	Place	Dates	Item
A.F.U. Bulletin	Edmonton	1941-1949	427
Alberta Business Review	Edmonton	1965	452
Alberta Farm Life	Edmonton	1969-1977	462
Alberta Farm Life	Edmonton	1977-	485
Alberta Farmer	Medicine Hat	1913-1914	748
Alberta Herold	Edmonton	1903-1915	343
Alberta Homestead	Edmonton	1908-1911	353
Calgary Rural Ad-viser	Calgary	1979-1981	211
Calgary Rural Week	Calgary	1981-1982	218
Canadai Magyar Farmer	Edmonton	1910-1921	357
Canadian Hungarian Farmer	Edmonton	1910-1921	357
Dairy Contact	Calgary	1976-1982	208
Dairy Contact	Edmonton	1982-	500
Deutsch-Canadischer Farmer	Calgary	1909-1912	140
F.U.A. Farmer	Edmonton	1949	427
Farmers Tribune	Alderson	1914	13
Farmers' Voice	Edmonton	1932-1934	415
Farmers' Word	Edmonton	1921	387
Farmerske Slovo	Edmonton	1921	387
Farmerskyi Holos	Edmonton	1932-1934	415
German-Canadian Farmer	Calgary	1909-1912	140
Great West	Edmonton	1907-1909	349
Homestead	Edmonton	1911-1913	353
Link and Mannville Empire	Vermilion	1922-1923	993
Market Examiner	Calgary	1917-1922	153
Market Examiner	Calgary	1954-1955	153
Market Examiner and Western Farm Journal	Calgary	1923-1954	153
Northern Alberta Farmer	Leduc	1977	690
Organized Farmer	Edmonton	1949-1971	427
Postup	Mundare	1915-1917	771
Progress	Mundare	1915-1917	771
Rocky View News and Market Examiner	Calgary	1956-1981	153
Rural Week	Calgary	1982-1983	218
Rural Weekly News and Rube's Farm Fun	Stony Plain	1912-1917	932
U.F.A.	Calgary	1922-1934	160
United Farmer	Calgary	1934-1936	160
Western Farm Leader	Calgary	1936-1954	181
Western Farmer	Calgary	1928-1931	164
Western Livestock and Agriculture News	Edmonton	1972-1982	473
Western Stockman	Calgary	1932	164
World of Beef and Stockman's Recorder	Calgary	1976-	209

Subject Index

Title	Place	Dates	Item

Business

Alberta Business	Edmonton	1978-1981	491
Alberta Business Review	Edmonton	1965	452
Business Reporter	Edmonton	1975-1977	479
Commerce News	Edmonton	1976	1067
Edmonton and Alberta Business	Edmonton	1981-1982	491
Edmonton Business	Edmonton	1982	491
Edmonton Free Press	Edmonton	1906-1907	1058
Financial News	Edmonton	1911-1913	361
Kupets	Edmonton	1936	422
Oil and Financial Review	Calgary	1929-1931	167
Westerner	Calgary	1923-1928	1051

Disabled

Spokesman	Edmonton	1972-	472

Feminist

Calgary Women's Newspaper	Calgary	1975-1981	206
On Our Way	Edmonton	1972-1975	475

Immigration

Central Albertan	Wetaskiwin	1910-1911	1025
New Country	Edmonton	1929	406
Novyi Krai	Edmonton	1929	406
Ouest canadien	Edmonton	1898-1900	338
Peace River Pilot	Peace River	1910	800
Pembina Outlook and Entwistle News	Entwistle	1910	519
Progrès albertain	Edmonton	1914-1915	374
Progrès albertain	Morinville	1913-1914	764
Red Deer Review	Red Deer	1894	831
Sunset News Bulletin	Calgary	1906	1048

Labour

Alberta Clarion	Calgary	1906	1048
Alberta Federationist	Calgary	1912-1913	144
Alberta Labor News	Edmonton	1920-1936	386
Alberta Labour	Edmonton	1963-1979	450

Subject Index

Title	Place	Dates	Item
Bond of Brotherhood	Calgary	1903-1904	129
Calgary Strike Bulletin	Calgary	1919	157
Calgary Typo News	Calgary	1935	177
Call	Calgary	1945-1952	186
Canadian Miner	Calgary	1931-1933	170
Deutsche Arbeiter Zeitung	Edmonton	1930-1931	411
Edmonton Free Press	Edmonton	1919-1920	384
Edmonton Strike Bulletin	Edmonton	1919	385
Farmers' Voice	Edmonton	1932-1934	415
Farmerskyi Holos	Edmonton	1932-1934	415
German Labor News	Edmonton	1930-1931	411
Great West	Edmonton	1907-1909	349
International Labor News	Edmonton	1923-1924	394
Labor Advocate	Edmonton	1960	1061
Labor Day Bulletin	Medicine Hat	1912	745
New Call	Calgary	1952	186
News-Advertiser	Edmonton	1947-1948	429
Nor'West Miner	Edmonton	1935-1939	418
Northwest Call	Calgary	1887	119
One Big Union Bulletin	Edmonton	1919	382
People's Weekly	Edmonton	1936-1952	386
Searchlight	Calgary	1919-1920	159
Southern Alberta Labor Bulletin	Lethbridge	1908-1913	696
Soviet	Edmonton	1919	381
Statesman	Edmonton	1919-1920	383
Statesman for Albertans	Edmonton	1917-1918	377
Typo News	Calgary	1935	177
Unemployed Bulletin	Calgary	1931-1932	1053
Union Laborer	Edmonton	1929	405
Wedge	Edmonton	1921	389
Western Miner	Calgary	1930-1931	170
Western Miner	Lethbridge	1930	700
Western Union Printer	Medicine Hat	1919-1923	749
Worker	Calgary	1936	178

Military

Title	Place	Dates	Item
Alberta Veteran	Calgary	1918-1920	155
Canadian Forces Base Cold Lake Courier	Cold Lake	1967-	287
Cold Lake Courier	Cold Lake	1959-1960	285
Roundup	Calgary	1968-	198
Sentinel and Military News	Calgary	1916	151
Western Illustrated News	Edmonton	1921-1922	390

Subject Index

Title	Place	Dates	Item

Oil Industry

Alberta Oil Examiner	Calgary	1926	163
Alberta Oil Review	Calgary	1915-1916	150
Black Diamond Press	Calgary	1913-1914	145
Canadian Western Standard	Calgary	1918	142
Natural Gas and Oil Record	Calgary	1913-1914	147
Oil and Financial Review	Calgary	1929-1931	167
Western Examiner	Calgary	1929-1949	165
Western Oil Examiner	Calgary	1927-1929	163
Western Oil Examiner	Calgary	1949-1958	165

Political-General

Canadian Field	Edmonton	1908-1910	354
Critic	Calgary	1902	128
Edmonton Saturday Mirror	Edmonton	1912-1913	365
Kanadiiskaia Niva	Edmonton	1908-1910	354
Liberty	Calgary	1922	161
Mirror	Edmonton	1912	365
New Pathway	Edmonton	1930-1933	410
Novyi Shliakh	Edmonton	1930-1933	410
Outlaw	Scott's Coulee	1896	888
Political World	Calgary	1934-1936	174

Political-Conservative

Advertiser and Central Alberta News	Lacombe	1898-1908	669
Claresholm Review	Claresholm	1904-1916	266
Edmonton Post	Edmonton	1899-1902	339
Fort Macleod Gazette	Fort Macleod	1882-1907	536
Lacombe Advertiser and Central Alberta News	Lacombe	1908-1909	669
Macleod Spectator	Fort Macleod	1912-1916	542
New Age	Wetaskiwin	1912-1913	1028
Nor'-Wester	Calgary	1884-1885	114
Rebel	Calgary	1937-1939	184
St. Paul Journal	St. Paul	1925-	883
St. Paul Tribune	St. Paul	1925-	883
Tory	Edmonton	1966	1063
Western Globe	Lacombe	1903-1938	670
Wetaskiwin Free Press	Wetaskiwin	1917-1941	1026

Subject Index

Title	Place	Dates	Item

Political-C.C.F. (Co-operative Commonwealth Federation)

People's Weekly	Edmonton	1936-1952	386
Progressive Student	Edmonton	1959-1960	1059

Political-Liberal

Acme News	Acme	1909-1914	1
Alberta Herold	Edmonton	1903-1915	343
Alberta Liberal	Edmonton	1961-1970	1064
Alberta Liberal	Edmonton	1970-1972	1065
Bassano News	Bassano	1910-1914	57
Camrose Canadian	Camrose	1908-	225
Canadian	Edmonton	1912-1919	364
Carlstadt Progress	Alderson	1911-1912	12
Castor Advance	Castor	1909-	252
Claresholm Review	Claresholm	1904-1916	266
Courrier de l'Ouest	Edmonton	1905-1916	347
Gazette	Lamont	1918-1920	680
Hardisty Enterprise	Hardisty	1908-1909	607
Kanadyiets	Edmonton	1912-1919	364
Mayerthorpe Times	Mayerthorpe	1931-1935	733
Nanton News	Nanton	1903-	780
New Alberta Liberal	Edmonton	1972-1978	1064
Postup	Mundare	1915-1917	771
Progress	Mundare	1915-1917	771
Recorder	Raymond	1917-1922	824
Stony Plain News	Stony Plain	1913-1914	933
Telegram-Tribune	Acme	1914	2
Tofield Advertiser	Tofield	1917-1918	968
Ukrainian Gazette	Edmonton	1933-1934	417
Ukrainska Gazeta	Edmonton	1933-1934	417
Vegreville Observer	Vegreville	1928-	987
Warner Record	Warner	1910-1916	1010
Wetaskiwin News	Wetaskiwin	1900	1019
Winnifred Record	Winnifred	1911-1912	1039

Political-Non-Partisan League

Alberta Non-Partisan	Calgary	1917-1919	152
Nutcracker	Calgary	1916-1917	152

Subject Index

Title	Place	Dates	Item

Political-Social Credit

Title	Place	Dates	Item
Alberta Challenge	Edmonton	1973	1066
Alberta Democrat	Calgary	1938	1054
Alberta Social Credit Chronicle	Calgary	1934-1936	175
Alliance Times	Alliance	1916-1939	16
Canadian Social Crediter	Edmonton	1944-1949	428
Canadian Social Crediter	Edmonton	1950-1959	434
Commonsense	Calgary	1937	183
Douglas Social Credit Advocate	Calgary	1934-1936	176
Focus	Edmonton	1959-	434
Newscene	Edmonton	1978-1979	1068
Social Credit	Edmonton	1937-1940	423
Social Credit Gazette	Edmonton	1935-1936	420
Social Credit Supplement	Calgary	1936-1938	175
Social Justice Advocate	Calgary	1934	176
Suspilnyi Kredit	Edmonton	1937-1940	423
Today and Tomorrow	Edmonton	1935-1944	421

Political-Socialist

Title	Place	Dates	Item
New Society	Edmonton	1911-1912	363
Moukari	Edmonton	1913-1915	366
Nova Hromada	Edmonton	1911-1912	363
Prairie Star	Edmonton	1975-1977	478
Soviet	Edmonton	1919	381

Political-Unionist

Title	Place	Dates	Item
Mannville Empire	Mannville	1910-1922	724

Political-United Farmers of Alberta (U.F.A.)

Title	Place	Dates	Item
Rural Weekly News and Rube's Farm Fun	Stony Plain	1912-1917	932
U.F.A.	Calgary	1922-1934	160
United Farmer	Calgary	1922-1934	160
Victoria Farmer	Camrose	1922-1924	226
Western Farm Leader	Calgary	1936-1954	181
Western Independent	Calgary	1919-1920	158

Subject Index

Title	Place	Dates	Item

Prohibitionist

Alberta Star	Edmonton	1930	409
Albertiis'ka Zoria	Edmonton	1930	409
Calgary Observer	Calgary	1904-1905	131
Renaissance	Edmonton	1930	409
Temperance Advocate	Ryley	1925	875
Vidrodzhennia	Edmonton	1930	409

Religious

Canadian Field	Edmonton	1908-1910	354
Druh Naroda	Edmonton	1926-1930	400
Kanadiiskaia Niva	Edmonton	1908-1910	354
Light	Mundare	1938-1949	772
People's Friend	Edmonton	1926-1930	400
Sonshine News	Edmonton	1981-	498
Svitlo	Mundare	1938-1949	772
West-Land	Edmonton	1908-1913	352
Western Catholic	Edmonton	1921-1965	388
Western Catholic Reporter	Edmonton	1965-	453

Sport

Calgary Sports Review	Calgary	1942	185
Clarion of Alberta	Edmonton	1908	351
Edmonton Sports Record	Edmonton	1939	425
Sports Guide	Calgary	1936-1940	180
Sports Review	Edmonton	1922	391
Western Sports Weekly	Edmonton	1968	459

Underground Press

Canada Goose	Edmonton	1968-1969	461
Poundmaker	Edmonton	1972-1975	476
Prairie Star	Edmonton	1975-1977	478
Ryce Street Fysh Markete	Edmonton	1967-1968	457

University

Business Reporter	Edmonton	1975-1977	479
Campus Lyfe	Edmonton	1971-1972	470
Demonstrator	Edmonton	1960	1060

Subject Index

Title	Place	Dates	Item
Gateway	Edmonton	1910-	359
Gauntlet	Calgary	1960-	195
Meliorist	Lethbridge	1967-	701
Portrait	Edmonton	1973-1975	477
Poundmaker	Edmonton	1972-1975	476
Progressive Student	Edmonton	1959-1960	1059
Summer Times	Edmonton	1976-	481
Tory	Edmonton	1966	1065

Veterans

Alberta Veteran	Calgary	1918-1920	155
Army and Navy News and Universal Weekly	Calgary	1918-1919	156
Civvy Street	Red Deer	1946-1948	838
Link and Mannville Empire	Vermilion	1922-1923	993
Western Illustrated News	Edmonton	1921-1922	390

Title Index

Title	Place	Dates	Item
40-Mile County Commentator	Forty Mile County	1971	563
A.F.U. Bulletin	Edmonton	1941-1949	427.1
Acadia Review	Cereal	1914	255.1
Acme News	Acme	1909-1914	1
Acme Sentinel	Acme	1914-1951	3.1
Actioneer	Stettler	1971-1981	926.1
Advance	Chauvin	1912	261
Advance and Southern Alberta Advertisers	Fort Macleod	1907-1909	538.2
Advertiser	Beaverlodge	1956-	66
Advertiser	Edmonton	1900	341
Advertiser	Granum	1920-1921	595
Advertiser	Sylvan Lake	1932-1933	950
Advertiser and Central Alberta News	Lacombe	1898-1908	669.1
Advocate	Athabasca	1982-	33
Advocate	Red Deer	1972-	834.4
Advocate Shopper	Red Deer County	1972-1978	830.1
AHCS News	Edmonton	1932-1933	472
Airdrie and District Echo	Airdrie	1975-1977	8.1
Airdrie and District Echo	Airdrie	1979-	8.3
Airdrie News	Airdrie	1908-1911	5
Airdrie Recorder	Airdrie	1921-1926	6
Alberta Advocate	Red Deer	1903-1907	834.2
Alberta Business	Edmonton	1978-1981	491.1
Alberta Business Review	Edmonton	1965	452
Alberta Challenge	Edmonton	1973	1066
Alberta Clarion	Calgary	1906	1048
Alberta Country Life	Edmonton	1954-1969	442
Alberta Democrat	Calgary	1938	1054
Alberta Deutsche Zeitung	Edmonton	1910-1913	360
Alberta Echo	Red Deer	1901-1903	834.1
Alberta Farm Journal and Edmonton Journal Weekly	Edmonton	1925-1932	396.4
Alberta Farm Life	Edmonton	1969-1977	462
Alberta Farm Life	Edmonton	1977-	485
Alberta Farmer	Medicine Hat	1913-1914	748
Alberta Farmer and Calgary Weekly Herald	Calgary	1918-1932	113.9
Alberta Federationist	Calgary	1912-1913	144
Alberta German Newspaper	Edmonton	1910-1913	360
Alberta Herald	Edmonton	1931	412
Alberta Herold	Edmonton	1903-1915	343
Alberta Herold	Edmonton	1931	412
Alberta Herold	Edmonton	1937-1939	424

Title Index

Title	Place	Dates	Item
Alberta Herold and Farmerfreund	Edmonton	1903-1915	343
Alberta Herold und Farmerfreund	Edmonton	1903-1915	343
Alberta Homestead	Edmonton	1908-1911	353.1
Alberta Illustrated News	Edmonton	1913-1914	372
Alberta Independent	Red Deer	1898-1899	833
Alberta Jewish Chronicle	Edmonton	1960-	446
Alberta Labor News	Edmonton	1920-1936	386.1
Alberta Labour	Edmonton	1963-1979	450
Alberta Liberal	Edmonton	1961-1970	1062
Alberta Liberal	Edmonton	1970-1971	1064
Alberta Livestock Journal	Calgary	1888	113.3
Alberta Mercury	Calgary	1930-1931	168
Alberta Non-Partisan	Calgary	1917-1919	152.2
Alberta Oil Examiner	Calgary	1926	163.1
Alberta Oil Review	Calgary	1915-1916	150
Alberta Oil Review and Industrial Record	Calgary	1915-1916	150
Alberta Plaindealer	Edmonton	1896-1900	336.2
Alberta Social Credit Chronicle	Calgary	1934-1936	175.1
Alberta Star	Cardston	1901-1911	240.2
Alberta Star	Edmonton	1930	409.2
Alberta Sun	Calgary	1925-1927	162
Alberta Sun	Edmonton	1899-1900	340
Alberta Sun	Leduc	1899	340
Alberta Tribune Daily Edition	Calgary	1895	122
Alberta Tribune Weekly Edition	Calgary	1895-1899	123.1
Alberta Veteran	Calgary	1918-1920	155
Albertan	Calgary	1899	126
Albertan	Calgary	1899-1902	123.2
Albertan	Calgary	1936-1980	127.3
Albertan and Alberta Tribune	Calgary	1899-1902	123.2
Albertan's South Side Shopper	Calgary	1957	193
Albertiis'ka Zoria	Edmonton	1930	409.2
Alderson News	Alderson	1915-1918	12.3
Alix Free Press	Alix	1909-1933	14.1
Alix Free Press	Alix	1948-1949	14.3
Alix Free Press	Alix	1951-1953	14.6
Alix Free Press Mirror News-Record	Alix	1933-1948	14.2
Alix Free Press Mirror News Record	Alix	1949-1950	14.4
Alix Promoter	Alix	1957-1959	15
Alix-Mirror Free Press	Alix	1950	14.5
Alliance Times	Alliance	1916-1939	16.1
Amisk Advocate	Amisk	1921-1951	20

Title Index

Title	Place	Dates	Item
Andrew Advocate	Andrew	1951-1953	23
Andrew News	Andrew	1951-1953	23
Andrew News	Andrew	1934-1935	22.1
Anthracite Chronicle	Canmore	1976	233
Argus	Alliance	1920	17
Army and Navy News and Universal Weekly	Calgary	1918-1919	156
Arrow	Altario	1919	18
Athabasca Advance	Athabasca	1956-1957	31
Athabasca Call	Athabasca	1975-1977	32
Athabasca Echo	Athabasca	1928-1970	30.1
Athabasca Echo	Athabasca	1978-	30.3
Athabasca Echo and Slave Lake Centennial Press	Athabasca	1971-1978	30.2
Athabasca Herald	Athabasca	1916-1919	28
Athabasca Herald	Athabasca	1920-1921	29
Athabasca Sun	Boyle	1968-1969	100.2
Athabasca Times	Athabasca	1913-1915	27
Aurora News	Stony Plain	1913-1914	933
Ayamewatikum Manito Sakihagan	Lac Ste. Anne	1900-1905	1078
B.D. Weekly	Brule	1922-1923	108
Banff Advocate and Rocky Mountains Park District Recorder	Banff	1918-1922	41
Banff Crag and Canyon	Banff	1957-	38.4
Banff Echoes	Banff	1893	36.1
Banff Mercury	Banff	1928	43
Banff News	Banff	1929-1951	44
Banff Summit News	Banff	1967-1970	45
Banner	Edmonton	1950	437
Banner Post	Manning	1978-	722.2
Barons Beacon	Barons	1909	1046
Barons Enterprise	Barons	1911-1912	48
Barons Globe	Barons	1919-1921	50
Barons Weekly	Barons	1918	49
Barrhead County Star	Barrhead	1971-1977	54
Barrhead Leader	Barrhead	1932-1969	52.1
Barrhead Leader	Barrhead	1976-	52.3
Barrhead News	Barrhead	1927-1931	51
Barrhead Star	Barrhead	1971-1977	54
Bashaw Record	Bashaw	1911-1913	55
Bashaw Star	Bashaw	1915-1959	56.1
Bashaw Star	Bashaw	1972-1973	56.4
Bashaw Star	Bashaw	1977-	56.6

Title Index

Title	Place	Dates	Item
Bashaw Star and Alix Promoter	Bashaw	1963-1972	56.3
Bashaw Star and Alix Promoter	Bashaw	1973-1977	56.5
Bashaw Star and the Alix Promoter	Bashaw	1959-1963	56.2
Bassano Herald	Bassano	1955-1959	61
Bassano Mail	Bassano	1913-1936	58
Bassano News	Bassano	1910-1914	57
Bassano Recorder	Bassano	1937-1945	59
Bassano Star	Bassano	1946-1947	60
Bassano Times	Bassano	1960-	62
Battle River Herald	Manning	1949-1954	721
Bawlf Banner	Bawlf	1947-1949	65
Bawlf Sun	Bawlf	1907	63
Bawlf Sun	Bawlf	1908-1930	64
Beacon	Calgary	1952-1962	189
Bear Hills Native Voice	Hobbema	1968-1972	631
Bear Hills Native Voice	Hobbema	1976-	632
Bear Lake Miner and Northern News	Edmonton	1933-1935	416.1
Beaverlodge Advertiser	Beaverlodge	1956-	66
Bee	Calgary	1903	130
Beiseker Times	Beiseker	1949-1953	68
Bellevue Times	Bellevue	1910-1918	69
Bellevue Times and Frank Vindicator	Bellevue	1910	69
Beverly Advertiser	Edmonton	1914	373
Beverly Page	Edmonton	1953-	440
Big Country News	Drumheller	1967-1978	332.1
Big Valley News	Big Valley	1916-1923	70
Biuletyn. Kongresu Polonii Kanadyjskiej Okreg Alberta	Edmonton	1957-	443.2
Biuletyn. Organizacji Polskich W Edmontonie	Edmonton	1956	443.1
Black Diamond Press	Calgary	1913-1914	145
Blackfalds Mercury	Blackfalds	1903	74
Blackie Recorder	Blackie	1921	75
Blairmore Enterprise	Blairmore	1910-1946	77.2
Blairmore Enterprise and Frank Vindicator	Blairmore	1909-1910	77.1
Blairmore Graphic	Blairmore	1946-1951	83
Blindman Valley Advertiser	Rimbey	1930-1936	855.1
Blue Diamond Weekly	Brule	1923	108
Bon Accord Herald	Bon Accord	1935-1938	85
Bond of Brotherhood	Calgary	1903-1904	129
Bonnyville Newscope	Bonnyville	1964	88
Bonnyville Nouvelle	Bonnyville	1935-1943	86

Title Index

Title	Place	Dates	Item
Bonnyville Nouvelle	Bonnyville	1967-1977	89.1
Bonnyville Nouvelle	Bonnyville	1980-	89.3
Bonnyville Nouvelle, Grande Centre Globe	Bonnyville	1978-1980	89.2
Bonnyville Sun	Grand Centre	1978-	581.2
Bonnyville Tribune	Bonnyville	1947-1960	87.1
Bonnyville Tribune	Bonnyville	1962-1964	87.3
Booster	Lloydminster	1959-	705
Booster	Waskatenau	1937-1940	1013
Border County Recorder	Milk River	1972	755
Bow City Star	Bow City	1913-1914	1047
Bow Island News	Bow Island	1954-1956	91
Bow Island Review	Bow Island	1910-1936	90
Bow River News	Arrowwood	1924-1927	1045
Bow Valley Advertiser	Calgary	1953-1959	190
Bow Valley Call	Gleichen	1910-1914	576.2
Bow Valley Resource	Arrowwood	1931-1936	24
Bow Valley Views	Canmore	1974-1975	231
Bowden Booster	Bowden	1937-1938	98
Bowden Eye Opener	Bowden	1976-	99
Bowden News	Bowden	1909-1912	95
Bowden Recorder	Bowden	1920	96
Bowden Reporter	Bowden	1905-1906	94
Bowden Times	Bowden	1923-1924	97
Bowness Bulletin	Calgary	1948-1951	1055.1
Bowness News	Calgary	1951-1952	1055.2
Bowness Review	Calgary	1963	1054
Boyle Beacon	Boyle	1949-1968	100.1
Boyle Star	Boyle	1970-1977	101
Brant Weekly	Brant	1917-1918	102
Bridgeland and Riverside Echo	Calgary	1930	1052
Brivais Latvietis	Edmonton	1948-1949	430
Brooks Banner	Brooks	1910-1912	105.1
Brooks Bulletin	Brooks	1910	104
Brooks Bulletin	Brooks	1912-	105.2
Bruce News	Bruce	1911-1915	106
Bruderheim Review	Bruderheim	1952-1953	107
Brüke	Medicine Hat	1945-1946	751
Brule District Weekly	Brule	1923	108
Buffalo Lake Wave	Buffalo Lake	1895	109
Bulletin	Barrhead	1961-1964	53
Bulletin	Edmonton	1880-1881	334.1

Title Index

Title	Place	Dates	Item
Bulletin of Polish Association of Edmonton	Edmonton	1956	443.1
Bulletin of the Canadian Polish Congress	Edmonton	1957-	443.2
Burdett Review	Burdett	1932-1935	112
Burdett Times	Burdett	1917-1918	111
Burdett Tribune	Burdett	1910-1911	110
Business Reporter	Edmonton	1975-1977	479
Buzzer, Mainly About Town	Fort Macleod	1911-1912	541
Calgarian	Calgary	1909	138
Calgary Advance	Calgary	1894	121
Calgary Albertan	Calgary	1924-1936	127.2
Calgary Albertan	Calgary	1980	127.4
Calgary Avenues	Calgary	1982	220
Calgary Canadian	Calgary	1918	136.4
Calgary Citizen	Calgary	1946-1951	187
Calgary Daily Herald	Calgary	1885-	115
Calgary Daily News	Calgary	1908-1910	136.2
Calgary Daily Tribune	Calgary	1893-1894	117.5
Calgary Eye Opener	Calgary	1911-1923	132.2
Calgary Herald	Calgary	1885-	115
Calgary Herald and Alberta Livestock Journal	Calgary	1888	113.3
Calgary Herald, Mining and Ranche Advocate and General Advertiser	Calgary	1883-1887	113.1
Calgary Home News	Calgary	1932-1933	172
Calgary Hungarian Courier	Calgary	1980-	214
Calgary Jewish News	Calgary	1962-	196
Calgary Mirror North Side Edition	Calgary	1981-	205.4
Calgary Mirror South Side Edition	Calgary	1981-	194.4
Calgary News	Calgary	1947-1948	188
Calgary News	Calgary	1978-1981	191.3
Calgary News Telegram	Calgary	1910-1918	136.3
Calgary North Hill News	Calgary	1976-1978	191.2
Calgary Observer	Calgary	1904-1905	131
Calgary Optimist	Calgary	1909-1910	141
Calgary Rural Ad-viser	Calgary	1979-1981	211
Calgary Rural Week	Calgary	1981-1982	218.1
Calgary Sports Review	Calgary	1942	185
Calgary Standard	Calgary	1912-1913	142.2
Calgary Strike Bulletin	Calgary	1919	157
Calgary Sun	Calgary	1979	212
Calgary Sun	Calgary	1980-	215

Title Index

Title	Place	Dates	Item
Calgary Sunday Standard	Calgary	1916-1917	142.4
Calgary Tribune	Calgary	1886-1895	116.2
Calgary Tribune	Calgary	1886-1888	117.1
Calgary Tribune	Calgary	1889-1893	117.4
Calgary Tribune	Calgary	1894-1895	117.6
Calgary Tribune and Bow River Advertiser	Calgary	1885-1886	116.1
Calgary Typo News	Calgary	1935	177.1
Calgary Weekly Herald	Calgary	1887-1888	113.2
Calgary Weekly Herald	Calgary	1893	113.5
Calgary Weekly Herald	Calgary	1894-1895	113.7
Calgary Weekly Herald and Alberta Livestock Journal	Calgary	1888-1892	113.4
Calgary Western Standard	Calgary	1917-1918	142.5
Calgary Women's Newspaper	Calgary	1975-1981	206
Call	Calgary	1945-1952	186.1
Calmar Review	Calmar	1975	223
Campus Lyfe	Edmonton	1971-1972	470
Camrose Booster	Camrose	1952-	227
Camrose Canadian	Camrose	1908-	225
Camrose Mail	Camrose	1906-1909	224
Canada Goose	Edmonton	1968-1969	461
Canada Magyar Farmer	Edmonton	1910-1921	357
Canadai Magyar Farmer	Edmonton	1910-1921	357
Canadian	Edmonton	1912-1919	364
Canadian Advocate	Lethbridge	1918-1925	698
Canadian Chinese Times	Calgary	1981-	217
Canadian Field	Edmonton	1908-1910	354
Canadian Forces Base Cold Lake Courier	Cold Lake	1967-	287
Canadian Hungarian Farmer	Edmonton	1910-1921	357
Canadian Miner	Calgary	1931-1933	170.2
Canadian Nation	Calgary	1918-1919	154
Canadian Social Crediter	Edmonton	1944-1949	428
Canadian Social Crediter	Edmonton	1950-1959	434.1
Canadian Ukraine	Edmonton	1976-1978	480
Canadian Western Jewish Times	Calgary	1914	149
Canadian Western Standard	Calgary	1918	142.6
Canmore Miner	Canmore	1975-1983	232
Canmore Times	Canmore	1931-1937	228
Canmore Times	Canmore	1966-1970	230
Capital	Three Hills	1979-	965.2
Carbon Chronicle	Carbon	1922-1927	238.1
Carbon Chronicle	Carbon	1929-1960	238.3

Title Index

Title	Place	Dates	Item
Carbon News	Carbon	1920-1922	237
Carbon Reporter	Carbon	1911-1913	235
Carbondale Advocate	Coleman	1908-1909	288.2
Cardston Chronicle	Cardston	1980-	246
Cardston Globe	Cardston	1911-1921	240.3
Cardston News	Cardston	1924-1925	240.5
Cardston News	Cardston	1925-1964	241
Cardston News	Cardston	1964-1966	242
Cardston Record	Cardston	1898-1901	240.1
Cardston Review	Cardston	1921-1924	240.4
Cardston Unlimited	Cardston	1967-1974	243
Carlstadt News	Alderson	1912-1915	12.2
Carlstadt Progress	Alderson	1911-1912	12.1
Carmangay Sun	Carmangay	1910-1937	247
Carseland Recorder	Carseland	1921-1923	248
Carstairs and District Community Press	Carstairs	1975-1977	250.2
Carstairs and District Community Press and Mountain View County News	Carstairs	1977-1980	250.3
Carstairs Community Press, Mountain View County News	Carstairs	1980-1985	250.4
Carstairs Journal	Carstairs	1905-1923	249
Carstairs News	Carstairs	1924-1975	250.1
Carstairs Reporter	Carstairs	1903	1055
Castor Advance	Castor	1909-	252
Cayley Advertiser	Cayley	1914	254
Cayley Hustler	Cayley	1909-1913	253
Central Alberta Ad-viser	Red Deer	1977-	841
Central Alberta Parkland News	Red Deer County	1979-	830.2
Central Albertan	Wetaskiwin	1910-1911	1025.2
Cereal Recorder	Cereal	1920-1947	256
Champion Chronicle	Champion	1919-1941	260.1
Champion News	Champion	1919-1920	259
Champion Spokesman	Champion	1914	257
Champion Weekly	Champion	1917-1919	258
Chauvin Chronicle	Chauvin	1914-1948	263
Chauvin Chronicle	Wainwright	1949-	1009.2
Chauvin Gazette	Chauvin	1912-1913	262
Chinook	Calgary	1906-1907	133
Chinook	High River	1904-1905	624
Chinook	Lethbridge	1972-1976	1082
Chinook Advance	Chinook	1914-1945	264
Chinook Belt Advertiser	Milk River	1960-1961	754
Chinook Belt Advertiser	Taber	1960-1961	955

Title Index

Title	Place	Dates	Item
Chinook Reporter	Lethbridge	1978-1981	702
Chronicle	Carbon	1927-1929	238.2
Chronicle	Champion	1941-1943	260.2
Chronicle	Crossfield	1907-1942	296
Chronicle	Raymond	1903-1907	824.1
Church and Home	Edmonton	1930-1961	408
Citizen	Edmonton	1953-1957	436.2
Citizen	Stettler	1909-1911	925
Civvy Street	Red Deer	1946-1948	838
Clairmont Independent	Clairmont	1916-1918	265
Clairmont Independent and Lake Saskatoon Journal	Clairmont	1916-1918	265
Claresholm Advertiser	Claresholm	1914-1916	267.1
Claresholm Local Press	Claresholm	1926-	268
Claresholm Review	Claresholm	1904-1916	266
Claresholm Review-Advertiser	Claresholm	1916-1928	267.2
Clarion	Canmore	1956-1961	229
Clarion	Edmonton	1950-1951	433
Clarion of Alberta	Edmonton	1908	351
Climber	Banff	1906	39
Clive Messenger	Clive	1919-1921	271
Clive News-Record	Clive	1914-1918	270
Clive Review	Clive	1919-1921	271
Cluny Recorder	Cluny	1921-1924	272
Clyde Bulletin	Clyde	1950-1952	273
Clyde Star	Clyde	1972-1973	274
Coaldale Flyer	Coaldale	1950-1958	276.1
Coaldale Flyer and the Lethbridge Northern News	Coaldale	1958-1959	276.2
Coaldale Times	Coaldale	1922-1927	275
Coalhurst News	Coalhurst	1928-1929	278
Cochrane Advocate	Cochrane	1909-1927	279
Cochrane Old Timer	Cochrane	1943-1972	280
Cochrane Times	Cochrane	1974-1984	281
Cold Lake Courier	Cold Lake	1959-1960	285
Cold Lake Herald	Cold Lake	1932	284
Cold Lake Sentinel	Cold Lake	1959	286
Cold Lake Sun	Grand Centre	1977-1978	581.1
Coleman Bulletin	Coleman	1912-1918	289
Coleman Bulletin and Crow's Nest Pass Advertiser	Coleman	1912-1918	289
Coleman Journal	Coleman	1921-1939	290.1
Coleman Journal	Coleman	1940-1972	290.3

Title Index

Title	Place	Dates	Item
Coleman Journal and Crows Nest Pass Advertiser	Coleman	1939-1940	290.2
Coleman Miner	Coleman	1908-1909	288.1
Coleman Miner	Coleman	1910-1911	288.3
Coleman Miner and Carbondale Advocate	Coleman	1909-1910	288.2
Coleman Review	Coleman	1972-1974	290.4
Colinton Clipper	Colinton	1951-1955	291
Commerce News	Edmonton	1976-	1067
Commonsense	Calgary	1937	183
Community Press	Sedgewick	1930-	890.2
Conservator	Fort Saskatchewan	1913-1922	559
Consort Enterprise	Consort	1912-1922	292.1
Consort Enterprise	Consort	1937-	292.3
Coronation Review	Coronation	1911-	293
County News	Ponoka County	1955-1976	816
County News	Strathcona County	1975-1976	939.2
County of Lamont Star	Lamont County	1969-1975	676.1
County of Lethbridge Sunny South News	Coaldale	1974-	276.4
County of Minburn Review	Minburn County	1965	758.1
County of Two Hills Review	Two Hills County	1963-1968	980.3
County of Two Hills Star	Two Hills County	1970-1977	981
County of Warner Review and Advertiser	Milk River	1958-1961	753.3
Courier	Carstairs	1982-	251
Courier	Smoky River Municipal District	1952-1953	908.1
Courrier de Falher	Falher	1967-1969	528
Courrier de L'Ouest	Edmonton	1905-1916	347
Coutts-Sweetgrass International Herald	Coutts	1911	1056
Cowley Chronicle and Lundbreck Advertiser	Cowley	1909-1910	294
Crag and Canyon	Banff	1900-1901	38.1
Crag and Canyon	Banff	1903-1957	38.3
Crag and Canyon and National Park Gazette	Banff	1901-1902	38.2
Craigmyle Gazette	Craigmyle	1921-1922	295
Critic	Calgary	1902	128
Croatian Herald	Calgary	1975-	207
Croix de Ste.-Anne	Lac Ste. Anne	1900-1905	1078
Crossfield Chronicle	Crossfield	1943-1948	298
Crossfield Chronicle	Crossfield	1948	299
Crossfield Chronicle	Crossfield	1949-1953	300
Cypress Courier	Forty Mile County	1971	563
Czar Clipper	Czar	1920-1951	301

Title Index

Title	Place	Dates	Item
Daily Advertiser	Drumheller	1937-1942	331
Daily Albertan	Calgary	1899-1902	123.2
Daily Bulletin	Drumheller	1933-1936	328
Daily Edmonton Bulletin	Edmonton	1903-1906	342.1
Daily Herald Tribune	Grande Prairie	1964-	586.3
Daily News	Calgary	1907-1908	136.1
Dairy Contact	Calgary	1976-1982	208
Dairy Contact	Edmonton	1982-	500
Danish Review	Calgary	1930-1934	169
Danske Revy	Calgary	1930-1934	169
Danskeren	Calgary	1930-1934	169
Daysland Commercial	Daysland	1930-1931	303
Daysland Press	Daysland	1907-1930	302
Daysland Sun	Daysland	1947-1953	304
Delburne and District Journal	Delburne	1967-1986	310
Delburne Independent	Delburne	1928	308
Delburne News	Delburne	1924-1926	306
Delburne Observer	Delburne	1927-1928	307
Delburne Progress	Delburne	1912-1922	305
Delburne Times	Delburne	1936-1967	309
Delia Times	Delia	1919-1960	312
Delia Times	Delia	1974	313
Demonstrator	Edmonton	1960	1060
Despertar	Edmonton	1972-198?	474
Deutsch-Canadier	Calgary	1909-1914	139
Deutsch-Canadier	Edmonton	1908-1909	355
Deutsch-Canadischer Farmer	Calgary	1909-1912	140
Deutsch Arbeiter Zeitung	Edmonton	1930-1931	411
Deutsche Canadische Farmer	Calgary	1909-1912	140
Devon Dispatch	Devon	1976-	315
Devonian	Devon	1949-1957	314
Diario	Edmonton	1982-	501
Diario Hispano	Edmonton	1982-	501
Didsbury Booster	Didsbury	1961-1974	318.1
Didsbury Booster and Mountain View County News	Didsbury	1974-1980	318.2
Didsbury Courier	Didsbury	1903	316
Didsbury Pioneer	Didsbury	1903-1974	317
Didsbury Pioneer and Mountain View County News	Didsbury	1980-1986	318.3
District Call	Edson	1921-1922	508
District News	Munson	1920	778.1
District News	Munson	1921	778.4

Title Index

Title	Place	Dates	Item
District News, Morrin News Section	Morrin	1921	770.2
District News, Munson News Section	Munson	1921	778.3
District Press	Andrew	1935-1946	22.2
Donalda Free Lance	Donalda	1915-1916	319
Donalda Recorder	Donalda	1920-1921	320
Donalda Review	Donalda	1921-1927	321
Douglas Social Credit Advocate	Calgary	1934-1936	176.2
Drayton Valley Banner	Drayton Valley	1965	1057
Drayton Valley Booster	Drayton Valley	1977	324
Drayton Valley Tribune	Drayton Valley	1954-1958	322
Drill	Frank	1904-1905	565
Druh Naroda	Edmonton	1926-1930	400
Drumheller Mail	Drumheller	1918-	327
Drumheller Review	Drumheller	1913-1934	325.1
Drumheller Review	Drumheller	1936-1940	325.4
Drumheller Standard	Drumheller	1917-1918	326
Drumheller Sun	Drumheller	1978-1979	332.2
Dzvin	Edmonton	1950-1951	433
Eagle Review	Two Hills County	1950-1963	980.2
Eagleview Post	Turner Valley	1981	979
East City News	Calgary	1974	204
East-Ender	Edmonton	1923-1924	397
Echo	High Level	1973-	614
Echo de Ste-Anne	Lac Ste Anne	1895	668.1
Echo de Ste-Anne	Lac Ste. Anne	1897	668.2
Eckville Examiner	Eckville	1949-	333
Edgerton Enterprise	Chauvin	1946-1948	263
Edgerton Enterprise	Wainwright	1949-	1009.2
Edmonton and Alberta Business	Edmonton	1981-1982	491.2
Edmonton Bulletin	Edmonton	1881-1923	334.2
Edmonton Bulletin	Edmonton	1924-1951	358.3
Edmonton Business	Edmonton	1982	491.3
Edmonton Capital	Edmonton	1909-1911	356.1
Edmonton Capital	Edmonton	1913-1914	356.3
Edmonton Daily Bulletin	Edmonton	1906-1923	342.2
Edmonton Daily Bulletin	Edmonton	1910-1915	358.1
Edmonton Daily Capital	Edmonton	1911-1913	356.2
Edmonton Evening Journal	Edmonton	1907-1909	344.2
Edmonton Examiner [North Editions]	Edmonton	1978-	490
Edmonton Examiner [South Editions]	Edmonton	1977-	486
Edmonton Examiner [West Editions]	Edmonton	1977-	487
Edmonton Free Press	Edmonton	1906-1907	1058
Edmonton Free Press	Edmonton	1919-1920	384

Title Index

Title	Place	Dates	Item
Edmonton Free Press	Edmonton	1961-1962	448
Edmonton Gazette	Edmonton	1965-1966	454
Edmonton Herald	Edmonton	1895-1896	337
Edmonton Journal	Edmonton	1911-	344.4
Edmonton Journal Farm Weekly	Edmonton	1924	396.2
Edmonton Journal Farm Weekly and Alberta Farm Journal	Edmonton	1924-1925	396.3
Edmonton News	Edmonton	1913-1919	371
Edmonton News	Edmonton	1958-1959	444
Edmonton News-Plaindealer	Edmonton	1912-1913	336.5
Edmonton Post	Edmonton	1912-1913	336.5
Edmonton Saturday Mirror	Edmonton	1899-1902	365.2
Edmonton Sports Record	Edmonton	1939	425
Edmonton Star	Edmonton	1971-1974	463.2
Edmonton Star and Alberta Farm Life	Edmonton	1969-1971	463.1
Edmonton Strike Bulletin	Edmonton	1919	385
Edmonton Sun	Edmonton	1951-1962	432.2
Edmonton Sun	Edmonton	1977-1978	488
Edmonton Sun	Edmonton	1978-	489
Edmonton Times	Edmonton	1977-	486
Edmonton Town Topics	Edmonton	1905-1909	346
Edmonton Weekly Journal	Edmonton	1923-1924	396.1
Edmonton Weekly Topics	Edmonton	1905-1909	346
Edmonton Weekly Town Topics	Edmonton	1905-1909	346
Edson Atom	Edson	1924	510
Edson Critic	Edson	1913	504.2
Edson Enterprise	Edson	1920	507
Edson Headlight	Edson	1922-1923	509
Edson Herald	Edson	1917	505
Edson Leader	Edson	1911-1913	503.1
Edson Leader	Edson	1917	503.3
Edson Leader	Edson	1953-	512
Edson News	Edson	1918	506
Edson Record	Edson	1910	502
Edson Semi-Weekly Critic	Edson	1913-1914	504.3
Edson-Jasper Signal	Edson	1928-1943	511.1
Elk Point Hunter	Elk Point	1961-1963	513
Elk Point Reflections	Elk Point	1979-1980	1069
Elk Point Sentinel	Elk Point	1979-1982	515
Elk Point Star	Elk Point	1972-1973	514
Elnora Advance	Elnora	1918-1933	516
Empress Express	Empress	1913-1936	517

Title Index

Title	Place	Dates	Item
Enchant Weekly	Enchant	1917-1918	518
English Express	Edmonton	1982-	499
Enterprise	Alliance	1939-	16.2
Enterprise	Leduc	1904-1906	688
Enterprise (Consort and Monitor)	Consort	1922-1937	292.2
Entwistle Enterprise	Entwistle	1912-1913	520
Erskine Review	Erskine	1912-1921	521
Erskine Times	Erskine	1922-1924	522
Etoile de St. Albert	St. Albert	1912-1913	878.1
Etoile de St. Albert	St. Albert	1914	878.2
Evansburg Pembina Herald	Pembina Municpal District	1952	806.1
Evening Chronicle	Edmonton	1907-1908	350
Evening Journal	Edmonton	1903-1907	344.1
Evening Journal	Edmonton	1909-1911	344.3
Evening Tribune	Calgary	1888	117.2
Evening Tribune and Bow River Advertiser	Calgary	1888	117.3
Examiner	Edmonton	1970-1971	467
Examiner	Spruce Grove	1981-	913.4
Examiner [North Edmonton Editions]	Edmonton	1978-	490
Examiner: Spruce Grove Edition	Spruce Grove	1979	913.2
Examiner, [West Edmonton Edition]	Edmonton	1977	487
Express	Falher	1973	529.3
Eye Opener	Calgary	1904-1911	132.1
Eye Opener	High River	1902-1903	623
F.U.A. Bulletin	Edmonton	1949	427.2
Fairplay	Calgary	1915-1918	1050
Fairview Post	Fairview	1940-1963	526.1
Fairview This Week	Fairview	1977-1978	527
Falher News	Falher	1967-1969	528
Falher News	Falher	1969-1972	529.1
Farm Business Trends	Edmonton	1949-1971	427.3
Farmers Tribune	Alderson	1914	13
Farmers' Voice	Edmonton	1932-1934	415
Farmers' Word	Edmonton	1921	387
Farmerfreund	Edmonton	1903-1915	343
Farmerske Slovo	Edmonton	1921	387
Farmerskyi Holos	Edmonton	1932-1934	415
Financial News	Edmonton	1911-1913	361
Five Village Weekly	Rocky View Municipal District	1975-1980	862.1
Flare	Black Diamond	1937-1946	73
Focus	Edmonton	1959-	434.2

Title Index

Title	Place	Dates	Item
Footnotes and News	Claresholm	1969-1973	269
Forestburg Advance	Forestburg	1916-1920	530
Forestburg Free Press	Forestburg	1947-1949	533
Forestburg Herald	Forestburg	1927-1933	532
Forestburg Home News	Forestburg	1920-1922	531
Fort Macleod Gazette	Fort Macleod	1882-1884	536.1
Fort McMurray Banner	Fort McMurray	1965-1967	548
Fort McMurray Express	Fort McMurray	1979-	553
Fort McMurray News Advertiser	Fort McMurray	1968-1970	1073
Fort McMurray Northern Star	Fort McMurray	1967-1969	550
Fort McMurray Sun	Fort McMurray	1969	1074
Fort McMurray Times	Fort McMurray	1969	1075
Fort McMurray Today	Fort McMurray	1974-	552
Fort Record	Fort Saskatchewan	1935-1951	560.3
Fort Record	Fort Saskatchewan	1978-1979	560.8
Fort Saskatchewan Herald	Fort Saskatchewan	1911	557
Fort Saskatchewan News	Fort Saskatchewan	1899	554
Fort Saskatchewan Record	Fort Saskatchewan	1931-1935	560.2
Fort Saskatchewan Record	Fort Saskatchewan	1952-1960	560.4
Fort Saskatchewan Recorder	Fort Saskatchewan	1911-1912	558
Fort Saskatchewan Reporter	Fort Saskatchewan	1903-1909	555
Fort Saskatchewan Star	Fort Saskatchewan	1972-1977	561
Fort Spitzee Signal	High River	1973-1974	626
Forty-Mile County Commentator	Forty Mile County	1971	563
Forum	Edmonton	1972-	472
Franco	Edmonton	1979-	458.2
Franco-albertain	Edmonton	1967-1979	458.1
Frank Paper	Frank	1905-1909	566
Frank Sentinel	Frank	1901-1903	564
Frank Vindicator	Frank	1910-1915	567
Free Lance	Calgary	1931	171
Free Lance	Innisfail	1898-1901	641
Free Lance	Innisfail	1902	642.1
Free Lance	Wetaskiwin	1897-1898	1018
Freelancer	Mayerthorpe	1978-	738
Free Latvian	Edmonton	1948-1949	430
Free Press	Wetaskiwin	1911-1917	1026.1
Free Press	Whitecourt	1982-1985	1034
Frontier Signal	Grande Prairie	1914-1916	585
Gadsby Gazette	Gadsby	1911	568
Gadsby Observer	Gadsby	1917-1918	569
Gadsby Recorder	Gadsby	1920-1922	570
Gadsby Weekly Bulletin	Stettler	1906-	923

Title Index

Title	Place	Dates	Item
Galahad Guardian	Galahad	1947-1949	572
Galahad Mail	Galahad	1917-1918	571
Garden City News	Magrath	1951	720
Garden City Times	Magrath	1941-1949	718
Gateway	Edmonton	1910-	359
Gateway	Jasper	1965-1969	658
Gauntlet	Calgary	1960-	195
Gazette	Lamont	1918-1922	680
Gazette	Olds	1978-	789.3
Gazette	Rocky Mountain House	1921-1923	859
Gazette	St. Albert	1966-1970	880.2
Gazette	St. Albert	1974-	880.4
Gazette	Stony Plain	1909-1910	929
Gazette and Alberta Live Stock Record	Fort Macleod	1894-1907	536.4
German-Canadian Farmer	Calgary	1909-1912	140
German Labor News	Edmonton	1930-1931	4111
Gibbons Herald	Gibbons	1951-1952	573
Gleichen Call	Gleichen	1907-1910	576.1
Gleichen Call	Gleichen	1914-1956	576.
Gleichen Chronicle	Gleichen	1905	575
Gleichen Echo	Gleichen	1903-1904	574
Gleichen Newspaper	Gleichen	1907-1910	576.1
Glendon Bulletin	Glendon	1952-1955	577
Glenwood Gleanings	Glenwood	1972-	578
Glow Worm	Edmonton	1923	398
Grand Centre Globe	Bonnyville	1967-1977	89.1
Grand Centre Press	Grand Centre	1962-1968	580
Grand Centre Times	Grand Centre	1959-1960	579
Grand Centre-Cold Lake-Bonnyville Sun.	Grand Centre	1978-	581.2
Grand Centre-Cold Lake Sun	Grand Centre	1977-1978	581.1
Grand Trunk Poplar Press	Evansburg	1979-	523
Grande Cache Mountaineer	Grande Cache	1970-	583
Grande Cache Star	Grande Cache	1970	582
Grande Prairie Booster	Grande Prairie	1972-1981	588.1
Grande Prairie Herald	Grande Prairie	1913-1939	584
Grande Prairie This Week	Grande Prairie	1981-	588.2
Granum Advertiser	Granum	1914	593
Granum Herald	Granum	1918-1919	594.2
Granum News	Granum	1910-1912	592
Granum News	Granum	1917-1918	594.1
Granum Press	Granum	1909-1910	591

Title Index

Title	Place	Dates	Item
Granum Times	Granum	1908	590
Graphic	Bow Island	1956-1960	92
Graphic	Bow Island	1960-1962	93
Grassy Lake Gazette	Grassy Lake	1911-1917	599
Grassy Lake News	Grassy Lake	1908-1909	596
Grassy Lake Pilot	Grassy Lake	1910-1911	589
Grassy Lake Record	Grassy Lake	1908-1909	596
Great West	Edmonton	1907-1909	349
Great West Saturday Night	Edmonton	1918	380
Great West Saturday Night Advance	Edmonton	1912-1913	370
Grimshaw Spotlight	Grimshaw	1956-1960	601
Grimshaw Voyageur	Grimshaw	1952-1953 ·	600
Grizzly Gazette	Swan Hills	1977-	947
Grouard News	Grouard	1912-1915	604
Grove Examiner	Spruce Grove	1974-1979	913.1
Grove Examiner	Spruce Grove	1979-1980	913.3
Guide to Citizenship, Prosperity and Happiness	Rocky Mountain House	1912-1917	856.2
Hand Hills Echo	Delia	1916-1918	311
Hanna Herald	Hanna	1912-1947	605.1
Hanna Herald and East Central Alberta News	Hanna	1947-	605.2
Hanna Leader	Hanna	1913	606
Hardisty Enterprise	Hardisty	1908-1909	607
Hardisty Mail	Hardisty	1910-1930	608
Hardisty World	Hardisty	1924-1952	609
Hat Air-Mail Weekly	Medicine Hat	1939-1940	750
Hay Lakes Review	Hay Lakes	1946-1949	611
Hay Lakes Times	Hay Lakes	1925-1931	610
Heisler Herald	Heisler	1947-1949	612
Heisler News	Forestburg	1927-1933	532
Herald Parklander	Hinton	1974-1976	627.3
Herald-Tribune	Grande Prairie	1939-1964	586.2
Herald-Tribune Rural Route	Grande Prairie	1972-	587
Herold	Edmonton	1928-1931	403
High Country Flare	Turner Valley	1979-1980	978
High Level Echo	High Level	1973-	614
High Prairie Progress	High Prairie	1956-1958	619.1
High Prairie Progress	High Prairie	1959-1963	619.3
High Prairie Reporter	High Prairie	1974-1975	621
High River Times	High River	1905-1975	625.1
Highway 43 Tribune	Onoway	1978-1979	794.1
Hinton Herald	Hinton	1955-1969	627.1

Title Index

Title	Place	Dates	Item
Hinton Herald Parklander	Hinton	1969-1974	627.2
Hlas Naroda	Blairmore	1932-1934	80
Holden Herald	Holden	1910-1943	633
Holden Herald	Holden	1944-1968	634
Holland Revue	Edmonton	1954	441
Holos Pravdy	Smoky Lake	1937-1960	904
Homestead	Edmonton	1911-1913	353.2
Hoodoo Highlander	Canmore	1976-1983	234
Hoofprints	Stettler	1906-	923
Hot Springs Record	Banff	1887	34
Hrvatski Vjesnik Hrvatskog Drustva Prijatelja Matice Hrvatske	Calgary	1975-	207
Hub	Westlock	1968-	1016
Hub (St. Albert Edition)	Westlock	1977	1016
Hughenden Herald	Hughenden	1920	636.2
Hughenden News	Hughenden	1916-1919	635
Hughenden Record	Hughenden	1921-1962	636.3
Hungarians of the West	Calgary	1982-	219
Huxley New Era	Huxley	1915	637
Huxley Recorder	Huxley	1920-1922	638
Hythe Headliner	Hythe	1973-1977	639
Independent	Calgary	1898	125
Independent Reformer	St. Paul	1945	885
Indian Advocate	Whitefish Lake	1897-1902	1035
Indochinese News	Calgary	1982-	221
Innisfail Booster	Innisfail	1954-	645
Innisfail Free Lance	Innisfail	1902-1908	642.2
Innisfail Independent	Innisfail	1909-1911	644
Innisfail Province	Innisfail	1927-	643.2
Innisfail Standard	Innisfail	1898-1899	640
Innisfail Star	Innisfail	1977	1077
Innisfree Banner	Innisfree	1950-1953	646
Innisfree Times	Mannville	1927-1929	725.2
International Labor News	Edmonton	1923-1924	394
Irma Independent	Irma	1934-1935	648
Irma Times	Irma	1922-1969	647.2
Irma Times	Viking	1969-1974	1000.2
Irricana Recorder	Irricana	1920	650
Irricana Review	Irricana	1911	649
Irvine Index	Irvine	1912-1913	651
Italian News	Calgary	1974-1975	202
Jarrow Journal	Jarrow	1911-1913	653
Jasper Booster	Jasper	1963-	657

Title Index

Title	Place	Dates	Item
Jasper Gateway	Jasper	1965-1969	658
Jasper Place Citizen	Edmonton	1950-1953	436.1
Jasper Place Review	Edmonton	1949-1951	431
Jasper Signal	Jasper	1927-1928	654
Jasper Totem	Jasper	1955-1967	656
Jewish Star [Calgary Edition]	Calgary	1980-	216
Jewish Star [Edmonton Edition]	Edmonton	1980-	495
Jornal Portugese	Edmonton	197?-1981	466
Journal ·	Big Valley	1924-1934	72
Journal	Wetaskiwin	1911-1912	1027.1
Kainai News	Stand Off	1968-	915
Kanadiiskaia Niva	Edmonton	1908-1910	354
Kanadiyska Ukraina	Edmonton	1976-1978	480
Kanadyiets	Edmonton	1912-1919	364
Katolytski Kartyny	Mundare	1938-1949	772
Kicking Horse Chronicles	Lake Louise	1961-1962	672
Kicking Horse News	Lake Louise	1962-1973	673
Killam News	Killam	1911-1930	659
Killam News	Killam	1946-1952	660
Kirken og Hjemmet	Edmonton	1930-1961	408
Korean Canadian Times	Edmonton	1981-	496
Korean Dong-Baung News	Calgary	1976	210
Kupets	Edmonton	1936	422
Labor Advocate	Edmonton	1960	1061
Labor Day Bulletin	Medicine Hat	1912	745
Lac La Biche Herald	Lac La Biche	1948-1968	662.1
Lac La Biche Herald	Lac La Biche	1974-1977	664.2
Lac La Biche Post	Lac La Biche	1968-	663
Lac La Biche Star	Lac La Biche	1970-1974	664.1
Lac La Biche Sun	Lac La Biche	1968-1969	662.2
Lac Ste Anne Advance	Lac Ste Anne County	1971	666
Lac Ste Anne Advance	Stony Plain	1971	937.2
Lac Ste Anne and Mayerthorpe Star	Mayerthorpe	1970-1972	737.1
Lac Ste Anne Chronicle	Lac Ste Anne County	1936-1968	665.1
Lac Ste Anne Chronicle	Lac Ste Anne County	1974-1977	667
Lac Ste Anne County Star	Whitecourt	1962-	1033
Lac Ste Anne Reporter	Stony Plain	1967-	937.2
Lac Ste Anne Star	Mayerthorpe	1970-1972	737.1
Lac Ste Anne Sun	Lac Ste Anne County	1968-1969	665.2

Title Index

Title	Place	Dates	Item
Lacombe Advertiser and Central Alberta News	Lacombe	1908-1909	669.2
Lacombe Globe	Lacombe	1938-	670.2
Lacombe Guardian	Lacombe	1913-1916	671
Lacombe Municipal News	Lacombe	1946-1955	1080
Lacombe Weekly Press	Lacombe	1899	1079
Lake Saskatoon Journal	Lake Saskatoon	1917-1918	674
Lakeside Leader	Slave Lake	1975-	903
Lakeview Wave	Lakeview	1911	675
Lamont Banner	Lamont	1946-1951	682
Lamont Bulletin	Lamont	1961-1963	684
Lamont County Star	Lamont County	1975-1977	676.2
Lamont Gazette	Fort Saskatchewan	1967-1969	560.6
Lamont Journal	Lamont	1951-1953	683
Lamont Times	Lamont	1907	678
Lamont Tribune	Lamont	1914-1916	679
Lamont Tribune	Lamont	1931-1941	681.2
Lamont Weekly News	Lamont	1907	678
Langdon Advance	Langdon	1911	685
Langdon Leader	Langdon	1911-1912	686
Latin Report	Edmonton	1976-1978	482
Leader	Barrhead	1969-1976	52.2
Leavings Star	Granum	1905	589
Leduc Record	Leduc	1903-1904	687
Legal Record	Legal	1948-1953	691
Lesser Slave Lake Scope	Slave Lake	1972-1973	901.2
Lesser Slave Lake Star	Slave Lake	1958-1960	899
Lethbridge Daily Herald	Lethbridge	1907-1926	694.1
Lethbridge Daily News	Lethbridge	1910-1912	695.1
Lethbridge Herald	Lethbridge	1905-1950	693
Lethbridge Herald	Lethbridge	1926-	694.2
Lethbridge News	Lethbridge	1885-1890	692.1
Lethbridge News	Lethbridge	1891-1900	692.3
Lethbridge News	Lethbridge	1905-1906	692.6
Lethbridge News	Lethbridge	1907-1910	692.8
Lethbridge News and Southern Alberta Irrigationist	Lethbridge	1905	692.5
Lethbridge News Weekly	Lethbridge	1913	695.3
Lethbridge Northern News	Picture Butte	1954-1958	812.2
Lethbridge Telegram	Lethbridge	1914-1919	697
Liberty	Calgary	1922	161
Light	Mundare	1938-1949	772
Link	Vermilion	1918-1922	993.1

Title Index

Title	Place	Dates	Item
Link and Mannville Empire	Vermilion	1922-1923	993.2
Lloydminster Daily Times	Lloydminster	1979-	706
Lloydminster Review	Lloydminster	1914	704
Lloydminster Times	Lloydminster	1905-1906	703.1
Lloydminster Times	Lloydminster	1914-1979	703.3
Lloydminster Times and District News	Lloydminster	1907-1914	703.2
Log	Lodgepole	1959-1961	707
Lomond Press	Lomond	1916-1926	708
Lomond Press	Lomond	1928	710
Lomond Weekly	Lomond	1917-1918	709
Lougheed Express	Lougheed	1912-1930	711
Lougheed Journal	Lougheed	1925-1950	712
Lougheed Leader	Sedgewick	1930-	890.2
Lousana Observer	Lousana	1922	713
Lousana Page	Delburne	1912-1922	305
Lunch News	Edmonton	1977	483
Lundbreck Advertiser	Cowley	1909-1910	294
M.D. Red Deer News	Red Deer	1945-1946	1084
Mackenzie Highway Pictorial	High Level	1979-1980	615.1
Mackenzie Highway Pictorial Review	High Level	1980-	615.2
Macklin Times	Macklin, Sask.	1962-1963	714
Macleod Advance	Fort Macleod	1899-1907	538.1
Macleod Advertiser	Fort Macleod	1909-1913	540
Macleod Argus	Fort Macleod	1939-1940	546
Macleod Chronicle	Fort Macleod	1908-1909	539.2
Macleod Gazette	Fort Macleod	1884-1887	536.2
Macleod Gazette	Fort Macleod	1907	536.5
Macleod Gazette	Fort Macleod	1931-	545
Macleod Gazette and Alberta Live Stock Record	Fort Macleod	1887-1894	536.3
Macleod News	Fort Macleod	1916-1919	543.1
Macleod Spectator	Fort Macleod	1912-1916	542
Macleod Times	Fort Macleod	1920	544.1
Macleod Times and Macleod Weekly News	Fort Macleod	1920-1930	544.2
Macleod Weekly News	Fort Macleod	1919-1920	543.2
Magrath Mirror	Magrath	1948-1951	719
Magrath News	Magrath	1929-1933	717
Magrath Pioneer	Magrath	1906-1915	715
Magrath Times	Magrath	1922-1923	716
Magyar Hirmondo	Calgary	1980-	214
Manning Banner Post	Manning	1966-1978	722.1
Mannville Empire	Mannville	1920-1922	724

Title Index

Title	Place	Dates	Item
Mannville Mirror	Mannville	1934-1946	726
Mannville Mirror	Mannville	1949-1965	729
Mannville News	Mannville	1923-1927	725.1
Mannville News and the Minburn and Innisfree Times	Mannville	1927-1929	725.2
Mannville Reflections	Mannville	1978-1980	731.1
Mannville Reflections	Mannville	1981-	731.3
Mannville Review	Mannville	1948-1949	728
Mannville Star	Mannville	1971-1973	730
Mannville Telegram	Mannville	1907-1909	723
Manville [sic] Empire	Mannville	1910-1922	724
Manville [sic] Reporter	Mannville	1935-1936	727
Manyberries Enterprise	Manyberries	1917-1919	732
Market Examiner	Calgary	1917-1922	153.1
Market Examiner	Calgary	1954-1955	153.3
Market Examiner and Western Farm Journal	Calgary	1923-1954	153.2
Mayerthorpe Free Press	Mayerthorpe	1950-1951	735
Mayerthorpe Merchant	Mayerthorpe	1939-1941	734
Mayerthorpe Review	Mayerthorpe	1951-1968	736
Mayerthorpe Star	Mayerthorpe	1972-1977	737.2
Mayerthorpe Times	Mayerthorpe	1931-1935	733
Mayerthorpe Times	Mayerthorpe	1950-1951	734
Mayerthorpe-Lac Ste Anne Star	Mayerthorpe	1970-1972	737.1
McMurray Courier	Fort McMurray	1970-1975	551
McMurray Northlander	Fort McMurray	1949-1952	547
McMurray Northlander	Fort McMurray	1966-1968	549
McMurray Times	Fort McMurray	1969	1075
Medicine Hat Advertiser	Medicine Hat	1939-1940	750
Medicine Hat Call	Medicine Hat	1912-1913	747
Medicine Hat Daily News	Medicine Hat	1910	743.1
Medicine Hat Daily News	Medicine Hat	1941-1949	743.3
Medicine Hat Daily Times	Medicine Hat	1888	740
Medicine Hat News	Medicine Hat	1894-1910	741
Medicine Hat News	Medicine Hat	1910-1941	743.2
Medicine Hat News	Medicine Hat	1910-1941	744.1
Medicine Hat News	Medicine Hat	1949-1971	743.4
Medicine Hat News	Medicine Hat	1981-	743.6
Medicine Hat Times	Medicine Hat	1885-1888	739.1
Medicine Hat Times	Medicine Hat	1888-1894	739.3
Medicine Hat Weekly News	Medicine Hat	1941-1955	744.2
Meliorist	Lethbridge	1967-	701
Merchant	Edmonton	1936	422

Title Index

Title	Place	Dates	Item
Mercury	Tofield	1918-1952	969
Mercury	Tofield	1962-	970.2
Meridian Booster	Lloydminster	1959-	705
Messaggero delle Praterie	Edmonton	1969-1977	465
Messaggero Italiano	Edmonton	1966	455
Midweeker	Red Deer	1977-1979	840
Mile Zero News	Grimshaw	1979-	603
Milk River Review	Milk River	1948-1954	753.1
Milk River Review	Milk River	1961	753.4
Milk River Review Tourist and Recreation Guide	Milk River	1962	753.6
Millet Bulletin	Millet	1946-1949	757
Minburn and Innisfree Times	Mannville	1927-1929	725.2
Minburn County Review	Minburn County	1965-1968	758.2
Minburn County Star	Minburn County	1973-1977	759
Minburn Sun	Minburn County	1968-1969	758.3
Mirror	Edmonton	1912	365.1
Mirror	Stony Plain	1915-1916	934
Mirror	Wabamun	1914-1915	1006
Mirror Journal	Mirror	1911-1929	761
Mirror Mail	Mirror	1925-1927	762
Mirror News Record	Alix	1951-1953	14.6
Mirror North Side	Calgary	1977-1980	205.2
Mirror South Side	Calgary	1977-1980	194.2
Moccasin Telegram	Fort Chipewyan	1976-1979	534
Mondo	Edmonton	1967-1969	456
Monitor News	Monitor	1915-1922	763
Morinville and Sturgeon Mirror	Morinville	1979-	767
Morinville Journal	Morinville	1948-1961	765
Morinville Journal	Morinville	1974-1977	766.2
Morinville Mirror	Morinville	1979-	767
Morinville Star	Morinville	1969-1973	766.1
Mormoratore	Calgary	1970-	200
Morning Albertan	Calgary	1902-1924	127.1
Morning Bulletin	Calgary	1980	127.4
Morning Bulletin	Edmonton	1915-1924	358.2
Morning Herald	Calgary	1885-	115
Morning News	Lethbridge	1912-1913	695.2
Morning Times	Medicine Hat	1912-1916	746
Morrin District News	Morrin	1920-1921	770.1
Morrin Recorder	Morrin	1920-1922	769
Moukari	Edmonton	1913-1915	366
Mountain Echoes	Banff	1888-1889	35

Title Index

Title	Place	Dates	Item
Mountain Merchandiser	Banff	1968	46
Mountaineer	Rocky Mountain House	1914	857
Mountaineer	Rocky Mountain House	1923-1950	860.1
Mountaineer	Rocky Mountain House	1957-1960	860.3
Mountaineer	Rocky Mountain House	1963-	860.5
Mundare Mirror	Mundare	1958-1961	774
Mundare Star	Mundare	1952-1953	773
Munson District News	Munson	1920-1921	778.2
Munson Mail	Munson	1912-1918	775
Munson News	Munson	1919-1920	777
Munson Times	Munson	1914-1915	776
Myrnam News	Myrnam	1936-1937	779
Nanton News	Nanton	1903-	780
Nasa Mladez	Blairmore	1932-1934	80
Nash Postup	Edmonton	1922-1929	393
National Park Gazette	Banff	1900	37
National Park Life	Banff	1888-1889	35
Nation's Ensign	Edmonton	1982-1983	494.2
Native Ensign	Edmonton	1980-1982	494.1
Native People	Edmonton	1968-1982	460
Natural Gas and Oil Record	Calgary	1913-1914	147
Neu-Kanadier	Coaldale	1954-1955	277
New Age	Wetaskiwin	1912-1913	1028
New Alberta Liberal	Edmonton	1972-1978	1065
New Bonnyville Tribune	Bonnyville	1964-1968	87.4
New Call	Calgary	1952	186.2
New Country	Edmonton	1929	406
New Pathway	Edmonton	1930-1933	410
New Raymond Recorder	Raymond	1950-1955	826.1
New Review	Drumheller	1934-1936	325.2
New Sarepta New Era	New Sarepta	1948-1949	781
New Society	Edmonton	1911-1912	363
New Stirling Star	Stirling	1910	927
News	Carbon	1912	236
News	Edmonton	1913-1915	367
News	Edmonton	1917-1922	379
News	Fort Chipewyan	1981-1983	535
News	Medicine Hat	1971-1981	743.5
News	Red Deer	1905-1920	835.1

Title Index

Title	Place	Dates	Item
News	Thorhild County	1974-1986	958
News Advertiser	Edmonton	1922-1923	392
News Advertiser	Vegreville	1950-1977	988.1
News and Alberta Irrigationist	Lethbridge	1900-1905	692.4
News Bulletin	Edmonton	1951	438
News Review	Coronation	1911	293
News, Sherwood Park	Sherwood Park	1977-1978	896.2
News-Advertiser	Edmonton	1947-1948	429
News-Advertiser	Wetaskiwin	1938-1983	1030
News-Advertiser Ad-Mart	Hinton	1962-1964	628
News-Plaindealer	Edmonton	1912	336.4
News-Record	Whitecourt	1914-1917	1031
Newscene	Edmonton	1978-1979	1068
Nisku News	Nisku	1981-1986	782
Noon News	Edmonton	1979	492
Nor-East Ad-Viser	Edmonton	1932	413
Nor' West Miner	Edmonton	1935-1950	416.2
Nor'-Wester	Calgary	1884-1885	114
North American Collector	Crossfield	1908	297
North American News	St. Albert	1899	876
North Country News	Hoadley	1920-1930	629
North Country Times	Hoadley	1950	630
North Edmonton Examiner	Edmonton	1978-	490
North Edmonton Star	Edmonton	1950-1951	435
North Hill Advocate	Calgary	1930	1052
North Hill News	Calgary	1954-1976	191.1
North Lethbridge Breeze and Milk River Review	Milk River	1961	753.5
North of the Athabasca	Barrhead	1932-1969	52.1
North Peace Pictorial	Peace River	1973-	805
North Side Mirror	Calgary	1975-1977	205.1
North Side Mirror	Calgary	1980-1981	205.3
North Star	Wetaskiwin	1900	1019
Northeast News	Vermilion	1978-1979	944
Northern Alberta Farmer	Leduc	1977	690
Northern Albertan	Wetaskiwin	1910	1025.1
Northern Banner	Fort McMurray	1959-1965	1072
Northern Echo	High Level	1969	613
Northern Echo	High Prairie	1945-1956	617
Northern Gazette	Peace River	1932-1939	803
Northern Herald	Lac La Biche	1941-1948	661
Northern Light	Athabasca	1908	25

Title	Place	Dates	Item
Northern Messenger	High Prairie	1974	622
Northern News	Athabasca	1909-1916	26
Northern Pioneer	Fort Vermilion	1976-	562
Northern Post	Waskatenau	1934-1935	1012
Northern Review	Fairview	1923-1924	524
Northern Review	Fairview	1929-1933	525
Northern Star	High Prairie	1955-1958	618
Northern Times	Picture Butte	1940-1941	811
Northern Tribune	Grande Prairie	1932-1939	586.1
Northerner	Grimshaw	1961-1962	602
Northland Calling	High Prairie	1945	616
Northland Free Press	Slave Lake	1972-1975	902
Northwest Call	Calgary	1887	119
Northwest Chronicle	Wetaskiwin	1904	1023
Northwest Review	Fort McMurray	1939-1940	1070
Nova Hromada	Edmonton	1911-1912	363
Novyi Krai	Edmonton	1929	406
Novyi Shliakh	Edmonton	1930-1933	410
Novyny	Edmonton	1913-1915	367
Novyny	Edmonton	1917-1922	379
Nuovo Mondo	Edmonton	1979-	493
Nutcracker	Calgary	1916-1917	152.1
Nyugati Magyarsa'g	Calgary	1982	219
Oil and Financial Review	Calgary	1929-1931	167
Oilfields Flare	Turner Valley	1947-1956	976
Okotoks Advance	Okotoks	1908-1914	784
Okotoks Observer	Okotoks	1914	785
Okotoks Review	Okotoks	1904-1914	783.3
Okotoks Review	Okotoks	1917-1970	783.5
Okotoks Review and Oilfields Record	Okotoks	1914-1917	783.4
Okotoks Times	Okotoks	1901-1917	783.1
Okotoks Weekly	Okotoks	1917-1918	786
Old Timer	Cochrane	1943-1972	280
Olde Towne Crier	Edmonton	1971-1973	471
Olds Gazette	Olds	1904-1960	789.1
Olds Gazette and Mountain View News	Olds	1960-1977	789.2
Olds Moose-Paper	Olds	1961	791
Olds News	Olds	1935-1944	790
Olds Optimist	Olds	1982-	792
Olds Oracle	Olds	1900-1904	788
Olds Star	Olds	1976-1977	1083
On Our Way	Edmonton	1972-1975	475
One Big Union Bulletin	Edmonton	1919	382

Title Index

Title	Place	Dates	Item
Onoway Tribune	Onoway	1980-1985	794.3
Onoway Westerner	Onoway	1949-1953	793
Opinion	Calgary	1982-	222
Optimist	Red Deer	1929-1943	836
Organized Farmer	Edmonton	1949-1971	427.3
Ostoroha	Wostok,	1912	1040
Ouest canadien	Edmonton	1898-1900	338
Ouest canadien	Edmonton	1911	362
Our Progress	Edmonton	1922-1929	393
Our Youth	Blairmore	1932-1934	80
Outlaw	Grassy Lake	1910	597
Outlaw	Scott's Coulee	1896	888
Oyen Echo	Oyen	1960	798
Oyen News	Oyen	1914-1935	795
Oyen Observer	Oyen	1956-1957	797
Packet	Millet	1909-1910	756
Panorama	Calgary	1968-1970	199
Parkland County Examiner	Parkland County	1977-1978	799
Parkland Review and Sylvan Lake News	Sylvan Lake	1960-1966	951.2
Parklander	Hinton	1976-	627.4
Pass Daily Herald	Blairmore	1933-1934	81
Pass Herald	Blairmore	1930-	79
Pass Promoter	Blairmore	1973-1978	84.1
Pass Promoter	Blairmore	1980-	84.3
Peace River Pilot	Peace River	1910	800
Peace River Record	Peace River	1914-1924	802.1
Peace River Record	Peace River	1926-1939	802.3
Peace River Record and Northern Review	Peace River	1924-1925	802.2
Peace River Record-Gazette	Peace River	1943-1955	804.2
Peace River Record with which is Amalgamated The Northern Gazette	Peace River	1939-1943	804.1
Peace River Standard and Farmers' Gazette	Peace River	1917-1922	801
Pembina Herald	Pembina Municipal District	1952-1968	806.2
Pembina Herald	Pembina Municipal District	1975-1977	808.2
Pembina News	Pembina Municipal District	1956-1965	807
Pembina News Advertiser	Pembina Municipal District	1956-1965	807
Pembina Outlook and Entwistle News	Entwistle	1910	519

Title Index

Title	Place	Dates	Item
Pembina Star	Pembina Municipal District	1970-1975	808.1
Penhold Journal	Penhold	1911	810
Penhold Reporter	Penhold	1903-1904	809
People's Friend	Edmonton	1926-1930	400
People's Weekly	Edmonton	1936-1952	386.2
Picture Butte Northern Times	Picture Butte	1940-1941	811
Picture Butte Progress	Picture Butte	1941-1954	812.1
Pincher City News	Pincher City	1908-1911	813
Pincher Creek Echo	Pincher Creek	1906-	814.2
Pioneer	Cochrane	1980-1982	282
Pioneer Post	Calgary	1887	118
Pisriverskyi Homin	Rycroft	1956-?	870
Plaindealer	Drumheller	1936-1941	330
Plaindealer	Edmonton	1900-1912	336.3
Plaindealer	Wildwood	1949-1950	1089
Plaindealer	Youngstown	1913-1936	1041
Political World	Calgary	1934-1936	174
Ponoka County News	Ponoka County	1955-1976	816
Ponoka Herald	Ponoka	1900-	817
Ponoka News and Advertiser	Ponoka	1949-	818
Port of Slave Lake Oiler	Slave Lake	1970-1972	901.1
Portrait	Edmonton	1973-1975	477
Post	Fairview	1953-	526.2
Post	Wetaskiwin	1904-1910	1024
Postup	Mundare	1915-1917	771
Poundmaker	Edmonton	1972-1975	476
Praerie Nyt	Calgary	1963-1965	197
Prairie	Calgary	1906	134
Prairie Illustrated	Calgary	1890-1891	120
Prairie Link	Edmonton	1981-	497
Prairie Rattler	Medicine Hat	1969-1976	752
Prairie Star	Edmonton	1975-1977	478
Prairies' Messenger	Edmonton	1969-1977	465
Pravda Naroda	Edmonton	1929	407
Press	Calgary	1912-1913	143
Problysk	Edmonton	1971	469
Progrès	Morinville	1909-1913	764.1
Progrès albertain	Edmonton	1914-1915	374
Progrès albertain	Morinville	1913-1914	764.2
Progress	High Prairie	1958-1959	619.2
Progress	Mundare	1915-1917	771
Progressive Student	Edmonton	1959-1960	1059

Title Index

Title	Place	Dates	Item
Promoter	Blairmore	1978-1980	84.2
Province	Innisfail	1906-1927	643.1
Provincial Standard	Calgary	1911-1912	142.1
Provost News	Provost	1917-	822
Provost Star	Provost	1910-1917	821
Radway Star	Radway	1950-1951	823
Rattler	Medicine Hat	1969-1976	752
Raymond Leader	Raymond	1911-1917	824.3
Raymond Recorder	Raymond	1923-1928	825.1
Raymond Recorder	Raymond	1929-1949	825.3
Raymond Recorder	Raymond	1955-1956	826.2
Raymond Recorder	Raymond	1957-1972	827
Raymond Review	Raymond	1965-	828
Raymond Rustler	Raymond	1907-1911	824.2
Raymond-Magrath Recorder	Raymond	1928-1929	825.2
Rebel	Calgary	1937-1939	184
Record	Fort Saskatchewan	1922-1931	560.1
Record	Fort Saskatchewan	1960-1967	560.5
Record	Fort Saskatchewan	1969-1978	560.7
Record	Fort Saskatchewan	1979-	560.9
Record and Lamont Gazette	Fort Saskatchewan	1967-1969	560.6
Record-Gazette	Peace River	1955-	804.3
Recorder	Altario	1921-1923	19
Recorder	Beiseker	1922-1924	67
Recorder	Raymond	1917-1922	824.4
Red Deer Ad-Viser	Red Deer	1946-1977	837
Red Deer Advocate	Red Deer	1907-1972	834.3
Red Deer County News	Red Deer County	1969-	829
Red Deer Gazette and Lacombe Advertiser	Red Deer	1898-1899	832
Red Deer News	Red Deer	1920-1926	835.2
Red Deer Review	Red Deer	1894	831
Red Deer Shopper	Red Deer	1979-	842
Redcliff Journal	Redcliff	1913	844
Redcliff Review	Redcliff	1910-1940	843
Redcliff Review	Redcliff	1976-1978	1085
Redcliff Tribune	Redcliff	1913	844
Redwater News	Redwater	1950-1951	846
Redwater News	Redwater	1953-1968	848.1
Redwater News	Redwater	1972-1974	850
Redwater News-Herald	Redwater	1951	846
Redwater News Daily Flashes	Redwater	1950	847
Redwater Recorder	Thorhild County	1967-1969	956
Redwater Review	Redwater	1949-1952	845

Title Index

Title	Place	Dates	Item
Redwater Star	Redwater	1970-1973	849
Redwater Sun	Redwater	1968-1969	848.2
Redwater Thorhild News	Thorhild County	1974-1986	958
Reflections	Mannville	1980-1981	731.2
Reflector	Mirror	1911	760
Regional Times	Lloydminster	1982	703.5
Renaissance	Edmonton	1930	409.1
Reporter	Edmonton	1964	451
Reporter	Stony Plain	1967-	937.2
Representative	Leduc	1907-	689
Retlaw Weekly	Retlaw	1917-1918	852
Review	Cereal	1915-1918	255.2
Review	Drumheller	1936	325.3
Review	Milk River	1954-1958	753.2
Ribstone Record	Hughenden	1919-1920	636.1
Rimbey Advance	Rimbey	1921-1922	854
Rimbey Pioneer	Rimbey	1919	853
Rimbey Record	Rimbey	1936-	855.2
Rimbey Record and Blindman Valley Advertiser	Rimbey	1930-1936	855.1
Rocky Mountain Capital	Rocky Mountain House	1918-1919	858.2
Rocky Mountain Courier	Banff	1914-1918	40
Rocky Mountain Courier	Banff	1922	42
Rocky Mountain Echo	Pincher Creek	1900-1906	814.1
Rocky Mountain Echoes	Banff	1893	36.2
Rocky Mountain House Capital	Rocky Mountain House	1918	858.1
Rocky Mountain House Capital	Rocky Mountain House	1919-1920	858.3
Rocky Mountain House Echo	Rocky Mountain House	1910-1912	856.1
Rocky Mountain House Mountaineer	Rocky Mountain House	1950-1957	860.2
Rocky Mountain House Mountaineer	Rocky Mountain House	1961-1963	860.4
Rocky View News and Market Examiner	Calgary	1956-1981	153.4
Rocky View Times	Airdrie	1977	9
Rocky View Times	Airdrie	1979-	10
Rocky View Times and Airdrie Echo	Airdrie	1977-1979	8.2
Rocky View-Five Village Weekly	Rocky View Municipal District	1981-	862.2

Title Index

Title	Place	Dates	Item
Rocky Weekly Press	Rocky Mountain House	1966-1967	861
Rockyford Budget	Rockyford	1921-1923	865
Rockyford Reporter	Rockyford	1918-1922	864
Rockyford Review	Rockyford	1949-1957	866
Rockyford (Alta.) Weekly	Rockyford	1917-1918	863
Rosalind Reporter	Rosalind	1948-1949	867
Rosebud Recorder	Rosebud Creek	1920-1925	868
Round-Up	Pincher Creek	1902	815
Roundup	Calgary	1968-	198
Rowley Recorder	Rowley	1921-1926	869
Rural Northwest and Edmonton Weekly Journal	Edmonton	1913-1916	368
Rural Route	Grande Prairie	1972-	587
Rural Week	Calgary	1982-1983	218.2
Rural Weekly News and Rube's Farm Fun	Stony Plain	1912-1917	932
Russian Life	Edmonton	1915-1918	375
Russian Voice	Edmonton	1913-1916	369
Russkyi Golos	Edmonton	1913-1916	369
Ryce Street Fysh Markete	Edmonton	1967-1968	457
Ryley Times	Ryley	1909-1916	872
Ryley Times	Ryley	1919-1924	873
Ryley Times	Ryley	1924-1925	874
Ryley Times	Tofield	1946-1952	969
Ryley Times	Tofield	1952-1967	970.2
Ryley Transcript	Vegreville	1927-1928	987.2
Sangudo Chronicle	Sangudo	1972-1973	887
Sangudo Star	Sangudo	1947-1948	886.1
Saturday Blade	Poplar Lake	1903	820
Saturday News	Edmonton	1905-1912	348
Scandinavian Centre News	Edmonton	1958-	445
Scope	Slave Lake	1973-	901.3
Scottish Standard	Calgary	1913-1914	146
Scree	Banff	1971	47
Searchlight	Calgary	1919-1920	159
Sedgewick Eagle	Sedgewick	1907-1909	889
Sedgewick Paper	Sedgewick	1907-1909	889
Sedgewick Review	Sedgewick	1918	891
Sedgewick Sentinel	Sedgewick	1908-1929	890.1
Semi-Weekly Albertan and The Alberta Tribune	Calgary	1899-1902	123.2
Semi-Weekly News	Lethbridge	1891	692.2
Sentinel	Acme	1951-1973	3.2

Title Index

Title	Place	Dates	Item
Sentinel	Fort Macleod	1894	537
Sentinel and Military News	Calgary	1916	151
Seventeenth Avenue	Calgary	1979-1981	213
Sexsmith Sentinel	Sexsmith	1949-1954	892
Sherwood Park Herald	Sherwood Park	1963-1968	893
Sherwood Park News	Sherwood Park	1976-1977	896.1
Sherwood Park News	Sherwood Park	1978-	896.3
Sherwood Park Star	Sherwood Park	1969-1977	895
Sherwood Park Sun	Sherwood Park	1964-1969	894
Sibbald Recorder	Sibbald	1920	897
Sibbald Times	Sibbald	1920-1922	898
Signal	Spirit River	1954-1959	910.2
Signal-Serving the Central Peace	Rycroft	1980-	871
Slave Lake Centennial Press	Slave Lake	1967-1970	900
Slovak Word	Blairmore	1910-1911	78
Slovak Word	Blairmore	1940	82
Slovenske Slovo	Blairmore	1910-1911	78
Slovenske Slovo	Blairmore	1940	82
Smoky Lake County Star	Smoky Lake	1974-1977	906.2
Smoky Lake Gazette	Smoky Lake	1948-1968	905.1
Smoky Lake Gazette	Smoky Lake	1974-1977	906.2
Smoky Lake Signal	Smoky Lake	1978-	907
Smoky Lake Star	Smoky Lake	1970-1974	906.1
Smoky Lake Sun	Smoky Lake	1968-1969	905.2
Smoky River Express	Falher	1972-1973	529.2
Smoky River Express	Falher	1973-	529.4
Smoky River News	Smoky River Municipal District	1953-1963	908.2
Social Credit	Edmonton	1937-1940	423
Social Credit Gazette	Edmonton	1935-1936	420
Social Credit Supplement	Calgary	1936-1938	175.2
Social Justice Advocate	Calgary	1934	176.1
Sonshine News	Edmonton	1981-	498
Source	Edmonton	1970-	468
South Calgary News	Calgary	1957	192
South East News	Edmonton	1953-1954	439
South Edmonton News	Edmonton	1894-1896	336.1
South Edmonton Sun	Edmonton	1949-1951	432.1
South Edmonton Sun	Edmonton	1962-1969	432.3
South Edmonton Times	Edmonton	1977-	486
South Edmonton Times Examiner	Edmonton	1977-	486
South Edmonton Weekly News	Edmonton	1940-1954	395.3
South Peace News	High Prairie	1964-	620

Title Index

Title	Place	Dates	Item
South Side Mirror	Calgary	1960-1977	194.1
South Side Mirror	Calgary	1980-1981	194.3
South Side Sun	Edmonton	1962	449
Southern Alberta Labor Bulletin	Lethbridge	1908-1913	696
Southern Alberta News	Lethbridge	1906-1907	692.7
Soviet	Edmonton	1919	381
Spectator	Edmonton	1932-1933	414
Spirit River Bulletin	Spirit River	1964-1969	911
Spirit River Echo	Spirit River	1917-1921	909
Spirit River Signal	Spirit River	1951-1954	910.1
Spirit River Signal	Spirit River	1959-1965	910.3
Spirit River Times	Spirit River	1916-1917	1086
Spokesman	Calgary	1932-1933	173
Spokesman	Edmonton	1972-	472
Sports Guide	Calgary	1936-1940	180
Sports Review	Edmonton	1922	391
Spotlight	Edmonton	1940-1954	426
Spruce Grove Reporter	Stony Plain	1967-	937.2
Spruce Grove Sentinel	Stony Plain	1967-	937.2
Spruce Grove Star	Spruce Grove	1970-1977	912
Square Shooter	Lethbridge	1922-1923	699
St. Albert and Sturgeon Gazette	St. Albert	1970-1974	880.3
St. Albert and Sturgeon Gazette	St. Albert	1974-	880.4
St. Albert Gazette	St. Albert	1949-1953	879
St. Albert Gazette	St. Albert	1961-1966	880.1
St. Albert News	St. Albert	1912-1914	877
St. Albert Star	St. Albert	1914	878.2
St. Albert Star	St. Albert	1972-1973	881
St. Albert-Sturgeon Gazette	St. Albert	1974-	880.4
St. Paul Canadian	St. Paul	1934-1935	884
St. Paul Journal	St. Paul	1925-	883.2
St. Paul Star	St. Paul	1920-1922	882
St. Paul Tribune	St. Paul	1925	883.1
Standard	Vermilion	1909-1921	992.1
Standard	Vermilion	1975-	992.3
Standard Enterprize	Standard	1920-1921	916
Standard Gazette	Standard	1921-1926	917
Star-Chronicle	Wainwright	1949	1009.1
Starland Reporter	Starland Municipal District	1950-1955	918
Statesman	Edmonton	1919-1920	383
Statesman for Albertans	Edmonton	1917-1918	377
Stavely Advertiser	Stavely	1914	921

Title	Place	Dates	Item
Stavely Advertiser	Stavely	1916-1965	922
Stavely Gazette	Stavely	1904-1905	919
Stavely Standard	Stavely	1909-1914	920
Stettler Actioneer	Stettler	1981	926.2
Stettler Gazette	Stettler	1909-1911	924
Stettler Independent	Stettler	1906-	923
Stoney Echo	Morley	1981-	768
Stony Plain Advertiser	Stony Plain	1910-1911	930.2
Stony Plain Advertiser	Stony Plain	1911-1913	931
Stony Plain Advertiser and Lac Ste Anne Reporter	Stony Plain	1909-1910	930.1
Stony Plain Herald	Stony Plain	1919-1920	935
Stony Plain News	Stony Plain	1913-1914	933
Stony Plain Reporter	Stony Plain	1945-1967	937.1
Stony Plain Sun	Stony Plain	1920-1938	936
Stony Plain Sun	Stony Plain Municipal District	1963-1967	928
Strathcolic	Edmonton	1899-1900	340
Strathcona Booster	Edmonton	1923-1925	395.1
Strathcona Chronicle	Edmonton	1904-1911	345
Strathcona County News	Strathcona County	1969-1975	939.1
Strathcona Plaindealer	Edmonton	1900-1912	336.3
Strathcona Plaindealer	Edmonton	1977-	484
Strathcona Wedge	Strathcona County	1967-1968	938
Strathcona Weekly News	Edmonton	1926-1939	395.2
Strathmore and Bow Valley Standard	Strathmore	1909-1929	940.1
Strathmore and Bow Valley Standard	Strathmore	1947-1955	940.3
Strathmore Standard	Strathmore	1929-1947	940.2
Strathmore Standard	Strathmore	1955-	940.4
Strome Despatch	Strome	1910-1929	941
Strome Star	Strome	1947-1950	942
Sturgeon and St. Albert Gazette	St. Albert	1974-	880.4
Sturgeon Gazette	St. Albert	1974-	880.4
Sturgeon Journal	Sturgeon Municipal District	1961-1968	943.1
Sturgeon Sun	Sturgeon Municipal District	1968-1969	943.2
Suburban Times	Edmonton	1957-1964	436.3
Summer Times	Edmonton	1976-	481
Sun Dance Echo	Stand Off	1964-1966	914
Sunday	Calgary	1974	203
Sunday Calgarian	Calgary	1962	1053
Sunday Sun	Calgary	1914	148

Title Index

Title	Place	Dates	Item
Sundre News-Advertiser	Sundre	1957	944
Sundre Round Up	Sundre	1960-1973	945.1
Sundre Round Up (1973)	Sundre	1973-1978	945.2
Sundre Round Up Publishing Ltd	Sundre	1978-	945.3
Sunny South News	Coaldale	1959-1974	276.3
Sunnyslope Sun	Acme	1909-1914	1
Sunset News Bulletin	Calgary	1906	1049
Survivance	Edmonton	1928-1967	404
Survivance des Jeunes	Edmonton	1934-194?	418
Suspilnyi Kredit	Edmonton	1937-1940	423
Svitlo	Mundare	1938-1949	772
Swalwell Recorder	Swalwell	1920	1087
Swan Hills Grizzly	Swan Hills	1977	946
Sylvan Lake News	Sylvan Lake	1935-1960	951.1
Sylvan Lake News	Sylvan Lake	1966-	951.3
Sylvan Lake Times	Sylvan Lake	1913-1914	948
Sylvan Lake World	Sylvan Lake	1922-1926	949
Taber Advertiser	Taber	1910-1911	953
Taber Free Press	Taber	1907-1910	952
Taber Times	Taber	1911-	954
Telegram	Edmonton	1969-1975	464
Telegram	Oyen	1939-1940	796
Telegram-Tribune	Acme	1914	2
Temperance Advocate	Ryley	1925	875
Temple City Tribune	Cardston	1964-1965	244
Thorhild County News	Thorhild County	1967-1969	956
Thorhild County Star	Thorhild County	1970-1977	957
Thorhild News	Thorhild	1972-1974	960
Thorhild Star	Thorhild County	1970-1977	957
Thorhild Sun	Thorhild	1968-1969	959.2
Thorhild Tribune	Thorhild	1949-1968	959.1
Thorsby Star	Thorsby	1970-1973	962
Three Hills Capital	Three Hills	1915-1979	965.1
Three Hills Herald	Three Hills	1911	963
Three Hills News	Three Hills	1922-1924	966
Three Hills Review	Three Hills	1915	964
Three Sisters Clarion	Canmore	1957-1961	229
Times	Big Valley	1923-1924	71
Times	Blairmore	1903-1911	76
Times	Edmonton	1893-1894	335
Times	Irma	1917-1969	647.1
Times	Medicine Hat	1903-1911	742.1
Times	Sylvan Lake	1913-1914	948

Title Index

Title	Place	Dates	Item
Times	Wetaskiwin	1958-1966	1022.2
Times	Wetaskiwin	1968-1979	1022.4
Times, Community Newspaper of the Foothills	High River	1975-	625.2
Times Regional	Lloydminster	1982-	703.6
Times Regional Weekly	Lloydminster	1979-1981	703.4
Times Semi-Weekly	Medicine Hat	1911-1912	742.2
Times-Reporter	Alderson	1911	11
Tiser	Calgary	1895-1896	124
Today and Tomorrow	Edmonton	1935-1944	421
Tofield Advertiser	Tofield	1917-1918	968
Tofield Mercury	Tofield	1918-1952	969
Tofield Mercury	Tofield	1952-1962	970.1
Tofield Standard	Tofield	1907-1917	967
Tofield Star	Tofield	1907-1917	967
Tory	Edmonton	1966	1063
Totem Pole	Jasper	1947-1948	655
Town Crier	Cochrane	1980-1982	283
Town Topics	Calgary	1906-1907	135
Town Topics	Edmonton	1905-1909	346
Town Topics	Edmonton	1926-1928	401
Travers Weekly	Travers	1917-1918	971
Triangle	Lamont County	1977-	677
Tribune	Bonnyville	1960-1962	87.2
Tribune	Lamont	1922-1931	681.1
Tribune	Onoway	1979-1980	794.2
Tribune	Redwater	1981-	851
Tri-City Observer (Black Diamond, Hartell and Turner Valley).	Turner Valley	1931	975.3
Tri-Neighbour Press	Airdrie	1972-1974	7
Trochu Times	Trochu	1911-1913	972
Trochu Tribune	Trochu	1911-1977	973
Trochu's Community Voice	Trochu	1977-	974
Truth of the People	Edmonton	1929	407
Turner Valley News	Turner Valley	1957-?	977
Turner Valley Observer and Black Diamond, Naptha and Hartell News	Turner Valley	1930-1931	975.2
Two Hills County Journal	Two Hills County	1974-	982
Two Hills County Star	Two Hills County	1970-1977	981
Two Hills County Times	Two Hills County	1980-1984	983
Two Hills Reporter	Two Hills County	1950	980.1
Two Hills Review	Two Hills County	1968	980.4
Two Hills Sun	Two Hills County	1968-1969	980.5

Title Index

Title	Place	Dates	Item
Two Hills County Journal	Two Hills County	1974-	982
Two Hills County Star	Two Hills County	1970-1977	981
Two Hills County Times	Two Hills County	1980-1984	983
Two Hills Reporter	Two Hills County	1950	980.1
Two Hills Review	Two Hills County	1968	980.4
Two Hills Sun	Two Hills County	1968-1969	980.5
Typo News	Calgary	1935	177.2
U.F.A.	Calgary	1922-1934	160.1
U.F.C. Bulletin	Calgary	1941	427.1
Ukrainian Catholic Pictorial	Mundare	1938-1949	772
Ukrainian Gazette	Edmonton	1933-1934	417
Ukrainian News	Edmonton	1932-	402.2
Ukrainian Record	Edmonton	1960-1963	447
Ukrainski Visti	Edmonton	1932-	402.2
Unemployed Bulletin	Calgary	1931-1932	1053
Union	Edmonton	1917-1929	378
Union Laborer	Edmonton	1929	405
United Farmer	Calgary	1934-1936	160.2
Universal Weekly	Calgary	1918-1919	156
Valhalla Star	Fort McMurray	1941	1071
Valley News	Acme	1953-1955	4
Valley News	Wimborne	1945-1953	1037
Valley Observer and Black Diamond, Naptha and Hartell News	Turner Valley	1929-1930	975.1
Valley Views	Canmore	1974-1975	231
Valley Views	Valleyview	1963-	985
Valleyview Times	Valleyview	1956-1962	984
Vauxhall Advance	Vauxhall	1978-	986
Vegreville Mirror	Vegreville	1961	989
Vegreville Mirror	Vegreville	1961-1965	990
Vegreville News Advertiser	Vegreville	1980-	988.3
Vegreville News Advertiser Ltd.	Vegreville	1977-1980	988.2
Vegreville Observer	Vegreville	1906-1927	987.1
Vegreville Observer	Vegreville	1928-	987.3
Vegreville Observer and Ryley Transcript	Vegreville	1927-1928	987.2
Vermilion River County Star	Vermilion River County	1973-1977	996
Vermilion River News	Vermilion River County	1961-1963	995
Vermilion Signal	Vermilion	1906-1910	991
Vermilion Standard	Vermilion	1921-1975	992.2
Veteran Eagle	Veteran	1972-1973	998

Title Index

Title	Place	Dates	Item
Veteran Post	Veteran	1933-1934	997
Victoria Farmer	Camrose	1922-1924	226
Vidrodzhennia	Edmonton	1930	409.1
Viking Gazette	Viking	1910-1911	999
Viking News	Viking	1913-1969	1000.1
Viking News	Viking	1974-1979	1000.3
Viking News and Irma Times	Viking	1969-1974	1000.2
Village Press	Carbon	1976-	239
Vilna Bulletin	Vilna	1955-1963	1003
Vilna Star	Vilna	1951-1953	1002
Voice of the Actioneer	Stettler	1981	926.2
Voice of the Nation	Blairmore	1932-1934	80
Voice of Truth	Smoky Lake	1937-1960	904
Vulcan Advocate	Vulcan	1913-	1005
Vulcan Review	Vulcan	1912-1914	1004
Wainwright Commercial	Wainwright	1933	1008.1
Wainwright Record	Wainwright	1933-1934	1008.2
Wainwright Star	Wainwright	1908-1949	1007
Wainwright Star-Chronicle	Wainwright	1949	1009.2
Warner Record	Warner	1910-1916	1010
Waskatenau World	Waskatenau	1949-1962	1014
Weasel Valley News	Brocket	1982-1983	103
Wedge	Edmonton	1921	389
Wednesday Review	Calgary	1971-1979	201
Weekender	Red Deer	1977-1979	839
Weekly Advance	Andrew	1931	21
Weekly Advertiser	Drumheller	1936	329
Weekly Albertan	Calgary	1902-1920	123.3
Weekly Chronicle	Fort Macleod	1908	539.1
Weekly Chronicle	Fort Saskatchewan	1910-1911	556
Weekly Herald	Calgary	1895-1918	113.8
Weekly News	Horburg	1920-1921	1076
Weekly Review	Viking	1978-	1001
Weekly Times	Medicine Hat	1888	739.2
Weekly Tribune	Edmonton	1935	419
West Edmonton Examiner	Edmonton	1977-	487
West-Ender	Calgary	1929-1930	166
Western Canada Enquirer	Calgary	1936-1938	179
Western Catholic	Edmonton	1921-1965	388
Western Catholic Reporter	Edmonton	1965-	453
Western Examiner	Calgary	1929-1949	165.1
Western Farm Leader	Calgary	1936-1954	181
Western Farmer	Calgary	1928-1931	164.1

Title Index

Title	Place	Dates	Item
Western Farmer and Weekly Albertan	Calgary	1921-1927	123.4
Western Globe	Lacombe	1903-1938	670.1
Western Homestead	Calgary	1907	137
Western Illustrated News	Edmonton	1921-1922	390
Western Independent	Calgary	1919-1920	158
Western Leader	Edson	1913-1917	503.2
Western Livestock and Agricultural News	Edmonton	1972-1982	473
Western Messenger	Thorsby	1937-1961	961
Western Miner	Calgary	1930-1931	170.1
Western Miner	Lethbridge	1930-1931	700
Western News	Edmonton	1925	399
Western News	Edmonton	1928-1931	402.1
Western Oil Examiner	Calgary	1927-1929	163.2
Western Oil Examiner	Calgary	1949-1958	165.2
Western Review	Drayton Valley	1965-	323
Western Sentinel	Calgary	1937	182
Western Signal	Edson	1946-1960	511.2
Western Sports Weekly	Edmonton	1968	459
Western Standard	Calgary	1913-1916	142.3
Western Star	Edson	1913	504.1
Western Star	Leslieville	1979	1081
Western Star and Okotoks Times	Okotoks	1903	783.2
Western Stockman	Calgary	1932	164.2
Western Union Printer	Medicine Hat	1919-1923	749
Western Weekly	Edmonton	1915	376
Western Weekly Supplement	Ponoka	1962-1968	819
Western Wheel	Okotoks	1976-	787
Westerner	Calgary	1923-1928	1051
Westerner	Sangudo	1948-1949	886.2
West-Land	Edmonton	1908-1913	352
Westlock News	Westlock	1957	1015.5
Westlock Witness	Westlock	1919-1922	1015.1
Westlock Witness	Westlock	1929-1949	1015.3
Westwind News	Cardston	1975-1979	245
Wetaskiwin Alberta Tribunen	Wetaskiwin	1914	1029
Wetaskiwin Breeze	Wetaskiwin	1901	1021
Wetaskiwin County News	Wetaskiwin	1966-1968	1017
Wetaskiwin Free Press	Wetaskiwin	1917-1939	1026.2
Wetaskiwin Journal	Wetaskiwin	1912-1914	1027.2
Wetaskiwin News	Wetakiwin	1900	1020
Wetaskiwin Times	Wetaskiwin County	1901-1958	1022.1
Wetaskiwin Times	Wetaskiwin	1966-1968	1022.3
Wetaskiwin Times	Wetaskiwin	1979-1983	1022.5

Title Index

Title	Place	Dates	Item
Whitecourt Echo	Whitecourt	1959-1969	1032
Whitecourt Star	Whitecourt	1962-	1033
Wideawake	Islay	1907	652
Wild Rose Chronicle	Vermilion	1978	1088
Willingdon Review	Willingdon	1951-1953	1036
Willingdon Times	Willingdon	1937-1938	1090
Winfield Gazette	Winfield	1939-1954	1038
Winnifred Record	Winnifred	1911-1912	1039
Witness	Waskatenau	1930-1934	1011
Witness	Westlock	1923-1929	1015.2
Witness	Westlock	1949-1957	1015.4
Worker	Calgary	1936	178
World of Beef and Stockman's Recorder	Calgary	1976-	209
Zakhidni Visti	Edmonton	1928-1931	402.1

Bibliography

A. Principle Sources Consulted 545
B. Checklists, Directories, and Union Lists of
   Newspapers 564
C. Newspaper Indexes 567

BIBLIOGRAPHY

For the convenience of the reader, the bibliography is divided into three sections:

A. Principal Sources Consulted
B. Checklists, Directories and Union Lists of Newspapers
C. Newpaper Indexes

A. Principal Sources Consulted

Items cited in the Guide are identified by a coded abbreviation.

ABU   Abu-Laban, Baha. *An olive branch on the family tree: the Arabs in Canada.* Toronto: McClelland and Stewart, 1980.

ACAD   Acadia Women's Institute. *Back over the trail: a history of the Huxley area.* Huxley, Alberta: the Institute, 1967

ACME   Acme and District Historical Society. *Acme memories.* Acme, Alberta: The Society, 1979

Alberta. Alberta Culture. Cultural Heritage Branch. *Profiles: ethno-cultural groups in Alberta.* [Edmonton; Calgary]: Cultural Heritage Branch, Alberta Culture, [1983?]

Alberta's local histories in The Historical Resources Library. 6th ed. Edmonton: The Library, 1986.

AGCL   *Alberta Government College / Libraries Union List of Serials.* 2d ed. [Edmonton: Alberta Government Libraries Council] 1984.

ALI   Alberta. Legislature Library. *Biographical register of the Alberta Legislature.* Edmonton: Alberta Legislatuur Library, 1970-. Unpublished.

ALB   *Alberta Report.* v.1(N 1973)- . Edmonton: Interwest Publications Ltd., 1973- To August 27, 1979 entitled *Saint John's Edmonton Report.*

ALC   Alcorn, Phyllis M., ed. *In the bend of the Battle: a history of Alliance and district.* Winnipeg: Intercollegiate Press, 1976.

Almanach franco-albertain. 1964- . Edmonton: Association canadienne française de l'Alberta, 1964- .

ANDE   Anderson, R.F. *Legacy: memories of yesteryear and today for tomorrow of Bowden and districts.* Bowden, Alberta.: Bowden Chamber of Commerce, 1979.

ANDR   Andrew Historical Society. *Dreams and destinies: Andrew and district.*
             Andrew, Alberta.: The Society, 1980.

APP   Appleby, Edna Hill. *Canmore: The story of an era.* Calgary, Alberta: E.
             Appleby, 1975.

ARN   Arndt, Karl J.R. and Mary E. Olson. *The German language press of the
             Americas, 1732-1968 / Die Deutschsprachige Press der Amerikas, 1732-
             1968.* Volume 2. München: Verlag Dokumentation Pullach, 1973.

             Artebise, Allan F.J. *Western Canada since 1870: a select bibliography and
             guide.* Vancouver: University of British Columbia, 1978.

             Askin, William R. "Labour unrest in Edmonton and district and its coverage
             by the Edmonton press: 1918-1919." M.A. Thesis, University of Alberta,
             1973.

             Aspects du passé franco-albertain: témoignages et études. Edmonton: Salon
             d'histoire de la francophonie albertaine, 1980.

             Athabasca Historical Society. *Athabasca Landing: an illustrated history.* A
             seventy-fifth anniversary project by the Athabasca Historical Society,
             David Gregory and Athabasca University. Athabasca, Alberta: The
             Society, c1986.

             Audley, Paul. *Canada's cultural industries: broadcasting, publishing,
             records and film.* Ottawa: Canadian Institute for Economic Policy, c 1983.

AY   *Ayers Directory of Newspapers and Periodicals.* 1880- . Philadelphia:
             Ayers, 1880- .

BARO   Barons History Book Club. *Wheat heart of the west: a history of Barons and
             district.* Barons, Alberta: Barons History Committee, 1972.

BARR   Barrhead History Book Committee. *The golden years.* Barrhead, Alberta:
             The Committee, 1978.

             Bassam, Bertha. *The first printers and newspapers in Canada.* Toronto:
             University of Toronto School of Library Science, 1968. (Monograph
             Series in Librarianship, 1)

BAT   Bates, Jane Eliza Woolf and Zina Woolf Hickman. *Founding of Cardston
             and vicinity.* Cardston, Alta.: s.n., 1974.

BER   Bercuson, David Jay. *Fools and wise men: the rise and fall of the one big
             union.* Toronto: McGraw Hill, 1978.

BLU   Blue, John. *Alberta past and present: historical and biographical.* Chicago:
             Pioneer Historical Publishing Co., 1924.

BOM   Bombak, Anna. "Ukrainian-Canadian newspapers published in Alberta from
            1909-1982: a bibliography." Non-thesis Project, Faculty of Library
            Science, University of Alberta, 1985.

BOU 1   Boudreau, Joseph A. *Alberta, Aberhart, and social credit.* Toronto: Holt,
            Rinehart and Winston, 1975.

BOU 2   _____. "Western Canada's enemy aliens in World War One." *Alberta
            Historical Review* Winter (1963):1-9.

BRO   Brown, Donald Edward. "A history of the Cochrane area." M.A. Thesis,
            University of Alberta, 1951.

BRU   Bruce, Charles. *News and the Southams.* Toronto: Macmillan of Canada,
            1968.

BUT   *The Butte stands guard: Stavely and district.* Stavely, Alberta: Stavely
            Historical Book Society, 1976.

BYR   Byron, David. *Alberta directory of members of the Canadian House of
            Commons, 1886-1986.* Unpublished.

            Calgary Printing Trades Union. *Local No. 1 Papers, 1935-1974.* Mss.
            (ACG:M 7211)

CA   Campbell, Alice A. *Milk River country.* Lethbridge, Alberta: Lethbridge
            Herald, 1959.

CAM 1   Campbell, Isabel M. *Grande Prairie, capital of the Peace.* Grande Prairie,
            Alberta: I.M. Campbell, 1968.

CAM 2   _____. *Pioneers of the Peace.* Grande Prairie, Alberta: Grande Prairie and
            District Oldtimer's Association, 1975.

CAMP   Campbell, Robert Eldon. *I would do it again: reminiscences of the Rockies.*
            Toronto: Ryerson Press, 1959.

CNLC   Canada. National Library of Canada. *Checklist of Canadian ethnic
            materials.* Compiled by Ruth Bogusis. Ottawa: The Library, 1981.

CNLR   _____. *Resources for native peoples studies.* Compiled by Nora T.
            Corley. Ottawa: The Library, 1984. (Research collections in Canadian
            libraries, 9)

CNLU   _____. *Union list of Canadian newspapers held by Canadian libraries.*
            Ottawa: The Library, 1977.

Canada. Royal Commission on Bilingualism and Biculturalism. *[Final report] v. 4. The cultural contribution of the other ethnic groups. Chapter VIII Section A: The ethnic press.* Ottawa: Information Canada, 1970.

Canada. Senate. Special Senate Committee on Mass Media. "Central brief of F.P. Publications Limited," R.S. Malone, President, and Bruce Laking, Secretary, Ottawa, January 22, 1970.

————. "Southam Press Ltd., brief," St. Clair Balfour, President, and Gordon N. Fisher, Vice-President and Managing Director, Ottawa, 1970.

————. *Mass Media.* Ottawa: Queen's Printer, 1970.

CAN   *Canadian Almanac and Directory.* 1847- . Toronto: Copp Clark, 1847- .

CANA   *Canadian Annual Review of Public Affairs.* 1-38 (1901-1938). Toronto: Annual Review Pub. Co., 1902-c1940.

CANC   *Canadian Community Publisher.* Ja/F, 1972-My, 1973. Toronto: Canadian Community Newspapers Association, Ja/F, 1972-My, 1973. Ctd. by *Publisher* (q.v.)

CANE   *Canadian Encyclopedia.* Edmonton: Hurtig, 1985.

CANP   *Canadian Parliamentary Guide.* 1862- . Ottawa: Normandin, 1862- .

          Canadian Press Association. *A history of Canadian journalism in several portions of the Dominion with a sketch of the Canadian Press Association 1859-1908.* Toronto: The Association, 1908.

CPP   *Canadian Printer and Publisher.* v.1(1892)- . Toronto: Maclean Hunter, 1892. To 1919 as *Printer and Publisher.* From Ap. 1974 unnumbered. Erratic numbering regularized in references.

CANW   *Canadian Weekly Publisher.* [v.48]-v.54no.11(Ja, 1965-D 1972). Toronto: Canadian Weekly Newspapers Association, 1965-1972. Ctd. by *Canadian Community Publisher* (q.v.)

CAWW   *Canadian Who's Who.* v.1(1910)- . Toronto: University of Toronto Press, 1910- .

CANF   *Canadien-français.* 1no.1-? (November 1915-19?). Edmonton: Société St. Jean Baptiste d'Edmonton, 1915-19? .

CARA 1   Caragata, Warren. *Alberta labour: a heritage untold.* Toronto: James Lorimer, 1979.

CARA 2   ————. *Research files compiled in writing Alberta labour: a heritage untold.* (AEPAA 80:218)

CARD   *CARD. Canadian Advertising Rates and Data.* v.1 (1928)- . Toronto: Maclean Hunter, 1928- .

CARDS   Cardston and District Historical Society. *Chief Mountain country: a history of Cardston and district.* Keith Shaw, ed. Cardston, Alberta: The Society, c1978.

CART   Carter, David J. *Behind Canadian barbed wire: alien refugee and prisoner of war camps in Canada, 1914-1946.* Calgary: Tumbleweed Press, 1980.

CAS   Cashman, A.W. *More Edmonton stories: the life and times of Edmonton, Alberta.* Edmonton: Institute of Applied Art, c1958.

CEN   *A century of memories: Okotoks and district, 1883-1983.* Okotoks, Alberta: Okotoks and District Historical Society, 1983.

CER   Central Women's Institute. *Down Cereal's memory trails.* Cereal, Alberta: The Institute, 1969?-1977.

CES   *See* Malycky, Alexander.

CHA   Chauvin, Ribstone and Districts History Book Committee. *Across the years.* The Committee, 1982.

       Christenson, Raymond Andrew. "The Calgary and Edmonton Railway and the Edmonton Bulletin." M.A. Thesis, University of Alberta, 1967.

CHU   Chubb, Jean and Hilda Milligan. *Leaves of yesteryear: a history of the Bon Accord district and the biographies of the men and women who pioneered the area.* Bon Accord, Alberta: Bon Accord F.W.U.A. (Local 502), 1969.

CL   Claresholm History Book Club. *Where the wheatlands meet the range.* Claresholm, Alberta: The Club, c1974.

CLA   Clark, Edith J. Lawrence. *Trails of Tail Creek Country.* Erskine, Alberta: 1968

CLAR   Clark, Thomas. "The Macleod Gazette." Canadian North-West Historical Society. *Publications.* 1no.4, pt. 1 (1928):48-49.

CLE   Cleverville Pioneer Club History Book Committee. *Cleverville-Champion, 1905-1970: A history of Champion and area.* Champion, Alberta: Champion History Book Committee, 1972.

COA   *Coaldale: gem of the west, 1900-1983.* Coaldale, Alberta: Coaldale Historical Society, 1983.

COCH   Cochrane and Area Historical Society. *Big Hill country: Cochrane and area.*
        Cochrane, Alberta: The Society, 1977.

COM   Comfort, Darlene. *Pass the McMurray salt please!* Fort McMurrary, 1975.

COR   Coronation Book Committee. *In the beginning: a history of Coronation,
        Throne, Federal and Fleet districts.* Coronation, Alberta: Coronation,
        Federal and Fleet Golden Age Club, 1979.

COU   Cousins, William James. "A History of the Crow's Nest Pass." M.A. Thesis,
        University of Alberta, 1952.

CRA   Craick, William Arnot. *A history of Canadian journalism. Vol. 2, Last years
        of the Canadian Press Association, 1908-1919.* Toronto: Ontario
        Publishing Co. Ltd., 1959.

CRO   Crossfield History Committee. *Prairie and goldenrod: Crossfield and area.*
        Crossfield, Alberta: The Committee, 1977.

CROW   Crowsnest Pass Historical Society. *Crowsnest and its people.* Coleman,
        Alberta: The Society, c1969.

CWNA   *CWNA Bulletin.* v.1no.1-v.47no.782 (Ja. 1919-D. 1964). Toronto: Canadian
        Weekly Newspapers Association, 1919-1964. Ctd. by *Canadian Weekly
        Publisher* (q.v.)

DAL   D'Albertanson, Leonard. *The story of Alberta Division, Canadian Weekly
        Newspapers Association.* Wainwright, Alberta: Wainwright Star-
        Chronicle, 1955.

DANK   Danky, James P., ed. *Native American Periodicals and Newspapers, 1828-
        1982.* Compiled by Maureen E. Hady in association with the State
        Historical Society of Wisconsin. Westport, Connecticut: Greenwood
        Press, 1984.

DATA   *Data, Alberta Weekly Newspapers: a guide reference book published for
        your convenience, listing member papers of Alberta Weekly Newspapers
        Association. 1965- .* Edmonton: Alberta Weekly Newspapers Association,
        1965- .

DAY   Daysland History Book Society. *Along the crocus trail: a history of
        Daysland and districts.* Daysland, Alberta: The Society, 1982.

        Dechêne, André M. "French participation in early Alberta." *Alberta
        Historical Review* 2(Autumn 1954): 11-27.

DEC   DeCoursey, Duke. *All in a lifetime: the Yellowknife years.* Squamish, B.C.:
        Parkview Publishing, 1986?

DEG 1   Degrâce, Eloi. *Index du Courrier de l'ouest (1905-1916)*. Edmonton: E. Degrâce, 1980.

DEG 2   _____. *Le Progrès (1909-1915): histoire et index*. Dartmouth, N.S.: E. Degrâce, 1983.

DEL   Delday, Eva. *Brooks, between the Red Deer and the Bow*. Edited by Pearl Thomas. Brooks, Alberta: E. Delday, c1975.

DELIA   *The Delia Craigmyle saga*. Lethbridge, Alberta: Southern Printing Co., 1970-.

DEM   Dempsey, Hugh A., ed. *The best of Bob Edwards*. Edmonton: Hurtig, 1975.

Den Otter, A.A. "A social history of the Alberta Coal Branch." M.A. Thesis, University of Alberta, 1967.

DEW   Dew, Ian F. *Bibliography of material relating to southern Alberta published to 1970*. Lethbridge: Learning Resources Centre, University of Lethbridge, 1975.

DICK 1   Dickson, Horatio Henry Lovat. *The ante-room*. Toronto: Macmillan, 1959. Chapter 9.

DICK 2   _____. "A pale shadow rising, 2." *The Review*. v.6no.5 (1976).

DON   *Donalda's roots and branches*. Donalda: U-Go Weavers History Book Committee, 1980.

DRE   Dreisziger, Nandor A.F. *Struggle and hope: the Hungarian experience*. Toronto: McClelland and Stewart, 1982.

DRUM   Drumheller Valley History Association. *The hills of home: Drumheller Valley*. Drumheller, Alberta: The Association, 1973.

EAR   *Early furrows: a story of our early pioneers in Provost, Hayter, Bodo, Alberta, and surrounding districts*. Provost, Alberta: Senior Citizens Club of Provost, 1977.

"Early Newspapers." *Alberta Historical Review*. 5no.1 (1957):31.

Edwards, Clifford Gordon. "The national policy as seen by the editors of the Medicine Hat newspapers: a western opinion." M.A. Thesis, University of Alberta, 1969.

EIG   *80 years of progress*. Westlock, Alberta: Westlock History Book Committee, 1984.

ELL   Elliott, Robbins L. "The Canadian labour press from 1867: a chronological
           annotated directory." *Canadian Journal of Economics and Political
           Science.* 14 (1948):220-248.

EMBR   Embree, David Grant. "The rise of the United Farmers of Alberta" M.A.
           Thesis, University of Alberta, 1956.

ENT   Entz, W. "The suppression of the German language press in September, 1918
           (with special reference to the secular German language papers in western
           Canada)." *Canadian Ethnic Studies.* v8no.2(1976):56-70.

FIN   Finlay, Charles M., ed. *History of Mannville and district.* [Mannville]:
           Mannville Old Timers' Association, 1961.

FLE   Fleming, Freeda, ed. *The days before yesterday: history of Rocky Mountain
           House district, 1799-1977.* Rocky Mountain House, Alberta: Rocky
           Mountain House Reunion Historical Society, 1977.

FOOK   Fooks, Georgia G. "A history of the Lethbridge Herald, 1905-1975." M.A.
           Thesis, Brigham Young University, 1975.

           Foran, Max. "Bob Edwards and social reform." *Alberta Historical Review.*
           21no.3 (Summer 1973):13-17.

FORA   _____. "The making of a booster: Wesley Fletcher Orr and nineteenth
           century Calgary." In Artibise, A.F.J., ed. *Town and city: aspects of
           Western Canadian urban development.* Regina: Canadian Plains
           Research, 1981. (Canadian Plains Studies, 10). pp. 289-308.

           Ford, A.R. "Canadian press." *Canadian Historical Review.* 23 (September
           1942):241-246.

FORT   Fort Macleod History Book Committee. *Fort Macleod: our colorful past. A
           history of the town of Fort Macleod from 1874 to 1924.* Fort Macleod,
           Alberta: The Committee, c1977.

           "Freedom of speech, press and assemblage." *Canadian Congress Journal.* 17
           (March 1938):9.

           Fremont, Donatien. *Les français dans l'ouest canadien.* Winnipeg: Les
           Editions de la Liberté, 1959.

           Friesen, John W. and Terry Lusty, eds. *The Metis of Canada: an annotated
           bibliography.* Toronto: OISE Press, 1980.

FUR   *Furrows of time: a history of Arrowwood, Shouldice, Mossleigh and Farrow,
           1883-1982.* [Arrowwood; Mossleigh]: Arrowwood-Mossleigh Historical
           Society, 1982.

GAE   Gaetz, Annie Louise. *The park country: a history of Red Deer and district.* Vancouver, B.C.: Wrigley Printing Co. Ltd., 1948.

GAL   Galbraith, Francis Wright. *Fifty years of newspaper work.* Red Deer, Alberta: [Red Deer Advocate] 1934.

GEL   Gellner, John and John Smerek. *The Czechs and Slovaks in Canada.* Toronto: University of Toronto Press, 1968.

GERS   Gershaw, F.W. *Saamis, the Medicine Hat.* Medicine Hat, Alberta: Val Marshall Printing Ltd. [1967]

GERW   Gerwin, Elizabeth Barbara. "A survey of the German-speaking population of Alberta." M.A. Thesis, University of Alberta, April 1938.

            Gerwing, A. James. "Newspaper accounts of the major educational reforms in Alberta, 1936." M.Ed. Thesis, University of Alberta, 1952.

GIL   Gilpin, John F. *Edmonton: gateway to the north.* Woodland Hills, California: Windsor Publications, c1984.

GILT   Gilt Edge Ladies Booster Club, Book Committee. *Buffalo trails and tails.* Edited by Melba Kitchen. Wainwright, Alberta: The Club, c1973.

GIS   Gish, Elmer Samuel. "A study of the history of the Rocky Mountain House area." M.A. Thesis, University of Alberta, 1952.

GLEA   *Gleanings after pioneers and progress.* Alix, Alberta: Alix-Clive Historical Club, 1981.

GLEI   Gleichen United Church Women. *The Gleichen call: a history of Gleichen and surrounding area, 1877-1968.* Gleichen, Alberta: Gleichen United Church Women, 1968.

GO   *Golden jubilee commemorating fifty years of picture history of Taber, Alberta, 1905-1955.* [Taber, Alberta: s.n., 1955].

GOL   Goldenberg, Susan. *The Thomson empire.* Toronto: Methuen, 1984.

            Gregorovich, Andrew. *Chronology of Ukrainian Canadian history.* Toronto: Ukrainian Canadian Committee, 1974.

GREG   Gregory, W., comp. *American newspapers: 1821-1936, a union list of files available in the United States and Canada.* New York: H.W. Wilson, 1937.

GUT   Gutkin, Harry. *Journey into our heritage: the story of the Jewish people in the Canadian west.* Toronto: Lester & Orpen Dennys, 1980.

HAG 1   Hagell, Edward. "The Lethbridge News." Canadian North-West Historical
        Society. *Publications.* 1no.4, pt.1 (1928):78-81.

HAG 2   Hagell, Edward and W.A. Buchanan. "The press." *Whoop-Up Country
        Chapter Newsletter.* 1 (January 1984):3-4.

HALL   Hall, Cecil T. *The golden years of Redcliff.* Redcliff, Alberta: 1982.

HAMB   Hambly, J.R. Stan, ed. *A light into the past: a history of Camrose, 1905-
        1980.* Camrose: Gospel Content Press, 1980.

HAR   Harrington, Kate, ed. *Sherwood Park, the first twenty-five years.* Compiled
        by the Twenty-Fifth Anniversary Committee. Henry Unrau, Coordinator.
        s.l.: Josten's National School Services Ltd., 1983.

HART   Hart, Edward John. *The Brewster story: from pack train to tour bus.* Banff,
        Alberta: Brewster Transport Co. Ltd., 1981.

        _____. "The History of the French-Speaking community of Edmonton,
        1795-1935." M.A. Thesis, University of Alberta, 1971.

HAT   Hattonford History Book Committee. *Bridging the years: a history of East-
        bank, Windfield, Hattonford and East Mahaska.* Hattonford, Alberta: The
        Committee, 1982.

HAY   Hayden, C.A. "Romance of the Calgary Herald." Canadian North-West His-
        torical Society. *Publications.* 1no4, pt.1 (1928):50-65.

HED   Hedley, Ralph. *East of the Beaver Hills: a history of Lamont, its people and
        their achievements, 1892-1955.* Edmonton: R. Hedley, 1955?

HEM   *Hemstitches and hackamores: a history of Holden and district.* Holden,
        Alberta: Holden Historical Society, 1984.

HENC   *Henderson's Calgary, Alberta, City Directory.* 1902- . [Winnipeg]:
        Henderson's Directories, 1902- .

HENE   *Henderson's Edmonton, Alberta, City Directory.* 1907- . [Winnipeg]:
        Henderson's Directories, 1907- .

HENW   *Henderson's Manitoba and Northwest Territories Gazetteer and Directory.*
        1881-1900; 1906. [Winnipeg]: Henderson's Directories, 1881-1906.

HIC   Hicken, J. Orvin, ed. and comp. *Round-up: Raymond 1901-1967.* Lethbridge,
        Alberta: Lethbridge Herald Co., 1967.

        Hill, Robert Clarke. "Social Credit and the press: the early Years." M.A.
        Thesis, University of Alberta, 1977.

Hlynka, Isydore. *The other Canadians: selected articles from the column of Ivan Harmata published in the Ukrainian Voice.* Winnipeg: Trident Press, 1973.

HRY   Hrynchuk, Audrey and Jean Klufas. *Memories: Redwater and district.* Redwater, Alberta: c1972.

INN   Innisfail and District Historical Society. *Candlelight years.* Innisfail, Alberta: The Society, 1973.

IRMA   Irma and District Historical Society. *Down memory lane: a history of Irma and district.* Irma, Alberta: The Society, 1985.

IRV   Irving, John A. *The social credit movement in Alberta.* Toronto: University of Toronto Press, 1959. (Social Credit in Alberta, no.10)

ISI   Isidore, Brother, F.S.C. "The Ukrainian Catholic press in Canada: its beginnings, aims, contributions, problems and role." M.A. Thesis, University of Ottawa, 1959.

JAR   Jardine, Rose and Harriet Austen, eds. *Many trails crossed here: a story of Oyen, Alberta, and the surrounding districts.* Oyen, Alberta: Oyen and District Historical Society, 1981.

JEN   Jensen, Bodil J. *Alberta's County of Mountain View: a history.* Didsbury?, Alberta: Mountain View County No. 17, 1983.

JOH   Johnston, Garth D. "Peace River Newspapers." In *I remember Peace River, Alberta, and adjacent districts 1914-1916, Part II.* Peace River, Alberta: Women's Institute, 1976. pp. 59-61.

Johnston, J. George. *The weeklies: biggest circulation in town.* Bolton, Ontario: Bolton Enterprise, 1972.

Kennedy, Fred. *Alberta was my beat: memoirs of a western newspaperman.* Calgary: Albertan, 1975.

KES   Kesterton, W.H. *A history of journalism in Canada.* Toronto: McClelland and Stewart Ltd., 1967. (Carleton Library, 36)

KIN   Kinette Club of Didsbury. History Book Committee. *Echoes of an era.* Didsbury, Alberta: Didsbury Booster, 1969.

KIRK   Kirkconnell, Watson. "Canada's foreign language press." *Canadians All.* 2no.2 (Spring 1944):42-44; 60-62.

KIRS   Kirschbaum, Joseph. *Slovaks in Canada.* Toronto: Canadian Ethnic Press Association of Ontario, 1967.

KLA Klassen, Henry C. "The Bond of Brotherhood and Calgary workingmen." In *Frontier Calgary town, city and region 1875-1914*, edited by Anthony W. Rasporich and Henry C. Klassen. Calgary: McClelland and Stewart West, 1975. pp. 267-271.

KNU Knupp, Lillian. *Life and legends: a history of the Town of High River.* Calgary: Sandstone Publishing, 1982.

    Krotki, Joanne E., comp. *Local histories of Alberta: an annotated bibliography.* 2d ed. Edmonton: Dept. of Slavic and East European Studies, University of Alberta and the Central and East European Studies Society of Alberta, 1983.

LAC *Lac La Biche: yesterday and today.* [Lac La Biche, Alberta: Lac La Biche Heritage Society, [1975]

LACO Lacombe Rural History Club. *Wagon trails to hard top: history of Lacombe and area.* Lacombe, Alberta: The Club, 1972.

LAM Lamerton Historical Society. *Land of the lakes: a story of settlement and development of the country west of Buffalo Lake.* Lamerton, Alberta: The Society, 1974.

LAN *The Landing Trail Post, fiftieth anniversary issue.* s.l: s.n., 1961.

LAND Landry, Charlotte. "Franco-Albertan newspapers, 1898-1982: a guide." Non-thesis Project, Faculty of Library Science, University of Alberta, 1984.

LANT *Lanterns on the prairie: Strome diamond jubilee, 1905-1980.* Strome, Alberta: Strome Senior Citizens Club, 1980.

    Lavkulich, Jolane A. "An annotated selective bibliography covering the period of Lethbridge history 1885-1913." Non-thesis Project, Faculty of Library Science, University of Alberta, 1982.

LED Leduc History Book Committee. *Leduc reflections, 1899-1981.* Leduc, Alberta: Lynard Publishers, 1981.

LEO Leonard, David, John E. McIsaac and Sheilagh Jameson. *A builder of the northwest: the life and times of Richard Secord, 1860-1935.* Edmonton: Richard Y. Secord, c1981.

LET *Let us not forget: aa hstory of Viking and district.* Viking, Alberta: Viking Historical Society, 1968.

LEW Lewis, Diane and John Pengelly. *Through the years: a sociological history of the Ardley, Delburne and Lousana areas.* Delburne, Alberta: History Book Committee, Anthony Henday Historical Society, 1980.

LIND   Lindstrom-Best, Varpu. "First press: a study of the Finnish-Canadian handwritten papers." In *Roots and realities among eastern and central Europeans*, edited by Martin L. Kovacs. Edmonton: Central and East European Studies Association of Canada, 1983. pp. 129-136.

Lobay, Danylo. "Ukrainian press in Canada." Translated and Revised by Olena Negrych. *Ukrainica Canadiana*. 14 (1967):17-32.

LO   *Lovell's Territories Directory of Manitoba and North West Territories for 1900-1901*. Winnipeg: John Lovell & Son, 1901 (Calgary: Glenbow Institute Archives, October, 1969).

LON   Long, H.G. "History of the news media in the Lethbridge Area." *Whoop-Up Country Chapter Newsletter*. 1 (January 1984):4-5.

LOV   Loveridge, D.M. *A historical directory of Manitoba newspapers, 1859-1978*. Winnipeg: University of Manitoba Press, 1981.

Lunn, A.J.E. "Bibliography of the history of the Canadian press." *Canadian Historical Review*. 22 (December 1941):416-433.

MacD   MacDonald, Christine, comp. *Historical directory of Saskatchewan Newspapers, 1878-1983*. Regina and Saskatoon: Saskatchewan Archives Board, 1984. (Saskatchewan Archives Reference Series, 4)

MacEwan, Grant. *Calgary Cavalcade: from fort to fortune*. Saskatoon, Saskatchewan: Western Producer Book Service, 1975.

MacE   _____. *Eye-Opener Bob: the story of Bob Edwards*. Edmonton: Institute of Applied Art, Ltd., 1957

MacG   MacGregor, James Grierson. *Edmonton: A History*. Edmonton: Hurtig, 1975.

_____. *A history of Alberta*. Edmonton: Hurtig, 1981.

Mackenzie, John David. *Country editor: relating sixty-seven years of newspaper life on a Scottish island and the Canadian prairie, 1901-1908*. Rothesay, Scotland: Printed by Bute Newspapers, 1968.

Macleod, Murdoch. "Papers tell south's history." *Lethbridge Herald*. February 1, 1974:13.

MACM   *Macmillan Dictionary of Canadian Biography*. Edited by W. Stewart Wallace. 4th ed., rev., enl. and updated by W. A. Mackay. Toronto: Macmillan of Canada, 1978.

Macpherson, R.G. "A trio of early western journals." *Canadian Magazine.*. 30no.6 (April 1908):550-2.

MAG   Magrath and District History Association. *Immigration builders.* Magrath,
           Alberta: The Association, 1974.

MAKU   Makuch, Andrij Borys. "In the populist tradition: organizing the Ukrainian
           farmer in Alberta, 1909-1935." M.A. Thesis, University of Alberta, 1983.

CES 1   Malycky, Alexander. "Bibliographical Issue." *Canadian Ethnic Studies.*
           1no.1 (April 1969).

CES 2   ———— "[Second] bibliographical issue." *Canadian Ethnic Studies.* 2no.1
           (June 1970).

CES 3   Maylcky, Alexander and H. Palmer. "Third bibliographical issue." *Canadian
           Ethnic Studies.* 5no.1-2 (April 1976).

           Malycky, Alexander. "German-Albertans: A bibliography." In *German-
           Canadian yearbook,* edited by Hartmut Froeschle. Toronto: Historical
           Society of Mecklenburg, Canada Inc. Bd.6 (1981) pt.1; Bd.7 (1983) pt.2.

           ————. *The German-Canadian press of Alberta.* Calgary: University of Cal-
           gary, [1978?].

MANN   Mannville and District Old Timers Society. *Trails to Mannville: a history of
           Mannville and district.* Mannville, Alberta: The Society, 1983.

MARD   Mardiros, Anthony. *William Irvine: the life of a prairie radical.* Toronto:
           Lorimer, 1979.

MARU   Marunchak, Michael H. *The Ukrainian Canadians: a history.* 2d ed. Winni-
           peg: Ukrainian Academy of Arts and Sciences (UVAN), 1982.

MCC   McCormack, A.R. "The origins and extent of western labour radicalism,
           1896-1919." Ph.D. Thesis, University of Western Ontario, 1973.

McI   McIntosh, William Andrew. "The United Farmers of Alberta, 1909-1920."
           M.A. Thesis, University of Calgary, 1971.

MK   *McKim's Canadian newspaper directory.* 1892-1945. Montreal: A. McKim,
           1892-1945.

           McLean, Elizabeth Margaret Mary. "Newspaper reaction to issues of domes-
           tic and foreign policy in Canada." Ph.D. Thesis, University of Alberta,
           1978.

           McMurtrie, Douglas Crawford. *The first printing in Alberta.* Chicago:
           Privately Printed, 1932.

MEE   Meeres, E.L. *Homesteads that nurtured a city: the history of Red Deer,
           1880-1905.* Red Deer, Alberta: Fletcher Printing, 1978.

MEER _____. *[History of Red Deer: a chronological account compiled from newspapers].* Unpublished typescript in Red Deer and District Archives.

Miller, James A. "The Alberta press and the conscription issue in the First World War, 1914-1918." M.A. Thesis, University of Alberta, 1974.

MOR Morgan, Henry. *Canadian men and women of the time: a hand-book of Canadian biography of living characters.* 2d ed. Toronto: Briggs, 1912.

MORR Morrow, James W. "The Medicine Hat Times." Canadian North-West Historical Society. *Publications.* 1no.4, pt.1 (1928):73-77.

MUN Mundare Historical Society. *Memories of Mundare: a history of Mundare and districts.* Mundare, Alberta: The Society, 1980.

Munson Women's Institute. *Munson and district.* Munson, Alberta: Munson Centennial Book Committee, 1967.

Myles, Eugenie. "They fought with ink." In *Alberta golden jubilee anthology,* edited by W.G. Hardy. Toronto: McClelland and Stewart, 1955. pp. 77-82.

NAN Nanton and District Historical Society. *Mosquito Creek roundup: Nanton-Parkland.* Nanton, Alberta: The Society, c1975.

Nichols, Mark Edgar. *CP: the story of the Canadian Press.* Toronto: Ryerson, 1948.

NIC Nicholson, Harold. *Heart of gold: Fairview 1928-1978.* [Edmonton: Bulletin Commercial] 1978.

NOL Nolan, Shelagh. "Bob Edwards of the Eye Opener." *Canada West.* 11no.2 (Summer 1981):7-11.

OLDS Olds Historical Committee. *A history of Olds and area.* Olds: The Committee, 1980.

OLD Olds Old Timers' Association. *See Olds first: a history of Olds and surrounding district.* Olds: The Association, 1968.

Orr, Wesley E. *Diaries, Letterbooks [and other papers]* Mss. (ACG)

OUR *Our Legacy: history of Smoky Lake and area.* Smoky Lake, Alberta: Smoky Lake and District Cultural and Heritage Society, 1983.

Painchaud, Robert P. "The Catholic Church and the movement of francophones to the Canadian prairies, 1870-1915." Ph.D. Thesis, University of Ottawa, 1976.

Palmer, Howard. *Land of the second chance: a history of ethnic groups in southern Alberta.* Lethbridge, Alberta: Lethbridge Herald, 1972.

PAP   Papen, Jean. "Georges S. Bugnet, homme de lettres canadien: sa vie, son oeuvre." M.A. Thesis, Université de Laval, 1967.

PAR   Parlby, Beatrice G., ed. *Pioneers and progress.* Alix, Alberta: Alix-Clive Historical Club.

Parry, David. *A century of Southam.* [Toronto: Southam Press, 1977].

Paulsen, Frank M. *Danish settlements on the Canadian prairies; folk traditions, immigrant experiences and local history.* Ottawa: National Museums of Canada, 1974

PEA   *Peace River Remembers: Peace River, Alberta and adjacent districts.* Peace River, Alberta: Sir Alexander Mackenzie Historical Society, 1984.

PEEL   Peel, Bruce Braden. *A bibliography of the prairie provinces to 1953, with biographical index.* 2d ed. Toronto: University of Toronto Press, 1973.

PEM   Pembina Lobstick Historical Society. *Foley trail: a history of Entwistle, Evansburg, and surrounding school districts.* s.l., The Society, 1984.

Philips, Grace A., ed. *Tales of Tofield.* Tofield, Alberta: Tofield Historical Society, 1969.

PON   Ponoka and District Historical Society. *Ponoka panorama.* Ponoka, Alberta: The Society, 1973.

PRA   *Prairie grass to mountain pass: history of the pioneers of Pincher Creek and district.* Pincher Creek, Alberta: Pincher Creek Historical Society, 1974.

Printer and Publisher See *Canadian Printer and Publisher*

PUB   *Publisher.* Ja. 1973- . Toronto: Canadian Community Newspapers Association, Ja. 1973- . Ctd. *Canadian Community Publisher* (q.v.)

RAI   Rainier-Bow City History Book Club. *Settlers along the Bow.* Bow City, Alberta: The Club, c1975.

REA   Ream, Peter T. *The Fort on the Saskatchewan: A resource book on Fort Saskatchewan and District.* [Fort Saskatchewan, s.n., 1974.]

REF   *Reflections of Sylvan Lake.* Sylvan Lake, Alberta: Sylvan Lake Historical Society, 1984.

REY   Reynolds, A. Bert. *"Siding 16": an early history of Wetaskiwin to 1930.* Wetaskiwin, Alberta: Wetaskiwin Alberta-R.C.M.P. Centennial Committee, 1975.

RIM   Rimbey History Committee. *History of Rimbey, Alberta: golden anniversary, 1902-1952; 50 years of progress.* Rimbey, Alberta: The Committee, 1952.

ROY   Royal Canadian Legion. Ladies Auxiliary. Ryley Branch, no. 192. Book Committee. *Beaver tales: history of Ryley and district.* Editor, Harriet C. Brown. Ryley, Alberta: The Auxiliary, c1978.

Rutherford. Paul. *The making of the Canadian Press.* Toronto: McGraw-Hill Ryerson Ltd., 1978. (McGraw-Hill Ryerson series in Canadian Sociology.)

—————. *A Victorian authority: the daily press in late nineteenth century Canada.* Toronto: University of Toronto Press, 1982.

SAM   Samis History Book Committee. *Memories of Samis and nearby districts.* Olds, Alberta: The Committee, 1985.

SCH   Schutz, Fred. *Pas-Ka-Poo; an early history of Rimbey and Upper Blindman Valley.* Edited by Jack Parry. Rimbey, Alberta: Rimbey Record, 1962.

Scratch, John Ronald. "The editorial reaction of the Alberta press to the Bennett government, 1930-1935." M.A. Thesis, University of Alberta, 1968.

Seager, Allen. "A Proletariat in wild rose country: the Alberta miners, 1905-1945." Ph.D. Thesis, York University, 1982.

SED   Sedgewick Historical Society. *Sedgewick Sentinel: a history of Sedgewick and surrounding districts.* Sedgewick, Alberta: The Society, 1982.

SHE   Sheep River Historical Society. *In the light of the flares: history of Turner Valley oilfields.* Turner Valley, Alberta: Society, 1979.

SMI   Smith, Bessie, ed. *The sunny side of the Neutrals: stories of Consort and district in Alberta, Canada.* Consort, Alberta: 1983.

SMIT   Smith, Jim. "The great newspaper war." *Canadian Golden West.* 13no.4 (1978):12-15.

STA   Stainton, Irene Hackett and Elizabeth Course Carlsson, eds. *Along the Victoria trail: Lamont and districts.* Edmonton: Lamont and District Historian, 1978.

STEE   Steele, C. Frank. *Prairie editor: the life and times of Buchanan of Lethbridge.* Toronto: Ryerson Press, 1961.

STEW   Stewart, Walter, ed. *Canadian Newspapers, The inside story.* Edmonton: Hurtig, 1980.

STON   Stony Plain and District Historical Society. *Along the fifth: a history of Stony Plain and district*. Stony Plain, Alberta: The Society, c1982.

STO   Stout, Clarence Howard. *Backtrack on old trails: memoirs of an international life of 91 years, 79 in Alberta*. Calgary: L. Stout, 1973.

Strathern, Gloria M. *Alberta, 1954-1979: a provincial bibliography*. Edmonton: Dept. of Printing Services, University of Alberta, 1982.

TAB   Taber Women's Institute. *Taber, yesterdy and today*. Taber, Alberta: Taber Times, 1953.

Tardif, Emile. *Saint Albert*. Edmonton: La Survivance Printing Ltd., 1961?

THO   Thomas, Jack, comp. *Silver sage*. Bow Island, Alberta: Bow Island Lions Club, 1972.

Thompson, John Herd. *The harvests of war: The prairie west, 1914-1918*. Toronto: McClelland and Stewart, 1978.

TIM   *The times of Irma, 1912-1972: a history of Irma and district*. Irma, Alberta: 1972.

TRE   *Treasured scales of the Kinsoo*. Cold Lake, Alberta: Historical Society of Cold Lake and District, 1980?

TRIB   *Tributaries of the Blindman*. Springdale, Alberta: 1972?

TRO   Trochu History Book Committee. *Remember when: the history of Trochu and district*. Trochu, Alberta: The Committee, 1975.

TUR   Turek, Victor. *The Polish-language press in Canada: its history and bibliographical list*. Toronto: Polish Alliance Press, 1962. (Polish Research Institute in Canada Studies, 4)

UKR   Ukrainian Pioneers' Association of Alberta. *Ukrainians in Alberta*. Edmonton: The Association, 1975-1981.

VEG   *Vegreville in review: a history of Vegreville and surrounding area, 1880-1980*. Vegreville, Alberta: Vegreville and District Historical Society, 1980.

VER   Vermilion Old Timers. *Vermilion memories*. Vermilion, Alberta: S. Carl Heckbert, 1967?

VIK   Viking Historical Society. *Let us not forget: a history of Viking and District*. [Viking, Alberta]: The Society, 1968.

VUL   Vulcan and District Historical Society. *Wheat country: a history of Vulcan and district*. Vulcan, Alberta: The Society, c1973.

WAD   Waddell, William S. "The Honorable Frank Oliver." M.A. Thesis, University of Alberta, 1950.

WAG   *Wagons to Wings.* Warner, Alberta: Warner and District Historical Society, 1985.

WAGO   *Wagon trails grown over: Sexsmith to the Smoky.* Sexsmith, Alberta: Sexsmith to the Smoky Historical Society, 1980.

WAR   Ward, Tom. *Cowtown: an album of early Calgary.* Calgary: McClelland and Stewart West, 1975.

WARN   Warner Old Timers' Association. *Warner pioneers.* Lethbridge, Alberta: Printed by the Lethbridge Herald, 1962.

WEC   *We came and we stayed: accounts of the pioneers, their descendants, and other residents of Bawlf, Alberta, and surrounding districts.* Compiled by Helen Lindroth. Camrose, Alberta: Gospel Contact Press, 1980.

WEI   Weinrich, Peter. *Social protest from the left in Canada, 1870-1970.* Toronto: University of Toronto, 1982.

WHE   *Where we crossed the creek and settled: Rockyford.* Rockyford, Alberta: Rockyford and District Book Society, 1980.

WHI   Whitlow, Alice. *Under the chinook arch: a history of Cayley and surrounding areas.* Cayley, Alberta: Women's Institute, 1979?

WW   *Who's Who and Why, 1912-1921.* Toronto: International Press, 1913-1922.

WWA1   *Who's Who in Alberta: A biographical directory.* 1968; 1974. Saskatoon: Lyone, 1968, 1974.

WWA2   *Who's Who in Alberta.* 1978/79. Edmonton: L.U.L. Publications, 1978?

WWAB   *Who's Who in Alberta business, finance and government: the key decision makers.* 1st. ed. (1984/85). Edmonton: Tridon Publications [1985?].

WWC   *Who's Who in Canada.* 16th (1922)- . Toronto: International Press, 1922- .

WWW   *Who's Who in Western Canada: A biographical directory of notable living men and women of western Canada.* v.1-2 (1911-1912). Vancouver: Canadian Press Associaiton, 1911-1912.

WILK   Wilk, Stephen William. *One day's journey.* 1st ed. Calgary: Alcraft Printing, 1963.

Williams, Stanley A. "Early newspapers in Alberta." Paper presented to the Amisk Waskahegan chapter of the Historical Society of Alberta, February 9, 1972. Photocopy provided by the Provincial Archives of Alberta.

Worth, Walter Holmes. "An analysis of the editorial treatment of education in the Alberta press." M.Ed. Thesis, University of Alberta.

WRIG   *Wrigley's Alberta Directory.* 1920; 1922. Vancouver: Wrigley's Directories Ltd., 1920, 1922.

YOU   Youngstown and District Historical Society. *Youngstown memories across the years, 1909-1983: stories of Youngstown, Alberta and surrounding districts.* Youngstown, Alberta: The Society, 1984.

Young, Charles H. *The Ukrainian Canadians.* Toronto: Nelson and Sons, 1931.

Zwicker, Barrie and Dick MacDonald, ed. *The news: inside the Canadian media.* Ottawa: Deneau Publishers, 1982.

B. Checklists, Directories and Union Lists of Newspapers

Alberta. Alberta Agriculture. *A guide to agricultural periodicals published in western Canada.* Edmonton: Print Media Branch, Alberta Agriculture, 1981. (AGDEX No. 003.1)

Alberta. Alberta Legislature Library. *Serials microform holdings.* Edmonton: The Library, September 1982.

Alberta. Provincial Archives of Alberta. *List of newspapers and news periodicals on microfilm at the provincial archives of Alberta.* Edmonton: The Archives, August 1982.

Alberta Government/College Libraries union list of serials. 2d ed. [Edmonton: Alberta Government Libraries Council] 1984.

Arndt, Karl J.R. and Mary E. Olson. *The German language press of the Americas, 1732-1968/Die Deutschsprachige Presse der Amerikas, 1732-1968.* v.2. Munchen: Verlag Dokumentation Pullach, 1973, pp. 227-229.

Ayers Directory of Newspapers and Periodicals. v.1- 1880-. Philadelphia: Ayers, 1880-.

Bombak, Anna. "Ukrainian-Canadian newspapers published in Alberta from 1909-1982: a bibliography." Non-thesis Project, Faculty of Library Science, University of Alberta, 1985.

Bush, Alfred L. and Robert S. Fraser. *American Indian periodicals in the Princeton University Library: a preliminary list.* Princeton: University of Princeton Library, 1970.

Calgary Public Library. *Periodicals and newspapers: 1984 catalogue.* Calgary: Calgary Public Library, May 1984.

Canada. Dept. of Indian Affairs and Northern Development. *List of Canadian native periodicals held by the INAC Library.* Ottawa: Dept. of Indian Affairs and Northern Development Library, 1983.

Canada. Library of Parliament. *Periodicals and newspapers in the collections of the Library of Parliament.* Ottawa: The Library, January 1984.

Canada. National Library of Canada. *Checklist of Canadian ethnic serials.* Comp. by Ruth Boguis. Ottawa: The Library, 1981.

————. *Resources for native peoples studies.* Comp. by Nora T. Corley. Ottawa: The Library, 1984. (Research collections in Canadian libraries; 9)

————. *Union list of Canadian newspapers held by Canadian libraries.* Ottawa: The Library, 1977.

Canadian Almanac and Directory, 1847- . Toronto: Copp Clark, 1847- .

"Canadian labour papers on microfilm available in the Dept. of Labour Library", *Labour Gazette* 59(6) June 1959:632-637.

Canadian Library Association. Microfilm Committee. *Canadian newspapers on microfilm catalogue.* Part I. (2 vols.). Ottawa: The Association, 1959+

————. *Canadian newspapers on microfilm, part 2, Canadian newspapers microfilmed by the Canadian Library Association and other producers.* Revised ed. Ottawa: The Library, 1969.

CARD. Canadian Advertising Rates and Data, v.1, 1928- . Toronto: Maclean-Hunter, 1928- .

Cukier, Golda. *Canadian Jewish periodicals: a revised listing.* Montreal: Collection of Jewish Canadiana, Jewish Public Library, 1978.

Danky, James P., ed. *Native American periodicals and newspapers 1828-1982.* Compiled by Maureen E. Hady in association with the State Historical Society of Wisconsin. Westport, Connecticut: Greenwood Press, 1984.

————. *Undergrounds: a union list of alternative periodicals in the libraries of the United States and Canada.* Madison, Wisconsin: State Historical Society of Wisconsin, 1974.

Data. Alberta weekly newspapers: a guide reference book published for your convenience listing member papers of Alberta Weekly Newspapers Association. 1965- . Edmonton: Alberta Weekly Newspapers Associaiton, 1965- .

Desbarats' Directory of Canada's Publications v.1-v.14 (1904-1932/33). Montreal: Desbarats' Advertising Agency, 1904-1932/33.

Duke, M.D., comp. *Agricultural periodicals published in Canada 1836-1960.* Ottawa: Dept. of Agriculture, 1962.

Elliott, Robins L. "The Canadian labour press from 1867: a chronological annotated directory." *Canadian Journal of Economics and Political Science* 14(1948):220-248.

Glazier, Kenneth M. *A list of newspapers in the University libraries of the Prairie universities of Canada.* Calgary: University of Calgary, 1974.

Glenbow-Alberta Institute. *Preliminary list of periodicals in the library of the Glenbow-Alberta Institute.* Calgary: The Institute, 1971.

Glenbow-Alberta Institute Archives. *Union List of newspapers.* Calgary: The Archives, 1982.

Gregory, W., comp. *American newspapers: 1821-1936, a union list of files available in the United States and Canada.* New York: H.W. Wilson, 1937.

Hann, R.G. et al, comps. *Primary sources in Canadian working class history, 1860-1930. Pt.2. Newspapers.* Kitchener, Ontario: Dumont Press, 1973.

Healey, M. Elma, comp. *Serials by and about native Americans.* Peterborough, Ontario: J. Bata Library, Trent University, 1982. (Bata biblio. no. 6)

Hewitt, A.R., comp. *Union list of commonwealth newspapers in London, Oxford and Cambridge.* London: Athlone Press, 1960.

Jaworsky, Stephen Jaroslaw. "Newspapers and periodicals of Slavic groups in Canada during the period of 1965-1969: An annotated bibliography". Ottawa: Faculty of Arts, University of Ottawa, 1971.

Landry, Charlotte. "Franco-Albertan Newspapers 1898-1982: a guide." Non-thesis project, Faculty of Library Science, University of Alberta, 1984.

Lehmann, Heinz. "Die Deutsche presses", in *Das Deutschtum in Westkanada.* Berlin: Junker und Dunnhaupt Verlag, 1939. pp. 319-325.

Loveridge, D.M. *A historical directory of Manitoba newspapers 1859-1978.* Winnipeg, Manitoba: University of Manitoba Press, 1981.

MacDonald, Christine, comp. *Historical directory of Saskatchewan newspapers, 1878-1983.* Regina and Saskatoon, Saskatchewan: Saskatchewan Archives Board, 1984.

Malycky, Alexander, ed. "Bibliographical issue". *Canadian Ethnic Studies* 1no.1 (April 1969).

_____ [Second] bibliographical issue". *Canadian Ethnic Studies* 2no.1 (June 1970).

————— and H. Palmer, eds. "Third bibliographical issue". *Canadian Ethnic Studies* 5no.1-2 (April 1976).

McKim's Canadian Newspaper Directory, 1892-1945. Montreal: A. McKim, 1892-1945.

Price, John A. "U.S. and Canadian Indian Publications." *Canadian Review of Sociology and Anthropology* 9no.2 (May 1972):150-162.

Rutkowski, Alan and Nadia Cyncar, comps. *Ukrainian serials: a checklist of Ukrainian journals, periodicals and newspapers in the University of Alberta Library.* Edmonton: Canadian Institute of Ukrainian Studies, 1983. (Canadian Institute of Ukrainian Studies. Research report no. 3)

Salmond, Margaret and Mary Alice Scott, comps. *Newspapers in the University of Alberta Libraries: a list of holdings.* Edmonton: University of Alberta Libraries, 1971. (Humanities and Social Sciences. Reference Dept. Pub. no. 2)

Smith, R. *Canadian newspapers in the University of British Columbia Library.* Vancouver: University of British Columbia Library, 1974. (Reference publication, 52)

Turek, Victor. *The Polish-language press in Canada: its history and a bibliographical list.* Toronto: Polish Alliance Press, 1962. (Studies (Polish Research Institute of Canada); 4)

United States. Library of Congress. *Newspapers in microform: foreign countries 1948-1972.* Washington, D.C.: The Library, 1973.

University of Calgary Library. *Newspaper list by title.* Calgary: The Library, January 1983.

Weres, Roman. *Directory of Ukrainian publishing houses, periodicals, bookstores, libraries and library collections of Ukrainica in diaspora.* Chicago: Ukrainian Bibliographical-Reference Center, 1976.

Woodsworth, Anne, comp. *The alternative press in Canada: a checklist of underground, revolutionary, radical and other alternative serials from 1960.* Toronto: University of Toronto Press, 1972.

C. Newspaper Indexes

Canadian News Index v.1, 1977- . Toronto: Micromedia Ltd., 1977- . 1977-1979 entitled *Canadian Newspaper Index.*

Degrâce, Eloi. *Index du Courrier de l'ouest (1905-1916).* Edmonton: [E. DeGrâce] 1980.

————. *L'Ouest canadien: Historique et Index (1898-1900).* Ottawa: Bibliotheque Nationale, 1979.

————. *Le Progrès (1909-1915): histoire et index.* Dartmouth, N.S.: E. Degrâce, 1983.

Edmonton Bulletin index 1880-1900. Compiled by the Alberta Folklore and Local History Project, directed by Robert E. Gard. [Edmonton: s.n., 1943-1946]. Typescript. Available at Bruce Peel Special Collections Library, University of Alberta.

Edmonton Public Library. *Local history index, subject keyword index [to the Edmonton Journal and the Alberta Report]* September 1979- . Edmonton: Edmonton Public Library, 1979- .

Index to Edmonton Journal. Prepared by the staff of the Reference unit of the Humanities and Social Sciences Library, University of Alberta. Edmonton: Humanities and Social Sciences Library, University of Alberta, January 1973-December 1980.

Marshalsay, Barbara, comp. *Lethbridge News and Macleod Gazette 1882-1900; a subject and biographical index.* Lethbridge: NW Associates, 1981.

Northern Titles: NWIC Index 1973- . Edmonton: Boreal Institute for Northern Studies, University of Alberta, 1973- .

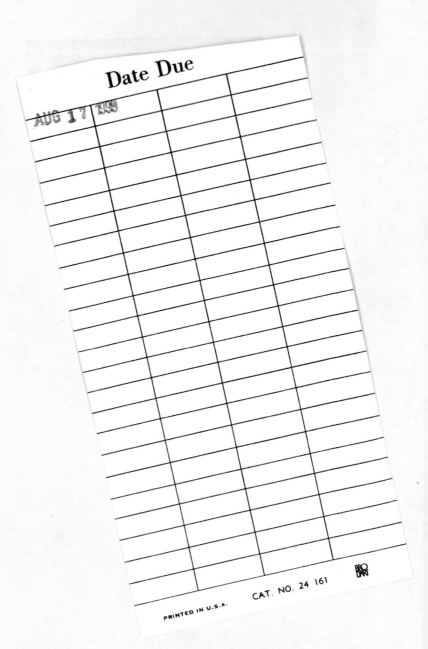

Date Due

AUG 17 1999

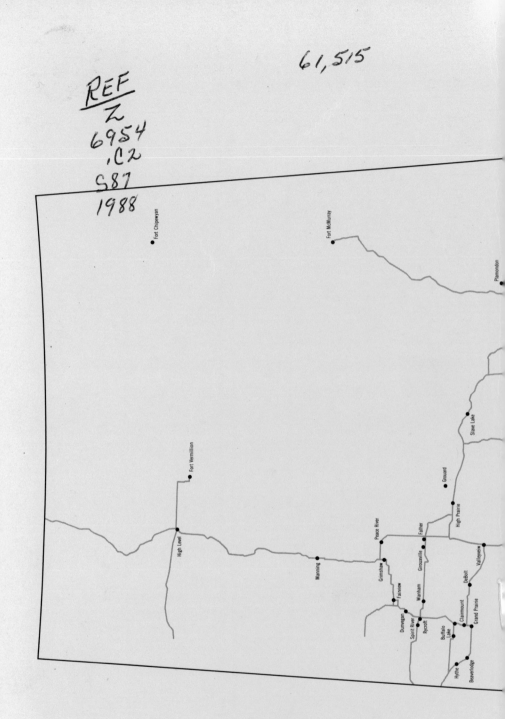